7 Large and Fast: Exploiting Memory Hierarchy

While *caches*, *translation lookaside buffers*, and *virtual memory* appear differe[nt] examining how they deal with the four questions: (1) Where can a block found? (3) What block is replaced on a miss? (4) How are writes handled? (*p.*

The challenge of memory hierarchies is that every change that improves the *miss* rate can also negatively affect performance: Increasing size decreases *capacity misses* but may also increase *access time*; increasing *associativity* decreases miss rate due to *conflict misses* but may also increase access time; and increasing *block size* may decrease miss rate yet also increase *miss penalty*. (*page 514*)

8 Interfacing Processors and Peripherals

Different bus characteristics allow the creation of buses optimized for a wide range of demands. In general, higher cost systems use wider and faster buses that are *synchronous*. In contrast, low-cost systems favor buses that are narrower, do not require intelligence among the devices, and are *asynchronous* so that low-speed devices can interface inexpensively. (*page 563*)

The performance of an I/O system, whether measured by bandwidth or latency, depends on all the elements in the path between the device and memory, including the operating system that generates the I/O commands. (*page 579*)

9 Parallel Processors

A key characteristic of programs for parallel machines is the frequency of *synchronization* and *communication*. Large-scale parallel machines have *distributed physical memory*; the higher bandwidth and lower overhead of local memory reward programs utilizing *locality*. (*page 634*)

A P P E N D I C E S

A Assemblers, Linkers, and the SPIM Simulator

Assembly language is a programming language. Its principal difference from high-level languages such as BASIC, Pascal, and C is that it provides only a few, simple types of data and control flow. Assembly language programs do not specify the type of value held in a variable, leaving the programmer to apply the appropriate operation. (*page A-13*)

B The Basics of Logic Design

C Mapping Control to Hardware

Independent of whether the control is represented as a finite state diagram or as a microprogram, the translation to hardware is similar: Each state or microinstruction asserts a set of control outputs and specifies how to choose the next state; next state function may be encoded in a finite state machine or with an explicit sequencer; control logic may be either ROMs or PLAs. (*page C-27*)

D Introducing C to Pascal Programmers

E Another Approach to Instruction Set Architecture: VAX

The differing goals for VAX and MIPS led to different architectures. The VAX goals, simple compilers and code density, led to powerful addressing modes, powerful instructions, and efficient instruction encoding. The MIPS goals were high performance via pipelining, ease of hardware implementation, and compatibility with optimizing compilers. These goals led to simple instructions, simple addressing modes, fixed-length instruction formats, and many registers. (*page E-4*)

Orthogonality is key to the VAX architecture; the opcode is independent of the addressing modes, which are independent of the data types and even the number of unique operands. Thus a few hundred operations expand to hundreds of thousands of instructions when accounting for the data types, operand counts, and addressing modes. (*page E-23*)

Computer Organization and Design

THE HARDWARE / SOFTWARE INTERFACE

Computer Organization and Design

THE HARDWARE/SOFTWARE INTERFACE

John L. Hennessy
Stanford University

David A. Patterson
University of California at Berkeley

With a contribution by
James R. Larus
University of Wisconsin

Morgan Kaufmann Publishers, Inc.
San Francisco, California

Senior Editor: Bruce M. Spatz
Production Manager: Yonie Overton
Editorial Coordinator: Douglas Sery
Copyediting: Steve Hiatt and Gary Morris
Text Design: Ross Carron Design
Illustration: Alexander Teshin Associates
Composition/Color Separation/Postscript
  Programming: Edward W. Sznyter, Babel Press
Cover Design: David Lance Goines
Additional Cover Mechanical Art: Patty King
Chapter Opener Illustrations: Jo Jackson
Indexing: Steve Rath
Proofreading: Gary Morris
Electronic Prepress: The Courier Connection
Printer: Courier Corporation

Morgan Kaufmann Publishers, Inc.
Editorial Office:
340 Pine Street, Sixth Floor
San Francisco, CA 94104

Advice, Praise, and Errors: Any correspondence related to this publication or intended for the authors should be addressed to the editorial offices of Morgan Kaufmann Publishers, Inc., Dept. P&H APE. Information regarding error sightings is encouraged. Any error sightings that are accepted for correction in subsequent printings will be rewarded by the authors with a payment of $1.00 (U.S.) per correction at the time of their implementation in a reprint. Electronic mail can be sent to errors@cs.berkeley.edu.

Instructor Support: For information on the SPIM software simulator and other instructor materials available to adoptors, please contact the editorial offices of Morgan Kaufmann Publishers, Inc.

Cataloging-in-Publication Data

Patterson, David A.
  Computer organization and design: the hardware/software interface
  / David A. Patterson, John L. Hennessy.
      p.   cm.
  Includes bibliographical references and index.
  ISBN 1-55860-281-X
      1. Computer organization. 2. Computers--Design and construction.
          3. Computer interfaces.   I. Hennessy, John L.   II. Title
          QA76.9.C643P37 1994
          004.2'2--dc20   94-17639
                                                                    CIP

TO LINDA AND ANDREA

Foreword

by Maurice V. Wilkes
Cambridge, England

This is an excellent time for a new book on computer design. During the last ten years the subject has undergone a marked renaissance. It has become less dependent on intuition and personal opinion, and more on measurement and rational analysis. The subtitle of the author's earlier book *Computer Architecture: A Quantitative Approach* makes this point.

Patterson and Hennessy played their part in these developments. Indeed, widespread public discussion of the new ideas may be said to have begun with the publication in 1980 of a paper by Patterson and Ditzel entitled "The Case for the Reduced Instruction Set Computer." The acronym RISC derives from this paper. Patterson proceeded to put RISC ideas into practice by developing the Berkeley RISC with the aid of a group of students. This design became the basis of the SPARC workstations. Hennessy applied his energies to the MIPS design project at Stanford and became one of the founders of the MIPS Computer company.

Like many seminal ideas, RISC is deceptively simple. The emphasis is not on the size of the instruction set, but on its nature; RISC instruction sets have made it possible to apply, in a single chip processor, subtle techniques for instruction level concurrency that were previously to be found only in large computers.

There is a lot more to computer design than is comprised in the RISC philosophy, as will be shown by a glance at the diagram entitled "The Five Classic Components of a Computer" which appears, with differing highlighting, at the head of various chapters of this book. But RISC has been a unifying influence. Another major unifying influence has been the need to work within the boundaries of a silicon chip, where there is never enough space and, if one thing goes in, another must go out. Performance depends critically on decisions taken at the chip level. No longer can system design be a subject divorced from computer implementation, a change which may have left some people high and dry, but which is nevertheless wholly to the good. Nor can system design be divorced from consideration of the software interface, a point which the authors bring out both in their subtitle and in their text.

The computer field, particularly on the software side, abounds with examples of new ideas that have found their way into industrial practice by being taught in universities and have thereby become part of the professional tool kit which graduating students have carried with them into industry. In hardware, it is often the other way round; teaching follows practice. This is another reason for welcoming a book by two engineers who can write of current practice with authority.

As I followed the authors through their unhurried chapters, I was conscious of the all-seeing eye of the evaluator pictured at the chapter heads. Ever watchful, she—I think it is a female eye, but I cannot be sure—seemed to be saying that every argument has another side, and that every insight gains by being put into perspective.

I think students will enjoy learning from this book; at least, I hope so and I give them my good wishes.

Contents

Preface

The most beautiful thing we can experience is the mysterious.
It is the source of all true art and science.

Albert Einstein
What I Believe, 1930

About This Book

We believe that learning in computer science and engineering should reflect the current state of the field, as well as introduce the principles that are shaping computing. We also feel that readers in every specialty of computing need to appreciate the organizational paradigms that determine the capabilities, performance, and, ultimately, the success of computer systems.

Modern computer technology requires professionals of every computing specialty to understand both hardware and software. The interaction between hardware and software at a variety of levels also offers a framework for understanding the fundamentals of computing. Whether your primary interest is computer science or electrical engineering, the central ideas in computer organization and design are the same. Thus, our emphasis in this book is to show the relationship between hardware and software and to focus on the concepts that are the basis for current computers.

Traditionally, the competing influences of assembly language, organization, and design have encouraged books that consider each area as a distinct subset. In our view, such distinctions have increasingly lost meaning as computer technology has advanced. To truly understand the breadth of our field, it is important to understand the interdependencies among these topics.

The audience for this book includes those with little experience in assembly language or logic design who need to understand basic computer organization, as well as readers with backgrounds in assembly language and/or logic design who want to learn how to design a computer or understand how a system works and why it performs as it does.

Relationship to CA:AQA

Many readers will be familiar with *Computer Architecture: A Quantitative Approach* (Morgan Kaufmann, 1990). Our motivation in writing that book was to describe the principles of computer architecture using solid engineering fundamentals and quantitative cost/performance tradeoffs. We used an approach that combined examples and measurements, based on commercial systems, to create realistic design experiences. Our goal was to demonstrate that computer architecture could be learned using scientific methodologies instead of a descriptive approach.

We've discovered that many people have used that book as a first introduction to the field. We've also learned that many institutions are now using this quantitative approach in more introductory computer organization courses. However, *Computer Architecture* was written at a more advanced level, for readers who already understood the basic principles.

A majority of the readers for *Computer Organization and Design: The Hardware/Software Interface* will not be or plan to become computer architects. However, the performance of future software systems will be dramatically affected by how well software designers understand the basic hardware techniques at work in a system. Thus, compiler writers, operating system designers, database programmers, and most other software engineers need a firm grounding in the principles presented in this book. Similarly, hardware designers must understand clearly the effects of their work on software applications.

Given these factors, we knew that this book had to be much more than a subset of the material in *Computer Architecture*. We've approached every topic in a new way. Topics shared between the books were written anew for this effort, while many other topics are presented here for the first time. To further ensure the uniqueness of *Computer Organization and Design*, we exchanged the writing responsibilities we assigned to ourselves for *Computer Architecture*. The topics that Hennessy covered in the first book were written by Patterson in this one, and vice versa. Several of our reviewers suggested that we call this book "Computer Organization: A Conceptual Approach" to emphasize the significant differences from our other book. It is our hope that the reader will find new insights in every section, as well as a more tractable introduction to the abstractions and principles at work in a modern computer.

Learning by Evolution

It is tempting for authors to present the latest version of a hardware concept and spend considerable time explaining how these often sophisticated ideas work. We decided instead to present each idea from its first principles, emphasizing the simplest version of an idea, how it works, and how it came to be. We believe that presenting the fundamental concepts first offers greater insight into why machines look the way they do today, as well as how they might evolve as technology changes.

To facilitate this approach, we have based the book upon the MIPS processor. It offers an easy to understand instruction set and can be implemented in a simple, straightforward manner. This allows readers to grasp an entire machine organization and to follow exactly how the machine implements its instructions. Throughout the text, we present the concepts before the details, building from simpler versions of ideas to more complex ones. Examples of this approach can be found in almost every chapter. Chapter 3 builds up to MIPS assembly language starting with one simple instruction type. The concepts and algorithms used in modern computer arithmetic are built up starting from the familiar grammar school algorithms in Chapter 4. Chapters 5 and 6 start from the simplest possible implementation of a MIPS subset and build to a fully pipelined version. Chapter 7 illustrates the abstractions and concepts in memory hierarchies by starting with the simplest possible cache and introducing virtual memory and TLBs as an extension of the concepts.

This evolutionary process is used extensively in Chapters 5 and 6, where the complete datapath and control for a processor are presented. Since learning is a visual process, we have included sequences of figures that contain progressively more detail or show a sequence of events within the machine. We have also used a second color to help readers follow the figures and sequences of figures.

Learning from this Book

Our objective of demonstrating first principles through the interrelationship of hardware and software is enhanced by several features found in each chapter. The Hardware/Software Interface sections are used to highlight these relationships. We've also included Big Picture sections for each chapter to remind readers of the major insights. We hope that these elements reinforce our goal of making this book equally valuable as a foundation for further study in both hardware and software courses.

To illustrate the relationship between high-level language and machine language and to describe the hardware algorithms, we have chosen C. It is widely used in compiler and operating system courses, it is widely used by computer professionals, and several facilities in the language make it suitable for describing hardware algorithms. For those who are familiar with Pascal rather than C, Appendix D provides a quick introduction to C for Pascal programmers and should be sufficient to understand the code sequences in the text.

We have tried to manage the pace of the presentation for readers of varying experience. Ideas that are not essential to a newcomer, but which may be of interest to the more advanced reader, are presented as Elaborations. When appropriate, advanced concepts have been saved for the exercise sets and enhanced with additional discussion as In More Depth sections. In addition, we found that the extent of background that students have in logic design varies widely. Thus, Appendix B provides all the necessary background for those readers not versed in the basics of logic design, as well as some slightly more sophisticated material for the more advanced student. Within a course, this material can be used in supplementary lectures or incorporated into the mainstream of the course, depending on the background of the students and the goals of the instructor.

We have also found that readers enjoy learning the history of the field, so the Historical Perspective sections include many photographs of important machines and little known stories about the ideas behind them. We hope that the perspective offered by these anecdotes and photographs will add a new dimension for our readers.

Course Syllabi and this Book

One particularly difficult issue facing instructors is the balance of assembly language programming with computer organization. We have written this book so that readers will learn more about organization and design, while still providing a complete introduction to assembly language. By using a RISC architecture, students can learn the basics of an instruction set and assembly language programming in less time than is typically reserved in the curriculum for CISC based assembly courses. Many instructors have also found that using a simulator, rather than running in native mode on a real machine, provides the experience of assembly language programming in substantially less time (and with less pain for the student).

Instructors may contact the publisher regarding the SPIM simulator of the MIPS processor. The XSPIM simulator developed by James R. Larus is retrievable via ftp (see page xxiii). Adaptations are also available in Windows and Macintosh formats. Although not identical, they offer the same general functionality. We feel this will enhance student opportunities for learning about computer organization (see Appendix A). Finally, stepwise derivation of assembly from a high-level language takes less study time than learning it from the ground up. Chapter 3 and Appendix A may be used together or separately, depending upon the reader's background. Chapter 3 provides the basics and can be supplemented with additional detail from Appendix A for a complete introduction to modern assembly language programming, including assemblers, linkers, and loaders. In the end, we hope this approach offers a more efficient treatment of assembly for most readers, while being sufficiently broad to support detailed lecture or laboratory coverage if an instructor wants more emphasis on assembly language programming.

For those courses intended to expose students to the important principles of computer organization, the chapters from 4 to 9 explain the key ideas. Chapter 4 explains the idea of number representation for both integers and floating-point numbers and shows how arithmetic algorithms work. Chapters 5 and 6 introduce key ideas in control and pipelining and can be covered at several levels. Chapter 7 introduces the principles of memory hierarchies, unifying the ideas of caching and virtual memory. Chapter 8 shows how I/O systems are organized and controlled, explaining the cooperative relationship between the hardware and the operating system. Finally, Chapter 9 uses examples to introduce the key principles used in multiprocessors.

For readers who want a greater emphasis on computer design, Chapters 4 through 6, together with Appendices B and C, provide that opportunity. For example, Chapter 4 explains a number of techniques used by computer designers to speed up addition and multiplication. Chapters 5 and 6 derive complete implementations of a MIPS subset using the arithmetic elements from Chapter 4 and a number of common datapath elements (such as register files and memories) that are explained in detail in Appendix B. Chapter 5 starts with a very simple implementation; a complete datapath and control unit are constructed for this organization. The implementation is then modified to derive a faster version where each instruction can take differing numbers of clock cycles. The control for this multicycle implementation is designed using two different methods in Chapter 5. Appendix C shows in detail how the control specifications are implemented using structured logic blocks. Chapter 6 builds on the single-clock cycle implementation created in Chapter 5 to show how pipelined machines are designed. The design is extended to show how hazards can be handled and how control for interrupts works. The student interested in computer design, is not only exposed to three different designs for the same instruction set, but can also see how these designs compare in terms of advantages and disadvantages.

Chapter Organization and Overview

Using these plans as the core, we developed the other chapters to introduce and support that core.

Many students remarked that they appreciated learning about the continuing rapid change in speed and capacity of hardware, as well as some of the history of computer development. This material is the focus of Chapter 1. It provides a perspective on how software or hardware will need to scale during the coming decades. Chapter 1 also introduces topics to be covered in later chapters.

Chapter 2 shows that time is the only safe measure of computer performance. It also relates common measurements used by hardware and software designers to the reliable measurement of time. The material in this chapter motivates the techniques discussed in Chapters 5, 6, and 7 and provides a framework for evaluating them.

Chapter 3 builds on the knowledge of a programming language to derive an assembly language, offering several rules of thumb that guide the designer of the assembly language. We chose the instruction set of a real computer, in this case MIPS, so that real compilers could be used by students to see the code that would be generated. We hide the delayed branch and load until Chapter 6 for pedagogical reasons. Fortunately, the MIPS assembler schedules both delayed branches and loads so the assembly language programmer can ignore these complexities without danger. Readers interested in seeing a very different approach to instruction set design should read Appendix E, which gives a short introduction to the VAX architecture using the same major programming example as in Chapter 3.

Although there is no consensus on what should be covered or what should be skipped in learning about computer arithmetic, we couldn't write Chapter 4 without reaching some conclusions of our own! We understand that the topics and depth of coverage vary greatly from one course to another, sometimes within the same department, depending upon the taste and background of the individual instructor. For example, some instructors feel it's essential that everyone learn multibit Booth algorithms, while others will skip signed multiplication. Our solution is to introduce all the central ideas in the chapter and to provide additional background for more advanced topics in the exercises. This allows one instructor to cover more advanced topics and assign exercises based on them, while another instructor may skip the material.

Chapters 5 and 6 show a realistic example of a processor in detail. Most readers appreciate having a real example to study, and a complete example provides the insight needed to see how all the pieces of a processor fit together for a pipelined and nonpipelined machine. To facilitate skipping some details on hardware implementation of control, we have included much of this material in Appendix C.

Just as Chapters 2 through 6 provide important background for readers with an interest in compilers, Chapters 7 and 8 provide vital background to anyone pursuing further work in operating systems or databases. Chapter 7 describes the principles of memory hierarchies, focusing on the commonality between virtual memory and caching. Chapter 7 emphasizes the role of the operating system and its interaction with the memory system.

Topics as diverse as operating systems, databases, graphics, and networking require an understanding of I/O systems organization as well as the major technical characteristics of devices that influence this organization. Chapter 8 focuses on the topic of how I/O systems are organized starting with bus organizations, working up to communication between the processor and I/O device, and finally to the management role of the operating system. While we emphasize the interfacing issues, especially between hardware and software, several other important topics are introduced. Many of these topics are useful not only in computer organization but as background in other areas. For example, the handshaking protocol, used to interface asynchronous I/O devices, has applications in any distributed system.

For some readers, this book may be their only overview of computer systems, so we have included a survey of parallel processing. Rather than the traditional catalog of characteristics for many parallel machines, we have tried to describe the underlying principles that will drive the designs of parallel processors for the next decade. This section includes a small running example to show different versions of the same program for different parallel architectures.

Because the book is intended as an introduction for readers with a variety of interests, we tried to keep the presentation flexible. The appendices on assembly language and logic design are one of the principle vehicles to allow such flexibility, as these are easily skipped by more advanced readers. The presence of the appendices has made it possible to use this book in a course that mixes EE and CS majors with fairly different backgrounds in logic design and software.

Assembly language programming is best learned by doing and in many cases will be done with the use of the simulator available with this book. Because of this, we invited Jim Larus, the creator of the SPIM simulator, to join us as a contributor of Appendix A. Appendix A describes the SPIM simulator and provides further details of the MIPS assembly language. In addition, it describes assemblers and linkers, which handle the translation of assembly language programs to executable machine language.

The logic design appendix is intended as a supplement to the material on computer organization rather than a comprehensive introduction to logic design. While many EE students in a computer organization course will have already had a course on logic design or digital electronics, we have found that CS majors in many institutions have not had much exposure to this area. The first few sections of Appendix B provide the necessary background. We include some material, such as the organization of memories and finite state machine control of a processor, in the mainstream material, since it is crucial to understanding computer organization.

Selection of Material

If you had no prior background and wanted to read from cover-to-cover, the following order makes sense: Chapters 1 and 2, Appendix D (if needed), Chapter 3, Appendices A and E, Chapter 4, Appendix B, Chapter 5, Appendix C, Chapters 6, 7, 8, and 9. Clearly, most readers skip material. We have worked to provide readers with flexibility in their approach to the material, without making the discussions redundant. The chapters have been written as self-contained units with cross-references to other chapters when related text or figures should be considered. The book has been used successfully in a variety of Beta courses with different goals and student backgrounds. Specific choice of materials as well as the sequence of presentation varied significantly among the Beta sites. Table 1 samples some of these differences.

Students	EE/CS soph/jr	CS jr/sr	CS soph/jr	EE sr/gr	EE/CS jr/sr	EE/CS jr/sr
Prerequisites	HLL	Assembly	Assembly HLL	Assembly Some logic	Assembly Digital fund.	Assembly Digital design
Term (in weeks)	10	14	15	10	16	10
1 Introduction	1	—	2	1	Reference	1
2 Performance	2	—	3	2	Reference	2
3 Instructions	3 (p)	4 (p)	4	3	1	3 (p)
4 Arithmetic	4	2	6	4	2/6	4
5 Processor	5	3	7	5 (p)	3/5	5
6 Pipelining	6	5	8 (p)	6	7	6
7 Memory	7	6	9	7	8	7
8 I/O	8	7	10	8	9	8 (p)
9 Parallel		8	11	9 (p)		
A Assembly	3	Reference				
B Logic	Reference	1	5			
C Control	Reference				4	
Other topics	VAX (App E)		1 C language		RISC machines	

Table 1 (p) = partial coverage or cursory. Numbers refer to the sequence of chapter coverage. Numbers separated by / indicates chapter was covered in parts out of sequence.

Concluding Remarks

In our last book we alternated the gender of a pronoun chapter by chapter. In this book we believe we have removed all such pronouns, except of course for specific people.

If you read the following acknowledgement section, you will see that we went to great lengths to correct mistakes. Since a book goes through many printings, we have the opportunity to make even more corrections. If you uncover any remaining, resilient bugs, please contact the publisher by electronic mail at errors@cs.berkeley.edu or by low-tech mail using the address found on the copyright page. The first person to report a technical error will be awarded a $1.00 bounty upon its implementation in future printings of the book!

Finally, like the last book there is no strict ordering of the authors' names. About half the time you will see Hennessy and Patterson, both in this book and in advertisements, and half the time you will see Patterson and Hennessy. You'll even find it listed both ways in bibliographic publications such as *Books In Print*. This again reflects the true collaborative nature of this book: Together we brainstormed about the ideas and method of presentation, then individually wrote about one-half of the chapters and acted as reviewer for every draft of the other. The page count suggests we again wrote almost exactly the same number of pages. Thus, we equally share the blame for what you are about to read.

Acknowledgements

We wish first to acknowledge the encouragement and suggestions offered by the readers of *Computer Architecture: A Quantitative Approach* and the reviewers of the proposal originally produced for this book. We would not have written this book without their support and directions.

Before we started this book, we received valuable comments on an outline of our ideas from

Alan Berenbaum, AT&T; **Douglas W. Clark**, Digital Equipment Corporation/Princeton University; **David Culler**, University of California at Berkeley; **Stephen J. Hartley**, University of Texas at San Antonio; **Monica Lam**, Stanford; **Daniel McCrackin**, McMaster University; **William R. Michalson**, Worcester Polytechnic Institute; **Yuval Tamir**, University of California at Los Angeles; **Philip A. Wilsey**, University of Cincinnati

The early comments from these reviewers convinced us that there was a need for a book with the goals we have used for this effort.

We'd like to express our appreciation to **Jim Larus** for his willingness in contributing his expertise on assembly language programming, as well as for welcoming readers of this book to use the simulator he developed and maintains at the University of Wisconsin.

Thanks go to about 50 students at Berkeley taking CS 152 during Spring semester 1992 and about 80 students at Stanford taking CS 182 during Winter Quarter 1992 for debugging the alpha version of the text. Professors **John**

Wawrzynek and **John Hennessy** taught the two courses. **Jeff Kuskin**, who served as the teaching assistant at Stanford, provided valuable advice and generated the original versions of a number of exercises that appear in this book.

In addition to the student comments, we appreciate the feedback from these reviewers of the alpha version:

> **Alan Berenbaum**, AT&T; **Douglas W. Clark**, Digital Equipment Corporation/Princeton University; **Rajan Chandra**, California State Polytechnic University at Pomona; **Edward W. Czeck**, Northeastern University; **Chris Edmondson**, Yurkanan University of Texas at Austin; **Robert Fowler**, University of Rochester; **Gideon Frieder**, George Washington University (Chapter 1); **Mark Hill**, University of Wisconsin at Madison; **Kai Li**, Princeton University; **Bart Locanthi**, AT&T (Chapter 8); **David Meyer**, Purdue University; **William R. Michalson**, Worcester Polytechnic Institute; **Mark Smotherman**, Clemson University ; **Evan Tick**, University of Oregon (careful review of figures); **Shlomo Weiss**, Tel Aviv University (Chapter 8); **Alan Zaring**, Ohio Wesleyan University (Chapter 9 and Appendix B)

Mark Smotherman's comments on the role of assembly language were especially helpful in deciding how to deal with this topic. Many of the reviewers provided helpful suggestions for exercises. **William Kahn** of UC Berkeley provided the material for the history section for the computer arithmetic chapter.

The Beta reviewers included:

> **David Douglas**, Thinking Machines (Chapter 9); **Alan Fekete**, University of Sydney; **Corinna Lee**, University of Toronto; **William R. Michalson** Worcester Polytechnic Institute; **Ned Okie**, Radford University; **Klaus Erik Schauser**, University of California at Berkeley; **Guri Sohi**, University of Wisconsin at Madison (Chapter 9); **Arun Somani**, University of Washington; **Philp Tromovitch**, SUNY at Stony Brook; **David Ward**, Brigham Young University; **James Van Orman**, Brigham Young University (who provided extensive figure review both in the Beta and for the final edition)

Special thanks go to **Doug Clark** for his inputs on both the Alpha and Beta versions. As with *Computer Architecture*, Doug provided a wealth of comments to us. His insights, as well as his persistence in urging us to simplify and improve the pedagogy, are deeply appreciated.

The Beta Edition was released for class testing in the Fall of 1992 by the following instructors and institutions:

> **Rajendra Boppana**, University of Texas at San Antonio; **Barry S. Fagin,** Dartmouth; **Michael Faiman**, Univ. of Illinois, Urbana–Champaign; **Mark A. Friedman,** Trinity College; **Anoop Gupta**, Stanford University; **Brian Harvey**, University of California at Berkeley; **Roy Jenevein**, University of Texas at Austin; **Corinna Lee**, University of Toronto; **Ned Okie**, Radford University; **Parameswaran Ramanathan,** University of Wisconsin at Madison; **Arun K. Somani,** University of Washington; **David M. Ward,** Brigham Young University; **John Wawrzynek,** University of California at Berkeley

We appreciate their adventurous spirit and thank them for their comments which helped improve the final text. We are especially appreciative to **Brian Harvey**, **Corinna Lee**, and **Ned Okie** for their extensive comments and to the students at Berkeley, Brigham Young, Radford, and Toronto for being especially diligent in completing their surveys. The surveys had an enormous impact on the first edition of this book. The teaching assistants at these institutions played a valuable role by collecting and forwarding surveys, as well as by providing feedback on sections or exercises that proved difficult for their classes. **Scott Bevan** at Brigham Young was especially helpful in getting comments and surveys back.

Many students reported bugs in the Beta Edition. Their comments were especially helpful. We would like to thank a group of students who were very diligent in finding and rapidly reporting bugs. These students were the first to report the greatest number of bugs:

> **Ernest Bailey**, Brigham Young University; **Wallace Chan**, University of Toronto; **Isaac Cheng**, University of California at Berkeley; **Jeff Clark**, Radford University; **Moored Fahim**, Radford University; **Xilin Jai**, Dartmouth College; **Guy Lemieux**, University of Toronto; **Cameron McNairy**, Brigham Young University; **Jose L. Urrusti**, University of Wisconsin; **James Van Orman**, Brigham Young University (who was the first reporter of 34 different bugs!); **John Yen**, University of California at Berkeley

We started writing this book in the Fall of 1991 and raced to stay ahead of the classes at Berkeley and Stanford that began in January. We completed the final chapter of the alpha edition in April 1992. After taking time to catch up with our postponed obligations, and to attend the Computer Architecture conference in Australia, we started the Beta Edition in late May, completing our revisions in July for the September printing. Inspired by comments on the Beta Edition from the classroom, we started writing again in October and finished in January 1993.

We wish to thank the extended Morgan Kaufmann family for agreeing to publish this book twice, under the able leadership of **Bruce Spatz** and the watchful eye of **Yonie Overton**. Composition, color separation, and postscript programming were provided by **Ed Sznyter** of Babel Press. **Ross Carron** designed the text. **Alexander Teshin Associates** served as the art source. **Gary Morris** was copyeditor and **Steve Rath** compiled the index. **David Lance Goines** joined us once more as the cover designer. We would also like to thank **Steve Hiatt**, **Sandra Popovich**, and **Sharilyn Hovind** for their contributions to the Beta Edition of the book.

David A. Patterson   **John L. Hennessy**

January 1993

The SPIM Simulator for the MIPS R2000/R3000

James R. Larus
University of Wisconsin

The SPIM S20 is a software simulator that runs assembly language programs for the MIPS R2000/R3000 RISC computers. SPIM can run files containing assembly language statements and read and run MIPS a.out files (when compiled and running on a system containing a MIPS processor). It is a self-contained system for running these programs and contains a debugger and interface to the operating system. SPIM is portable; it has run on a DECStation 3100/5100, Sun 3, Sun 4, PC/RT, IBM RS/6000, HP Bobcat, HP Snake, and Sequent. Students can generate code for a simple, clean, orthogonal computer, regardless of the machine used. SPIM comes with complete source code and documentation of all instructions.

SPIM has a simple terminal style and a flashy X-windows interface. SPIM also includes an optional extension by Anne Rogers and Scott Rosenberg of Princeton that performs a cycle-by-cycle MIPS simulation that exposes the hardware pipeline. Contact Morgan Kaufmann for information on available UNIX, Windows, and Macintosh formats.

Retrieval of the SPIM by FTP

spim and xspim are available for anonymous ftp from ftp.cs.wisc.edu in the file pub/spim/spim.tar.Z (which is a compressed tar file).

For those unfamiliar with anonymous ftp, here are the steps to follow to get a copy of spim and xspim:

1. ftp to ftp.cs.wisc.edu from your computer:

   % ftp ftp.cs.wisc.edu

2. The ftp server will respond and ask you to login. login as anonymous and use your email address as a password:

   Name (ftp.cs.wisc.edu:larus): anonymous
   331 Guest login ok, send login or email address as password
   Password:

3. The server will then print a welcome message. Change to the directory containing spim:

ftp> cd pub/spim

4. Set binary mode for the transfer (since the file is compressed):

ftp> binary

5. Copy the file to your machine:

ftp> get spim.tar.Z

6. Exit the ftp program:

ftp> quit

7. Uncompress and untar the file:

% uncompress spim.tar.Z
% tar xvf spim.tar

If the uncompression fails, you probably forgot to set binary (step 4). Try again. Read the directions in the file README.

Computer
Abstractions
and Technology

*Civilization advances by extending
the number of important operations
which we can perform without
thinking about them.*

Alfred North Whitehead
An Introduction to Mathematics, 1911

1.1 Introduction

Welcome to this book! We're delighted to have this opportunity to convey the excitement of the world of computer systems. This is not a dry and dreary field, where progress is glacial and where new ideas atrophy from neglect. No! Computer systems have a vital and synergistic relationship to an important industry—responsible for 5% to 10% of the gross national product of the United States—and this unusual industry embraces innovation at a breathtaking rate. In the last decade there have been a half-dozen new machines whose introduction appeared to revolutionize the computing industry; these revolutions were cut short only because someone else built an even better computer.

This race to innovate has led to unprecedented progress since computing's inception in the late 1940s. Had the transportation industry kept pace with the computer industry, for example, today we could travel coast to coast in 30 seconds for 50 cents. Take just a moment to contemplate how such an improvement would change society—living in Tahiti while working in San Francisco, going to Moscow for an evening at the Bolshoi ballet—and you can appreciate the implications of such a change.

Computers have led to a third revolution for civilization, with the information revolution taking its place alongside the agricultural and the industrial revolutions. The resulting multiplication of humankind's intellectual strength and reach naturally has affected the sciences as well. There is now a new vein of scientific investigation, with computational scientists joining theoretical and experimental scientists in the exploration of new frontiers in astronomy, biology, chemistry, physics, ...

The computer revolution continues. Each time the cost of computing improves by another factor of 10, the opportunities for computers multiply. Applications that were economically infeasible suddenly become practical. In the recent past, the following applications were "computer science fiction."

- *Automatic teller machines:* A computer placed in the wall of banks to distribute and collect cash was a ridiculous concept in the 1950s, when the cheapest computer cost at least $500,000 and was the size of a car.

- *Computers in automobiles:* Until microprocessors improved dramatically in price and performance in the early 1980s, computer control of cars was ludicrous. Today, computers reduce pollution and improve fuel efficiency via engine controls and increase safety through the prevention of dangerous skids and through the inflation of air bags to protect occupants in a crash.

- *Laptop computers:* Who would have dreamed that advances in computer systems would lead to laptop computers, allowing students to bring computers to coffeehouses and on airplanes?

- *Human genome project:* The cost of computer equipment to map human DNA sequences in the 1990s will be hundreds of millions of dollars. It's unlikely that anyone would have considered this project had the computer costs been 10 to 100 times higher, as they would have been 10 to 20 years ago.

Such hardware advances have allowed programmers to create infinitely useful software, and explain why computers are omnipresent. Today's science fiction computer applications include electronic libraries, the cashless society, automated intelligent highways, and genuinely ubiquitous computing—a pervasiveness which precludes the need to carry computers because they will be everywhere. Clearly, advances in this technology now affect almost every aspect of our society.

Successful programmers have always been concerned about the performance of their programs, because getting results to the user quickly is critical in creating successful software. In the 1960s and 1970s, a primary constraint on computer performance was the size of the computer's memory. Thus programmers often followed a simple credo: Minimize memory space to make programs fast. In the last decade advances in computer design and memory technology have greatly reduced the importance of small memory size. Programmers interested in performance now need to understand the issues that have replaced the simple memory model of the 1960s: the hierarchical nature of memories and the parallel nature of processors. Programmers who seek to build competitive versions of compilers, operating systems, databases, and even applications will therefore need to increase their knowledge of computer organization.

We are honored to have the opportunity to explain what's inside this revolutionary machine, unraveling the software below your program and the hardware under the covers of your computer. By the time you finish this book, you will understand the secrets of programming a computer in its native tongue, the internal organization of computers and how it affects performance of your programs, and even how you would go about designing a computer of your own.

This first chapter lays the foundation for the rest of the book. It introduces the basic ideas and definitions, places the major components of software and hardware in perspective, and introduces integrated circuits, the technology that fuels the computer revolution.

1.2   Below Your Program

In Paris they simply stared when I spoke to them in French; I never did succeed in making those idiots understand their own language.

Mark Twain, *The Innocents Abroad,* 1869

To actually speak to an electronic machine, you need to send electrical signals. The easiest signals for machines to understand are *on* and *off,* and so the machine alphabet is just two letters. Just as the 26 letters of the English alphabet do not limit how much can be written, the two letters of the computer alphabet do not limit what computers can do. The two symbols for these two letters are the numbers 0 and 1, and we commonly think of the machine language as numbers in base 2, or *binary numbers.* We refer to each "letter" as a *binary digit* or *bit.* Computers are slaves to our commands; hence, the name for an individual command is *instruction.* Instructions, which are just collections of bits that the computer understands, can be thought of as numbers. For example, the bits

```
1000110010100000
```

tell one computer to add two numbers. Chapter 3 explains why we use numbers for instructions *and* data; we don't want to steal that chapter's thunder, but using numbers for both instructions and data is a foundation of computing.

The first programmers communicated to computers in binary numbers, but this was so tedious that they quickly invented new notations that were closer to the way humans think. At first these notations were translated to binary by hand, but this process was still tiresome. Using the machine to help program the machine, the pioneers invented programs to translate from symbolic notation to binary. The first of these programs was named an *assembler*. This program translates a symbolic version of an instruction into the binary version. For example, the programmer would write

```
add A,B
```

and the assembler would translate this notation into

```
1000110010100000
```

This instruction tells the computer to add the two numbers A and B. The name coined for this symbolic language, still used today, is *assembly language*.

Although a tremendous improvement, assembly language is still far from the notation a scientist might like to use to simulate fluid flow or that an accountant might use to balance the books. Assembly language requires the programmer to write one line for every instruction that the machine will follow, forcing the programmer to think like the machine.

Such low-level thinking inspired a simple question: If we can write a program to translate from assembly language to binary instructions to simplify programming, what prevents us from writing a program that translates from some higher level notation down to assembly language?

The answer was: nothing. Although more challenging to create than an assembler, this higher level translator was plausible.

Programmers today owe their productivity, and their sanity, to this observation. Programs that accept this more natural notation are called *compilers*, and the languages they *compile* are called *high-level programming languages*. They enable a programmer to write this high-level language statement:

```
A + B
```

The compiler would compile it into this assembly language statement:

```
add A,B
```

The assembler would translate this statement into the binary instruction that tells the computer to add the two numbers A and B:

```
1000110010100000
```

Figure 1.1 shows the relationships among these programs and languages.

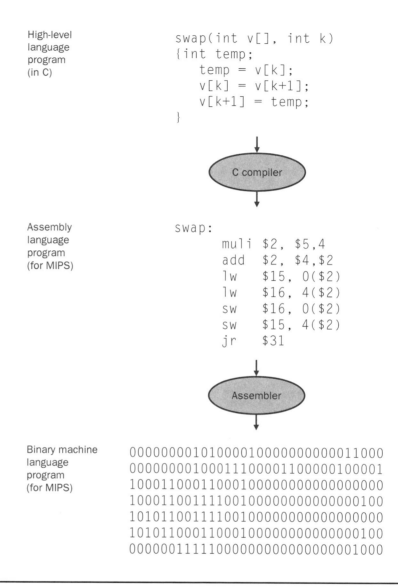

High-level
language
program
(in C)

```
swap(int v[], int k)
{int temp;
    temp = v[k];
    v[k] = v[k+1];
    v[k+1] = temp;
}
```

C compiler

Assembly
language
program
(for MIPS)

```
swap:
    muli $2, $5,4
    add  $2, $4,$2
    lw   $15, 0($2)
    lw   $16, 4($2)
    sw   $16, 0($2)
    sw   $15, 4($2)
    jr   $31
```

Assembler

Binary machine
language
program
(for MIPS)

```
00000000101000010000000000011000
00000000100011100001100000100001
10001100011000100000000000000000
10001100111100100000000000000100
10101100111100100000000000000000
10101100011000100000000000000100
00000011111000000000000000001000
```

FIGURE 1.1   C program compiled into assembly language and then assembled into binary machine language. Although the translation from high-level language to binary machine language is shown in two steps, some compilers cut out the middleman and produce binary machine language directly. These languages and this program are examined in more detail in Chapter 3.

High-level programming languages offer several important benefits. First, they allow the programmer to think in a more natural language, using English words and algebraic notation, resulting in programs that look much more like text than like tables of cryptic symbols (see Figure 1.1). Moreover, they allow languages to be designed according to their intended use. Hence, Fortran was designed for scientific computation, Cobol for business data processing, Lisp for symbol manipulation, and so on. The second advantage of programming languages is improved programmer productivity. One of the few areas of widespread agreement in software development is that it takes less time to develop programs when they are written in languages that require fewer lines to express an idea. Conciseness is a clear advantage of high-level languages over assembly language. The final advantage is that programming languages allow programs to be independent of the computer on which they were developed, since compilers and assemblers can translate high-level language programs to the binary instructions of any machine. These advantages are so strong that today little programming is done in assembly language.

As programming matured, many of its practitioners saw that reusing programs was much more efficient than writing everything from scratch. Hence programmers began to pool potentially widely used routines into libraries. One of the first of these *subroutine libraries* was for inputting and outputting data, which included, for example, routines to control printers, such as ensuring paper is in the printer before printing can begin. Such software controlled other input/output devices, such as magnetic disks, magnetic tapes, and displays. It soon became apparent that a set of programs could be run more efficiently if there was a separate program that supervised running those programs. As soon as one program completed, the supervising program would start the next program in the queue, thereby avoiding delays. These supervising programs, which soon included the input/output subroutine libraries, are the basis for what we call *operating systems* today. Operating systems are programs that manage the resources of a computer for the benefit of the programs that run on that machine.

Software came to be categorized by its use. Software that provides services that are commonly useful is called *systems software*. Operating systems, compilers, and assemblers are examples of systems software. In contrast to programs aimed at programmers, *applications software* or just *applications* is the name given to programs aimed at computer users, such as spreadsheets or text editors. Figure 1.2 shows the classical drawing mapping the hierarchical layers of software and hardware.

This simplified view has some problems. Should we really place compilers in the systems software level in Figure 1.2? Compilers produce programs at both the applications *and* the systems level, and applications programs don't normally call on the compiler while they are running. A more realistic view of the nature of systems appears in Figure 1.3. It shows that software does not

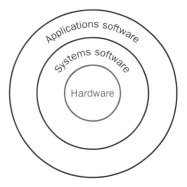

FIGURE 1.2 A simplified view of hardware and software as hierarchical layers, classically shown as concentric rings building up from the core of hardware to the software closest to the user.

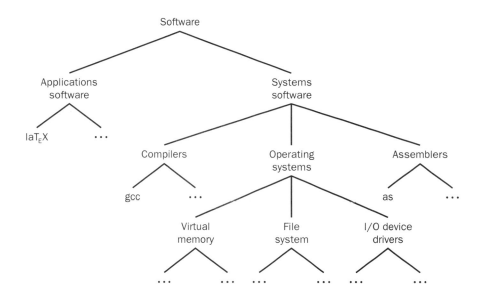

FIGURE 1.3 An example of the decomposability of computer systems. The terms in the middle of the chart, such as LaT$_E$X and gcc, are examples of Unix programs. The terms lower in the chart, such as virtual memory, will be introduced in Chapters 7 and 8.

consist of monolithic layers, but is composed of many programs that build on one another. Like the strands of a thick rope, each time you look carefully at what appears to be a single strand you find it is really composed of many finer components.

1.3   Under the Covers

Now that we have looked below your program to uncover the underlying software, let's open the covers of the computer to learn about the underlying hardware.

Figure 1.4 shows a typical workstation with keyboard, mouse, screen, and a box containing even more hardware. What is not visible in the photograph is a network that connects the workstation to printers and disks. This photograph reveals two of the key components of computers: *input devices*, such as the keyboard and mouse, and *output devices*, such as the screen and printers. As the names suggest, input feeds the computer and output is the result of computation sent to the user. Some devices, such as networks and disks, provide both input and output to the computer.

Chapter 8 describes input/output (I/O) devices in more detail, but let's take an introductory tour through the computer hardware, starting with the external I/O devices.

Anatomy of a Mouse

I got the idea for the mouse while attending a talk at a computer conference. The speaker was so boring that I started daydreaming and hit upon the idea.

Doug Engelbart

Although many users now take mice for granted, the idea of a pointing device such as a mouse is less than 30 years old. Engelbart showed the first demonstration of a system with a mouse on a research prototype in 1967. The Alto, which was the inspiration for all workstations as well as for the Macintosh, included a mouse as its pointing device in 1973. By the 1980s, all workstations and many personal computers included this device, and new user interfaces based on graphics displays and mice became popular. The mouse is actually quite simple, as the photograph in Figure 1.5 shows.

The mechanical version consists of a large ball that is mounted in such a way that it makes contact with a pair of wheels, one positioned on the *x*-axis and the other on the *y*-axis. These wheels either turn mechanical counters or turn a slotted wheel, through which a light-emitting diode (LED) shines on a

FIGURE 1.4 Photograph of a workstation. The cathode ray tube (CRT) screen is the primary output device, and the keyboard and mouse are the primary input devices. Photo courtesy of Silicon Graphics.

FIGURE 1.5 Photograph of the inside of a mechanical mouse. Mouse courtesy of Logitech.

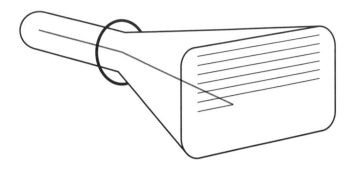

FIGURE 1.6   A CRT display. A beam is shot by an electronic gun through the vacuum onto a phosphor-coated screen. The steering coil at the neck of the CRT aims the gun. Raster scan systems, used in television and in almost all computers, paint the screen a line at a time as a series of dots, or pixels. The screen is refreshed 30 to 60 times per second.

photosensor. In either scheme, moving the mouse rolls the large ball, which turns the x-wheel or the y-wheel or both, depending on whether the mouse is moved in the vertical, horizontal, or diagonal direction. Although there are many styles of interfaces for these pointing devices, moving each wheel essentially increments or decrements counters somewhere in the system. The counters serve to record how far the mouse has moved and in which direction.

Through the Looking Glass

Through computer displays I have landed an airplane on the deck of a moving carrier, observed a nuclear particle hit a potential well, flown in a rocket at nearly the speed of light and watched a computer reveal its innermost workings.

Ivan Sutherland, the "father" of computer graphics, quoted in "Computer Software for Graphics," *Scientific American*, 1984

The most fascinating I/O device is probably the graphics display. Based on television technology, a *raster cathode ray tube* (CRT) *display* scans an image one line at a time, 30 to 60 times per second (Figure 1.6). At this *refresh rate*, few people notice a flicker on the screen. The image is composed of a matrix of picture elements, or *pixels*, which can be represented as a matrix of bits, called a *bit map*. Depending on the size of screen and resolution, the display matrix ranges in size from 512×340 to 1560×1280 pixels. The simplest display has 1 bit per pixel, allowing it to be black or white. For displays that support over 100 different shades of black and white, sometimes called *gray-scale* displays, 8 bits per pixel are required. A color display might use 8 bits for

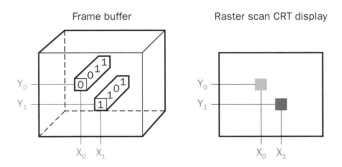

FIGURE 1.7 Each coordinate in the frame buffer on the left determines the shade of the corresponding coordinate for the raster scan CRT display on the right. Pixel (X_0,Y_0) contains the bit pattern 0011, which is a lighter shade of gray on the screen than the bit pattern 1101 in pixel (X_1,Y_1).

each of the three primary colors (red, blue, and green), for 24 bits per pixel, permitting millions of different colors to be displayed.

The hardware support for graphics consists mainly of a *raster refresh buffer*, or *frame buffer*, to store the bit map. The image to be represented on-screen is stored in the frame buffer, and the bit pattern per pixel is read out to the graphics display at the refresh rate. Figure 1.7 shows a frame buffer with 4 bits per pixel.

The goal of the bit map is to faithfully represent what is on the screen. The challenges in graphics systems arise because the human eye is very good at detecting even subtle changes on the screen. For example, when the screen is being updated, the eye can detect the inconsistency between the portion of the screen that has changed and that which hasn't.

Opening the Box

If we open the box containing the computer, we see a fascinating board of thin green plastic, covered with dozens of small gray or black rectangles. Figure 1.8 shows the contents of the workstation in Figure 1.4. The board is shown vertically on the left, with a tape reader and floppy disk drive shown on the right. The small rectangles on the board contain the devices that drive our advancing technology, *integrated circuits* or *chips*. The board is composed of three pieces: the piece connecting to the I/O devices mentioned above, the memory, and the processor. The *memory* is where the programs are kept when they are running; it also contains the data needed by the running programs. In Figure 1.8, memory is found on the eight small boards that are attached

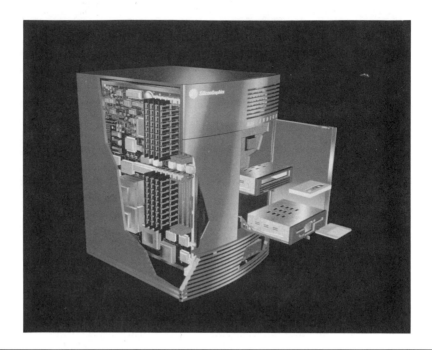

FIGURE 1.8 Inside a workstation. An exploded view of a workstation. The vertical board on the left is a printed cicuit board (PC board) that contains most of the electronics of the computer; Figure 1.11 is an overhead photograph of that board, rotated 90 degrees. The eight small boards attached to the main board contain the memory chips. The processor is below the memory boards; Figure 1.18 is a photograph of the processor. To the right of the PC board in this workstation is a tape reader and a floppy disk drive. Photo courtesy of Silicon Graphics.

perpendicularly toward the front of the large board. Each small memory board contains 18 integrated circuits. The *processor* is the active part of the board, following the instructions of the programs to the letter. It adds numbers, tests numbers, signals I/O devices to activate, and so on. Occasionally, people call the processor the *CPU*, for the more bureaucratic sounding *central processor unit*. The processor is the large square below the bottom memory boards and to the left in Figure 1.8.

Descending even lower into the hardware, Figure 1.9 reveals details of the processor in Figure 1.8. The processor comprises two main components: datapath and control, the respective brawn and brain of the processor. The *datapath* performs the arithmetic operations, and *control* tells the datapath, memory, and I/O devices what to do according to the wishes of the instructions of the program. Chapters 4 and 5 explain the datapath and control for a straightforward implementation, and Chapter 6 describes the changes needed for a higher performance design.

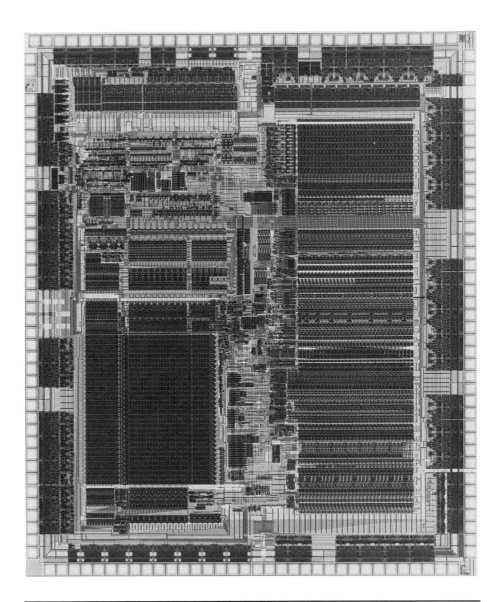

FIGURE 1.9 Inside the processor chip used on the board shown in Figure 1.8. The right-hand side of the chip is the datapath. The upper-left-hand side is the control unit. The lower left contains the portion of the memory system called the Translation Lookaside Buffer, which we discuss in Chapter 7. This chip is called the MIPS R3000. Photo courtesy of MIPS Technology, Inc.

We have now identified the major components of any computer. When we come to an important point in this book, a point so important that we hope you will remember it forever, we emphasize it by identifying it as a "Big Picture" item. We have about a dozen Big Pictures in this book, with the first being the five components of a computer.

The Big Picture

The five classic components of a computer are input, output, memory, datapath, and control, with the last two sometimes combined and called the processor. Figure 1.10 shows the standard organization of a computer. This organization is independent of hardware technology: You can place every piece of every computer, past and present, into one of these five categories.

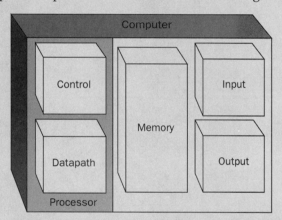

FIGURE 1.10   The organization of a computer, showing the five classic components. The processor gets instructions and data from memory; input writes data to memory, and output reads data from memory. Control sends the signals that determine the operations of the datapath, memory, input, and output.

Descending into the depths of any component of the hardware reveals insights into the machine. We have done this for the processor, so let's try memory. The board in Figure 1.11 contains two kinds of memories: DRAM and cache. *DRAM* stands for *dynamic random access memory*. Several DRAMs are used together to contain the instructions and data of a program. In contrast to sequential access memories such as magnetic tapes, the *RAM* portion of the term DRAM means that memory accesses take the same amount of time no matter what portion of the memory is read. *Cache* memory consists of a small,

FIGURE 1.11 Close-up of workstation processor board. This board uses the MIPS R4000 processor, which is located on the right edge of the board in the middle. The R4000 contains high-speed cache memories on the processor chip. The main memory is contained on the small boards that are perpendicular to the motherboard in the upper left corner. The DRAM chips are mounted on these boards (called *SIMMs* for Single In-line Memory Module) and then plugged into the connectors. The connectors at the bottom of the photograph are for external I/O devices, such as the network (Ethernet), keyboard, and CRT display. Photo courtesy of Silicon Graphics.

fast memory that acts as a buffer for the DRAM memory. (The nontechnical definition of *cache* is a safe place for hiding things.)

The careful reader may have noticed a common theme in both the software and the hardware descriptions: delving into the depths of hardware or software reveals more information or, conversely, lower level details are hidden to offer a simpler model at higher levels. The use of such layers or *abstractions* is a principal technique for designing very sophisticated computer systems.

One of the most important abstractions is the interface between the hardware and the lowest level software. Because of its importance, it is given a special name: the *instruction set architecture*, or simply *architecture*, of a machine. The instruction set architecture includes anything programmers need to know to make a binary machine language program work correctly, including instructions, I/O devices, and so on. (The components of an architecture are discussed in Chapters 3, 4, 7, and 8.)

This standardized interface allows computer designers to talk about functions independently from the hardware that performs them. For example, we can talk about the functions of a digital clock—keeping time, displaying the time, setting the alarm—independently from the clock hardware—quartz crystal, LED displays, plastic buttons. Computer designers distinguish architecture from an *implementation* of an architecture along the same lines: an implementation is hardware that obeys the architecture abstraction. These ideas bring us to another Big Picture.

The Big Picture

Both hardware and software consist of hierarchical layers, with each lower layer hiding details from the level above. This principle of *abstraction* is the way both hardware designers and software designers cope with the complexity of computer systems. One key interface between the levels of abstraction is the *instruction set architecture*: the interface between the hardware and low-level software. This abstract interface enables many *implementations* of varying cost and performance to run identical software.

A Safe Place for Data

I think Silicon Valley was misnamed. If you look back at the dollars shipped in products in the last decade, there has been more revenue from magnetic disks than from silicon. They ought to rename the place Iron Oxide Valley.

Al Hoagland, one of the pioneers of magnetic disks, 1982

Thus far we have seen how to input data, compute using the data, and display data. If we were to lose power to the computer, however, everything would be lost, because the memory inside the computer is *volatile*; that is, it forgets when it loses power. In contrast, a cassette tape for a stereo doesn't forget the recorded music when you turn off the power. This is because the tape is magnetic and is thus a *nonvolatile* memory technology. To distinguish between the memory used to hold programs while they are running and this nonvolatile memory used to store programs between runs, the term *primary memory* or *main memory* is used for the former and *secondary memory* for the latter. The DRAMs of Figure 1.11 are the main memory of that computer.

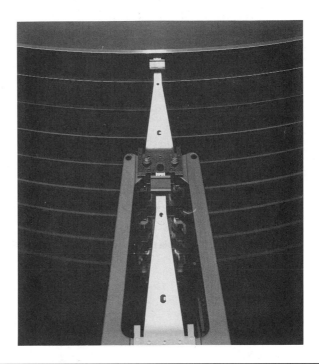

FIGURE 1.12 Photograph of a disk showing ten disk platters and the read/write heads.
Photo courtesy of Storage Technology Corp.

Magnetic disks have dominated secondary memory since 1965. As Figure 1.12 shows, a magnetic hard disk consists of a collection of platters, which rotate on a spindle at 3600 to 5400 revolutions per minute. The metal platters are covered with magnetic recording material on both sides, similar to the material found on a cassette tape. Disk diameters vary by a factor of 10, and have been shrinking over the years. They range from 10.25 to 1.3 inches, with disks of less than 1 inch in diameter to be available in the near future. Traditionally, the widest disks have the highest performance, and the smallest disks have the lowest cost. To read and write information, a movable *arm* containing a small electromagnetic coil called a *read/write head* is located just above each surface. The use of mechanical components means that access times for magnetic disks are much slower than for DRAMs: disks typically take 5 to 20 milliseconds, while DRAMs take 50 to 150 nanoseconds—making DRAMs about 100,000 times faster.

There are two major types of magnetic disks: floppy disks and hard disks. The basic concept at work in these disks is the same: a rotating platter coated with a magnetic recording material. The primary differences arise because the floppy disk is made of a mylar substance that is flexible, while the hard disk uses metal. Floppy disks can be removed and carried around, while most hard disks today are not removable. Another removable medium is magnetic tape, which is cheaper than magnetic disks but slower still: It can take seconds to find data on a magnetic tape.

In conclusion, the primary characteristics of magnetic disks versus main memory are

- Nonvolatility, because they are magnetic.

- Slower access time, because they are mechanical devices.

- Lower cost for the same storage capacity, because the production costs for a given amount of storage are lower than for integrated circuits.

Communicating to Other Computers

There is an old network saying: Bandwidth problems can be cured with money. Latency problems are harder because the speed of light is fixed—you can't bribe God.

David Clark, MIT

We've explained how we can input, compute, display, and save data, but there is still one missing item found in today's computers: computer networks. Just as the processor shown in Figure 1.10 on page 16 is connected to memory and I/O devices, networks connect whole computers, allowing computer users to extend the power of computing by including communication. Networks have become so popular that they are the backbone of current computer systems; a new machine without an optional network interface would be ridiculed. Networked computers have several major advantages:

- *Communication*: Information is exchanged between computers at high speeds.

- *Resource sharing*: Rather than each machine having its own I/O devices, devices can be shared by computers on the network.

- *Nonlocal access*: By connecting computers over long distances, users need not be near the computer they are using.

Networks vary in length and performance, with the cost of communication increasing according to both the speed of communication and the distance that information travels. Perhaps the most popular network is the *Ethernet*. Its length is limited to about a kilometer, and it takes at least a second to send 1 million bytes of data. The network itself uses the same material that is used to connect households to cable television. Its length and speed makes the Ethernet useful to connect computers on the same floor of a building; hence, it is an example of what is generically called a *local area network*.

1.4 Integrated Circuits: Fueling Innovation

I thought [computers] would be a universally applicable idea, like a book is. But I didn't think it would develop as fast as it did, because I didn't envision we'd be able to get as many parts on a chip as we finally got. The transistor came along unexpectedly. It all happened much faster than we expected.

J. Presper Eckert, co-inventor of ENIAC, speaking in 1991.

Processors and memory have improved at an incredible rate because computer designers have long embraced the latest in electronic technology to try to win the race of designing a better computer. Figure 1.13 shows the technologies that have been used over time, with an estimate of the relative performance per unit cost for each technology. This section explores the technology that has fueled the computer industry since 1975 and will continue to do so for the foreseeable future. Since this technology shapes what computers will be able to do and how quickly they will evolve, we believe all computer professionals should be familiar with the basics of integrated circuits.

A *transistor* is simply an on/off switch controlled by electricity. The *integrated circuit* combined dozens to hundreds of transistors into a single chip. To describe the tremendous increase in the number of transistors from hundreds to millions, the adjectives *very large scale* are added to the term, creating the abbreviation *VLSI* for *very large scale integrated circuit.*

This rate of increasing integration has been remarkably stable. Figure 1.14 shows the growth in DRAM capacity since 1977. The industry has consistently quadrupled capacity every three years, resulting in an increase in excess of 1000 times in just over 15 years! This remarkable rate of advance in cost/performance and capacity of integrated circuits governs the design of hardware *and* software, underscoring the need to understand this technology.Let's start at the beginning. The manufacture of a chip begins with *silicon*, a substance found in sand. Because silicon does not conduct electricity well, it is called a *semiconductor*. With a special chemical process, it is possible to add materials to silicon that allow tiny areas to transform into one of three devices:

- Excellent conductors of electricity (similar to copper or aluminum wire)

- Excellent insulators from electricity (like plastic sheathing or glass)

- Areas that can conduct *or* insulate under special conditions (as a switch)

Transistors fall in the last category. A VLSI circuit, then, is just millions of combinations of conductors, insulators, and switches manufactured in a single, small package.

Year	Technology used in computers	Relative cost/performance
1951	Vacuum tube	1
1965	Transistor	35
1975	Integrated circuit	900
1990	Very large scale integrated circuit	400,000

FIGURE 1.13 Relative cost/performance of technologies used in computers over time.
(Source: Computer Museum, Boston)

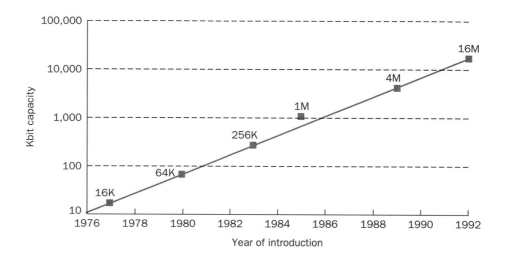

FIGURE 1.14 Growth of capacity per DRAM chip over time. The *y*-axis is measured in K bits, where K = 1024 (2^{10}). The DRAM industry has quadrupled capacity every three years, a 60% increase per year, for more than 15 years. The one exception was the 1M bit DRAM, which arrived a year earlier than expected. This 4×-every-3-years rule of thumb is called the *DRAM growth rule*.

The manufacturing process for integrated circuits is critical to the cost of the chips and hence important to computer designers. The process starts with a silicon crystal ingot, which looks remarkably like a large sausage. Today ingots are between 5 and 8 inches in diameter and about 12 inches long. An ingot is finely sliced into *wafers* no more than 0.1 inch thick. These wafers then go through a series of steps, during which patterns of chemicals are placed on each wafer, creating the transistors, conductors, and insulators discussed above.

A single microscopic flaw in the wafer itself or in one of the dozens of patterning steps can result in that area of the wafer failing. These *defects*, as they

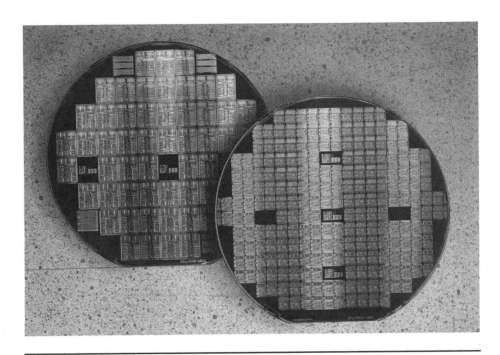

FIGURE 1.15 Photograph of a 6-inch wafer containing MIPS R4000 processors on the left and a 6-inch wafer containing MIPS R3000 processors on the right. The number of R3000 dies per wafer on the right at 100% yield is 210. Each die is 0.8 cm by 0.9 cm and contains about 125,000 transistors. Figure 1.9 on page 15 is a photomicrograph of one of these R3000 dies. The number of R4000 dies per wafer on the left at 100% yield is 59. The die size is 1.5 cm by 1.1 cm, and each die contains about 1.3 million transistors. A close-up of one R4000 die is seen in Figure 1.16. The dozen partially rounded chips at the boundaries of the R3000 wafer are useless; they are included because it's easier to create the masks used to pattern the silicon. The "empty" rectangles in both wafers contain test circuits used to rapidly test the full wafer. The MIPS R4000 wafer has 4 additional test circuits at the "corners." Photo courtesy of IDT.

are called, make it virtually impossible to manufacture a perfect wafer. To cope with imperfection, several strategies have been used, the simplest of which is to place many independent components on a single wafer. The wafer is then chopped up or *diced* into these components, called *dies* or *chips*. Dicing enables you to discard only those dies that were unlucky enough to contain the flaws, rather than the whole wafer. This concept is quantified by the *yield* of a process, which is defined as the percentage of good dies from the total number of dies on the wafer. Figure 1.15 is a photograph of two wafers containing single-chip processors before they have been diced. The wafer on the right contains copies of the chip shown in Figure 1.9. Figure 1.16 shows an individual die of the left-hand wafer. Figures 1.17 and 1.18 (on page 25) show the packaged parts for each die.

FIGURE 1.16 Photograph of an R4000 die. The die size is 1.5 cm by 1.1 cm, and each die contains about 1.3 million transistors. The right-hand side of the die contains the datapath for the integer portion of the processor. The left-hand side contains the datapath for the floating point processor, which we discuss in Chapter 4. The control is in the middle of the die. The two large blocks on the top of the die are the caches, which are discussed in Chapter 7. Photo courtesy of MIPS Technology, Inc.

Note that there are many more of the smaller dies per wafer than the larger dies: There are 210 dies in the 6-inch wafer on the right of Figure 1.15 but only 59 of the larger dies in the wafer on the left. Since a wafer costs about the same

FIGURE 1.17 Photograph of the packaged part of a die in Figure 1.9, the MIPS R3000.
Photo courtesy of MIPS Technology, Inc.

FIGURE 1.18 Photograph of three different versions of the R4000 processor, shown in die form at left. To reduce the cost of the part, a smaller package is used in lower end systems, while a large package is used in servers and multiprocessors. The large package has over 400 pins, while the small has about 150 pins. The pins allow a wider path between the main memory and the processor, allowing faster transfers of data and the addressing of larger memories. Photo courtesy of MIPS Technology, Inc.

no matter what is on it, fewer dies mean higher costs. Costs are increased further because a larger die is much more likely to contain a defect and thus fail to work. Hence die costs rise very fast with increasing die area. (Exercises 1.46 through 1.52 explore wafer costs in more detail.) Clearly, computer designers must be familiar with the technology they are using to be sure that the added cost of larger chips is justified by enhanced performance.

Computer designers must know both hardware *and* software technologies to build competitive computers. Silicon is the medium in which computer designers work, so they must understand the foundations of integrated circuit costs and performance. Designers must also learn the principles of the software that most strongly affect computer hardware, namely, compilers and operating systems.

1.5   Fallacies and Pitfalls

The purpose of a section on fallacies and pitfalls, which will be found in every chapter, is to explain some commonly held misconceptions that you might encounter. We call such misbeliefs *fallacies*. When discussing a fallacy, we try to give a counterexample. We also discuss *pitfalls*, or easily made mistakes. Often pitfalls are generalizations of principles that are true in a limited context. The purpose of these sections is to help you avoid making these mistakes in the machines you may design or use.

Fallacy: Computers have been built in the same, old-fashioned way for far too long, and this antiquated model of computation is running out of steam.

For an antiquated model of computation, it surely is improving quickly. Figure 1.19 plots the top performance per year of workstations between 1987 and 1992. (Chapter 2 explains the proper way to measure performance.) The graph shows a line indicating an improvement of 54% per year. In contrast to the statement above, computers are improving in performance faster today than at any time in their history.

Pitfall: Ignoring the inexorable progress of hardware when planning a new machine.

Suppose you plan to introduce a machine in three years, and you claim the machine will be a terrific seller because it's three times as fast as anything available today. Unfortunately, the machine will probably sell poorly, because the average performance growth rate for the industry will yield machines with the same performance. For example, assuming a 50% yearly growth rate in performance, a machine with performance x today can be expected to have performance $1.5^3 x = 3.4x$ in three years. Your machine would have no per-

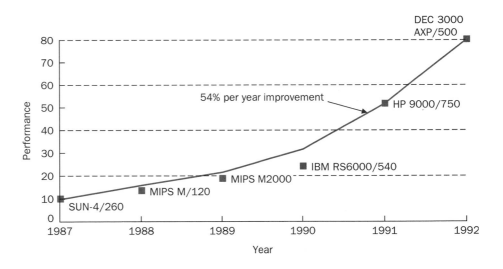

FIGURE 1.19 Performance increase of workstations, 1987–92. Here performance is given as approximately the number of times faster than the VAX-11/780, a commonly used yardstick. The colored line plots a rate of improvement of 54% per year; hence, a performance rating of 10 in one year must be followed by a rating of 15.4 (1.54 × 10) the following year and 23.7 (1.54 × 15.4) the year after. (These performance numbers are for the integer SPEC benchmarks; see Chapter 2, section 2.5 for more details on SPEC.)

formance advantage! Many projects within computer companies are canceled, either because they ignore this rule or because the project is completed late and the performance of the delayed machine is below the industry average. This phenomenon may occur in any industry, but rapid improvements in cost/performance make it a major concern in the computer industry.

Pitfall: Trying to predict price, performance, or price/performance more than five years into the future in this rapidly moving field.

Figure 1.20 is from a 1974 book based on a government study that predicted the cost/performance of computers in the 1980s. Conventional wisdom was that the largest machines had the best cost/performance. This may have been true at the time, but it hasn't been true for more than a decade. Unforeseen innovations between 1974 and 1991 include workstations, improved compilers, and reduced instruction set computers (see Chapter 3, section 3.14, Historical Perspective and Further Reading). In 1990 the Sun SPARCstation achieved a price/performance about 10 times better than these predictions, with the following year's HP model 750 workstation at an even better price/performance. Another way of calibrating the inaccuracy of the prediction is that we would have to extend the curve to the year 2010 before finding computers with the

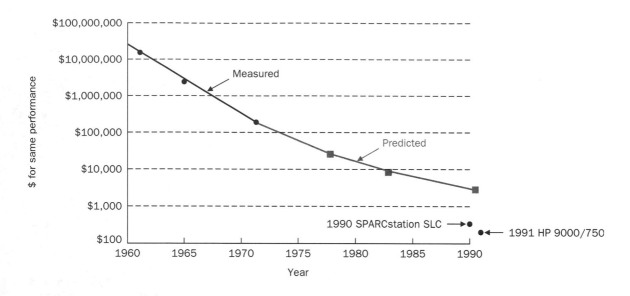

FIGURE 1.20   Prediction of computer price/performance in 1980s made in 1974. The *y*-axis is actually labeled $/MIPS. Although Turn recognized that large-scale integrated circuits would impact the cost/performance relationship, he predicted that it would further improve the cost/performance advantage of large machines instead of allowing small and inexpensive machines to match the performance of large machines. From Rein Turn, *Computers in the 1980s* (New York: Columbia University Press, 1974): Figure 8, p. 80.

cost/performance of a SPARCstation, and to add another 5 years to reach the level of cost/performance of the HP machine.

1.6   Concluding Remarks

Where ... the ENIAC is equipped with 18,000 vacuum tubes and weighs 30 tons, computers in the future may have 1,000 vacuum tubes and perhaps weigh just 1-1/2 tons.

Popular Mechanics, March 1949, p. 258

Although it is difficult to predict exactly what level of cost/performance computers will have in the future, it's a safe bet that they will be much better than they are today. To participate in these advances, computer designers and programmers must understand a wider variety of issues.

Both hardware and software designers construct computer systems in hierarchical layers, with each lower layer hiding details from the level above. This principle of abstraction is fundamental to understanding today's computer systems, but it does not mean that designers can limit themselves to knowing a single technology. Perhaps the most important example of abstraction is the interface between hardware and low-level software, called the *instruction set architecture*. Maintaining the instruction set architecture as a constant enables many implementations of that architecture—presumably varying in cost and performance—to run identical software. On the downside, the architecture may preclude introducing innovations that require the interface to change.

Key technologies for processors in the 1990s are compilers and silicon. Clearly, to participate you must understand some of the characteristics of both. Equal in importance to an understanding of integrated circuit technology is an understanding of the expected rates of technological change. One example of this relationship is the DRAM tradition of a fourfold capacity increase every three years. While silicon fuels the rapid advance of hardware, new ideas in the organization of computers have multiplied price/performance. Two of the key ideas are exploiting parallelism in the processor, typically via pipelining, and exploiting locality of accesses to a memory hierarchy, typically via caches.

Roadmap for this Book

At the bottom of these abstractions are the five classic components of a computer: datapath, control, memory, input, and output (Figure 1.21). These five components also serve as the framework for the rest of the chapters in this book:

- *Datapath:* Chapters 4, 5, and 6
- *Control:* Chapters 5 and 6
- *Memory:* Chapter 7
- *Input:* Chapter 8
- *Output:* Chapter 8

Chapter 6 describes how processor pipelining exploits parallelism, and Chapter 7 describes how the memory hierarchy exploits locality. The remaining chapters provide the introduction and the conclusion to this material. Chapter 2 covers performance and thus describes how to evaluate the whole computer. Chapter 3 describes instruction sets—the interface between compilers and the machine—and emphasizes the role of compilers and programming languages in using the features of the instruction set. Chapter 9 concludes this coverage with a discussion on parallel processors.

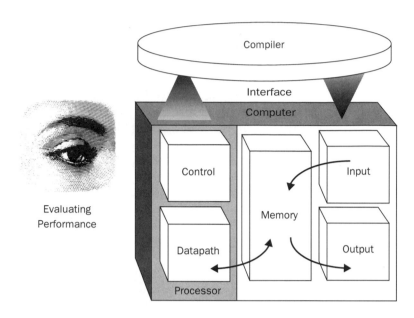

FIGURE 1.21 The organization of a computer, showing the five classic components. To help the reader keep all this in perspective, the five components of a computer are shown on the front page of the following chapters, with the portion of interest to that chapter highlighted.

1.7   Historical Perspective and Further Reading

An active field of science is like an immense anthill; the individual almost vanishes into the mass of minds tumbling over each other, carrying information from place to place, passing it around at the speed of light.

Lewis Thomas, "Natural Science," in *The Lives of a Cell*, 1974

A section devoted to an historical perspective closes each chapter in the text. We may trace the development of an idea through a series of machines or describe some important projects, and we provide references for the reader interested in probing further. This section provides historical background on some of the key ideas presented in this opening chapter. Its purpose is to give you the human story behind the technological advances and to place achieve-

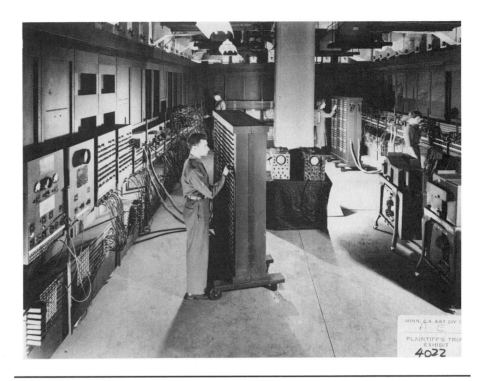

FIGURE 1.22 ENIAC, the world's first general-purpose electronic computer. Note the court tag in the lower, right hand corner; this is from the patent case mentioned on page 33. Photo courtesy of Charles Babbage Institute, University of Minnesota.

ments in their historical context. By understanding the past, you may be better able to understand the forces that will shape computing in the future.

The First Electronic Computers

J. Presper Eckert and John Mauchly at the Moore School of the University of Pennsylvania built what is widely accepted to be the world's first operational electronic, general-purpose computer. This machine, called ENIAC (Electronic Numerical Integrator and Calculator), was funded by the United States Army and became operational during World War II, but was not publicly disclosed until 1946. ENIAC was a general-purpose machine used for computing artillery firing tables. This *U*-shaped computer was 80 feet long by 8.5 feet high and several feet wide (Figure 1.22). Each of the twenty 10-digit registers was 2 feet long. In total, ENIAC used 18,000 vacuum tubes.

In size, ENIAC was two orders of magnitude bigger than machines built today, yet it was more than four orders of magnitude slower, performing 1900 additions per second. ENIAC provided conditional jumps and was programmable, clearly distinguishing it from earlier calculators. Programming was done manually by plugging cables and setting switches, and data was entered on punched cards. Programming for typical calculations required from half an hour to a whole day. ENIAC was a general-purpose machine, limited primarily by a small amount of storage and tedious programming.

In 1944, John von Neumann was attracted to the ENIAC project. The group wanted to improve the way programs were entered and discussed storing programs as numbers; von Neumann helped crystallize the ideas and wrote a memo proposing a stored-program computer called EDVAC (Electronic Discrete Variable Automatic Computer). Herman Goldstine distributed the memo and put von Neumann's name on it, much to the dismay of Eckert and Mauchly, whose names were omitted. This memo has served as the basis for the commonly used term *von Neumann computer*. Several early pioneers in the computer field believe that this term gives too much credit to von Neumann, who wrote up the ideas, and too little to the engineers, Eckert and Mauchly, who worked on the machines. For this reason, the term does not appear elsewhere in this book.

In 1946, Maurice Wilkes of Cambridge University visited the Moore School to attend the latter part of a series of lectures on developments in electronic computers. When he returned to Cambridge, Wilkes decided to embark on a project to build a stored-program computer named EDSAC (for Electronic Delay Storage Automatic Calculator). EDSAC, shown in Figure 1.23, became operational in 1949 and was the world's first full-scale, operational, stored-program computer [Wilkes 1985]. (A small prototype called the Mark I, built at the University of Manchester in 1948, might be called the first operational stored-program machine.) Section 3.4 in Chapter 3 explains the stored-program concept.

In 1947, Eckert and Mauchly applied for a patent on electronic computers. The dean of the Moore School, by demanding that the patent be turned over to the university, may have helped Eckert and Mauchly conclude that they should leave. Their departure crippled the EDVAC project, delaying completion until 1952.

Goldstine left to join von Neumann at the Institute for Advanced Study (IAS) at Princeton in 1946. Together with Arthur Burks, they issued a report based on the memo written earlier [Burks 1946].The paper was incredible for the period; reading it today, one would never guess this landmark paper was written more than 45 years ago, because it discusses most of the architectural concepts seen in modern computers. This paper led to the IAS machine built by Julian Bigelow. It had a total of 1024, 40-bit words and was roughly 10 times faster than ENIAC. The group thought about uses for the machine, published

FIGURE 1.23 EDSAC in 1949 was the first full-scale stored-program computer. Wilkes is the person in the front, kneeling and wearing glasses. Photo courtesy of The Computer Museum, Boston.

a set of reports, and encouraged visitors. These reports and visitors inspired the development of a number of new computers.

Recently, there has been some controversy about the work of John Atanasoff, who built a small-scale electronic computer in the early 1940s. His machine, designed at Iowa State University, was a special-purpose computer that was never completely operational. Mauchly briefly visited Atanasoff before he built ENIAC. The presence of the Atanasoff machine, together with delays in filing the ENIAC patents (the work was classified and patents could not be filed until after the war) and the distribution of von Neumann's EDVAC paper, were used to break the Eckert-Mauchly patent. Though controversy still rages over Atanasoff's role, Eckert and Mauchly are usually given credit for building the first working, general-purpose, electronic computer [Stern 1980].

Another early machine that deserves some credit was a special-purpose machine built by Konrad Zuse in Germany in the late 1930s and early 1940s. Although Zuse had the design for a programmable computer ready, the German government decided not to fund scientific investigations taking more than two years, because the bureaucrats expected the war would be won by that deadline.

While work on ENIAC went forward, Howard Aiken was building an electromechanical computer called the Mark-I at Harvard. He followed the Mark-I with a relay machine, the Mark-II, and a pair of vacuum tube machines, the Mark-III and Mark-IV. In contrast to earlier machines like EDSAC, which used a single memory for instructions and data, the Mark-III and Mark-IV had separate memories for instructions and data. The machines were regarded as reactionary by the advocates of stored-program computers; the term *Harvard architecture* was coined to describe machines with separate memories. This term is used today in a different sense to describe machines with a single main memory but with separate caches for instructions and data.

The Whirlwind project was begun at MIT in 1947 and was aimed at applications in real-time radar signal processing. Although it led to several inventions, its most important innovation was magnetic core memory. Whirlwind had 2048, 16-bit words of magnetic core. Magnetic cores served as the main memory technology for nearly 30 years.

Commercial Developments

In December 1947, Eckert and Mauchly formed Eckert-Mauchly Computer Corporation. Their first machine, the BINAC, was built for Northrop and was shown in August 1949. After some financial difficulties, their firm was acquired by Remington-Rand, where they built the UNIVAC I (universal automatic computer), designed to be sold as a general-purpose computer (Figure 1.24). First delivered in June 1951, UNIVAC I sold for about $1 million and was the first successful commercial computer—48 systems were built! This early machine, along with many other fascinating pieces of computer lore, may be seen at the Computer Museum in Boston, Massachusetts.

IBM had been in the punched card and office automation business but didn't start building computers until 1950. The first IBM computer, the IBM 701, shipped in 1952, and eventually 19 units were sold. In the early 1950s, many people were pessimistic about the future of computers, believing that the market and opportunities for these "highly specialized" machines were quite limited.

In 1964, after investing $5 billion, IBM made a bold move with the announcement of the System/360. An IBM spokesman said the following at the time:

We are not at all humble in this announcement. This is the most important product announcement that this corporation has ever made in its history. It's not a computer in any previous sense. It's not a product, but a line of products . . . that spans in performance from the very low part of the computer line to the very high.

FIGURE 1.24 UNIVAC I, the first commercial computer in the United States. It correctly predicted the outcome of the 1952 presidential election, but its initial forecast was withheld from broadcast because experts doubted the use of such early results. Photo courtesy of the Charles Babbage Institute, University of Minnesota.

Moving the idea of the architecture abstraction into commercial reality, IBM announced six implementations of the System/360 architecture that varied in price and performance by a factor of 25. Figure 1.25 shows these models. IBM bet its company on the success of a *computer family*, and IBM won. The System/360 and its successors dominated the large computer market.

About a year later Digital Equipment Corporation (DEC) unveiled the PDP-8, the first commercial *minicomputer* shown in Figure 1.26. This small machine was a breakthrough in low-cost design, allowing DEC to offer a computer for under $20,000. Minicomputers were the forerunners of microprocessors, with Intel inventing the first microprocessor in 1971—the Intel 4004, shown in Figure 1.27 (on page 38) as a photomicrograph.

In 1963 came the announcement of the first *supercomputer*. This came not from the large companies nor even from the high tech centers. Seymour Cray led the design of the Control Data Corporation CDC 6600 in Minnesota. This machine developed many ideas that are beginning to be found in the latest microprocessors. Cray later left CDC to form Cray Research Inc., in Wisconsin. In 1976 he announced the Cray-1 (Figure 1.28 on page 39). This machine was simultaneously the fastest in the world, the most expensive, and the computer with the best cost/performance for scientific programs.

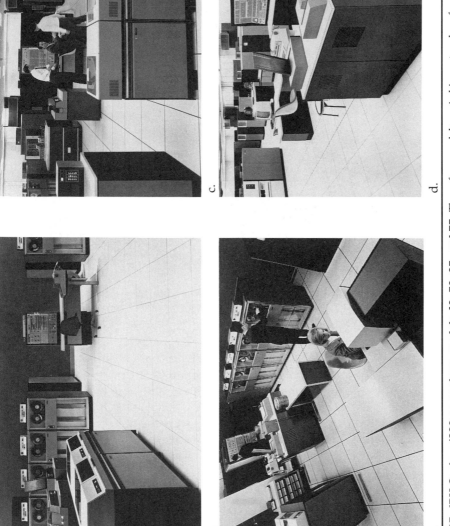

a.

b.

c.

d.

FIGURE 1.25 IBM System/360 computers: models 40, 50, 65, and 75. These four models varied in cost and performance by a factor of almost 10. The clock rate, range of memory sizes, and approximate price for only the processor and memory of average size: (a) Model 40,1.6 MHz, 32 KB–256 KB, and $225,000; (b) Model 50, 2.0 MHz, 128 KB–256 KB, and $550,000; (c) Model 65, 5.0 MHz, 256 KB–1 MB, and $1,200,000; and (d) Model 75, 5.1 MHz, 256 KB–1 MB, $1,900,000. Adding I/O devices typically increased the price by factors of 1.8 to 3.5, with higher factors for cheaper models. Photos courtesy of International Business Machines Corporation.

FIGURE 1.26 The DEC PDP-8, the first commercial minicomputer, announced in 1965.
Among other uses, the PDP-8 was used to stage the musical *A Chorus Line*. Photo courtesy of Digital Equipment Corporation, Corporate Photo Library.

While Seymour Cray was creating the world's most expensive computer, other designers around the world were looking at using the microprocessor to create a computer so cheap that you could have it at home. There is no single fountainhead for the *personal computer*, but in 1977 the Apple II (Figure 1.29 on page 39) of Steve Jobs and Steve Wozniak set standards for low cost, high volume, and high reliability that defined the personal computer industry. But even with a four-year head start, Apple's personal computers finished second in popularity. The IBM Personal Computer, announced in 1981, became the best selling computer of any kind; its success made the Intel 80x86 the most popular microprocessor and made the Microsoft Disk Operating System (MS-DOS) the most popular operating system. In 1990 Microsoft sold 12 million copies of DOS—2 million more than the best selling record album of 1990—even though DOS costs ten times as much!

FIGURE 1.27   Microphotograph of the Intel 4004 from 1971, the first microprocessor.
Contrast this microprocessor, with just 2300 transistors and 0.3 by 0.4 cm in size, with the micro-processor in Figure 1.16 on page 24. Photo courtesy of Intel Corp.

Computer Generations

Since 1952, there have been thousands of new computers using a wide range of technologies and having widely varying capabilities. To put these developments in perspective, the industry has tended to group computers into generations. This classification is often based on the implementation technology used in each generation, as shown in Figure 1.30 (on page 40). Typically, each *computer generation* is eight to ten years in length, although the length and birth years—especially of recent generations—are debated. By convention, the first generation is taken to be commercial electronic computers, rather than the mechanical or electromechanical machines that preceded them.

The fifth generation may well be defined on two fronts: portable communications/computing devices at the low end and parallel computers at the high end. Some computers of the future will be much more personal and portable: They will combine laptop computers, cellular phones, and pagers to provide electronic assistance that will be so valuable that no one will leave

FIGURE 1.28 Cray 1, the first commercial vector supercomputer in 1976. This machine had the unusual distinction of being both the fastest computer for scientific applications and the computer with the best price/performance for those applications. Viewed from the top, the computer looks like the letter C. Photo courtesy of Cray Research, Inc.

FIGURE 1.29 Shown here, the Apple IIC Plus. The success of the original Apple, designed by Steve Wozniak, defined the personal computer industry in 1977 and set standards of cost and reliability for the industry. Photo courtesy of Apple Computer, Inc.

Generation	Dates	Technology	Principal new product
1	1950–1959	Vacuum tubes	Commercial, electronic computer
2	1960–1968	Transistors	Cheaper computers
3	1969–1977	Integrated circuit	Minicomputer
4	1978–199?	LSI and VLSI	Personal computers and workstations
5	199?–20??	Microprocessor?	Personal portable computing devices and parallel processors?

FIGURE 1.30 Computer generations are usually determined by the change in dominant implementation technology. Typically, each generation offers the opportunity to create a new class of computers and for new computer companies to be created. Many researchers believe that parallel processing at the high end and portable computers at the low end will be the basis for the fifth computer generation.

Year	Name	Size (cu. ft.)	Power (watts)	Performance (adds/sec)	Memory (KB)	Price	Price/ performance vs. UNIVAC	Adjusted price (1991 $)	Price/ performance vs. UNIVAC
1951	UNIVAC I	1000	124,500	1,900	48	$1,000,000	1	$4,533,607	1
1964	IBM S360/ model 50	60	10,000	500,000	64	$1,000,000	263	$3,756,502	318
1965	PDP-8	8	500	330,000	4	$16,000	10,855	$59,947	13,135
1976	Cray-1	58	60,000	166,000,000	32,768	$4,000,000	21,842	$7,675,591	51,604
1981	IBM PC	1	150	240,000	256	$3,000	42,105	$3,702	154,673
1991	HP 9000/ model 750	2	500	50,000,000	16,384	$7,400	3,556,188	$7,400	16,122,356

FIGURE 1.31   Characteristics of key commercial computers since 1950, in actual dollars and in 1991 dollars adjusted for inflation. (Source: The Computer Museum, Boston, and Producer Price Index for Industrial Commodities.) In contrast to Figure 1.25, in this figure the price of the IBM S360 model 50 includes I/O devices.

home without them. Parallel computers with tens to thousands of nodes, each with the power of a workstation connected by very high-speed networks, are already replacing traditional supercomputers and mainframes at some installations (see Chapter 9). The amazing possibility of the fifth generation is that the same microprocessor architecture will be driving both the high-end parallel machines and the low-end portable computers, possibly with different implementations aimed at high performance or low power.

Figure 1.31 summarizes the key characteristics of some machines mentioned in this section. After adjusting for inflation, price/performance has improved by more than 16 million in 40 years. Readers interested in computer history should consult *Annals of the History of Computing*, a journal devoted to the history of computing. Several books describing the early days of computing have also appeared, many written by the pioneers themselves.

To Probe Further

Bell, C. G. [1984]. "The mini and micro industries," *IEEE Computer* 17:10 (October) 14–30.

An insider's personal view of the computing industry, including computer generations.

Burks, A. W., H. H. Goldstine, and J. von Neumann [1946]. "Preliminary discussion of the logical design of an electronic computing instrument," Report to the U.S. Army Ordnance Department, p. 1; also appears in *Papers of John von Neumann*, W. Aspray and A. Burks, eds., MIT Press, Cambridge, Mass., and Tomash Publishers, Los Angeles, Calif., 1987, 97–146.

A classic paper explaining computer hardware and software before the first stored-program computer was built. It simultaneously explained computers to the world and was a source of controversy because the first draft did not give credit to Eckert and Mauchly.

Goldstine, H. H. [1972]. *The Computer: From Pascal to von Neumann*, Princeton University Press, Princeton, N.J.

A personal view of computing by one of the pioneers who worked with von Neumann.

Hennessy, J. L., and D. A. Patterson [1990]. "Performance and Cost," Chapter 2 of *Computer Architecture: A Quantitative Approach*, Morgan Kaufmann Publishers, San Mateo, Calif.

This chapter contains much more detail on the cost of integrated circuits and explains the reasons for the difference between price and cost.

Public Broadcasting System [1992]. *The Machine That Changed the World*, videotapes.

These five one-hour programs include rare footage and interviews with pioneers of the computer industry.

Slater, R. [1987]. *Portraits in Silicon*, MIT Press, Cambridge, Mass.

Short biographies of 31 computer pioneers.

Stern, N. [1980]. "Who invented the first electronic digital computer?" *Annals of the History of Computing* 2:4 (October) 375–76.

A historian's perspective on Atanasoff vs. Eckert and Mauchly.

Wilkes, M. V. [1985]. *Memoirs of a Computer Pioneer*, MIT Press, Cambridge, Mass.

A personal view of computing by one of the pioneers.

1.8 Exercises

The relative time ratings of exercises are shown in square brackets after each exercise number. On average, an exercise rated [10] will take you twice as long as one rated [5]. Sections of the text that should be read before attempting an exercise will be given in angled brackets, e.g., <§1.4> means you should have read section 1.4, Integrated Circuits: Fueling Innovation, to help you solve this exercise. If the solution to an exercise depends on others, they will be listed in curly brackets, e.g., {ex. 1.50} means that you should answer exercise 1.50 before trying this exercise.

Exercises 1.1 to 1.26   Find the word or phrase from the list below that best matches the description in the following questions. Use the letters to the left of words in the answer. Each answer should be used only once.

a	abstraction	n	DRAM (dynamic random access memory)
b	assembler	o	implementation
c	binary number	p	instruction
d	bit	q	instruction set architecture
e	cache	r	integrated circuit
f	CPU (central processor unit)	s	memory
g	chip	t	operating system
h	compiler	u	processor
i	computer family	v	semiconductor
j	control	w	supercomputer
k	datapath	x	transistor
l	defect	y	VLSI (very large scale integrated circuit)
m	die	z	yield

1.1 [2] Specific abstraction that the hardware provides the low-level software.

1.2 [2] Active part of the computer, following the instructions of the programs to the letter: It adds numbers, tests numbers, and so on.

1.3 [2] Another name for processor.

1.4 [2] Approach to the design of hardware or software; the system consists of hierarchical layers, with each lower layer hiding details from the level above.

1.5 [2] Base 2 number.

1.6 [2] Binary digit.

1.7 [2] Collection of implementations of the same instruction set architecture; they are available at the same time and vary in price and performance.

1.8 [2] Component of the processor that performs arithmetic operations.

1.9 [2] Component of the processor that tells the datapath, memory, and I/O devices what to do according to the instructions of the program.

1.10 [2] Hardware that obeys the instruction set architecture abstraction.

1.11 [2] High performance machine, costing more than $1 million.

1.12 [2] Individual command to a computer.

1.13 [2] Integrated circuit commonly used to construct main memory.

1.14 [2] Integrates dozens to hundreds of transistors into a single chip.

1.15 [2] Integrates hundreds of thousands to millions of transistors into a single chip.

1.16 [2] Location of programs when they are running, containing the data needed as well.

1.17 [2] Microscopic flaw in a wafer.

1.18 [2] Nickname for a die or integrated circuit.

1.19 [2] On-off switch controlled by electricity.

1.20 [2] Percentage of good dies from the total number of dies on the wafer.

1.21 [2] Program that manages the resources of a computer for the benefit of the programs that run on that machine.

1.22 [2] Program that translates a symbolic version of an instruction into the binary version.

1.23 [2] Program that translates from a higher level notation to assembly language.

1.24 [2] Rectangular component that results from dicing a wafer.

1.25 [2] Small, fast memory that acts as a buffer for the main memory.

1.26 [2] Substance that does not conduct electricity well.

Exercises 1.27 to 1.44 Using the categories in the table below, classify the following examples. Use the letters to the left of words in the answer. Unlike the previous exercises, answers in this table may be used more than once.

a	applications software		f	output device
b	high-level programming language		g	personal computer
c	input device		h	semiconductor
d	integrated circuit		i	supercomputer
e	minicomputer		j	systems software

1.27 [1] Apple II

1.28 [1] Assembler

1.29 [1] Compiler

1.30 [1] Cray 1

1.31 [1] DRAM

1.32 [1] Fortran

1.33 [1] IBM PC

1.34 [1] Keyboard

1.35 [1] Microprocessor

1.36 [1] Mouse

1.37 [1] Operating system

1.38 [1] Pascal

1.39 [1] PDP-8

1.40 [1] Printer

1.41 [1] Cathode Ray Tube Display

1.42 [1] Silicon

1.43 [1] Spreadsheet

1.44 [1] Text editor

1.45 [10] In a magnetic disk, the disks containing the data are constantly rotating. On average it should take half a revolution for the desired data on the disk to spin under the read/write head. Assuming that the disk is rotating at 3600 revolutions per minute, what is the average time for the data to rotate under the disk head? What is the time if the disk were spinning at 5400 RPM?

In More Depth

Our approach in this book is to include optional sections in exercises, leaving it up to the instructor whether to cover the material in class, leave students to read it on their own, or skip the material altogether. This first example gives more information on the cost of integrated circuits and is used in Exercises 1.46 to 1.52.

The cost of an integrated circuit can be expressed in three simple equations:

$$\text{cost per die} \quad = \quad \frac{\text{cost per wafer}}{\text{dies per wafer} \times \text{yield}}$$

$$\text{dies per wafer} \quad \approx \quad \frac{\text{wafer area}}{\text{die area}}$$

$$\text{yield} \quad = \quad \frac{1}{\left(1 + \text{defects per area} \times \text{die area}/2\right)^{2}}$$

The first equation is straightforward to derive. The second is an approximation, since it does not subtract the area near the border of the round wafer that cannot accommodate the rectangular dies. The final equation is based on years of empirical observations of yields at integrated circuit factories, with the exponent related to the number of critical processing steps in the manufacturing process.

1.46 [10] Combine the three equations above to determine the cost per die in terms of die area. If you ignore constants, what is the approximate relationship between cost and die area?

1.47 [15] Compare the estimate of the number of dies per wafer calculated in the formula above to the actual number given in the caption of Figure 1.15 on page 23. Propose a formula that gives a more accurate estimate of the number of dies per wafer and give an explanation of your formula.

1.48 [10] What is the approximate cost of a die in the wafer shown at left in Figure 1.15 on page 23? Assume that a 6-inch wafer costs $750 and that the defect density is 2 per square centimeter. Use the number of dies per wafer given in the figure caption.

1.49 [10] This is the same as exercise 1.48, but use the wafer shown at right in Figure 1.15 on page 23 instead of the left-hand wafer.

Exercises 1.50 to 1.52 DRAM chips have significantly increased in die size with each generation, yet yields have stayed about the same (43% to 48%). Figure 1.32 shows key statistics for DRAM production over the years.

| Capacity (K bits) | 64 | 256 | 1024 | 4096 | 16384 |
Year	1980	1983	1985	1989	1992
Die Area (sq. cm.)	0.16	0.24	0.42	0.65	0.97
Wafer Diameter (inches)	5	5	6	6	8
Yield	48%	46%	45%	43%	48%

FIGURE 1.32 History of DRAM capacity, die size, wafer size, and yield. Provided by Howard Dicken of DM Data Inc. of Scottsdale, Arizona.

1.50 [5] Given the increase in die area of DRAMS, what parameter must improve to maintain yield?

1.51 [10] {ex. 1.50} Derive a formula for the improving parameter found in Exercise 1.50 from the other parameters.

1.52 [10] <§1.4> {ex. 1.50, 1.51} Using the formula in the answer to Exercise 1.51, what is the calculated improvement in that parameter between 1980 and 1992?

2

The Role of
Performance

Time discovers truth.

Seneca
Moral Essays, 22 A.D.

The Five Classic Components of a Computer

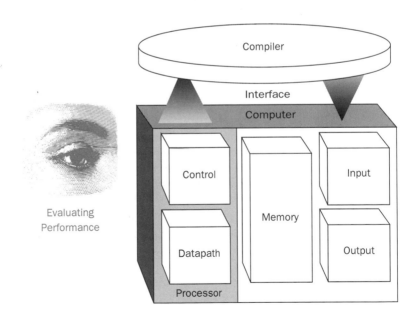

2.1   Introduction

This chapter discusses how to measure, report, and summarize performance and describes the major factors that determine the performance of a computer. A primary reason for examining performance is that hardware performance is often key to the effectiveness of an entire system of hardware and software. Assessing the performance of such a system can be quite challenging. The scale and intricacy of modern software systems, together with the wide range of performance improvement techniques employed by hardware designers, have made performance assessment much more difficult. It is simply impossible to sit down with an instruction set manual and a significant software system and determine how fast the software will run on the machine. In fact, for different types of applications, different performance metrics may be appropriate and different aspects of a computer system may be the most significant in determining overall performance.

Of course, in trying to choose among different computers, performance is almost always an important attribute. Accurately measuring and comparing different machines is critical to purchasers, and therefore to designers. The people selling computers know this as well. Often, salespeople would like you to see their machine in the best possible light, whether or not this light accurately reflects the needs of the purchaser's application. In some cases, claims are made about computers that don't provide useful insight for any real applications. Hence, understanding how best to measure performance and the limitations of performance measurements is important in selecting a machine.

Our interest in performance, however, goes beyond issues of assessing performance only from the outside of a machine. To understand why a piece of software performs as it does, why one instruction set can be implemented to perform better than another, or how some hardware feature affects performance, we need to understand what determines the performance of a machine. For example, to improve the performance of a software system, we may need to understand what factors in the hardware contribute to the overall system performance and the relative importance of these factors. These factors may include how well the program uses the instructions of the machine, how well the underlying hardware implements the instructions, and how well the memory and I/O systems perform. Understanding how to determine the performance impact of these factors is crucial to understanding the motivation behind the design of particular aspects of the machine, as we will see in the chapters that follow.

The rest of this section describes different ways in which performance can be determined. In section 2.2 we describe the metrics for measuring perfor-

Airplane	Passenger capacity	Cruising range (miles)	Cruising speed (m.p.h.)	Passenger throughput (passengers x m.p.h.)
Boeing 737-100	101	630	598	60,398
Boeing 747	470	4150	610	286,700
BAC/Sud Concorde	132	4000	1350	178,200
Douglas DC-8-50	146	8720	544	79,424

FIGURE 2.1 The capacity, range, and speed for a number of commercial airplanes. The last column shows the rate at which the airplane transports passengers, which is the capacity times the cruising speed (ignoring range and take-off and landing times).

mance from the viewpoint of both a computer user and a designer. In section 2.3 we look at how these metrics are related and present the classical processor performance equation, which we will use throughout the text. Section 2.4 describes some popular performance metrics and why they are inadequate. Sections 2.5 and 2.6 describe how best to choose benchmarks to evaluate machines and how to accurately summarize the performance of a group of programs. Finally, in section 2.7 we'll examine some of the many pitfalls that have trapped designers and those who analyze and report performance.

Defining performance

When we say one computer has better performance than another, what do we mean? Although this question might seem simple, an analogy with passenger airplanes shows how subtle the question of performance can be. Figure 2.1 shows some typical passenger airplanes, together with their cruising speed, range, and capacity. If we wanted to know which of the planes in this table had the best performance, we would first need to define performance. For example, considering different measures of performance we see that the plane with the highest cruising speed is the Concorde, the plane with the longest range is the DC-8, and the plane with the largest capacity is the 747. Let's suppose we define performance in terms of speed. This still leaves two possible definitions. You could define the fastest plane as the one with the highest cruising speed, taking a single passenger from one point to another in the least time. However, if you were interested in transporting 450 passengers from one point to another, the 747 would clearly be the fastest, as the last column of the figure shows. Similarly, we can define computer performance in several different ways.

If you were running a program on two different workstations, you'd say that the faster one is the workstation that gets the job done first. However, if you were running a computer center that had two large timeshared computers running jobs submitted by many users, you'd say that the faster computer was the one that completed the most jobs during a day. As an individual computer user, you are interested in reducing *response time*—the time between the start and completion of a task—also referred to as *execution time*. Computer center managers are interested in increasing *throughput*—the total amount of work done in a given time.

To illustrate the application of new ideas, specific examples are used throughout this text. We highlight the example and then provide an answer. Try working out the answer yourself, or—if you feel unsure about the material—just follow along. The examples that appear are similar in type to the problems that you will have an opportunity to tackle in the exercises at the end of each chapter. Here's our first example:

Do the following changes to a computer system increase throughput, decrease response time, or both?

1.   Replacing the processor in a computer with a faster version.

2.   Adding additional processors to a system that uses multiple processors for separate tasks—for example, handling an airline reservations system.

Decreasing response time almost always improves throughput. Hence, in case 1, both response time and throughput are improved. In case 2, no one task gets work done faster, so only throughput increases. If, however, the demand for processing in the second case were larger than the throughput, the system might force requests to queue up. In this case, increasing the throughput could also improve response time. Thus, in many real computer systems, changing either execution time or throughput often affects the other.

In discussing the performance of machines, we will be primarily concerned with response time for the first few chapters. (In Chapter 8 on input/output systems we will discuss throughput-related measures.) To maximize performance, we want to minimize response time or execution time for some task. Thus we can relate performance and execution time for a machine X:

$$\text{Performance}_X = \frac{1}{\text{Execution time}_X}$$

This means that for two machines X and Y, if the performance of X is greater than the performance of Y, we have

$$\text{Performance}_X > \text{Performance}_Y$$

$$\frac{1}{\text{Execution time}_X} > \frac{1}{\text{Execution time}_Y}$$

$$\text{Execution time}_Y > \text{Execution time}_X$$

That is, the execution time on Y is longer than that on X, if X is faster than Y.

In discussing a computer design, we often want to relate the performance of two different machines quantitatively. We will use the phrase "X is n times faster than Y" to mean

$$\frac{\text{Performance}_X}{\text{Performance}_Y} = n$$

If X is n times faster than Y, then the execution time on Y is n times longer than it is on X:

$$\frac{\text{Performance}_X}{\text{Performance}_Y} = \frac{\text{Execution time}_Y}{\text{Execution time}_X} = n$$

Example

If machine A runs a program in 10 seconds and machine B runs the same program in 15 seconds, how much faster is A than B?

Answer

We know that A is n times faster than B if

$$\frac{\text{Performance}_A}{\text{Performance}_B} = n$$

or

$$\frac{\text{Execution time}_B}{\text{Execution time}_A} = n$$

Thus the performance ratio is

$$\frac{15}{10} = 1.5$$

and A is therefore 1.5 times faster than B.

In the above example, we could also say that machine B is 1.5 times *slower than* machine A, since

$$\frac{\text{Performance}_A}{\text{Performance}_B} = 1.5$$

means that

$$\frac{\text{Performance}_A}{1.5} = \text{Performance}_B$$

For simplicity, we will normally use the terminology *faster than* when we try to compare machines quantitatively. Because performance and execution time are reciprocals, increasing performance requires decreasing execution time. To avoid the potential confusion between the terms *increasing* and *decreasing*, we usually say *improve performance* or *improve execution time* when we mean "increase performance" and "decrease execution time."

2.2   Measuring Performance

Time is the measure of computer performance: the computer that performs the same amount of work in the least time is the fastest. Program *execution time* is measured in seconds per program. But time can be defined in different ways, depending on what we count. The most straightforward definition of time is called *wall-clock time*, *response time*, or *elapsed time*. This is the total time to complete a task, including disk accesses, memory accesses, input/output (I/O) activities, operating system overhead—everything. However, computers are often timeshared, and a processor may work on several programs simultaneously. In such cases, the system may try to optimize throughput rather than attempt to minimize the elapsed time for one program. Hence, we often want to distinguish between the elapsed time and the time that the processor is working on our behalf. *CPU execution time* or simply *CPU time*, which recognizes this distinction, is the time the CPU spends computing for this task and does not include time spent waiting for I/O or running other programs. (Remember, though, that the response time experienced by the user will be the elapsed time of the program, not the CPU time.) CPU time can be further divided into the CPU time spent in the program, called *user CPU time*, and the CPU time spent in the operating system performing tasks on behalf of the program, called *system CPU time*. Differentiating between system and user CPU time is difficult to do accurately, because it is often hard to assign responsibility for operating system activities to one user program rather than another.

The breakdown of the elapsed time for a task is reflected in the UNIX time command, which in one case returned

$$90.7u\ 12.9s\ 2:39\ 65\%$$

User CPU time is 90.7 seconds, system CPU time is 12.9 seconds, elapsed time is 2 minutes and 39 seconds (159 seconds), and the percentage of elapsed time that is CPU time is

$$\frac{90.7 + 12.9}{159} = 0.65$$

or 65%. More than a third of the elapsed time in this example was spent waiting for I/O, running other programs, or both. Sometimes we ignore system CPU time when examining CPU execution time because of the inaccuracy of operating systems' self-measurement and the inequity of including system CPU time when comparing performance between machines with different operating systems. On the other hand, system code on some machines is user code on others, and no program runs without some operating system running on the hardware, so a case can be made for using the sum of user CPU time and system CPU time as the measure of program execution time.

For consistency, we maintain a distinction between performance based on elapsed time and that based on CPU execution time. We will use the term *system performance* to refer to elapsed time on an *unloaded* system, and use *CPU performance* to refer to *user* CPU time. We will concentrate on CPU performance in this chapter, although our discussions of how to summarize performance can be applied to either elapsed time or to CPU time measurements.

Although as computer users we care about time, when we examine the details of a machine it's convenient to think about performance in other metrics. In particular, computer designers may want to think about a machine by using a measure that relates to how fast the hardware can perform basic functions. Almost all computers are constructed using a clock that runs at a constant rate and determines when events take place in the hardware. These discrete time intervals are called *clock cycles* (or ticks, clock ticks, clock periods, clocks, cycles). Designers refer to the length of a *clock period* both as the time for a complete *clock cycle* (e.g., 10 nanoseconds, or 10 ns) and as the *clock rate* (e.g., 100 megahertz, or 100 MHz), which is the inverse of the clock period. In the next section, we will formalize the relationship between the clock cycles of the hardware designer and the seconds of the computer user.

2.3 Relating the Metrics

Users and designers often examine performance using different metrics. If we could relate these different metrics, we could determine the effect of a design change on the performance as seen by the user. Since we are confining ourselves to CPU performance at this point, the bottom-line performance measure is CPU execution time. A simple formula relates the most basic metrics (clock cycles and clock cycle time) to CPU time:

$$\text{CPU execution time for a program} = \text{CPU clock cycles for a program} \times \text{Clock cycle time}$$

Alternatively, because clock rate and clock cycle time are inverses:

$$\text{CPU execution time for a program} = \frac{\text{CPU clock cycles for a program}}{\text{Clock rate}}$$

This formula makes it clear that the hardware designer can improve performance by reducing either the length of the clock cycle or the number of clock cycles required for a program. As we will see in this chapter and later in Chapters 5, 6, and 7, the designer often faces a trade-off between the number of clock cycles needed for a program and the length of each cycle. Many techniques that decrease the number of clock cycles also increase the clock cycle time.

Example

Our favorite program runs in 10 seconds on computer A, which has a 100 MHz clock. We are trying to help a computer designer build a machine, B, that will run this program in 6 seconds. The designer has determined that a substantial increase in the clock rate is possible, but this increase will affect the rest of the CPU design, causing machine B to require 1.2 times as many clock cycles as machine A for this program. What clock rate should we tell the designer to target?

Answer

Let's first find the number of clock cycles required for the program on A:

$$\text{CPU time}_A = \frac{\text{CPU clock cycles}_A}{\text{Clock rate}_A}$$

$$10 \text{ seconds} = \frac{\text{CPU clock cycles}_A}{100 \times 10^6 \frac{\text{cycles}}{\text{second}}}$$

$$\text{CPU clock cycles}_A = 10 \text{ seconds} \times 100 \times 10^6 \frac{\text{cycles}}{\text{second}} = 1000 \times 10^6 \text{cycles}$$

CPU time for B can be found using this equation:

$$\text{CPU time}_B = \frac{1.2 \times \text{CPU clock cycles}_A}{\text{Clock rate}_B}$$

$$6 \text{ seconds} = \frac{1.2 \times 1000 \times 10^6 \text{cycles}}{\text{Clock rate}_B}$$

$$\text{Clock rate}_B = \frac{1.2 \times 1000 \times 10^6 \text{cycles}}{6 \text{ seconds}} = \frac{200 \times 10^6 \text{cycles}}{\text{second}} = 200 \text{ MHz}$$

Machine B must therefore have twice the clock rate of A to run the program in 6 seconds.

Hardware Software Interface

Throughout this text, you will see sections called Hardware Software Interfaces. These sections highlight important interactions between some aspect of the software (typically a program, compiler, or the operating system) and some hardware aspect of the computer. In addition to highlighting such interactions, they remind the reader that hardware and software design decisions interact in many different ways.

The equations in our previous examples do not include any reference to the number of instructions needed for the program. However, since the compiler clearly generated instructions to execute, and the machine had to execute the instructions to run the program, the execution time must depend on the number of instructions in a program. One way to think about execution time is that it equals the number of instructions executed multiplied by the average time per instruction. Therefore, the number of clock cycles required for a program can be written as

$$\text{CPU clock cycles} = \text{Instructions for a program} \times \frac{\text{Average clock cycles}}{\text{per instruction}}$$

The term *clock cycles per instruction*, which is the average number of clock cycles each instruction takes to execute, is often abbreviated as CPI. Since different instructions may take different amounts of time depending on what they do, CPI is an average of all the instructions executed in the program. CPI provides one way of comparing two different implementations of the same instruction set architecture, since the instruction count required for a program will, of course, be the same.

Example

Suppose we have two implementations of the same instruction set architecture. Machine A has a clock cycle time of 10 ns (nanoseconds) and a CPI of 2.0 for some program, and machine B has a clock cycle time of 20 ns and a CPI of 1.2 for the same program. Which machine is faster for this program, and by how much?

Answer

We know that each machine executes the same number of instructions for the program; let's call this number I. First, find the number of processor clock cycles for each machine:

$$\text{CPU clock cycles}_A = I \times 2.0$$

$$\text{CPU clock cycles}_B = I \times 1.2$$

Now we can compute the CPU time for each machine:

$$\text{CPU time}_A = \text{CPU clock cycles}_A \times \text{Clock cycle time}_A$$
$$= I \times 2.0 \times 10 \text{ ns} = 20 \times I \text{ ns}$$

Likewise, for B:

$$\text{CPU time}_B = I \times 1.2 \times 20 \text{ ns} = 24 \times I \text{ ns}$$

Clearly, machine A is faster. The amount faster is given by the ratio of the execution times:

$$\frac{\text{CPU performance}_A}{\text{CPU performance}_B} = \frac{\text{Execution time}_B}{\text{Execution time}_A} = \frac{24 \times I \text{ ns}}{20 \times I \text{ ns}} = 1.2$$

We can conclude that machine A is 1.2 times faster than machine B for this program.

We can now write this basic performance equation in terms of instruction count (the number of instructions executed by the program), CPI, and clock cycle time:

$$\text{CPU time} = \text{Instruction count} \times \text{CPI} \times \text{Clock cycle time}$$

or

$$\text{CPU time} = \frac{\text{Instruction count} \times \text{CPI}}{\text{Clock rate}}$$

These formulas are particularly useful because they separate the three key factors that affect performance. We can use these formulas to compare two different implementations or to evaluate a design alternative if we know its impact on these three parameters.

How can we determine the value of these factors in the performance equation? We can measure the CPU execution time by running the program, and the clock cycle time is usually published as part of the documentation for a machine. The instruction count and CPI can be more difficult to obtain. Of course, if we know the clock rate and CPU execution time, we need only the instruction count or the CPI to determine the other.

We can measure the instruction count by using software tools that profile the execution or by using a simulator of the architecture. Since the instruction count depends on the architecture, but not on the exact implementation, we can measure the instruction count without knowing all the details of the implementation. The CPI, however, depends on a wide variety of design details in the machine, including both the memory system and the processor structure (as we will see in Chapters 5, 6, and 7), as well as on the mix of instruction types executed in an application. CPI varies by application, as well as among implementations with the same instruction set.

Designers often obtain CPI by a detailed simulation of an implementation. Sometimes it is possible to compute the CPU clock cycles by looking at the different types of instructions and using their individual clock cycle counts. In such cases, the following formula is useful:

$$\text{CPU clock cycles} = \sum_{i=1}^{n} (\text{CPI}_i \times \text{C}_i)$$

The Big Picture

Figure 2.2 shows the basic measurements at different levels in the computer and what is being measured in each case. We can see how these factors are combined to yield execution time measured in seconds:

$$\text{Time} = \text{Instructions} \times \frac{\text{Clock cycles}}{\text{Instruction}} \times \frac{\text{Seconds}}{\text{Clock cycle}}$$

Always bear in mind that the only complete and reliable measure of computer performance is time. For example, changing the instruction set to lower the instruction count may lead to an organization with a slower clock cycle time that offsets the improvement in instruction count. Similarly, because CPI depends on instruction mix, the code that executes the fewest number of instructions may not be the fastest.

Components of performance	Units of measure
CPU execution time for a program	Seconds for the program
Instruction count	Instructions executed for the program
Clock cycles per instruction (CPI)	$\dfrac{\text{Average clock cycles}}{\text{Instruction}}$
Clock cycle time	$\dfrac{\text{Seconds}}{\text{Clock cycle}}$

FIGURE 2.2 The basic components of performance and how each is measured.

where C_i is the count of the number of instructions of class i executed, CPI_i is the average number of cycles per instruction for that instruction class, and n is the number of instruction classes. Remember that overall CPI for a program will depend on both the number of cycles for each instruction type and the frequency of each instruction type in the program execution. Thus, both the hardware used to execute a program and the program's characteristics affect the observed CPI.

Example

A compiler designer is trying to decide between two code sequences for a particular machine. The hardware designers have supplied the following facts:

Instruction class	CPI for this instruction class
A	1
B	2
C	3

For a particular high-level-language statement, the compiler writer is considering two code sequences that require the following instruction counts:

	Instruction counts for instruction class		
Code sequence	A	B	C
1	2	1	2
2	4	1	1

Which code sequence executes the most instructions? Which will be faster? What is the CPI for each sequence?

Answer

Sequence 1 executes $2 + 1 + 2 = 5$ instructions. Sequence 2 executes $4 + 1 + 1 = 6$ instructions. So sequence 1 executes fewer instructions.

We can use the equation for CPU clock cycles based on instruction count and CPI to find the total number of clock cycles for each sequence:

$$\text{CPU clock cycles} = \sum_{i=1}^{n} (\text{CPI}_i \times \text{C}_i)$$

This yields:

$$\text{CPU clock cycles}_1 = (2 \times 1) + (1 \times 2) + (2 \times 3) = 2 + 2 + 6 = 10 \text{ cycles}$$

$$\text{CPU clock cycles}_2 = (4 \times 1) + (1 \times 2) + (1 \times 3) = 4 + 2 + 3 = 9 \text{ cycles}$$

So code sequence 2 is faster, even though it actually executes one extra instruction. Since code sequence 2 takes fewer overall clock cycles but has more instructions, it must have a lower CPI. The CPI values can be computed by

$$\text{CPI} = \frac{\text{CPU clock cycles}}{\text{Instruction count}}$$

$$\text{CPI}_1 = \frac{\text{CPU clock cycles}_1}{\text{Instruction count}_1} = \frac{10}{5} = 2$$

$$\text{CPI}_2 = \frac{\text{CPU clock cycles}_2}{\text{Instruction count}_2} = \frac{9}{6} = 1.5$$

The above example shows the danger of using only one factor (instruction count) to assess performance. When comparing two machines, you must look at all three components, which combine to form execution time. If some of the factors are identical, like the clock rate in the above example, performance can be determined by comparing all the nonidentical factors. However, since CPI varies by instruction mix, both instruction count and CPI must be compared, even if clock rates are identical. Exercises 2.14 through 2.17 explore this further by asking you to evaluate a series of machine and compiler enhancements that affect clock rate, CPI, and instruction count. In the next section, we'll examine a common performance measurement that does not incorporate all the terms and can thus be misleading.

2.4   Popular Performance Metrics

A number of popular measures have been devised in attempts to create a standard measure of computer performance. One result has been that simple metrics, valid in a limited context, have been heavily misused. All proposed alternatives to the use of time as the performance metric have led eventually to misleading claims, distorted results, or incorrect interpretations. In this section we discuss two of the most commonly used and abused metrics.

MIPS and What's Wrong with It

One alternative to time as the metric is MIPS, or *million instructions per second*. For a given program, MIPS is simply

$$\text{MIPS} = \frac{\text{Instruction count}}{\text{Execution time} \times 10^6} = \frac{\text{Instruction count}}{\text{CPU clocks} \times \text{Cycle time} \times 10^6}$$

$$= \frac{\text{Instruction count} \times \text{Clock rate}}{\text{Instruction count} \times \text{CPI} \times 10^6} = \frac{\text{Clock rate}}{\text{CPI} \times 10^6}$$

Thus

$$\text{MIPS} = \frac{\text{Clock rate}}{\text{CPI} \times 10^6}$$

This last formula shows that MIPS is a measure of the instruction execution rate for a particular machine. This MIPS measurement is also called *native MIPS* to distinguish it from some alternative definitions of MIPS that we will look at shortly.

We can relate MIPS to execution time by using this formula:

$$\text{Execution time} = \frac{\text{Instruction count} \times \text{CPI}}{\text{Clock rate}}$$

$$= \frac{\text{Instruction count}}{\dfrac{\text{Clock rate}}{\text{CPI} \times 10^6} \times 10^6} = \frac{\text{Instruction count}}{\text{MIPS} \times 10^6}$$

Thus

$$\text{Execution time} = \frac{\text{Instruction count}}{\text{MIPS} \times 10^6}$$

Since MIPS is an instruction execution rate, MIPS specifies performance inversely to execution time; faster machines have a higher MIPS rating. The good news about MIPS is that it is easy to understand, and faster machines mean bigger MIPS, which matches intuition.

There are three problems with using MIPS as a measure for comparing machines. First, MIPS specifies the instruction execution rate but does not depend on the instruction set. We cannot compare computers with different instruction sets using MIPS, since the instruction counts will certainly differ. Second, MIPS varies between programs on the same computer; thus a machine cannot have a single MIPS rating. Finally and most importantly, MIPS can vary inversely with performance! There are many examples of this anomalous behavior; one is given below.

Example

Consider the machine with three instruction classes and CPI measurements from the last example on page 58. Now suppose we measure the code for the same program from two different compilers and obtain the following data:

Code from	Instruction counts (in millions) for each instruction class		
	A	**B**	**C**
Compiler 1	5	1	1
Compiler 2	10	1	1

Assume that the machine's clock rate is 100 MHz. Which code sequence will execute faster according to MIPS? According to execution time?

Answer

We can use the following equation to find MIPS:

$$\text{MIPS} = \frac{\text{Clock rate}}{\text{CPI} \times 10^6}$$

$$\text{MIPS} = \frac{100 \text{ MHz}}{\text{CPI} \times 10^6}$$

To find overall CPI for each compiler, we start with the following:

$$\text{CPI} = \frac{\text{CPU clock cycles}}{\text{Instruction count}}$$

We can use an earlier formula for CPU clock cycles:

$$\text{CPU clock cycles} = \sum_{i=1}^{n} (\text{CPI}_i \times \text{C}_i)$$

After substituting into the first formula, we get:

$$\text{CPI} = \frac{\sum_{i=1}^{n} (\text{CPI}_i \times \text{C}_i)}{\text{Instruction count}}$$

We use this formula to compute the CPI values for the two code sequences:

$$\text{CPI}_1 = \frac{(5 \times 1 + 1 \times 2 + 1 \times 3) \times 10^6}{(5 + 1 + 1) \times 10^6} = \frac{10}{7} = 1.428$$

$$\text{MIPS}_1 = \frac{100 \text{ MHz}}{1.428 \times 10^6} = 70.0$$

$$\text{CPI}_2 = \frac{(10 \times 1 + 1 \times 2 + 1 \times 3) \times 10^6}{(10 + 1 + 1) \times 10^6} = \frac{15}{12} = 1.25$$

$$\text{MIPS}_2 = \frac{100 \text{ MHz}}{1.25 \times 10^6} = 80.0$$

Hence, the code produced by Compiler 2 has a higher MIPS rating. Now let's compute execution time using the formula:

$$\text{CPU time} = \frac{\text{Instruction count} \times \text{CPI}}{\text{Clock rate}}$$

$$\text{CPU time}_1 = \frac{(5 + 1 + 1) \times 10^6 \times 1.43}{100 \times 10^6} = \frac{7 \times 1.43}{100} = 0.10 \text{ seconds}$$

$$\text{CPU time}_2 = \frac{(10 + 1 + 1) \times 10^6 \times 1.25}{100 \times 10^6} = \frac{12 \times 1.25}{100} = 0.15 \text{ seconds}$$

So, Compiler 1 is clearly faster—contrary to what we would conclude from looking at MIPS!

We could also compute the performance ratio from the MIPS measurements and the instruction counts, using the formula from above:

$$\text{Execution time} = \frac{\text{Instruction count}}{\text{MIPS} \times 10^6}$$

Thus

$$\text{CPU time}_1 = \frac{7 \times 10^6}{69.9 \times 10^6} = 0.10 \text{ seconds}$$

$$\text{CPU time}_2 = \frac{12 \times 10^6}{80.0 \times 10^6} = 0.15 \text{ seconds}$$

As examples such as this show, MIPS can fail to give a true picture of performance—*even* when comparing two versions of the same program on the same machine. One particularly misleading definition of MIPS is *peak MIPS*. Peak MIPS is obtained by choosing an instruction mix that minimizes the CPI, even if that instruction mix is totally impractical. In the example above, the peak MIPS ratings are the same for both machines: 100 MIPS. To achieve a 100 MIPS rating with a 100 MHz clock, the CPI for the program must be 1. But the only program that can have a CPI of 1, is a program consisting solely of type A instructions! Thus peak MIPS tells us very little about the machine: it does not indicate the actual MIPS rating, nor does it give any indication of actual performance. In addition, the instruction mix used for peak MIPS may be totally useless. Although peak MIPS is an essentially useless measure, many computer manufacturers have announced products using peak MIPS as a metric, often neglecting to include the word "peak"!

If we were trying to compare two machines with dissimilar instruction sets, MIPS would be even more misleading, since the number of instructions required could be very different; we'll see some examples of this in the next chapter. To compensate for this weakness, many people have chosen a definition of MIPS that is relative to some agreed-upon reference machine. *Relative MIPS* is defined as follows:

$$\text{Relative MIPS} = \frac{\text{Time}_{\text{reference}}}{\text{Time}_{\text{unrated}}} \times \text{MIPS}_{\text{reference}}$$

where

$\text{Time}_{\text{reference}}$ = Execution time of a program on the reference machine

$\text{Time}_{\text{unrated}}$ = Execution time of the same program on machine to be rated

$\text{MIPS}_{\text{reference}}$ = Agreed-upon MIPS rating of the reference machine

Relative MIPS tracks execution time *only* for a given program and a given input. Even when these are identified, it becomes harder to find a reference machine on which to run programs as the machine ages. (In the 1980s the dominant reference machine was the VAX-11/780, which was called a 1-MIPS machine and is now hard to find in operation.) Moreover, should the older machine be run with the newest release of the compiler and operating system, or should the software be fixed so the reference machine does not become faster over time? There is also the temptation to generalize from a relative MIPS rating obtained using one benchmark to a general statement about relative performance, even though there can be wide variations in performance of two machines across a complete set of benchmarks.

In summary, the advantage of relative MIPS is small, since execution time, program, and program input still must be known to obtain meaningful information, just as it would if seconds were used. Furthermore, although no one would consider publishing an execution time without specifying the program and its input, nearly everyone who chooses to use relative MIPS eventually succumbs to the temptation either to publish MIPS ratings without additional information or to replace relative MIPS with native or peak MIPS.

MFLOPS and What's Wrong with It

Another popular alternative to execution time is *million floating-point operations per second*, abbreviated *megaFLOPS* or *MFLOPS* but always pronounced "megaflops." The formula for MFLOPS is simply the definition of the acronym:

$$\text{MFLOPS} = \frac{\text{Number of floating-point operations in a program}}{\text{Execution time} \times 10^6}$$

A *floating-point operation* is an addition, subtraction, multiplication, or division operation applied to a number represented in a single or a double precision floating-point representation. Such data items are heavily used in scientific calculations and are specified in programming languages using key words like *float*, *real*, *double*, or *double precision*. Chapter 4 discusses extensively both representation and operations on floating-point numbers.

Clearly, a MFLOPS rating is dependent on the program. Different programs require the execution of different numbers of floating-point operations. Since MFLOPS were intended to measure floating-point performance, they are not applicable outside that range. Compilers, as an extreme example, have a MFLOPS rating near 0 no matter how fast the machine is, because compilers rarely use floating-point arithmetic.

Because it is based on operations in the program rather than on instructions, MFLOPS has a stronger claim than MIPS to being a fair comparison between different machines. The key to this claim is that the same program running on different computers may execute a different number of instructions but will always execute the same number of floating-point operations. Unfortunately, MFLOPS is not dependable because the set of floating-point operations is not consistent across machines, and the number of actual floating-point operations performed may vary. For example, the Cray-2 has no divide instruction, while the Motorola 68882 has divide, square root, sine, and cosine. Thus several floating-point operations are needed on the Cray-2 to perform a floating-point division; whereas, on the Motorola 68882, a call to the sine routine, which would require performing several floating-point operations on most machines, would require only one operation.

Another potential problem is that the MFLOPS rating changes according not only to the mixture of integer and floating-point operations but to the mixture of fast and slow floating-point operations. For example, a program with 100% floating-point adds will have a higher rating than a program with 100% floating-point divides. The solution to both these problems is to define a method of counting the number of floating-point operations in a high-level language program. This counting process can also weigh the operations, giving more complex operations larger weights, allowing a machine to achieve a high MFLOPS rating even if the program contains many floating-point divides. These MFLOPS might be called *normalized MFLOPS*. Of course, because of the counting and weighting, these normalized MFLOPS may be very different from the actual rate at which a machine executes floating-point operations.

Like any other performance measure, the MFLOPS rating for a single program cannot be generalized to establish a single performance metric for a computer. The use of the same term to refer to everything from peak performance (the maximum MFLOPS rate possible for any code segment), to the MFLOPS rate for one benchmark, to a normalized MFLOPS rating only increases the confusion. The worst of these variants of MFLOPS, peak MFLOPS, is unrelated to actual performance; the best variant is redundant to execution time, our principal measure of performance. Yet, unlike execution time, it is tempting to characterize a machine with a single MFLOPS rating without naming the program or input.

2.5   Choosing Programs to Evaluate Performance

A computer user who runs the same programs day in and day out would be the perfect candidate to evaluate a new computer. The set of programs run would form a *workload*. To evaluate two computer systems, a user would simply compare the execution time of the workload on the two machines. However, most users are not in this situation. Instead, they must rely on other methods that measure the performance of a candidate machine, hoping that the methods will reflect how well the machine will perform with the user's workload. This is usually done by evaluating the machine using a set of *benchmarks*, or programs chosen to measure performance. The benchmarks form a workload that the user hopes will predict the performance of the actual workload.

Today it is widely understood that the best type of programs to use for benchmarks are real applications. These may be applications that the user employs regularly or simply applications that are typical. For example, in an environment where the users are primarily engineers, one might use a set of benchmarks containing several typical engineering or scientific applications. If the user community were primarily software development engineers, the best benchmarks would probably include such applications as a compiler or document processing system. Using real applications as benchmarks makes it much more difficult to find simple ways to speed up the execution of the benchmark. Should we find such techniques, they are likely to help not only the benchmark, but other applications as well.

The use of benchmarks whose performance depends on very small code segments encourages optimizations in either the architecture or compiler that target these segments. The compiler optimizations might recognize special code fragments and generate an instruction sequence that is particularly efficient for this code fragment. Likewise, a designer might try to make some sequence of instructions run especially fast, because the sequence occurs in a benchmark. Recently, several companies have introduced compilers that take a specific option (e.g., the name of the benchmark or a code describing it uniquely) for certain well-known benchmarks. Whether the compiler would produce good code, or even *correct* code, when real application programs use these switches, is an open question.

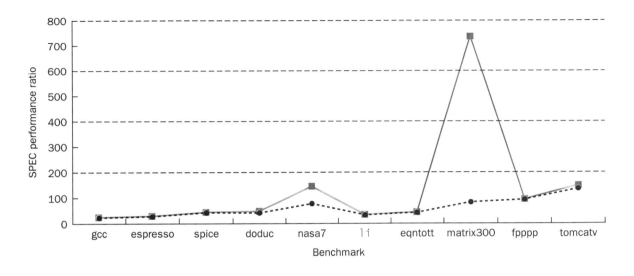

FIGURE 2.3   SPEC performance ratios for the IBM Powerstation 550 using two different compilers. The higher numbers on matrix300 (and nasa7) result from applying an optimization technique to these two kernel-oriented benchmarks. For the enhanced compiler, special flags are passed to the compiler for both nasa7 and matrix300, which are not used for the other benchmarks. In both programs, the compiler transforms the program by blocking the matrix operations that are in the inner loops. These blocking transformations substantially lower the number of memory accesses required and transform the inner loops from having high cache miss rates to having almost negligible cache miss rates. Interestingly, the original motivation for including matrix300 was to exercise the computer's memory system; however, this optimization basically reorganizes the program to minimize memory usage. This data appeared in two SPEC reports during the fall and winter of 1991.

Small programs or programs that spend almost all their execution time in a very small code fragment are especially vulnerable to such efforts. For example, the SPEC processor benchmark suite was chosen to use primarily real applications (see section 2.9 for a further discussion of SPEC). However, the first release of SPEC suite included a benchmark called matrix300, which consists solely of a series of matrix multiplications. In fact, 99% of the execution time is in a single line of this benchmark. The fact that so much time is spent in one line doing the same computation many times has led several companies to purchase or develop special compiler technology to improve the running time of this benchmark. Figure 2.3 shows the performance ratios (inverse to execution time) for one machine with two different compilers. The enhanced compiler has essentially no effect on the running time of eight of the nine benchmarks, but it improves performance on matrix300 by a factor of more than nine. On matrix300, therefore, the program runs 729.8 times faster using the enhanced compiler than the reference time obtained from a VAX-11/780— but the more typical performance of the machine is much slower. The other programs run from just over 30 times faster to just over 140 times faster. A user expecting a program to run 700 times faster than it does on a VAX-11/780 would likely be very disappointed! In 1992, there was a new release of the SPEC benchmark suite and matrix300 was dropped.

So why doesn't everyone run real programs to measure performance? Small benchmarks are attractive when beginning a design, since they are small enough to compile and simulate easily, even by hand. They are especially tempting when designers are working on a novel machine because compilers may not be available until much later. Small benchmarks are also more easily standardized than large programs, hence numerous published results are available for small benchmark performance, but few for large ones.

Although the use of such small benchmarks early in the design process may be justified, there is no valid rationale for using them to evaluate working computer systems. In the past, it was hard to obtain large applications that could be easily ported to a machine, but this is no longer true. Using small programs as benchmarks was an attempt to make fair comparisons among different machines, but use of anything less than real programs after initial design studies is likely to give misleading results and lure the designer astray.

Once we have selected a set of suitable benchmarks and obtained performance measurements, we can write a performance report. The guiding principle in reporting performance measurements should be *reproducibility*—one should list everything another experimenter would need to duplicate the results. This must include the version of the operating system, compilers, and the input, as well as the machine configuration. As an example, we include the system description section of a SPEC benchmark report in Figure 2.4.

2.6 Comparing and Summarizing Performance

Once we have selected programs to use as benchmarks and agreed on whether we are measuring response time or throughput, you might think that performance comparison would be straightforward. However, we must still decide how to summarize the performance of a group of benchmarks. Although summarizing a set of measurements results in less information, marketers and even users often prefer to have a single number to compare performance. The key question is, How should a summary be computed? Figure 2.5, which is abstracted from an article about summarizing performance, illustrates some of the difficulties facing such efforts.

Hardware	
Model number:	Powerstation 550
CPU:	41.67 MHz POWER 4164
FPU:	Integrated
Number of CPUs:	1
Cache size per CPU:	64K data/8K instruction
Memory:	64 MB
Disk subsystem:	2 – 400 MB SCSI
Network interface:	NA
Software	
O/S type and rev:	AIX v3.1.5
Compiler rev:	AIX XL C/6000 Ver. 1.1.5 AIX XL Fortran Ver. 2.2
Other software:	None
File system type:	AIX
Firmware level:	NA
System	
Tuning parameters:	None
Background load:	None
System state:	Multiuser (single-user login)

FIGURE 2.4 System description of the machine used to obtain the higher performance results in Figure 2.3. A footnote attached to the entry for the Fortran compiler states: "AIX XL Fortran Alpha Version 2.2 used for testing." Although no tuning parameters are indicated, additional footnotes describe a number of special flags passed to the compilers for the benchmarks.

	Computer A	Computer B
Program 1 (seconds)	1	10
Program 2 (seconds)	1000	100
Total time (seconds)	1001	110

FIGURE 2.5 Execution times of two programs on two different machines. Taken from Figure 1 of Smith [1988].

Using our definition of *faster*, the following statements hold for the program measurements in Figure 2.5:

- A is 10 times faster than B for program 1.

- B is 10 times faster than A for program 2.

Taken individually, each of these statements is true. Collectively, however, they present a confusing picture—the relative performance of computers A and B is unclear.

Total Execution Time: A Consistent Summary Measure

The simplest approach to summarizing relative performance is to use total execution time of the two programs. Thus

$$\text{B is } \frac{1001}{110}$$

or 9.1 times faster than A for programs 1 and 2.

This summary tracks execution time, our final measure of performance. If the workload consists of running programs 1 and 2 an equal number of times, this statement would predict the relative execution times for the workload on each machine.

The average of the execution times that tracks total execution time is the *arithmetic mean* (AM):

$$\text{AM} = \frac{1}{n} \sum_{i=1}^{n} \text{Time}_i$$

where Time_i is the execution time for the ith program of a total of n in the workload. Since it is the mean of execution times, a smaller mean indicates a smaller average execution time and thus improved performance.

The arithmetic mean tracks execution time by assuming that the programs in the workload are each run an equal number of times. Is that the right workload? If not, we can assign a weighting factor w_i to each program to indicate the frequency of the program in that workload. If, for example, 20% of the tasks in the workload were program 1 and 80% of the tasks in the workload were program 2, then the weighting factors would be 0.2 and 0.8. By summing the products of weighting factors and execution times, we can obtain a clear picture of the performance of the workload. This is called the *weighted arithmetic mean*. One method of weighting programs is to choose weights so that the execution time of each benchmark is equal on the machine used as the base. We will explore the weighted mean in more detail in Exercises 2.25 and 2.26.

2.7   Fallacies and Pitfalls

Cost/performance fallacies and pitfalls have ensnared many a computer architect, including ourselves. Accordingly, this section suffers no shortage of relevant examples. We start with a pitfall that has trapped many designers and reveals an important relationship in computer design.

Pitfall: Expecting the improvement of one aspect of a machine to increase performance by an amount proportional to the size of the improvement.

This pitfall has visited designers of both hardware and software. A simple design problem illustrates it well. Suppose a program runs in 100 seconds on a machine, with multiply operations responsible for 80 seconds of this time. How much do I have to improve the speed of multiplication if I want my program to run five times faster?

The execution time of the program after I make the improvement is given by the following simple equation:

Execution time after improvement =

$$\left(\frac{\text{Execution time affected by improvement}}{\text{Amount of improvement}} + \text{Execution time unaffected} \right)$$

For this problem:

$$\text{Execution time after improvement} = \frac{80 \text{ seconds}}{n} + (100 - 80 \text{ seconds})$$

Since we want the performance to be five times faster, the new execution time should be 20 seconds, giving

$$20 \text{ seconds} = \frac{80 \text{ seconds}}{n} + 20 \text{ seconds}$$

$$0 = \frac{80 \text{ seconds}}{n}$$

That is, there is no amount by which we can enhance multiply to achieve a fivefold increase in performance, if multiply accounts for only 80% of the workload. The performance enhancement possible with a given improvement is limited by the amount that the improved feature is used. This concept is referred to as *Amdahl's Law*. We'll see some other implications of this relationship in Exercises 2.32 through 2.35.

A common theme in hardware design is a corollary of Amdahl's Law: *Make the common case fast*. This simple guideline reminds us that in many cases the frequency with which one event occurs may be much higher than another. Amdahl's Law reminds us that the opportunity for improvement is affected by how much time the event consumes. Thus, making the common case fast will tend to enhance performance better than optimizing the rare case. Ironically, the common case is often simpler than the rare case and hence is often easier to enhance.

Fallacy: Hardware-independent metrics predict performance.

Because accurately predicting and comparing performance is so difficult, many designers and researchers have tried to devise methods to assess performance that do not rely on measurements of execution time. These methods are

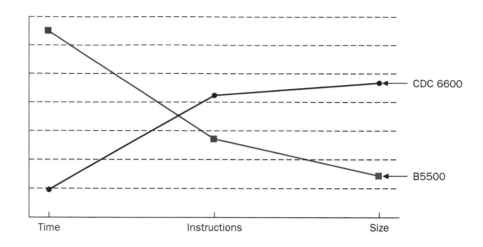

FIGURE 2.6 As found on the cover of *Assessing the Speed of Algol 60* by B. A. Wichmann. The graph shows relative execution time, instruction count, and code size of programs written in Algol 60 for the Burroughs B5500 and the CDC 6600. The results are normalized to a reference machine, with a higher number indicating slower performance. The CDC 6600 was designed later than the B5500 and had a shorter clock cycle, but that accounts for only part of the difference. The CDC 6600 and B5500 are discussed further in the Historical Perspective sections of Chapters 1 and 3.

frequently employed when designers compare different instruction sets to factor out the effects of different implementations or software systems and arrive at conclusions about the performance obtainable for different instruction sets.

One such method, which has been used in the past, is to use code size as a measure of speed. With this method, the instruction set architecture with the smallest program is fastest. The size of the compiled program is, of course, important when memory space is at a premium, but it is not the same as performance. In fact, today, the fastest machines tend to have instruction sets that lead to larger programs but can be executed faster with less hardware.

Evidence of the fallacy of using code size to measure speed can be found on the cover of the well-known book, shown in Figure 2.6. The CDC 6600's programs are over three times as big, yet the CDC machine runs Algol 60 programs almost six times *faster* than the Burroughs B5500, a machine designed for Algol 60.

Compiler writers sometimes use code size to choose between two different code segments on the same architecture. While this is less misleading than trying to compare code size across architectures, the accuracy of predicting performance from code size can vary widely.

Pitfall: Comparing computers using only one or two of three performance metrics: clock rate, CPI, and instruction count.

The processor performance equation shows why such comparisons can mislead. Again, Figure 2.6 provides an example: the CDC 6600 executes almost 1.5 times as many instructions as the Burroughs B5500, yet it is 6.5 times faster. Another example comes from increasing the clock rate while making design decisions that also result in a high overall CPI that offsets the clock rate advantage. The Intergraph Clipper C100 had a clock rate of 33 MHz and a performance of 33 *peak MIPS*—the maximum performance rate for some sequence of instructions. Yet the Sun 4/280, with half the clock rate and half the peak MIPS rating, ran programs faster. Since the Clipper's instruction count is about the same as the Sun's, the former machine's CPI must be more than double that of the latter.

Pitfall: Using peak performance to compare machines.

When the Intel i860 was announced in February 1989, the product announcement used the peak performance of the processor to compare performance against other machines. The i860 was able to execute up to two floating-point operations and one integer operation per clock. With a clock rate target of 50 MHz the i860 was claimed to offer 100 MFLOPS and 150 MOPS (millions of operations per second). The first i860-based systems (using 40-MHz parts) became available for benchmarking during the first quarter of 1991. By comparison, a MIPS machine based on a 33-MHz R3000 processor, available at about the same time, had a peak performance of about 16 MFLOPS and 33 MOPS. Although the peak performance claims might suggest that the i860-based machine was more than five times faster than the R3000-based machine, the SPEC benchmarks showed that the R3000-based machine was actually about 15% faster!

Fallacy: Synthetic benchmarks predict performance.

Synthetic benchmarks are artificial programs that are constructed to try to match the characteristics of a large set of programs. The goal is to create a single benchmark program where the execution frequency of statements in the benchmark matches the statement frequency in a large set of benchmarks. Whetstone and Dhrystone are the most popular synthetic benchmarks. Whetstone was based on measurements of ALGOL programs in a scientific and engineering environment. It was later converted to FORTRAN and became popular. Dhrystone, which was inspired by Whetstone, was created as a benchmark for systems programming environments and was based on a set of published frequency measurements. Dhrystone was originally written in Ada and later converted to C, after which it became popular.

One major drawback of synthetic benchmarks is that no user would ever run a synthetic benchmark as an application, because these programs don't compute anything a user would find remotely interesting. Furthermore, because synthetic benchmarks are not real programs, they usually do not reflect program behavior, other than the behavior considered when they were created. Finally, compiler and hardware optimizations can inflate performance of these benchmarks, far beyond what the same optimizations would achieve on real programs. Of course, because these benchmarks are not natural programs, they may not reward optimizations of behavior that occur in real programs. Here are some examples of how Dhrystone may distort the importance of various optimizations:

- Optimizing compilers can easily discard 25% of the Dhrystone code; examples include loops that are executed only once, making the loop overhead instructions unnecessary. To address these problems, the authors of the benchmark "require" both optimized and unoptimized code to be reported. In addition, they "forbid" the practice of inline-procedure expansion optimization, because Dhrystone's simple procedure structure allows elimination of all procedure calls at almost no increase in code size.

- One C compiler appears to include optimizations targeted just for Dhrystone. If the proper option flag is set at compile time, the compiler turns the portion of the C version of this benchmark that copies a variable-length string of bytes (terminated by an end-of-string symbol) into a loop that transfers a fixed number of words, assuming the source and destination of the string is word-aligned in memory. Although an estimated 99.70% to 99.98% of typical string copies could *not* use this optimization, this single change can make a 20% to 30% improvement in Dhrystone's overall performance.

The small size and simplistic structure of synthetic benchmarks makes them especially vulnerable to this type of activity.

Pitfall: Using the arithmetic mean of normalized execution times to predict performance.

This pitfall has trapped many researchers, including one of the authors. An inviting method of presenting machine performance is to normalize execution times to a reference machine, similar to the relative MIPS rating discussed earlier, and then take the average of the normalized execution times. However, if we average the normalized execution time values with an arithmetic mean, the result will depend on the choice of the machine we use as a reference. For example, in Figure 2.7 the execution times from Figure 2.5 are normalized to both A and B, and the arithmetic mean is computed. When we normalize to A, the arithmetic mean indicates that A is faster than B by $5.05/1$, which is the inverse ratio of the execution times. When we normalize to B, we conclude that B *is faster by exactly the same ratio*. Clearly, both these results cannot be correct!

	Time on A	Time on B	Normalized to A		Normalized to B	
			A	**B**	**A**	**B**
Program 1	1	10	1	10	0.1	1
Program 2	1000	100	1	0.1	10	1
Arithmetic mean	500.5	55	1	5.05	5.05	1
Geometric mean	31.6	31.6	1	1	1	1

FIGURE 2.7 Execution times from Figure 2.5 normalized to each machine. While the arithmetic means vary when we normalize to either A or B, the geometric means are consistent, independent of normalization.

The difficulty arises from the use of the arithmetic mean of ratios. Instead, normalized results should be combined with the *geometric* mean. The formula for the geometric mean is

$$\sqrt[n]{\prod_{i=1}^{n} \text{Execution time ratio}_i}$$

where *Execution time ratio*$_i$ is the execution time, normalized to the reference machine, for the ith program of a total of n in the workload. Note the following:

$$\prod_{i=1}^{n} a_i \text{ means the product: } a_1 \times a_2 \times \ldots \times a_n$$

The geometric mean is independent of which data series we use for normalization because it has the property

$$\frac{\text{Geometric mean } (X_i)}{\text{Geometric mean } (Y_i)} = \text{Geometric mean} \left(\frac{X_i}{Y_i}\right)$$

meaning that taking either the ratio of the means or the means of the ratios produces the same results. Thus the geometric mean produces the same result whether we normalize to A or B, as we can see in the bottom row of Figure 2.7 .When execution times are normalized, only a geometric mean can be used to consistently summarize the normalized results.

Fallacy: The geometric mean of execution-time ratios tracks total execution time.

The advantage of the geometric mean is that it is independent of the running times of the individual programs, and it doesn't matter which machine is used for normalization. However, the drawback to using geometric means of execution times is that they violate our fundamental principle of performance measurement—they do not predict execution time. The geometric means in

Figure 2.7 suggest that for programs 1 and 2 the performance is the same for machines A and B. Yet, the arithmetic mean of the execution times, which we know tracks total execution time, suggests that machine B is 9.1 times faster than machine A! If we use total execution time as the performance measure, A and B would have the same performance only for a workload that ran the first program 100 times more often than the second program.

In general, *no workload* for three or more machines will match the performance predicted by the geometric mean of normalized execution times. The ideal solution is to measure a real workload and weight the programs according to their frequency of execution. If this can't be done, normalizing so that equal time is spent on each program on some machine at least makes the relative weightings explicit and predicts execution time of a workload with that mix. If results must be normalized to a specific machine, first summarize performance with the proper weighted measure and *then* do the normalizing.

2.8 Concluding Remarks

Although we have focused on performance and how to evaluate it in this chapter, designing only for performance without considering cost is unrealistic. All computer designers must balance performance and cost. Of course, there exists a domain of *high-performance design,* in which performance is the primary goal and cost is secondary. Much of the supercomputer industry designs in this fashion. At the other extreme is *low-cost design*, where cost takes precedence over performance. Computers like the low-end IBM PC clones belong here. Between these extremes is *cost/performance design*, in which the designer balances cost against performance. Examples from the workstation industry typify the kinds of trade-offs that designers in this region must live with.

We have seen in this chapter that there is a reliable method of determining and reporting performance, using the execution time of real programs as the metric. This execution time is related to other important measurements we can make by the following equation:

$$\frac{\text{Seconds}}{\text{Program}} = \frac{\text{Instructions}}{\text{Program}} \times \frac{\text{Clock cycles}}{\text{Instruction}} \times \frac{\text{Seconds}}{\text{Clock cycles}}$$

We will use this equation and its constituent factors many times. Remember, though, that individually the factors do not determine performance: Only the product, which equals execution time, is a reliable measure of performance.

Of course, simply knowing this equation is not enough to guide the design or evaluation of a computer. We must understand how the different aspects of a design affect each of these key parameters. This involves a wide variety of issues from the effects of instruction set design on dynamic instruction count, to the impact of pipelining and memory systems on CPI, to the interaction between the technology and organization that determine the clock rate. The art of computer design lies not in plugging numbers into a performance equation, but in accurately determining how design alternatives will affect performance and cost.

Most computer users care about both cost and performance, and while understanding the relationship among aspects of a design and its performance is challenging, determining the cost of various design features is often a more difficult problem. The cost of a machine is affected not only by the cost of the components, but by the costs of labor to assemble the machine, of research and development overhead, of sales and marketing, and of the profit margin. Finally, because of the rapid change in implementation technologies, the most cost-effective choice today is often sub-optimal in six months or a year.

Computer designs will always be measured by cost and performance and finding the best balance will always be the art of computer design, just as in any engineering task.

2.9 Historical Perspective and Further Reading

From the earliest days of computing, designers have specified performance goals—ENIAC was to be 1000 times faster than the Harvard Mark I, and the IBM Stretch (7030) was to be 100 times faster than the fastest machine then in existence. What wasn't clear, though, was how this performance was to be measured.

The original measure of performance was the time required to perform an individual operation, such as addition. Since most instructions took the same execution time, the timing of one was the same as the others. As the execution times of instructions in a machine became more diverse, however, the time required for one operation was no longer useful for comparisons. To take these differences into account, an *instruction mix* was calculated by measuring the relative frequency of instructions in a computer across many programs. Multiplying the time for each instruction by its weight in the mix gave the user the *average instruction execution time*. (If measured in clock cycles, average instruction execution time is the same as average CPI.) Since instruction sets were similar, this was a more precise comparison than add times. From average instruction execution time, then, it was only a small step to MIPS. MIPS had the virtue of being easy to understand, hence it grew in popularity.

The development of *relative* MIPS as a popular performance measurement demonstrates that benchmarking does not necessarily evolve in a logical fashion. In the 1970s, MIPS was being used as a way to compare the performance of IBM 360/370 implementations. Because the measure was used to compare identical architectures (and hence identical instruction counts), it was a valid metric. The notion of relative MIPS came along as a way to extend the easily understandable MIPS rating. In 1977, when the VAX-11/780 was ready to be announced, DEC ran small benchmarks that were also run on an IBM 370/158. IBM marketing referred to the 370/158 as a 1-MIPS computer and, since the programs ran at the same speed, DEC marketing called the VAX-11/780 a 1-MIPS computer.

The popularity of the VAX-11/780 made it a popular reference machine for relative MIPS, especially since relative MIPS for a 1-MIPS reference machine is easy to calculate. If a machine was five times faster than the VAX-11/780, its rating for that benchmark would be 5 relative MIPS. The 1-MIPS rating was widely believed for four years until Joel Emer of DEC measured the VAX-11/780 under a timesharing load. Emer found that the actual VAX-11/780 MIPS rate was 0.5. Subsequent VAXs that run 3 million VAX instructions per second for some benchmarks were therefore called 6-MIPS machines because they run 6 times faster than the VAX-11/780. In the late 1980s, DEC began using *VAX units of performance* (VUP), meaning performance relative to that of the VAX-11/780, so 6 relative MIPS became 6 VUPs.

The 1970s and 1980s marked the growth of the supercomputer industry, which was defined by high performance on floating-point-intensive programs. Average instruction time and MIPS were clearly inappropriate metrics for this industry; hence the invention of MFLOPS. Unfortunately, customers quickly forgot the program used for the rating, and marketing groups decided to start quoting peak MFLOPS in the supercomputer performance wars.

As processors were becoming more sophisticated and relied on memory hierarchies and pipelining, a single execution time for each instruction no longer existed; neither execution time nor MIPS, therefore, could be calculated from the instruction mix and the manual. While it might seem obvious today that the right thing to do would have been to develop a set of real applications that could be used as standard benchmarks, this was a difficult task until relatively recent times. Variations in operating systems and language standards made it hard to create large programs that could be moved from machine to machine simply by recompiling. Instead, the next step was benchmarking using synthetic programs. The Whetstone synthetic program was created by measuring scientific programs written in Algol 60 (see Curnow and Wichman's [1976] description). This program was converted to Fortran and was widely used to characterize scientific program performance. Whetsone performance is typically quoted in Whetstones per second—the number of executions of one iteration of the Whetsone benchmark! Dhrystone was developed much more recently (see Weicker's [1984] description and methodology).

About the same time Whetstone was developed, the concept of *kernel benchmarks* gained popularity. Kernels are small, time-intensive pieces from real programs that are extracted and then used as benchmarks. This approach was developed primarily for benchmarking high-end machines, especially supercomputers. Livermore Loops and Linpack are the best known examples. The Livermore Loops consist of a series of 21 small loop fragments. Linpack consists of a portion of a linear algebra subroutine package. Kernels are best used to isolate the performance of individual features of a machine and to explain the reasons for differences in the performance of real programs. Because scientific applications often use small pieces of code that execute for a long period of time, characterizing performance with kernels is most popular in this application class. Although kernels help illuminate performance, they often overstate the performance on real applications. For example, today's supercomputers often achieve a high percentage of their peak performance on such kernels. However, when executing real applications, the performance often is only a small fraction of the peak performance.

Another misstep on the way to developing better benchmarking methods, was the use of toy programs as benchmarks. Such programs typically have between 10 and 100 lines of code and produce a result the user already knows before running the toy program. Programs like Sieve of Erastosthenes, Puzzle, and Quicksort are popular because they are small, easy to compile, and run on almost any computer. These programs became quite popular in the early 1980s, when universities were engaged in designing the early RISC machines. The small size of these programs made it easy to compile and run them on simulators. Unfortunately, your authors have to admit that they played a role in popularizing such benchmarks, by using them to compare performance and even collecting sets of such programs for distribution. Even more unfortunately, some people continue to use such benchmarks—much to our embarrassment! However, we can report that we have learned our lesson and we now understand that the best use of such programs is as beginning programming assignments.

Almost every issue that involves measuring and reporting performance has been controversial, including the question of how to summarize performance. The methods used have included the arithmetic mean of normalized performance, the harmonic mean of rates, the geometric mean of normalized execution time, and the total execution time. Several references listed in the next section discuss this question, including Smith's [1988] article, whose proposal is the approach used in section 2.6.

A promising development in performance evaluation was the formation of the System Performance Evaluation Cooperative, or SPEC, group in 1988. SPEC comprises representatives of many computer companies—the founders being Apollo/Hewlett-Packard, DEC, MIPS, and Sun—who have agreed on a set of real programs and inputs that all will run. It is worth noting that SPEC couldn't have come into being before portable operating systems and the popularity of high-level languages. Now compilers, too, are accepted as a proper part of the performance of computer systems and must be measured in any evaluation.

History teaches us that while the SPEC effort is useful with current computers, it will not meet the needs of the next generation without changing. In 1991, a throughput measure was added, based on running multiple versions of the benchmark. It is most useful for evaluating timeshared usage of a uniprocessor or a multiprocessor. Other system benchmarks that include OS– and I/O–intensive activities have also been added. Another change, motivated in part by the kind of results shown in Figure 2.3, was the decision to drop matrix300 and to add more benchmarks. One result of the difficulty in finding benchmarks was that the initial version of the SPEC benchmarks (called SPEC89) contained six floating-point benchmarks but only four integer benchmarks. Calculating a single SPECMark, using the geometric mean of execution times normalized to a VAX-11/780, meant that this measure favored machines with strong floating-point performance.

In 1992, a new benchmark set (called SPEC92) was introduced. It incorporated additional benchmarks, dropped matrix300, and provided separate means (SPECINT and SPECFP) for integer and floating-point programs. To address the lack of good benchmarks for supercomputing applications, an effort similar to SPEC, called the Perfect Club, was created by the University of Illinois. Like the SPEC benchmark set, the Perfect Club benchmarks consist of a selection of real applications, aimed at the scientific and engineering environments.

Creating and developing such benchmark sets has become difficult and time-consuming. Although SPEC was initially created as a good faith effort by a group of companies, it became important to competitive marketing and sales efforts. The selection of benchmarks and the rules for running them are made by representatives of the companies that compete by advertising test results. Conflicts between the companies' perspectives and those of consumers naturally arise. Perhaps in the future the decisions about such performance benchmarks should be made by, or at least include, a neutral group.

To Probe Further

Curnow, H. J., and B. A. Wichman [1976]. "A synthetic benchmark," *The Computer J.* 19 (1): 80.

Describes the first major synthetic benchmark, Whetstone, and how it was created.

Flemming, P. J., and J. J. Wallace [1986]. "How not to lie with statistics: The correct way to summarize benchmark results," *Comm. ACM* 29:3 (March) 218–21.

Describes some of the underlying principles in using different means to summarize performance results.

McMahon, F. M. [1986]. "The Livermore FORTRAN kernels: A computer test of numerical performance range," Tech. Rep. UCRL-55745, Lawrence Livermore National Laboratory, Univ. of California, Livermore, Calif. (December).

Describes the Livermore Loops—a set of Fortran kernel benchmarks.

Smith, J. E. [1988]. "Characterizing computer performance with a single number," *Comm. ACM* 31:10 (October) 1202–06.

Describes the difficulties of summarizing performance with just one number and argues for total execution time as the only consistent measure.

SPEC [1989]. "SPEC Benchmark Suite Release 1.0," Santa Clara, Calif., October 2, 1989.

Describes the SPEC benchmark suite.

Weicker, R. P. [1984]. "Dhrystone: A synthetic systems programming benchmark," *Comm. ACM* 27:10 (October) 1013–30.

Describes the Dhrystone benchmark and its construction.

Exercises

2.1 [5] <§2.1> We wish to compare the performance of two different systems: S1 and S2. System S1 costs $10,000 and System 2 costs $15,000. The following measurements have been made on these systems:

Program	Time on S1	Time on S2
1	10 seconds	5 seconds
2	3 seconds	4 seconds

We say one machine is more *cost effective* than another if the ratio of performance divided by cost is higher.

One user cares only about the performance of program 1. Which machine is more cost effective for running only program 1? By how much?

2.2 [5] <§2.1> Another user is concerned with throughput of the systems in Exercise 2.1, as measured with an equal workload of programs 1 and 2. Which system has better performance for this workload? By how much? Which system is more cost effective for this workload? By how much?

2.3 [10] <§2.1> Yet another user has the following requirements for the systems discussed in Exercise 2.1: Program 1 must be executed 200 times each hour. Any remaining time can be used for running program 2. If the system has enough performance to execute program 1 the required number of times per hour, performance is measured by the throughput for program 2. Which system is faster for this workload? Which system is more cost effective?

2.4 [5] <§2.2–2.3> Consider the two systems and programs in Exercise 2.1. The following additional measurements were made:

Program	Instructions executed on S1	Instructions executed on S2
1	20×10^6	16×10^6

Find the instruction execution rate (instructions per second) for each machine when running program 1.

2.5 [5] <§2.2–2.3> If the clock rate of system S1 in Exercise 2.1 is 20 MHz and the clock rate of system S2 in Exercise 2.1 is 30 MHz, find the clock cycles per instruction (CPI) for program 1 on both systems using the data in exercises 2.1 and 2.4.

2.6 [5] <§2.2–2.3> {ex. 2.5} Assuming the CPI for program 2 on each machine in Exercise 2.1 is the same as the CPI for program 1 found in Exercise 2.5, find the instruction count for program 2 running on each machine using the executions times from Exercise 2.1.

2.7 [5] <§2.2–2.3> Consider two different implementations, M1 and M2, of the same instruction set. There are four classes of instructions (A, B, C, and D) in the instruction set.

M1 has a clock rate of 50 MHz. The average number of cycles for each instruction class on M1 is as follows:

Class	CPI for this class
A	1
B	2
C	3
D	4

M2 has a clock rate of 75 MHz. The average number of cycles for each instruction class on M2 is as follows:

Class	CPI for this class
A	2
B	2
C	4
D	4

Assume peak performance is defined as the fastest rate that a machine could execute an instruction sequence chosen to maximize that rate. What are the peak performances of M1 and M2 expressed as instructions per second?

2.8 [10] <§2.2–2.3> If the number of instructions executed in a certain program is divided equally among the classes of instructions in Exercise 2.7, how much faster is M2 than M1?

2.9 [5] <§2.2–2.3> {ex. 2.8} Assuming the CPI values from Exercise 2.7 and the instruction distribution from Exercise 2.8, at what clock rate would M1 have the same performance as the 75-MHz version of M2?

2.10 [10] <§2.2–2.4> We are interested in two implementations of a machine, one with and one without special floating-point hardware.

Consider a program, P, with the following mix of operations:

floating-point multiply	10%
floating-point add	15%
floating-point divide	5%
Integer instructions	70%

Machine MFP (Machine with Floating Point) has floating-point hardware and can therefore implement the floating-point operations directly. It requires the following number of clock cycles for each instruction class:

floating-point multiply	6
floating-point add	4
floating-point divide	20
Integer instructions	2

Machine MNFP (Machine with No Floating Point) has no floating-point hardware and so must emulate the floating-point operations using integer instructions. The integer instructions all take 2 clock cycles. The number of integer instructions needed to implement each of the floating-point operations is as follows:

floating-point multiply	30
floating-point add	20
floating-point divide	50

Both machines have a clock rate of 100 MHz. Find the native MIPS ratings for both machines.

2.11 [10] <§2.2–2.4> If the machine MFP in Exercise 2.10 needs 300,000,000 instructions for this program, how many integer instructions does the machine MNFP require for the same program?

2.12 [5] <§2.2–2.4> {ex. 2.11} Assuming the instruction counts from Exercise 2.11, what is the execution time (in seconds) for the program in Exercise 2.10 run on MFP and MNFP?

2.13 [5] <§2.4> {ex. 2.12} Assuming that each floating-point operation counts as 1, and that MFP executes 300,000,000 instructions, find the MFLOPS rating for both machines in Exercise 2.10.

2.14 [10] <§2.3–2.4> You are the lead designer of a new processor. The processor design and compiler are complete and now you must decide whether to produce the current design as it stands or spend additional time to improve it.

You discuss this problem with your hardware engineering team and arrive at the following options:

a. *Leave the design as it stands.* Call this base machine *Mbase*. It has a clock rate of 50 MHz, and the following measurements have been made using a simulator:

Instruction class	CPI	Frequency
A	2	40%
B	3	25%
C	3	25%
D	5	10%

b.   *Optimize the hardware.* The hardware team claims that it can improve the processor design to give it a clock rate of 60 MHz. Call this machine *Mopt*. The following measurements were made using a simulator for Mopt:

Instruction class	CPI	Frequency
A	2	40%
B	2	25%
C	3	25%
D	4	10%

What is the CPI for each machine?

2.15 [5] <§2.3–2.4> {ex. 2.14} What are the native MIPS ratings for Mbase and MOpt in Exercise 2.14?

2.16 [10] <§2.3–2.4> {ex. 2.14} How much faster is Mopt in Exercise 2.14 than Mbase?

2.17 [5] <§2.3–2.4> The compiler team has heard about the discussion to enhance the machine discussed in Exercises 2.14 –2.16 . The compiler team proposes to improve the compiler for the machine to further enhance performance. Call this combination of the improved compiler and the base machine Mcomp. The instruction improvements from this enhanced compiler have been estimated as follows:

Instruction class	Percentage of instructions executed vs. base machine
A	90%
B	90%
C	85%
D	95%

For example, if the base machine executed 500 class A instructions, Mcomp would execute 0.9×500 = 450 class A instructions for the same program.

What is the CPI for Mcomp?

2.18 [5] <§2.3–2.4> {ex. 2.14, 2.17} Using the data of Exercise 2.14, how much faster is Mcomp than Mbase?

2.19 [10] <§2.3–2.4> {ex. 2.14, 2.17, 2.18} The compiler group points that it is possible to implement both the hardware improvements of Exercise 2.14 and the compiler enhancements described in Exercise 2.17. If *both* the hardware and compiler improvements are implemented, yielding machine *Mboth*, how much faster is Mboth than Mbase?

2.20 [10] <§2.3–2.4> {ex. 2.14, 2.17, 2.18, 2.19} You must decide whether to incorporate the hardware enhancements suggested in Exercise 2.14 or the compiler enhancements of Exercise 2.17 (or both) to the base machine described in Exercise 2.14. You estimate that the following time would be required to implement the optimizations described in Exercises 2.14, 2.17, and 2.19:

Optimization	Time to implement	Machine name
Hardware	6 months	Mopt
Compiler	6 months	Mcomp
Both	8 months	Mboth

Recall from Chapter 1 that CPU performance improves by approximately 50% per year, or about 3.4% per month. Assuming that the base machine has performance equal to that of its competitors, which optimizations (if any) would you choose to implement?

2.21 [5] <§2.4, 2.6> The table below shows the number of floating-point operations executed in two different programs and the runtime for those programs on three different machines:

Program	Floating-point operations	Execution time in seconds		
		Computer A	Computer B	Computer C
Program 1	10,000,000	1	10	20
Program 2	100,000,000	1000	100	20

Which machine is fastest according to total execution time? How much faster is it than the other two machines?

2.22 [5] <§2.4, 2.6> Find the MFLOPS ratings for each program on each machine in Exercise 2.21, assuming that each floating-point operation counts as 1 FLOP.

2.23 [5] <§2.6, 2.7> You wonder how the performance of the three machines in Exercise 2.22 would compare using other means to normalize performance.

Which machine is fastest by the geometric mean?

2.24 [15] <§2.6, 2.7> {ex. 2.23} Find a workload for the two programs of Exercise 2.21 that will produce the same performance summary using total execution time of the workload as the geometric mean of performance computed in

Exercise 2.23. Give the workload as a percentage of executions of each program for the pairs of machines: A and B, B and C, and A and C.

2.25 [15] <§2.6, 2.7> One user has told you that the two programs in Exercises 2.22–2.23 constitute the bulk of his workload, but he does not run them equally. The user wants to determine how the three machines compare when the workload consists of different mixes of these two programs. You know you can use the arithmetic mean to find the relative performance.

Suppose the total number of FLOPS executed in the workload is equally divided among the two programs. That is, program 1 is run 10 times as often as program 2. Find which machine is fastest for this workload and by how much. How does this compare with the total execution time for a workload with equal numbers of program executions?

2.26 [15] <§2.6, 2.7> An alternative weighting to that of Exercise 2.25 is to assume that equal amounts of time will be spent running each program on some machine. Which machine is fastest using the data of Exercise 2.21 and assuming a weighting that generates equal execution time for each benchmark on machine A? Which machine is fastest if we assume a weighting that generates equal execution time for each benchmark on machine B? How do these results compare with the unweighted performance summaries?

2.27 [15] <§2.6> If performance is expressed as a rate, then a higher rating and a higher average indicate better performance. When performance is expressed as a rate, the average that tracks total execution time is the *harmonic mean* (HM):

$$\text{HM} = \frac{n}{\displaystyle\sum_{i=1}^{n} \frac{1}{\text{Rate}_i}}$$

Each Rate_i is $1/\text{Time}_i$, where Time_i is the execution time for the ith of n programs in the workload. Prove that the harmonic mean of a set of rates tracks execution time by showing that it is the inverse of the arithmetic mean of the corresponding execution times.

2.28 [3 hours] <§2.5> Pick two computers, A and B, and run the Dhrystone benchmark and some substantial C program, such as the C compiler, calling this program P. Try running the two programs using no optimization and maximum optimization. Then calculate the following performance ratios:

a. Unoptimized Dhrystone on machine A versus unoptimized Dhrystone on machine B.

b. Unoptimized P on A versus unoptimized P on B.

c. Optimized Dhrystone on A versus optimized Dhrystone on B.

d. Optimized P on A versus optimized P on B.

e. Unoptimized Dhrystone versus optimized Dhrystone on machine A.

f. Unoptimized P versus optimized P on A.

g. Unoptimized Dhrystone versus optimized Dhrystone on B.

h. Unoptimized P versus optimized P on B.

We want to explore whether Dhrystone accurately predicts the performance of other C programs. If Dhrystone does predict performance, then the following equations should be true about the ratios:

```
(a) = (b) and (c) = (d)
```

If Dhrystone accurately predicts the value of compiler optimizations for real programs, then

```
(e) = (f) and (g) = (h)
```

Determine which of the above relationships hold. For the situations where the relationships are not close, try to find the explanation. Do features of the machines, the compiler optimizations, or the differences between P and Dhrystone explain the answer?

2.29 [3 hours] <§2.5> Perform the same experiment as in Exercise 2.33, replacing Dhrystone with Whetstone and choosing a floating-point program written in Fortran to replace P.

2.30 [4 hours] <§2.4> Devise a program in C or Pascal that determines the peak MIPS rating for a computer. Run it on two machines to calculate the peak MIPS. Now run a real C or Pascal program such as a compiler on the two machines. How well does peak MIPS predict performance of the real program?

2.31 [4 hours] <§2.4> Devise a program in C or Fortran that determines the peak MFLOPS rating for a computer. Run it on two machines to calculate the peak MFLOPS. Now run a real floating-point program on both machines. How well does peak MFLOPS predict performance of the real floating-point program?

In More Depth: Amdahl's Law

Amdahl's Law is sometimes given in another form that yields the speedup. *Speedup* is the measure of how a machine performs after some enhancement relative to how it previously performed. Thus, if some feature yields a speedup ratio of 2, performance with the enhancement is twice that before the enhancement. Hence, we can write

$$\text{Speedup} = \frac{\text{Performance after improvement}}{\text{Performance before improvement}}$$

$$= \frac{\text{Execution time before improvement}}{\text{Execution time after improvement}}$$

The earlier version of Amdahl's Law was given as

Execution time after improvement =

$$\left(\frac{\text{Execution time affected by improvement}}{\text{Amount of improvement}} + \text{Execution time unaffected} \right)$$

For the following problems, suppose we enhance a machine making all floating-point instructions run *five times faster*. Let's look at how speedup behaves when we incorporate the faster floating-point hardware.

2.32 [5] <§2.7> If the execution time of some benchmark before the floating-point enhancement is 10 seconds, what will the speedup be if half of the 10 seconds is spent executing floating-point instructions?

2.33 [10] <§2.7> We are looking for a benchmark to show off the new floating-point unit described above, and we want the overall benchmark to show a speedup of 3. One benchmark we are considering runs for 100 seconds with the old floating-point hardware. How much of the initial execution time would floating-point instructions have to account for to show an overall speedup of 3 on this benchmark?

2.34 [10] <§2.7> Assuming that we make floating point five times faster, plot the speedup from this change, versus the fraction of time in the original program spent doing floating-point operations on a graph of the following form:

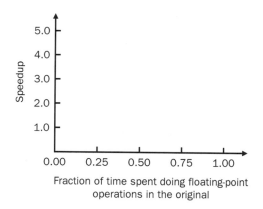

Fraction of time spent doing floating-point
operations in the original

2.35 [20] <§2.7> Amdahl's Law is often written as overall speedup as a function of two variables: the size of the enhancement (or amount of improvement) and the fraction of the original execution time that the enhanced feature is being used. Derive this form of the equation from the two equations above.

3

Instructions:
Language of
the Machine

I speak Spanish to God,
Italian to women,
French to men,
and German to my horse.

Charles V, King of France
1337–1380

The Five Classic Components of a Computer

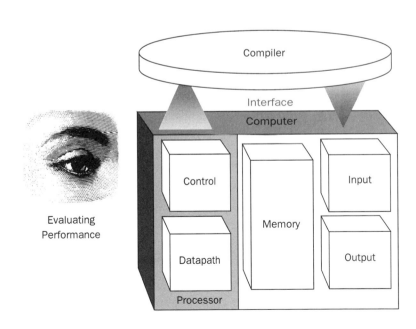

3.1   Introduction

To command a computer's hardware, you must speak its language. The words of a machine's language are called *instructions*, and its vocabulary is called an *instruction set*. In this chapter you will see the instruction set of a real computer, both in the form written by humans and in the form read by the machine. Starting from a notation that looks like a restricted programming language, we refine it step-by-step until you see the real language of a real computer.

You might think that the languages of machines would be as diverse as those of humans, but in reality machine languages are quite similar, more like regional dialects than like independent languages. Hence once you learn one, it is easy to pick up others. This similarity occurs because all computers are constructed from hardware technologies based on similar underlying principles and because there are a few basic operations that all machines must provide. Moreover, computer designers have a common goal: to find a language that makes it easy to build the hardware and the compiler while maximizing performance and minimizing cost. This goal is time-honored; the following quote was written before you could buy a computer, and it is as true today as it was in 1947.

> *It is easy to see by formal-logical methods that there exist certain [instruction sets] that are in abstract adequate to control and cause the execution of any sequence of operations . . . . The really decisive considerations from the present point of view, in selecting an [instruction set], are more of a practical nature: simplicity of the equipment demanded by the [instruction set], and the clarity of its application to the actually important problems together with the speed of its handling of those problems.*

> Burks, Goldstine, and von Neumann, 1947

The "simplicity of the equipment" is as valuable a consideration for the machines of the 1990s as it was for those of the 1950s. The goal of this chapter is to teach an instruction set that follows this advice, showing both how it is represented in the hardware and the relationship between high-level programming languages and this more primitive one. We are using the C programming language. Readers familiar with another language should refer to Appendix D for a short comparison of C with Pascal.

By learning how instructions are represented, you will also discover the secret of computing: the stored-program concept. And you will exercise your "foreign language" skills by writing assembly programs and running them on the simulator that comes with this book. We conclude with a look at the historical evolution of instruction sets and an overview of other machine dialects.

The chosen instruction set comes from MIPS Computer Company and is typical of instruction sets designed since the early 1980s. We reveal the MIPS instruction set a piece at a time, giving the rationale along with the machine structures. This step-by-step tutorial weaves the components with their explanations, making assembly language more palatable. To keep the overall picture in mind, each section ends with a figure summarizing the MIPS instruction set revealed thus far, highlighting the portions presented in that section.

3.2 Operations of the Computer Hardware

There must certainly be instructions for performing the fundamental arithmetic operations.

Burks, Goldstine, and von Neumann, 1947

Every computer must be able to perform arithmetic. The MIPS notation

```
add a, b, c
```

instructs a computer to add the two variables b and c and to put their sum in a.

This notation is rigid in that each MIPS arithmetic instruction must always have exactly three variables. For example, suppose we want to place the sum of variables b, c, d, and e into variable a. The following sequence of instructions adds the variables:

```
add a, b, c    # The sum of b and c is placed in a.
add a, a, d    # The sum of b, c and d is now in a.
add a, a, e    # The sum of b, c, d and e is now in a.
```

Thus it takes three instructions to take the sum of four variables.

The words to the right of the sharp symbol (#) on each line above are *comments* for the human reader, and they are ignored by the computer. Note that unlike other programming languages, each line of this language can contain, at most, one instruction. Another difference is that comments terminate at the end of a line.

The natural number of operands for an operation like addition is three: the two numbers being added together and a placeholder for the sum. Requiring every instruction to have exactly three operands, no more and no less, conforms to the philosophy of keeping the hardware simple. Hardware for a variable number of operands is more complicated than hardware for a fixed

MIPS assembly language

Category	Instruction	Example	Meaning	Comments
Arithmetic	add	add a,b,c	a = b + c	Always 3 operands
	subtract	sub a,b,c	a = b - c	Always 3 operands

FIGURE 3.1 MIPS architecture revealed in section 3.1. The real machine operands will be unveiled in the next section. Highlighted portions in such summaries show MIPS structures introduced in this section; for this first figure, all is new.

number. This situation illustrates the first of four underlying principles of hardware design:

Principle 1: Simplicity favors regularity.

We can now show, in the two examples that follow, the relationship of programs written in programming languages to programs in this more primitive notation. Figure 3.1 summarizes the portions of MIPS described in this section.

Example

This segment of a C program contains the five variables a, b, c, d, and e:

```
a = b + c;
d = a - e;
```

(Reminder: We are using the C programming language; readers familiar with another language should refer to Appendix D for a short comparison of C with Pascal.) The translation from C to MIPS instructions is performed by the *compiler*. Show the MIPS code produced by the C compiler.

Answer

The C compiler could produce

```
add a, b, c
sub d, a, e
```

These instructions are symbolic representations of what the processor understands; they are called *assembly language* instructions.

Example	A more complex C statement contains the five variables f, g, h, i, and j:

f = (g + h) - (i + j);

What would the C compiler produce?

Answer	The statement might be compiled into the following three MIPS instructions:

```
add t0,g,h  # temporary variable t0 contains g+h
add t1,i,j  # temporary variable t1 contains i+j
sub f,t0,t1 # f gets t0-t1, or (g+h)-(i+j)
```

Note that the compiler created two new variables, t0 and t1, to express the program in the restricted three-operands-per-instruction notation of the machine.

3.3   Operands of the Computer Hardware

Unlike programs in high-level languages, the operands of arithmetic instructions cannot be any variables; they must be from a limited number of special locations called *registers*. Registers are the bricks of computer construction, for registers are primitives used in hardware design that are also visible to the programmer when the computer is completed. The size of a register in the MIPS architecture is 32 bits; groups of 32 bits occur so frequently that they are given the name *word* in the MIPS architecture.

One major difference between the variables of a programming language and registers is the limited number of registers, typically between 16 and 32 on current computers. MIPS has 32 registers, using the notation $0, $1, ... , $31 to represent them. (See section 3.14 for the history of the number of registers.) The reason for this limit may be found in the second of our four underlying principles of hardware technology:

Principle 2: Smaller is faster.

A very large number of registers would increase the clock cycle time simply because it takes electronic signals longer when they must travel farther. Guidelines such as "smaller is faster" are not absolutes; 31 registers may not be faster than 32. Yet the truth behind such observations causes computer designers to take them seriously. In this case, the designer must balance the craving of programs for more registers with the designer's desire to keep the clock cycle fast.

Chapters 5 and 6 show the central role that registers play in hardware construction; as we shall see in this chapter, effective use of registers is a key to program performance.

Example

It is the compiler's job to associate program variables with registers. Take, for instance, the C statement from our earlier example:

```
f = (g + h) - (i + j);
```

The variables f, g, h, i, and j can be assigned to the registers $16, $17, $18, $19, and $20, respectively. What is the compiled MIPS assembly code?

Answer

The compiled program is

```
add $8,$17,$18    # register $8 contains g+h
add $9,$19,$20    # register $9 contains i+j
sub $16,$8,$9     # f gets $8-$9, or (g+h)-(i+j)
```

Registers $8 and $9 correspond to t0 and t1 in the earlier example.

Programming languages have simple variables that contain single data elements as in these examples, but they also have more complex data structures such as arrays. These complex data structures can contain many more data elements than there are registers in a machine. How can a computer represent and access such large structures?

Recall the five components of a computer introduced in Chapter 1 and depicted on the second page of this chapter (page 93). The processor can store only a small amount of data in registers, but computer memory contains millions of data elements. Hence data structures, like arrays, are kept in memory.

As explained above, arithmetic operations occur only on registers in MIPS; thus MIPS must include instructions that transfer data between memory and registers. Such instructions are called *data transfer* instructions. To access a word in memory, the instruction must supply its *address*. Memory is really just a large, single-dimensional array, with the address acting as the index to that array. Addresses start at 0. For example, in Figure 3.2, the address of the third data element is 2, and the value of Memory[2] is 1000.

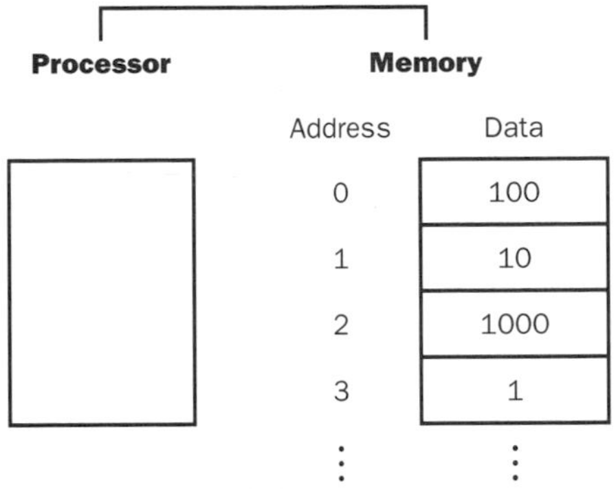

FIGURE 3.2 Memory addresses and contents of memory at those locations. This is a simplification of the MIPS addressing; Figure 3.3 shows MIPS addressing for sequential words in memory.

The data transfer instruction that moves data from memory to a register is called *load*. The format of the load instruction is the name of the operation followed by the register to be loaded, then the start address of the array, and finally a register that contains the index of the element of the array to be loaded. Thus the memory address of the array element is formed by the sum of the constant portion of the instruction and a register. The MIPS name for this instruction is `lw`, standing for *load word*.

Example

Assume that A is an array of 100 elements and that the compiler has associated the variables g, h, and i with the registers $17, $18, and $19. Let's also assume that the array starts at address Astart. Translate this C statement:

    g = h + A[i];

Answer

The C assignment statement becomes

```
lw      $8,Astart($19)      # Temporary reg $8 gets A[i]
add     $17,$18,$8          # g = h + A[i]
```

The load instruction lw adds the starting address of the array A (named Astart here) to the index i in register $19 to form the address of element A[i]. The register added to the address is therefore called the *index register*. The processor then reads the value from memory at that address and places it into register $8, which is used as a temporary variable. The following *add* instruction can operate on the value in $8 (which equals A[i]) since it is in a register. The instruction adds A[i] to h and puts the sum in the register corresponding to g.

Hardware Software Interface In addition to associating variables with registers, it is up to the compiler to allocate data structures like arrays to locations in memory. The compiler can then place the proper starting address into the data transfer instructions.

Since 8-bit *bytes* are useful in many programs, the MIPS architecture addresses individual bytes. The address of a word is therefore actually the same as one of the 4 bytes in a word. Hence, addresses of sequential words differ by 4. Figure 3.3 shows the actual addresses for Figure 3.2. (Appendix A, section A-9 on page A-45, shows the two ways to number bytes in a word.)

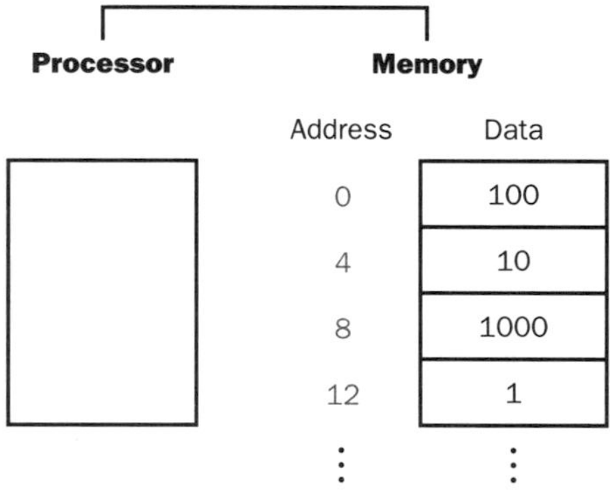

FIGURE 3.3 Actual MIPS memory addresses and contents of memory for those words. The changed addresses are highlighted to contrast to Figure 3.2.

Byte addressing also affects the index i. To get the proper byte address in the code above, register $19 must have $4 \times i$ so that the sum of $19 and Astart will select A[i] and not A[i/4].

The instruction complementary to load is called *store*; it transfers data from a register to memory. The format of a store is similar to that of a load: the name of the operation, followed by the register to be stored, then the starting address of the array, and finally a register that contains the index to the element of the array to be stored. The MIPS name is sw, standing for *store word*. Once again, the MIPS address is specified in part by a constant and in part by a register.

Example

Assume the variables g and h are associated with the registers $17 and $18. To accommodate the byte addresses of MIPS, assume that register $19 now has the value $4 \times i$. Chapter 4 explains how to multiply in MIPS; for now assume the multiplication has already occurred. What is the MIPS assembly code for the C statement below?

```
A[i] = h + A[i];
```

Answer

The C assignment statement becomes

```
lw   $8,Astart($19)      # Temporary reg $8 gets A[i]
add  $8,$18,$8           # Temporary reg $8 gets h+A[i]
sw   $8,Astart($19)      # Stores h+A[i] back into A[i]
```

Instead of placing the sum of h and A[i] into register $17, as in the prior example, the sum is placed into temporary register $8 and then stored back into A[i].

These are the instructions that transfer words between memory and registers in the MIPS architecture. Other brands of computers use instructions in addition to load and store to transfer data; these alternatives are described in section 3.8. Figure 3.4 summarizes the portions of MIPS described in this section.

MIPS operands

Name	Example	Comments
32 registers	$0, $1, $2, . . . , $31	Fast locations for data. In MIPS, data must be in registers to perform arithmetic.
2^{30} memory words	Memory[0], Memory[4], . . . , Memory[4294967292]	Accessed only by data transfer instructions in MIPS. MIPS uses byte addresses, so sequential words differ by 4. Memory holds data structures, such as arrays, and spilled registers.

MIPS assembly language

Category	Instruction	Example	Meaning	Comments
Arithmetic	add	add $1,$2,$3	$1 = $2 + $3	3 operands; data in registers
	subtract	sub $1,$2,$3	$1 = $2 - $3	3 operands; data in registers
Data transfer	load word	lw $1,100($2)	$1 = Memory[$2+100]	Data from memory to register
	store word	sw $1,100($2)	Memory[$2+100] = $1	Data from register to memory

FIGURE 3.4 MIPS architecture revealed through section 3.3. Highlighted portions show MIPS structures introduced in this section.

Hardware Software Interface

Many programs have more variables than machines have registers. Consequently, the compiler tries to keep the most frequently used variables in registers and places the rest in memory, using loads and stores to move variables between registers and memory. The process of putting less commonly used variables (or those needed later) into memory is called *spilling* registers.

The hardware principle relating size and speed suggests that memory must be slower than registers since registers are smaller. This is indeed the case; data accesses are faster if data is kept in registers instead of memory. Moreover, data in registers is easier to manipulate. A MIPS arithmetic instruction can read two registers, operate on them, and write the result. A MIPS data transfer instruction only reads one operand or writes one operand, without operating on them. Thus data in MIPS registers are both faster to access and easier to use. To achieve highest performance, MIPS compilers must use registers efficiently.

Elaboration: A series of instructions can be used to extract a byte from a word, so load word and store word are sufficient for transferring bytes as well as words. Some programs use bytes frequently, however, so the full MIPS architecture has explicit instructions to load and store bytes. For the same reason, the full MIPS instruction set also has explicit instructions to load and store 16-bit quantities, called *halfwords*. We cover only a subset of the MIPS instructions in this book to keep the instruction set as easy to understand as possible. Hence we omit byte and halfword data transfer instructions from the text, although section A.10 starting on page A-47 includes the full instruction set.

3.4 Representing Instructions in the Computer

We are now ready to explain the difference between the way humans instruct machines and the way machines see instructions. But first, let's quickly review how a machine represents numbers.

Humans are taught to think in base 10, but numbers may be represented in any base. For example, 123 base 10 = 1111011 base 2.

Numbers are kept in computer hardware as a series of high and low electronic signals, and so they are considered base 2 numbers. (Just as base 10 numbers are called *decimal* numbers, base 2 numbers are called *binary* numbers.) A single digit of a binary number is thus the "atom" of computing, for all information is composed of binary digits or *bits*. This fundamental building block can be one of two values, which can be thought of as several alternatives: high or low, on or off, true or false, or 1 or 0.

Instructions are also kept in the computer as a series of high and low electronic signals and may be represented as numbers. In fact, each piece of an instruction can be considered as an individual number, and placing these numbers side by side forms the instruction. For example, the MIPS instruction

    add $8,$17,$18

is represented as the following combination of decimal numbers:

0	17	18	8	0	32

Each of these segments of an instruction is called a *field*. The first and last fields (containing 0 and 32 in this case) in combination tell the MIPS computer that this instruction performs addition. The second field gives the number of the register that is the first source operand of the addition operation ($17) and the third field gives the other source operand for the addition ($18). The fourth field contains the number of the register that is to receive the sum ($8). The fifth field is unused in this instruction, so it is set to 0. Thus this instruction adds register $17 to register $18 and places the sum in register $8.

Of course, this instruction can also be represented as fields of binary numbers as opposed to decimal:

000000	10001	10010	01000	00000	100000
6 bits	5 bits	5 bits	5 bits	5 bits	6 bits

This layout of the instruction is called the *instruction format*. As you can see from counting the number of bits, this MIPS instruction takes exactly 32 bits— the same size as a data word. In keeping with our design principle that simplicity favors regularity, all MIPS instructions are 32 bits long.

MIPS fields are given names to make them easier to discuss:

op	rs	rt	rd	shamt	funct
6 bits	5 bits	5 bits	5 bits	5 bits	6 bits

Here is the meaning of each name of the fields in MIPS instructions:

- *op*: operation of the instruction
- *rs*: the first register source operand
- *rt*: the second register source operand
- *rd*: the register destination operand; it gets the result of the operation
- *shamt*: shift amount (This term is explained in Chapter 4; you will not need it until then.)
- *funct*: function; this field selects the variant of the operation in the op field

A problem occurs when an instruction needs longer fields than those shown above. For example, the load instruction must specify two registers and an address. If the address were to use one of the 5-bit fields in the format above, the address within the load instruction would be limited to only 2^5 or 32 memory locations. This is too small to be a useful data address.

Hence we have a conflict between the desire to keep all instructions the same length and the desire to have a single instruction format. This leads us to the third hardware design principle:

Principle 3: Good design demands compromise.

The compromise chosen by the MIPS designers is to keep all instructions the same length, thereby requiring different kinds of instruction formats for different kinds of instructions. For example, the format above is called the

Instruction	Format	op	rs	rt	rd	shamt	funct	address
add	R	0	reg	reg	reg	0	32	n.a.
sub	R	0	reg	reg	reg	0	34	n.a.
lw	I	35	reg	reg	n.a.	n.a.	n.a.	address
sw	I	43	reg	reg	n.a.	n.a.	n.a.	address

FIGURE 3.5 MIPS instruction encoding. In the table above, reg means a register number between 0 and 31, address means a 16-bit address, and n.a. (not applicable) means this field does not appear in this format. Note that add and sub instructions have the same value in the op field; the hardware uses the funct field to decide whether to add or subtract.

R-type (for register). A second type of instruction format is called *I-type* and is used by the data transfer instructions. The fields of this format are

op	rs	rt	address
6 bits	5 bits	5 bits	16 bits

Let's take a look at the load instruction from page 101:

```
lw    $8,Astart($19)# Temporary reg $8 gets A[i]
```

Here, 19 is placed in the rs field, 8 is placed in the rt field, and Astart, the name of the starting address for the array A, is placed in the address field. Note that the meaning of the rt field has changed for this instruction: in a load instruction, the rt field specifies the register to receive the result of the operation.

Although multiple formats complicate the hardware, we can reduce the complexity by keeping the formats similar. For example, the first three fields of the R-type and I-type formats have the same names, with the fourth field in I-type equal to the length of the last three fields of R-type.

In case you were wondering, the formats are distinguished by the values in the first field: each format is assigned a set of values in the first field (op) so that the hardware knows whether to treat the last half of the instruction as three fields (R-type) or as a single field (I-type). This distinguishing field (op) is traditionally known as the *opcode*. Figure 3.5 shows the numbers used in each field for the MIPS instructions covered so far.

Example

We can now take an example all the way from what the programmer writes to what the machine executes. Using the register assignments from the prior example on page 101, including that register $19 has the value $4 \times i$, the C statement:

```
A[i] = h + A[i];
```

is compiled into:

```
lw    $8,Astart($19)    # Temporary reg $8 gets A[i]
add   $8,$18,$8         # Temporary reg $8 gets h + A[i]
sw    $8,Astart($19)    # Stores h + A[i] back into A[i]
```

What is the MIPS machine language code for these three instructions?

Answer

For convenience, let's first represent the machine language instructions using decimal numbers. We need to pick the starting location or *address* for array A. Assume the location is 1200 in base 10 (or 0000 0100 1011 0000 base 2). Here are the three instructions:

op	rs	rt	(rd)	(shamt)	address/ funct
35	19	8		1200	
0	18	8	8	0	32
43	19	8		1200	

The lw instruction is identified by 35 (see Figure 3.5) in the first field (op). The index register $19 is specified in the second field (rs), and the destination register $8 is specified in the third field (rt). The starting address of the array is found in the final field (address). The add instruction that follows is specified with 0 in the first field (op) and 32 in the last field (funct). The three register operands ($18, $8, and $8) are found in the second, third, and fourth fields, respectively. The sw instruction is identified with 43 in the first field. The rest of this final instruction is identical to the lw instruction. The binary equivalent to the decimal form is

100011	10011	01000	0000 0100 1011 0000		
000000	10010	01000	01000	00000	100000
101011	10011	01000	0000 0100 1011 0000		

Note the similarity of the binary representations of the first and last instructions. The only difference is found in the third bit from the left.

As we shall see in Chapters 5 and 6, the similarity of the binary representations of related instructions simplifies hardware design. These instructions are another example of regularity in the MIPS architecture. Figure 3.6 summarizes the portions of MIPS described in this section.

MIPS operands

Name	Example	Comments
32 registers	$0, $1, $2, . . . , $31	Fast locations for data. In MIPS, data must be in registers to perform arithmetic. MIPS register $0 always equals 0.
2^{30} memory words	Memory[0], Memory[4], . . . , Memory[4294967292]	Accessed only by data transfer instructions in MIPS. MIPS uses byte addresses, so sequential words differ by 4. Memory holds data structures, such as arrays, and spilled registers.

MIPS assembly language

Category	Instruction	Example	Meaning	Comments
Arithmetic	add	add $1,$2,$3	$1 = $2 + $3	3 operands; data in registers
	subtract	sub $1,$2,$3	$1 = $2 − $3	3 operands; data in registers
Data transfer	load word	lw $1,100($2)	$1 = Memory[$2+100]	Data from memory to register
	store word	sw $1,100($2)	Memory[$2+100] = $1	Data from register to memory

MIPS machine language

Name	Format	Example						Comments
add	R	0	2	3	1	0	32	add $1,$2,$3
sub	R	0	2	3	1	0	34	sub $1,$2,$3
lw	I	35	2	1		100		lw $1,100($2)
sw	I	43	2	1		100		sw $1,100($2)
Field size		6 bits	5 bits	5 bits	5 bits	5 bits	6 bits	All MIPS instructions 32 bits
Format R	R	op	rs	rt	rd	shamt	funct	Arithmetic instruction format
Format I	I	op	rs	rt		address		Data transfer format

FIGURE 3.6 MIPS architecture revealed through section 3.4. Highlighted portions show MIPS structures introduced in this section.

Today's computers are built on two key principles:

1. Instructions are represented as numbers; and
2. Programs can be stored in memory to be read or written just like numbers.

This is the *stored-program* concept; its invention let the computing genie out of its bottle. Figure 3.7 shows the power of the concept; specifically, memory can contain the C code for an editor program, the corresponding compiled machine code, the text that the compiled program is using, and even the compiler that generated the machine code.

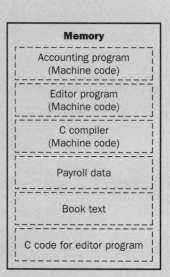

FIGURE 3.7 The stored-program concept. Stored programs allow a computer that performs accounting to become, in the blink of an eye, a computer that helps an author write a book. The switch happens simply by loading memory with programs and data and then telling the computer to begin executing at a given location in memory. Treating instructions in the same way as data greatly simplifies both the memory hardware and the software of computer systems. Specifically, the memory technology needed for data can also be used for programs, and programs like compilers, for instance, can translate code written in a notation far more convenient for humans into code that the machine can understand.

Hardware Software Interface

Recall from Chapter 1 that the symbolic representation of instructions is called the *assembly language* of a computer. To avoid confusion between the symbolic and numerical forms of programs, we traditionally call the numerical equivalent that the machine executes the *machine language*. The translation from assembly language to machine language is called *assembly*, and the program that translates is called an *assembler*. Figure 3.8 shows the translation hierarchy: A C program is first translated into an assembly language program by the compiler, then the assembler translates the assembly language program into machine language. The program that places the machine language program into memory for execution is called a *loader* (see section A.4 on page A-19).

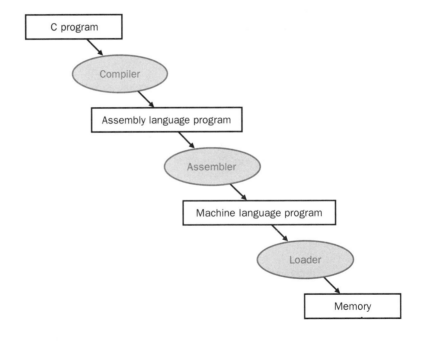

FIGURE 3.8 A translation hierarchy. A high-level language program is first compiled into an assembly language program and then assembled into a machine language program. The loader then places the machine code into the proper memory locations for execution by the processor.

Assembly language is obviously a great improvement over writing numbers. In addition to replacing symbols with numbers, assemblers treat common variations of machine language instructions as if they were instructions in their own right.

For example, the MIPS hardware makes sure that register $0 always has the value 0. That is, whenever register $0 is used, it supplies a 0, and the programmer cannot change the value of register $0. Register $0 is used to create the assembly language instruction move that copies the contents of one register to another. Thus the MIPS assembler accepts this instruction even though it is not found in the MIPS architecture:

```
move $8,$18        # register $8 gets register $18
```

The assembler converts this assembly language instruction into the machine language equivalent of the following instruction:

```
add  $8,$0,$18     # register $8 gets 0 + register $18
```

The MIPS assembler effectively increases the number of instructions available to the assembly language programmers and to compilers. These instructions need not be implemented in hardware; however, their appearance in assembly language simplifies programming. Such instructions are called *pseudoinstructions*.

Elaboration: Representing decimal numbers in base 2 gives an easy way to represent positive integers in computer words. Chapter 4 explains how negative numbers can be represented, but for now take our word that a 32-bit word can represent integers between -2^{31} and $+2^{31} - 1$ or $-2,147,483,648$ to $+2,147,483,647$. Such integers are called *two's complement* numbers.

3.5 Instructions for Making Decisions

The utility of an automatic computer lies in the possibility of using a given sequence of instructions repeatedly, the number of times it is iterated being dependent upon the results of the computation. When the iteration is completed a different sequence of [instructions] is to be followed, so we must, in most cases, give two parallel trains of [instructions] preceded by an instruction as to which routine is to be followed. This choice can be made to depend upon the sign of a number (zero being reckoned as plus for machine purposes). Consequently, we introduce an [instruction] (the conditional transfer [instruction]) which will, depending on the sign of a given number, cause the proper one of two routines to be executed.

Burks, Goldstine, and von Neumann, 1947

What distinguishes a computer from a simple calculator is its ability to make decisions. Based on the input data and the values created during the computation, different instructions are executed. Decision making is commonly represented in programming languages using the *if* statement, sometimes combined with *goto* statements and labels. MIPS includes two decision making instructions, similar to an *if* statement with a *goto*:

```
beq register1, register2, L1
```

This instruction means go to the statement labeled L1 if the value in register1 equals the value in register2. The mnemonic stands for *branch equal*. The second instruction is

```
bne register1, register2, L1
```

It means go to the statement labeled L1 if the value in register1 does *not* equal the value in register2. The mnemonic stands for *branch not equal*. These two instructions are called *conditional branches*.

Example

In the following C code segment, f, g, h, i, and j are variables:

```
        if (i == j) goto L1;
        f = g + h;
   L1:  f = f - i;
```

Assuming that the five variables correspond to five registers $16 through $20, what is the compiled MIPS code?

Answer

The compiled program is

```
        beq $19,$20, L1    # goto L1 if i equals j
        add $16,$17,$18    # f = g + h (skipped if i equals j)
   L1:  sub $16,$16,$19    # f = f - i (always executed).
```

Instructions are stored in memory in stored-program computers; hence, instructions must have memory addresses just like other words in memory. The label L1 thus corresponds to the address of the subtract instruction. Notice that the assembler relieves the compiler or the assembly language programmer from the tedium of calculating branch addresses, just as it does for calculating data addresses for loads and stores (see section A.1 on page A-3 in Appendix A or the example on page 106).

Hardware Software Interface

Compilers frequently create branches and labels when they do not appear in the programming language. Using the same variables and registers from the previous example, the C code:

```
                if (i == j) f = g + h; else f = g - h;
```

```
        bne    $19,$20,Else    # goto Else if i ≠ j
        add    $16,$17,$18     # f = g + h (skipped if i ≠ j)
        j      Exit            # go to Exit
Else:   sub    $16,$17,$18     # f = g - h (skipped if i = j)
Exit:
```

Figure 3.9 shows the form of the C code that the compiler must translate into MIPS code. The second instruction above performs the "then" part of the *if* statement and the fourth instruction performs the "else" part. When i ≠ j, the first instruction branches to the label Else, going around the "then" part. To avoid executing the fourth instruction when i = j, we must branch around it to the label Exit. This introduces another kind of branch, sometimes called an *unconditional branch*. This instruction says that the machine always follows the branch. To distinguish between conditional and unconditional branches, the MIPS name for this type of instruction is *jump*, abbreviated as j.

Decisions are important both for choosing between two alternatives—found in *if* statements—and for iterating a computation—found in loops. The same assembly instructions are the building blocks in both cases.

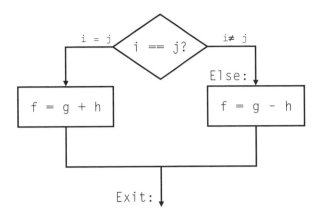

FIGURE 3.9 Illustration of the options in the if statement above. The left box corresponds to the "then" part of the *if* statement and the right box corresponds to the "else" part.

Example

Here is a loop in C:

```
Loop:  g = g + A[i];
       i = i + j;
       if (i != h) goto Loop;
```

Assume A is an array of 100 elements and that the compiler associates the variables g, h, i, and j to the registers $17, $18, $19, and $20, respectively. Let's assume that the array starts at Astart. Remember that byte addressing means we will need to multiply the index i by 4 before we can use it in the load instruction. Let's assume that 4 has already been placed in register $10 and that the MIPS instruction mult (further described in Chapter 4), is available for multiplies. What is the MIPS assembly code corresponding to this C segment?

Answer   It becomes the following assembly language code:

```
Loop:   mult $9,$19,$10      # Temporary reg $9 = i*4
        lw   $8,Astart($9)   # Temporary reg $8 = A[i]
        add  $17,$17,$8      # g = g + A[i]
        add  $19,$19,$20     # i = i + j
        bne  $19,$18, Loop   # goto Loop if i ≠ h
```

Since the body of the loop modifies i, we must multiply its value by 4 each time through the loop. (Section 3.11 shows how to avoid these multiplies when writing loops like this one.)

Hardware Software Interface

Of course, programmers don't normally write loops with gotos, so it is up to the compiler to translate traditional loops into assembly language. This C segment:

```
while (save[i]==k)
    i = i + j;
```

could be translated into the MIPS instructions below, assuming that i, j, and k correspond to registers $19, $20, and $21, the array save starts at Sstart, and register $10 contains 4.

```
Loop:   mult $9,$19,$10      # Temporary reg $9 = i*4
        lw   $8,Sstart($9)   # Temporary reg $8 = save[i]
        bne  $8,$21, Exit    # goto Exit if save[i] ≠ k
        add  $19,$19,$20     # i = i + j
        j    Loop            # goto Loop
Exit:
```

(See Exercise 3.11 for an optimization of this sequence.)

The test for equality or inequality is probably the most popular test, but sometimes it is useful to see if a variable is less than another variable. For example, a *for* loop may want to test to see if the index variable is less than 0. Such comparisons are accomplished in MIPS with an instruction that compares two registers and sets a third register to 1 if the first is less than the second; otherwise, it is set to 0. The instruction is called *set on less than* or slt. For example,

```
slt    $8, $19, $20
```

means that register $8 is set to 1 if the value in register $19 is less than the value in register $20; otherwise, register $8 is set to 0.

<table>
<tr><td>

Hardware

Software

Interface

</td><td>

MIPS compilers use the slt, beq, bne, and the fixed value of 0 in register $0 to create all relative conditions. For example, let's take a look at the code to test if variable a (corresponding to register $16) is less than variable b ($17), branching to Less if the condition holds. Assume that $1 is an available temporary register. The first step is to use the set on less than instruction and the temporary register:

</td></tr>
</table>

```
        slt    $1,$16,$17    #   $1 gets 1 if $16<$17 (a<b)
```

Register $1 is set to 1 if a is less than b. Hence, a branch to see if register $1 is not equal to 0 will give us the effect of branching if a is less than b. Register $0 always contains 0, so this final test is accomplished using the bne instruction and comparing register $1 to register $0:

```
    bne $1,$0, Less      # go to Less if $1≠$0
                         #   (that is, if a < b)
```

This pair of instructions, slt and bne, implements a branch on less than, and, in fact, the MIPS assembler converts blt (branch on less than) into exactly these two instructions. Note again how an assembler can create instructions that are not implemented by the hardware. Heeding von Neumann's warning about the simplicity of the "equipment," the MIPS architecture doesn't include blt because it is too complicated; either it would stretch the clock cycle time or this instruction would take extra clock cycles per instruction. Two faster instructions are more useful.

To support such pseudoinstructions, the assembler must have a temporary register which can be used without fear of altering the program. Since compilers allocate registers, the MIPS compiler writers have promised to abstain from using register $1 so that it can be used by the MIPS assembler.

Most programming languages have a *case* or *switch* statement that allows the programmer to select one of many alternatives depending on a single value. One way to implement switch is via a sequence of conditional tests, turning the *switch* statement into a chain of *if-then-else* statements. But sometimes the alternatives may be efficiently encoded as a table of addresses of alternative instruction sequences, and the program needs only to index the *jump address table* and then jump to the appropriate sequence. To support such situations, computers like MIPS include a *Jump register* instruction (jr), meaning an unconditional jump to the address specified in a register.

Example

This C version of a case statement is called a *switch statement*. The following C code chooses among four alternatives depending on whether k has the value 0, 1, 2, or 3. Assume the six variables f through k correspond to six registers $16 through $21 and that register $10 contains 4. What is the corresponding MIPS code?

```
switch (k) {
       case 0:    f = i + j;  break;  /* k = 0 */
       case 1:    f = g + h;  break;  /* k = 1 */
       case 2:    f = g - h;  break;  /* k = 2 */
       case 3:    f = i - j;  break;  /* k = 3 */
}
```

Answer

The following MIPS assembly language will work, provided four words in memory, starting at location JumpTable, have addresses corresponding to the labels L0, L1, L2, and L3, respectively. Since we are using the variable k to index into this array of words, we must first multiply by 4 to turn k into its byte address equivalent.

```
Loop: mult $9,$10,$21     # Temporary reg $9 = k*4
      lw    $8,JumpTable($9)  # Temp reg $8 = JumpTable[k]
      jr    $8            # jump based on register $8
L0: add   $16,$19,$20     # k=0 so f gets i + j
      j     Exit          # end of this case so goto Exit
L1: add   $16,$17,$18     # k=1 so f gets g + h
      j     Exit          # end of this case so goto Exit
L2: sub   $16,$17,$18     # k=2 so f gets g - h
      j     Exit          # end of this case so goto Exit
L3: sub   $16,$19,$20     # k=3 so f gets i - j
Exit:                     # end of switch statement
```

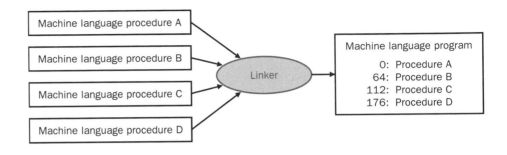

FIGURE 3.10 A linker allows separate compilation and assembly of portions of a whole program. It finds the addresses in the machine language procedures and corrects the addresses to refer to the actual memory locations.

Hardware Software Interface

What we have presented so far suggests that a single change to one line of one procedure requires compiling and assembling the whole program. Complete retranslation is a terrible waste of computing resources. This is particularly true for standard library routines, because programmers would be compiling and assembling routines that by definition almost never change. An alternative is to compile and assemble each procedure independently, so that a change to one line would require compiling and assembling only one procedure. This alternative implies a new systems program that would take all the independently assembled machine language programs and "stitch" them together.

The challenge for this program is to place the independent modules end to end, fix the cross-references between modules, and, finally, to alter any addresses within these independent modules to make them refer to the new instruction addresses. Figure 3.10 shows an example. Such references occur in branch instructions, jump instructions, and data addresses, so the job of this program is much like that of an editor: It finds the old addresses and replaces them with the new addresses. Editing gives rise to the name of the program: *link editor* or *linker* for short. The reason a linker makes sense is that it is much faster to "patch" code than it is to recompile and reassemble. Many operating systems combine the linker with the loader, giving rise to the name *linking loader*. Sections A.3 on page A-17 and A.4 on page A-19 describe linkers and loaders in more detail.

MIPS operands

Name	Example	Comments
32 registers	$0, $1, $2, . . . , $31	Fast locations for data. In MIPS, data must be in registers to perform arithmetic. MIPS register $0 always equals 0. Register $1 is reserved for the assembler to handle pseudoinstructions.
2^{30} memory words	Memory[0], Memory[4], . . . , Memory[4294967292]	Accessed only by data transfer instructions in MIPS. MIPS uses byte addresses, so sequential words differ by 4. Memory holds data structures, such as arrays, and spilled registers.

MIPS assembly language

Category	Instruction	Example	Meaning	Comments
Arithmetic	add	add $1,$2,$3	$1 = $2 + $3	3 operands; data in registers
	subtract	sub $1,$2,$3	$1 = $2 – $3	3 operands; data in registers
Data transfer	load word	lw $1,100($2)	$1 = Memory[$2+100]	Data from memory to register
	store word	sw $1,100($2)	Memory[$2+100] = $1	Data from register to memory
Conditional Branch	branch on equal	beq $1,$2,L	if ($1 == $2) go to L	Equal test and branch
	branch on not eq.	bne $1,$2,L	if ($1 != $2) go to L	Not equal test and branch
	set on less than	slt $1,$2,$3	if ($2 < $3) $1=1; else $1=0	Compare less than; for beq,bne
Unconditional jump	jump	j 10000	go to 10000	Jump to target address
	jump register	jr $31	go to $31	For switch statements

MIPS machine language

Name	Format	Example						Comments
add	R	0	2	3	1	0	32	add $1,$2,$3
sub	R	0	2	3	1	0	34	sub $1,$2,$3
lw	I	35	2	1	100			lw $1,100($2)
sw	I	43	2	1	100			sw $1,100($2)
beq	I	4	1	2	100			beq $1,$2,100
bne	I	5	1	2	100			bne $1,$2,100
slt	R	0	2	3	1	0	42	slt $1,$2,$3
j	J	2	10000					j 10000 (see section 3.7)
jr	R	0	31	0	0	0	8	jr $31
Field size		6 bits	5 bits	5 bits	5 bits	5 bits	6 bits	All MIPS instructions 32 bits
Format R	R	op	rs	rt	rd	shamt	funct	Arithmetic instruction format
Format I	I	op	rs	rt	address			Data transfer, branch format

FIGURE 3.11 MIPS architecture revealed through section 3.5. Highlighted portions show MIPS structures introduced in this section. The J format, used for jump instructions, is explained in section 3.7.

Figure 3.11 summarizes the portions of MIPS described in this section.

Elaboration: Readers who might have heard about delayed branches, covered in Chapter 6, should not worry: The MIPS assembler makes them invisible to the assembly language programmer.

3.6   Supporting Procedures in Computer Hardware

A procedure or subroutine is one way that programmers structure programs, both to make them easier to understand and to allow code to be reused. An instruction set must provide a way to jump to a procedure and then return from the procedure to the instruction just after the calling point. Programmers must also have conventions governing how to pass parameters and how to support the nesting of procedure calls.

First, let's look at the primitive operations that support procedures. MIPS provides an instruction that jumps to an address and simultaneously saves the address of the following instruction in register $31. The *jump-and-link* instruction (jal) is simply written

                 jal   ProcedureAddress

The *link* portion of the name means that a link is formed to the calling site to allow the procedure to return to the proper address. This link, stored in register $31, is called the *return address*.

We already have an instruction to do the return jump:

                 jr $31

The Jump register instruction, useful in the *switch* statement, jumps to the address stored in register $31—which is just what we want.

Implicit in the instruction set is the need to have a register to hold the address of the current instruction being executed. The jal instruction just increments this register to point to the next instruction before saving it in register $31, and jr $31 simply copies $31 into that register. For historical reasons, this register is almost always called the *program counter*, abbreviated *PC*, although a more sensible name would have been *Instruction Address register*. MIPS follows tradition and calls it the PC.

Suppose a procedure wanted to call another procedure. Then the programmer would need to save the old value of register $31, since the new jal would clobber the old return address. This is an example of where we need to spill registers to memory, as mentioned in the Hardware Software Interface on page 102.

Since procedures can call procedures that call procedures, and so on, the ideal data structure for spilling registers is a *stack*—a last-in-first-out queue. A stack needs a pointer to the top of the stack to show where the next procedure should place the registers to be spilled or where old register values can be found. The top of the stack is adjusted by the number of registers that are saved or restored. Stacks are so popular that they have their own buzzwords for transferring data to and from the stack: Placing data onto the stack is called a *push*, and removing data from the stack is called a *pop*.

Example

Assume procedure A has invoked procedure B, that procedure B is about to call procedure C, and that C calls no more procedures. Figure 3.12 on page 122 shows the steps we must perform. Before calling C, procedure B must save its return address on the stack. The stack pointer, register $29, is adjusted to point to the new top of stack. Procedure C is then called, and the jal instruction changes register $31 to contain C's return address. After procedure C returns to procedure B, the old return address is restored from the stack into register $31. The stack pointer is then changed back to the old top-of-stack location. What is the essential MIPS code to implement this calling protocol?

Answer

Below is the basic MIPS assembly code segment. Assume that register $29 contains the pointer to the top of the stack and one register, say $24, already has the value to adjust the top of stack. Recall that the MIPS assembly convention is to list labels on the left, indent the instruction to the right of the labels, and follow these with an optional comment that starts with the sharp symbol (#).

```
A:...
   ...
   jal  B            # call B & save return address in $31
   ...
B:...
   ...               # now ready to call C
   add  $29,$29,$24  # adjust stack to make room
                     # for next item
   sw   $31, 0($29)  # save the return address
   jal  C            # call C & save return address in
                     # $31; return from C to next instr
   lw   $31, 0($29)  # restore B's return address...
   sub  $29,$29,$24  # adjust stack to pop
                     # B's return address
```

```
        ...
   jr    $31              # return to routine that called B
C:...
        ...
   jr    $31              # return to routine that called C
```

A calls B using `jal`, saving the address of the following instruction in register $31. Before B calls C, the stack pointer is adjusted and register $31 is saved. Procedure B then calls C, saving the address again in $31. Since procedure C calls no other procedure, it skips storing its return address on the stack. When C is finished, it returns to B by executing the Jump register instruction using register $31, which in turn invokes the load instruction that follows the jump and link instruction in B. This load restores the proper return address into $31, and the subtract adjusts the stack the other direction. When B is finished, it returns to A using `jr` with register $31, returning to the instruction just after the `jal` in procedure A.

In addition to return addresses, we need a convention that governs passing the arguments, or *parameters*, passed to a procedure. The MIPS software convention is to put parameters in registers $4 through $7. If a procedure needs to call another procedure, these parameter registers can be saved and restored from the stack just like return addresses. In general, if a procedure modifies registers used by the current routine, there must be a convention for saving and restoring registers across procedure calls. The two standard conventions are:

1. *Caller save.* The calling procedure (caller) is responsible for saving and restoring any registers that must be preserved across the call. The called procedure (callee) can then modify any register without constraint.

2. *Callee save.* The callee is responsible for saving and restoring any registers that it might use. The caller uses registers without worrying about restoring them after a call.

Sections 3.9 and 3.10 use callee save, and Exercises 3.28 and 3.29 treat the subject in depth. Note that conventions are not generally limited to a single language. This allows compiled procedures written originally in Fortran to call procedures written originally in C, and vice versa.

Figure 3.13 summarizes the portions of MIPS described in this section.

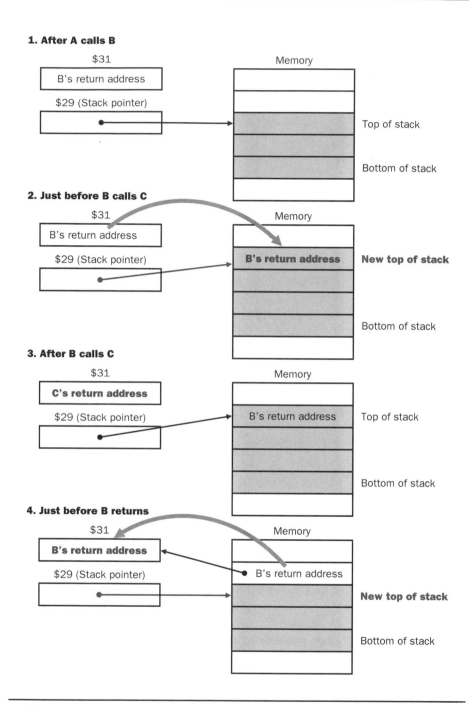

FIGURE 3.12 Saving and restoring the return address on the stack. Procedure calls are nested. Since B calling C will clobber register $31, we must save the current value on the stack. Register $29 is the stack pointer that points to an area of memory containing the top of the stack, which is shown in color. Boldface color indicates items that have changed from the previous step.

MIPS operands

Name	Example	Comments
32 registers	$0, $1, $2, . . . , $31	Fast locations for data. In MIPS, data must be in registers to perform arithmetic. MIPS register $0 always equals 0. Register $1 is reserved for the assembler to handle pseudoinstructions.
2^{30} memory words	Memory[0], Memory[4], . . . , Memory[4294967292]	Accessed only by data transfer instructions. MIPS uses byte addresses, so sequential words differ by 4. Memory holds data structures, such as arrays, and spilled registers, such as those saved on procedure calls.

MIPS assembly language

Category	Instruction	Example	Meaning	Comments
Arithmetic	add	add $1,$2,$3	$1 = $2 + $3	3 operands; data in registers
	subtract	sub $1,$2,$3	$1 = $2 – $3	3 operands; data in registers
Data Transfer	load word	lw $1,100($2)	$1 = Memory[$2+100]	Data from memory to register
	store word	sw $1,100($2)	Memory[$2+100] = $1	Data from register to memory
Conditional Branch	branch on equal	beq $1,$2,L	if ($1 == $2) go to L	Equal test and branch
	branch on not eq.	bne $1,$2,L	if ($1 != $2) go to L	Not equal test and branch
	set on less than	slt $1,$2,$3	if ($2 < $3) $1=1; else $1=0	Compare less than; for beq,bne
Unconditional Jump	jump	j 10000	go to 10000	Jump to target address
	jump register	jr $31	go to $31	For switch, procedure return
	jump and link	jal 10000	$31 = PC + 4; go to 10000	For procedure call

MIPS machine language

Name	Format	Example						Comments
add	R	0	2	3	1	0	32	add $1,$2,$3
sub	R	0	2	3	1	0	34	sub $1,$2,$3
lw	I	35	2	1	100			lw $1,100($2)
sw	I	43	2	1	100			sw $1,100($2)
beq	I	4	1	2	100			beq $1,$2,100
bne	I	5	1	2	100			bne $1,$2,100
slt	R	0	2	3	1	0	42	slt $1,$2,$3
j	J	2	10000					j 10000 (see section 3.7)
jr	R	0	31	0	0	0	8	jr $31
jal	J	3	10000					jal 10000 (see section 3.7)
Field size		6 bits	5 bits	5 bits	5 bits	5 bits	6 bits	All MIPS instructions 32 bits
Format R	R	op	rs	rt	rd	shamt	funct	Arithmetic instruction format
Format I	I	op	rs	rt	address			Data transfer, branch format

FIGURE 3.13 MIPS architecture revealed through section 3.6. Highlighted portions show MIPS structures introduced in this section. The J format, used for jump and jump-and-link instructions, is explained in section 3.7.

Elaboration: What if there are more than four parameters? The MIPS convention is to place the extra parameters on the stack. The procedure then expects the first four parameters to be in registers $4 through $7 and the rest in memory, addressable via the stack pointer.

Parameters are passed in registers to make calls fast. Another challenge in making fast calls is avoiding saving and restoring registers. A MIPS software convention is to consider some registers as caller saved (not preserved across procedure call) and others as callee saved (preserved across procedure call). The compiler allocates short-lived values to the former category of registers and long-lived values to the latter, thereby reducing register saves and restores. Figure A.9 on page A-23 shows the convention.

A final point to mention is that by historical precedent, stacks "grow" from higher addresses to lower addresses. Figure 3.12 follows this convention, with the higher addresses being at the bottom of the drawing. This convention means that you push values onto the stack by subtracting from the stack pointer. Adding to the stack pointer shrinks the stack, thereby popping values off the stack.

3.7   Other Styles of MIPS Addressing

Designers of the MIPS architecture provided two more ways of accessing operands. The first is to make it faster to access small constants and the second is to make branches more efficient.

Constant or Immediate Operands

Many times a program will use a constant in an operation—for example, incrementing an index to point to the next element of an array, counting iterations of a loop, or adjusting a stack in a nested procedure call. In fact, in two programs which have been studied, more than half of the arithmetic instructions have a constant as an operand: in the C compiler gcc, 52% of arithmetic operands are constant, in the circuit simulation program spice, it is 69%.

With the instructions given so far, we would have to load a constant from memory to use it. (The constants would have been placed in memory when the program was loaded.) For example, to add the constant 4 to register $29, we could use the code

```
lw    $24, AddrConstant4($0)    # $24 = constant 4
add   $29,$29,$24               # $29 = $29 + $24 ($24 = 4)
```

assuming that AddrConstant4 is the memory address of the constant 4.

An alternative that avoids memory accesses is to offer new versions of the arithmetic instructions in which one operand is a constant, with the novel constraint that this constant is kept inside the instruction itself. Following the recommendation urging regularity, we use the same format for these instructions as for the data transfer instructions. In fact, the *I* in the name of the I-type format is for *immediate*, the traditional name for this type of operand. The MIPS field containing the constant is 16 bits long.

Example

The add instruction that has one constant operand is called *add immediate* or addi. To add 4 to register 29 we just write

```
addi    $29,$29,4          # $29 = $29 + 4
```

What is the corresponding MIPS machine code?

Answer

This instruction is the following machine code (using decimal numbers):

op	rs	rt	immediate
8	29	29	4

In binary it is

op	rs	rt	immediate
001000	11101	11101	0000 0000 0000 0100

Immediate or constant operands are also popular in comparisons. Since register $0 always has 0, we can already compare to 0. To compare to other values, there is an immediate version of the set on less than instruction. To test if register $18 is less than the constant 10, we can just write:

```
slti    $8,$18,10          # $8 = 1 if $18 < 10
```

Similar to the prior example on page 115 (Hardware Software Interface), this instruction is followed by bne $8,$0 to branch if register $18 is less than the constant 10.

Immediate addressing illustrates the final hardware design guideline, first mentioned in Chapter 2:

Principle 4: Make the common case fast.

Constant operands occur frequently, and by making constants part of arithmetic instructions they are much faster than if they were loaded from memory.

Although constants are frequently short and fit into the 16-bit field, sometimes they are too big. The MIPS instruction set includes the instruction *load upper immediate* (lui) specifically to set the upper 16 bits of a constant in a register, allowing a subsequent instruction to specify the lower 16 bits of the constant. Figure 3.14 shows the operation of lui.

The machine language version of `lui $8, 255`:

001111	00000	01000	0000 0000 1111 1111

Contents of register 8 after executing `lui $8, 255`:

0000 0000 1111 1111	0000 0000 0000 0000

FIGURE 3.14 The effect of the lui instruction. The instruction `lui` transfers the rightmost 16 bits of the drawing into the leftmost 16 bits of the register, filling the lower 16 bits with zeros. As we shall see in Chapter 4, this is like multiplying the constant by 2^{16} before loading it into the register.

Example

What is the MIPS assembly code to load this 32-bit constant into register $16?

        0000 0000 0011 1101 0000 1001 0000 0000

Answer

First we would load the upper 16 bits, which is 61 in decimal, using `lui`:

        lui $16, 61   # 61 decimal = 0000 0000 0011 1101 binary

The value of register $16 afterward is

        0000 0000 0011 1101 0000 0000 0000 0000

The next step is to add the lower 16 bits, whose decimal value is 2304:

        addi $16, $16, 2304 # 2304 decimal = 0000 1001 0000 0000

The final value in register $16 is the desired value:

        0000 0000 0011 1101 0000 1001 0000 0000

Hardware Software Interface

Either the compiler or the assembler must break large constants into pieces and then reassemble them into a register. As you might expect, this size restriction may be a problem for memory addresses in loads and stores as well as for constants in immediate instructions. If this job falls to the assembler, as it does for MIPS software, then the assembler must have a temporary register available in which to create the long values. This is another use for register $1, which was reserved to allow the assembler to expand the set of branch instructions that it accepted (see the Hardware Software Interface on page 115). This means that the assembly language programmer can let the assembler handle large constants and large addresses.

Addressing in Branches and Jumps

The simplest addressing is found in the MIPS jump instructions. They use the final MIPS instruction format, called the *J-type*, which consists of 6 bits for the operation field and the rest of the bits for the address field. Thus,

```
j       10000           # goto location 10000
```

is assembled into this format:

2	10000
6 bits	26 bits

where the value of the jump opcode is 2 and the jump address is 10000.

Unlike the jump instruction, the conditional branch instruction must specify two operands in addition to the branch address. Thus,

```
bne     $8,$21,Exit     # goto Exit if $8 ≠ $21
```

is assembled into this instruction, leaving only 16 bits for the branch address:

5	8	21	Exit
6 bits	5 bits	5 bits	16 bits

If addresses of the program had to fit in this 16-bit field, it would mean that no program could be bigger than 2^{16}, which is far too small to be a realistic option today. An alternative would be to specify a register that would always be added to the branch address, so that a branch instruction would calculate the following:

$$PC = register + branch\ address$$

This allows the program to be as large as 2^{32} and still be able to use conditional branches, solving the branch address size problem. The question is then, which register?

The answer comes from seeing how conditional branches are used. Conditional branches are found in loops and in *if* statements, so they tend to branch to a nearby instruction. For example, almost half of all conditional branches in gcc and spice go to locations less than 16 instructions away. Since the program counter (PC) contains the address of the current instruction, we can branch within 2^{16} of the current instruction if we use the PC as the register to be added to the address. Almost all loops and *if* statements are much smaller than 2^{16}, so the PC is the ideal choice. This form of branch addressing is called *PC-relative addressing*. As we shall see in Chapter 5, it is convenient for the hardware to increment the PC early to point to the next instruction. Hence the MIPS address is actually relative to the address of the following instruction (PC + 4) as opposed to the current instruction (PC).

Like most recent machines, MIPS uses PC-relative addressing for all conditional branches because the destination of these instructions is likely to be close to the branch. On the other hand, jump-and-link instructions invoke procedures that have no reason to be near the call, and so they normally use other forms of addressing. Hence MIPS offers long addresses for procedure calls by using the J-type format for both jump and jump-and-link instructions.

Example

The *while* loop on page 114 was compiled into this MIPS assembler code:

```
Loop:   mult  $9,$19,$10      # Temporary reg $9 = i*4
        lw    $8,Sstart($9)    # Temporary reg $8 = save[i]
        bne   $8,$21, Exit     # goto Exit if save[i] ≠ k
        add   $19,$19,$20      # i = i + j
        j     Loop             # goto Loop
Exit:
```

If we assume that the loop is placed at location 80000 in memory and that the address Sstart refers to location 1000, what is the MIPS machine code for this loop?

Answer

The assembled instructions and their addresses would look like this:

80000	0	19	10	9	0	24
80004	35	9	8		1000	
80008	5	8	21		8	
80012	0	19	20	19	0	32
80016	2			80000		
80020	. . .					

Remember that MIPS uses byte addresses, so addresses of sequential words differ by 4, the number of bytes in a word. The bne instruction on the third line adds 8 bytes to the address of the *following* instruction (80012), specifying the branch destination relative to that instruction (8) instead of using the full address (80020). The jump instruction on the last line does use the full address (80000), corresponding to the label Loop. (The first line is a simplified version of the MIPS multiply instruction; see page 179 in Chapter 4 for details.)

Hardware Software Interface

Nearly every conditional branch is to a nearby location, but occasionally it branches far away, farther than can be represented in the 16 bits of the conditional branch instruction. The assembler comes to the rescue just as it did with large addresses or constants: it inserts an unconditional jump to the branch target, and the condition is inverted so that the branch decides whether to skip the jump. For example, a branch on register $18 being equal to register $19 such as

```
        beq    $18,$19, L1
```

can be replaced by this pair of instructions that offers a much greater branching distance:

```
        bne    $18,$19, L2
        j      L1
L2:
```

We have seen two new forms of addressing in this section. Multiple forms of addressing are generically called *addressing modes*. The MIPS addressing modes are

1. *Register addressing,* where the operand is a register;

2. *Base* or *displacement addressing,* where the operand is at the memory location whose address is the sum of a register and an address in the instruction;

3. *Immediate addressing,* where the operand is a constant within the instruction itself; and

4. *PC-relative addressing,* where the address is the sum of the PC and a constant in the instruction.

Figure 3.15 shows how operands are identified for each addressing mode. The next section expands this list to show addressing modes found in other styles of computers.

Figure 3.16 shows the MIPS architecture that is revealed in Chapter 3. The remaining hidden portion of MIPS deals mainly with arithmetic, covered in the next chapter.

Elaboration: Since all MIPS instructions are 4 bytes long, MIPS stretches the distance of the branch by having PC-relative addressing refer to the number of *words* to the next instruction instead of the number of bytes. Thus the 16-bit field can branch four times as far by interpreting the field as a relative word address rather than as a relative byte address.

The 26-bit field in jump instructions is also a word address, meaning that it represents a 28-bit byte address. Since the PC is 32 bits, 4 bits must come from someplace else. The MIPS jump instruction replaces only the lower 28 bits of the PC, leaving the upper 4 bits of the PC unchanged. The loader and linker must be careful to avoid placing a program across an address boundary of 256 MB (64 million instructions), for otherwise a jump must be replaced by a Jump register instruction and other instructions to load the full 32-bit address into a register.

3.8   Alternatives to the MIPS Approach

Designers of instruction sets sometimes provide more powerful operations than those found in MIPS. The goal is generally to reduce the number of instructions executed by a program. The danger is that this reduction can occur at the cost of simplicity, increasing the time a program takes to execute because the instructions are slower. This slowness may be the result of a slower clock cycle time or of requiring more clock cycles than a simpler sequence (see section 2.8 on page 76). The following sections present several methods of reducing the number of executed instructions by using more powerful ways of

1. Register addressing

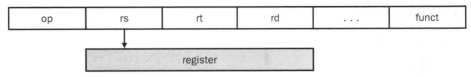

2. Base addressing

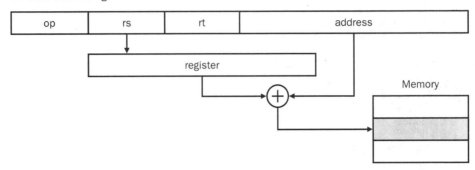

3. Immediate addressing

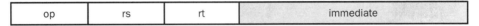

4. PC-relative addressing

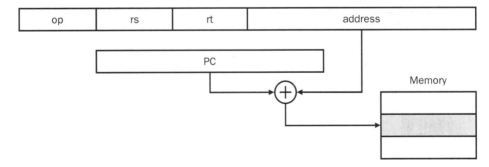

FIGURE 3.15 Illustration of the four MIPS addressing modes. The operands are shaded in color. The operands of modes 2 and 4 are locations in memory, whereas the operand for mode 1 is a register. For mode 3 the operand is 16 bits of the instruction itself.

MIPS operands

Name	Example	Comments
32 registers	$0, $1, $2, . . . , $31	Fast locations for data. In MIPS, data must be in registers to perform arithmetic. MIPS register $0 always equals 0. Register $1 is reserved for the assembler to handle pseudoinstructions and large constants.
2^{30} memory words	Memory[0], Memory[4], . . . , Memory[4294967292]	Accessed only by data transfer instructions. MIPS uses byte addresses, so sequential words differ by 4. Memory holds data structures, such as arrays, and spilled registers, such as those saved on procedure calls.

MIPS assembly language

Category	Instruction	Example		Meaning	Comments
Arithmetic	add	add	$1,$2,$3	$1 = $2 + $3	3 operands; data in registers
	subtract	sub	$1,$2,$3	$1 = $2 – $3	3 operands; data in registers
	add immediate	addi	$1,$2,100	$1 = $2 + 100	Used to add constants
Data Transfer	load word	lw	$1,100($2)	$1 = Memory[$2+100]	Data from memory to register
	store word	sw	$1,100($2)	Memory[$2+100] = $1	Data from register to memory
	load upper imm.	lui	$1,100	$1 = 100 * 2^{16}	Loads constant in upper 16 bits
Conditional Branch	branch on equal	beq	$1,$2,100	if ($1 == $2) go to PC+4+100	Equal test; PC relative branch
	branch on not eq.	bne	$1,$2,100	if ($1 != $2) go to PC+4+100	Not equal test; PC relative
	set on less than	slt	$1,$2,$3	if ($2 < $3) $1=1; else $1=0	Compare less than; for beq,bne
	set less than imm.	slti	$1,$2,100	if ($2 < 100) $1=1; else $1=0	Compare less than constant
Uncondi-tional Jump	jump	j	10000	go to 10000	Jump to target address
	jump register	jr	$31	go to $31	For switch, procedure return
	jump and link	jal	10000	$31 = PC + 4; go to 10000	For procedure call

MIPS machine language

Name	Format	Example						Comments
add	R	0	2	3	1	0	32	add $1,$2,$3
sub	R	0	2	3	1	0	34	sub $1,$2,$3
addi	I	8	2	1	100			addi $1,$2,100
lw	I	35	2	1	100			lw $1,100($2)
sw	I	43	2	1	100			sw $1,100($2)
lui	I	15	0	1	100			lui $1,100
beq	I	4	1	2	100			beq $1,$2,100
bne	I	5	1	2	100			bne $1,$2,100
slt	R	0	2	3	1	0	42	slt $1,$2,$3
slti	I	10	2	1	100			slti $1,$2,100
j	J	2	10000					j 10000
jr	R	0	31	0	0	0	8	jr $31
jal	J	3	10000					jal 10000
Field size		6 bits	5 bits	5 bits	5 bits	5 bits	6 bits	All MIPS instructions 32 bits
Format R	R	op	rs	rt	rd	shamt	funct	Arithmetic instruction format
Format I	I	op	rs	rt	address/immediate			Transfer, branch, imm. format
Format J	J	op	target address					Jump instruction format

FIGURE 3.16 MIPS architecture revealed in Chapter 3. Highlighted portions show portions from this section.

Autoincrement addressing (not found in MIPS)

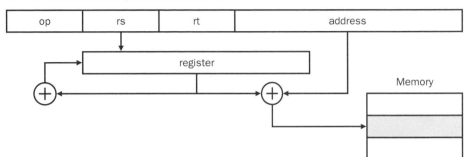

FIGURE 3.17 Illustration of autoincrement addressing mode. The operand is shaded in color.

accessing operands and by using more powerful operations. Appendix E describes the VAX architecture, an example of such an alternative approach.

Autoincrement and Autodecrement

Imagine the case of a code sequence marching through an array of words in memory. A frequent pair of operations would be loading a word and then incrementing the Index register to point to the next word. The idea of *autoincrement* addressing is to have a new version of data transfer instructions that will automatically increment the Index register to point to the next word each time data is transferred. Since the MIPS architecture uses byte addresses and words are 4 bytes, this new form would be equivalent to this pair of MIPS instructions:

```
lw      $8,Sstart($19)      # reg $8 gets S[$19]
addi    $19,$19,4           # $19 = $19 + 4
```

They would be replaced by a single *hypothetical* instruction, *not* found in MIPS, that might look like this:

```
lw+     $8,Sstart($19)      # reg $8=S[$19]; $19 = $19+4
```

Using the same notation as Figure 3.15, Figure 3.17 shows autoincrement addressing.

Sometimes programs will march through memory in the other direction, and so *autodecrement* address may be provided as well. Autoincrement and autodecrement addressing are also useful for stacks, since they are equivalent to primitives for push and pop.

Memory-Based Operands for Operations

Another attempt to reduce the number of instructions executed also combines loads with arithmetic instructions, but in this case the idea is to have a version of the arithmetic instruction that can specify one of its operands to be in memory. The goal is to replace this pair of MIPS instructions

```
lw     $8,Astart($19)        # Temporary reg $8 gets A[$19]
add    $16,$17,$8            # $16 = $17 + A[i]
```

with a single add instruction that adds memory operand A[$19]directly to register $17 and then places the sum in register $16. This *hypothetical* instruction, *not* found in MIPS, might look like this:

```
addm   $16,$17, Astart($19)  # $16=$17+Memory[$19+Astart]
```

Incorporating this instruction, thereby disregarding the advice on regularity, means longer instructions to hold both a memory address field and the three register fields, and probably leads to multiple sizes of instructions. In the VAX architecture, each operand can be a register or a memory location, and the address of a memory operand can use more than a dozen different addressing modes. Since many instructions have three memory addresses per instruction, this combination leads to a large number of instruction lengths.

Complex Operations

The examples of more sophisticated operations above all dealt with ways of accessing operands. Another path to a more powerful instruction set is making the operations themselves more complex than the simple arithmetic primitives we have seen so far. Following this approach, the computer designer looks for instruction sequences that happen frequently and replaces them with a single instruction, hoping to improve performance by reducing the number of executed instructions. The designers of the VAX followed this approach; see Appendix E. One example would be a single instruction that does everything needed to call a procedure, including saving registers and adjusting the stack. (The Fallacy on page 147 explains the reasons not to do this.)

Let's look at another example. The *for* loop found in most programming languages allows the programmer to specify the starting value of the loop index, the ending value, and the amount the index should be incremented. Some machines provide an *increment-compare-and-branch* instruction to try to match the needs of a *for* loop. Assuming that we want to increment register $19, compare to register $20, and then branch as long as register $19 is less, we would need the following MIPS instructions:

```
Loop: ...
        addi    $19,$19,1        # $19 = $19 + 1
        slt     $8, $19,$20      # $8 = 1 if $19 < $20
        bne     $8,$0,Loop       # $8 ≠ 0 means $19 < $20,
                                 #    so goto Loop if $8 ≠ $0
```

A single instruction replacing these three would specify the register to be incremented, the register to be compared, and the branch address. This *hypothetical* instruction, once again *not* found in MIPS, might look like this:

```
icb    $19,$20,Loop# $19=$19+1; if $19<$20 then goto Loop
```

Hardware Software Interface

In addition to going against the advice of simplicity, such sophisticated operations may not *exactly* match what the compiler needs to produce. For example, suppose that instead of incrementing by 1 the compiler wanted to increment by 4, or instead of branching on less than, the compiler wanted to branch if the index was less than or equal to the limit. Then the instruction just described would be a mismatch. When faced with such objections, the instruction set designer might then generalize the operation, adding another operand to specify the increment and perhaps an option on which branch condition to use. Then the danger is that a common case, say, incrementing by 1, will be slower than a sequence of simple operations.

The path toward operation complexity is thus fraught with peril. To avoid these problems, designers have moved toward simpler instructions. Section 3.12 demonstrates the pitfalls of complexity.

3.9 An Example to Put It All Together

One danger of showing assembly language code in snippets is that the reader has no idea what a full assembly language program looks like. In this section and the next we derive the MIPS code from a procedure written in C. Section 3.10 uses this code in a longer example.

Let's start with the code for the procedure swap in Figure 3.18. (The Pascal version of this procedure is found on page D-8 in Appendix D.) This procedure simply swaps two locations in memory. When translating from C to assembly language, we follow these general steps:

```
swap(int v[], int k)
{
  int temp;
  temp = v[k];
  v[k] = v[k+1];
  v[k+1] = temp;
}
```

FIGURE 3.18 A C procedure that swaps two locations in memory. This procedure will be used in the sorting example in the next section. Appendix D shows the C and Pascal versions of this procedure side by side (page D-8).

1. Allocate registers to program variables.

2. Produce code for the body of the procedure.

3. Preserve registers across the procedure invocation.

This section describes the swap procedure in these three pieces, concluding by putting all the pieces together.

Register Allocation

As mentioned on page 121, the MIPS convention on parameter passing is to use registers $4, $5, $6, and $7. Since swap has just two parameters, v and k, they will be found in registers $4 and $5. The only other variable is temp, which we associate with register $15. This register allocation corresponds to the variable declarations in the first half of the swap procedure.

Code for the Body of the Procedure

The remaining lines of C code in swap are

```
temp = v[k];
v[k] = v[k+1];
v[k+1] = temp;
```

A *simplistic* view is to translate them into these five MIPS instructions:

```
add    $2, $4,$5    # reg $2 = v + k
                    # reg $2 has the address of v[k]
lw     $15, 0($2)   # reg $15 (temp) = v[k]
lw     $16, 1($2)   # reg $16 = v[k+1]
                    # refers to next element of v
sw     $16, 0($2)   # v[k] = reg $16
sw     $15, 1($2)   # v[k+1] = reg $15 (temp)
```

Note that the register $2 contains the base of array, and we use the constant part of the instruction to select the element of the array. The code is *not* that simple, however. Recall that the memory address for MIPS refers to the *byte* address, and so words are really 4 bytes apart; both the index and the address are wrong! Hence we need to multiply the index k by 4 before adding it to the address, and we must increment the address of v[k] by 4 instead of by 1 to get the address of v[k+1]. *Forgetting that sequential word addresses differ by 4 instead of by 1 is a common mistake in assembly language programming.*

We assume an instruction that can multiply by a small constant for now (muli), but we'll cover the real instructions in Chapter 4. We must also change the address from 1 to 4 in the data transfers that refer to v[k+1], since sequential words are 4 bytes apart. The new version has the changes highlighted:

```
muli    $2, $5,4        # reg $2 = k * 4
add     $2, $4,$2       # reg $2 = v + (k*4)
                        # reg $2 has the address of v[k]
lw      $15, 0($2)      # reg $15 (temp) = v[k]
lw      $16, 4($2)      # reg $16 = v[k+1]
                        # refers to next element of v
sw      $16, 0($2)      # v[k] = reg $16
sw      $15, 4($2)      # v[k+1] = reg $15 (temp)
```

Now we have allocated storage and written the code to perform the operations of the procedure. The only missing code is the code that preserves registers across the routine that calls swap.

Preserving Registers Across Procedure Invocation

Let's use callee save as our convention. Since we are changing registers $2, $15, and $16, we must first make room on the stack to save their original values. Register $29 contains the stack pointer, and we need to adjust it by 3×4 or 12 bytes before we save the three words:

```
addi    $29, $29, -12
```

The adjustment is negative because the MIPS convention is for the stack to grow from higher addresses to lower addresses. Now we save the old values:

```
sw      $2, 0($29)      # save $2 on stack
sw      $15, 4($29)     # save $15 on stack
sw      $16, 8($29)     # save $16 on stack
```

At the end of the procedure we just restore the registers via three loads and then adjust the stack in the other direction. Since swap calls no procedures, we skip saving and restoring the return address in register $31. We just place a Jump register instruction at the end of the code to return.

Saving registers			
swap:	addi	$29, $29, -12	# make room on stack for 3 reg
	sw	$2, 0($29)	# save $2 on stack
	sw	$15, 4($29)	# save $15 on stack
	sw	$16, 8($29)	# save $16 on stack
Procedure body			
	muli	$2, $5, 4	# reg $2 = k * 4
	add	$2, $4, $2	# reg $2 = v + (k*4)
			# reg $2 has the address of v[k]
	lw	$15, 0($2)	# reg $15 (temp) = v[k]
	lw	$16, 4($2)	# reg $16 = v[k+1]
			# refers to next element of v
	sw	$16, 0($2)	# v[k] = reg $16
	sw	$15, 4($2)	# v[k+1] = reg $15 (temp)
Restoring registers			
	lw	$2, 0($29)	# restore $2 from stack
	lw	$15, 4($29)	# restore $15 from stack
	lw	$16, 8($29)	# restore $16 from stack
	addi	$29, $29, 12	# restore stack pointer
Procedure return			
	jr	$31	# return to calling routine

FIGURE 3.19 MIPS assembly code of the procedure swap in Figure 3.18 on page 136.

The Full Procedure

We are now ready for the whole routine. To make it easier to follow, we identify each block of code with its purpose in the procedure in Figure 3.19. This simple example shows the power of writing in high-level programming languages versus assembly language: 8 lines of C code became 17 lines of MIPS assembly code.

3.10 A Longer Example

To ensure that the reader appreciates the rigor of programming in assembly language, we'll try a second, longer example. In this case we'll build a routine that calls the swap procedure from section 3.9. This program sorts an array of 10,000 integers. Figure 3.20 shows the C version of the program, and the Pascal version is found on page D-8 in Appendix D. Once again we present this procedure in several steps, concluding with the full procedure.

```
int v[10000];

sort (int v[], int n)
{
    int i, j;
    for (i = 0; i < n; i = i+1) {
        for (j = i-1; j>=0 && v[j]>v[j+1]; j = j-1) {
            swap(v,j);
        }
    }
}
```

FIGURE 3.20 A C procedure that performs a bubble sort on the array v. For readers unfamiliar with C, the three parts of the first *for* statement are the initialization that happens before the first iteration (i = 0), the test if the loop should iterate again (i < n), and the operation that happens at the end of each iteration (i = i + 1). Appendix D shows the C and Pascal versions of this procedure side by side (page D-8).

Register Allocation

The two parameters of the procedure sort, v and n, are in the parameter registers $4 and $5, and we assign register $19 to i and register $17 to j.

Code for the Body of the Procedure

The procedure body consists of two nested *for* loops and a call to swap which includes parameters. Let's unwrap the code from the outside to the middle.

The Outer Loop

The first translation step is the first *for* loop:

```
for (i = 0; i < n; i = i+1) {
```

Recall that the C *for* statement has three parts: initialization, loop test, and iteration increment. It takes just one instruction to initialize i to 0, the first part of the *for* statement:

```
        add   $19, $0, $0    # i = 0
```

It also takes just one instruction to increment i, the last part of the for:

```
        addi $19, $19, 1     # i = i + 1
```

The loop should be exited if i < n is *not* true, or, said another way, should be exited if $i \geq n$. This test takes two instructions:

```
for1tst:slt $8, $19, $5     # reg $8 = 0 if $19 ≥ $5 (i≥n)
        beq $8, $0, exit1    # go to exit1 if $19 ≥ $5 (i≥n)
```

The set on less than instruction sets register $8 to 1 if $19 < $5 and 0 otherwise. Since we want to test if $19 ≥ $5, we branch if register $8 is zero. The bottom of the loop just jumps back to the loop test:

```
          j    for1tst        # jump to test of outer loop
exit1:
```

The skeleton code of the first *for* loop is then:

```
          add  $19, $0, $0    # i = 0
for1tst:slt  $8, $19, $5      #  reg $8 = 0 if $19 ≥ $5 (i≥n)
          beq  $8, $0, exit1  # go to exit1 if $19 ≥ $5 (i≥n)
          . . .
          (body of first for loop)
          . . .
          addi $19, $19, 1    # i = i + 1
          j    for1tst        # jump to test of outer loop
exit1:
```

Voila! Exercise 3.11 explores writing faster code for similar loops.

The Inner Loop

The second *for* loop looks like this in C:

```
    for (j = i-1; j>=0 && v[j]>v[j+1]; j = j-1) {
```

The initialization portion of this loop is again one instruction:

```
          addi $17, $19, -1   # j = i - 1
```

and the decrement of j is also one instruction:

```
          addi $17, $17, -1   # j = j - 1
```

The loop test has two parts. We exit the loop if either condition fails, so the first test must exit the loop if it fails (j < 0):

```
for2tst:slti $8, $17, 0       # reg $8 = 1 if $17 < 0 (j < 0)
          bne  $8, $0, exit2  # go to exit2 if $17 < 0 (j < 0)
```

This branch will skip over the second condition test. If it doesn't skip, j ≥ 0.

The second test exits if v[j]>v[j+1] is *not* true, or exits if v[j] ≤ v[j+1]. First we create the address by multiplying j by 4 (since we need a byte address) and add it to the base address of v:

```
          muli $15, $17,4     # reg $15 = j * 4
          add  $16, $4,$15    # reg $16 = v + (j*4)
```

Now we load v[j]:

```
          lw   $24, 0($16)    # reg $24 = v[j]
```

Since we know that the second element is just the following word, we add 4 to the address in register $16 to get v[j+1]:

```
        lw    $25, 4($16)     # reg $25 = v[j+1]
```

The test of v[j] ≤ v[j+1] is the same as v[j+1]≥v[j], so the two instructions of the exit test are

```
        slt   $8, $25, $24    # reg $8 = 0 if $25 ≥ $24
        beq   $8, $0,exit2    # go to exit2 if $25 ≥ $24
```

The bottom of the loop jumps back to the full loop test:

```
        j     for2tst         # jump to test of inner loop
```

Combining the pieces together, the second *for* loop looks like this:

```
        addi $17, $19, -1     # j = i - 1
for2tst:slti $8, $17, 0       #  reg $8 = 1 if $17 < 0 (j<0)
        bne  $8, $0, exit2    # go to exit2 if $17 < 0 (j<0)
        muli $15, $17,4       # reg $15 = j * 4
        add  $16, $4,$15      # reg $16 = v + (j*4)
        lw   $24, 0($16)      # reg $24 = v[j]
        lw   $25, 4($16)      # reg $25 = v[j+1]
        slt  $8, $25, $24     #  reg $8 = 0 if $25 ≥ $24
        beq  $8, $0, exit2    # go to exit2 if $25 ≥ $24
            . . .
        (body of second for loop)
            . . .
        addi $17, $17, -1     # j = j - 1
        j    for2tst          # jump to test of inner loop
exit2:
```

The Procedure Call

The next step is the body of the second *for* loop:

```
    swap(v,j);
```

Calling swap is easy enough:

```
    jal    swap
```

Passing Parameters

The problem comes when we want to pass parameters, because the sort procedure needs the values in registers $4 and $5, yet the swap procedure needs to have its parameters placed in those same registers. One solution is to copy the parameters for sort into other registers earlier in the procedure, making registers $4 and $5 available for the call of swap.We first copy $4 and $5 into $18 and $20 during the procedure:

```
    move   $18, $4           # copy parameter $4 into $18
    move   $20, $5           # copy parameter $5 into $20
```

(Remember that move is a pseudoinstruction provided by the assembly for the convenience of the assembly language programmer: see page 110.) Then we pass the parameters to swap with these two instructions:

```
move    $4, $18        # first swap parameter is v
move    $5, $17        # second swap parameter is j
```

Preserving Registers Across Procedure Invocation

The only remaining code is the saving and restoring of registers using the callee save convention. Clearly we must save the return address in register $31, since sort calls another procedure. The other registers we have used are $15, $16, $17, $18, $19, $20, $24, and $25. The prologue of the sort procedure is then:

```
addi    $29,$29,-36     # make room on stack for 9 reg
sw      $15, 0($29)     # save $15 on stack
sw      $16, 4($29)     # save $16 on stack
sw      $17, 8($29)     # save $17 on stack
sw      $18,12($29)     # save $18 on stack
sw      $19,16($29)     # save $19 on stack
sw      $20,20($29)     # save $20 on stack
sw      $24,24($29)     # save $24 on stack
sw      $25,28($29)     # save $25 on stack
sw      $31,32($29)     # save $31 on stack
```

The tail of the procedure simply reverses all these instructions, then adds a jr to return.

The Full Procedure

Now we put all the pieces together in Figure 3.21, being careful to replace references to registers $4 and $5 in the *for* loops with references to registers $18 and $20. Once again to make the code easier to follow, we identify each block of code with its purpose in the procedure. In this example, 11 lines of the sort procedure in C became the 44 lines in the MIPS assembly language.

Elaboration: Copying $18 into $4 in the passing parameters section was unnecessary, since that was the old value of $4, but it is good practice to save all the parameters if you are going to call another procedure. We could also streamline the procedure call overhead by using a combination of callee and caller, save for procedures that don't call other procedures, such as swap. Exercises 3.28 and 3.29 explore these options.

3.11 Arrays versus Pointers

A challenging topic for any new programmer is understanding pointers. Comparing assembly code which uses arrays and array indices to the assembly code which uses pointers offers insight into that difference. This section shows C and MIPS assembly versions of two procedures to clear a sequence of words in memory: one using array indices and one using pointers. Figure 3.22 shows the two C procedures.

Let's start with the array version, clear1, focusing on the body of the loop and ignoring the procedure linkage code. We assume that the two parameters array and size are found in the registers $4 and $5, and that i is allocated to register $2.

The initialization of i, the first part of the *for* loop, is straightforward:

```
move    $2,$0        # i = 0 (register $0 = 0)
```

To set array[i] to 0 we must first get its address. Start by multiplying i by 4 to get the byte address:

```
loop1:  muli   $14,$2, 4    # $14 = i * 4
```

Since the starting address of the array is in a register, we must add it to the index to get the address of array[i] using an add instruction:

```
add     $3,$4,$14    # $3 = address of array[i]
```

Finally we can store 0 in that address:

```
sw    $0, 0($3)       # array[i] = 0
```

This is the end of the body of the loop, so the next step is to increment i:

```
addi $2,$2,1          # i = i + 1
```

The loop test checks if i is less than size:

```
slt   $6,$2,$5        # $6 = (i < size)
bne   $6,$0,loop1     # if (i < size) go to loop1
```

We have now seen all the pieces of the procedure. Here is the MIPS code for clearing an array using indices:

```
        move $2,$0         # i = 0
loop1:  muli $14,$2,4      # $14 = i * 4
        add  $3,$4,$14     # $3 = address of array[i]
        sw   $0, 0($3)     # array[i] = 0
        addi $2,$2,1       # i = i + 1
        slt  $6,$2,$5      # $6 = (i < size)
        bne  $6,$0,loop1   # if (i < size) go to loop1
```

Saving registers			
	sort:	addi $29,$29, -36	# make room on stack for 9 reg
		sw $15, 0($29)	# save $15 on stack
		sw $16, 4($29)	# save $16 on stack
		sw $17, 8($29)	# save $17 on stack
		sw $18,12($29)	# save $18 on stack
		sw $19,16($29)	# save $19 on stack
		sw $20,20($29)	# save $20 on stack
		sw $24,24($29)	# save $24 on stack
		sw $25,28($29)	# save $25 on stack
		sw $31,32($29)	# save $31 on stack
Procedure body			
Move parameters		move $18, $4	# copy parameter $4 into $18
		move $20, $5	# copy parameter $5 into $20
Outer loop	forltst:	add $19, $0, $0	# i = 0
		slt $8, $19, $20	# reg $8 = 0 if $19 ≥ $20 (i≥n)
		beq $8, $0, exit1	# go to exit1 if $19 ≥ $20 (i≥n)
Inner loop	for2tst:	addi $17, $19, -1	# j = i - 1
		slti $8, $17, 0	# reg $8 = 1 if $17 < 0 (j<0)
		bne $8, $0, exit2	# go to exit2 if $17 < 0 (j<0)
		muli $15, $17, 4	# reg $15 = j * 4
		add $16, $18, $15	# reg $16 = v + (j*4)
		lw $24, 0($16)	# reg $24 = v[j]
		lw $25, 4($16)	# reg $25 = v[j+1]
		slt $8, $25, $24	# reg $8 = 0 if $25 ≥ $24
		beq $8, $0, exit2	# go to exit2 if $25 ≥ $24
Pass parameters and call		move $4, $18	# 1st parameter of swap is v
		move $5, $17	# 2nd parameter of swap is j
		jal swap	
Inner loop		addi $17, $17, -1	# j = j - 1
		j for2tst	# jump to test of inner loop
Outer loop	exit2:	addi $19, $19, 1	# i = i + 1
		j forltst	# jump to test of outer loop
Restoring registers			
	exit1:	lw $15, 0($29)	# restore $15 from stack
		lw $16, 4($29)	# restore $16 from stack
		lw $17, 8($29)	# restore $17 from stack
		lw $18,12($29)	# restore $18 from stack
		lw $19,16($29)	# restore $19 from stack
		lw $20,20($29)	# restore $20 from stack
		lw $24,24($29)	# restore $24 from stack
		lw $25,28($29)	# restore $25 from stack
		lw $31,32($29)	# restore $31 from stack
		addi $29,$29, 36	# restore stack pointer
Procedure return			
		jr $31	# return to calling routine

FIGURE 3.21 MIPS assembly version of procedure sort in Figure 3.20 on page 139.

```
clear1(int array[], int size)
{
  int i;
  for (i = 0; i < size; i = i + 1)
      array[i] = 0;
}


clear2(int *array, int size)
{
  int *p;
  for (p = &array[0]; p < &array[size]; p = p + 1)
      *p = 0;
}
```

FIGURE 3.22 Two C procedures for setting an array to all zeros. Clear1 uses indexes while clear2 uses pointers. The second procedure needs some explanation for those unfamiliar with C. The address of a variable is indicated by "&" and referring to the object pointed to by a pointer is indicated by "*". The declarations declare that array and p are pointers to integers. The first part of the *for* loop in clear2 assigns the first element of array to the pointer p. The second part of the *for* loop tests to see if the pointer is pointing to the last element of array. Incrementing a pointer by one, in the last part of the *for* loop, means moving the pointer to the next sequential object of its declared size. Since p is a pointer to integers, the compiler will generate MIPS instructions to increment p by 4, the number of bytes in a MIPS integer. The assignment in the loop places 0 in the object pointed to by p.

(This code works as long as size is greater than 0.)

The second procedure allocates the two parameters array and size to the registers $4 and $5 and allocates p to register $2. The code for the second procedure starts with assigning the pointer p to the first element of the array:

```
        move    $2,$4       # p = address of array[0]
```

The next code is the body of the *for* loop, which simply stores 0 into p:

```
loop2:  sw      $0,0($2)    # Memory[p] = 0
```

This is all of the body of the loop, so the next code is the iteration increment, which changes p to point to the next word:

```
        addi    $2,$2,4     # p = p + 4
```

Incrementing a pointer by 1 means moving the pointer to the next sequential object in C. Since p is a pointer to integers, the compiler increments p by 4.

The loop test is next. The first step is calculating the address of the last element of array. Start with multiplying size by 4 to get its byte address:

```
        muli    $14,$5,4    # $14 = size * 4
```

and then we add the product to the starting address of the array to get the address of the last element of the array:

```
add     $3,$4,$14     # $3 = address of array[size]
```

The loop test is simply to see if p is less than the last element of array:

```
slt     $6,$2,$3      # $6 = (p < array[size])
bne     $6,$0,loop2   # if (p<array[size]) go to loop2
```

With all the pieces completed we can show a pointer version of the code to zero an array:

```
        move    $2,$4         # p = address of array[0]
loop2:  sw      $0,0($2)      # Memory[p] = 0
        addi    $2,$2,4       # p = p + 4
        muli    $14,$5,4      # $14 = size * 4
        add     $3,$4,$14     # $3 = address of array[size]
        slt     $6,$2,$3      # $6 = (p < array[size])
        bne     $6,$0,loop2   # if (p<array[size]) go to loop2
```

As in the first example, this code assumes size is greater than 0.

Note that this program calculates the address of the end of the array every iteration of the loop even though it does not change. A faster version of the code moves this calculation outside the loop:

```
        move    $2,$4         # p = address of array[0]
        muli    $14,$5,4      # $14 = size * 4
        add     $3,$4,$14     # $3 = address of array[size]
loop2:  sw      $0,0($2)      # Memory[p] = 0
        addi    $2,$2,4       # p = p + 4
        slt     $6,$2,$3      # $6 = (p < array[size])
        bne     $6,$0,loop2   # if (p<array[size]) go to loop2
```

Comparing the two code sequences side by side illustrates the difference between array indices and pointers (the changes introduced by the pointer version are highlighted):

```
       move $2,$0        # i = 0                 move $2,$4        # p = & array[0]
loop1: muli $14,$2,4     # $14 = i * 4           muli $14,$5,4     # $14 = size * 4
       add  $3,$4,$14    # $3 =& array[i]        add  $3,$4,$14    # $3 = & array[size]
       sw   $0, 0($3)    # array[i] = 0   loop2: sw   $0,0($2)     # Memory[p] = 0
       addi $2,$2,1      # i = i + 1             addi $2,$2,4      # p = p + 4
       slt  $6,$2,$5     # $6 = (i < size)       slt  $6,$2,$3     # $6=(p<&array[size])
       bne  $6,$0,loop1  # if () go to loop1     bne  $6,$0,loop2  # if () go to loop2
```

The version on the left must have the multiply and add inside the loop because i is incremented and each address must be recalculated from the new index while the memory pointer version increments the pointer p directly. This reduces the instructions executed per iteration from 6 to 4. Many modern compilers will optimize the C code in clear1 to produce code similar to the assembly code above on the right-hand side.

3.12 | Fallacies and Pitfalls

Fallacy: More powerful instructions mean higher performance.

Perhaps the most famous counterexample is an instruction in the VAX architecture that supported an elaborate procedure call mechanism in a single instruction. This single instruction automatically saved the following items on the stack: the return address, the number of parameters, any registers that would be modified by the procedure, and the old value of the stack pointer.

In addition, the call instruction updated the stack pointer and did some other bookkeeping before jumping to the procedure. The VAX also had an instruction very similar to jal in MIPS. People found that using compiler conventions on parameter passing and register saving and replacing the sophisticated call instruction by simpler instructions like jal had the following effect: it made programs run 1.2 times faster by *avoiding* the powerful instruction! Clearly moving procedure call into hardware means you can't tailor the overhead to the program, and is overkill in most cases.

Pitfall: Writing in assembly language in order to obtain the highest performance,

At one time compilers for programming languages produced naive instruction sequences; the increasing sophistication of compilers means the gap between compiled code and code produced by hand is closing fast. In fact, to compete with current compilers, the assembly language programmer needs to thoroughly understand the concepts in Chapters 6 and 7 on processor pipelining and memory hierarchy.

This battle between compilers and assembly language coders is one situation in which humans are losing ground. For example, C offers the programmer a chance to give a hint to the compiler about which variables should be kept in registers versus spilled to memory. When compilers were poor at register allocation, such hints were vital to performance. In fact, some C textbooks spent a fair amount of time giving examples to effectively use register hints. Today's C compilers generally ignore such hints because the compiler does a better job at allocation than the programmer.

As a specific counterexample, we ran the MIPS assembly language programs in Figures 3.19 and 3.21 to compare performance to the C programs in Figures 3.18 and 3.20. Figure 3.23 shows the results. As you can see, the compiled program is 1.5 times faster than the assembled program. The compiler generally was able to create assembly language code that was tailored exactly

Language	Time
Assembly	37.9 seconds
C	25.3 seconds

FIGURE 3.23 Performance Comparison of the C and assembly language version of the sort and swap procedures in sections 3.9 and 3.10. The size of the array to be sorted was increased to 10,000 elements. The programs were run on a DECsystem 5900 with 128 MB of main memory and a 40-MHz R3000 processor using version 4.2a (Revision 47) of the Ultrix operating system. The C compiler was run with the –O option.

to these conditions, while the assembly language program was written in a slightly more general fashion to make it easier to modify and understand. The specific improvements of the C compiler were a more streamlined procedure linkage convention and changing the address calculations to move the multiply outside the inner loop.

Even if the battle isn't lost yet, the dangers of writing in assembly language are longer time spent coding and debugging, the loss in portability, and the difficulty of maintaining such code. One of the few widely accepted axioms of software engineering is that coding takes longer if you write more lines, and it clearly takes many more lines to write a program in assembly language than in C. And once it is coded, the next danger is that it will become a popular program. Such programs always live longer than expected, meaning that someone will have to update the code over several years and make it work with new releases of operating systems and new models of machines. Writing in higher level language instead of assembly language not only allows future compilers to tailor the code to future machines, it also makes the software easier to maintain, and allows the program to run on more brands of computers.

Pitfall: Forgetting that sequential word addresses in machines with byte addressing do not differ by 1.

The first version of our `swap` code on page 136 made this mistake. Many an assembly language programmer has toiled over errors made by assuming that the address of the next word can be found by incrementing the address in a register by 1 instead of by the word size in bytes. Forewarned is forearmed!

3.13   Concluding Remarks

Less is more.

Robert Browning, *Andrea del Sarto*, 1855

The two principles of the *stored-program* computer are the use of instructions that are indistinguishable from numbers and the use of alterable memory for programs. These principles allow a single machine to aid environmental scientists, financial advisers, and novelists in their specialties. The selection of a set of instructions that the machine can understand demands a delicate balance among the number of instructions needed to execute a program, the number of clock cycles needed by an instruction, and the speed of the clock. Four principles guide the designers of instruction sets in making that delicate balance:

1. *Smaller is faster.* The desire for speed is the reason that MIPS has 32 registers rather than many more.

2. *Simplicity favors regularity.* Regularity motivates many features of the MIPS instruction set: keeping all instructions a single size, always requiring three register operands in arithmetic instructions, and keeping the register fields in the same place in each instruction format.

3. *Good design demands compromise.* One MIPS example was the compromise between providing for larger addresses and constants in instructions and keeping all instructions the same length.

4. *Make the common case fast.* Examples of making the common MIPS case fast include PC-relative addressing for conditional branches and immediate addressing for constants.

Above this machine level is assembly language, a language that humans can read. The assembler translates it into the binary numbers that machines can understand, and it even "extends" the instruction set by creating symbolic instructions that aren't in the hardware. For instance, constants or addresses that are too big are broken into properly sized pieces, common variations of instructions are given their own name, and so on.

The MIPS instructions we have covered so far are listed in Figure 3.24. Each category is associated with constructs that appear in programming languages:

- The arithmetic instructions correspond to the operations found in assignment statements.

- Data transfer instructions are most likely to occur when dealing with data structures like arrays.

- The conditional branches are used in *if* statements and in loops.

- The unconditional jumps are used in procedure calls and returns and also for *case/switch* statements.

More of the MIPS instruction set is revealed in Chapter 4, after we explain computer arithmetic. Appendix A (section A.10 on page A-47) describes the full MIPS architecture.

Instruction category	MIPS examples	HLL correspondence	Frequency	
			gcc	spice
Arithmetic	add, sub, addi	Operations in assignment statements	48%	50%
Data transfer	lw, sw, lui	References to data structures such as arrays	33%	41%
Conditional branch	beq, bne, slt, slti	*If* statements and loops	17%	8%
Jump	j, jr, jal	Procedure calls, returns, and *case/switch* statements	2%	1%

FIGURE 3.24 MIPS instruction categories, examples, correspondence to high-level program language constructs, and percentage of MIPS instructions executed by category for two programs, gcc and spice. Figure 3.16 on page 132 shows more details of the MIPS architecture revealed in this chapter, and Figure 4.46 on page 248 shows the percentage of the individual MIPS instructions executed.

These instructions are not born equal; the popularity of the few dominates the many. For example, Figure 3.24 shows the popularity of each class of instructions for two programs, gcc and spice. The varying popularity of instructions plays an important role in the chapters on performance, datapath, control, and pipelining.

3.14 Historical Perspective and Further Reading

accumulator: Archaic term for register. On-line use of it as a synonym for "register" is a fairly reliable indication that the user has been around quite a while . . . .

Eric Raymond, *The New Hacker's Dictionary*, 1991

Hardware was precious in the earliest stored-program computers. As a consequence, computer pioneers could not afford the number of registers found in today's machines. In fact, these machines had a single register for arithmetic instructions. Since all operations would accumulate in a single register, it was called the *accumulator,* and this style of instruction set is given the same label. For example, EDSAC in 1949 had a single accumulator.

The three-operand format of the MIPS suggests that a single register is at least two registers shy of our needs. Having the accumulator as both a source operand *and* as the destination of the operand fills part of the shortfall, but it still leaves us one operand short. That final operand is found in memory. Accumulator machines have the memory-based operand-addressing mode suggested earlier. It follows that the add instruction of an accumulator instruction set would look like this:

```
add    200
```

This instruction means add the accumulator to the word in memory at address 200 and place the sum back into the accumulator. No registers are specified because the accumulator is known to be both a source and a destination of the operation.

Example

What is the accumulator-style assembly code for this C code?

```
A = B + C;
```

Answer

It would be translated into the following instructions in an accumulator instruction set:

```
load    AddressB     # Acc = Memory[AddressB],
        #                 or Acc = B
add     AddressC     # Acc = B + Memory[AddressC],
        #                 or Acc = B+C
store AddressA       # Memory[AddressA] = Acc,
        #                 or A = B+C
```

All variables in a program are in memory in accumulator machines, instead of in registers as we saw for MIPS. One way to think about this is that variables are always spilled to memory in this style of machine. As you may imagine, it takes many more instructions to execute a program with a single-accumulator architecture. (See Exercises 3.25 and 3.26 for other comparative examples.)

The next step in the evolution of instruction sets was the addition of registers dedicated to specific operations. Hence, registers might be included to act as indices for array references in data transfer instructions, to act as separate accumulators for multiply or divide instructions, and to serve as the top-of-stack pointer. Perhaps the best known example of this style of instruction set is found in the Intel 8086, the computer at the core of the IBM Personal Computer. This style of instruction set is labeled *extended accumulator* or *dedicated register* or *special-purpose register*. Like the single-register accumulator machines, one operand may be in memory for arithmetic instructions. Like the MIPS architecture, however, there are also instructions where all the operands are registers.

The generalization of the dedicated register machine allows all the registers to be used for any purpose, hence the name *general-purpose register*. MIPS is an example of a general-purpose register machine. This style of instruction set may be further divided into those that allow one operand to be in memory as

Machine	Number of general-purpose registers	Architectural style	Year
EDSAC	1	accumulator	1949
IBM 701	1	accumulator	1953
CDC 6600	8	load-store	1963
IBM 360	16	register-memory	1964
DEC PDP-8	1	accumulator	1965
DEC PDP-11	8	register-memory	1970
DEC VAX	16	register-memory, memory-memory	1977
Motorola 68000	16	register-memory	1980
MIPS	32	load-store	1985
SPARC	32	load-store	1987

FIGURE 3.25 Number of general-purpose registers in popular machines over the years.

found in accumulator machines, called a *register-memory* architecture, and those that demand that operands always be in registers, called either a *load-store* or a *register-register* machine. The first load-store machine was the CDC 6600 in 1963, considered by many to be the first supercomputer. MIPS is a more recent example of a load-store machine. Perhaps the best known register-memory instruction set is the IBM 360 architecture, first announced in 1964. This instruction set is still at the core of IBM's mainframe computers—responsible for a large part of the business of the largest computer company in the world. Register-memory architectures were the most popular in the 1960s and the first half of the 1970s. Figure 3.25 shows a history of the number of registers in some popular computers.

Digital Equipment Corporation's VAX architecture took memory operands one step further in 1977. It allowed any combination of registers and memory operands to be used in an instruction. A style of machine in which all operands can be in memory is called *memory-memory*. (In truth the VAX instruction set, like almost all other instruction sets since the IBM 360, is a hybrid since it also has general-purpose registers; see Appendix E.)

Example

What is the memory-memory style assembly code for this C code?

```
A = B + C;
```

Answer

It would be translated into the following instructions in a memory-memory instruction set:

```
add   AddressA,AddressB,AddressC
```

(See Exercises 3.25 and 3.26 for more comparative examples.)

While MIPS has a single 32-bit add instruction, the VAX has many versions of a 32-bit add to specify the number of operands and whether an operand is in memory or is in a register. In addition, each memory operand can be accessed with more than 10 addressing modes. This combination of address modes and register, versus memory, operands means that there are thousands of variants of a VAX add instruction. Clearly this variability makes VAX implementations more challenging.

When memory was scarce, it was also important to keep programs small, so machines like the Intel 8086, IBM 360, and VAX had variable-length instructions, both to match the varying operand specifications and to minimize code size. Intel 8086 instructions are from 1 to 5 bytes long, IBM 360 instructions are 2, 4, or 6 bytes long, and VAX instruction lengths are anywhere from 1 to 54 bytes. If instruction memory space becomes precious once again, such techniques could return to popularity.

In the 1960s, a few companies followed a radical approach to instruction sets. In the belief that it was too hard for compilers to utilize registers effectively, these companies abandoned registers altogether! Instruction sets were based on a *stack model* of execution, like that found in the older Hewlett-Packard hand-held calculators. Operands are pushed on the stack from memory or popped off the stack into memory. Operations take their operands from the stack and then place the result back onto the stack. In addition to simplifying compilers by eliminating register allocation, stack machines lent themselves to compact instruction encoding, thereby removing memory size as an excuse not to program in high-level languages.

Example

What is the stack-style assembly code for this C code?

```
A = B + C;
```

Answer

It would be translated into the following instructions in a stack instruction set:

```
push AddressC   # Top=Top+4;Stack[Top]=Memory[AddressC]
push AddressB   # Top=Top+4;Stack[Top]=Memory[AddressB]
add             # Stack[Top-4]=Stack[Top]
                # + Stack[Top-4];Top=Top-4;
pop  AddressA   # Memory[AddressA]=Stack[Top];
                #   Top=Top-4;
```

To get the proper byte address, we use 4 to adjust the stack. The downside of stacks as compared to registers is that it is hard to reuse data that has been fetched or calculated without repeatedly going to memory. (See Exercises 3.25 and 3.26 for other comparative examples.)

In the 1960s little systems software was written in high-level languages. For example, virtually every commercial operating system before UNIX was programmed in assembly language, and more recently even OS/2 was originally programmed at that same low level. Some people blamed the instruction sets rather than the programming languages and the compiler technology. Hence a machine design philosophy called *high-level language computer architecture* was advocated, with the goal of making the hardware more like the programming languages. More efficient programming languages and compilers, plus expanding memory, doomed this movement to a historical footnote. The Burroughs B5000 was the commercial fountainhead of this philosophy, but today there is no significant commercial descendent of this 1960s radical.

This language-oriented design philosophy was replaced in the 1980s by *RISC*, which stands for *reduced instruction set computer*. Improvements in programming languages, compiler technology, and memory size meant that less programming was being done at the assembly level, so instruction sets could be measured by how well compilers used them as opposed to how well assembly language programmers used them.

For the reasons discussed earlier in this chapter, it was difficult both for the compiler to use the more complex operations and for the instruction set designer to avoid making such instructions so general that they were slower than simple instruction sequences. Virtually all new instruction sets since 1982 have followed this RISC philosophy of fixed instruction lengths, load-store instruction set, limited addressing modes, and limited operations. MIPS, Sun SPARC, Hewlett Packard HPPA, IBM Power PC, and DEC Alpha are all examples of RISC architectures.

To Probe Further

Hennessy, J. L., and D. A. Patterson [1990]. *Computer Architecture: A Quantitative Approach*, Morgan Kaufmann Publishers, San Mateo, Calif.

Chapters 3 and 4 describe Intel 80x86, IBM 360, VAX, and a generic RISC machine. The book also includes measurements of the frequency of instructions and operands. Appendix E surveys four RISC architectures: MIPS, SPARC, 88000, and i860.

Kane, G. and J. Heinrich [1992]. *MIPS RISC Architecture*, Prentice Hall, Englewood Cliffs, N.J.

This book describes the MIPS architecture in greater detail than Appendix A.

Levy, H., and R. Eckhouse [1989]. *Computer Programming and Architecture: The VAX*, Digital Press, Boston.

This book concentrates on the VAX, but also includes descriptions of the Intel 80x86, IBM 360, and CDC 6600.

Wakerly, J. [1989]. *Microcomputer Architecture and Programming*, Wiley, New York.

The Motorola 680x0 is the main focus of the book, but it covers the Intel 80x86 as well.

Exercises

Appendix A describes the MIPS simulator that is helpful for these exercises.

3.1 [3] <§3.2, 3.9> In some cases a simple instruction set like MIPS can synthesize instructions found in richer instruction sets such as the VAX. The following VAX instruction decrements register $5:

```
decl $5 # register $5 = $5 - 1
```

The operation is described in the comment of the instruction to help explain the operation. What is the single MIPS instruction, or if it cannot be represented in a single instruction, the shortest sequence of MIPS instructions, that performs the same operation?

3.2 [3] <§3.2, 3.9> This is the same as Exercise 3.1, except this VAX instruction clears register $5:

```
clrl $5 # register $5 = 0
```

3.3 [3] <§3.3, 3.9> This is the same as Exercise 3.1, except this VAX instruction clears memory location 1000:

```
clrl 1000            # memory[1000] = 0
```

3.4 [5] <§3.2, 3.5, 3.9> This is the same as Exercise 3.1, except this VAX instruction adds 1 to register $5, placing the sum back in register $5, compares the sum to register $6, and then branches to L1 if $5 < $6:

```
aoblss $6, $5,L1      # $5 = $5 + 1; if ($5<$6) goto L1
```

3.5 [5] <§3.2, 3.5, 3.9> This is the same as Exercise 3.1, except this VAX instruction subtracts 1 from register $5, placing the difference back in register $5, and then branches to L1 if $5 > 0:

```
sobgtr $5,L1           # $5 = $5 - 1; if ($5 > 0) goto L1
```

3.6 [5] <§3.7> Show the single MIPS instruction or minimal sequence of instructions for this C statement:

```
a = b + 100;
```

Assume a corresponds to register $11 and b corresponds to register $12.

3.7 [10] <§3.7> Show the single MIPS instruction or minimal sequence of instructions for this C statement:

```
x[10] = x[11] + c;
```

Assume c corresponds to register $13 and the array x begins at memory location 4,000,000$_{ten}$.

3.8 [10] <§3.2, 3.3, 3.5, 3.7> The following program tries to copy words from the address in register $4 to the address in register $5, counting the number of words copied in register $2. The program stops copying when it finds a word equal to 0. You do not have to preserve the contents of registers $3, $4, and $5. This terminating word should be copied but not be counted.

```
loop: lw      $3,0($4)     # Read next word from source
      addi    $2,$2,1      # Increment count words copied
      sw      $3,0($5)     # Write to destination
      addi    $4,$4,1      # Advance pointer to next source
      addi    $5,$5,1      # Advance pointer to next dest
      bne     $3,$0,loop   # Loop if word copied ≠ zero
```

There are multiple bugs in this MIPS program. Fix them and turn in a bug-free version of this program. Like many of the exercises in this chapter, the easiest way to write MIPS programs is to use the simulator described in Appendix A. (The preface describes how to get a copy of this program.)

3.9 [15] <§3.4> Using the MIPS program in Exercise 3.8 (with bugs intact), determine the instruction format for each instruction and the decimal values of each instruction field.

3.10 [10] <§3.2, 3.3, 3.5, 3.7> {ex. 3.8} Starting with the corrected program in the answer to Exercise 3.8, write the C code segment that might have produced this code. Assume variable `source` corresponds to register $4, the variable `destination` corresponds to register $5, and the variable `count` corresponds to register $2. Show variable declarations, but assume that source and destination have been initialized to the proper addresses.

3.11 [10] <§3.5> This C segment

```
while (save[i] == k)
        i = i + j;
```

on page 114 uses both a conditional branch and an unconditional jump each time through the loop. Only poor compilers would produce code with this loop overhead. Rewrite the assembly code so that it uses at most one branch or jump each time through the loop. If the number of iterations of the loop is 10, what is the number of instructions executed before and after the optimization?

3.12 [3] <§3.5> There are six relative conditions between the values of two registers. Assuming that variable i corresponds to register $19 and variable j to $20, show the MIPS code for the condition corresponding to this C code:

```
if (i == j) goto L1;
```

3.13 [3] <§3.5> This is the same as Exercise 3.12, except use this C code:

```
if (i != j) goto L1;
```

3.14 [3] <§3.5> This is the same as Exercise 3.12, except use this C code:

```
if (i < j) goto L1;
```

3.15 [3] <§3.5> This is the same as Exercise 3.12, except use this C code:

```
if (i <= j) goto L1;
```

3.16 [3] <§3.5> This is the same as Exercise 3.12, except use this C code:

```
if (i > j) goto L1;
```

3.17 [3] <§3.5> This is the same as Exercise 3.12, except use this C code:

```
if (i >= j) goto L1;
```

3.18 [5] <3.5, 3.7> The instruction

```
beq $2,$3,L1
```

will compare the contents of $2 and $3 and branch to L1 if they are equal. Unfortunately, there is no single instruction that can be used to compare $2 with an immediate value such as 14. Look at the format for branch instructions and explain why. Write a sequence of MIPS instructions that will branch to L1 if $2 is equal to 14. Hint: It only takes two instructions.

3.19 [30] <§3.5> Consider the following fragment of C code:

```
for (i=0; i<=100; i=i+1)
            {a[i] = b[i] + c;}
```

Assume that a and b are arrays of words at addresses 1500 and 2000, respectively. Register $15 is associated with variable i and $16 with c. Write the code for MIPS. How many instructions are executed during the running of this code? How many memory data references will be made during execution?

3.20 [10] <§3.13> When designing memory systems, it becomes useful to know the frequency of memory reads versus writes as well as the frequency of accesses for instructions versus data. Using the average instruction-mix information for MIPS for the program gcc in Figure 3.24 on page 150, find

a.   the percentage of *all* memory accesses that are for *data* (vs. instructions)

b.   the percentage of *all* memory accesses that are reads (vs. writes). Assume that two-thirds of data transfers are loads.

3.21 [10] <§3.13> This is the same as Exercise 3.20, but replace the program gcc with spice.

3.22 [15] <§3.13> Suppose we have made the following measurements of average CPI for instructions:

Arithmetic	1.0 clock cycles
Data transfer	1.4 clock cycles
Conditional branch	1.7 clock cycles
Jump	1.2 clock cycles

Compute the effective CPI for MIPS. Average the instruction frequencies for gcc and spice in Figure 3.24 on page 150 to obtain the instruction mix.

3.23 [20] <§3.9> Several researchers have suggested that adding a register–memory addressing mode to a load/store machine might be useful. The idea is to replace sequences of

```
lw      $8,addr($3)
add     $2,$2,$8
```

by

```
addm    $2,addr($3)
```

Assume the new instruction will cause the clock cycle to increase by 10%. Use the instruction frequencies for the *gcc* benchmark from Figure 3.24 on page 150, and assume that two-thirds of the moves are loads and the rest are stores. Assume the new instruction affects only the clock speed and not the CPI. What percentage of the loads must be eliminated for the machine with the new instruction to have at least the same performance?

3.24 [10] <§3.9> Using the information in Exercise 3.23, write a multiple instruction sequence in which a load of $8 followed immediately by the use of $8—in, say, an add—could not be replaced by a single instruction of the form proposed.

In More Depth:
Comparing Instruction Sets of Different Styles

For the next three exercises, your task is to compare the memory efficiency of four different styles of instruction sets for two code sequences. The architecture styles are

- *Accumulator*

- *Memory–Memory*: All three operands of each instruction are in memory.

- *Stack*: All operations occur on top of the stack. Only push and pop access memory, and all other instructions remove their operands from the stack and replace them with the result. The implementation uses a stack for the top two entries; accesses that use other stack positions are memory references.

- *Load-Store*: All operations occur in registers, and register-to-register instructions have three operands per instruction. There are 16 general-purpose registers, and register specifiers are 4 bits long.

To measure memory efficiency, make the following assumptions about all four instruction sets:

- The opcode is always 1 byte (8 bits).

- All memory addresses are 2 bytes (16 bits).

- All data operands are 4 bytes (32 bits).

- All instructions are an integral number of bytes in length.

There are no other optimizations to reduce memory traffic, and the variables a, b, c, and d are initially in *memory*.

Using the assembly language mnemonics from section 3.14, write the best equivalent assembly language code for the high-level language fragments given.

3.25 [15] <§3.14> Write the four code sequences for

```
a = b + c;
```

For each code sequence, calculate the instruction bytes fetched and the memory-data bytes transferred. Which architecture is most efficient as measured by code size? Which architecture is most efficient as measured by total memory bandwidth required (code + data)?

3.26 [20] <§3.14> Write the four code sequences for

```
a = b + c;
b = a + c;
d = a - b;
```

For each code sequence, calculate the instruction bytes fetched and the memory-data bytes transferred (read or written). Which architecture is most efficient as measured by code size? Which architecture is most efficient as measured by total memory bandwidth required (code + data)? If the answers are not the same, why are they different?

3.27 [5] <§3.14> Sometimes architectures are characterized according to the typical number of memory addresses per instruction. Commonly used terms are 0-, 1-, 2-, and 3-addresses per instruction. Associate the names above with each category.

In More Depth:
Register Conventions and Procedure Overhead

Caller and callee save (page 121) are strategies to save and restore registers across procedure calls. MIPS software uses a combination of the two strategies, saving only registers $16 to $23 and $30 across procedure calls if they are modified. This compiler convention reduces the amount of code to be written, lowers the cost of calls, and standardizes linkage to simplify calling procedures written in different languages. In fact, some compilers use alternative names for the registers to reflect their different uses. Figure A.9 on page A-23 lists all register conventions and the alternative names.

3.28 [15] <§3.9, A.6> Rewrite the swap procedure in Figure 3.19 on page 138 using the conventions in Figure A.9 on page A-23 to reduce the saving and restoring of registers. What is the change in number of instructions executed in the new version?

ASCII value	Character	ASCII value	Character	ASCII value	Character	ASCII value	Character	ASCII value	Character
32	space	51	3	70	F	89	Y	108	l
33	!	52	4	71	G	90	Z	109	m
34	"	53	5	72	H	91	[	110	n
35	#	54	6	73	I	92	\	111	o
36	$	55	7	74	J	93	]	112	p
37	%	56	8	75	K	94	^	113	q
38	&	57	9	76	L	95	_	114	r
39	'	58	:	77	M	96	`	115	s
40	(	59	;	78	N	97	a	116	t
41	)	60	<	79	O	98	b	117	u
42	*	61	=	80	P	99	c	118	v
43	+	62	>	81	Q	100	d	119	w
44	,	63	?	82	R	101	e	120	x
45	-	64	@	83	S	102	f	121	y
46	.	65	A	84	T	103	g	122	z
47	/	66	B	85	U	104	h	123	{
48	0	67	C	86	V	105	i	124		
49	1	68	D	87	W	106	j	125	}
50	2	69	E	88	X	107	k	126	~

FIGURE 3.26 ASCII representation of characters. Values not shown include values useful in formatting characters. For example, 9 represents a tab character and 13 represents a carriage return. Other useful ASCII values are 8 for backspace and 0 for Null, the value the programming language C uses to terminate the end of a string.

3.29 [15] <§3.10, A.6> Rewrite the sort procedure Figure 3.21 on page 144 using the conventions in Figure A.9 on page A-23 to reduce the saving and restoring of registers. What is the change in number of instructions executed in the new version (not including the call of swap)?

In More Depth: Characters and Strings

While many programs work primarily with numbers, others work with characters. Most computers today use 8-bit bytes to represent characters, with the American Standard Code for Information Interchange (ASCII) being the representation that nearly everyone follows. Figure 3.26 summarizes ASCII.

Because of the popularity of strings in some programs, MIPS provides special instructions to move bytes. Load byte (lb) loads a byte from memory, placing it in the rightmost 8 bits of a register; the other 24 bits are set to 0. Store byte (sb) takes a byte from the rightmost 8 bits of a register and writes it to memory. Thus the sequence

```
lb $3,0($4)    # Read byte from source
sb $3,0($5)    # Write byte to destination
```

copies a byte.

Characters are normally combined into strings, which have a variable number of characters. C uses the convention that a string is terminated by a byte with the value 0.

3.30 [10] Compute the decimal byte values that form the null-terminated ASCII representation of the string (the "s" in "bits" is the last character).

```
A byte is 8 bits.
```

3.31 [20] {ex. 3.8} Write a procedure, bcopy, in MIPS assembler language. The bcopy procedure takes two arguments: a pointer to a null-terminated source string in register $4 and a pointer to the destination string in register $5. It returns a count of the total number of non-null characters in the string in register $2. Hint: Look at the program copy in Exercise 3.8 for ideas. The easiest way to write a MIPS program is to use the simulator described in Appendix A.

3.32 [30] {ex. 3.8, 3.31}Both the program in the answer to Exercise 3.8 and the program in the answer to Exercise 3.31 copy bytes. Under what circumstances do they behave in exactly the same way? Assuming those circumstances hold, write formulas for the number of instructions executed for both programs as a function of the number of bytes copied. Describe what a hybrid program would have to do to determine when to invoke the faster copying program as a procedure. (The instructions you need to do this are described in the next chapter.)

3.33 [30] Write a program in MIPS assembly language to convert an ASCII decimal string to an integer. Your program should expect register $4 to hold the address of a null-terminated string containing some combination of the digits 0 through 9. Your program should compute the integer value equivalent to this string of digits, then place the number in register $2. Your program need not handle negative numbers. If a non-digit character appears anywhere in the string, your program should stop with the value –1 in register $2.

For example, if register $4 points to a sequence of three bytes 50_{ten}, 52_{ten}, 0_{ten} (the null-terminated string "24"), then when the program stops, register $2 should contain the value 24_{ten}. (The subscript "ten" means base 10.)

3.34 [20] Write a procedure, bfind, in MIPS assembler language. The procedure should take a single argument which is a pointer to a null-terminated string in register $4. The bfind procedure should locate the first b character in the string and return its address in register $2. If there are no b's in the string, then bfind should return a pointer to the null character at the end of the string.

For example, if the argument to bfind points to the string "imbibe," then the return value will be a pointer to the third character of the string.

3.35 [20] {ex. 3.33} Write a procedure, bcount, in MIPS assembler language. The bcount procedure takes a single argument, which is a pointer to a string in register $4, and it returns a count of the total number of b characters in the string in register $2. You must use your bfind procedure in Exercise 3.34 in your implementation of bcount.

3.36 [30] Write a procedure, itoa, that will convert an integer argument into an ASCII decimal string. The procedure should take two arguments: the first is an integer in register $4 and the second is the address at which to write a result string in register $5. Then itoa should convert its first argument to a null-terminated decimal ASCII string and store that string at the given result location. The return value from itoa, in register $2, should be a count of the number of non-null characters stored at the destination.

In More Depth: The Single Instruction Computer

The computer architecture in this book, MIPS, has one of the simpler instruction sets in existence. However, it is possible to imagine even simpler instruction sets. In this assignment you are to consider a hypothetical machine called SIC, for *Single Instruction Computer*. As its name implies, SIC has only one instruction: Subtract and Branch if Negative, or sbn for short. The sbn instruction has three operands, each consisting of the address of a word in memory:

```
sbn a,b,c # Mem[a] = Mem[a] - Mem[b];if (Mem[a]<0) goto c
```

The instruction will subtract the number in memory location b from the number in location a and place the result back in a, overwriting the previous value. If the result is greater than or equal to 0, the computer will take its next instruction from the memory location just after the current instruction. If the result is less than 0, the next instruction is taken from memory location c. SIC has no registers and no instructions other than sbn.

Although it has only one instruction, SIC can imitate many of the operations of more complex instruction sets by using clever sequences of sbn instructions. For example, here is a program to copy a number from location a to location b:

```
start:   sbn temp,temp,.+1      # Sets temp to zero
         sbn temp,a,.+1         # Sets temp to -a
         sbn b,b,.+1            # Sets b to zero
         sbn b,temp,.+1         # Sets b to -temp, which is a
```

In the program above, the notation .+1 means "the address after this one," so that each instruction in this program goes on to the next in sequence whether or not the result is negative. We assume Temp to be the address of a spare memory word that can be used for temporary results.

3.37 [10] Write a SIC program to add a and b, leaving the result in a and leaving b unmodified.

3.38 [20] Write a SIC program to multiply a by b, putting the result in c. Assume that memory location one contains the number 1. Assume a and b are > 0 and that it's OK to modify a or b. Hint: What does this program compute?

```
c = 0; while (b > 0) {b = b - 1; c = c + a;}
```

4

Arithmetic for Computers

*Numerical precision
is the very soul
of science.*

Sir D'arcy Wentworth Thompson,
On Growth and Form, 1917

The Five Classic Components of a Computer

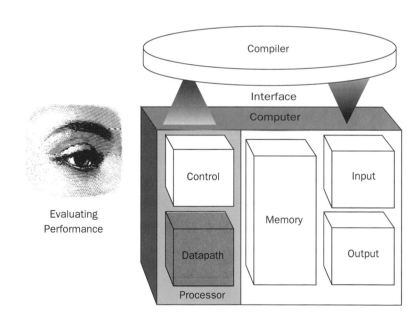

4.1 Introduction

Computer words are composed of bits; thus words can be represented as binary numbers. Although the natural numbers 0, 1, 2, and so on can be represented either in decimal or binary form, what about the other numbers that commonly occur? For example,

- How are negative numbers represented?

- What is the largest number that can be represented by a computer word?

- What happens if an operation creates a number bigger than can be represented?

- What about fractions and real numbers?

And underlying all these questions is a mystery: How does hardware really add, subtract, multiply, or divide numbers?

The goal of this chapter is to unravel this mystery, including representation of numbers, arithmetic algorithms, hardware that follows these algorithms, and the implications of all this for instruction sets. These insights may even explain quirks that you have already encountered with computers. (Readers who are familiar with signed binary numbers may wish to skip the next two sections and go to Section 4.4 on page 179.)

4.2 Negative Numbers

> *minus infinity*: *The smallest [number that can be represented in a particular type of variable], not necessarily or even usually the simple negation of plus infinity.*
>
> Eric Raymond, *The New Hacker's Dictionary*, 1991

Numbers can be represented in any base; humans prefer base ten and, as we examined in Chapter 3, base two is best for computers. Because we will frequently be dealing with both decimal and binary numbers, to avoid confusion we will subscript decimal numbers with *ten* and binary numbers with *two*.

In any number base the value of ith digit d is

$$d \times base^i$$

where i starts at 0 and increases from right to left. This leads to an obvious way to number the bits in the word: Simply use the power of the base for that bit. For example,

$$1011_{two}$$

represents

$$(1 \times 2^3) + (0 \times 2^2) + (1 \times 2^1) + (1 \times 2^0)_{ten}$$
$$= (1 \times 8) + (0 \times 4) + (1 \times 2) + (1 \times 1)_{ten}$$
$$= 8 + 0 + 2 + 1_{ten}$$
$$= 11_{ten}$$

Hence the bits are numbered 0, 1, 2, 3, ... from *right to left* in a word. The drawing below shows the numbering of bits within a MIPS word and the placement of the number 1011_{two}:

31 30 29 28	27 26 25 24	23 22 21 20	19 18 17 16	15 14 13 12	11 10 9 8	7 6 5 4	3 2 1 0
0 0 0 0	0 0 0 0	0 0 0 0	0 0 0 0	0 0 0 0	0 0 0 0	0 0 0 0	1 0 1 1

(32 bits wide)

Since words are drawn vertically as well as horizontally, leftmost and rightmost may be unclear. Hence, the phrase *least significant bit* is used to refer to the rightmost bit (bit 0 above) and *most significant bit* to the leftmost bit (bit 31).

The MIPS word is 32 bits long, so we can represent 2^{32} different 32-bit patterns. It is natural to let these combinations represent the numbers from 0 to $2^{32} - 1$ ($4{,}294{,}967{,}295_{ten}$):

$$0000\ 0000\ 0000\ 0000\ 0000\ 0000\ 0000\ 0000_{two} = 0_{ten}$$
$$0000\ 0000\ 0000\ 0000\ 0000\ 0000\ 0000\ 0001_{two} = 1_{ten}$$
$$0000\ 0000\ 0000\ 0000\ 0000\ 0000\ 0000\ 0010_{two} = 2_{ten}$$
$$...$$
$$1111\ 1111\ 1111\ 1111\ 1111\ 1111\ 1111\ 1101_{two} = 4{,}294{,}967{,}293_{ten}$$
$$1111\ 1111\ 1111\ 1111\ 1111\ 111\ \ 1111\ 1110_{two} = 4{,}294{,}967{,}294_{ten}$$
$$1111\ 1111\ 1111\ 1111\ 1111\ 1111\ 1111\ 1111_{two} = 4{,}294{,}967{,}295_{ten}$$

Computer programs calculate both positive and negative numbers, so we need a representation that distinguishes the positive from the negative. This representation should be divided as evenly as possible, since it would be awkward to be able to represent, say, 2000_{ten} but not -2000_{ten}. Since a 32-bit word has an even number of bit patterns, balanced representation seems straightforward. It's not. The reason is that we need to represent zero *plus* an equal number of positive and negative numbers. The alternative to unbalanced positives and negatives is having two bit patterns to represent 0. The cure of two bit patterns that are different but both represent 0 is worse than the disease of unbalance, so 32-bit computers use the following unbalanced convention:

```
0000 0000 0000 0000 0000 0000 0000 0000two=    0ten
0000 0000 0000 0000 0000 0000 0000 0001two=    1ten
0000 0000 0000 0000 0000 0000 0000 0010two=    2ten
. . .

0111 1111 1111 1111 1111 1111 1111 1101two=  2,147,483,645ten
0111 1111 1111 1111 1111 1111 1111 1110two=  2,147,483,646ten
0111 1111 1111 1111 1111 1111 1111 1111two=  2,147,483,647ten
1000 0000 0000 0000 0000 0000 0000 0000two= -2,147,483,648ten
1000 0000 0000 0000 0000 0000 0000 0001two= -2,147,483,647ten
1000 0000 0000 0000 0000 0000 0000 0010two= -2,147,483,646ten
. . .

1111 1111 1111 1111 1111 1111 1111 1101two= -3ten
1111 1111 1111 1111 1111 1111 1111 1110two= -2ten
1111 1111 1111 1111 1111 1111 1111 1111two= -1ten
```

The positive half of the numbers, from 0 to $2,147,483,647_{ten}$ ($2^{31}-1$), use the same representation as before. The following bit pattern ($1000\ldots0000_{two}$) represents the most negative number $-2,147,483,648_{ten}$ (-2^{31}). It is followed by a declining set of negative numbers: $-2,147,483,647_{ten}$ ($1000\ldots0001_{two}$) down to -1_{ten} ($1111\ldots1111_{two}$). There is, therefore, just one negative number, $-2,147,483,648_{ten}$, that has no corresponding positive number. This convention for representing signed binary numbers is called *two's complement* representation. It ensures that $x + (-x) = 0$.

In addition to a single 0, two's complement representation has the advantage that all negative numbers have a 1 in the most significant bit. Consequently, hardware need test only this bit to see if a number is positive or negative (with 0 considered positive). This particular bit is often called the *sign* bit. By recognizing the role of the sign bit, we can represent positive and negative numbers in terms of the bit value times a power of 2 (here xi means the *i*th bit of x):

$$(x31 \times -2^{31}) + (x30 \times 2^{30}) + (x29 \times 2^{29}) + \ldots + (x1 \times 2^1) + (x0 \times 2^0)$$

The sign bit is multiplied by -2^{31} and the rest of the bits are then multiplied by positive versions of their respective base values.

Example   What is the decimal value of this 32-bit two's complement number?

```
1111 1111 1111 1111 1111 1111 1111 1100two
```

Answer

Substituting into the bit values in the formula above:

$$(1 \times -2^{31}) + (1 \times 2^{30}) + (1 \times 2^{29}) + \ldots + (1 \times 2^2) + (0 \times 2^1) + (0 \times 2^0)$$
$$= -2^{31} + 2^{30} + 2^{29} + \ldots + 2^2$$
$$= -2{,}147{,}483{,}648_{ten} + 2{,}147{,}483{,}644_{ten}$$
$$= -4_{ten}$$

Hardware Software Interface

Unlike the numbers discussed above, memory addresses naturally start at 0 and continue to the largest address. Put another way, negative addresses make no sense. Thus, programs want to deal sometimes with numbers that can be positive or negative and sometimes with numbers that can be only positive. Programming languages reflect this distinction. C, for example, names the former *integers* (declared as int in the program) and the latter *unsigned integers* (unsigned int).

Comparison instructions must deal with this dichotomy. Sometimes a bit pattern with a 1 in the most significant bit represents a negative number and, of course, is less than any positive number, which must have a 0 in the most significant bit. With unsigned integers, on the other hand, a 1 in the most significant bit represents a number that is *larger* than any that begins with a 0. MIPS offers two versions of the set-on-less-than comparison to handle these alternatives. *Set on less than* (slt) and *set on less than immediate* (slti) work with signed integers. Unsigned integers are compared using *set on less than unsigned* (sltu) and *set on less than immediate unsigned* (sltiu).

Example

Suppose register $16 has the binary number

```
1111 1111 1111 1111 1111 1111 1111 1111two
```

and that register $17 has the binary number

```
0000 0000 0000 0000 0000 0000 0000 0001two
```

What are the values of registers $8 and $9 after these two instructions?

```
slt    $8, $16, $17 # signed comparison
sltu   $9, $16, $17 # unsigned comparison
```

Answer

The value in register $16 represents -1 if it is an integer and $4{,}294{,}967{,}295_{ten}$ if it is an unsigned integer. The value in register $17 represents 1 in either case. Then register $8 has the value 1, since $-1_{ten} < 1_{ten}$, and register $9 has the value 0, since $4{,}294{,}967{,}295_{ten} > 1_{ten}$.

Before going on to addition and subtraction, let's examine a few shortcuts when working with two's complement numbers. The first shortcut is a quick way to negate a binary number. Simply invert every 0 to 1 and every 1 to 0, then add 1 to the result. This shortcut is based on the observation that the number represented by inverting each bit is off by 1 from the two's complement negative of the number.

Example

Negate 2_{ten}, and then check the result by negating -2_{ten}.

Answer

$$2_{ten} = 0000\ 0000\ 0000\ 0000\ 0000\ 0000\ 0000\ 0010_{two}$$

Negating this number by inverting the bits and adding 1:

$$
\begin{aligned}
&\ 1111\ 1111\ 1111\ 1111\ 1111\ 1111\ 1111\ 1101_{two} \\
+&1_{two} \\
\hline
=&\ 1111\ 1111\ 1111\ 1111\ 1111\ 1111\ 1111\ 1110_{two} \\
=&-2_{ten}
\end{aligned}
$$

Going the other direction,

$$1111\ 1111\ 1111\ 1111\ 1111\ 1111\ 1111\ 1110_{two}$$

is first inverted and then incremented:

$$
\begin{aligned}
&\ 0000\ 0000\ 0000\ 0000\ 0000\ 0000\ 0000\ 0001_{two} \\
+&1_{two} \\
\hline
=&\ 0000\ 0000\ 0000\ 0000\ 0000\ 0000\ 0000\ 0010_{two} \\
=&2_{ten}
\end{aligned}
$$

The second shortcut tells us how to convert a binary number represented in n bits to a number represented with more than n bits. For example, the immediate field in the load, store, branch, add, and set-on-less-than instructions contains a two's complement 16-bit number, representing $-32{,}768_{ten}$ (-2^{15}) to $32{,}767_{ten}(2^{15}-1)$. To add the immediate field to a 32-bit register, the machine must convert that 16-bit number to its 32-bit equivalent. The shortcut is to take the most significant bit from the smaller quantity, the sign bit, and replicate it to fill the new bits of the larger quantity. The old bits are simply copied into the right portion of the new word. This shortcut is commonly called *sign exten-sion*.

Example

Convert 16-bit binary versions of 2_{ten} and -2_{ten} to 32-bit binary numbers.

Answer

The 16-bit binary version of the number 2 is

$$0000\ 0000\ 0000\ 0010_{two} = 2_{ten}$$

It is converted to a 32-bit number by making 16 copies of the value in the most significant bit (0) and placing that in the left-hand half of the word. The right half gets the old value:

$$0000\ 0000\ 0000\ 0000\ 0000\ 0000\ 0000\ 0010_{two} = 2_{ten}$$

Let's negate the 16-bit version of 2 using the earlier shortcut. Thus,

$$0000\ 0000\ 0000\ 0010_{two}$$

becomes

$$
\begin{array}{r}
1111\ 1111\ 1111\ 1101_{two} \\
+\qquad\qquad\qquad\quad 1_{two} \\
\hline
=\quad 1111\ 1111\ 1111\ 1110_{two}
\end{array}
$$

Creating a 32-bit version of the negative number means copying the sign bit 16 times and placing it on the left:

$$1111\ 1111\ 1111\ 1111\ 1111\ 1111\ 1111\ 1110_{two} = {-2}_{ten}$$

This trick works because positive two's complement numbers can be thought of as having an infinite number of 0s on the left and negative numbers have an infinite number of 1s. Placing a two's complement number in a word merely chops off those bits to make the number fit in a word, and sign extension restores them.

The main point of this section is that we need to represent both positive and negative integers within a computer word and, although there are pros and cons to any option, the overwhelming choice for the last 25 years has been two's complement. Figure 4.1 shows the additions to the MIPS assembly language revealed in this section. (MIPS machine language is illustrated on the endpapers of this book.)

MIPS operands

Name	Example	Comments
32 registers	$0, $1, $2, . . . ,$31	Fast locations for data. In MIPS, data must be in registers to perform arithmetic. MIPS register $0 always equals 0. Register $1 is reserved for the assembler to handle pseudoinstructions and large constants.
2^{30} memory words	Memory[0], Memory[4], . . . , Memory[4294967292]	Accessed only by data transfer instructions. MIPS uses byte addresses, so sequential words differ by 4. Memory holds data structures, such as arrays, and spilled registers, such as those saved on procedure calls.

MIPS assembly language

Category	Instruction		Example	Meaning	Comments
Arithmetic	add	add	$1,$2,$3	$1 = $2 + $3	3 operands; data in registers
	subtract	sub	$1,$2,$3	$1 = $2 – $3	3 operands; data in registers
	add immediate	addi	$1,$2,100	$1 = $2 + 100	Used to add constants
Data transfer	load word	lw	$1,100($2)	$1 = Memory[$2+100]	Data from memory to register
	store word	sw	$1,100($2)	Memory[$2+100] = $1	Data from register to memory
	load upper imm.	lui	$1,100	$1 = 100 × 2^{16}	Loads constant in upper 16 bits
Conditional branch	branch on equal	beq	$1,$2,100	if ($1 == $2) go to PC+4+100	Equal test; PC relative branch
	branch on not eq.	bne	$1,$2,100	if ($1 != $2) go to PC+4+100	Not equal test; PC relative
	set on less than	slt	$1,$2,$3	if ($2 < $3) $1 = 1; else $1 = 0	Compare less than; 2's comp.
	set less than imm.	slti	$1,$2,100	if ($2 < 100) $1 = 1; else $1 = 0	Compare < constant; 2's comp.
	set on less than unsigned	sltu	$1,$2,$3	if ($2 < $3) $1 = 1; else $1 = 0	Compare less than; unsigned numbers
	set less than imm. unsigned	sltiu	$1,$2,100	if ($2 < 100) $1 = 1; else $1 = 0	Compare less than constant; unsigned numbers
Unconditional jump	jump	j	10000	go to 10000	Jump to target address
	jump register	jr	$31	go to $31	For switch, procedure return
	jump and link	jal	10000	$31 = PC + 4; go to 10000	For procedure call

FIGURE 4.1 MIPS architecture revealed thus far. Color indicates portions from this section added to the MIPS architecture revealed in Chapter 3 (Figure 3.16 on page 132). MIPS machine language is illustrated in the endpapers of this book.

Elaboration: Two's complement gets its name from the rule that the sum of an n-bit number and its negative is 2^n, hence the complement or negation of a two's complement number x is $2^n - x$. One obvious alternative representation to two's complement uses the leftmost bit as the sign, with the other 31 bits representing the number. This *sign and magnitude* representation has the drawback of having positive and negative 0. In addition, it is harder to design an adder for sign and magnitude, as we shall see shortly. A third alternative is called *one's complement*. The negative of a one's complement is found by inverting each bit, from 0 to 1 and from 1 to 0. This representation is similar to two's complement except that it has two 0s: $00 \ldots 00_{two}$ is positive 0 and $11 \ldots 11_{two}$ is negative 0. The most negative number $10 \ldots 000_{two}$ represents $-2{,}147{,}483{,}647_{ten}$ and so the positives and negatives are balanced. A final notation, which we will look at when we discuss floating point, is to make the most negative value be $00 \ldots 000_{two}$ and the most positive value be $11 \ldots 11_{two}$, with 0 typically having the value $10 \ldots 00_{two}$. This is called a *biased* notation, for it biases the number such that the number plus the bias is non-negative.

As a final point, in order to save space, many programs display numbers using a higher base than binary that converts easily to binary. Since almost all computer data sizes are multiples of 4, *hexadecimal* (base 16) numbers are popular. The 16 hexadecimal digits are 0, 1, 2, 3, 4, 5, 6, 7, 8, 9, a, b, c, d, e, and f. C uses the notation $0xnnnn$ to represent a hexadecimal number. In this book, we will use either the subscript *hex* or the C notation.

4.3   Addition and Subtraction

Subtraction: Addition's Tricky Pal

> No. 10, Top Ten Courses for Athletes at a Football Factory
> David Letterman et al., *Book of Top Ten Lists*, 1990

Addition is just what you would expect in computers. Digits are added bit by bit from right to left, with carries passed to the next digit to the left, just as you would do by hand. Subtraction uses addition: The appropriate operand is simply negated before being added.

Example   Let's try adding 6_{ten} to 7_{ten} and then subtracting 6_{ten} from 7_{ten}.

Answer

$$
\begin{array}{rll}
 & 0000\ 0000\ 0000\ 0000\ 0000\ 0000\ 0000\ 0111_{two} & = 7_{ten} \\
+ & 0000\ 0000\ 0000\ 0000\ 0000\ 0000\ 0000\ 0110_{two} & = 6_{ten} \\
\hline
= & 0000\ 0000\ 0000\ 0000\ 0000\ 0000\ 0000\ 1101_{two} & = 13_{ten}
\end{array}
$$

The 4 bits to the right have all the action; Figure 4.2 shows the sums and carries. The carries are shown in parentheses, with the arrows showing how they are passed.

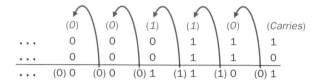

FIGURE 4.2 Binary addition, showing carries from right to left. The rightmost bit adds 1 to 0, resulting in the sum of this bit being 1 and the carry out from this bit being 0. Hence, the operation for the second digit to the right is 0+1+1. This generates a 0 for this sum bit and a carry out of 1. The third digit is the sum of 1+1+1, resulting in a carry out of 1 and a sum bit of 1. The fourth bit is 1+0+0, yielding a 1 sum and no carry.

Subtracting 6_{ten} from 7_{ten} can be done directly:

$$
\begin{array}{rl}
  & 0000\ 0000\ 0000\ 0000\ 0000\ 0000\ 0000\ 0111_{two} = 7_{ten} \\
- & 0000\ 0000\ 0000\ 0000\ 0000\ 0000\ 0000\ 0110_{two} = 6_{ten} \\
\hline
= & 0000\ 0000\ 0000\ 0000\ 0000\ 0000\ 0000\ 0001_{two} = 1_{ten}
\end{array}
$$

or via addition using the two's complement representation of –6:

$$
\begin{array}{rl}
  & 0000\ 0000\ 0000\ 0000\ 0000\ 0000\ 0000\ 0111_{two} = 7_{ten} \\
+ & 1111\ 1111\ 1111\ 1111\ 1111\ 1111\ 1111\ 1010_{two} = -6_{ten} \\
\hline
= & 0000\ 0000\ 0000\ 0000\ 0000\ 0000\ 0000\ 0001_{two} = 1_{ten}
\end{array}
$$

The one complexity in computer addition is the possibility of the sum being too large to represent properly. No matter how numbers are represented, it's possible that the sum of two 32-bit numbers will be too large to represent in 32 bits. This event is called *overflow*.

For example, the sum of these two signed numbers is too large for 32 bits:

$$
\begin{array}{rl}
  & 0111\ 1111\ 1111\ 1111\ 1111\ 1111\ 1111\ 1111_{two} = 2{,}147{,}483{,}647_{ten} \\
+ & 0000\ 0000\ 0000\ 0000\ 0000\ 0000\ 0000\ 0010_{two} = 2_{ten} \\
\hline
= & 1000\ 0000\ 0000\ 0000\ 0000\ 0000\ 0000\ 0001_{two} = -2{,}147{,}483{,}647_{ten}
\end{array}
$$

The sum of $2{,}147{,}483{,}647_{ten} + 2$ should be $2{,}147{,}483{,}649_{ten}$, but instead we get the *negative* value $-2{,}147{,}483{,}647_{ten}$. The problem is that we need 33 bits to represent $2{,}147{,}483{,}649_{ten}$ in two's complement notation, but the word size is only 32 bits. Therefore, the result has only the lower 32 bits of the actual sum.

Overflow can also occur in subtraction. For example, to subtract 2 from $-2{,}147{,}483{,}647_{ten}$, we convert 2 to –2 and add it to $-2{,}147{,}483{,}647_{ten}$:

Operation	Operand A	Operand B	Result
A + B	≥ 0	≥ 0	< 0
A + B	< 0	< 0	≥ 0
A − B	≥ 0	< 0	< 0
A − B	< 0	≥ 0	≥ 0

FIGURE 4.3 Overflow conditions for addition and subtraction.

$$
\begin{array}{rcr}
1000\ 0000\ 0000\ 0000\ 0000\ 0000\ 0000\ 0001_{two} &=& -2{,}147{,}483{,}647_{ten} \\
+1111\ 1111\ 1111\ 1111\ 1111\ 1111\ 1111\ 1110_{two} &=& -2_{ten} \\
\hline
=0111\ 1111\ 1111\ 1111\ 1111\ 1111\ 1111\ 1111_{two} &=& 2{,}147{,}483{,}647_{ten}
\end{array}
$$

Once again, the result of $-2{,}147{,}483{,}647_{ten} - 2$ should be $-2{,}147{,}483{,}649_{ten}$, but we cannot represent that result in 32 bits so we get the wrong *positive* value of $2{,}147{,}483{,}647_{ten}$.

When can overflow occur? When adding operands with different signs, overflow cannot occur. The reason is the sum must be no larger than one of the operands. For example, $-10 + 4 = -6$. Since the operands fit in 32 bits and the sum is no larger than an operand, the sum must fit in 32 bits as well. Therefore no overflow can occur when adding positive and negative operands.

There are similar restrictions to the occurrence of overflow during subtract, but it's just the opposite principle: When the signs of the operands are the *same*, overflow cannot occur. To see this, remember that $x - y = x + (-y)$, because we subtract by negating the second operand and then add. So, when we subtract operands of the same sign we end up by *adding* operands of *different* signs. From the prior paragraph, we know that overflow cannot occur in this case.

Having examined when overflow cannot occur, we still haven't answered how to detect when it does occur. As we saw in the examples above, adding or subtracting two 32-bit numbers can yield a result that needs 33 bits to be fully expressed. The lack of a 33rd bit means that when overflow occurs the sign bit is being set with the *value* of the result instead of the proper sign of the result: Since we need just one extra bit, only the sign bit can be wrong. That is, overflow occurs when adding two positive numbers and the sum is negative, or vice versa. And overflow occurs in subtraction when we subtract a negative number from a positive number and get a negative result, or when we subtract a positive number from a negative number and get a positive result. Figure 4.3 shows the combination of operations, operands, and results that indicate an overflow. (Exercise 4.29 gives a shortcut for detecting overflow more simply in hardware.)

Hardware Software Interface	The machine designer must decide how to handle arithmetic overflows. Although some languages like C leave the decision up to the machine designer, languages like Ada, Fortran, and Lisp require that the program be notified. The programmer or the programming environment must then decide what to do when overflow occurs.

MIPS detects overflow with an *exception*, also called an *interrupt* on many computers. An exception or interrupt is essentially an unplanned procedure call. The address of the instruction that overflowed is saved in a register, and the computer jumps to a predefined address to invoke the appropriate routine for that exception. The interrupted address is saved so that in some situations the program can continue after corrective code is executed (see Chapter 7). MIPS includes a register called *exception program counter* (*EPC*) to contain the address of the instruction that caused the exception. The instruction *move from system control* (mfc0) is used to copy EPC into a register so that MIPS software has the option of returning to the offending instruction via a Jump register instruction. Chapter 5, section 5.6 covers exceptions in more detail; Chapters 7 and 8 also describe situations where exceptions and interrupts occur.

We have just seen how to detect overflow for two's complement numbers in a machine. What about unsigned integers? Clearly, unsigned integers exist that are too large to be represented in 32 bits, but they are normally *not* considered to overflow. The reason is that unsigned integers are commonly used for memory addresses and, unlike natural numbers, they *do* have a finite limit in that memories are finite. In our MIPS machine, the maximum memory that a user can address directly is $4,294,967,296_{ten}$ or 2^{32} bytes.

The machine designer must therefore provide a way to ignore overflow in some cases and to recognize it in others. The MIPS solution is to have two kinds of arithmetic instructions to recognize the two choices:

- add (add), add immediate (addi) and subtract (sub) cause exceptions on overflow, and

- add unsigned (addu), add immediate unsigned (addiu), and subtract unsigned (subu) do *not* cause exceptions on overflow.

Because C ignores overflows, the MIPS C compilers will always generate the unsigned versions of the arithmetic instructions addu, addiu, and subu. The MIPS Ada compilers, however, pick the appropriate arithmetic instructions, depending on the type of the operands.

The main point of this section is that, independent of the representation, the finite word size of computers means that arithmetic operations can create results that are too large to fit in this fixed word size. It's easy to detect overflow in natural numbers, although these are almost always ignored because programs don't want to detect overflow for address arithmetic, the most common use of natural numbers. Two's complement presents a greater challenge, yet some software systems require detection of overflow, so today all machines have a way to detect it. Figure 4.4 shows the additions to the MIPS architecture from this section.

Elaboration: In the preceding text, we said that you copy EPC into a register via `mfc0` and then return to the interrupt code via Jump register. This leads to an interesting question: How can you use Jump register to return to the interrupted code and yet restore the original values of all registers? You either restore the old registers first, thereby destroying your return address from EPC, or you restore all registers but the one with the return address so that you can jump—meaning an exception would result in changing one register at any time in the program execution! Neither option is satisfactory. To rescue the hardware from this dilemma, MIPS programmers agreed to reserve registers $26 and $27 for the operating system; these registers are *not* restored on exceptions. Just as the MIPS compilers avoid using register $1 so that the assembler can use it as a temporary register (see the Hardware Software Interface on page 115 in Chapter 3), compilers also abstain from using registers $26 and $27 to make them available for the operating system. Exception routines place the return address in one of these registers and then use Jump register to restore the address.

4.4 Logical Operations

Insanity is often the logic of an accurate mind overtaxed.

Oliver Wendell Holmes, *The Autocrat of the Breakfast Table*, 1858

Although the first computers concentrated on full words, it soon became clear that it was useful to operate on fields of bits within a word or even on individual bits. Examining characters within a word, each of which are stored as 8 bits, is one example of such an operation. It follows that instructions were added to simplify, among other things, the packing and unpacking of bits into words.

One class of such operations is called *shifts*. They move all the bits in a word to the left or right, filling the emptied bits with 0s. For example, if register $16 contained

MIPS operands

Name	Example	Comments
32 registers	$0, $1, $2, . . . ,$31	Fast locations for data. In MIPS, data must be in registers to perform arithmetic. MIPS register $0 always equals 0. Register $1 is reserved for the assembler to handle pseudoinstructions and large constants.
2^{30} memory words	Memory[0], Memory[4], . . . , Memory[4294967292]	Accessed only by data transfer instructions. MIPS uses byte addresses, so sequential words differ by 4. Memory holds data structures, such as arrays, and spilled registers, such as those saved on procedure calls.

MIPS assembly language

Category	Instruction	Example	Meaning	Comments
Arithmetic	add	add $1,$2,$3	$1 = $2 + $3	3 operands; exception possible
	subtract	sub $1,$2,$3	$1 = $2 – $3	3 operands; exception possible
	add immediate	addi $1,$2,100	$1 = $2 + 100	+ constant; exception possible
	add unsigned	addu $1,$2,$3	$1 = $2 + $3	3 operands; no exceptions
	subtract unsigned	subu $1,$2,$3	$1 = $2 – $3	3 operands; no exceptions
	add immediate unsigned	addiu $1,$2,100	$1 = $2 + 100	+ constant; no exceptions
	Move from coprocessor reg.	mfc0 $1,$epc	$1 = $epc	Used to get copy of Exception PC
Data transfer	load word	lw $1,100($2)	$1 = Memory[$2+100]	Data from memory to register
	store word	sw $1,100($2)	Memory[$2+100] = $1	Data from register to memory
	load upper imm.	lui $1,100	$1 = 100 × 2^{16}	Loads constant in upper 16bits
Conditional branch	branch on equal	beq $1,$2,100	if ($1 == $2) go to PC+4+100	Equal test; PC relative branch
	branch on not eq.	bne $1,$2,100	if ($1 != $2) go to PC+4+100	Not equal test; PC relative
	set on less than	slt $1,$2,$3	if ($2 < $3) $1 = 1; else $1 = 0	Compare less than; 2's comp.
	set less than imm.	slti $1,$2,100	if ($2 < 100) $1 = 1; else $1 = 0	Compare < constant; 2's comp.
	set less than uns.	sltu $1,$2,$3	if ($2 < $3) $1 = 1; else $1 = 0	Compare less than; natural no.
	set l. t. imm. uns.	sltiu $1,$2,100	if ($2 < 100) $1 = 1; else $1 = 0	Compare < constant; natural
Uncondi-tional jump	jump	j 10000	go to 10000	Jump to target address
	jump register	jr $31	go to $31	For switch, procedure return
	jump and link	jal 10000	$31 = PC + 4; go to 10000	For procedure call

FIGURE 4.4 MIPS architecture revealed thus far. Color indicates the portions revealed since Figure 4.1 on page 174. MIPS machine language is illustrated on the endpapers of this book.

$$0000\ 0000\ 0000\ 00000\ 000\ 0000\ 0000\ 0000\ 1101_{two}$$

and the instruction to shift left by 8 was executed, the new value would look like this:

$$0000\ 0000\ 0000\ 0000\ 0000\ 0000\ 1101\ 0000\ 0000_{two}$$

To complement a shift left, there is a shift right. The two MIPS shift instructions are called *shift left logical* (sll) and *shift right logical* (srl). To perform the operation above, assuming that the result should go in register $10:

```
sll    $10,$16,8    # reg $10 = reg $16 << 8 bits
```

In Chapter 3, we delayed explaining the *shamt* field in the R format. It stands for *shift amount* and is used in shift instructions. Hence, the machine language version of the instruction above is

op	rs	rt	rd	shamt	funct
0	0	16	10	8	0

The encoding of sll is 0 in both the op and funct fields, rd contains $10, rt contains $16, and shamt contains 8. The rs field is unused, and thus is set to 0.

Another useful operation that isolates fields is *AND*. (We capitalize the word to avoid confusion between the operation and the English conjunction.) AND is a bit-by-bit operation that leaves a 1 in the result only if both bits of the operands are 1. For example, if register $10 still contains

0000 0000 0000 0000 0000 1101 0000 0000$_{two}$

and register $9 contains

0000 0000 0000 0000 0011 1100 0000 0000$_{two}$

then, after executing the MIPS instruction

```
and $8,$9,$10        # reg $8 = reg $9 & reg $10
```

the value of register $8 would be

0000 0000 0000 0000 0000 1100 0000 0000$_{two}$

As you can see, AND can be used to apply a mask to a set of bits to force 0s where there is a 0 in the mask. To place a value into one of these seas of 0s, there is the complement to AND called *OR*. It is a bit-by-bit operation that places a 1 in the result if either operand bit is a 1. To elaborate, if the registers $9 and $10 are unchanged from the preceding example, the result of the MIPS instruction

```
or $8,$9,$10         # reg $8 = reg $9 | reg $10
```

is this value in register $8

0000 0000 0000 0000 0011 1101 0000 0000$_{two}$

Logical Operations	C Operators	MIPS Instructions
Shift Left	<<	sll
Shift Right	>>	srl
AND	&	and, andi
OR	|	or, ori

FIGURE 4.5 Logical operations and their corresponding operations in C and MIPS.

Figure 4.5 shows the logical C operations and the corresponding MIPS instructions. Constants are useful in logical operations as well as in arithmetic operations, so MIPS also provides the instructions *and immediate* (andi) and *or immediate* (ori). This section describes the logical operations AND, OR, and shift found in every computer today. Figure 4.6 summarizes the MIPS instructions for those operations.

Elaboration: Since andi and ori normally work with unsigned integers, the immediates are treated as unsigned integers as well, meaning that they are expanded to 32 bits by adding leading 0s instead of sign extension. The MIPS assembler creates 32-bit constants with the pair of instructions lui and ori; see Chapter 3, pages 125–126 for an example of creating 32-bit constants using lui and addi.

4.5   Constructing an Arithmetic Logic Unit

> *ALU n. [Arthritic Logic Unit or (rare) Arithmetic Logic Unit] A random-number generator supplied as standard with all computer systems.*
>
> Stan Kelly-Bootle, *The Devil's DP Dictionary*, 1981

The *arithmetic logic unit* or *ALU* is the brawn of the computer, the device that performs the arithmetic operations like addition and subtraction or logical operations like AND and OR. This section constructs an ALU from the four hardware building blocks shown in Figure 4.7 (see Appendix B for more details on these building blocks). Cases 1, 2, and 4 in Figure 4.7 all have two inputs. We will sometimes use versions of these components with more than two inputs, confident that the reader can generalize from this simple example. (In any case, Appendix B provides examples with more inputs.)

MIPS operands

Name	Example	Comments
32 registers	$0, $1, $2, . . . ,$31	Fast locations for data. In MIPS, data must be in registers to perform arithmetic. MIPS register $0 always equals 0. Register $1 is reserved for the assembler to handle pseudoinstructions and large constants.
2^{30} memory words	Memory[0], Memory[4], . . . , Memory[4294967292]	Accessed only by data transfer instructions. MIPS uses byte addresses, so sequential words differ by 4. Memory holds data structures, such as arrays, and spilled registers, such as those saved on procedure calls.

MIPS assembly language

Category	Instruction	Example	Meaning	Comments
Arithmetic	add	add $1,$2,$3	$1 = $2 + $3	3 operands; exception possible
	subtract	sub $1,$2,$3	$1 = $2 – $3	3 operands; exception possible
	add immediate	addi $1,$2,100	$1 = $2 + 100	+ constant; exception possible
	add unsigned	addu $1,$2,$3	$1 = $2 + $3	3 operands; no exceptions
	subtract unsigned	subu $1,$2,$3	$1 = $2 – $3	3 operands; no exceptions
	add imm. unsign.	addiu $1,$2,100	$1 = $2 + 100	+ constant; no exceptions
	Move fr. copr. reg.	mfc0 $1,$epc	$1 = $epc	Used to get of Exception PC
Logical	and	and $1,$2,$3	$1 = $2 & $3	3 reg. operands; Logical AND
	or	or $1,$2,$3	$1 = $2 | $3	3 reg. operands; Logical OR
	and immediate	andi $1,$2,100	$1 = $2 & 100	Logical AND reg, constant
	or immediate	ori $1,$2,100	$1 = $2 | 100	Logical OR reg, constant
	shift left logical	sll $1,$2,10	$1 = $2 << 10	Shift left by constant
	shift right logical	srl $1,$2,10	$1 = $2 >> 10	Shift right by constant
Data transfer	load word	lw $1,100($2)	$1 = Memory[$2+100]	Data from memory to register
	store word	sw $1,100($2)	Memory[$2+100] = $1	Data from register to memory
	load upper imm.	lui $1,100	$1 = 100 × 2^{16}	Loads constant in upper 16bits
Conditional branch	branch on equal	beq $1,$2,100	if ($1 == $2) go to PC+4+100	Equal test; PC relative branch
	branch on not eq.	bne $1,$2,100	if ($1 != $2) go to PC+4+100	Not equal test; PC relative
	set on less than	slt $1,$2,$3	if ($2 < $3) $1 = 1; else $1 = 0	Compare less than; 2's comp.
	set less than imm.	slti $1,$2,100	if ($2 < 100) $1 = 1; else $1 = 0	Compare < constant; 2's comp.
	set less than uns.	sltu $1,$2,$3	if ($2 < $3) $1 = 1; else $1 = 0	Compare less than; natural num.
	set l. t. imm. uns.	sltiu $1,$2,100	if ($2 < 100) $1 = 1; else $1 = 0	Compare < constant; natural num.
Unconditional jump	jump	j 10000	go to 10000	Jump to target address
	jump register	jr $31	go to $31	For switch, procedure return
	jump and link	jal 10000	$31 = PC + 4; go to 10000	For procedure call

FIGURE 4.6 MIPS architecture revealed thus far. Color indicates the portions since Figure 4.4 on page 180. MIPS machine language is illustrated on the endpapers of this book.

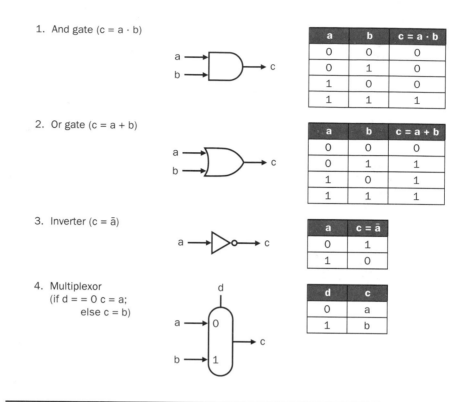

1. And gate ($c = a \cdot b$)

a	b	$c = a \cdot b$
0	0	0
0	1	0
1	0	0
1	1	1

2. Or gate ($c = a + b$)

a	b	$c = a + b$
0	0	0
0	1	1
1	0	1
1	1	1

3. Inverter ($c = \bar{a}$)

a	$c = \bar{a}$
0	1
1	0

4. Multiplexor
   (if $d == 0$ $c = a$;
   else $c = b$)

d	c
0	a
1	b

FIGURE 4.7 Four hardware building blocks used to construct an arithmetic logic unit. The name of the operation and an equation describing it appear on the left. In the middle is the symbol for the block we will use in the drawings. On the right are tables that describe the outputs in terms of the inputs. Using the notation from Appendix B, a . b means "a AND b," a + b means "a OR b," and a line over the top (e.g., $\bar{a}$) means invert.

Because the MIPS word is 32 bits wide, we need a 32-bit-wide ALU. Let's assume that we will connect 32 1-bit ALUs to create the desired ALU. We'll therefore start by constructing a 1-bit ALU.

A 1-bit ALU

The logical operations are easiest, because they map directly onto the hardware components in Figure 4.7. The 1-bit logical unit for AND and OR looks like this:

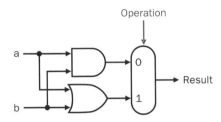

The multiplexor on the right then selects *a AND b* or *a OR b*, depending on whether the value of *Operation* is 0 or 1. The line that controls the multiplexor is shown in color to distinguish it from the lines containing data. Notice that we have renamed the control and output lines of the multiplexor to give them names that reflect the function of the ALU.

The next function to include is addition. From Figure 4.2 on page 176 we can deduce the inputs and outputs of a single-bit adder. First, an adder must have two inputs for the operands and a single-bit output for the sum. There must be a second output to pass on the carry, called *CarryOut*. Since the CarryOut from the neighbor adder must be included as an input, we need a third input. This input is called *CarryIn*. Figure 4.8 shows the inputs and the outputs of a 1-bit adder. Since we know what addition is supposed to do, we can specify the outputs of this "black box" based on its inputs, as Figure 4.9 demonstrates.

From Appendix B, we know that we can express the output functions CarryOut and Sum as logical equations, and these equations can in turn be implemented with the building blocks in Figure 4.7. Let's do CarryOut; the table below shows the values of the inputs when CarryOut is a 1:

Inputs		
a	b	CarryIn
0	1	1
1	0	1
1	1	0
1	1	1

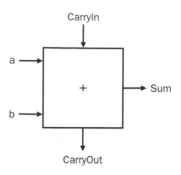

FIGURE 4.8 A 1-bit adder. This adder is called a full adder; it is also called a (3,2) adder because it has 3 inputs and 2 outputs. An adder with only the a and b inputs is called a (2,2) adder or half adder.

Inputs			Outputs		
a	**b**	**CarryIn**	**CarryOut**	**Sum**	**Comments**
0	0	0	0	0	$0 + 0 + 0 = 00_{two}$
0	0	1	0	1	$0 + 0 + 1 = 01_{two}$
0	1	0	0	1	$0 + 1 + 0 = 01_{two}$
0	1	1	1	0	$0 + 1 + 1 = 10_{two}$
1	0	0	0	1	$1 + 0 + 0 = 01_{two}$
1	0	1	1	0	$1 + 0 + 1 = 10_{two}$
1	1	0	1	0	$1 + 1 + 0 = 10_{two}$
1	1	1	1	1	$1 + 1 + 1 = 11_{two}$

FIGURE 4.9 Input and output specification for a 1-bit adder.

We can turn this truth table into a logical equation, as explained in Appendix B (Recall that a + b means "a OR b" and that a · b means "a AND b".):

$$CarryOut = (b \cdot CarryIn) + (a \cdot CarryIn) + (a \cdot b) + (a \cdot b \cdot CarryIn)$$

If a · b · CarryIn is true, then one of the other three terms must also be true, so we can leave out this last term corresponding to the fourth line of the table. We can thus simplify the equation to

$$CarryOut = (b \cdot CarryIn) + (a \cdot CarryIn) + (a \cdot b)$$

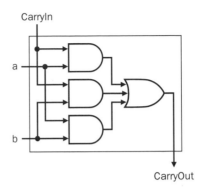

Carryln

a

b

CarryOut

FIGURE 4.10 Adder hardware for the carry out signal. The rest of the adder hardware is the logic for the Sum output given in the equation above.

Figure 4.10 shows that the hardware within the adder black box for CarryOut consists of three AND gates and one OR gate. The three AND gates correspond exactly to the three parenthesized terms of the formula above for CarryOut, and the OR gate sums the three terms.

The Sum bit is set when exactly one input is 1 or when all three inputs are 1. The Sum results in a messier Boolean equation (recall that $\overline{a}$ means NOT a):

$$\text{Sum} = (a \cdot \overline{b} \cdot \overline{\text{CarryIn}}) + (\overline{a} \cdot b \cdot \overline{\text{CarryIn}})$$

$$+ (\overline{a} \cdot \overline{b} \cdot \text{CarryIn}) + (a \cdot b \cdot \text{CarryIn})$$

The drawing of the logic for the Sum bit in the adder black box is left as an exercise for the reader (see Exercise 4.30).

Figure 4.11 shows a 1-bit ALU derived by combining the adder with the earlier components. Sometimes designers also want the ALU to perform a few more simple operations, such as generating 0. The easiest way to add an operation is to expand the multiplexor controlled by the Operation line and, for this example, to connect 0 directly to the new input of that expanded multiplexor.

A 32-bit ALU

Now that we have completed the 1-bit ALU, the full 32-bit ALU is created by connecting adjacent "black boxes." Using xi to mean the ith bit of x, Figure 4.12 shows a 32-bit ALU. Just as a single stone can cause ripples to radiate to the shores of a quiet lake, a single carry out of the least significant bit (Result0) can ripple all the way through the adder, causing a carry out of

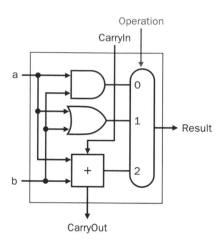

FIGURE 4.11 A 1-bit ALU that performs AND, OR, and addition (see Figure 4.10).

the most significant bit (Result31). Hence, the adder created by directly linking the carries of 1-bit adders is called a *ripple carry* adder. We'll see a faster way to connect the 1-bit adders later.

Subtraction is the same as adding the negative version of an operand, and this is how adders perform subtraction. Recall that the shortcut for negating a two's complement number is to invert each bit (sometimes called the *one's complement*) and then add 1 (see page 174, Elaboration). In order to invert each bit, we simply add a 2:1 multiplexor that chooses between b and $\bar{b}$, as Figure 4.13 shows.

Suppose we connect 32 of these 1-bit ALUs, as we did in Figure 4.12. The added multiplexor gives the option of b or its inverted value, depending on Binvert, but this is only one step in negating a two's complement number. Notice that the least significant bit still has a CarryIn signal, even though it's unnecessary for addition. What happens if we set CarryIn to 1 instead of 0? The adder will then calculate a + b + 1. By selecting the inverted version of b, we get exactly what we want:

$$a + \bar{b} + 1 = a + (\bar{b} + 1) = a + (-b) = a - b$$

The simplicity of the hardware design of a two's complement adder helps explain why two's complement representation has become the universal standard for integer computer arithmetic.

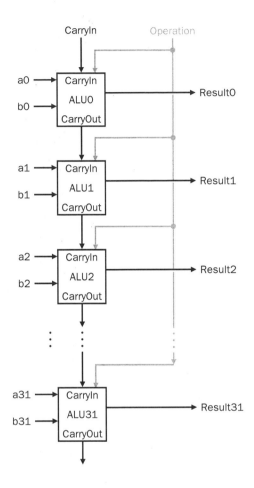

FIGURE 4.12 A 32-bit ALU constructed from 32 1-bit ALUs. CarryOut of the less significant bit is connected to the CarryIn of the more significant bit. This organization is called ripple carry.

Tailoring the 32-bit ALU to MIPS

This set of operations—add, subtract, AND, OR— is found in the ALU of almost every computer. But the design of the ALU is incomplete. If we look at Figure 4.6 on page 183, we see that the operations of most MIPS instructions can be performed by this ALU. One instruction that still needs support is the set-on-less-than instruction. Recall that the operation produces 1 if Rs < Rt, and 0 otherwise. Consequently, set on less than will set all but the least significant bit to 0, with the least significant bit set according to the comparison.

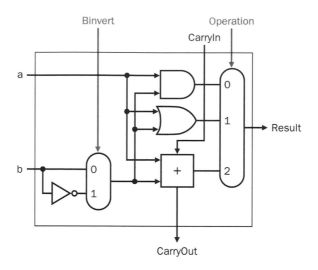

FIGURE 4.13 A 1-bit ALU that performs AND, OR, and addition on a and b or a and $\overline{b}$. By selecting b (Binvert = 1) and setting CarryIn to 1, we get two's complement subtraction of b from a instead of addition of b to a.

Thus, we need to expand the multiplexor to bring a value for the less than comparison for each bit of the ALU. Figure 4.14 shows the new 1-bit ALU with the expanded multiplexor. What remains to consider is how to compare and set the least significant bit for set-on-less-than instructions.

What happens if we subtract Rt from Rs? If the difference is negative, then Rs < Rt since

$$(Rs - Rt) < 0$$
$$\Rightarrow ((Rs - Rt) + Rt) < (0 + Rt)$$
$$\Rightarrow (0 + Rs) < (0 + Rt)$$
$$\Rightarrow Rs < Rt$$

Then we want the least significant bit of set on less than to be a 1 if the difference is negative and a 0 if it's positive. It would seem that this corresponds exactly to the sign-bit values: 1 means negative and 0 means positive. Following this line of argument, we need only connect the sign bit from the adder output to the least significant bit to get what we want.

Unfortunately, the Result output from the most significant ALU bit for the less operation is *not* the output of the adder; the ALU output for the less operation is the input value Less. Thus, we need a new ALU for the most significant bit which makes the adder output available in addition to the standard result

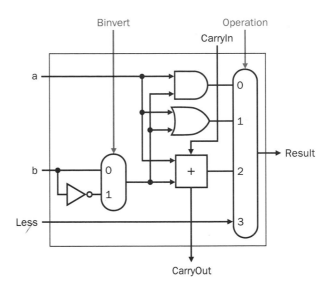

FIGURE 4.14 A 1-bit ALU that performs AND, OR, and addition on a and b or $\overline{b}$. It includes a direct input that is connected to perform the set-on-less-than operation (see Figure 4.16).

output. Figure 4.15 shows the design, with this new adder output line called Set. As long as we need a special ALU for the most significant bit, we added the overflow detection logic since it is also associated with that bit.

Unfortunately, the test of less than is a little more complicated than just described because of overflow; Exercise 4.25 on page 261 explores what must be done. Figure 4.16 shows the final organization of the 32-bit ALU.

Notice that every time we want the ALU to subtract, we set both CarryIn and Binvert to 1. For adds or logical operations, we want both control lines to be 0. We can therefore simplify control of the ALU by combining the CarryIn and Binvert to a single control line called *Bnegate*.

To further tailor the ALU to the MIPS instruction set, we must support conditional branch instructions. These instructions branch either if two registers are equal or if they are unequal. The easiest way to test equality with the ALU is to subtract b from a and then test to see if the result is 0, since

$$(a - b = 0) \Rightarrow a = b$$

Thus, if we add hardware to test if the result is 0, we can test for equality. The simplest way is to OR all the outputs together and then send that signal through an inverter:

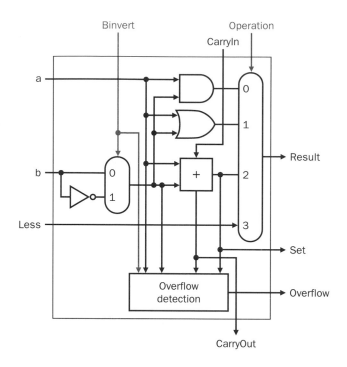

FIGURE 4.15 A 1-bit ALU for the most significant bit. It includes a direct output from the adder for the less than comparison called Set.

$$\text{Zero} = \overline{(\text{Result31} + \text{Result30} + \ldots + \text{Result2} + \text{Result1} + \text{Result0})}$$

Figure 4.17 shows the revised 32-bit ALU.

Now that we have seen what is inside a 32-bit ALU, we will use the universal symbol for a complete ALU, as shown in Figure 4.18. The 3 ALU Operation lines, consisting of the combination of the 1-bit Bnegate line and the 2-bit Operation line, make the ALU perform the desired operation: add, subtract, AND, OR, or set on less than. Figure 4.19 shows the ALU control lines and the corresponding ALU operation.

Carry Lookahead

The next question is, "How quickly can this ALU add two 32-bit operands?" We can determine the a and b inputs, but the CarryIn input depends on the operation in the adjacent 1-bit adder. If we trace all the way through the chain of dependencies, we get to the least significant

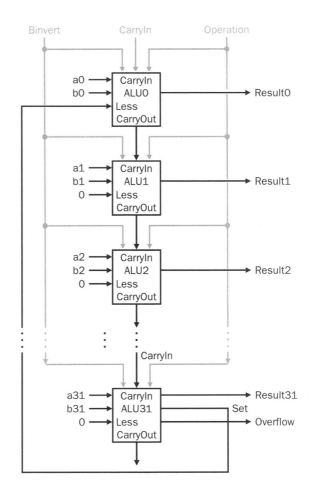

FIGURE 4.16 A 32-bit ALU constructed from the 31 1-bit ALUs found in Figure 4.14 and one 1-bit ALU found in Figure 4.15. The *Less* inputs are connected to 0 except for the least significant bit, and that is connected to the *Set* output of the most significant bit. If the ALU performs a – b and we select the input 3 in the multiplexor in Figures 4.14 and 4.15, then Result =0, 001 if a < b and 0, and 000 otherwise. (The carryout of the most significant bit is useful in multiword additions as carryin of upperwords.)

bit, so the most significant bit of the sum must wait for the sequential evaluation of the 32 1-bit adders. This sequential chain reaction is too slow to be used in time-critical hardware. There are a variety of schemes to anticipate the carry so that the worst-case scenario is a function of the $\log_2$ of the number of bits in the adder. These anticipatory signals are

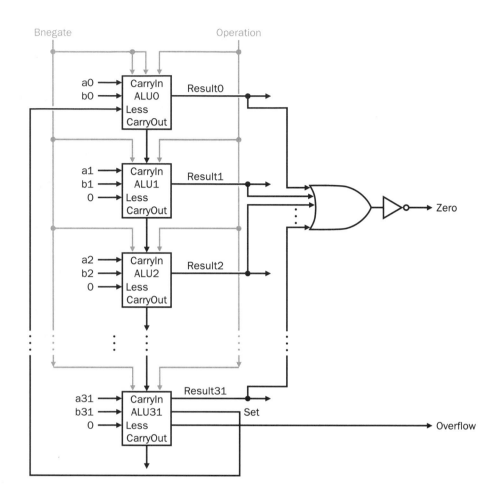

FIGURE 4.17 The final 32-bit ALU. This adds a Zero detector to Figure 4.16, using the 1-bit ALU.

faster because they go through fewer gates in sequence, but it takes many more gates in parallel to anticipate the proper carry.

Appendix B mentions that any equation can be represented in two levels of logic, since the only external inputs are the two operands and the CarryIn to the least significant bit of the adder. In theory, we could calculate the CarryIn values to all the remaining bits of the adder in just two levels of logic.

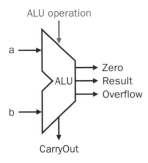

FIGURE 4.18 The symbol commonly used to represent an ALU, as shown in Figure 4.17.
This symbol is also used to represent an adder, so it is normally labeled either with *ALU* or *Adder*.
The control lines labeled ALUOperation include the Operation and Bnegate lines from
Figure 4.17; their values and the ALU operation are found in Figure 4.19.

ALU Control lines	Function
000	And
001	Or
010	Add
110	Subtract
111	Set-on-less-than

**FIGURE 4.19 The values of the three ALU Control lines Bnegate and Operation and the
corresponding ALU operations.**

For example, the CarryIn for bit 2 of the adder is the CarryOut of bit 1 of the
adder, so the formula is

$$CarryIn2 = (b1 \cdot CarryIn1) + (a1 \cdot CarryIn1) + (a1 \cdot b1)$$

Similarly, CarryIn1 is defined as

$$CarryIn1 = (b0 \cdot CarryIn0) + (a0 \cdot CarryIn0) + (a0 \cdot b0)$$

Substituting the definition of CarryIn1 for the first equation results in this formula, where ci means CarryIni:

$$c2 = (a1 \cdot a0 \cdot b0) + (a1 \cdot a0 \cdot c0) + (a1 \cdot b0 \cdot c0)$$
$$+ (b1 \cdot a0 \cdot b0) + (b1 \cdot a0 \cdot c0) + (b1 \cdot b0 \cdot c0) + (a1 \cdot b1)$$

You can imagine how the equation expands as we get to higher bits in the
adder; this complexity is reflected in the cost of the hardware for fast carry,
making this simple scheme prohibitively expensive for wide adders.

Most fast-carry schemes limit the complexity of the equations to simplify the hardware, while still making substantial improvements over ripple carry. One such scheme is a *carry-lookahead adder*. The first step is to factor out some common terms from these complex logic equations. Two important factors are called *generate* (gi) and *propagate* (pi):

$$gi = ai \cdot bi$$

$$pi = ai + bi$$

The two terms are well-named:

   gi is true if bit i of the adder *generates* a CarryOut independent of CarryIn;

   pi is true if bit i of the adder *propagates* a CarryIn to a CarryOut.

The $CarryIn_i$ is a 1 if either g_{i-1} is 1 or both p_{i-1} is 1 and $CarryIn_{i-1}$ is 1. Using propagate and generate we can express the CarryIn signals more economically; let's show it for 4 bits:

$$c1 = g0 + (p0 \cdot c0)$$

$$c2 = g1 + (p1 \cdot g0) + (p1 \cdot p0 \cdot c0)$$

$$c3 = g2 + (p2 \cdot g1) + (p2 \cdot p1 \cdot g0) + (p2 \cdot p1 \cdot p0 \cdot c0)$$

$$c4 = g3 + (p3 \cdot g2) + (p3 \cdot p2 \cdot g1) + (p3 \cdot p2 \cdot p1 \cdot g0)$$
$$+ (p3 \cdot p2 \cdot p1 \cdot p0 \cdot c0)$$

These equations just represent common sense: $CarryIn_i$ is a 1 if some earlier adder generates a carry and all intermediary adders propagate a carry.

Even this simplified form leads to large equations and, hence, considerable logic even for a 16-bit adder. In Chapter 1, we said computer systems cope with complexity by using levels of abstraction. Let's try abstraction here. First we consider this 4-bit adder with its carry-lookahead logic as a single building block. Then we must have two choices: either we just connect these abstractions in ripple carry fashion or we create carry-lookahead signals for them.

We'll need carry lookahead at the higher level to run fast. To perform carry lookahead for 4-bit adders, we need propagate and generate signals at this higher level. Here they are for the four 4-bit adder blocks:

$$P0 = p3 \cdot p2 \cdot p1 \cdot p0$$

$$P1 = p7 \cdot p6 \cdot p5 \cdot p4$$

$$P2 = p11 \cdot p10 \cdot p9 \cdot p8$$

$$P3 = p15 \cdot p14 \cdot p13 \cdot p12$$

That is, the propagate signal for the 4-bit abstraction (Pi) is true only if each of the bits in the group will propagate a carry. Similarly, the generate signal for the 4-bit abstraction (Gi) is true only if all of the bits will generate a carry from the most significant bit of the group:

$$G0 = g3 + (p3 \cdot g2) + (p3 \cdot p2 \cdot g1) + (p3 \cdot p2 \cdot p1 \cdot g0)$$

$$G1 = g7 + (p7 \cdot g6) + (p7 \cdot p6 \cdot g5) + (p7 \cdot p6 \cdot p5 \cdot g4)$$

$$G2 = g11 + (p11 \cdot g10) + (p11 \cdot p10 \cdot g9) + (p11 \cdot p10 \cdot p9 \cdot g8)$$

$$G3 = g15 + (p15 \cdot g14) + (p15 \cdot p14 \cdot g13) + (p15 \cdot p14 \cdot p13 \cdot g12)$$

Then the equations at this higher level of abstraction for a 16-bit adder are very similar to those before:

$$C1 = G0 + (P0 \cdot c0)$$

$$C2 = G1 + (P1 \cdot G0) + (P1 \cdot P0 \cdot c0)$$

$$C3 = G2 + (P2 \cdot G1) + (P2 \cdot P1 \cdot G0) + (P2 \cdot P1 \cdot P0 \cdot c0)$$

$$C4 = G3 + (P3 \cdot G2) + (P3 \cdot P2 \cdot G1) + (P3 \cdot P2 \cdot P1 \cdot G0)$$
$$+ (P3 \cdot P2 \cdot P1 \cdot P0 \cdot c0)$$

Exercises 4.31 to 4.35 explore the speed differences between these carry schemes, different notations for multi-bit propagate and generate signals, and the design of a 64-bit adder.

Summary

The primary point of this section is that the traditional ALU can be constructed from a multiplexor and a few gates that are replicated 32 times. To make it more useful to the MIPS architecture, we expand the traditional ALU with hardware to test if the result is 0, detect overflow, and perform the basic operation for set on less than.

Elaboration: The logic equation for the Sum output of the full adder on page 187 can be expressed more simply by using a more powerful gate than AND and OR. An *exclusive OR* gate is true if the two operands disagree; that is,

$$x \neq y \Rightarrow 1 \text{ and } x = y \Rightarrow 0$$

In some technologies, exclusive OR is more efficient than two levels of AND and OR gates. Using the symbol $\oplus$ to represent exclusive OR, here is the new equation:

$$\mathsf{Sum} = \mathsf{a} \oplus \mathsf{b} \oplus \mathsf{CarryIn}$$

We have now accounted for all but one of the arithmetic and logical operations for the MIPS instruction set: the ALU in Figure 4.18 omits support of shift instructions. It would be possible to widen the ALU multiplexor to include a left shift by 1 bit or right shift by 1 bit. But hardware designers have created a circuit called a *barrel shifter*, which can shift from 1 to 31 bits in no more time than it takes to add two 32-bit numbers, so shifting is normally done outside the ALU.

4.6

Multiplication

Multiplication is vexation, Division is as bad;
The rule of three doth puzzle me, And practice drives me mad.

Anonymous, *Elizabethan manuscript,* 1570

With the construction of the ALU and explanation of addition, subtraction, and shifts, we are ready to build the more vexing operation of multiply.

But first let's review the multiplication of decimal numbers in longhand to remind ourselves of the steps and the names of the operands. For reasons that will become clear shortly, we limit this decimal example to using only the digits 0 and 1. Multiplying 1000_{ten} by 1001_{ten}:

```
Multiplicand              1000ten
Multiplier          x     1001ten
                          1000
                         0000
                        0000
                       1000
Product                1001000ten
```

The first operand is called the *multiplicand* and the second the *multiplier*. The final result is called the *product*. As you may recall, the algorithm learned in grammar school is to take the digits of the multiplier one at a time from right to left, multiplying the multiplicand by the single digit of the multiplier and placing the intermediate product at the appropriate place to the left of the earlier results.

The first observation is that the number of digits in the product is considerably larger than the number in either the multiplicand or the multiplier. In fact, if we ignore the sign bits, the length of an n-bit multiplicand and an m-bit multiplier is a product that is $n+m$ bits long. Hence, like add, multiply must cope with overflow, because we normally want a 32-bit product as the result of multiplying two 32-bit numbers.

In this example we restricted the decimal digits to 0 and 1. With only two choices, each step of the multiplication is simple:

Just place a copy of the multiplicand (1 × multiplicand) in the proper place if the multiplier digit is a 1, or

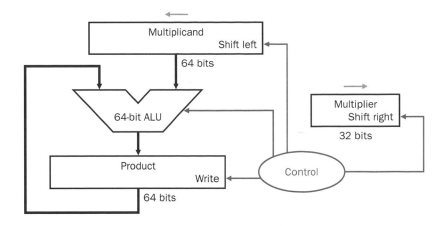

FIGURE 4.20 First version of the multiplication hardware. The Multiplicand register, ALU, and Product register are all 64 bits wide, with only the Multiplier register containing 32 bits. The 32-bit multiplicand starts in the right half of the Multiplicand register, and is shifted left 1 bit on each step. The multiplier is shifted in the opposite direction at each step. The algorithm starts with the product initialized to 0. Control decides when to shift the Multiplicand and Multiplier registers and when to write new values into the Product register.

place 0 (0 × multiplicand) if the digit is 0.

Although the decimal example above happened to use only 0 and 1, multiplication of binary numbers must always use 0 and 1, and thus always offers only these two choices.

   Now that we have reviewed the basics of multiplication, the traditional next step is to provide the highly optimized multiply hardware. We break with tradition in the belief that the reader will gain better understanding by seeing the evolution of the multiply hardware and algorithm through three generations. The rest of this section presents successive refinements of the hardware and the algorithm until we have a version that you would really find in a computer. For now, let's assume that we are multiplying only positive numbers.

First Iteration of the Multiplication Algorithm and Hardware

The initial design mimics the algorithm we learned in grammar school; the hardware is shown in Figure 4.20. We have drawn the hardware so that data flows from top to bottom to more closely resemble the paper-and-pencil method.

   Let's assume that the multiplier is in the 32-bit Multiplier register and that the 64-bit Product register is initialized to 0. Since the basic algorithm shifts the

Multiplicand register left one digit each step so that it can be added to that step, moving the 32-bit multiplicand value from being aligned on the right to aligned on the left, we use a 64-bit Multiplicand register with the multiplicand starting in the right half of the register and 0 in the left half. This register is shifted left 1 bit each step to align the multiplicand with the sum being accumulated in the 64-bit Product register.

Figure 4.21 shows the three basic steps needed for each bit. The least signif-

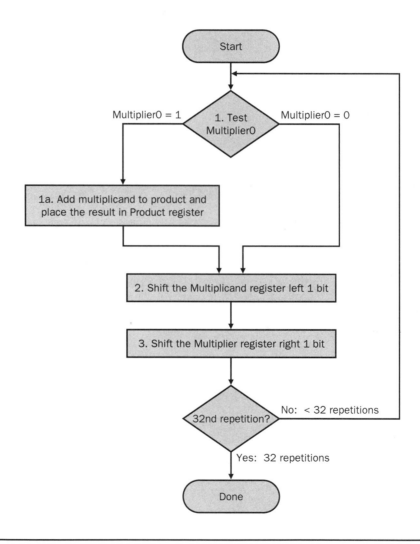

FIGURE 4.21 The first multiplication algorithm, using the hardware shown in Figure 4.20. If the least significant bit of the multiplier is 1, add the multiplicand to the product. If not, go to the next step. Shift the multiplicand left and the multiplier right in the next two steps. These three steps are repeated 32 times.

icant bit of the multiplier (Multiplier0) determines whether the multiplicand is added to the Product register. The left shift in step 2 has the effect of moving the intermediate operands to the left, just as when multiplying by hand. The shift right in step 3 gives us the next bit of the multiplier to examine in the following iteration. These three steps are repeated 32 times to obtain the product.

Example

Using 4-bit numbers to save space, multiply $2_{ten} \times 3_{ten}$ or $0010_{two} \times 0011_{two}$.

Answer

Figure 4.22 shows the value of each register for each of the steps labeled according to Figure 4.21, with the final value of $0000\ 0110_{two}$ or 6_{ten}. Color is used to indicate the register values that change on that step, and the bit circled is the one examined to determine the operation of the next step.

Iteration	Step	Multiplier	Multiplicand	Product
0	Initial Values	0010	0000 0010	0000 0000
1	1a: 1 =>Prod=Prod+Mcand	0011	0000 0010	0000 0010
	2: Shift left Multiplicand	0011	0000 0100	0000 0010
	3: Shift right Multiplier	0001	0000 0100	0000 0010
2	1a: 1 =>Prod=Prod+Mcand	0001	0000 0100	0000 0110
	2: Shift left Multiplicand	0001	0000 1000	0000 0110
	3: Shift right Multiplier	0000	0000 1000	0000 0110
3	1: 0 =>no operation	0000	0000 1000	0000 0110
	2: Shift left Multiplicand	0000	0001 0000	0000 0110
	3: Shift right Multiplier	0000	0001 0000	0000 0110
4	1: 0 =>no operation	0000	0001 0000	0000 0110
	2: Shift left Multiplicand	0000	0010 0000	0000 0110
	3: Shift right Multiplier	0000	0010 0000	0000 0110

FIGURE 4.22 Multiply example using first algorithm in Figure 4.21.

If each step took a clock cycle, this algorithm would require almost 100 clock cycles to multiply. The relative importance of arithmetic operations like multiply varies with the program, but addition and subtraction may be anywhere from 5 to 100 times more popular than multiply. Accordingly, in many appli-

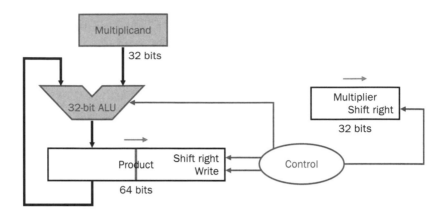

FIGURE 4.23 Second version of the multiplication hardware. Compare to the first version in Figure 4.20. The Multiplicand register, ALU, and Multiplier register are all 32 bits wide, with only the Product register left at 64 bits. Now the product is shifted right. These changes are highlighted in color.

cations, multiply can take multiple clock cycles without significantly affecting performance. Yet Amdahl's Law (see Chapter 2, page 71) reminds us that even a moderate frequency for a slow operation can limit performance.

Second Iteration of the Multiplication Algorithm and Hardware

Computer pioneers recognized that half of the bits of the multiplicand in the first algorithm were always 0, so only half could contain useful bit values. A full 64-bit ALU thus seemed wasteful and slow since half of the adder bits were adding 0 to the intermediate sum.

The original algorithm shifts the multiplicand left with 0s inserted in the new positions, so the least significant bits of the product can never change after they are formed. Instead of shifting the multiplicand left, they wondered, what if we shift the *product* to the *right*? Now the multiplicand would be fixed relative to the product, and since we are adding only 32 bits, the adder need be only 32 bits wide. Figure 4.23 shows how this change halves the widths of both the ALU and the multiplicand.

Figure 4.24 shows the multiply algorithm inspired by this observation. This algorithm starts with the 32-bit Multiplicand and 32-bit Multiplier registers set to their named values and the 64-bit Product register set to 0. This algorithm

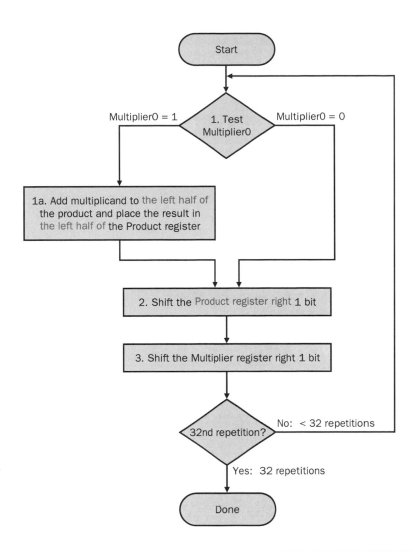

FIGURE 4.24 The second multiplication algorithm, using the hardware in Figure 4.23. In this version, the Product register is shifted right instead of shifting the Multiplicand. Color type shows the changes from Figure 4.21.

only forms a 32-bit sum, so only the left half of the 64-bit Product register is changed during the addition.

Iteration	Step	Multiplier	Multiplicand	Product
0	Initial Values	0011	0010	0000 0000
1	1a: 1 =>Prod=Prod+Mcand	0011	0010	0010 0000
	2: Shift right Product	0011	0010	0001 0000
	3: Shift right Multiplier	0001	0010	0001 0000
2	1a: 1 =>Prod=Prod+Mcand	0001	0010	0011 0000
	2: Shift right Product	0001	0010	0001 1000
	3: Shift right Multiplier	0000	0010	0001 1000
3	1: 0 =>no operation	0000	0010	0001 1000
	2: Shift right Product	0000	0010	0000 1100
	3: Shift right Multiplier	0000	0010	0000 1100
4	1: 0 =>no operation	0000	0010	0000 1100
	2: Shift right Product	0000	0010	0000 0110
	3: Shift right Multiplier	0000	0010	0000 0110

FIGURE 4.25 Multiply example using second algorithm in Figure 4.24.

Example

Multiply $0010_{two} \times 0011_{two}$ using the algorithm in Figure 4.24.

Answer

Figure 4.25 above shows the revised 4-bit example, again giving 0000 0110_{two}.

Final Version of the Multiplication Algorithm and Hardware

The final observation of the frugal computer pioneers was that the Product register had wasted space that matched exactly the size of the multiplier: As the wasted space in the product disappears, so do the bits of the multiplier. In response, the third version of the multiplication algorithm combines the rightmost half of the product with the multiplier. Figure 4.26 shows the hardware. The least significant bit of the 64-bit Product register (Product0) now is the bit to be tested.

The algorithm starts by assigning the multiplier to the right half of the Product register, placing 0 in the upper half. Figure 4.27 shows the new steps.

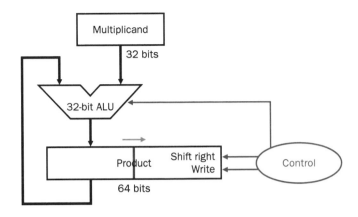

FIGURE 4.26 Third version of the multiplication hardware. Comparing to the second version in Figure 4.23 on page 202, the separate Multiplier register disappeared. The multiplier is placed instead in the right half of the Product register.

Example

Multiply $0010_{two} \times 0011_{two}$ using the algorithm in Figure 4.27.

Answer

Figure 4.28 below shows the revised 4-bit example for the final algorithm.

Signed Multiplication

So far we have dealt with positive numbers. The simplest way to convert this algorithm to signed numbers is to first convert the multiplier and multiplicand to positive numbers and then remember the original signs. The algorithms should then be run for 31 iterations, leaving the signs out of the calculation. As we learned in grammar school, we need negate the product only if the original signs disagree.

Booth's Algorithm

A more elegant approach to multiplying signed numbers is called *Booth's algorithm*. It starts with the observation that with the ability to both add and subtract there are multiple ways to compute a product. Suppose we want to multiply 2_{ten} by 6_{ten} or 0010_{two} by 0110_{two}:

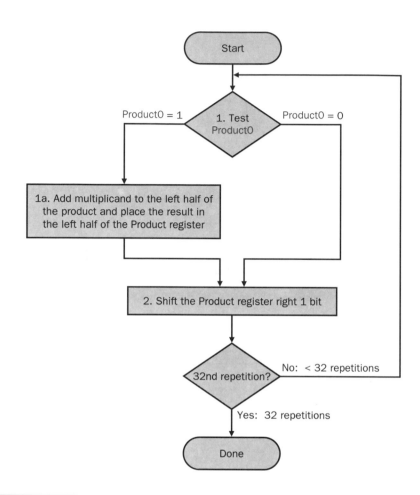

FIGURE 4.27 The third multiplication algorithm. It needs only two steps because the Product and Multiplier registers have been combined. Color type shows changes from Figure 4.24.

$$0010_{two}$$
$$\times \quad 0110_{two}$$

```
+      0000  shift (0 in multiplier)
+      0010  add (1 in multiplier)
+     0010    add (1 in multiplier)
+    0000     shift (0 in multiplier)

   00001100_two
```

Iteration	Step	Multiplicand	Product
0	Initial Values	0010	0000 0010
1	1a: 1 =>Prod=Prod+Mcand	0010	0010 0011
	2: Shift right Product	0010	0001 0001
2	1a: 1 =>Prod=Prod+Mcand	0010	0011 0001
	2: Shift right Product	0010	0001 1000
3	1: 0 =>no operation	0010	0001 1000
	2: Shift right Product	0010	0000 1100
4	1: 0 =>no operation	0010	0000 1100
	2: Shift right Product	0010	0000 0110

FIGURE 4.28 Multiply example using third algorithm in Figure 4.27.

Booth observed that an ALU that could add or subtract could get the same result in more than one way. For example, since

$$6_{ten} = -2_{ten} + 8_{ten} \text{, or}$$
$$0110_{two} = -0010_{two} + 1000_{two}$$

we could replace a string of 1s in the multiplier with an initial subtract when we first see a 1 and then later add for the bit *after* the last one. For example,

```
                0010_two
    x           0110_two
    +         0000  shift (0 in multiplier)
    -         0010  sub (first 1 in multiplier)
    +        0000   shift (middle of string of 1s)
    +       0010    add (prior step had last 1)
            00001100_two
```

Booth invented this approach in a quest for speed, believing that shifting was faster than addition. Indeed, for some patterns his algorithm would be faster; it's our good fortune that it handles signed numbers as well, and we'll prove this later. The key to Booth's insight is in his classifying groups of bits into the beginning, the middle, or the end of a run of 1s:

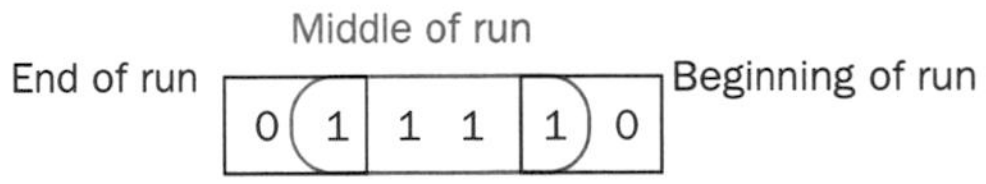

Of course, a string of 0s already avoids arithmetic, so we can leave these alone.

If we are limited to looking at just 2 bits, we can then try to match the situation in the preceding drawing, according to the value of these 2 bits:

Current bit	Bit to the right	Explanation	Example
1	0	Beginning of a run of 1s	00001111000_{two}
1	1	Middle of a run of 1s	00001111000_{two}
0	1	End of a run of 1s	00001111000_{two}
0	0	Middle of a run of 0s	00001111000_{two}

Booth's algorithm changes the first step of the algorithm in Figure 4.27—looking at 1 bit of the multiplier and then deciding whether to add the multiplicand—to looking at 2 bits of the multiplier. The new first step, then, has four cases, depending on the values of the 2 bits. Let's assume that the pair of bits examined consists of the current bit and the bit to the right—which was the current bit in the previous step. The second step is still to shift the product right. The new algorithm is then

1. Depending on the current and previous bits, do one of the following:

   00: a. Middle of a string of 0s, so no arithmetic operation.

   01: b. End of a string of 1s, so add the multiplicand to the left half of the product.

   10: c. Beginning of a string of 1s, so subtract the multiplicand from the left half of the product.

   11: d. Middle of a string of 1s, so no arithmetic operation.

2. As in the previous algorithm, shift the Product register right 1 bit.

Now we are ready to begin the operation, shown in Figure 4.29. It starts with a 0 for the mythical bit to the right of the rightmost bit for the first stage. The table below compares the two algorithms, with Booth's on the right. Note that Booth's operation is now identified according to the values in the 2 bits. By the fourth step the two algorithms have the same values in the Product register.

The one other requirement is that shifting the product right must preserve the sign of the intermediate result, since we are dealing with signed numbers. The solution is to extend the sign when the product is shifted to the right. Thus, step 2 of the first iteration turns 1110 0111 0_{two} into 1111 0011 1_{two} instead of

Itera-tion	Multi-plicand	Original algorithm		Booth's algorithm	
		Step	Product	Step	Product
0	0010	Initial Values	0000 0110	Initial Values	0000 0110 0
1	0010	1: 0 => no operation	0000 0110	1a: 00 => no operation	0000 0110 0
	0010	2: Shift right Product	0000 0011	2: Shift right Product	0000 0011 0
2	0010	1a: 1 => Prod = Prod + Mcand	0010 0011	1c: 10 =>Prod = Prod – Mcand	1110 0011 0
	0010	2: Shift right Product	0000 0001	2: Shift right Product	1111 0001 1
3	0010	1a: 1 => Prod = Prod + Mcand	0011 0001	1d: 11 => no operation	1111 0001 1
	0010	2: Shift right Product	0001 1000	2: Shift right Product	1111 0000 1
4	0010	1: 0 => no operation	0001 1000	1b: 01 =>Prod = Prod + Mcand	0001 1000 1
	0010	2: Shift right Product	0000 1100	2: Shift right Product	0000 1100 0

FIGURE 4.29 Comparing algorithm in Figure 4.27 and Booth's algorithm for positive numbers.

$0111\ 0011\ 1_{two}$. This shift is called an *arithmetic right shift* to differentiate it from a logical right shift.

Example

Let's try Booth's algorithm with negative numbers: $2_{ten} \times -3_{ten} = -6_{ten}$ or $0010_{two} \times 1101_{two} = 1111\ 1010_{two}$.

Answer

Figure 4.30 shows the steps. Our example computes multiply 1 bit at a time, but it is possible to generalize Booth's algorithm to look at multiple bits for faster multiplies (see Exercise 4.39).

Iteration	Step	Multiplicand	Product
0	Initial Values	0010	0000 1101 0
1	1.c: 10 => Prod = Prod – Mcand	0010	1110 1101 0
	2: Shift right Product	0010	1111 0110 1
2	1.b: 01 => Prod = Prod + Mcand	0010	0001 0110 1
	2: Shift right Product	0010	0000 1011 0
3	1.c: 10 => Prod = Prod – Mcand	0010	1110 1011 0
	2: Shift right Product	0010	1111 0101 1
4	1.d: 11 => no operation	0010	1111 0101 1
	2: Shift right Product	0010	1111 1010 1

FIGURE 4.30 Booth's algorithm with negative multiplier example.

	Booth's observation about replacing arithmetic by shifts can
Hardware	be applied when multiplying by constants. Some compilers
Software	replace multiplications by short constants with a series of
Interface	shifts, adds, and subtracts. Because 1 bit to the left represents
	a number twice as large in base 2, shifting the bits left has the
	same effect as multiplying by a power of 2, so almost every
	compiler will substitute a left shift for a multiplication by a
	constant that is a power of 2.

Example   Let's multiply 5_{ten} by 2_{ten} using a left shift by 1.

Answer   Given that

$$101_{two} = (1 \times 2^2) + (0 \times 2^1) + (1 \times 2^0)_{ten} = 4 + 0 + 1_{ten} = 5_{ten}$$

if we shift left one bit we get

$$1010_{two} = (1 \times 2^3) + (0 \times 2^2) + (1 \times 2^1) + (0 \times 2^0)_{ten}$$
$$= 8 + 0 + 2 + 0_{ten} = 10_{ten}$$

and

$$5 \times 2^1{}_{ten} = 10_{ten}$$

Hence the MIPS `sll` instruction can be used for multiplies by powers of 2.

For real multiplies, MIPS provides a separate pair of 32-bit registers to contain the 64-bit product, called *Hi* and *Lo*. To produce a properly signed or unsigned product, MIPS has two instructions: multiply (`mult`) and multiply unsigned (`multu`). To fetch the normal 32-bit product, the programmer uses *move from lo* (mflo). The MIPS assembler allows multiply instructions to specify three registers, issuing the `mflo` instructions to place the products into registers.

Both multiply instructions ignore overflow, so it is up to the software to check to see if the product is too big to fit in 32 bits. To avoid overflow, Hi must be 0 for `multu` or must be the replicated sign of Lo for `mult`. The instruction *move from hi* (mfhi) transfers Hi to a register to test for overflow.

Now that we have seen Booth's algorithm work, we are ready to see *why* it works for two's complement signed integers. Let a be the multiplier and b be the multiplicand and we'll use a_i to refer to bit i of a. Recasting Booth's algorithm in terms of the bit values of the multiplier yields this table:

a_i	a_{i-1}	Operation
0	0	Do nothing
0	1	Add b
1	0	Subtract b
1	1	Do nothing

Instead of representing Booth's algorithm in tabular form, we can represent it as the expression:

$$(a_{i-1} - a_i)$$

where the value of the expression means the following actions:

$$\begin{aligned} 0 \quad & \text{do nothing,} \\ +1 \quad & \text{add } b, \\ -1 \quad & \text{subtract } b. \end{aligned}$$

Since we know that shifting of the multiplicand left with respect to the Product register can be considered multiplying by a power of 2, Booth's algorithm can be written as the sum:

$$\begin{aligned} & (a_{-1} - a_0) \times b \\ + \quad & (a_0 - a_1) \times b \times 2^1 \\ + \quad & (a_1 - a_2) \times b \times 2^2 \\ & \cdots \\ + \quad & (a_{29} - a_{30}) \times b \times 2^{30} \\ + \quad & (a_{30} - a_{31}) \times b \times 2^{31} \end{aligned}$$

We can simplify this sum by noting that

$$- a_i \times 2^{i-1} + a_i \times 2^i = (-a_i + 2a_i) \times 2^{i-1} = (2a_i - a_i) \times 2^{i-1} = a_i \times 2^{i-1}$$

and by factoring out b from each term:

$$b \times ((a_{31} \times -2^{31}) + (a_{30} \times 2^{30}) + (a_{29} \times 2^{29}) + \ldots + (a_1 \times 2^1) + (a_0 \times 2^0))$$

The long formula in parentheses to the right of the first multiply operation is simply the two's complement representation of *a* (see page 170.) Thus the sum is further simplified to

$$b \times a$$

Hence Booth's algorithm does in fact perform two's complement multiplication of *a* and *b*.

Summary

Multiplication is accomplished by a simple shift and add hardware, derived from the paper-and-pencil method learned in grammar school. Compilers even replace multiplications by powers of 2 with shift instructions. Signed multiplication is more challenging, with Booth's algorithm rising to the challenge with essentially a clever factorization of the two's complement number representation of the multiplier.

Elaboration: The original reason for Booth's algorithm was speed, because early machines could shift faster than they could add. The hope was that this encoding scheme would increase the number of shifts. This algorithm is sensitive to particular bit patterns, however, and may actually increase the number of adds or subtracts. For example, bit patterns that alternate 0 and 1, called *isolated 1s*, will cause the hardware to add or subtract at each step. If all combinations occur with uniform distribution, then on average there is no savings. Greater advantage comes from performing multiple bits per step, which we explore in Exercise 4.39.

4.7 Division

Divide et impera.

Latin for "Divide and rule," Ancient political maxim cited by Machiavelli, 1532

The reciprocal operation of multiply is divide, an operation that is even less frequent and even more quirky. It even offers the opportunity to perform a mathematically invalid operation: dividing by 0.

Let's start with an example of long division using decimal numbers to recall the names of the operands and the grammar school division algorithm. For reasons similar to those in the previous section, we limit the decimal digits to just 0 or 1. The example is dividing $1,001,010_{ten}$ by 1000_{ten}:

$$
\begin{array}{r}
1001_{ten} \quad \text{Quotient} \\
\text{Divisor } 1000_{ten} \overline{\big)\ 1001010_{ten}} \quad \text{Dividend} \\
-1000 \\
\hline
10 \\
101 \\
1010 \\
-1000 \\
\hline
10_{ten} \qquad \text{Remainder}
\end{array}
$$

The two operands *(dividend* and *divisor)* and the result *(quotient)* of divide are accompanied by a second result called the *remainder*. Here is another way to express the relationship between the components:

$$\text{Dividend} = \text{Quotient} \times \text{Divisor} + \text{Remainder}$$

where the Remainder is smaller than the Divisor. Infrequently, programs use the divide instruction just to get the remainder, ignoring the quotient. Note that the size of the dividend is limited by the sum of the sizes of the divisor and quotient.

The basic grammar school division algorithm tries to see how big a number can be subtracted, creating a digit of the quotient on each attempt. Our carefully selected decimal example uses only the numbers 0 and 1, so it's easy to figure out how many times the divisor goes into the portion of the dividend: it's either 0 times or 1 time. Binary numbers contain only 0 or 1, so binary division is restricted to these two choices, thereby simplifying binary division.

Once again textbooks traditionally jump to the refined division hardware, and once again we abandon tradition to offer insight into how that hardware evolved. The next three subsections examine three versions of the divide algorithm, refining the hardware requirements as we go. Let's assume that both the dividend and divisor are positive and hence the quotient and the remainder are nonnegative.

First Iteration of the Division Algorithm and Hardware

Figure 4.31 shows hardware to mimic our grammar school algorithm. We start with the 32-bit Quotient register set to 0. Each step of the algorithm needs to move the divisor to the right one digit, so we start with the divisor placed in the left half of the 64-bit Divisor register and shift it right one bit each step to align it with the dividend.

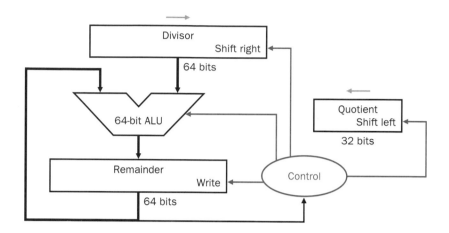

FIGURE 4.31 First version of the division hardware. The Divisor register, ALU, and Remainder register are all 64 bits wide, with only the Quotient register being 32 bits. The 32-bit divisor starts in the left half of the Divisor register and is shifted right 1 bit on each step. The remainder is initialized with the dividend. Control decides when to shift the Divisor and Quotient registers and when to write the new value into the Remainder register.

Figure 4.32 shows three steps of the first division algorithm. Unlike a human, the computer isn't smart enough to know in advance whether the divisor is smaller than the dividend. It must first subtract the divisor in step 1; remember that this is how we performed the comparison in the set-on-less-than instruction. If the result is negative, the next step is to restore the original value by adding the divisor back to the remainder (step 2b). The remainder and quotient will be found in their namesake registers after the iterations are complete.

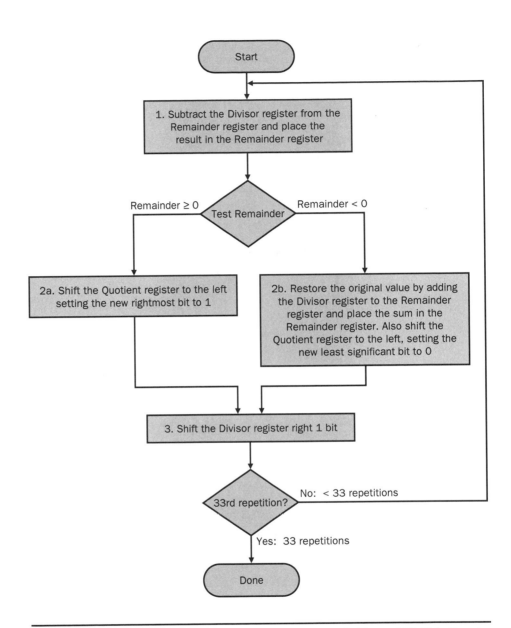

FIGURE 4.32 The first division algorithm, using the hardware in Figure 4.31. If the Remainder is positive, the divisor did go into the dividend, so step 2a generates a 1 in the quotient. A negative Remainder after this step means that the divisor did not go into the dividend, so step 2b generates a 0 in the quotient and adds the divisor to the remainder, thereby reversing the subtraction of step 1. The final shift, in step 3, aligns the divisor properly, relative to the dividend for the next iteration. These steps are repeated 33 times; the reason for the apparent extra step will become clear in the next version of the algorithm.

Example

Using a 4-bit version of the algorithm to save pages, let's try dividing 7_{ten} by 2_{ten} or $0000\ 0111_{two}$ by 0010_{two}.

Answer

Figure 4.33 shows the value of each register for each of the steps, with the quotient being 3_{ten} and the remainder 1_{ten}. Notice that the test in step 2 of whether the remainder is positive or negative simply tests whether the sign bit of the Remainder register is a 0 or 1. The surprising requirement of this algorithm is that it takes n + 1 steps to get the proper quotient and remainder.

Iteration	Step	Quotient	Divisor	Remainder
0	Initial Values	0000	0010 0000	0000 0111
1	1: Rem = Rem – Div	0000	0010 0000	0110 0111
	2b: Rem<0 => +Div, sll Q, Q0 = 0	0000	0010 0000	0000 0111
	3: shift Div right	0000	0001 0000	0000 0111
2	1: Rem = Rem – Div	0000	0001 0000	0111 0111
	2b: Rem < 0 => +Div, sll Q, Q0 = 0	0000	0001 0000	0000 0111
	3: shift Div right	0000	0000 1000	0000 0111
3	1: Rem = Rem – Div	0000	0000 1000	0111 1111
	2b: Rem < 0 => +Div, sll Q, Q0 = 0	0000	0000 1000	0000 0111
	3: shift Div right	0000	0000 0100	0000 0111
4	1: Rem = Rem – Div	0000	0000 0100	0000 0011
	2a: Rem ≥ 0 => sll Q, Q0 = 1	0001	0000 0100	0000 0011
	3: shift Div right	0001	0000 0010	0000 0011
5	1: Rem = Rem – Div	0001	0000 0010	0000 0001
	2a: Rem ≥ 0 => sll Q, Q0 = 1	0011	0000 0010	0000 0001
	3: shift Div right	0011	0000 0001	0000 0001

FIGURE 4.33 Division example using first algorithm in Figure 4.32.

Second Version of the Division Algorithm and Hardware

Once again the frugal computer pioneers recognized that, at most, half the divisor has useful information, and so both the divisor and ALU could potentially be cut in half. Shifting the remainder to the left instead of shifting the divisor to the right produces the same alignment and accomplishes the goal of simplifying the hardware necessary for the ALU and the divisor. Figure 4.34 shows the simplified hardware for the second version of the algorithm.

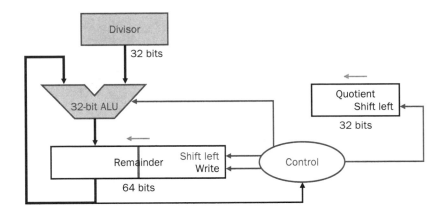

FIGURE 4.34 Second version of the division hardware. The Divisor register, ALU, and Quotient register are all 32 bits wide, with only the Remainder register left at 64 bits. Compared to Figure 4.31, the ALU and Divisor registers are halved and the remainder is shifted left. These changes are highlighted.

The second improvement comes from noticing that the first step of the current algorithm cannot produce a 1 in the quotient bit; if it did, then the quotient would be too large for the register. By switching the order of the operations to shift and then subtract, one iteration of the algorithm can be removed. Figure 4.35 shows the changes in this refined division algorithm. The remainder is now found in the left half of the Remainder register.

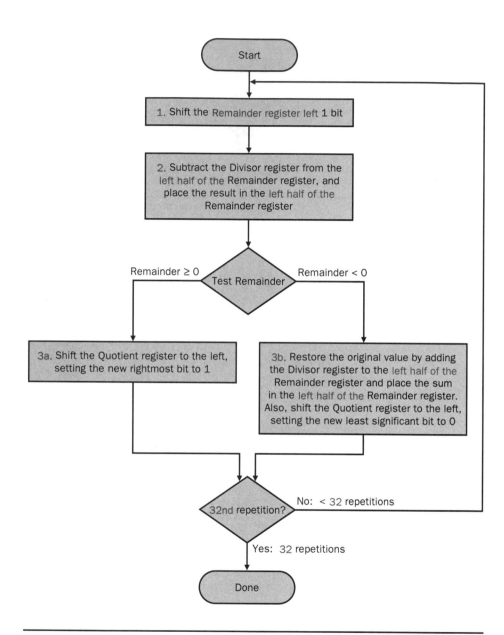

FIGURE 4.35 The second division algorithm, using the hardware in Figure 4.34. Unlike the first algorithm in Figure 4.32, only the left half of the remainder is changed, and the remainder is shifted left instead of the divisor being shifted right. Color type shows the changes from Figure 4.32.

Example   Divide 0000 0111$_{two}$ by 0010$_{two}$ using the algorithm in Figure 4.35.

Answer   The answer is summarized in Figure 4.36.

Iteration	Step	Quotient	Divisor	Remainder
0	Initial Values	0000	0010	0000 0111
1	1: shift Rem left	0000	0010	0000 1110
	2: Rem = Rem − Div	0000	0010	⓪110 1110
	3b: Rem < 0 => +Div, sll Q, Q0 = 0	0000	0010	0000 1110
2	1: shift Rem left	0000	0010	0001 1100
	2: Rem = Rem − Div	0000	0010	⓪111 1100
	3b: Rem < 0 => +Div, sll Q, Q0 = 0	0000	0010	0001 1100
3	1: shift Rem left	0000	0010	0011 1000
	2: Rem = Rem − Div	0000	0010	⓪001 1000
	3a: Rem ≥ 0 => sll Q, Q0 = 1	0001	0010	0001 1000
4	1: shift Rem left	0001	0010	0011 0000
	2: Rem = Rem − Div	0001	0010	⓪001 0000
	3a: Rem ≥ 0 => sll Q, Q0 = 1	0011	0010	0001 0000

FIGURE 4.36 Division example using second algorithm in Figure 4.35.

Final Version of the Division Algorithm and Hardware

With the same insight and motivation as in the third version of the multiplication algorithm, computer pioneers saw that the Quotient register could be eliminated by shifting the bits of the quotient into the Remainder instead of shifting in 0s as in the preceding algorithm. Figure 4.37 shows the third version of the algorithm. We start the algorithm by shifting the Remainder left as before. Thereafter, the loop contains only two steps because the shifting of the Remainder register shifts both the remainder in the left half and the quotient in the right half (see Figure 4.38). The consequence of combining the two registers and the new order of the operations in the loop is that the remainder will be shifted left one time too many. Thus the final correction step must shift back only the remainder in the left half of the register.

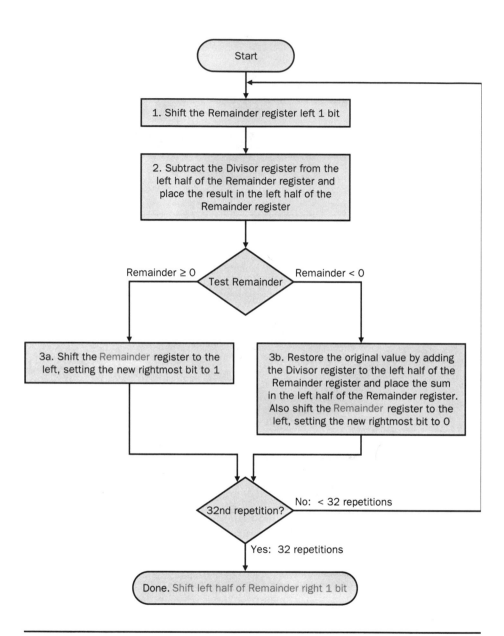

FIGURE 4.37 The third division algorithm has just two steps. The Remainder register shifts left, combining steps 1 and 3 in Figure 4.35 on page 218.

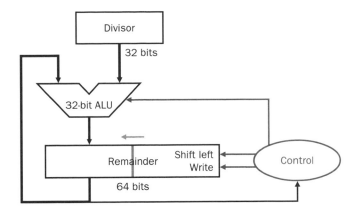

FIGURE 4.38 Third version of the division hardware. This version combines the Quotient register with the right half of the Remainder register.

Example

Use the third version of the algorithm to divide $0000\ 0111_{two}$ by 0010_{two}.

Answer

Figure 4.39 shows how the quotient is created in the bottom of the Remainder register and how both are shifted left in a single operation.

Iteration	Step	Divisor	Remainder
0	Initial Values	0010	0000 0111
	Shift Rem left 1	0010	0000 1110
1	1: Rem = Rem − Div	0010	⓪110 1110
	2b: Rem < 0 => +Div, sll R, R0 = 0	0010	0001 1100
2	1: Rem = Rem − Div	0010	⓪111 1100
	2b: Rem < 0 => +Div, sll R, R0 = 0	0010	0011 1000
3	1: Rem = Rem − Div	0010	⓪001 1000
	2a: Rem ≥ 0 => sll R, R0 = 1	0010	0011 0001
4	1: Rem = Rem − Div	0010	⓪001 0001
	2a: Rem ≥ 0 => sll R, R0 = 1	0010	0010 0011
	Shift left half of Rem right 1	0010	0001 0011

FIGURE 4.39 Division example using third algorithm in Figure 4.37.

Signed Division

So far we have ignored signed numbers in division. The simplest solution is to remember the signs of the divisor and dividend and then negate the quotient if the signs disagree.

The one complication is that we must also set the sign of the remainder. Remember that the following equation must always hold:

$$Dividend = Quotient \times Divisor + Remainder$$

To understand how to set the sign of the remainder, let's look at the example of dividing all the combinations of 7_{ten} by 2_{ten}. The first case is easy:

$$+7 \div +2: \text{ Quotient} = +3, \text{ Remainder} = +1$$

Checking the results:

$$7 = 3 \times 2 + (+1) = 6 + 1$$

If we change the sign of the dividend, the quotient must change as well:

$$-7 \div +2: \text{ Quotient} = -3$$

Rewriting our basic formula to calculate the remainder:

$$\text{Remainder Dividend} - \text{Quotient} \times \text{Divisor}$$
$$= -7 - (+3 \times -2) = -7 - (-6) = -1$$

So,

$$-7 \div +2: \text{ Quotient} = -3, \text{ Remainder} = -1$$

Checking the results again:

$$-7 = -3 \times 2 + (-1) = -6 - 1$$

The reason the answer isn't a quotient of -4 and a remainder of $+1$, which would also fit this formula, is that the quotient and remainder must have the same absolute values no matter what the signs of the dividend and divisor. Clearly if $-(x \div y) \neq (-x) \div y$, programming would be an even greater challenge!

We calculate the other combinations by following the same logic:

$$+7 \div -2: \text{ Quotient} = -3, \text{ Remainder} = +1$$

$$-7 \div -2: \text{ Quotient} = +3, \text{ Remainder} = -1$$

Notice that a nonzero remainder always has the same sign as the dividend. So the correctly signed division algorithm makes the sign of the remainder the same as the dividend, and the quotient is negated if the signs of the operands are opposite.

| **Hardware Software Interface** | The observant reader will recognize that the same hardware can be used for both multiply and divide. The only requirement is a 64-bit register that can shift left or right and a 32-bit ALU that adds or subtracts. For example, MIPS uses the 32-bit Hi and 32-bit Lo registers for both multiply and divide. As we might expect from the algorithm above, Hi contains the remainder and Lo contains the quotient after the |

divide instruction. To handle both signed integers and unsigned integers, MIPS has two instructions: *divide* (`div`) and *divide unsigned* (`divu`). The MIPS assembler allows divide instructions to specify three registers, issuing the `mflo` and `mfhi` instructions to place the results into registers.

MIPS divide instructions ignore overflow, so software must determine if the quotient is too large. In addition to overflow, division can also result in an improper calculation: division by 0. Some machines distinguish these two anomalous events. MIPS software must check the divisor to discover division by 0 as well as overflow.

Summary

The commonality hardware support for multiply and divide allows MIPS to provide a single pair of 32-bit registers that are used both for multiply and divide. Figure 4.40 summarizes the additions to the MIPS architecture for the last two sections.

Elaboration: The reason for needing an extra iteration for the first algorithm and the early shift in the second and third algorithms involves the placement of the dividend in the Remainder register. We expect to have a 32-bit quotient and a 32-bit divisor, but each is really a 31-bit integer plus a sign bit. The product would be 31+31, or 62 bits plus a single sign bit; the hardware can then support only a 63-bit dividend. Given that registers are normally powers of 2, this means we must place the 63-bit dividend properly in the 64-bit Remainder register. If we place the 63 bits to the right, we need to run the algorithm for an extra step to get to that last bit. A better solution is to shift early, thereby saving a step of the algorithm.

MIPS operands

Name	Example	Comments
32 registers	$0, $1, $2, . . . , $31, Hi, Lo	Fast locations for data. In MIPS, data must be in registers to perform arithmetic. MIPS register $0 always equals 0. Register $1 is reserved for the assembler to handle pseudoinstructions and large constants. Hi and Lo are 32-bit registers containing the results of multiply and divide.
2^{30} memory words	Memory[0], Memory[4], . . . , Memory[4294967292]	Accessed only by data transfer instructions. MIPS uses byte addresses, so sequential words differ by 4. Memory holds data structures, such as arrays, and spilled registers, such as those saved on procedure calls.

MIPS assembly Language

Category	Instruction	Example	Meaning	Comments
Arithmetic	add	add $1,$2,$3	$1 = $2 + $3	3 operands; exception possible
	subtract	sub $1,$2,$3	$1 = $2 – $3	3 operands; exception possible
	add immediate	addi $1,$2,100	$1 = $2 + 100	+ constant; exception possible
	add unsigned	addu $1,$2,$3	$1 = $2 + $3	3 operands; no exceptions
	subtract unsigned	subu $1,$2,$3	$1 = $2 – $3	3 operands; no exceptions
	add imm. unsign.	addiu $1,$2,100	$1 = $2 + 100	+ constant; no exceptions
	Move fr. copr. reg.	mfc0 $1,$epc	$1 = $epc	Used to get Exception PC
	multiply	mult $2,$3	Hi, Lo = $2 × $3	64-bit signed product in Hi, Lo
	multiply unsigned	multu $2,$3	Hi, Lo = $2 × $3	64-bit unsigned product in Hi, Lo
	divide	div $2,$3	Lo = $2 / $3, Hi = $2 mod $3	Lo = quotient, Hi = remainder
	divide unsigned	divu $2,$3	Lo = $2 / $3, Hi = $2 mod $3	Unsigned Quotient and Rem.
	Move from Hi	mfhi $1	$1 = Hi	Used to get copy of Hi
	Move from Lo	mflo $1	$1 = Lo	Used to get copy of Lo
Logical	and	and $1,$2,$3	$1 = $2 & $3	3 reg. operands; Logical AND
	or	or $1,$2,$3	$1 = $2 | $3	3 reg. operands; Logical OR
	and immediate	andi $1,$2,100	$1 = $2 & 100	Logical AND reg, constant
	or immediate	ori $1,$2,100	$1 = $2 | 100	Logical OR reg, constant
	shift left logical	sll $1,$2,10	$1 = $2 << 10	Shift left by constant
	shift right logical	srl $1,$2,10	$1 = $2 >> 10	Shift right by constant
Data transfer	load word	lw $1,100($2)	$1 = Memory[$2+100]	Data from memory to register
	store word	sw $1,100($2)	Memory[$2+100] = $1	Data from register to memory
	load upper imm.	lui $1,100	$1 = 100 × 2^{16}	Loads constant in upper 16 bits
Conditional branch	branch on equal	beq $1,$2,100	if ($1 == $2) go to PC+4+100	Equal test; PC relative branch
	branch on not eq.	bne $1,$2,100	if ($1 != $2) go to PC+4+100	Not equal test; PC relative
	set on less than	slt $1,$2,$3	if ($2 < $3) $1 = 1; else $1 = 0	Compare less than; 2's comp.
	set less than imm.	slti $1,$2,100	if ($2 < 100) $1 = 1; else $1 = 0	Compare < constant; 2's comp.
	set less than uns.	sltu $1,$2,$3	if ($2 < $3) $1 = 1; else $1 = 0	Compare less than; natural no.
	set l. t. imm. uns.	sltiu $1,$2,100	if ($2 < 100) $1 = 1; else $1 = 0	Compare < constant; natural
Unconditional jump	jump	j 10000	go to 10000	Jump to target address
	jump register	jr $31	go to $31	For switch, procedure return
	jump and link	jal 10000	$31 = PC + 4; go to 10000	For procedure call

FIGURE 4.40 MIPS architecture revealed thus far. Color indicates the portions revealed since Figure 4.6 on page 183. MIPS machine language is illustrated on the endpapers of this book.

4.8 Floating Point

Speed gets you nowhere if you're headed in the wrong direction.

American proverb

In addition to signed and unsigned integers, programming languages include numbers to represent numbers with fractions, which are called *reals* in mathematics. Here are some examples of reals:

$3.14159265\ldots_{\text{ten}}$ (pi)

$2.71828\ldots_{\text{ten}}$ (e)

0.000000001_{ten} or $1.0_{\text{ten}} \times 10^{-9}$ (seconds in a nanosecond)

$3{,}155{,}760{,}000_{\text{ten}}$ or $3.15576_{\text{ten}} \times 10^{9}$ (seconds in a century)

Notice that in the last case, the number didn't represent a small fraction, but it was bigger than we could represent with a signed integer. The alternative notation for the last two numbers is called *scientific notation*, which has a single digit to the left of the decimal point. A number in scientific notation that has no leading 0s is called a *normalized* number, which is the usual way to write it. For example, $1.0_{\text{ten}} \times 10^{-9}$ is in normalized scientific notation, but $0.1_{\text{ten}} \times 10^{-8}$ and $10.0_{\text{ten}} \times 10^{-10}$ are not.

Just as we can show decimal numbers in scientific notation, we can also show binary numbers in scientific notation:

$1.0_{\text{two}} \times 2^{-1}$

The binary base replaces the decimal base so that we can adjust the exponent by 1 to keep the binary number in normalized form.

Computer arithmetic that supports such numbers is called *floating point*, because it represents numbers in which the decimal point is not fixed, as it is for integers. The programming language C uses the name *float* for such numbers. Just as in scientific notation, numbers are represented as a single digit to the left of the decimal point. In binary, the form is

$1.\text{xxxxxxxxx}_{\text{two}} \times 2^{\text{yyyy}}$

(Although the computer represents the exponent in base 2 as well as the rest of the number, to simplify the notation we'll show the exponent in decimal.)

A standard scientific notation for reals in normalized form offers three advantages. It simplifies exchange of data that includes floating-point numbers; it simplifies the floating-point arithmetic algorithms to know that numbers will always be in this form; and it increases the accuracy of the numbers that can be stored in a word, since the unnecessary leading 0s are replaced by real numbers to the right of the decimal point.

| **Hardware Software Interface** | Practicality dictates that floating-point numbers be compatible with the size of a word. Representation of a MIPS floating-point number is shown below, where *s* is the sign of the floating-point number (1 meaning negative), *exponent* is the value of the 8-bit exponent field (including the sign of the exponent), and *significand* is the 23-bit number in the fraction. |

This is called *sign and magnitude* representation, since the sign has a separate bit from the rest of the number.

31	30	29	28	27	26	25	24	23	22	21	20	19	18	17	16	15	14	13	12	11	10	9	8	7	6	5	4	3	2	1	0
s		exponent							significand																						

1 bit   8 bits   23 bits

In general, floating point numbers are of the form:

$$(-1)^S \times F \times 2^E$$

F involves the value in the significand field and E involves the value in the exponent field; the exact relationship to these fields will be spelled out soon.

The designer of arithmetic must find a compromise between the size of the significand and the size of the exponent, because a fixed word size means you must take a bit from one to add a bit to the other. This trade-off is between accuracy and range: Increasing the size of the significand enhances the number of bits to represent the significand, but increasing the size of the exponent increases the range of numbers that can be represented. As our guideline from Chapter 3 reminds us, good design demands compromise.

These chosen sizes of exponent and significand give MIPS computer arithmetic an extraordinary range. Fractions as small as $2.0_{ten} \times 10^{-38}$ and numbers as large as $2.0_{ten} \times 10^{38}$ can be represented in a computer. Alas, extraordinary differs from infinite, so it is still possible for numbers to be too large. Thus, overflow interrupts can occur in floating-point arithmetic as well as in integer arithmetic. Notice that *overflow* here means that the exponent is too large to be represented in the exponent field.

Floating point offers a new kind of exceptional event as well. Just as programmers will want to know when they have calculated a number that is too large to be represented, they will want to know if the fraction they are calculating has become so small that it cannot be represented; either event could result in a program giving incorrect answers. This situation occurs when the negative exponent is too large to fit in the exponent field. To contrast it from overflow, some people call this event *underflow*.

To reduce the chances of underflow or overflow, most programming languages offer a notation that has a larger exponent. In C this is called *double*, and operations on doubles are called *double precision* floating-point arithmetic; *single precision* floating-point is the name of the earlier format. MIPS double precision allows numbers almost as small as $2.0_{ten} \times 10^{-308}$ and almost as large as $2.0_{ten} \times 10^{308}$.

Hardware Software Interface	The representation of a double precision floating-point number takes two MIPS words, as shown below, where *s* is still the sign of the number, *exponent* is the value of the 11-bit exponent field, and *significand* is the 52-bit number in the fraction.

31	30	29	28	27	26	25	24	23	22	21	20	19	18	17	16	15	14	13	12	11	10	9	8	7	6	5	4	3	2	1	0
s	exponent											significand																			

1 bit   11 bits   20 bits

significand (cont'd)

32 bits

These formats go beyond MIPS. They are part of the *IEEE 754 floating-point standard*, found in virtually every computer invented since 1980. This standard has greatly improved both the ease of porting floating-point programs and the quality of computer arithmetic.

To pack even more bits into the significand, IEEE 754 makes the leading 1 bit of normalized binary numbers implicit. Hence, the significand is actually

24 bits long in single precision (implied 1 and a 23-bit fraction), and 53 bits long in double precision (1+52). Since 0 has no leading 1, it is given the reserved exponent value 0 so that the hardware won't attach a leading 1 to it. Thus $00\ldots00_{two}$ represents 0; the representation of the rest of the numbers uses the form from before with the hidden 1 added:

$$(-1)^S \times (1 + \text{significand}) \times 2^E$$

where the bits of the significand represent the fraction between 0 and 1 and E specifies the value in the exponent field, to be given in detail shortly. If we number the bits of the significand from *left to right* s1, s2, s3, $\ldots$, then the value is

$$(-1)^S \times (1 + (s1 \times 2^{-1}) + (s2 \times 2^{-2}) + (s3 \times 2^{-3}) + (s4 \times 2^{-4}) + \ldots) \times 2^E$$

The designers of IEEE 754 also wanted a floating-point representation that could be easily processed by integer operations. This is why the sign is in the most significant bit, allowing a test of less than, greater than, or equal to 0 to be performed quickly. Placing the exponent before the significand simplifies integer sorting of floating-point numbers, since numbers with bigger exponents look larger than numbers with smaller exponents, as long as they have the same sign.

Negative exponents pose a challenge to simplified sorting. If we use two's complement or any other notation in which negative exponents have a 1 in the most significant bit of the exponent field, a negative exponent will look like a big number. For example, $1.0_{two} \times 2^{-1}$ would be represented as

31	30	29	28	27	26	25	24	23	22	21	20	19	18	17	16	15	14	13	12	11	10	9	8	7	6	5	4	3	2	1	0
0	1	1	1	1	1	1	1	1	0	0	0	0	0	0	0	0	0	0	0	0	0	0	0	0	0	0	0	0	0	0	0 . . .

(Remember that the leading 1 is implicit in the significand.) The value $1.0_{two} \times 2^{+1}$ would look like the smaller binary number:

31	30	29	28	27	26	25	24	23	22	21	20	19	18	17	16	15	14	13	12	11	10	9	8	7	6	5	4	3	2	1	0
0	0	0	0	0	0	0	0	1	0	0	0	0	0	0	0	0	0	0	0	0	0	0	0	0	0	0	0	0	0	0	0 . . .

The desirable notation must therefore represent the most negative exponent as $00\ldots00_{two}$ and the most positive as $11\ldots11_{two}$. This is called *biased notation*, with the bias being the number subtracted from the normal, unsigned representation to determine the real value.

IEEE 754 uses a bias of 127 for single precision, so -1 is represented by the bit pattern of the value $-1+127_{ten}$ or $126_{ten} = 0111\ 1110_{two}$, and $+1$ is represented by $1+127$ or $128_{ten} = 1000\ 0000_{two}$. This means that the value represented by a floating-point number is really

$$(-1)^s \times (1 + \text{significand}) \times 2^{(\text{exponent}-\text{bias})}$$

The exponent bias for single precision is 127 and for double precision is 1023.

Example

Show the IEEE 754 binary representation of the numbers -0.75_{ten} in single and double precision.

Answer

The number -0.75_{ten} is also $-3/4_{ten}$ or $-3/2^2_{ten}$. It is also represented by the fraction $-11_{two}/2^2_{ten}$ or -0.11_{two}. In scientific notation the value is $-0.11_{two} \times 2^0$ and in normalized scientific notation it is $-1.1_{two} \times 2^{-1}$.

The general representation for a single precision number is

$$(-1)^S \times (1 + \text{significand}) \times 2^{(\text{exponent}-127)}$$

and so we add the bias 127 to the exponent of $-1.1_{two} \times 2^{-1}$

$$(-1)^1 \times (1 + .1000\ 0000\ 0000\ 0000\ 0000\ 000_{two}) \times 2^{(126)}$$

The single precision, binary representation of -0.75_{ten} is then

31	30	29	28	27	26	25	24	23	22	21	20	19	18	17	16	15	14	13	12	11	10	9	8	7	6	5	4	3	2	1	0
1	0	1	1	1	1	1	1	0	1	0	0	0	0	0	0	0	0	0	0	0	0	0	0	0	0	0	0	0	0	0	0

1 bit   8 bits   23 bits

The double precision representation is

$$(-1)^1 \times (1 + .1000000000000000000000000000$$
$$0000000000000000000000000_{two}) \times 2^{(1022)}$$

31	30	29	28	27	26	25	24	23	22	21	20	19	18	17	16	15	14	13	12	11	10	9	8	7	6	5	4	3	2	1	0
0	0	1	1	1	1	1	1	1	1	1	0	1	0	0	0	0	0	0	0	0	0	0	0	0	0	0	0	0	0	0	0

1   11   20

0	0	0	0	0	0	0	0	0	0	0	0	0	0	0	0	0	0	0	0	0	0	0	0	0	0	0	0	0	0	0	0

32

Example

What decimal number is represented by this word?

31	30	29	28	27	26	25	24	23	22	21	20	19	18	17	16	15	14	13	12	11	10	9	8	7	6	5	4	3	2	1	0
1	1	0	0	0	0	0	0	1	0	1	0	0	0	0	0	0	0	0	0	0	0	0	0	0	0	0	0	0	0	0	0 . . .

Answer

The sign bit is 1, the exponent field contains 129, and the significand field contains $1 \times 2^{-2} = 1/4$ or 0.25. Using the basic equation:

$$(-1)^s \times (1 + \text{significand}) \times 2^{(\text{exponent–bias})}$$

$$= (-1)^1 \times (1 + 0.25) \times 2^{(129-127)}$$
$$= -1 \times 1.25 \times 2^2$$
$$= -1.25 \times 4$$
$$= -5.0$$

In the next sections we will give the algorithms for floating-point addition and multiplication. At their core, they use the corresponding integer operations on the significands, but extra bookkeeping is necessary to handle the exponents and normalize the result. We first give an intuitive derivation of the algorithms in decimal, and then give a more detailed, binary version in the figures.

Elaboration: In an attempt to increase range without removing bits from the significand, some computers before the IEEE 754 standard used a base other than 2. For example, the IBM 360 and 370 mainframe computers use base 16. Since changing the IBM exponent by 1 means shifting the significand by 4 bits, "normalized" base 16 numbers can have up to 3 leading bits of 0s. Hexadecimal digits mean that up to 3 bits must be dropped from the significand, which leads to surprising problems in the accuracy of floating-point arithmetic, as noted in the Historical Perspective section on page 249.

Floating-Point Addition

Let's add numbers in scientific notation by hand to illustrate the problems in floating-point addition: $9.999_{ten} \times 10^1 + 1.610_{ten} \times 10^{-1}$. Assume that we can store only four decimal digits of the significand and two decimal digits of the exponent.

Step 1. To be able to add these numbers properly, we must align the decimal point of the number with the smaller exponent. Hence, we need a form of the smaller number, $1.610_{ten} \times 10^{-1}$, that matches the larger exponent. We obtain this by observing that there are multiple representations of an unnormalized floating-point number in scientific notation:

$$1.610_{ten} \times 10^{-1} = 0.1610_{ten} \times 10^{0} = 0.01610_{ten} \times 10^{1}$$

The number on the right is the version we desire, since its exponent matches the exponent of the larger number $9.999_{ten} \times 10^{1}$. Thus, the first step shifts the significand of the smaller number to the right until its corrected exponent matches that of the larger number. But we can represent only four decimal digits so, after shifting, the number is really:

$$0.016_{ten} \times 10^{1}$$

Step 2. Next comes the addition of the significands:

$$
\begin{array}{r}
9.999_{ten} \\
+ \quad 0.016_{ten} \\
\hline
10.015_{ten}
\end{array}
$$

The sum is $10.015_{ten} \times 10^{1}$

Step 3. This sum is not in normalized scientific notation, so we need to correct it. Again, there are multiple representations of this number; we pick the normalized form:

$$10.015_{ten} \times 10^{1} = 1.0015_{ten} \times 10^{2}$$

Thus, after the addition we may have to shift the sum to put it into normalized form, adjusting the exponent appropriately. This example shows shifting to the right, but if one number were positive and the other were negative it would be possible for the sum to have many leading 0s, requiring left shifts. Whenever the exponent is increased or decreased, we must check for overflow or underflow—that is, we must make sure that the exponent still fits in its field.

Step 4. Since we assumed that the significand can be only 4 digits long (excluding the sign), we must round the number. In our grammar school algorithm, the rules truncate the number if the digit to the right of the desired point is between 0 and 4 and add 1 to the digit if the number to the right is between 5 and 9. The number

$$1.0015_{ten} \times 10^{2}$$

is rounded to four digits in the significand to

$$1.002_{ten} \times 10^2$$

since the fourth digit to the right of the decimal point was between 5 and 9. Notice that if we have bad luck on rounding, such as adding 1 to a string of 9s, the sum may no longer be normalized and we would need to perform step 3 again.

Figure 4.41 shows the algorithm for binary floating-point addition that follows this decimal example. Steps 1 and 2 are similar to the example just discussed: adjust the significand of the number with the smaller exponent and then add the two significands. Step 3 normalizes the results, forcing a check for overflow or underflow. The test for overflow and underflow in step 3 depends on the precision of the operands. For single precision, the maximum exponent is 127 and the minimum exponent is –126. The limits for double precision are 1023 and –1022.

For simplicity, we will show truncation in step 4, one of four rounding options in IEEE 754 floating point. The accuracy of floating-point calculations depends a great deal on the accuracy of rounding so, although it is easy to follow, truncation leads away from accuracy.

Example

Try adding the numbers 0.5_{ten} and -0.4375_{ten} in binary using the algorithm in Figure 4.41.

Answer

Let's first look at the binary version of the two numbers in normalized scientific notation, assuming that we keep 4 bits of precision:

$$\begin{aligned}0.5_{ten} &= 1/2_{ten} &= 1/2^1{}_{ten} \\ &= 0.1_{two} &= 0.1_{two} \times 2^0 &= 1.000_{two} \times 2^{-1} \\ -0.4375_{ten} &= -7/16_{ten} &= -7/2^4{}_{ten} \\ &= -0.0111_{two} &= -0.0111_{two} \times 2^0 &= -1.110_{two} \times 2^{-2}\end{aligned}$$

Now we follow the algorithm:

Step 1. The significand of the smaller number ($-1.11_{two} \times 2^{-2}$) is shifted right until its exponent matches the larger number:

$$-1.110_{two} \times 2^{-2} = -0.111_{two} \times 2^{-1}$$

Step 2. Add the significands:

$$1.0_{two} \times 2^{-1} + (-0.111_{two} \times 2^{-1}) = 0.001_{two} \times 2^{-1}$$

Step 3. Normalize the sum, checking for overflow or underflow:

$$0.001_{two} \times 2^{-1} = 0.010_{two} \times 2^{-2} = 0.100_{two} \times 2^{-3}$$
$$= 1.000_{two} \times 2^{-4}$$

Since $127 \geq -4 \geq -126$, there is no overflow or underflow. (The biased exponent would be $-4+127$ or 123, which is between 0 and 255, the smallest and largest biased exponents.)

Step 4. Round the sum:

$$1.000_{two} \times 2^{-4}$$

The sum already fits in 4 bits, so there is no need to round.
  This sum is then

$$1.000_{two} \times 2^{-4} = 0.0001000_{two} = 0.0001_{two}$$
$$= 1/2^4{}_{ten} \quad = 1/16_{ten} \quad = 0.0625_{ten}$$

This sum is what we would expect from adding 0.5_{ten} to -0.4375_{ten}.

Many machines dedicate hardware to run floating-point operations as fast as possible. Figure 4.42 sketches the basic organization of hardware for floating-point addition.

Floating-Point Multiplication

Now that we have explained floating-point addition, let's try floating-point multiplication. We start by multiplying decimal numbers in scientific notation by hand: $1.110_{ten} \times 10^{10} \times 9.200_{ten} \times 10^{-5}$. Assume that we can store only four digits of the significand and two digits of the exponent.

Step 1. Unlike addition, we calculate the exponent of the product by simply adding the exponents of the operands together:

New exponent = $10 + (-5) = 5$

Let's do this with the biased exponents as well to make sure we obtain the same result. $10 + 127 = 137$ and $-5 + 127 = 122$, so

New exponent = $137 + 122 = 259$

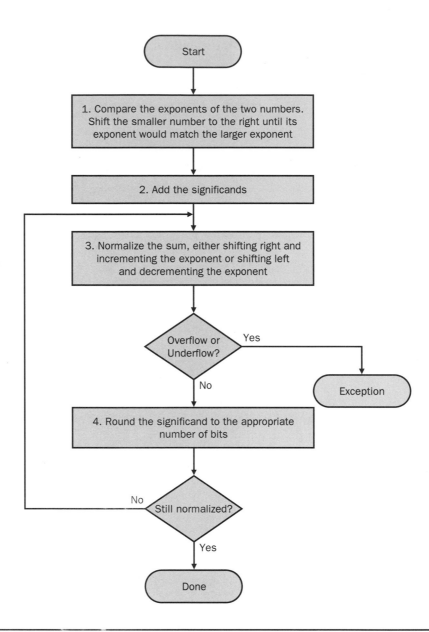

FIGURE 4.41 Floating-point addition. The normal path is to execute steps 3 and 4 once, but if rounding causes the sum to be unnormalized, we must repeat step 3.

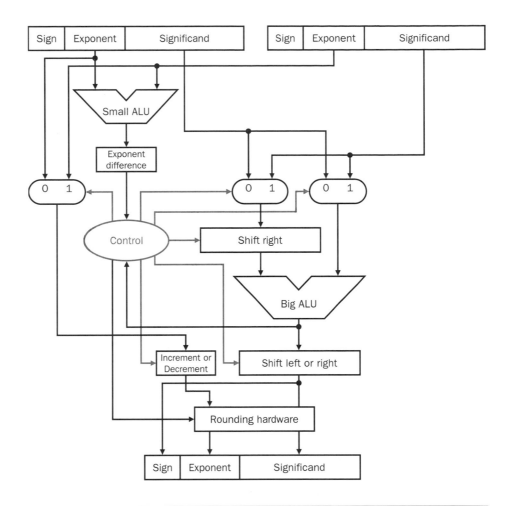

FIGURE 4.42 Block diagram of an arithmetic unit dedicated to floating-point addition. The steps of Figure 4.41 correspond to each block, from top to bottom. First the exponent of one operand is subtracted from the other using the small ALU to determine which is larger and by how much. This difference controls the three multiplexors; from left to right they select the larger exponent, the significand of the smaller number, and the significand of the larger number. The smaller significand is shifted right and then the significands are added together using the big ALU. The normalization step then shifts the sum left or right and increments or decrements the exponent. Rounding then creates the final result.

This result is too large for the 8-bit exponent field, so something is amiss! The problem is with the bias, because we are adding the biases as well as the exponents:

New exponent = $(10 + 127) + (-5 + 127) = (5 + 2 \times 127) = 259$

Accordingly, to get the correct biased sum when we add biased numbers, we must subtract the bias from the sum:

New exponent = $137 + 122 - 127 = 259 - 127 = 132 = (5 + 127)$

and 5 is indeed the exponent we calculated initially.

Step 2. Next comes the multiplication of the significands:

$$
\begin{array}{r}
1.110_{ten} \\
\times \quad 9.200_{ten} \\
\hline
0000 \\
0000 \\
2220 \\
9990 \\
\hline
10212000_{ten}
\end{array}
$$

There are three digits to the right of the decimal for each operand, so the decimal point is placed six digits from the right in the product significand:

10.212000_{ten}

Assuming that we can keep only three digits to the right of the decimal point, the product is 10.212×10^5.

Step 3. This product is unnormalized, so we need to correct it. Again, there are multiple representations of this number, so we must pick the normalized form:

$10.212_{ten} \times 10^5 = 1.0212_{ten} \times 10^6$

Thus, after the multiplication, the product can be shifted right one digit to put it in normalized form, adding 1 to the exponent. At this point, we can check for overflow and underflow. Underflow may occur if both operands are small—that is, if both have large negative exponents.

Step 4. We assumed that the significand is only four digits long (excluding the sign), so we must round the number. The number

$1.0212_{ten} \times 10^6$

is rounded to four digits in the significand to

$1.021_{ten} \times 10^6$.

Step 5. The sign of the product depends on the signs of the original operands. If they are both the same, the sign is positive; otherwise it's negative. Hence the sum is

$$+1.021_{ten} \times 10^6.$$

The sign of the sum in the addition algorithm was determined by addition of the significands, but in multiplication the sign of the product is determined by the signs of the operands.

Once again, as Figure 4.43 shows, multiplication of binary floating-point numbers is quite similar to the steps we have just completed. We start with calculating the new exponent of the product by adding the biased exponents, being sure to subtract one bias to get the proper result. Next is multiplication of significands, followed by an optional normalization step. The size of the exponent is checked for overflow or underflow, and then the product is rounded. If rounding leads to further normalization, we once again check for exponent size. Finally, set the sign bit to 1 if the signs of the operands were different (negative product) or to 0 if they were the same (positive product).

Example

Let's try multiplying the numbers 0.5_{ten} and -0.4375_{ten} using the steps in Figure 4.43.

Answer

In binary, the task is multiplying $1.000_{two} \times 2^{-1}$ by $-1.110_{two} \times 2^{-2}$.

Step 1. Adding the exponents without bias:

$$-1 + (-2) = -3$$

or, using the biased representation:

$$(-1 + 127) + (-2 + 127) - 127 = (-1 - 2) + (127 + 127 - 127)$$
$$= -3 + 127 = 124$$

Step 2. Multiplying the significands:

$$
\begin{array}{r}
1.000_{two} \\
\times \quad 1.110_{two} \\
\hline
0000 \\
1000 \\
1000 \\
1000 \\
\hline
1110000_{two}
\end{array}
$$

The product is $1.110000_{two} \times 2^{-3}$, but we need to keep it to 4 bits, so it is $1.110_{two} \times 2^{-3}$.

Step 3. Now we check the product to make sure it is normalized and then check the exponent for overflow or underflow. The product is already normalized and, since $127 \geq -3 \geq -126$, there is no overflow or underflow. (Using the biased representation, $255 \geq 124 \geq 0$, so the exponent fits.)

Step 4. Rounding the product makes no change:

$$1.110_{two} \times 2^{-3}$$

Step 5. Since the signs of the original operands differ, make the sign of the product negative. Hence the product is

$$-1.110_{two} \times 2^{-3}$$

Converting to decimal to check our results:

$$-1.110_{two} \times 2^{-3} = -0.001110_{two} = -0.00111_{two}$$
$$= -7/2^5{}_{ten} = -7/32_{ten} = -0.21875_{ten}$$

The product of 0.5_{ten} and -0.4375_{ten} is indeed -0.21875_{ten}.

Hardware Software Interface

MIPS supports the IEEE single precision and double precision formats with these instructions:

- Floating-point *addition, single* (add.s) and *addition, double* (add.d)

- Floating-point *subtraction, single* (sub.s) and *subtraction,*

- Floating-point *multiplication, single* (mul.s) and *multiplication, double* (mul.d)

- Floating-point *division, single* (div.s) and *division, double* (div.d)

- Floating-point *comparison, single* (c.x.s) and *comparison, double* (c.x.d), where x may be *equal* (eq), *not equal* (neq), *less than* (lt), *less than or equal* (le), *greater than* (gt), or *greater than or equal* (ge)

- Floating-point *branch, true* (bc1t) and *branch, false* (bc1f). Floating-point comparison sets a bit to true or false, depending on the comparison con-

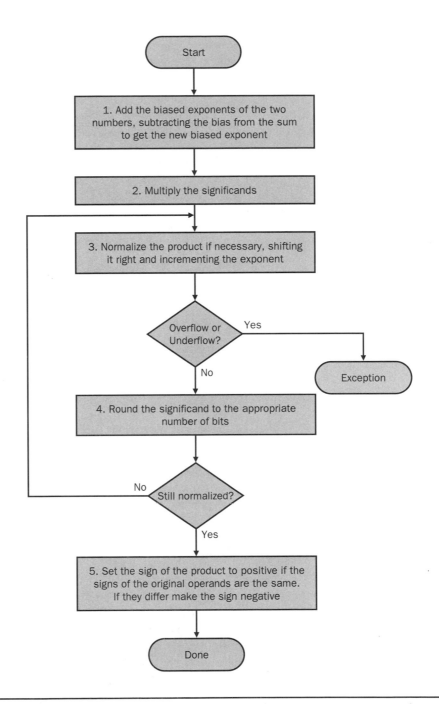

FIGURE 4.43 Floating-point multiplication. The normal path is to execute steps 3 and 4 once, but if rounding causes the sum to be unnormalized, we must repeat step 3.

dition, and a floating-point branch then decides whether or not to branch, depending on the condition.

One issue that computer designers face in supporting floating-point arithmetic is whether to use the same registers used by the integer instructions or to add a special set for floating point. Because programs normally perform integer operations and floating-point operations on different data, separating the registers will only slightly increase the number of instructions needed to execute a program. The major impact is to create a separate set of data transfer instructions to move data between floating-point registers and memory. The MIPS designers decided to add separate floating-point registers—called $f0, $f1, $f2, . . .—used either for single precision or double precision, and hence included in separate loads and stores for single precision and double precision floating-point registers: l.s, s.s, l.d, and s.d. Thus, the MIPS code to load two single precision numbers from memory, add them, and then store the sum might look like this:

```
l.s    $f4,x($29)   # Load 32-bit F.P. number into F4
l.s    $f6,y($29)   # Load 32-bit F.P. number into F6
add.s  $f2,$f4,$f6  # F2 = F4 + F6 single precision
s.s    $f2,z($29)   # Store 32-bit F.P. number from F2
```

Figure 4.40 summarizes the floating point portion of the MIPS architecture revealed in Chapter 4, with the additions to support floating point shown in color.

Elaboration: Only 16 of the 32 MIPS floating-point registers can be used for single precision operations: $f0, $f2, $f4, . . . , $f30. Double precision is computed using pairs of these registers. The odd number floating-point registers are used only to load and store the right half of 64-bit floating-point numbers.

Accurate Arithmetic

Unlike integers, which can represent exactly every number between the smallest and largest number, floating-point numbers are normally approximations for a number they can't really represent. The reason is that an infinite variety of real numbers exists between, say, 0 and 1, but no more than 2^{53} can be represented exactly in double precision floating point. The best we can do is get the floating-point representation close to the actual number. Thus, IEEE 754 offers several modes of rounding to let the programmer pick the desired approximation.

MIPS floating-point operands

Name	Example	Comments
32 floating-point regs	$f0, $f1, $f2, . . . , $f31	MIPS floating pointer registers are used in pairs for double precision numbers.Odd numbered registers cannot be used for arithmetic or branch, just for data transfer of the right "half" of double precision register pairs.
2^{30} memory words	Memory[0], Memory[4], . . . , Memory[4294967292]	Accessed only by data transfer instructions. MIPS uses byte addresses, so sequential words differ by 4. Memory holds data structures, such as arrays, and spilled registers, such as those saved on procedure calls.

MIPS floating-point assembly language

Category	Instruction	Example	Meaning	Comments
Arithmetic	FP add single	add.s $f2,$f4,$f6	$f2 = $f4 + $f6	Floating-Pt. add (single prec.)
	FP subtract single	sub.s $f2,$f4,$f6	$f2 = $f4 − $f6	Floating-Pt. sub (single prec.)
	FP multiply single	mul.s $f2,$f4,$f6	$f2 = $f4 × $f6	Floating-Pt. multiply (s. prec.)
	FP divide single	div.s $f2,$f4,$f6	$f2 = $f4 / $f6	Floating-Pt. divide (s. prec.)
	FP add double	add.d $f2,$f4,$f6	$f2 = $f4 + $f6	Floating-Pt. add (double prec.)
	FP subtr. double	sub.d $f2,$f4,$f6	$f2 = $f4 − $f6	Floating-Pt. sub (double prec.)
	FP mult. double	mul.d $f2,$f4,$f6	$f2 = $f4 × $f6	Floating-Pt. multiply (d. prec.)
	FP divide double	div.d $f2,$f4,$f6	$f2 = $f4 / $f6	Floating-Pt. divide (d. prec.)
Data transfer	load word copr. 1	lwc1 $f1,100($2)	$f1 = Memory[$2+100]	32-bit data to FP register
	store word copr. 1	swc1 $f1,100($2)	Memory[$2+100] = $f1	32-bit data to memory
Conditional branch	branch on FP true	bc1t 100	if (cond==1) go to PC+4+100	PC relative branch if FP cond.
	branch on FP false	bc1f 100	if (cond==0) go to PC+4+100	PC relative branch if not cond.
	FP compare single (eq,ne,lt,le,gt,ge)	c.lt.s $f2,$f4	if ($f2 < $f4) cond=1; else cond=0	Floating-Pt. compare less than single precision
	FP comp. double (eq,ne,lt,le,gt,ge)	c.lt.d $f2,$f4	if ($f2 < $f4) cond=1; else cond=0	Floating-Pt. compare less than double precision

MIPS floating-point machine language

Name	Format			Example				Comments
add.s	R	17	16	6	4	2	0	add.s $f2,$f4,$f6
sub.s	R	17	16	6	4	2	1	sub.s $f2,$f4,$f6
mul.s	R	17	16	6	4	2	2	mul.s $f2,$f4,$f6
div.s	R	17	16	6	4	2	3	div.s $f2,$f4,$f6
add.d	R	17	17	6	4	2	0	add.d $f2,$f4,$f6
sub.d	R	17	17	6	4	2	1	sub.d $f2,$f4,$f6
mul.d	R	17	17	6	4	2	2	mul.d $f2,$f4,$f6
div.d	R	17	17	6	4	2	3	div.d $f2,$f4,$f6
lwc1	I	49	2	1	100			lwc1 $f1,100($2)
swc1	I	57	2	1	100			swc1 $f1,100($2)
bc1t	I	17	8	1	100			bc1t 100
bc1f	I	17	8	0	100			bc1f 100
c.lt.s	R	17	16	4	2	0	60	c.lt.s $f2,$f4
c.lt.d	R	17	17	4	2	0	60	c.lt.d $f2,$f4
Field size		6 bits	5 bits	5 bits	5 bits	5 bits	6 bits	All MIPS instructions 32 bits

FIGURE 4.44 MIPS floating point architecture revealed thus far. See Appendix A, section A.10 on page A-47 for more detail.

Rounding sounds simple enough, but to round accurately requires the hardware to include extra bits in the calculation. In the preceding examples, we were vague on the number of bits that an intermediate representation can occupy, but clearly if every intermediate result had to be truncated to the exact number of digits, there would be no opportunity to round. IEEE 754, therefore, always keeps 2 extra bits on the right during intermediate calculations, called *guard* and *round*, respectively. Let's do a decimal example to illustrate the value of these extra digits.

Example

Add $2.56_{ten} \times 10^0$ to $2.34_{ten} \times 10^2$ assuming that we have three significant decimal digits. Round to the nearest decimal number with three significant decimal digits, first with guard and round digits and then without them.

Answer

First we must shift the smaller number to the right to align the exponents, so $2.56_{ten} \times 10^0$ becomes $0.0256_{ten} \times 10^2$. Since we have guard and round digits, we are able to represent the two least significant digits when we align exponents. The guard digit holds 5 and the round digit holds 6. The sum is

$$
\begin{array}{r}
2.3400_{ten} \\
+ \quad 0.0256_{ten} \\
\hline
2.3656_{ten}
\end{array}
$$

Thus the sum is $2.3656_{ten} \times 10^2$. Since we have two digits to round, we want values 0 to 49 to round down and 51 to 99 to round up, with 50 being the tie breaker. Rounding the sum up with three significant digits yields $2.37_{ten} \times 10^2$.

Doing this *without* guard and round digits drops two digits from the calculation. The new sum is then

$$
\begin{array}{r}
2.34_{ten} \\
+ \quad 0.02_{ten} \\
\hline
2.36_{ten}
\end{array}
$$

The answer is $2.36_{ten} \times 10^2$, off by 1 in the last digit from the sum obtained above.

Since the worst case for rounding would be when the actual number is halfway between two floating-point representations, accuracy in floating point is normally measured in terms of the number of bits in error in the least significant bits of the significand; the measure is called the number of *units in the last place* or *ulp*. If a number was off by 2 in the least significant bits, it would be called off by 2 ulps. IEEE 754 guarantees that the computer uses the number that is within one-half ulp.

Summary

The big picture below reinforces the stored program concept from Chapter 3; the meaning of the information cannot be determined just by looking at the bits, for the same bits can represent a variety of objects. This section shows that computer arithmetic is finite and thus can disagree with natural arithmetic. For example, the IEEE standard 754 floating-point representation

$$(-1)^S \times (1 + \text{significand}) \times 2^{(\text{exponent–bias})}$$

is almost always an approximation of the real number. Computer systems and programmers at times must take care to minimize this gap between computer arithmetic and arithmetic in the real world.

The Big Picture

Bit patterns have no inherent meaning. They may represent signed integers, unsigned integers, floating-point numbers, instructions, and so on. What is represented depends on the instruction that operates on the bits in the word.

The major difference between computer numbers and numbers in the real world is that computer numbers have limited size, hence limited precision; it's possible to calculate a number too big or too small to be represented in a word. Programmers must remember these limits and write programs accordingly.

Elaboration: The IEEE 754 floating-point standard is filled with little widgets to help the programmer try to maintain accuracy, like the toggle switches in an airline cockpit. We'll cover a few here, but take a look at the references at the end of section 4.11 to learn more.

There are four rounding modes: always round up (toward $+\infty$), always round down (toward $-\infty$), truncate, and round to nearest even. The final mode determines what to do if the number is exactly halfway in between. The Internal Revenue Service always rounds 0.50 dollars up, possibly to the benefit of the IRS. A more equitable way would be to round up this case half the time and round down the other half. IEEE 754 says that if the bit to the left of the halfway case is odd, add 1; if it's even, truncate. This method always creates a 0 in the least significant bit, giving the rounding mode its name.

Two extra digits are always enough for the first three rounding modes. To always obtain the right rounding for the last case, the standard has a third bit in addition to guard and round; it is set whenever there are nonzero bits to the right of the round bit. This *sticky* bit allows the computer to see the difference between $0.50\ldots00_{ten}$ and $0.50\ldots01_{ten}$ when rounding. The sticky bit might be set, for example, during addition, when the smaller number is shifted to the right.

The goal of such modes is to allow the machine to get the same results as if the intermediate results were calculated to infinite precision and then rounded.

Other features of IEEE 754 are special symbols to represent unusual events. For example, instead of interrupting on a divide by 0, you can set the result to a bit pattern representing $+\infty$ or $-\infty$; the largest exponent is reserved for these special symbols. When the programmer prints the results, the program will print an infinity symbol. It even has a symbol for the result of invalid operations, such as 0/0 or subtracting infinity from infinity. This symbol is *NaN*, for *Not A Number*. Finally, in an attempt to squeeze every last bit of precision from a floating-point operation, the standard allows some numbers to be represented in unnormalized form. Rather than having a gap between 0 and the smallest normalized number, IEEE allows *denormalized numbers*. They have the same exponent as zero but a nonzero significand. They allow a number to degrade in significance until it becomes 0, called *gradual underflow*.

Here are the encodings of IEEE 754 floating-point numbers:

Single precision		Double precision		Object represented
Exponent	Significand	Exponent	Significand	
0	0	0	0	0
0	nonzero	0	nonzero	Denormalized number
1 to 254	anything	1 to 2046	anything	Floating Point number
255	0	2047	0	Infinity
255	nonzero	2047	nonzero	NaN (Not A Number)

The possibility of an occasional unnormalized operand has given headaches to floating-point designers who are trying to build fast floating-point units. Hence many computers cause an exception if an operand is denormalized, letting software complete the operation.

4.9   Fallacies and Pitfalls

Thus mathematics may be defined as the subject in which we never know what we are talking about, nor whether what we are saying is true.

Bertrand Russell, *Recent Words on the Principles of Mathematics*, 1901

Arithmetic fallacies and pitfalls generally stem from the difference between the limited precision of computer arithmetic and the unlimited precision of natural arithmetic.

Pitfall: Forgetting that floating-point addition is not associative. (Hence $x + (y + z) \neq (x + y) + z$.)

Given the great range of numbers that can be represented in floating point, problems occur when adding two large numbers of opposite signs plus a small number. For example, suppose $x = -1.5_{ten} \times 10^{38}$, $y = 1.5_{ten} \times 10^{38}$, and $z = 1.0$, and that these are all single precision numbers. Then

$$x + (y + z) = -1.5_{ten} \times 10^{38} + (1.5_{ten} \times 10^{38} + 1.0)$$
$$= -1.5_{ten} \times 10^{38} + (1.5_{ten} \times 10^{38}) = 0.0$$
$$(x + y) + z = (-1.5_{ten} \times 10^{38} + 1.5_{ten} \times 10^{38}) + 1.0$$
$$= (0.0_{ten}) + 1.0 = 1.0$$

Since floating-point numbers have limited precision and result in approximations of real results, $1.5_{ten} \times 10^{38}$ is so much larger than 1.0_{ten} that $1.5_{ten} \times 10^{38} + 1.0$ is still $1.5_{ten} \times 10^{38}$. That's why the sum of x, y, and z is 0.0 or 1.0, depending on the order of the floating-point additions.

Fallacy: Just as a left shift instruction can replace an integer multiply by a power of 2, a right shift is the same as an integer division by a power of 2.

Recall that a binary number x, where xi means the ith bit, represents the number:

$$\ldots + (x3 \times 2^3) + (x2 \times 2^2) + (x1 \times 2^1) + (x0 \times 2^0)$$

Shifting the bits of x right by n bits would seem to be the same as dividing by 2^n. And this *is* true for unsigned integers. The problem is with signed integers. For example, suppose we want to divide -5_{ten} by 4_{ten}; the quotient should be -1_{ten}. The two's complement representation of -5_{ten} is

1111 1111 1111 1111 1111 1111 1111 1011$_{two}$

According to this fallacy, shifting right by 2 should divide by 4_{ten} (2^2):

0011 1111 1111 1111 1111 1111 1111 1110$_{two}$

With a 0 in the sign bit, this result is clearly wrong. The value created by the shift right is actually $1{,}073{,}741{,}822_{ten}$ instead of -1_{ten}.

Perhaps the solution would be to have an arithmetic right shift (see page 208) that extends the sign bit to the right instead of shifting in 0s. A 2-bit arithmetic shift right of -5_{ten} produces

1111 1111 1111 1111 1111 1111 1111 1110$_{two}$

The result is -2_{ten} instead of -1_{ten}; close, but no cigar.

Concluding Remarks

Computer arithmetic is distinguished from paper-and-pencil arithmetic by the constraints of limited precision. This limit may result in invalid operations through calculating numbers larger than the predefined limits. Such anomalies, called overflow or underflow, may result in exceptions or interrupts, emergency events similar to unplanned subroutine calls. Chapter 5 discusses exceptions in more detail. Floating-point arithmetic has the added challenge of being an approximation of real numbers, and care needs to be taken to ensure that the computer number selected is the representation closest to the actual number. The challenges of imprecision and limited representation are part of the inspiration for the field of numerical analysis.

Over the years computer arithmetic has become largely standardized, greatly enhancing the portability of programs. Two's complement binary integer arithmetic and IEEE 754 binary floating-point arithmetic are found in the vast majority of computers sold today. For example, every desktop computer sold since this book was first printed follows these conventions.

A side effect of the stored program computer is that bit patterns have no inherent meaning. The same bit pattern may represent a signed integer, unsigned integer, floating-point number, instruction, and so on. It is the instruction that operates on the word that determines its meaning.

With the explanation of computer arithmetic in this chapter comes a description of much more of the MIPS instruction set. Figure 4.45 lists the MIPS instructions covered in Chapters 3 and 4. For the rest of the book, we concentrate on the left-hand side of the table—the integer instruction set excluding multiply and divide. Figure 4.46 on page 248 gives the popularity of each of these instructions for two programs: gcc and spice. Note that the double precision floating point is much more popular than single precision for this running of the spice program—supporting evidence for the decision by MIPS designers to offer 16 separate double precision floating-point registers.

Core MIPS instructions	Name	Format	Integer multiply and divide + floating-point instructions	Name	Format
add	add	R	multiply	mult	R
add immediate	addi	I	multiply unsigned	multu	R
add unsigned	addu	R	divide	div	R
add immediate unsigned	addiu	I	divide unsigned	divu	R
subtract	sub	R	move from hi	mfhi	R
subtract unsigned	subu	R	move from lo	mflo	R
and	and	R	move from system control (EPC)	mfc0	R
and immediate	andi	I	floating-point add single	add.s	R
or	or	R	floating-point add double	add.d	R
or immediate	ori	I	floating-point subtract single	sub.s	R
shift left logical	sll	R	floating-point subtract double	sub.d	R
shift right logical	srl	R	floating-point multiply single	mul.s	R
load upper immediate	lui	I	floating-point multiply double	mul.d	R
load word	lw	I	floating-point divide single	div.s	R
store word	sw	I	floating-point divide double	div.d	R
branch on equal	beq	I	load word to floating-point single	l.s	I
branch on not equal	bne	I	load word to floating-point double	l.d	I
jump	j	J	store word to floating-point single	s.s	I
jump and link	jal	J	store word to floating-point double	s.d	I
jump register	jr	R	branch on floating-point true	bc1t	I
set less than	slt	R	branch on floating-point false	bc1f	I
set less than immediate	slti	I	floating-point compare single	c.x.s	R
set less than unsigned	sltu	R	(x = eq, neq, lt, le, gt, ge)		
set less than immediate unsigned	sltiu	I	floating-point compare double (x = eq, neq, lt, le, gt, ge)	c.x.d	R

FIGURE 4.45 The MIPS instruction set covered so far. This book concentrates on the instructions in the left column. Appendix A, section A.10 gives the full MIPS instruction set.

Core MIPS	Name	gcc	spice	Multiply and divide + FP	Name	gcc	spice
add	add	0%	0%	multiply	mult	0%	0%
add imm.	addi	0%	0%	multiply unsigned	multu	0%	0%
add unsigned	addu	8%	13%	divide	div	0%	0%
add imm. uns.	addiu	16%	6%	divide unsigned	divu	0%	0%
subtract	sub	0%	0%	move from hi	mfhi	0%	0%
subtract unsigned	subu	1%	1%	move from lo	mflo	0%	0%
and	and	2%	1%	move from system control	mfc0	0%	0%
and imm.	andi	2%	1%	f.p. add single	add.s	0%	0%
or	or	2%	0%	f.p. add double	add.d	0%	5%
or imm.	ori	0%	1%	f.p. subtract single	sub.s	0%	0%
shift left logical	sll	8%	6%	f.p. subtract double	sub.d	0%	3%
shift right logical	srl	2%	1%	f.p. multiply single	mul.s	0%	0%
load upper imm.	lui	2%	0%	f.p. multiply double	mul.d	0%	6%
load word	lw	22%	11%	f.p. divide single	div.s	0%	0%
store word	sw	11%	5%	f.p. divide double	div.d	0%	3%
branch on equal	beq	8%	5%	load word to f.p. single	l.s	0%	0%
branch on not eq.	bne	8%	1%	load word to f.p. double	l.d	0%	15%
jump	j	0%	0%	store word to f.p. single	s.s	0%	3%
jump and link	jal	1%	1%	store word to f.p. double	s.d	0%	6%
jump register	jr	1%	1%	branch on f.p. true	bc1t	0%	1%
set less than	slt	3%	1%	branch on f.p. false	bc1f	0%	1%
set less than imm.	slti	1%	0%	f.p. compare single	c.x.s	0%	0%
set less than uns.	sltu	1%	0%	(x = eq, neq, lt, le, gt, ge)			
set less t. imm. uns.	sltiu	1%	0%	f.p. compare double	c.x.d	0%	2%
Column Total		100%	55%	Column Total		0%	45%

FIGURE 4.46 The frequency of the MIPS instructions for two programs, gcc and spice. (Calculated from "pixie" output of the full MIPS instruction set and then converted to equivalent instructions from the MIPS subset in the table.)

4.11   Historical Perspective and Further Reading

Gresham's Law ("Bad money drives out Good") for computers would say "The Fast drives out the Slow even if the Fast is wrong."

W. Kahan, 1992

At first it may be hard to imagine a subject of less interest than the correctness of computer arithmetic or its accuracy and harder still to understand why a subject so old and mathematical should be so controversial. Computer arithmetic is as old as computing itself, and some of the subject's earliest notions, like the economical re-use of registers during serial multiplication and division, still command respect today. Maurice Wilkes [1985] recalled a conversation about that notion during his visit to the United States in 1946, before the earliest stored-program machine had been built:

> . . . a project under von Neumann was to be set up at the Institute of Advanced Studies in Princeton . . . Goldstine explained to me the principal features of the design, including the device whereby the digits of the multiplier were put into the tail of the accumulator and shifted out as the least significant part of the product was shifted in. I expressed some admiration at the way registers and shifting circuits were arranged . . . and Goldstine remarked that things of that nature came very easily to von Neumann.

> There is no controversy here; it can hardly arise in the context of exact integer arithmetic so long as there is general agreement on what integer the correct result should be. However, as soon as approximate arithmetic enters the picture, so does controversy, as if one person's *negligible* must be another's *everything*.

The First Dispute

Floating-point arithmetic kindled disagreement before it was ever built. John von Neumann refused to include it in the machine he built at Princeton. In an influential report coauthored in 1946 with H. H. Goldstine and A. W. Burks, he gave the arguments for and against floating point. In favor:

> . . . to retain in a sum or product as many significant digits as possible and . . . to free the human operator from the burden of estimating and inserting into a problem "scale factors"—multiplication constants which serve to keep numbers within the limits of the machine.

Floating point was excluded for several reasons:

> There is, of course, no denying the fact that human time is consumed in arranging for the introduction of suitable scale factors. We only argue

that the time consumed is a very small percentage of the total time we will spend in preparing an interesting problem for our machine. The first advantage of the floating point is, we feel, somewhat illusory. In order to have such a floating point, one must waste memory capacity which could otherwise be used for carrying more digits per word. It would therefore seem to us not at all clear whether the modest advantages of a floating binary point offset the loss of memory capacity and the increased complexity of the arithmetic and control circuits.

The argument seems to be that most bits devoted to exponent fields would be bits wasted. Experience has proved otherwise.

One software approach to accommodate reals without floating-point hardware was called *floating vectors*; the idea was to compute at runtime one scale factor for a whole array of numbers, choosing the scale factor so that the array's biggest number would barely fill its field. By 1951, James H. Wilkinson had used this scheme extensively for matrix computations. The problem proved to be that a program might encounter a very large value, and hence the scale factor must accommodate these rare large numbers. The common numbers would thus have many leading 0s, since all numbers had to use a single scale factor. Accuracy was sacrificed because the least significant bits had to be lost on the right to accommodate leading 0s. This wastage became obvious to practitioners on early machines that displayed all their memory bits as dots on cathode ray tubes (like TV screens), because the loss of precision was visible. Where floating point deserved to be used, no practical alternative existed.

Thus true floating-point hardware became popular because it was useful. By 1957, floating-point hardware was almost ubiquitous. A decimal floating-point unit was available for the IBM 650; and soon the IBM 704, 709, 7090, 7094 . . . series would offer binary floating-point hardware for double as well as single precision. As a result, everybody had floating point, but every implementation was different.

Diversity Versus Portability

Since roundoff introduces some error into almost all floating-point operations, to complain about another bit of error seems picayune. So for twenty years nobody complained much that those operations behaved a little differently on different machines. If software required clever tricks to circumvent those idiosyncracies and finally deliver results correct in all but the last several bits, such tricks were deemed part of the programmer's art. For a long time, matrix computations mystified most people who had no notion of error analysis; perhaps this continues to be true. That may be why people are still surprised that numerically stable matrix computations depend upon the quality of arithmetic in so few places, far fewer than are generally supposed. Books by Wilkinson and widely used software packages like LINPACK and

EISPACK sustained a false impression, widespread in the early 1970s, that a modicum of skill sufficed to produce *portable* numerical software.

Portable here means that the software is distributed as source-code in some standard language to be compiled and executed on practically any commercially significant machine, and that it will then perform its task as well as any other program performs that task on that machine. Insofar as numerical software has often been thought to consist entirely of machine-independent mathematical formulas, its portability has often been taken for granted; the mistake in that presumption will become clear shortly.

Packages like LINPACK and EISPACK cost so much to develop—over a hundred dollars per line of Fortran delivered—that they could not have been developed without U. S. government subsidy; their portability was a precondition for that subsidy. But nobody thought to distinguish how various components contributed to their cost. One component was algorithmic—devise an algorithm that deserves to work on at least one computer despite its roundoff and over/underflow limitations. Another component was the software engineering effort required to achieve and confirm portability to the diverse computers commercially significant at the time; this component grew more onerous as ever more diverse floating-point arithmetics blossomed in the 1970s. And yet scarcely anybody realized how much that diversity inflated the cost of such software packages.

A Backward Step

Early evidence that somewhat different arithmetics could engender grossly different software development costs was presented in 1964. It happened at a meeting of SHARE, the IBM mainframe users' group, at which IBM announced System/360, the successor to the 7094 series. One of the speakers described the tricks he had been forced to devise to achieve a level of quality for the S/360 library that was not quite so high as he had previously achieved for the 7094.

Part of the trouble could have been foretold by von Neumann had he still been alive. In 1948 he and Goldstine had published a lengthy error analysis so difficult and so pessimistic that hardly anybody paid attention to it. It did predict correctly, however, that computations with larger arrays of data would probably fall prey to roundoff more often. IBM S/360s had bigger memories than 7094s, so data arrays could grow bigger, and they did. To make matters worse, the S/360s had narrower single precision words (32 bits versus 36) and used a cruder arithmetic (hexadecimal or base 16 versus binary or base 2) with consequently poorer worst-case precision (21 significant bits versus 27) than old 7094s. Consequently, software that had almost always provided (barely) satisfactory accuracy on 7094s too often produced inaccurate results when run on S/360s. The quickest way to recover adequate accuracy was to replace old codes' single precision declarations with double precision before recompilation for the S/360. This practice exercised S/360 double precision far more than had been expected.

The early S/360s' worst troubles were caused by lack of a guard digit in double precision. This lack showed up in multiplication as a failure of identities like 1.0 * x = x, because multiplying x by 1.0 dropped x's last hexadecimal digit (4 bits). Similarly, if x and y were very close but had different exponents, subtraction dropped off the last digit of the smaller operand before computing x − y. This last aberration in double precision undermined a precious theorem that single precision then (and now) honored: If 1/2 ≤ x/y ≤ 2, then no rounding error can occur when x − y is computed; it must be computed exactly.

Innumerable computations had benefited from this minor theorem, most often unwittingly, for several decades before its first formal announcement and proof. We had been taking all this stuff for granted.

The identities and theorems about exact relationships that persisted, despite roundoff, with reasonable implementations of approximate arithmetic were not appreciated until they were lost. Previously, all that had been thought to matter were precision (how many significant digits were carried) and range (the spread between over/underflow thresholds). Since the S/360s' double precision had more precision and wider range than the 7094s', software was expected to continue to work at least as well as before. But it didn't.

Programmers who had matured into program managers were appalled at the cost of converting 7094 software to run on S/360s. A small subcommittee of SHARE proposed improvements to the S/360 floating point. This committee was surprised and grateful to get a fair part of what they asked for from IBM, including all-important guard digits. By 1968, these had been retrofitted to S/360s in the field at considerable expense; worse than that was customers' loss of faith in IBM's infallibility. IBM employees who can remember the incident still shudder.

The People Who Built the Bombs

Seymour Cray has been associated for decades with the CDC and Cray computers that were, when he built them, the world's biggest and fastest. He has always understood what his customers wanted most: *speed*. And he gave it to them even if, in so doing, he also gave them arithmetics more *interesting* than anyone else's. Among his customers have been the great government laboratories like those at Livermore and Los Alamos, where nuclear weapons were designed. The challenges of "interesting" arithmetics were pretty tame to people who had to overcome Mother Nature's challenges.

Perhaps all of us could learn to live with arithmetic idiosyncrasy if only one computer's idiosyncracies had to be endured. Instead, when accumulating different computers' different anomalies, software dies the Death of a Thousand Cuts. Here is an example from Cray's machines:

```
if (x == 0.0)   y = 17.0 else y = z/x
```

Could this statement be stopped by a divide-by-0 error? On a CDC 6600 it could. The reason was a conflict between the 6600's adder, where x was compared with 0.0, and the multiplier and divider. The adder's comparison examined x 's leading 13 bits, which sufficed to distinguish zero from normal nonzero floating-point numbers x. The multiplier and divider examined only 12 leading bits. Consequently, tiny numbers x existed that were nonzero to the adder but zero to the multiplier and divider! To avoid disasters with these tiny numbers, programmers learned to replace statements like the one above by

```
if (1.0*x == 0.0)   y = 17.0 else y = z/x
```

But this statement is unsafe to use in would-be portable software because it malfunctions obscurely on *other* computers designed by Cray, the ones marketed by Cray Research, Inc. If x is so huge that 2.0 * x would overflow, then 1.0 * x may overflow too! This happens because Cray computers check the product's exponent for overflow *before* the product's exponent has been normalized, just to save the delay of a single AND gate. In case you think the statement above is safe to use now for portable software, since computers of the CDC 6600 era are no longer commercially significant, you should be warned that it can lead to overflow on a Cray computer even if z is almost as tiny as x; the trouble here is that the Cray computes not z/x but z * (1/x), and the reciprocal can overflow even though the desired quotient is unexceptionable. A similar difficulty troubles the Intel i860s used in its massively parallel computers. The would-be programmer of portable code faces countless dilemmas like these whenever trying to program for the full range of existing computers.

Rounding error anomalies that are far worse than the over/underflow anomaly just discussed also affect Cray computers. The worst error comes from the lack of a guard digit in add/subtract, an affliction of IBM S/360s. Further bad luck for software is occasioned by the way Cray economized his multiplier; about one-third of the bits that normal multiplier arrays generate have been left out of his multipliers because they would contribute less than a unit to the last place of the final Cray-rounded product. Consequently, a Cray's multiplier errs by almost a bit more than might have been expected. This error is compounded when division takes three multiplications to improve an approximate reciprocal of the divisor and then multiply the numerator by it. Square root compounds a few more multiplication errors. The fast way drove out the slow, even though the fast was occasionally slightly wrong.

Making the World Safe for Floating Point, or Vice Versa

William Kahan was an undergraduate at the University of Toronto in 1953 when he learned to program its Ferranti-Manchester Mark 1 computer. Because he entered the field early, Kahan became acquainted with a wide range of devices and a large proportion of the personalities active in computing; the numbers of both were small at that time. He has performed computations on slide rules, desktop mechanical calculators, tabletop analog differential analyzers, and so on; he used all but the earliest electronic computers and calculators mentioned in this book.

Kahan's desire to deliver reliable software led to an interest in error analysis that intensified during two years of postdoctoral study in England, where he became acquainted with Wilkinson. In 1960, he resumed teaching at Toronto, where an IBM 7090 had been acquired, and was granted free reign to tinker with its operating system, Fortran compiler, and runtime library. (He denies that he ever came near the 7090 hardware with a soldering iron but admits asking to do so.) One story from that time illuminates how misconceptions and numerical anomalies in computer systems can incur awesome hidden costs.

A graduate student in aeronautical engineering used the 7090 to simulate the wings he was designing for short takeoffs and landings. He knew such a wing would be difficult to control if its characteristics included an abrupt onset of stall, but he thought he could avoid that. His simulations were telling him otherwise. Just to be sure that roundoff was not interfering, he had repeated many of his calculations in double precision and gotten results much like those in single; his wings had stalled abruptly in both precisions. Disheartened, the student gave up.

Meanwhile Kahan replaced IBM's logarithm program (ALOG) with one of his own, which he hoped would provide better accuracy. While testing it, Kahan re-ran programs using the new version of ALOG. The student's results changed significantly; Kahan approached him to find out what had happened.

The student was puzzled. Much as the student preferred the results produced with the new ALOG—they predicted a gradual stall—he knew they must be wrong because they disagreed with his double precision results. The discrepancy between single and double precision results disappeared a few days later when a new release of IBM's double precision arithmetic software for the 7090 arrived. (The 7090 had no double precision hardware.) He went on to write a thesis about it and to build the wings; they performed as predicted. But that is not the end of the story.

In 1963, the 7090 was replaced by a faster 7094 with double precision floating-point hardware but with otherwise practically the same instruction set as the 7090. Only in double precision and only when using the new hardware did the wing stall abruptly again. A lot of time was spent to find out why. The 7094 hardware turned out, like the superseded 7090 software and the subsequent early S/360s, to lack a guard bit in double precision. Like so many programmers on those machines and on Cray's, the student discovered a trick to compensate for the lack of a guard digit; he wrote the expression (0.5 - x) + 0.5

in place of `1.0 - x`. Nowadays we would blush if we had to explain why such a trick might be necessary, but it solved the student's problem.

Meanwhile the lure of California was working on Kahan and his family; they came to Berkeley and he to the University of California. An opportunity presented itself in 1974 when accuracy questions induced Hewlett Packard's calculator designers to call in a consultant. The consultant was Kahan, and his work dramatically improved the accuracy of HP calculators, but that is another story. Fruitful collaboration with congenial co-workers, however, fortified him for the next and crucial opportunity.

It came in 1976, when John F. Palmer at Intel was empowered to specify the "best possible" floating-point arithmetic for all of Intel's product line. The 8086 was imminent, and an 8087 floating-point coprocessor for the 8086 was contemplated. (A *coprocessor* is simply an additional chip that accelerates a portion of the work of a processor; in this case, it accelerated floating-point computation.) Palmer had obtained his Ph.D. at Stanford a few years before and knew who to call for counsel of perfection—Kahan. They put together a design that obviously would have been impossible only a few years earlier and looked not quite possible at the time. But a new Israeli team of Intel employees led by Rafi Navé felt challenged to prove their prowess to Americans and leaped at an opportunity to put something impossible on a chip—the 8087. By now, floating-point arithmetics that had been merely diverse among mainframes had become anarchic among microprocessors, one of which might be host to a dozen varieties of arithmetic in ROM firmware or software. Robert G. Stewart, an engineer prominent in IEEE activities, got fed up with this anarchy and proposed that the IEEE draft a decent floating-point standard. Simultaneously, word leaked out in Silicon Valley that Intel was going to put on one chip some awesome floating point well beyond anything its competitors had in mind. The competition had to find a way to slow Intel down, so they formed a committee to do what Stewart requested.

Meetings of this committee began in late 1977 with a plethora of competing drafts from innumerable sources and dragged on into 1985 when IEEE Standard 754 for Binary Floating Point was made official. The winning draft was very close to one submitted by Kahan, his student Jerome T. Coonen, and Harold S. Stone, a professor visiting Berkeley at the time. Their draft was based on the Intel design, with Intel's permission of course, as simplified by Coonen. Their harmonious combination of features, almost none of them new, had at the outset attracted more support within the committee and from outside experts like Wilkinson than any other draft, but they had to win nearly unanimous support within the committee to win official IEEE endorsement, and that took time.

In 1980, Intel became tired of waiting and released the 8087 for use in the IBM PC. In 1982, Motorola announced its 68881, which found a place in Sun 3s and Macintosh IIs; Apple had been a supporter of the proposal from the beginning. Another Berkeley graduate student, George S. Taylor, had soon designed a high-speed implementation of the proposed standard for an early super-minicomputer (ELXSI 6400). The standard was becoming de facto before its final draft's ink was dry.

An early rush of adoptions gave the computing industry the false impression that IEEE 754, like so many other standards, could be implemented easily by following a standard recipe. Not true. Only the enthusiasm and ingenuity of its early implementors made it look easy. In fact, to implement IEEE 754 correctly demands extraordinarily diligent attention to detail; to make it run fast demands extraordinarily competent ingenuity of design. Had the industry's engineering managers realized this, they might not have been so quick to affirm that, as a matter of policy, "We conform to all applicable standards."

Today the computing industry is enmeshed in a host of standards that evolve continuously as technology changes. The floating-point standards IEEE 754/854 (they are practically the same) stand in somewhat splendid isolation only because nobody wishes to repeat the protracted wrangling that surrounded their birth when, with unprecedented generosity, the representatives of hardware interests acceded to the demands of those few who represented the interests of mathematical and numerical software. Unfortunately, the compiler-writing community was not represented adequately in the wrangling, and some of the features didn't balance language and compiler issues against other points. That community has been slow to make IEEE 754's unusual features available to the applications programmer. Humane exception handling is one such unusual feature; directed rounding another. Without compiler support, these features could atrophy.

At present, IEEE 754/854 have been implemented to a considerable degree of fidelity in at least part of the product line of every North American computer manufacturer except Cray Research Inc., and that company has recently announced that it too will conform "to some degree" by the mid 1990s to ease the transfer of data files and portable software between CRAYs and the workstations through which CRAY users have come to access their machines nowadays.

In 1989, the Association for Computing Machinery, acknowledging the benefits conferred upon the computing industry by IEEE 754, honored Kahan with the Turing Award. On accepting it, he thanked his many associates for their diligent support, and his adversaries for their blunders. So . . . not all errors are bad.

To Probe Further

Readers interested in learning more about floating point will find two publications by David Goldberg [1990, 1991] good starting points; they abound with pointers to further reading. Several of the stories told above come from Kahan [1972, 1983]. The latest word on the state of the art in computer arithmetic is often found in the *Proceedings* of the latest IEEE-sponsored Symposium on Computer Arithmetic, held every two or three years; the tenth was held in 1991.

Burks, A. W., H. H. Goldstine, and J. von Neumann [1946]. "Preliminary discussion of the logical design of an electronic computing instrument," *Report to the U.S. Army Ordnance Dept.,* p. 1; also in *Papers of John von Neumann,* W. Aspray and A. Burks, eds., MIT Press, Cambridge, Mass., and Tomash Publishers, Los Angeles, Calif. (1987) 97–146.

This classic paper includes arguments against floating-point hardware.

Goldberg, D. [1990]. "Computer Arithmetic," *Appendix A of Computer Architecture: A Quantitative Approach,* J. L. Hennessy and D. A. Patterson, Morgan Kaufmann Publishers, San Mateo, Calif.

A more advanced introduction to integer and floating-point arithmetic, with emphasis on hardware. It covers pages 168 to 225 of this book in just 10 pages, leaving another 45 pages for advanced topics.

Goldberg, D. [1991]. "What every computer scientist should know about floating-point arithmetic," ACM *Computing Surveys* V23#1, pp. 5–48.

Another good introduction to floating-point arithmetic by the same author, this time with emphasis on software.

Kahan, W. [1972]. "A survey of error-analysis," in *Info. Processing 71* (Proc. IFIP Congress 71 in Ljubljana), vol. 2, pp. 1214–39, North-Holland Publishing, Amsterdam.

This survey is a source of stories on the importance of accurate arithmetic.

Kahan, W. [1983]. "Mathematics written in sand," *Proc. Amer. Stat. Assoc. Joint Summer Meetings of 1983, Statistical Computing Section,* pp. 12–26.

The title refers to silicon, and is another source of stories illustrating the importance of accurate arithmetic.

Koren, I. [1993]. *Computer Arithmetic Algorithms,* Prentice Hall, Englewood Cliffs, N.J.

A recent textbook aimed at seniors and first year graduate students that explains fundamental principles of basic arithmetic, as well as complex operations such as logarithmic and trigonometric functions.

Wilkes, M. V. [1985]. *Memoirs of a Computer Pioneer,* MIT Press, Cambridge, Mass.

This computer pioneer's recollections include the derivation of the standard hardware for multiply and divide developed by von Neumann.

4.12   Exercises

Never give in, never give in, never, never, never—in nothing, great or small, large or petty—never give in....

Winston Churchill, Address at Harrow School, October 29, 1941

4.1 [15] <§3, 4.2, 4.8> The Big Picture on page 243 mentions that bits have no inherent meaning. Given the bit pattern

1000 1111 1110 1111 1100 0000 0000 0000

What does it represent, assuming that it is

a. a two's complement integer?

b. an unsigned integer?

c. a single precision floating-point number?

d. a MIPS instruction?

4.2 [10] <§4.2, 4.4, 4.8> This exercise is similar to Exercise 4.1, but this time use the bit pattern

0000 0000 0000 0000 0000 0000 0000 0000

4.3 [3] <§4.2> Convert 512_{ten} into a 32-bit two's complement binary number.

4.4 [3] <§4.2> Convert $-1,023_{ten}$ into a 32-bit two's complement binary number.

4.5 [5] <§4.2> Convert $-4,000,000_{ten}$ into a 32-bit two's complement binary number.

4.6 [5] <§4.2> What decimal number does this two's complement binary number represent: $1111\ 1111\ 1111\ 1111\ 1111\ 1110\ 0000\ 1100_{two}$?

4.7 [5] <§4.2> What decimal number does this two's complement binary number represent: $1111\ 1111\ 1111\ 1111\ 1111\ 1111\ 1111\ 1111_{two}$?

4.8 [5] <§4.2> What decimal number does this two's complement binary number represent: $0111\ 1111\ 1111\ 1111\ 1111\ 1111\ 1111\ 1111_{two}$?

4.9 [5] <§4.2> What binary number does this hexadecimal number represent: $7fff\ fffa_{hex}$? What decimal number does it represent?

4.10 [5] <§4.2> What hexadecimal number does this binary number represent: $1100\,1010\,1111\,1110\,1111\,1010\,1100\,1110_{two}$?

4.11 [5] <§4.8> Using the notation in the Hardware Software Interface sections on pages 226 and 227, show the MIPS binary floating-point formats in single precision and double precision for 10_{ten}.

4.12 [5] <§4.8> This exercise is similar to Exercise 4.11, but this time replace the number 10_{ten} with 10.5_{ten}.

4.13 [10] <§4.8> This exercise is similar to Exercise 4.11, but this time replace the number 10_{ten} with 0.1_{ten}.

4.14 [10] <§4.10> For the program gcc (Figure 4.46 on page 248), find the 10 most frequently executed MIPS instructions. List them in order of popularity, from most used to least used. Show the rank, name, and percentage of instructions executed for each instruction. If there is a tie for a given rank, list all instructions that tie with the same rank, even if this results in more than 10 instructions.

4.15 [10] <§4.10> This exercise is similar to Exercise 4.14, but this time replace the program gcc with the program spice.

4.16 <§4.10> {§4.14, 4.15} These questions examine the relative frequency of instructions in different programs.

a. [5] Which instructions are found in both the answer to Exercise 4.14 *and* in the answer to Exercise 4.15?

b. [5] What percentage of gcc instructions executed is due to the instructions identified in Exercise 4.16a?

c. [5] What percentage of gcc instructions executed is due to the instructions identified in Exercise 4.14?

d. [5] What percentage of spice instructions executed is due to the instructions identified in Exercise 4.16a?

e. [5] What percentage of spice instructions executed is due to the instructions identified in Exercise 4.15?

4.17 [10] <§4.10> {ex. 4.14, 4.15, 4.16} If you were designing a machine to execute the MIPS instruction set, what are the five instructions that you would try to make as fast as possible, based on the answers to Exercises 4.14 through 4.16? Give your rationale.

4.18 [15] <§2, 4.10> Using Figure 4.46 on page 248, calculate the average clock cycles per instruction (CPI) for the program gcc. Figure 4.47 gives the average

Instruction category	Average CPI
Loads and stores	01.4
Conditional branch	01.8
Jumps	01.2
Integer multiply	10.0
Integer divide	30.0
Floating-point add and subtract	02.0
Floating-point multiply, single precision	04.0
Floating-point multiply, double precision	05.0
Floating-point divide, single precision	12.0
Floating-point divide, double precision	19.0

FIGURE 4.47 CPI for MIPS instruction categories.

CPI per instruction category, taking into account cache misses and other effects. Assume that instructions omitted from the table have a CPI of 1.0.

4.19 [15] <§2, 4.10> This exercise is similar to Exercise 4.18, but this time replace the program gcc with the program spice.

4.20 [5] <§4.2> Why doesn't MIPS have a subtract immediate instruction?

4.21 [10] <§4.2> Find the shortest sequence of MIPS instructions to determine the absolute value of a two's complement integer. Convert this instruction (accepted by the MIPS assembler):

```
abs     $10,$11
```

This instruction means that register $10 has a copy of register $11 if register $11 is positive, and the two's complement of register $11 if $11 is negative.

4.22 [10] <§4.3> Find the shortest sequence of MIPS instructions to determine if there is a carry out from the addition of two registers, say registers $11 and $12. Place a 0 or 1 in register $10 if carry out is 0 or 1, respectively.

4.23 [15] <§4.3> {ex. 4.22} Find the shortest sequence of MIPS instructions to perform double precision integer addition. Assume that one 64-bit, two's complement integer is in registers $12 and $13 and another is in registers $14 and $15. The sum is to be placed in registers $10 and $11. In this example the most significant word of the 64-bit integer is found in the even-numbered registers, and the least significant word is found in the odd-numbered registers.

4.24 [20] <§4.6> Find the shortest sequence of MIPS instructions to perform double precision integer *multiplication*. Assume that one 64-bit, *unsigned* integer is in registers $12 and $13 and another is in registers $14 and $15. The 128-bit product is to be placed in registers $8, $9, $10 and $11. The most significant word is found in the lower numbered registers, and the least significant word is found in the higher numbered registers in this example. Hint: Write out the formula for $(a \times 2^{32} + b) \times (c \times 2^{32} + d)$.

4.25 [15] <§4.5> The ALU supported set on less than (slt) using just the sign bit of the adder. Let's try a set-on-less-than operation using the values -7_{ten} and 6_{ten}. To make it simpler to follow the example, let's limit the binary representations to 4 bits: 1001_{two} and 0110_{two}.

$$1001_{\text{two}} - 0110_{\text{two}} = 1001_{\text{two}} + 1010_{\text{two}} = 0011_{\text{two}}$$

This result would suggest that $-7 > 6$, which is clearly wrong. Hence we must factor in overflow in the decision. Modify the 1-bit ALU in Figure 4.15 on page 192 to handle slt correctly. Make your changes on a photocopy of this figure to save time.

4.26 [15] <§4.4> Some computers have explicit instructions to extract an arbitrary field from a 32-bit register and place it in the least significant bits of a register. The figure below shows the desired operation:

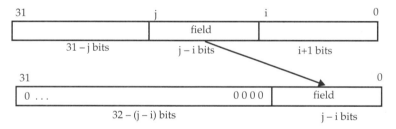

Find the shortest sequence of MIPS instructions that extracts a field for the constant values $i = 7$ and $j = 19$ from register $16 and places it in register $17.

In More Depth: Logical Instructions

The full MIPS instruction set has two more logical operations not mentioned thus far: xor and nor. The operation xor stands for exclusive OR, and nor stands for not OR. The table that follows defines these operations on a bit-by-bit basis. These instructions will be useful in the following two exercises.

a	b	a xor b	a nor b
0	0	0	1
0	1	1	0
1	0	1	0
1	1	0	0

4.27 [15] <§4.4> Show the minimal MIPS instruction sequence for a new instruction called `swap` that exchanges two registers. After the sequence completes, the Destination register has the original value of the Source register, and the Source register has the original value of the Destination register. Convert this instruction:

```
swap r10,r20
```

The hard part is that this sequence *must use only these two registers!* Hint: Try to use the new logical instructions: What is the value of (0 xor A)? (B xor B)?

4.28 [5] <§4.4> Show the minimal MIPS instruction sequence for a new instruction called `not` that takes the one's complement of a Source register and places it in a Destination register. Convert this instruction (accepted by the MIPS assembler):

```
not r10,r20
```

Hint: Try to use the new logical instructions.

4.29 [20] <§4.5> A simple check for overflow during addition is to see if the CarryIn to the most significant bit is *not* the same as the CarryOut of the most significant bit. Prove that this check is the same as in Figure 4.3 on page 177.

4.30 [10] <§4.5> Draw the gates for the Sum bit of an adder, given the equation on page 187.

4.31 [5] <§4.5> Rewrite the equations on page 197 for a carry lookahead logic for a 16-bit adder using a new notation. First use the names for the CarryIn signals of the individual bits of the adder. That is, use $c4$, $c8$, $c12$, ... instead of $C1$, $C2$, $C3$, ... Also, let $P_{i,j}$ mean a propagate signal for bits i to j, and $G_{i,j}$ mean a generate signal for bits i to j. For example, the equation

$$C2 = G1 + (P1 \cdot G0) + (P1 \cdot P0 \cdot c0)$$

can be rewritten as

$$c8 = G_{7,4} + (P_{7,4} \cdot G_{3,0}) + (P_{7,4} \cdot P_{3,0} \cdot c0)$$

This more general notation is useful in creating wider adders.

4.32 [15] <§4.5> {ex. 4.31} Write the equations for a carry lookahead logic for a *64-bit* adder using the new notation from Exercise 4.31 and using 16-bit adders as building blocks.

4.33 [10] <§4.5> Now calculate the relative performance of adders. Assume that hardware corresponding to any equation containing only OR or AND terms, such as the equations for pi and gi on page 192, takes one time unit T. Equations that consist of the OR of several AND terms, such as the equations for c1, c2, c3, and c4 on page 192, take 2T. Calculate the numbers and performance ratio for 4-bit adders for both ripple carry and carry lookahead. If the terms in equations are further defined by other equations, then add the appropriate delays for those intermediate equations, and continue recursively until the actual input bits of the adder are used in an equation.

4.34 [15] <§4.5> {ex. 4.33} This exercise is similar to Exercise 4.33, but this time calculate the relative speeds of a 16-bit adder using ripple carry only, ripple carry of 4-bit groups that use carry lookahead, and the carry lookahead scheme on page 197.

4.35 [15] <§4.5> {ex. 4.32, 4.33, 4.34} This exercise is similar to Exercises 4.33 and 4.34, but this time calculate the relative speeds of a 64-bit adder using ripple carry only, ripple carry of 4-bit groups that use carry lookahead, ripple carry of 16-bit groups that use carry lookahead, and the carry-lookahead scheme from Exercise 4.32.

In More Depth: Carry Save Adders

The adder in Figure 4.8 on page 186 is called a (3,2) adder because each stage adds 3 bits and produces 2 output bits. This piece of hardware is simple and fast; the problem comes from trying to get the CarryIn signal calculated in a timely fashion. When we are just adding two numbers together, there is little we can do with this observation, but when we are adding more than two operands, it is possible to reduce the cost of the carry. Perhaps the most likely case would be when trying to multiply more quickly by using many adders to add many numbers in a single clock cycle. Compared to the multiply algorithm in Figure 4.27 on page 206, such a scheme could multiply more than 10 times faster.

Assume we want to add four 4-bit numbers *a*, *b*, *e*, and *f*. Figure 4.48 shows how to use (3,2) adders to form two independent sums, called C′ and S′. Note that the C′ is shifted left 1 bit relative to S′. This technique of delaying carry propagation until the end of a sum of numbers is called *carry save addition*. To get the actual sum of these four numbers, we need to add C′ and S′ together using a normal adder.

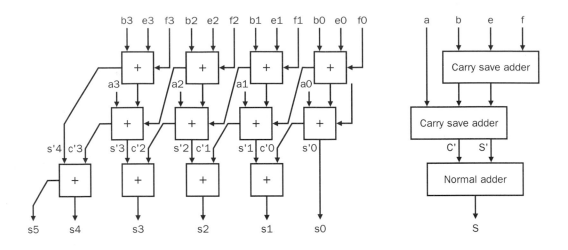

FIGURE 4.48 Carry save addition of four 4-bit numbers. The details are shown on the left, with the individual signals in lower case, and the higher level blocks are on the right in upper case. Note that the sum of 4 n-bit numbers can take n+2 bits.

4.36 [5] <§4.5> Assume the time delay through each 1-bit (3,2) adder is 2T. Calculate the time of adding four 4-bit numbers using three ripple carry adders versus the time using the carry save scheme in Figure 4.48.

4.37 [10] <§4.5> {ex. 4.33, 4.34, 4.36} Calculate the delays to add four 16-bit numbers using full carry lookahead adders versus carry save with a carry lookahead adder forming the final sum. The time unit T in Exercises 4.33 and 4.36 are the same.

4.38 [20] <§4.5, 4.6> {ex. 4.33, 4.34, 4.36, 4.37} Combinational multipliers refer to using many adders to try to reduce the time of multiplication. This exercise estimates the cost and speed of a combinational multiplier to multiply two 16-bit numbers. Assume that you have 16 intermediate terms M15, M14, . . . , M0, called *partial products*, that contain the multiplicand ANDed with multiplier bits m15, m14, . . . , m0. First show the block organization of the 16-bit carry save adders to add these 16 terms, as shown on the right in Figure 4.48. Then calculate the delays to add these 16 numbers. Compare this time to the iterative multiplication scheme in Figure 4.27 on page 206 but only assume 16 iterations using a 16-bit adder that has full carry lookahead whose speed was calculated in Exercise 4.34.

4.39 [30] <§4.6> The original reason for Booth's algorithm was to reduce the number of operations by avoiding operations when there were strings of 0s and 1s. Revise the algorithm on page 208 to look at 3 bits at a time and compute the multiplicand 2 bits at a time. Fill in the following table to determine the 2-bit Booth encoding:

Current bits		Previous bit	Operation	Reason
a_{i+1}	a_i	a_{i-1}		
0	0	0		
0	0	1		
0	1	0		
0	1	1		
1	0	0		
1	0	1		
1	1	0		
1	1	1		

Assume that you have both the multiplicand and $2 \times$ multiplicand already in registers. Explain the reason for the operation on each line, and show a 6-bit example that runs faster using this algorithm. Hint: Try dividing to conquer; see what the operations would be in each of the eight cases in the table using a 2-bit Booth algorithm, and then optimize the pair of operations.

4.40 [30] <§4.6, 4.7> The division algorithm in Figure 4.37 on page 220 is called *restoring division*, since each time the result of subtracting the divisor from the dividend is negative you must add the divisor back into the dividend to restore the original value. Recall that shift left is the same as multiplying by 2. Let's look at the value of the left half of the Remainder again, starting with step 3b of the divide algorithm and then going to step 2:

$$(\text{Remainder} + \text{Divisor}) \times 2 - \text{Divisor}$$

This value is created from restoring the Remainder by adding the Divisor, shifting the sum left, and then subtracting the Divisor. Simplifying the result we get

$$\text{Remainder} \times 2 + \text{Divisor} \times 2 - \text{Divisor} = \text{Remainder} \times 2 + \text{Divisor}$$

Based on this observation, write a *nonrestoring division* algorithm using the notation of Figure 4.37 that does not add the Divisor to the Remainder in step 3b. Show that your algorithm works by dividing $0000\ 0111_{two}$ by 0010_{two}.

4.41 [5] <§4.8> Add $6.42_{ten} \times 10^1$ to $9.51_{ten} \times 10^2$, assuming that you have only three significant digits, first with guard and round digits and then without them.

4.42 [5] <§4.8> This exercise is similar to Exercise 4.41, but this time use the numbers $8.76_{ten} \times 10^1$ and $1.47_{ten} \times 10^2$.

4.43 [25] <§4.8> Derive the floating-point algorithm for division as we did for addition and multiplication on pages 230 through 240. First divide $1.110_{ten} \times 10^{10}$ by $1.100_{ten} \times 10^{-5}$, showing the same steps that we did in the example starting on page 232. Then derive the floating-point division algorithm using a format similar to the multiplication algorithm in Figure 4.43 on page 239.

4.44 [30] <§4.8> The Elaboration on page 243 explains the four rounding modes of IEEE 754 and the extra bit, called the *sticky bit*, needed in addition to the 2 bits called *guard* and *round*. Guard is the first bit, round is the second bit, and sticky represents whether the remaining bits are 0 or not. Fill in the following table with logical equations that are functions of guard(g), round(r), and sticky(s) for the result of a floating-point addition that creates Sum. Let p be the proper number of bits in the significand for a given precision and Sum_p be the pth most significant bit of Sum. A blank box means that the p most significant bits of the sum are correctly rounded. If you place an equation in a box, a false equation means that the p bits are correctly rounded; a true equation means add 1 to the pth most significant bit of Sum.

Rounding mode	Sum $\geq$ 0	Sum < 0
Toward −		
Toward +		
Truncate		
Nearest Even		

4.45 [30] <§4.5> If you have access to a computer containing a MIPS processor, write a loop in assembly language that sets registers $26 and $27 to an initial value, and then loop for several seconds, checking the contents of these registers. Print the values if they change. See the Elaboration on page 179 for an explanation of why they change. Can you find a reason for the particular values you observe?

5

The Processor:
Datapath
and Control

In a major matter,
no details are small.

French Proverb

The Five Classic Components of a Computer

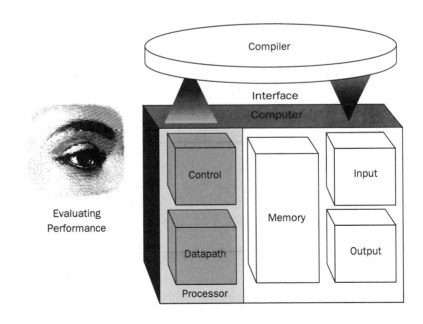

5.1   Introduction

In Chapter 2, we saw that the performance of a machine was determined by three key factors: instruction count, clock cycle time, and clock cycles per instruction. The compiler and the instruction set architecture, which we examined in Chapters 3 and 4, determine the instruction count required for a given program. However, both the clock cycle time and the number of clock cycles per instruction are determined by the implementation of the processor. In this chapter, we construct the datapath and control unit for two different implementations of the MIPS instruction set.

We will be designing an implementation that includes the core of the MIPS instruction set, including:

- The memory-reference instructions *load word* (lw) and *store word* (sw)

- The arithmetic-logical instructions add, sub, and, or, and slt

- The branch equal instruction (beq); and the jump instruction (j), which we add last.

This subset does not include all the integer instructions (for example, multiply and divide are missing), nor does it include any floating-point instructions. However, the key principles used in creating a datapath and designing the control will be illustrated. The implementation of the remaining instructions is similar.

In examining the implementation, we will have the opportunity to see how the instruction set architecture determines many aspects of the implementation, and how the choice of various implementation strategies affects the clock rate and CPI for the machine. Many of the key design principles introduced in earlier chapters can be illustrated by looking at the implementation. This includes the guidelines *Make the common case fast* and *Simplicity favors regularity*. In addition, most of the concepts used to implement the MIPS subset in this chapter and the next are the same ideas that are used to construct a broad spectrum of computers, from high-performance machines to general-purpose microprocessors to special-purpose processors used with increasing frequency in products ranging from VCRs to automobiles.

An Overview of the Implementation

In Chapters 3 and 4, we looked at a core subset of MIPS instructions, including the integer arithmetic-logical instructions, the memory-reference instructions, and the branch instructions. Much of what needs to be done to implement these instructions is the same, independent of the exact type of instruction. For every instruction, the first two steps are identical:

1. Send the program counter (PC) to a memory that contains the code to fetch the instruction.

2. Read one or two registers using fields of the instruction to select the registers to read. For a load instruction we need to read only one register, but all other instructions require that we read two registers.

After these two steps, the actions required to complete the instruction depend on the instruction type. However, for each of the three instruction types (memory-reference, arithmetic-logical, and branches), the actions are largely the same, independent of the exact opcode. Even across different instruction classes there are some similarities. For example, all instruction types use the ALU after reading the registers. The memory reference instructions use the ALU for an effective address calculation, the arithmetic-logical instructions for the opcode execution, and branches for comparison. As we can see, the simplicity and regularity of the instruction set simplifies the implementation by making the execution of many of the instruction types similar.

After using the ALU, the actions required to complete the different instruction types differ. A memory-reference instruction will need to access the memory containing the data to complete a store or get a word that is being loaded. An arithmetic-logical instruction must write the data from the ALU back into a register. Lastly, for a branch instruction, we may need to change the next instruction address based on the comparison. Figure 5.1 shows the high-level view of a MIPS implementation. In the remainder of the chapter, we refine this view to fill in the details, which requires that we add further functional units, increase the number of connections between units, and, of course, add a control unit to control what actions are taken for different instruction types. Before we begin to create a more complete implementation, we need to discuss a few principles of logic design.

A Word about Logic Conventions and Clocking

To discuss the design of a machine, we must decide how the logic implementing the machine will operate and how the machine is clocked. This section reviews a few key ideas in digital logic that we will use extensively in this chapter. The reader who has little or no background in digital logic will find it helpful to read through Appendix B before continuing.

Within a logic design, it is often convenient for the designer to change the mapping between a logically true or false signal and the high or low voltage level. Thus, in some parts of a design, a signal that is logically asserted may actually be an electrically low signal, while in others an electrically high signal is

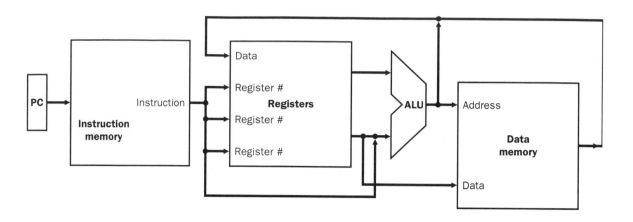

FIGURE 5.1 An abstract view of the implementation of the MIPS subset showing the major functional units and the major connections between them. All instructions start by using the program counter to supply the instruction address to the instruction memory. After the instruction is fetched, the register operands used by an instruction are specified by fields of that instruction. Once the register operands have been fetched, they can be operated on to compute a memory address (for a load or store), to compute an arithmetic result (for an integer arithmetic-logical instruction), or a compare (for a branch). If the instruction is an arithmetic-logical instruction, the result from the ALU must be written to the Result register. If the operation is a load or store, the ALU result is used as an address to either store a value from the registers or load a value from memory into the registers. The result from the ALU or memory is written back into the register file. Branches require the use of the ALU output to determine the next instruction address, which requires some control logic, as we will see.

asserted. To maintain consistency we will use the word *asserted* to indicate a signal that is logically high and *assert* to specify that a signal should be driven logically high.

The functional units in the MIPS implementation consist of two different types of logic elements: elements that contain state and elements that operate on data values. The elements that operate on data values are all *combinational*, which means that their outputs depend only on the current inputs. Given the same input, a combinational element always produces the same output. The ALU shown in Figure 5.1 and discussed in detail in Chapter 4 is a combinational element. Given a set of inputs, it always produces the same output, because it has no internal storage.

Other elements in the design are not combinational, but instead contain *state*. An element contains state if it has some internal storage. We call these elements *state elements*, because, if we pulled the plug on the machine, we could restart it by loading the state elements with the values they contained before we pulled the plug. Furthermore, if we saved and restored the state elements, it would be as if the machine had never lost power. Thus, these state elements completely characterize the machine. In Figure 5.1, the instruction and data memories as well as the registers are all examples of state elements.

A state element has at least two inputs and one output. The required inputs are the data value, which is to be written, and the clock, which determines when the data input value is stored. The output provides the value that was written in the previous clock. For example, the simplest state element is a D-type flip-flop (see Appendix B), which has exactly these two inputs (a value and a clock) and one output. In addition to flip-flops, our MIPS implementation also uses two other types of state elements: memories and registers, both of which appear in Figure 5.1. The clock is used only to determine when the state element should be written; a state element can be read at any time.

Logic components that contain state are also called *sequential*, because their outputs depend on both their inputs and the contents of the internal state. For example, the output from the functional unit representing the registers depends on both the register numbers supplied and on what was written into the registers previously. The operation of both the combinational and sequential elements and their construction are discussed in more detail in Appendix B.

A *clocking methodology* defines when signals can be read and when they can be written. It is important to distinguish the timing of reads from writes, because, if a signal is written at the same time it is read, the value of the read could correspond to the old value, the newly written value, or even some mix of the two! Needless to say, computer designs cannot tolerate this unpredictability. A clocking methodology is designed to prevent this circumstance.

For simplicity, we will assume an *edge-triggered* clocking methodology. An edge-triggered clocking methodology means that any values stored in the machine are updated only on a clock edge. Thus, the state elements all update their internal storage on the clock edge. Because only state elements can store a data value, any collection of combinational logic must have its inputs coming from a set of state elements and its outputs written into a set of state elements. The inputs are values that came from a previous clock cycle, while the outputs are values that will be used in a following clock cycle. Figures 5.2 and 5.3 show two examples. In the simpler example shown in Figure 5.2, the block of combinational logic operates in a single clock cycle. In this case, all signals must propagate from state element 1, through the combinational logic, and to state element 2 in the time of one clock cycle, and state element 2 can be written at the end of every clock cycle. The time necessary for the signals to reach state element 2 defines the length of the clock cycle.

The second example requires several clock cycles for the signals to propagate from state element 1 through the combinational logic to state element 2. In this case, the signal that controls the writing of the second state element must be controlled so that the internal storage in the state element is not updated on every clock, but only on certain clocks. The state element is still up-

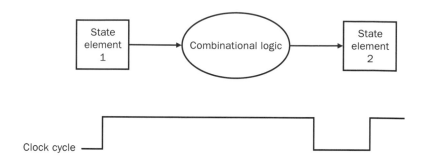

FIGURE 5.2 Combinational logic, state elements, and the clock are closely related. In a synchronous digital system, the clock determines when elements with state will write values into internal storage. Any inputs to a state element must reach a stable value (that is, have reached a value from which they will not change until after the clock edge) before the active clock edge causes the state to be updated.

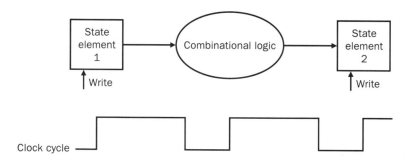

FIGURE 5.3 State element 2 is not written on every clock, but only on a clock edge when the write signal is also asserted. This organization can be used to allow the combinational logic block to take several clock cycles to propagate from the inputs at state element 1. The output of state element 1 also must not change during the time the signal is propagating through the combinational logic. Thus, state element 1 must also have a controlled write signal. If, for example, it requires two clock periods to propagate through the combinational logic, then the write control for state element 1 must be deasserted during the clock cycle that precedes the clock cycle in which state element 2 is written.

dated on a clock edge, but only if the write signal is also asserted, as shown in Figure 5.3. For this to work properly, it is critical that the output of state element 1 also does not change during the clock cycles in which the signal is propagating through the combinational logic. Both state elements will require write signals and these signals must be coordinated so that the clocking methodolo-

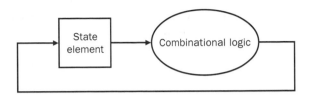

FIGURE 5.4 An edge-triggered methodology allows a state element to be read and written in the same clock cycle without creating a race that could lead to indeterminate data values. Of course, the clock cycle still must be long enough so that the input values are stable when the active clock edge occurs.

gy is consistent. This type of state element will be used extensively in the multicycle design that we will explore in the second half of this chapter. For simplicity, we do not show the write signal when a state element is updated on every active clock edge. Although we will not show the clock signal explicitly, remember that all state elements have the clock as an input.

An edge-triggered methodology allows us to read the contents of a register, send the value through some combinational logic, and write the register in the same clock cycle, as shown in Figure 5.4. It doesn't matter whether we assume that all writes take place on the rising clock edge or on the falling clock edge, since the inputs to the combinational logic block cannot change except on the chosen clock edge. In Appendix B we briefly discuss additional timing constraints (such as set-up and hold times) as well as other timing methodologies.

Nearly all of these state and logic elements will have inputs and outputs that are 32 bits wide, since that is the width of most of the data handled by the processor. We will make it clear whenever a unit has an input or output that is other than 32 bits in width. The figures will indicate *buses*, which are signals wider than 1 bit, with thicker lines. Arrows help clarify the direction of the flow of data between elements. Color indicates a control signal as opposed to a signal that carries data; this distinction will become clearer as we proceed through this chapter.

The MIPS Subset Implementation

We will start with a simple implementation that uses a single long clock cycle for every instruction and follows the general form of Figure 5.1. In this first design, every instruction begins execution on one clock edge and completes execution on the next clock edge.

While easier to understand, this approach is not really practical, since it would be slower than an implementation that allows different instruction types to take different numbers of clock cycles, each of which could be shorter. After designing the control for this simple machine, we will look at an implementation that uses multiple clock cycles for each instruction. This implementation is more realistic but also requires more complex control. In this chapter, we will take the specification of the control to the level of logic equations and finite state machine specifications. From either representation, a modern computer-aided design (CAD) system can synthesize a hardware implementation. Before closing the chapter, we will discuss how exceptions (mentioned in Chapter 4) are implemented.

5.2   Building a Datapath

A reasonable way to start a datapath design is to examine the major components required to execute each type of MIPS instruction. Let's start by looking at which datapath elements each instruction needs and build up the sections of the datapath for each instruction type from these elements. When we show the datapath elements initially, we will also show their control signals. After that, we will not include the control signals in the actual datapath until section 5.3, when we add the control unit.

The first element we will need is a place to store the instructions of a program. A memory unit, which is a state element, is used to hold and supply instructions given an address, as shown in Figure 5.5. The address of the instruction must also be kept in a state element, which we call the program counter, also shown in Figure 5.5. Lastly, we will need an adder to increment the PC to the address of the next instruction. This adder, which is combinational, can be built from the ALU we designed in the last chapter simply by wiring the control lines so that the control always specifies an add operation. We will draw this ALU with the label *Add*, as in Figure 5.5, to indicate that it has been permanently made an adder and cannot perform the other ALU functions.

To execute any instruction, we must start by fetching the instruction from memory. To prepare for executing the next instruction, we must also increment the program counter so that it points at the next instruction, 4 bytes later. The datapath for this step, shown in Figure 5.6, uses the three elements from Figure 5.5.

Now let's consider the R-format instructions. They all read two registers, perform an ALU operation on the contents of the registers, and write the result. We call these instructions either *R-type instructions* or *arithmetic-logical instructions* (since they perform arithmetic or logical operations). This instruction class includes add, sub, and, or, and slt; recall that a typical instance of such an instruction is add $1, $2, $3, which reads $2 and $3 and writes $1. The processor's 32 registers are stored in a structure called a *register file*. A register

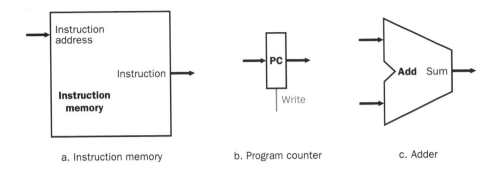

a. Instruction memory   b. Program counter   c. Adder

FIGURE 5.5 Two state elements are needed to store and access instructions, and an adder is needed to compute the next instruction address. The state elements are the instruction memory and the program counter. The instruction memory need only provide read access, because the datapath does not write instructions. (We will need to write the instruction memory when we load the program; this is not hard to add, and we ignore it for simplicity.) Since the instruction memory unit can only be read, we do not include a read control signal; this simplifies the design. Control signals, such as the write signal on the PC, are shown in color. The program counter is a 32-bit register that will be written under the control of a write signal. The adder is an ALU wired to always perform an add of its two 32-bit inputs and place the result on its output.

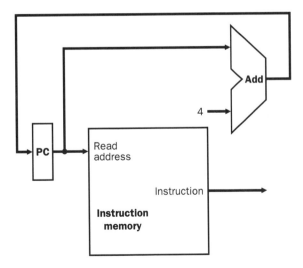

FIGURE 5.6 A portion of the datapath used for fetching instructions and incrementing the program counter. The fetched instruction is used by other parts of the datapath.

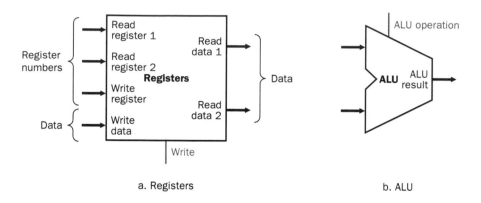

a. Registers   b. ALU

FIGURE 5.7 The two elements needed to implement R-format ALU operations are the register file and the ALU.
The register file contains all the registers and provides two read ports and one write port. The register file always provides the contents of the registers corresponding to the Read register inputs on the outputs, while the writes must be explicitly controlled with the write control signal. The inputs carrying the register number to the register file are all 5 bits wide, whereas the lines carrying data values are 32 bits wide. (The design of multiported register files is discussed in section B.5 of Appendix B.) The operation to be performed by the ALU is controlled with the ALU operation signal, which will be 3 bits wide, using the ALU designed in the previous chapter (see Figure 4.18). We will need the Zero detection output of the ALU shortly to implement branches, and we will add it then. The overflow output will not be needed until section 5.6, when we discuss exceptions; we omit it until then.

file is a collection of registers in which any register can be read or written by specifying the number of the register in the file. The register file contains the register state of the machine. In addition, we will need an ALU to operate on the values read from the registers.

Because the R-format instructions have three register operands, we will need to read two data words from the register file and write one data word into the register file for each instruction. For each data word to be read from the registers, we need an input to the register file that specifies the register number to be read and an output from the register file that will carry the value that has been read from the registers. To write a data word, we will need two inputs: one to specify the register number to be written and one to supply the data to be written into the register. Thus, we need a total of four inputs (three for register numbers and one for data) and two outputs (both for data), as shown in Figure 5.7. The register file always outputs the contents of whatever register numbers are on the Read register inputs. Writes, however, are controlled by the write control signal, which must be asserted for a write to occur when the clock input falls. The register number inputs are 5 bits wide to specify 1 of 32 registers ($32 = 2^5$), whereas the data input and two data outputs are each 32 bits wide. The ALU takes two 32-bit inputs and produces a 32-bit re-

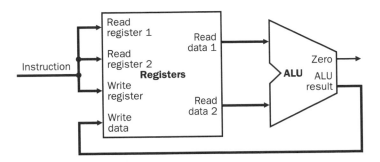

FIGURE 5.8 The datapath for R-type instructions. The ALU discussed in Chapter 4 can be controlled to provide all the basic ALU functions required for R-type instructions.

sult. The ALU, shown in Figure 5.7, is controlled by the 3-bit signal described in Chapter 4.

The datapath for these R-type instructions, which uses the register file and the ALU of Figure 5.7, is shown in Figure 5.8. Since the register numbers come from fields of the instruction, we show the instruction, which comes from Figure 5.6, as connected to the register inputs of the register file.

Next, consider the MIPS load and store instructions, which have the general form: `lw $1,offset_value($2)` or `sw $1,offset_value($2)`. These instructions compute a memory address by adding the base register ($2) to the 16-bit signed, offset field contained in the instruction. If the instruction is a store, the value to be stored must also be read from the register file ($1). If the instruction is a load, the value read from memory must be written into the register file in the specified register ($1). Thus, we will need both the register file and the ALU, which are required for R-format instructions and shown in Figure 5.7. In addition, we will need a unit to sign-extend the 16-bit offset field in the instruction to a 32-bit signed value, and a data memory unit to read from or write to. The data memory must be written on store instructions; hence, it has both read and write control signals, as well as an input for the data to be written into memory. Figure 5.9 shows these two elements.

Figure 5.10 shows how to combine these elements to build the datapath for a load word or a store word instruction, assuming that the instruction has already been fetched. The register number inputs for the register file come from fields of the instruction, as does the offset value, which after sign extension becomes the second ALU input.

The `beq` instruction has three operands, two registers that are compared for equality, and a 16-bit offset used to compute the branch target address relative

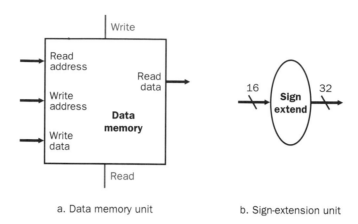

a. Data memory unit   b. Sign-extension unit

FIGURE 5.9 The two units needed to implement loads and stores are the data memory unit and the sign-extension unit, in addition to the register file and ALU of Figure 5.7. The memory unit is a state element with inputs for the read address, write address, and the write data, and a single output for the read result. There are separate read and write controls, although only one of these may be asserted on any given clock. The sign-extension unit has a 16-bit input that is sign-extended into a 32-bit result appearing on the output (see Chapter 4, page 172).

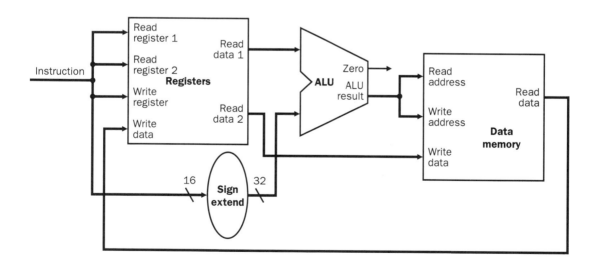

FIGURE 5.10 The datapath for a load or store that does a register access. It is followed by a memory address calculation, then a read or write from memory, and a write into the register file if the instruction is a load.

to the branch instruction address. Its form is `beq $1,$2,offset`. To implement this instruction, we must compute the branch target address by adding the sign-extended offset field of the instruction to the PC. As noted in an Elaboration in Chapter 3, there are two details in the instruction set architecture to which we must pay attention.

- The instruction set architecture specifies that the base for the branch address calculation is the address of the instruction following the branch. Since we compute PC + 4 (the address of the next instruction) in the instruction fetch datapath, it is easy to use this value as the base for computing the branch target address.

- The architecture also states that the offset field is shifted left 2 bits so that it is a word offset; this shift is helpful because it increases the effective range of the offset field by a factor of 4.

To deal with the latter complication, we will need to shift the offset field by two. This is done in the datapath figures beginning with Figure 5.11, which shows the branch datapath. (Later on we will also need to adjust jump offsets.)

In addition to computing the branch target address, we must also determine whether the next instruction is the instruction that follows sequentially or the instruction at the branch target address. When the condition is true (i.e., the operands are equal), the branch target address becomes the new PC, and we say that the branch is *taken*. If the operands are not equal, the incremented PC should replace the current PC (just as for any other normal instruction); in this case, we say that the branch is *not taken*.

Thus, the branch must do two operations: compute the branch target address and compare the register contents. To compute the branch target address, we will need a sign-extension unit, just like that in Figure 5.9, and an adder. We must also modify the instruction fetch portion of the datapath. To perform the compare, we need to use the register file shown in Figure 5.7 to supply the two register operands (although we will not need to write into the register file). In addition, the comparison can be done using the ALU we designed in Chapter 4. Since that ALU provides an output signal that indicates whether the result was 0, we can send the two register operands to the ALU with the control set to do a subtract. If the Zero signal out of the ALU unit is asserted, we know that the two values are equal. Although the Zero output always signals if the result is 0, we will be using it only to implement the equal test of branches. Later, we will show exactly how to connect the control signals of the ALU for use in the datapath. The datapath for a branch combines these elements, as shown in Figure 5.11.

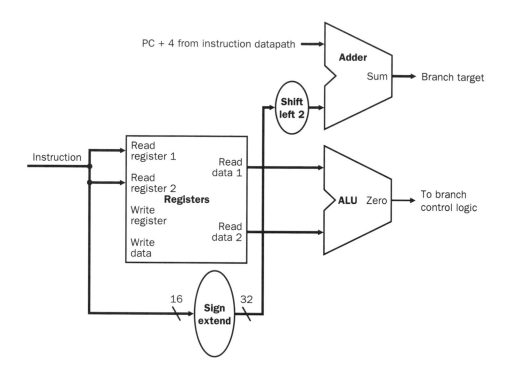

FIGURE 5.11 The datapath for a branch uses an ALU for evaluation of the branch condition and a separate adder for computing the branch target as the sum of the incremented PC and the sign-extended, lower 16 bits of the instruction (the branch displacement), shifted left 2 bits. The unit labeled *Shift left 2* performs the shift adding 00_{two} to the bottom of the sign-extended offset field. Since we know that the offset was sign-extended from 16 bits, the shift will throw away only "sign bits." Control logic is used to decide whether the incremented PC or branch target should replace the PC, based on the Zero output of the ALU.

The jump instruction operates by replacing a portion of the PC with the lower 26 bits of the instruction shifted left by two bits. This shift is accomplished simply by concatenating 00 to the jump offset.

Now that we have examined the datapaths needed for the individual instruction types, we can combine them into a single datapath and add the control to complete the implementation. The datapaths shown in Figures 5.6, 5.8, 5.10, and 5.11 will be the building blocks for two different implementations. In the next section we will create an implementation that uses a single clock cycle for every instruction. In section 5.4, we will look at an implementation that uses multiple clock cycles for every instruction.

5.3 A Simple Implementation Scheme

In this section, we look at what might be thought of as the simplest possible implementation of our MIPS subset. We build this simple datapath and control by assembling the datapath segments of the last section and adding control lines as needed. This simple implementation covers *load word* (lw), *store word* (sw), *branch equal* (beq), and the arithmetic-logical instructions add, sub, and, or, and slt. We will later enhance the design to include a *jump* instruction (j).

Creating a Single Datapath

Suppose we were going to build a datapath from the pieces we looked at in Figures 5.6, 5.8, 5.10, and 5.11. The simplest datapath might attempt to execute all instructions in one clock cycle. This means that no datapath resource can be used more than once per instruction and that any element needed more than once must be duplicated. We therefore need a memory for instructions separate from one for data. While some of the functional units will need to be duplicated when the individual datapaths of the previous section are combined, many of the elements can be shared by different instruction flows. To share a datapath element between two different instruction types, we may need to allow multiple connections to the input of an element and have a control signal select among the inputs. This is commonly done with a device called a *multiplexor*, although this device might better be called a *data selector*. The multiplexor, which was introduced in the last chapter (Figure 4.7 on page 184), selects from among several inputs based on the setting of its control lines.

Example

The arithmetic-logical (or R-type) instruction datapath of Figure 5.8 on page 279 and the memory instruction datapath of Figure 5.10 on page 280 are quite similar. The key differences are

- The second input to the ALU unit is either a register (if it's an R-type instruction) or the sign-extended lower half of the instruction (if it's a memory instruction).

- The value written into the Result register comes from the ALU (for an R-type instruction) or the memory (for a load).

Show how to combine the two datapaths using multiplexors, without duplicating the functional units that are in common in Figures 5.8 and 5.10. Ignore the control of the multiplexors.

Answer

To combine the two datapaths and use only a single register file and an ALU, we must support two different sources for the second ALU input, as well as two different sources for the data stored into the register file. Thus, one multiplexor is placed at the ALU input and another at the data input to the register file. Figure 5.12 shows the combined datapath.

The instruction fetch portion of the datapath, shown in Figure 5.6 on page 277, can easily be added to the datapath in Figure 5.12. Figure 5.13 shows the result. The combined datapath includes a memory for instructions and a separate memory for data. This combined datapath requires both an adder and an ALU, since the adder is used to increment the PC, while the other ALU is used for executing the instruction in the same clock cycle.

Now we can combine all the pieces to make a simple datapath for the MIPS architecture by adding the datapath for branches from Figure 5.11. Figure 5.14 shows the datapath we obtain by composing the separate pieces. The branch instruction uses the main ALU for comparison of the register operands, so we

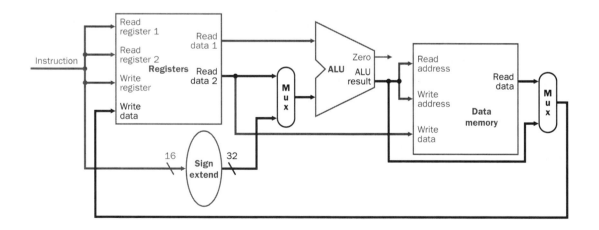

FIGURE 5.12 Combining the datapaths for the memory instructions and the R-type instructions. This example shows how a single datapath can be assembled from the pieces. The multiplexors and their connections are highlighted.

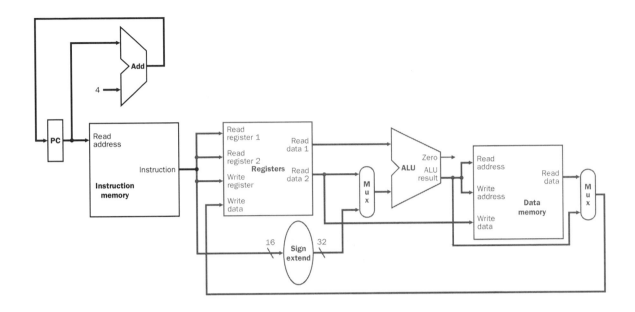

FIGURE 5.13 The instruction fetch portion of the datapath from Figure 5.6 is appended to the datapath of Figure 5.12 that handles memory and ALU instructions. The addition is highlighted. The result is a datapath that supports many operations of the MIPS instruction set—branches and jumps are the major missing pieces.

must keep the adder in Figure 5.11 for computing the branch target address. An additional multiplexor is required to select either the sequentially following instruction address (PC + 4) or the branch target address to be written into the PC. Because the PC will be written with one of these two values on every clock, we do not need an explicit write control signal.

Now that we have completed this simple datapath, we can add the control unit. The control unit must be able to take inputs and generate a write signal for each state element, the selector control for each multiplexor, and the ALU control. The ALU control is different in a number of ways, and it will be useful to design it first before we design the rest of the control unit.

The ALU Control

Recall from Chapter 4 that the ALU has three control inputs. Only five of the possible eight input combinations are used. Figure 4.19 on page 195 showed the five following combinations:

ALU control input	Function
000	And
001	Or
010	Add
110	Subtract
111	Set-on-less-than

Depending on the instruction type, the ALU will need to perform one of these five functions. For load and store instructions, we use the ALU to compute the memory address by addition. For the R-type instructions, the ALU needs to perform one of five actions (subtract, add, AND, OR, or set-on-less-than), depending on the value of the 6-bit funct (or function) field in the low-order

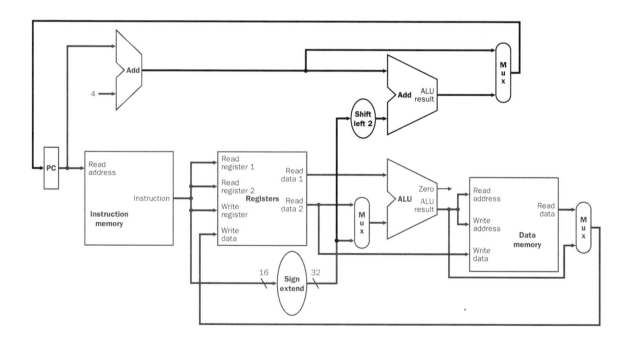

FIGURE 5.14 The simple datapath for the MIPS architecture combines the elements required by the different instruction classes. This datapath can execute the basic instructions (load/store word, ALU operations, and branches) in a single clock cycle. The additions to Figure 5.13, which are needed to implement branches, are highlighted.

Instruction opcode	ALUOp	Instruction operation	Function code	Desired ALU action	ALU control input
LW	00	load word	XXXXXX	add	010
SW	00	store word	XXXXXX	add	010
Branch equal	01	branch equal	XXXXXX	subtract	110
R-type	10	add	100000	add	010
R-type	10	subtract	100010	subtract	110
R-type	10	AND	100100	and	000
R-type	10	OR	100101	or	001
R-type	10	set-on-less-than	101010	set-on-less-than	111

FIGURE 5.15 This table shows how the ALU control bits are set depending on the ALUOp control bits and the different function codes for the R-type instruction The opcode, listed in the first column, determines the setting of the ALUOp bits. All the encodings are shown in binary. Notice that when the ALUOp code is 00 or 01, the output fields do not depend on the function code field; in this case, we say that we "don't care" about the value of the function code, and the function field is shown as XXXXXX. When the ALUOp value is 10, then the function code is used to set the ALU control input.

bits of the instruction (see Chapter 3, page 104). For branch equal, the ALU must perform a subtraction.

We can generate the 3-bit ALU control input using a small control unit that has as inputs the function field of the instruction and a 2-bit control field, which we call ALUOp. ALUOp indicates whether the operation to be performed should be add (00) for loads and stores, subtract (01) for beq, or the operation encoded in the function field (10). The output of the ALU control unit is a 3-bit signal that directly controls the ALU by generating one of the five 3-bit combinations shown on the previous page. In Figure 5.15 we show how to set the ALU control inputs based on the 2-bit ALUOp control and the 6-bit function code. For completeness, the relationship between the ALUOp bits and the instruction opcode is also shown. Later in this chapter we will see how the ALUOp bits are generated from the main control unit.

There are several different ways to implement the mapping from the 2-bit ALUOp field and the 6-bit function code field to the three ALU operation control bits. Because only a small number of the 64 possible values of the function field are of interest and the function field is used only when the ALUOp bits equal 10, we can use a small piece of logic that recognizes the subset of possible values and causes the correct setting of the ALU control bits. As a step in designing this logic, it is useful to create a truth table for the interesting combinations of the function code field and the ALUOp bits as we've done in Figure 5.16 ; this truth table shows how the 3-bit ALU control is set depending on these two input fields. Since the full truth table is very large ($2^8 = 256$ entries) and the ALU control is unused for most of these input combinations, we show only the truth table entries for which the ALU control is needed.

| ALUOp | | Function code | | | | | | Operation |
ALUOp1	ALUOp0	F5	F4	F3	F2	F1	F0	
0	0	X	X	X	X	X	X	010
X	1	X	X	X	X	X	X	110
1	X	X	X	0	0	0	0	010
1	X	X	X	0	0	1	0	110
1	X	X	X	0	1	0	0	000
1	X	X	X	0	1	0	1	001
1	X	X	X	1	0	1	0	111

FIGURE 5.16 The truth table for the three ALU control bits (called Operation) as a function of the ALUOp and function code field. Only the entries for which the ALU control is not all zeroes are shown. Some don't care entries have been added. For example, the ALUOp does not use the encoding 11, so the truth table can contain entries 1X and X1, rather than 10 and 01. Also, when the function code field is used, the first two bits (F5 and F4) of these instructions are always 10, so they are don't care terms and are replaced with XX in the truth table.

Throughout this chapter, we will use this practice of showing only the truth table entries that have nonzero output values. (This practice has a disadvantage that we will discuss shortly.)

Because in many instances we do not care about the values of some of the inputs and to keep the tables compact, we also include "don't care" terms. A don't care term in this truth table (represented by an X) indicates that the output is true, independent of the value of the corresponding input. For example, when the ALUOp bits are 00, as in the first line of the table in Figure 5.16, we always set the ALU control to 010, independent of the function code. In this case, then, the function code inputs will be don't cares in this line of the truth table. Later, we will see examples of another type of don't care term. The reader unfamiliar with the concept of don't care terms should see Appendix B for more information.

Once the truth table has been constructed, it can be optimized and then turned into gates. This process is completely mechanical. Optimization takes advantage of the don't cares in the table.

A logic block that implements the ALU control function will have three distinct outputs (called Operation2, Operation1, and Operation0), each corresponding to one of the three bits of the ALU control. The logic function for each output is constructed by combining all the truth table entries that set that particular output. For example, the low-order bit of the ALU control (Operation0) is set by the last two entries of the truth table in Figure 5.16. Thus, the truth table for Operation0 will have these two entries. In addition, looking at the truth tables for each output individually allows us to minimize the logic required by exploiting commonalities among the terms associated with an output. Figure 5.17 shows the truth tables for each of the three ALU control bits.

ALUOp		Function code fields					
ALUOp1	ALUOp0	F5	F4	F3	F2	F1	F0
X	1	X	X	X	X	X	X
1	X	X	X	X	X	1	X

a. The truth table for Operation2 = 1. This table corresponds to the left bit of the Operation field in Figure 5.16.

ALUOp		Function code fields					
ALUOp1	ALUOp0	F5	F4	F3	F2	F1	F0
0	X	X	X	X	X	X	X
X	X	X	X	X	0	X	X

b. The truth table for Operation1 = 1.

ALUOp		Function code fields					
ALUOp1	ALUOp0	F5	F4	F3	F2	F1	F0
1	X	X	X	X	X	X	1
1	X	X	X	1	X	X	X

c. The truth table for Operation0 = 1.

FIGURE 5.17 The truth tables for the three ALU control lines. Only the entries for which the output is 1 are shown. The bits in each field are numbered from right to left starting with 0; thus, F5 is the most significant bit of the function field and F0 is the least significant bit. Similarly, the names of the signals corresponding to the 3-bit operation code supplied to the ALU are Operation2, Operation1, and Operation0 (with the last being the least significant bit). Thus, the truth table above shows the input combinations for which the ALU control should be 010, 001, 110, or 111 (the combinations 011, 100, and 101 are not used). The ALUOp bits are named ALUOp1 and ALUOp0. The three output values depend on the 2-bit ALUOp field and, when that field is equal to 10, the 6-bit function code in the instruction. Accordingly, when the ALUOp field is not equal to 10, we don't care about the function code value (it is represented by an X). See Appendix B for more background on don't cares.

We have also taken advantage of the common structure in each truth table to incorporate additional don't cares. For example, the five lines in the truth table of Figure 5.16 that set Operation1 are reduced to just two entries in Figure 5.17. A logic minimization program will use the don't care terms to reduce the number of gates and the number of inputs to each gate in a logic gate realization of these truth tables.

From the simplified truth table in Figure 5.17, we can generate the logic shown in Figure 5.18, which we call the *ALU control block*. This process is straightforward and can be done with a computer-aided design (CAD) program. An example of how the logic gates can be derived from the truth tables is given in the legend to Figure 5.18.

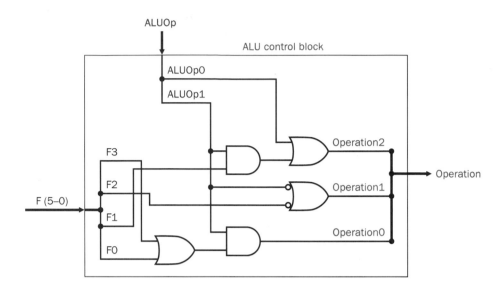

FIGURE 5.18 The ALU control block generates the three ALU control bits, based on the function code and ALUOp bits. This logic is generated directly from the truth table in Figure 5.17. Only 4 of the 6 bits in the function code are actually needed as inputs, since the upper 2 bits are always don't cares. Let's examine how this logic relates to the truth table of Figure 5.17. Consider the Operation2 output, which is generated by two lines in the truth table for Operation2. The second line is the AND of two terms (F1 = 1 and ALUOp1 = 1); the top two-input AND gate corresponds to this term. The other term that causes Operation2 to be asserted is simply ALUOp0. These two terms are combined with an OR gate whose output is Operation2. The outputs Operation0 and Operation1 are derived in similar fashion from the truth table.

This ALU control logic is simple because there are only three outputs, and only a few of the possible input combinations need to be recognized. If a large number of possible ALU function codes had to be transformed into ALU control signals, this simple method would not be efficient. Instead, one could use a decoder, a memory, or a structured array of logic gates. These techniques are described in detail in Appendices B and C.

Elaboration: In general, a logic equation and truth table representation of a logic function are equivalent. (We discuss this in further detail in Appendix B.) However, when a truth table only specifies the entries that result in nonzero outputs, it may not completely describe the logic function. A full truth table completely indicates all don't care entries. For example, the encoding 11 for ALUOp always generates a don't care in the output. Thus, a complete truth table would have XXX in the output portion for all entries with 11 in the ALUOp field. These don't care entries allow us to replace the

Field	0	rs	rt	rd	shamt	funct
Bit positions	31–26	25–21	20–16	15–11	10–6	5–0

a. R-type instruction

Field	35 or 43	rs	rt	address
Bit positions	31–26	25–21	20–16	15–0

b. Load or store instruction

Field	4	rs	rt	address
Bit positions	31–26	25–21	20–16	15–0

c. Branch instruction

FIGURE 5.19 The three instruction classes (R-type, load and store, and branch) use two different instruction formats. The jump instructions use another format, which we will discuss shortly. **a.** Instruction format for R-format instructions, which all have an opcode of 0. These instructions have three register operands: rs, rt, and rd. Fields rs and rt are sources, and rd is the destination. The ALU function is in the field funct and is decoded by the ALU control design in the previous section. The instructions with this form that we implement are add, sub, and, or, and slt. The shamt field is used only for shifts; we will ignore it. **b.** Instruction format for load (opcode=35) and store (opcode=43) instructions. The register rs is the base register that is added to the 16-bit address field to form the memory address. For loads, rt is the destination register for the loaded value. For stores, rt is the source register whose value should be stored into memory. **c.** Instruction format for branch equal (opcode=4). The registers rs and rt are the source registers that are compared for equality. The 16-bit address field is shifted and added to the PC to compute the branch target address.

ALUOp field 10 and 01 with 1X and X1, respectively. Incorporating the don't care terms and minimizing the logic is both complex and error-prone and, thus, is better left to a program.

Designing the Main Control Unit

Now that we have described how to design an ALU that uses the function code and a 2-bit signal as its control inputs, we can return to looking at the rest of the control. To start this process, let's identify all the control lines and the required instruction components for the datapath we constructed in Figure 5.14 on page 286. To understand how buses should be added to route the instruction pieces to the datapath, it is useful to review the formats of the three instruction types: the R-type, branch, and load/store instructions. These formats are shown in Figure 5.19.

There are several major observations about this instruction format that we will rely on:

■ The op field, also called the *opcode*, is always contained in bits 31–26. We will refer to this field as Op[5-0].

- The two registers to be read are always specified by the rs and rt fields, at positions 25–21 and 20–16. This is true for the R-type instructions, branch equal, and for store.

- The base register for load and store instructions is always in bit positions 25–21 (rs).

- The 16-bit offset for branch equal, load, and store is always in positions 15–0.

- The destination register is in one of two places. For a load it is in bit positions 20–16 (rt), while for an R-type instruction it is in bit positions 15–11 (rd). Thus, we will need to add a multiplexor to select which field of the instruction is used to indicate the register number to be written.

Using this information, we can add the instruction labels and extra multiplexor (for the Write register number input of the register file) to the simple datapath. Figure 5.20 shows these additions plus the ALU control block, the write signals for state elements, the read signal for the data memory, and the control signals for the multiplexors. Since all the multiplexors have two inputs, they each require a single control line.

Figure 5.20 shows the seven single-bit control lines plus the 2-bit ALUOp control signal. We have already defined how the ALUOp control signal works, and it is useful to define what the seven other control signals do informally before we determine how to set these control signals during instruction execution. Figure 5.21 describes the function of these seven control lines.

Now that we have looked at the function of each of the control signals, we can look at how to set them. The control unit can set all but one of the control signals, based solely on the opcode field of the instruction. The PCSrc control line is the exception. That control line should be set if the instruction is branch on equal (a decision that the control unit can make) *and* the Zero output of the ALU, which is used for equality comparison, is true. To generate the PCSrc signal, we will need to AND together a signal from the control unit, which we call *Branch*, with the Zero signal out of the ALU.

These nine control signals can now be set on the basis of six input signals to the control unit, which are the opcode bits. The datapath with the control unit and the control signals are shown in Figure 5.22.

Before we try to write a set of equations or a truth table for the control unit, it will be useful to try to define the control function informally. Because the setting of the control lines depends only on the opcode, we define whether each control signal should be 0, 1, or don't care (X), for each of the opcode fields of interest. Figure 5.23 defines how the control signals should be set for each opcode; this information follows directly from Figures 5.15, 5.21, and 5.22.

With the information contained in Figures 5.21 and 5.23, we can design the control unit logic, but before we do that, let's look at how each instruction uses

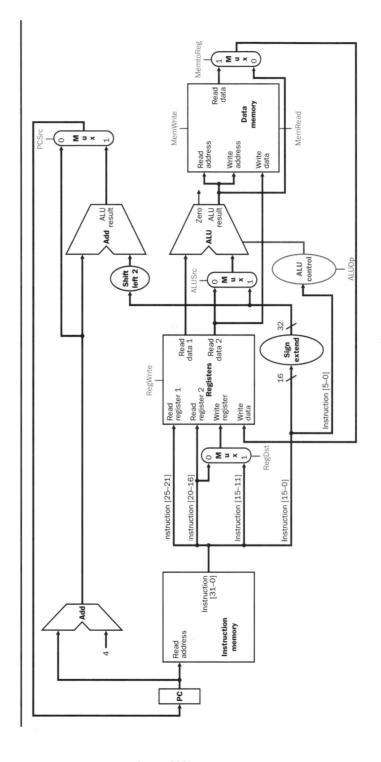

FIGURE 5.20 The datapath of Figure 5.14 with all necessary multiplexors and all control lines identified. The control lines are shown in color. The ALU control block has also been added

Signal name	Effect when deasserted	Effect when asserted
MemRead	None	Data memory contents at the read address are put on read data output.
MemWrite	None	Data memory contents at address given by write address is replaced by value on write data input.
ALUSrc	The second ALU operand comes from the second register file output.	The second ALU operand is the sign-extended lower 16-bits of the instruction.
RegDst	The register destination number for the Write register comes from the rt field.	The register destination number for the Write register comes from the rd field.
RegWrite	None	The register on the Write register input is written into with the value on the write data input.
PCSrc	The PC is replaced by the output of the adder that computes the value of PC + 4.	The PC is replaced by the output of the adder that computes the branch target.
MemtoReg	The value fed to the register write data input comes from the ALU.	The value fed to the register write data input comes from the data memory.

FIGURE 5.21 The function of each of the seven control signals. When the 1-bit control to a two-way multiplexor is asserted, the multiplexor selects the input corresponding to 1. Otherwise, if the control is deasserted, the multiplexor selects the 0 input. Remember that the state elements all have the clock as an implicit input and that the clock is used in controlling writes. The clock is never gated externally to a state element, since this can create timing problems. (See Appendix B for further discussion of this problem.)

the datapath. In the next few figures, we show the flow of three different instruction types through the datapath. The asserted control signals and active datapath elements are highlighted in each of these. Note that a multiplexor whose control is 0 has a definite action, even if its control line is not highlighted. Multiple-bit control signals are highlighted if any constituent signal is asserted.

Let's begin with an R-type instruction, such as add $x, $y, $z. Rather than looking at the entire datapath as one piece of combinational logic, it is easier to think of an instruction executing in a series of steps, focusing our attention on the portion of the datapath associated with each step. The four steps to execute an R-type instruction are

1. An instruction is fetched from the instruction memory and the PC is incremented. Figure 5.24 shows this first step. The active units and asserted control lines are highlighted; those that are asserted in later steps of an R-type instruction are in gray, and those in light gray are those not active for an R-type instruction in any step. The same format is followed for the next three steps.

2. Two registers, $y and $z, are read from the register file as shown in Figure 5.25 on page 298. The main control unit computes the setting of the control lines during this step also.

3. The ALU operates on the data read from the register file, using the

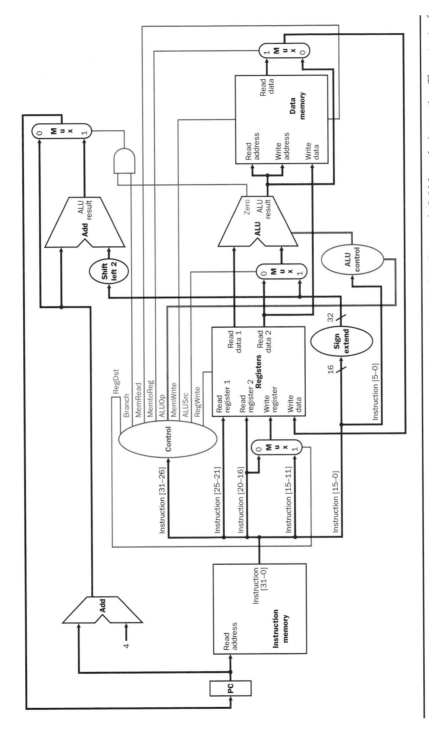

FIGURE 5.22 The simple datapath with the control unit. The input to the control unit is the 6-bit opcode field from the instruction. The outputs of the control unit consist of three 1-bit signals that are used to control multiplexors (RegDst, ALUSrc, and MemtoReg), three signals for controlling read and writes in the register file and data memory (RegWrite, MemRead, and MemWrite), a 1-bit signal used in determining whether to possibly branch (Branch), and a 2-bit control signal for the ALU (ALUOp). An AND gate is used to combine the branch control signal and the Zero output from the ALU; the AND gate output controls the selection of the next PC.

Instruction	RegDst	ALUSrc	Memto-Reg	Reg Write	Mem Read	Mem Write	Branch	ALUOp1	ALUOp0
R-format	1	0	0	1	0	0	0	1	0
lw	0	1	1	1	1	0	0	0	0
sw	X	1	X	0	0	1	0	0	0
beq	X	0	X	0	0	0	1	0	1

FIGURE 5.23 The setting of the control lines is completely determined by the opcode fields of the instruction. The first row of the table corresponds to the R-format instructions (add, subtract, and, or, and slt). For all instructions, the source register fields are rs and rt and the destination register field is rd; this defines how the signals ALUSrc and RegDst are set. Furthermore, an R-type instruction writes a register (RegWrite = 1), but neither reads nor writes data memory. The ALUOp field for R-type instructions is set to 10 to indicate that the ALU control should be generated from the funct field. The second and third rows of this table give the control signal settings for lw and sw. These ALUSrc and ALUOp fields are set to perform the effective address calculation. The MemRead and MemWrite are set to perform the memory access. Finally, RegDst and RegWrite are set for a load to cause the result to be stored into the rt register. The branch instruction is similar to an R-format operation, since it sends the rs and rt registers to the ALU. The ALUOp field for branch is set for a subtract (ALU control = 01), which is used to test for comparison. Notice that the MemtoReg field is irrelevant when the RegWrite signal is 0—since the register is not being written, the value of the data on the register data write port is not used. Thus, the entry MemtoReg in the last two rows of the table is replaced with X for don't care. This type of don't care must be added by the designer, since it depends on knowledge of how the datapath works. Don't cares can also be added to RegDst when RegWrite is 0.

function code (bits 5–0 of the instruction) to generate the ALU function. Figure 5.26 on page 299 shows the operation of this step.

4. The result from the ALU is written into the register file using bits 15–11 of the instruction to select the destination register ($x). Figure 5.27 on page 300 shows the final step added to the previous three.

Remember that this implementation is combinational. That is, it is not really a series of four distinct steps. The datapath really operates in a single clock cycle, and the signals within the datapath can vary unpredictably during the clock cycle. The signals stabilize roughly in the order of the steps given above, because the flow of information follows this order. Thus, Figure 5.27 shows not only the action of the last step, but essentially the operation of the entire datapath when the clock cycle actually ends.

We can illustrate the execution of a load word, such as lw $x, offset($y), in a style similar to Figure 5.27. Figure 5.28 on page 301 shows the active functional units and asserted control lines for a load. We can think of a load instruction as operating in five steps (similar to the R-type executed in four):

1. An instruction is fetched from the instruction memory and the PC is incremented.

2. A register ($y) value is read from the register file.

3. The ALU computes the sum of the value read from the register file and the sign-extended lower 16 bits of the instruction (offset).

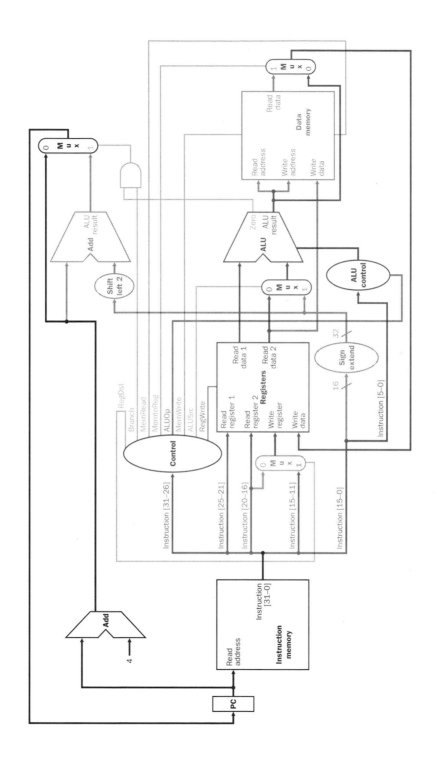

FIGURE 5.24 The first step of an R-type instruction performs a fetch from instruction memory and increments the PC. The portions active in this step are highlighted; the light gray portions are not active in any step, while those in between are active on later steps.

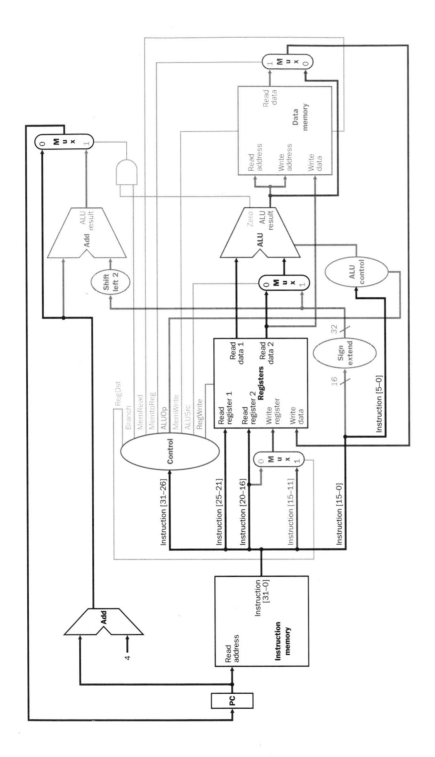

FIGURE 5.25 The second phase in the execution of R-type instructions reads the two source registers from the register file. The main control unit also uses the opcode field to determine the control line setting. These units become active in addition to the units active during the instruction fetch portion, shown in Figure 5.24.

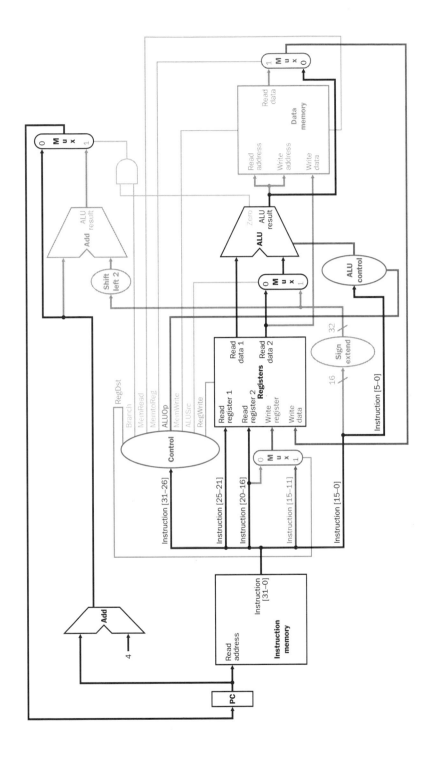

FIGURE 5.26 The third phase of execution for R-type instructions involves the ALU operating on the register data operands. The control line values are all set and the ALU control has been computed. The ALU operates on the data.

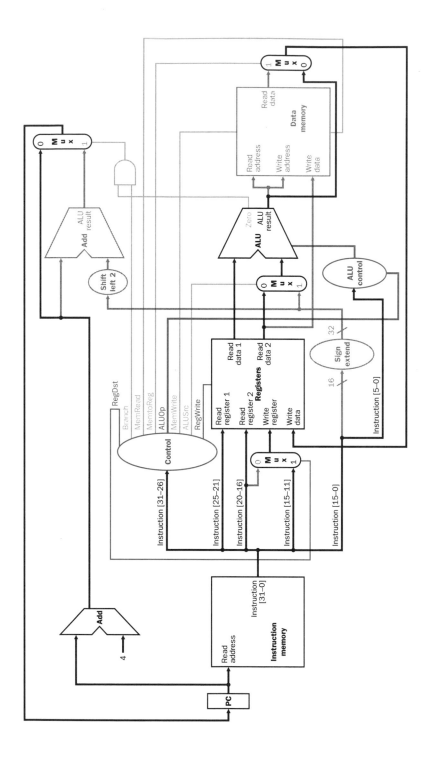

FIGURE 5.27 The final step in an R-type instruction, writing the result, is added to the active units shown for the previous three steps in Figure 5.26 on page 299. The PC is also updated at the end of this phase. Because the datapath is combinational, this step shows all the active units and asserted control lines when they are stable.

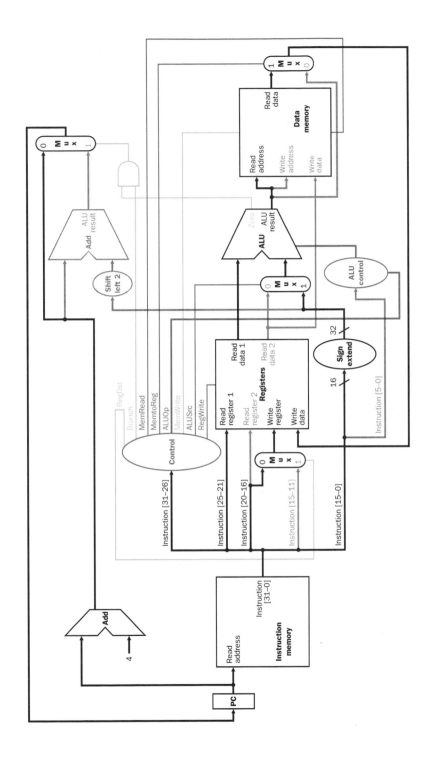

FIGURE 5.28 The operation of a load instruction with the simple datapath control scheme. A store instruction would operate very similarly. The main difference would be that the memory control would indicate a write rather than a read, the second register value read would be used for the data to store, and the operation of writing the data memory value to the register file would not occur.

4. The sum from the ALU is used as the address for the data memory.

5. The data from the memory unit is written into the register file; the register destination is given by bits 20–16 of the instruction ($x).

Finally, we can illustrate the operation of the branch-on-equal instruction, such as beq $x,$y,offset, in the same fashion. It operates much like an R-format instruction, but the ALU output is used to determine whether the PC is written with PC + 4 or the branch target address. Figure 5.29 shows the four steps in execution:

1. An instruction is fetched from the instruction memory and the PC is incremented.

2. Two registers, $x and $y, are read from the register file.

3. The ALU performs a subtract on the data values read from the register file. The value of PC + 4 is added to the sign-extended lower 16 bits of the instruction (offset); the result is the branch target address.

4. The Zero result from the ALU is used to decide which adder result to store into the PC.

In the next section, we will examine machines that are truly sequential, namely, those in which each of these steps is a distinct clock cycle.

Now that we have seen how the instructions operate in steps, let's continue with the control implementation. The control function can be precisely defined using the contents of Figure 5.23. The outputs are the control lines, the input is the 6-bit opcode field, Op [5–0]. Thus, we can create a truth table for each of the outputs. Before doing so, let's write down the encoding for each of the opcodes of interest in Figure 5.23, both as a decimal number and as a series of bits that are input to the control unit:

Name	Opcode in decimal	Opcode in binary					
		Op5	Op4	Op3	Op2	Op1	Op0
R-format	0_{ten}	0	0	0	0	0	0
lw	35_{ten}	1	0	0	0	1	1
sw	43_{ten}	1	0	1	0	1	1
beq	4_{ten}	0	0	0	1	0	0

Using this information, we can now describe the logic in the control unit in one large truth table that combines all the outputs as in Figure 5.30. It com-

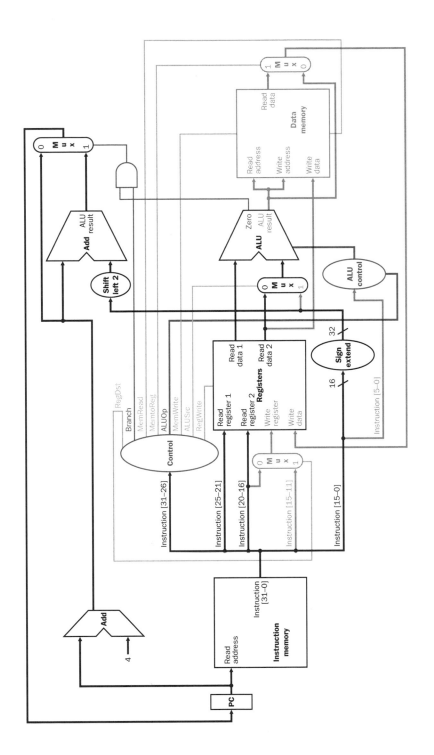

FIGURE 5.29 The datapath in operation for a branch equal instruction. After using the register file and ALU to perform the compare, the Zero output is used to select the next program counter from between the two candidates.

	R-format		lw	sw	beq
Inputs	Op5	0	1	1	0
	Op4	0	0	0	0
	Op3	0	0	1	0
	Op2	0	0	0	1
	Op1	0	1	1	0
	Op0	0	1	1	0
Outputs	RegDst	1	0	X	X
	ALUSrc	0	1	1	0
	MemtoReg	0	1	X	X
	RegWrite	1	1	0	0
	MemRead	0	1	0	0
	MemWrite	0	0	1	0
	Branch	0	0	0	1
	ALUOp1	1	0	0	0
	ALUOp0	0	0	0	1

FIGURE 5.30 The control function for the simple one-clock implementation is completely specified by this truth table. The top half of the table gives the combinations of input signals that correspond to the four opcodes that determine the control output settings. (Remember that Op [5–0] corresponds to bits 31–26 of the instruction, which is the opcode field.) The bottom portion of the table gives the outputs. Thus, the output RegWrite is asserted for two different combinations of the inputs. If we consider only the four opcodes shown in this table, then we can simplify the truth table by using don't cares in the input portion. For example, we can detect an R-format instruction with the equation $\overline{\text{Op5}} \cdot \overline{\text{Op2}}$, since this is sufficient to distinguish the R-format instructions from lw, sw, and beq. We do take advantage of this simplification, since the rest of the MIPS opcodes are used in a full implementation.

pletely specifies the control function, and we can implement it directly in gates in the same way that we implemented the ALU control unit.

Implementing this simple control function with an unstructured collection of gates is reasonable because the control function is neither complex nor large. However, if most of the 64 possible opcodes were used and there were many more control lines, the number of gates would be much larger and each gate could have many more inputs. Since any function can be computed in two levels of logic, another way to implement a logic function is with a structured two-level logic array. Figure 5.31 shows such an implementation. It uses an array of AND gates followed by an array of OR gates. This structure is called a *programmable logic array (PLA)*. A PLA is one of the most common ways to implement a control function. We will return to the topic of using structured logic elements to implement control later in this chapter; further discussion of this topic also appears in Appendices B and C.

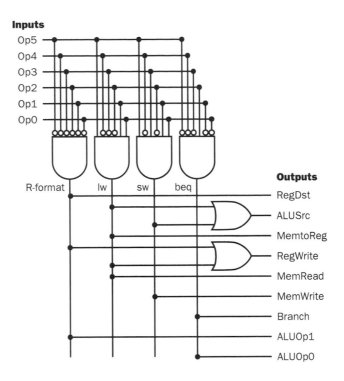

Inputs

Outputs

FIGURE 5.31 The structured implementation of the control function as described by the truth table in Figure 5.30. The structure, called a programmable logic array (PLA) uses an array of AND gates followed by an array of OR gates. The inputs to the AND gates are the function inputs and their inverses (bubbles indicate inversion of a signal). The inputs to the OR gates are the outputs of the AND gates (or, as a degenerate case, the function inputs and inverses). The output of the OR gates is the function outputs.

Example

Figure 5.22 includes the implementation of many of the instructions we looked at in Chapter 3. One class of key instructions missing is that of the jump instructions. Show how to extend the implementation of Figure 5.22 to include the jump instruction. Describe how to set any new control lines.

Answer

The jump instruction looks somewhat like a branch instruction but computes the target PC differently and is not conditional. Like a branch, the low-order 2 bits of a jump address are always 00_{two}. The next lower 26 bits of this 32-bit address come from the 26-bit immediate field in the instruction, as shown in Figure 5.32. The upper 4 bits of the address that should replace the PC come from the current PC. Thus, we can implement a jump by storing into the PC the concatenation of

- the upper four bits of the current PC (these are bits 31–28),

- the 26-bit immediate field of the jump instruction, and

- the bits 00_{two}.

Figure 5.33 on page 307 shows the addition of the control for `jmp` added to Figure 5.22. An additional multiplexor is used to select the source for the new PC value, which is either the incremented PC (PC + 4), the branch target PC, or the jump target PC. One additional control signal is needed for the additional multiplexor. This control signal, called jump, is asserted only when the instruction is a jump—that is, when the opcode is 2.

Field	2	address
Bit positions	31–26	25–0

FIGURE 5.32 Instruction format for the jump instruction (opcode = 2). The destination address for a jump instruction is formed by concatenating the upper 4 bits of the current PC to the 26-bit address field in the jump instruction and adding 00 as the two low-order bits.

What's Wrong with a Single-Cycle Implementation

By definition, the clock cycle must have the same length for every instruction in this single-cycle design, and the CPI (see Chapter 2) will therefore be 1. Of course, the clock cycle is determined by the longest possible path in the machine. This path is almost certainly a load instruction, which uses five functional units in series: the instruction memory, the register file, the ALU, the data memory, and the register file. Although the CPI is 1, the overall performance of a single clock implementation is not likely to be very good, since several of the instruction types could fit in a shorter clock cycle.

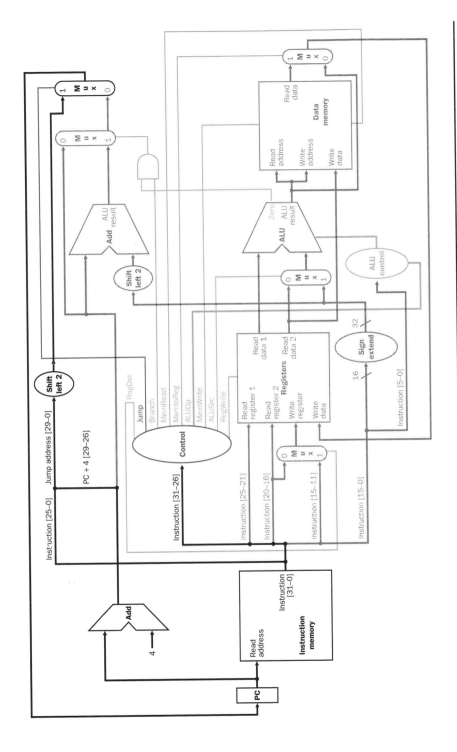

FIGURE 5.33 The simple control and datapath are extended to handle the jmp instruction. An additional multiplexor (at the upper right) is used to choose between the branch target or the sequential instruction following this one. This multiplexor is controlled by the jump control signal. The jump target address actually uses the value of PC [31–28] for the jump target address rather than the value of these bits after the PC has been incremented by 4. This makes a difference only if the increment of the PC by 4 causes one of the high-order 4 bits to change. For simplicity, we ignore this detail and use the incremented PC as the source for the upper 4 bits.

Example

Assume that the operation time for the major functional units in this implementation are

■ Memory units: 10 ns,

■ ALU and adders: 10 ns,

■ Register file (read or write): 5 ns.

Assuming that the multiplexors, control unit, PC accesses, sign-extension unit, and wires have no delay, which of the following implementations would be faster and by how much?

1. An implementation in which every instruction operates in one clock cycle of a fixed length.

2. An implementation where every instruction executes in one clock cycle using a variable-length clock, which for each instruction is only as long as it needs to be. (Such an approach is not terribly practical, but it will allow us to see what is being sacrificed when all the instructions must execute in a single clock of the same length.)

Use the instruction mix for gcc that appears in Chapter 4, Figure 4.46 on page 248 to determine the performance of the alternatives.

Answer

Let's start by comparing the CPU execution times. Recall from Chapter 2 that

$$\text{CPU execution time} = \text{Instruction count} \times \text{CPI} \times \text{Clock cycle time}$$

Since CPI must be 1, we can simplify this to

$$\text{CPU execution time} = \text{Instruction count} \times \text{Clock cycle time}$$

We need only find the clock cycle time for the two implementations. The critical path for the different instruction types is as follows:

Instruction type	Functional units used by the instruction type				
R-format	Instruction fetch	Register access	ALU	Register access	
Load word	Instruction fetch	Register access	ALU	Memory access	Register access
Store word	Instruction fetch	Register access	ALU	Memory access	
Branch	Instruction fetch	Register access	ALU		
Jump	Instruction fetch				

Using these critical paths, we can compute the required length for each instruction type:

Instruction type	Instruction memory	Register read	ALU operation	Data memory	Register write	Total
R-format operations	10	5	10	0	5	30 ns
Load word	10	5	10	10	5	40 ns
Store word	10	5	10	10		35 ns
Branch	10	5	10	0		25 ns
Jump	10					10 ns

So the clock cycle for a machine with a single clock for all instructions is 40 ns, but a machine with a variable clock will have a cycle between 10 ns and 40 ns.

We can find the average clock cycle length for a machine with a variable-length clock using the information above and an instruction frequency distribution. This distribution can be computed from Chapter 4's Figure 4.46 by summing the individual frequencies into categories: 22% loads, 11% stores, 49% R-format operations, 16% branches, and 2% jumps.

Thus, the average time per instruction with a variable clock is

$$\text{CPU clock cycle} = 40 \times 22\% + 35 \times 11\% + 30 \times 49\% + 25 \times 16\% + 10 \times 2\%$$

$$= 31.6 \text{ ns}$$

Since the variable clock implementation has a shorter average clock cycle, it is clearly faster. Let's find the performance ratio:

$$\frac{\text{CPU performance}_{\text{variable clock}}}{\text{CPU performance}_{\text{single clock}}} = \frac{\text{CPU Execution time}_{\text{single clock}}}{\text{CPU Execution time}_{\text{variable clock}}}$$

$$= \frac{\text{IC} \times \text{CPU clock cycle}_{\text{single clock}}}{\text{IC} \times \text{CPU clock cycle}_{\text{variable clock}}}$$

$$\frac{\text{CPU performance}_{\text{variable clock}}}{\text{CPU performance}_{\text{single clock}}} = \frac{\text{CPU clock cycle}_{\text{single clock}}}{\text{CPU clock cycle}_{\text{variable clock}}}$$

$$= \frac{40}{31.6} = 1.27$$

The variable clock implementation would be 1.27 times faster. Unfortunately, implementing a variable-speed clock for each instruction type is extremely difficult, and the overhead for such an approach could be larger than any advantage gained. As we will see in the next section, an alternative is to use a shorter clock cycle that does less work and then vary the number of *clock cycles* for the different instruction types.

The penalty for using the single-clock-cycle design with a fixed clock cycle is nontrivial, but might be considered acceptable for this small instruction set. However, if we tried to implement the floating-point unit or an instruction set with more complex instructions, or to use more sophisticated implementation techniques, this single-clock-cycle design wouldn't work well at all. Let's look at an example with floating point.

Example

Suppose we have a floating-point unit that requires 20 ns for a floating-point add time and 60 ns for a floating-point multiply. All the other functional unit times are as in the previous example, and a floating-point instruction is like an arithmetic-logical instruction, except that it uses the floating point ALU rather than the main ALU. Using the instruction distribution for spice from Chapter 4, Figure 4.46 on page 248, find the performance ratio between an implementation in which the clock cycle is different for each instruction type and an implementation in which all instructions have the same clock cycle time. Assume that

■ Double-precision loads and stores take the same time as 32-bit loads and stores.

■ FP branch takes the same time as an integer branch.

■ FP subtract and compare take the same time as FP add.

■ FP divide takes the same time as FP multiply.

Answer

From the previous example, we know that

$$\frac{\text{CPU performance}_{\text{variable clock}}}{\text{CPU performance}_{\text{single clock}}} = \frac{\text{CPU clock cycle}_{\text{single clock}}}{\text{CPU clock cycle}_{\text{variable clock}}}$$

The cycle time for the single-cycle machine will be equal to the longest instruction timing, which is floating-point multiply. The time for a floating-point multiply, and thus the clock cycle, is $10 + 5 + 60 + 5 = 80$ ns .

Consider a machine whose instructions have different cycle times. The time for a floating-point add instruction is $10 + 5 + 20 + 5 = 40$ ns . If we sum up the individual instruction frequencies in Figure 4.46, we get 26% loads, 14% stores, 31% R-format, 8% branches, 2% jumps, and 19% floating-point operations (of which 9% are multiplies or divides, and 10% are adds, subtracts, or compares). Thus, the average clock length will be

$$\text{CPU clock cycle} = 40 \times 26\% + 35 \times 14\% + 30 \times 31\% + 25 \times 8\%$$

$$+ 10 \times 2\% + 80 \times 9\% + 40 \times 10\% = 38.0 \text{ ns}$$

The improvement in performance is

$$\frac{\text{CPU performance}_{\text{variable clock}}}{\text{CPU performance}_{\text{single clock}}} = \frac{\text{CPU clock cycle}_{\text{single clock}}}{\text{CPU clock cycle}_{\text{variable clock}}}$$

$$= \frac{80}{38} = 2.11$$

A variable clock would allow us to improve performance by more than two times.

Similarly, if we had a machine with more powerful operations and addressing modes, instructions could vary from three or four functional unit delays to tens or hundreds of functional unit delays. In addition, because we must assume that the clock cycle is equal to the worst-case delay for all instructions, we can't use implementation techniques that reduce the delay of the common case but do not improve the worst-case cycle time. For example, such a restriction would make a cache useless in this machine! A single-cycle implementation thus violates our key design principle of making the common case fast. In addition, with this single-cycle implementation, each functional unit can be used only once per clock; therefore, some functional units must be duplicated, raising the cost of the implementation.

We can avoid these difficulties by using implementation techniques that have a shorter clock cycle—derived from the basic functional unit delays— and that require multiple clock cycles for each instruction. The next section explores this alternative implementation scheme. In Chapter 6, we'll look at another implementation technique, called pipelining, that uses a datapath very similar to the one in this section. Pipelining overlaps the execution of multiple instructions to further increase performance.

5.4   A Multiple Clock Cycle Implementation

In an earlier example, we broke each instruction into a series of steps corresponding to the functional unit operations that were needed. We can use these steps to create a *multicycle implementation*. In a multicycle implementation, each *step* in the execution will take one clock cycle. The multicycle implementation allows a functional unit to be used more than once per instruction, as long as it is used on different clock cycles. This can help reduce the amount of hardware required. The ability to allow instructions to take different numbers of clock cycles and the ability to share functional units within the execution of a single instruction are the major advantages of a multicycle design. Figure 5.34 shows the abstract version of the multicycle datapath. Comparing this to the datapath for the single-cycle version shown in Figure 5.14 on page 286, we can see the following differences:

- A single memory unit is used for both instructions and data.

- A register is used to save the instruction after it is read. This *Instruction register* (IR) is required because the memory may be re-used to access data later in the instruction execution.

There is a single ALU, rather than an ALU and two adders.

Because several functional units are shared for different purposes, we need both to add multiplexors and to expand existing multiplexors. Since one memory is used for both instructions and data, we need a multiplexor to select between the two sources for a memory address, namely the PC (for instruction access) and the ALU result (for data access). Sharing the ALU requires the introduction of a multiplexor for the first ALU input, which can be either a register or the PC, and a change in the multiplexor on the second ALU input from a two-way to a four-way multiplexor, which requires two additional inputs: the constant 4 (used to increment the PC) and the sign-extended and shifted offset field used in the branch address computation. Figure 5.35 shows

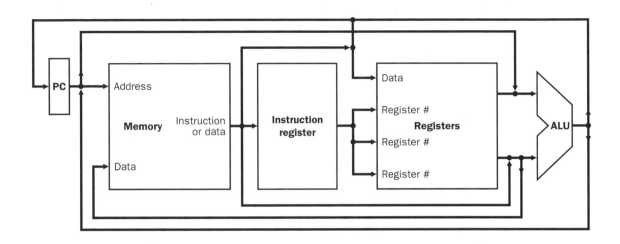

FIGURE 5.34 The high-level view of the multicycle datapath. This picture shows the key elements of the datapath: a shared memory unit, a single ALU shared among instructions, and the datapaths to connect these shared units.

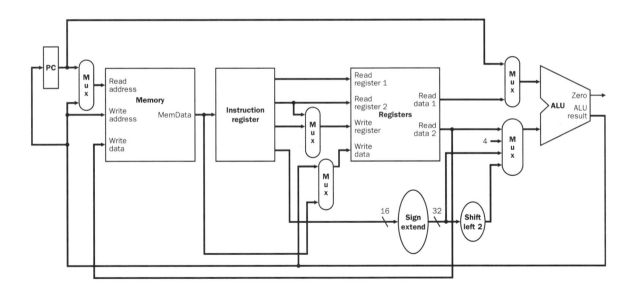

FIGURE 5.35 Multistate datapath for MIPS handles all basic instructions. The additions versus the single-clock data-path include a multiplexor for the memory read address, a multiplexor for the top ALU input, and an expansion of the multiplexor on the bottom ALU input to a four-way selector. These small additions allow us to remove two adders and a memory unit.

the details of the datapath with these additional multiplexors. Altogether, by introducing a register and three multiplexors, we are able to reduce the number of memory units from two to one and eliminate two adders. Since registers and multiplexors are fairly small, this could yield a substantial reduction in the hardware cost.

Because the datapath shown in Figure 5.35 takes multiple clock cycles per instruction, it will require a different set of control signals. We will need a write signal for each of the state elements: the memory, the PC, the general-purpose registers, and the Instruction register. We will also need a read signal for the memory. We can use the ALU control unit from earlier examples (Figures 5.17 and 5.18) to control the ALU here as well. Finally, each of the two-input multiplexors requires a single control line, while the four-input multiplexor requires two control lines. Figure 5.36 shows the datapath of Figure 5.35 with these control lines added. After we look at the sequencing of instructions we will see that additional control signals will be required to implement some instructions, specifically branches; these signals will control when the PC is written and what value is written into the PC.

Before examining the steps to execute each instruction, it is useful to state informally what effect the control signals, which we have added, have when they are asserted and deasserted (just as we did for the single-cycle design in Figure 5.21 on page 294). Figure 5.37 shows what each control signal does when it is asserted and deasserted. The single-bit control signals appear in table a of the figure, and the two-bit control signals ALUSelB and ALUOp are defined in table b.

Elaboration: To reduce the number of signal lines interconnecting the functional units, designers can use *shared buses*. A shared bus is a set of lines that connect multiple units; in most cases, they include multiple sources that can place data on the bus and multiple readers of the value. Just as we reduced the number of functional units for the datapath, we can reduce the number of buses interconnecting these units by sharing the buses. For example, there are five sources coming to the ALU; however, only two of them are needed at any one time. Thus, a pair of buses can be used to hold values that are being sent to the ALU. Rather than placing a large multiplexor in front of the ALU, a designer can use a shared bus and then ensure that only one of the sources is driving the bus at any point.

Breaking the Instruction Execution into Clock Cycles

Given this datapath, we now need to look at what should happen in each clock cycle of the multicycle execution, since this will determine what additional datapath elements (temporary registers, for example) and what addi-

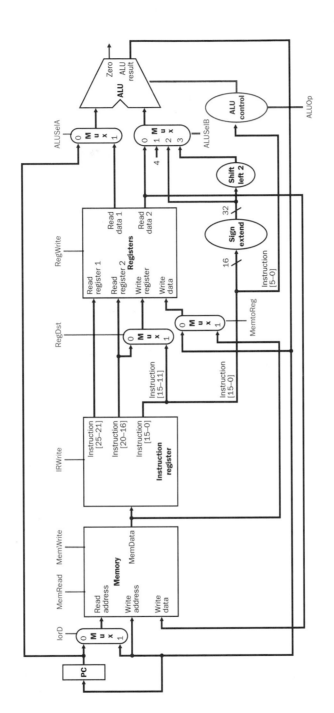

FIGURE 5.36 The multicycle datapath with the control lines shown. The signals ALUOp and ALUSelB are 2-bit control signals, while all the other control lines are 1-bit signals. The MemRead signal has been moved to the top of the memory unit to simplify the figures.

Signal name	Effect when deasserted	Effect when asserted
MemRead	None	Contents of memory at the read address are put on read data output.
MemWrite	None	Memory contents at the write address is replaced by value on write data input.
ALUSelA	The first ALU operand is the PC.	The first ALU operand comes from the register given by the rs field.
RegDst	The register destination number for the register write comes from the rt field.	The register destination number for the register write comes from the rd field.
RegWrite	None	The register given by Write register number is written with the value on the write data input.
MemtoReg	The value fed to the register write data input comes from the ALU.	The value fed to the register write data input comes from the Data memory.
IorD	The PC is used to supply the address to the memory unit.	The output of the ALU is used to supply the address to the memory unit.
IRWrite	None	The value from the memory unit is written into the Instruction register (IR).

a. The actions of the 1-bit control signals are defined.

Signal name	Value	Effect
ALUSelB	00	The second input to the ALU comes from the register given by the rt field.
	01	The second input to the ALU is the constant 4.
	10	The second input to the ALU is the sign-extended lower 16 bits of the IR.
	11	The second input to the ALU is the sign-extended and shifted lower 16 bits of the IR.
ALUOp	00	The ALU performs an add operation.
	01	The ALU performs a subtract operation.
	10	The function code field of the instruction determine the ALU operation.

b. The actions of the 2-bit control signals are defined.

FIGURE 5.37 The action caused by the setting of each control signal. Table a describes the 1-bit control signals, while table b describes the 2-bit signals. Only those control lines that affect multiplexors have an action when they are 0. This information is similar to tha in Figure 5.21 on page 294 for the single-cycle datapath, but adds the new control lines (ALU-SelA, IorD, IRWrite, and ALUSelB) and removes control lines that are no longer used or have been replaced (Jump, Branch, and ALUSrc).

tional control signals may be needed. We will need to introduce a register to hold a signal value whenever the following two conditions hold:

1. The signal is computed in one clock cycle and used in another; and

2. The inputs to the functional block that outputs this signal can change before the signal is written into a state element.

For example, we need to store the instruction into the Instruction register, because the functional unit (the memory) that produces the value changes its output before we complete all uses of the fields of the instruction. On the other hand, when the ALU is used in an R-type instruction, we need not store its output, even though we will not use the output until the next clock. This is because the output of the ALU does not change (that is, it is *stable*) during the clock cycle when it is written into the register file. The ALU output is stable because the inputs to the ALU come from the register file, and the output of the register file is determined by the rs and rt fields of the Instruction register, which is stable because it is a state element written only once per instruction execution. Thus, the functional units from the register file through the ALU constitute one block of combinational logic, whose inputs come from the Instruction register (a state element), and whose output is written into the register file (also a state element). This structure looks like the structure we saw abstractly in Figure 5.3 on page 274. Although the single-cycle implementation always used state elements that were written every clock (as in Figure 5.4 on page 275), our multicycle implementation will write the state element selectively, as in Figure 5.3.

Our goal in breaking the execution into clock cycles should be to balance the amount of work done in each cycle, so that we minimize the clock cycle time. We can break the execution into five steps, each taking one clock cycle, which will be roughly balanced in length. For example, we will restrict each step to contain at most one ALU operation, or one register file access, or one memory access. With this restriction, the clock cycle could be as short as the longest of these operations.

In the single-cycle datapath each instruction must use a set of datapath elements to carry out its execution. Many of the datapath elements operate in series, using the output of another element as an input. Some datapath elements operate in parallel; for example, the PC is incremented and the instruction is read at the same time. A similar situation exists in the multicycle datapath. All the operations listed in one step occur in parallel within one clock cycle, while successive steps operate in series in different clock cycles. The limitation of one ALU operation, one memory access, or one register file access determines what can fit in one step. The five execution steps and their actions are given below.

1. Instruction fetch step:

Fetch the instruction from memory and increment the program counter.

```
IR = Memory[PC];
PC = PC + 4;
```

Operation: Send the PC to the memory as the address, perform a read, and fetch the instruction into the Instruction register (IR), where it will be stored. To implement this step, we will need to assert the control signals MemRead and IRWrite, and set IorD to 0 to select the PC as the source of the address. We also increment the PC by 4 in this stage, which requires setting the ALUSelB signal to 01, the ALUSelA signal to 0, and ALUOp to 00 (to make the ALU add). Finally, we will also want to store the incremented instruction address back into the PC; we will add this path and control, when we have determined the full control for the PC, including branches. The increment of the PC and the instruction memory access can occur in parallel.

2. Instruction decode and register fetch step:

In the previous step and in this one, we do not yet know what the instruction is, so we can perform only actions that are either applicable to all instructions (such as fetching the instruction in step 1), or are not harmful, in case the instruction isn't what we think it might be. Thus, in this step we can read the two registers indicated by the rs and rt instruction fields, since it isn't harmful to read them even if it isn't necessary. The register contents may be needed in later stages, so we name them *A* and *B* in the following description. The register outputs need not be saved in a temporary register, since the register number inputs (and thus the register data outputs) are not changed throughout the execution of the instruction.

We will also compute the branch target address with the ALU, which also is not harmful because we can ignore the value if the instruction turns out not to be a branch. Because we do not know whether this instruction is a branch (let alone whether the branch should be taken) and because we need to use the ALU for other purposes in later steps, we must save the computed branch target address into a new register that we name *Target*. (We'll show the revised datapath and control once we have completed all five steps.)

Performing these "optimistic" actions early has the benefit of decreasing the number of clock cycles needed to execute an instruction. We can do these optimistic actions early because of the regularity of the instruction formats. For instance, if the instruction has two register inputs, they are always in the rs and rt fields; and if the instruction is a branch, the offset is always the low-order 16 bits:

```
A = Register[IR[25-21]];
B = Register[IR[20-16]];
Target = PC + (sign-extend (IR[15-0]) << 2);
```

Operation: Access the register file to read the registers using the rs and rt fields; this does not require setting any control lines. Compute the branch target address and store the address in Target. This requires setting ALUSelB to the value 11 (so that the offset field is both sign-extended and shifted), ALU-SelA to 0, and ALUOp to 00. In addition to adding the Target register, we will need to add a write control line for this register, which must be asserted during this step. The register accesses and computation of branch target occur in parallel.

After this clock cycle, determining the action to take can depend on the instruction contents.

3. Execution, memory address computation, or branch completion:

This is the first cycle during which the datapath operation is determined by the instruction type. In all cases, the ALU is operating on the operands prepared in the previous step, performing one of three functions, depending on the instruction type. We name the ALU result *ALUoutput* for use in later stages. Since the ALU inputs are stable, this value need not be saved in a register. However, any signals set in this cycle that affect the ALU result must be held constant until the ALU results are written into a register or are no longer needed. We specify the action to be taken depending on the instruction class:

Memory reference:

```
ALUoutput = A + sign-extend (IR[15-0]);
```

Operation: The ALU is adding the operands to form the memory address. This requires setting ALUSelA to 1, which will use the first register file output as the first ALU input, and setting ALUSelB to 10, which will cause the output of the sign-extension unit to be used for the second ALU input. The ALUOp signals will need to be set to 00, forcing the ALU to add.

Arithmetic-logical instruction (R-type):

```
ALUoutput =  A op B;
```

Operation: The ALU is performing the operation specified by the opcode on the two registers read in the previous cycle. This requires setting ALUSelA = 1 and setting ALUSelB = 00, which together cause the register file outputs to be used as the ALU inputs. The ALUOp signals will need to be set to 10, so that the function code is used to determine the ALU control signal settings.

Branch:

```
if (A == B) PC = Target;
```

Operation: The ALU is used to do the equal comparison between the two registers read in the previous step. The Zero signal out of the ALU is used to determine whether or not to branch. This requires setting ALUSelA = 1 and setting ALUSelB = 00, just as for an R-type instruction. The ALUOp signals will need to be set to 01 to perform the subtract used for equality testing. A write signal will need to be triggered for updating the PC if the Zero output of the ALU is asserted. This will be specified later when we add the PC control.

4. Memory access or R-type instruction completion step:

During this step, loads and stores access memory and arithmetic-logical operations write their result. We name the output of the memory *memory-data*, though it need not correspond to a register, since its output will be stable during the next clock cycle when it is written into a register.

Memory reference:

```
memory-data = Memory [ALUoutput];
       or
Memory [ALUoutput] = B;
```

Operation: If the instruction is a load, data returns from memory, and we call the value memory-data. If the instruction is a store, then the data is written into memory. In either case, the address used is the one computed during the previous step and named ALUoutput. The ALU control signals set in the previous cycle must be held stable during this cycle. For a store, the source operand, which we named B, was read in the step that occurred two clock cycles earlier. The signal MemRead (for a load) or MemWrite (for store) will need to be asserted. In addition, the signal IorD is set to 1 to force the memory address to come from the ALU, rather than the PC.

Arithmetic-logical instruction (R-type):

```
Reg[IR[15-11]] = ALUoutput;
```

Operation: Place the result of the ALU operation into the Result register. The signal RegDst must be set to 1 to force the rd (bits 15–11) field to be used to select the register to write. RegWrite must be asserted, and MemtoReg must be set to 0, so that the output of the ALU is written (as opposed to the memory data output). The signals ALUSelA, ALUSelB, and ALUOp do not change from the previous clock cycle. Recall that because writes are edge-tiggered, the write of the rd register cannot affect the data currently being read, even if the register destination is also an instruction source register.

5. Write-back step:

```
Reg[IR[20-16]] = memory-data;
```

Operation: Write the load data from memory into the register file. Here we set MemtoReg = 1, to write the result from memory, and RegWrite, to cause a write, and we make RegDst = 0, to choose the rt (bits 20–16) field as the regis-

Step name	Action for R-type instructions	Action for memory-reference instructions	Action for branches
Instruction fetch	IR = Memory[PC] PC = PC + 4;		
Instruction decode/ register fetch	A = Registers[IR[25−21]] B = Registers[IR[20−16]] Target = PC + (sign-extend (IR[15−0]) << 2)		
Execution, address computation, or branch completion	ALUoutput = A op B	ALUoutput = A + sign-extend (IR[15−0])	if (A == B) then PC = Target
Memory access or R-type completion	Reg[IR[15−11]] = ALUoutput	memory-data = Memory[ALUoutput] or Memory [ALUoutput] = B	
Write-back		Reg[IR[20−16]] = memory-data	

FIGURE 5.38 Summary of the steps taken to execute any instruction type. Instructions take from 3 to 5 execution steps. The first two steps are independent of the instruction type. After these steps, an instruction takes from 1 to 3 more cycles to complete, depending on the instruction type.

ter number. Again, the ALUSelA, ALUSelB, and ALUOp signals must be held stable until the end of this cycle.

This five-step sequence is summarized in Figure 5.38. From this sequence we can determine what the control must do on each clock cycle. However, before we can design the control unit, we must add the PC write control and multiplexors necessary to select the correct value to write into the PC, as well as the Target register and its control. Since implementing the jump instruction requires dealing with the same two capabilities, let's also incorporate the control for the jump instruction at the same time. Including the jump instruction, there are three possible sources for the value to be written into the PC. These are

- The ALUoutput, which is the source when the PC is incremented for a sequential instruction fetch.

- The Target register, which is the source when the instruction is a taken conditional branch. We will also need a signal to write the register, called TargetWrite.

- The lower 26 bits of the Instruction register (IR) shifted left by two and concatenated with the upper 4 bits of the PC, which is the source when the instruction is a jump.

We encode these three possible sources using a 2-bit control signal, PCSource. The three possibilities above are encoded as 00, 01, and 10, corresponding to the sources ALUoutput (00), Target (01), and the IR (10). The signal PCSource then controls a 3-input multiplexor.

As we observed when we implemented the single-cycle control, the PC is written in two different ways. If the instruction is not a conditional branch (`beq`), the PC is written unconditionally. If the instruction is a conditional branch, the incremented PC is replaced with the value in Target, only if the ALU output signal Zero is also asserted. Thus, we need two PC write signals, which we will call PCWrite and PCWriteCond. The PCWriteCond signal and the Zero signal from the ALU are combined with an AND gate, which then is combined with PCWrite to create a write signal for the PC.

Figure 5.39 shows the complete multicycle datapath and control unit, including the additional control signals, Target register, and multiplexor for implementing the PC updating. Figure 5.40 shows the effects of these additional control signals; together with Figure 5.37 these tables define the effects of all the control signals in the multicycle datapath of Figure 5.39.

Defining the Control

Now that we have determined what the control signals are and when they must be asserted, we can implement the control unit. To design the control unit for the single-cycle datapath, we used a set of truth tables that specified the setting of the control signals based on the instruction type; then we mapped those truth tables to the logic gates shown in Figure 5.31. For the multicycle datapath, the control is more complex because the instruction is executed in a series of steps. The control for the multicycle datapath must specify both the signals to be set in any step and the next step in the sequence.

In this subsection and in section 5.5, we will look at two different techniques to specify the control. The first technique is based on finite state machines that are usually represented graphically. The second technique, called *microprogramming*, uses a programming representation for control. Both of these techniques represent the control in a form that allows the detailed implementation—using gates, ROMs, or PLAs—to be synthesized by a CAD system. In this chapter, we will focus on the design of the control and its representation in these two forms. For those interested in how these control specifications are translated into actual hardware, Appendix C continues the development of this chapter, translating the multicycle control unit to a detailed hardware implementation. The key ideas of control can be grasped from this chapter without examining the material in the Appendix. However, if you want to get down to the bits, Appendix C can show you how to do it!

The first method we use to specify the multicycle control is a *finite state machine*. A finite state machine consists of a set of states and directions on how to change states. The directions are defined by a *next-state function*, which maps the current state and the inputs to a new state. When we use a finite state machine for control, each state also specifies a set of outputs that are asserted when the machine is in that state. The implementation of a finite state machine

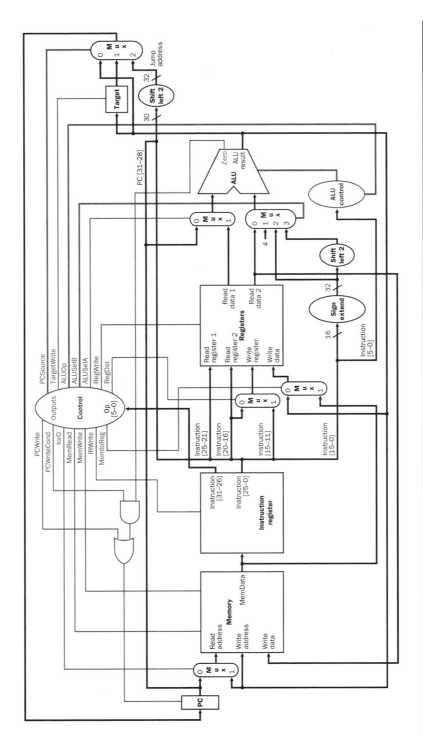

FIGURE 5.39 This is the complete datapath for the multicycle implementation together with the necessary control lines. The control lines of Figure 5.36 are attached to the control unit, and the control and datapath elements needed to effect changes to the PC are included. The major additions from Figure 5.36 include: the Target register (in the upper right-hand corner), the three-input multiplexor used to select the source of a new PC value (at the top right), two gates used to combine the PC write signals, and the control signals PCSource, PCWrite, PCWriteCond, and TargetWrite. The PCWriteCond signal is ANDed with the Zero output of the ALU to decide whether a branch should be taken; the resulting signal is ORed with the control signal PCWrite, to generate the actual write control signal for the PC. In addition, the output of the IR is rearranged to send the lower 26 bits (the jump address) to the logic used to select the next PC. These 26 bits are concatenated with the high-order 4 bits of the current PC, and then shifted 2 bits to the left (this is equivalent to just concatenating two low-order 0 bits).

Signal name	Effect when deasserted	Effect when asserted
PCWrite	None	The PC is written; the source is controlled by PCSource.
PCWriteCond	None	The PC is written *if* the Zero output from the ALU is also active.
TargetWrite	None	The output of the ALU is written into the register Target.

a. The actions of the additional 1-bit control signals are defined.

Signal name	Value	Effect
PCSource	00	The ALU output is sent to the PC for writing.
	01	The contents of the register Target are sent to the PC for writing.
	10	The jump target address (PC + 4[29–26] concatenated with IR[25–0] and shifted left two bits) is sent to the PC for writing.

b. The actions of the additional 2-bit control signal, PCSource, are defined.

FIGURE 5.40 The effect of the control signals, which determine how the PC is written. Table a describes the 1-bit control signals, which control writing of the PC and the Target register. Table b describes the 2-bit signal that determines the source of a value written into the PC. This information together with the contents of Figure 5.37 define the operation of all the control signals in the multicycle datapath.

usually assumes that all outputs that are not explicitly asserted are deasserted, and the correct operation of the datapath often depends on the fact that a signal is deasserted. For example, the RegWrite signal should be asserted only when a register is to be written; when it is not explicitly asserted, it must be deasserted.

Multiplexor controls are slightly different, since they select one of the inputs whether they are 0 or 1. Thus, in the finite state machine, we always specify the setting of all the multiplexor controls that we care about. When we implement the finite state machine with logic, setting a control to 0 may be the default and thus may not require any gates. A simple example of a finite state machine appears in Appendix B, and readers unfamiliar with the concept of a finite state machine should examine Appendix B before proceeding.

The finite state control essentially corresponds to the five steps of execution shown on pages 317 through 321; each state in the finite state machine will take one clock cycle. The finite state machine will consist of several parts. Since the first two steps of execution are identical for every instruction, the initial two states of the finite state machine will be common for all instructions. Steps 3 through 5 differ, depending on the opcode. After the execution of the last step for a particular instruction type, the finite state machine will return to the initial state to begin fetching the next instruction. Figure 5.41 shows this

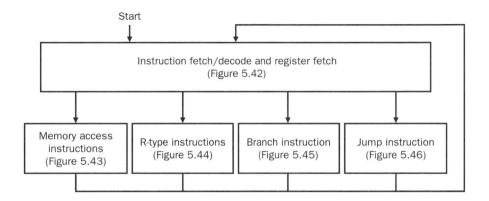

FIGURE 5.41 The high-level view of the finite state machine control. The first steps are independent of the instruction type; then a series of sequences that depend on the instruction opcode are used to complete each instruction type. After completing the actions needed for that instruction type, the control returns to fetch a new instruction. Each box in this Figure may represent one to several states. The arc labeled Start marks the state in which to begin when the first instruction is to be fetched.

abstracted representation of the finite state machine. To fill in the details of the finite state machine, we will first expand the instruction fetch and decode portion, then we will show the states (and actions) for the different instruction types.

We show the first two states of the finite state machine in Figure 5.42, using a traditional graphic representation. We number the states to simplify the explanation, though the numbers are arbitrary. State 0, corresponding to step 1, is the starting state of the machine.

The signals that are asserted in each state are shown within the state. The arcs between states define the next state, and are labeled with conditions that select a specific next state when multiple next states are possible. After state 1, the signals asserted may depend on the type of instruction. Thus, the finite state machine has four arcs exiting state 1, corresponding to the four instruction types: memory reference, R-type, branch on equal, and jump. This process of branching to different states depending on the instruction is called *decoding*, since the choice of the next state, and hence the actions that follow, depend on the instruction type.

The portion of the finite state machine needed to implement the memory reference instructions is shown in Figure 5.43. For the memory-reference instructions, the first state after fetching the instruction and registers computes the memory address (state 2). To compute the memory address, the ALU input

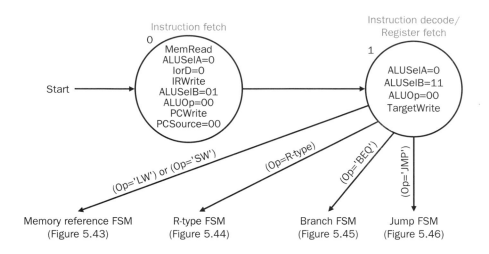

FIGURE 5.42 The instruction fetch and decode portion of every instruction is identical.
These states correspond to the top box in the abstract finite state machine in Figure 5.41. In the
first state we assert a number of signals to cause the memory to read an instruction and write it
into the Instruction register (MemRead and IRWrite), and we set IorD to 0 to choose the PC as the
address source. The signals PCWrite, PCSource, ALUSelA, ALUOp, and ALUSelB are set to compute PC + 4 and store it into the PC. In the next state, we compute the branch target address by
setting ALUSelB to 11 (causing the shifted and sign-extended lower 16 bits of the IR to be sent to
the ALU), setting ALUSelA to 0 and ALUOp to 00; we store the result in the Target register (using
TargetWrite). There are four next states that depend on the type of the instruction, which is
known during this state. If the instruction is either lw or sw, we go to one state, while the other
arcs handle single instruction opcodes. The control unit input, called *op*, is used to determine
which of these arcs to follow.

multiplexors must be set so that the first input is the register corresponding to
rs, while the second input is the sign-extended displacement field. After the
memory address calculation, the memory should be read or written; this requires two different states. If the instruction opcode is lw, then state 3 (corresponding to the step Memory access) does the memory read (MemRead is
asserted). If it is sw, state 5 does a memory write (MemWrite is asserted). In
both states 3 and 5, the signal IorD is set to 1 to force the memory address to
come from the ALU. After performing a write, the instruction sw has completed execution, and the next state is state 0. However, if the instruction is a load,
another state (state 4) is needed to write the result from the memory into the
register file.

The memory is kept in read mode with the same address (by asserting
MemRead and IorD). These signals must be kept asserted across states because
the output of the ALU and the memory are not saved in a register. If the con-

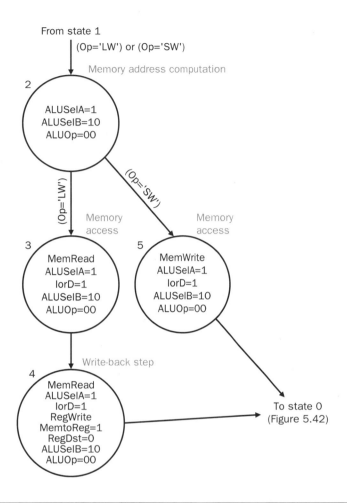

FIGURE 5.43 The finite state machine for controlling memory-reference instructions has four states. These states correspond to the box labeled "Memory access instructions" in Figure 5.41. After performing a memory address calculation, a separate sequence is needed for load and for store. The setting of the control signals ALUSelA, ALUSelB, and ALUOp is used to cause the memory address computation. These signals must be kept stable until the value is written into a register (if a load) or into memory (if a store).

trol values changed, the output of the ALU and memory would change, and the value stored as a result of the load would be incorrect. With these values stable, setting the multiplexor controls MemtoReg = 1 and RegDst = 0 will send the memory output to be written into the register file, using rd as the reg-

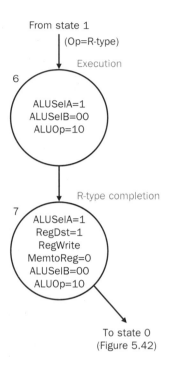

From state 1
(Op=R-type)

Execution

6

ALUSelA=1
ALUSelB=00
ALUOp=10

R-type completion

7

ALUSelA=1
RegDst=1
RegWrite
MemtoReg=0
ALUSelB=00
ALUOp=10

To state 0
(Figure 5.42)

FIGURE 5.44 R-type instructions can be implemented with a simple two-state finite state machine. These states correspond to the box labeled *R-type Instructions* in Figure 5.41. The first state causes the ALU operation to occur, while the second state causes the ALU result to be written in the register file. The signals dealing with the ALU are stable during both cycles. The three additional signals asserted during state 7 cause the ALU output to be written into the register specified by the rd field of the Instruction register.

ister number. After this state, corresponding to the Write-back step, the next state is state 0.

To implement the R-type instructions requires a two-state finite state machine corresponding to the steps Execute and R-type completion. Figure 5.44 shows this two-state portion of the finite state machine. State 6 asserts ALUSelA and leaves the ALUSelB signals deasserted; this forces the two registers that were read from the register file to be used as inputs to the ALU. Setting ALUOp to 10 causes the ALU control unit to use the function code to set the ALU control signals. In state 7, RegWrite is asserted to cause the register to write, and RegDst is asserted to cause the rd field to be used as the register number of the destination.

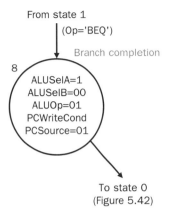

From state 1

(Op='BEQ')

Branch completion

8

ALUSelA=1
ALUSelB=00
ALUOp=01
PCWriteCond
PCSource=01

To state 0
(Figure 5.42)

FIGURE 5.45 The branch instruction requires a single state machine. The first three outputs that are asserted cause the ALU to compare the registers (ALUSelA, ALUSelB, and ALUOp), while the signals PCSource and PCWriteCond perform the conditional write if the branch condition is true.

For branches, only a single additional state is necessary, because they complete execution during the third step of instruction execution. During this state, the control signals that cause the ALU to compare the two register values must be set, and the signals that cause the PC to be written conditionally with the address in the Target register are also set. To perform the comparison requires that we assert ALUSelA and set the ALUOp value to 01 (forcing a subtract). To control the writing of the PC, we assert PCWriteCond and set PCSource to 01, which will cause the value in the Target register to be written into the PC if the Zero bit out of the ALU is asserted. Figure 5.45 shows this single state machine.

The last instruction type is jump; like branch, it requires only a single state (shown in Figure 5.46) to complete its execution. In this state, the signal PCWrite is asserted to cause the PC to be written. By setting PCSource to 10, the value supplied for writing will be the lower 26 bits of the Instruction register with 00_{two} concatenated combined with the upper 4 bits of the PC.

We can now put these pieces of the finite state machine together to form a specification for the control unit, as shown in Figure 5.47 on page 332. In each state, the signals that are asserted are shown. The next-state function depends on the opcode bits of the instruction, so we label the arcs corresponding to the next state function simply with the instruction opcode test they use on the input to the control unit (which is the opcode field of the IR). Given this imple-

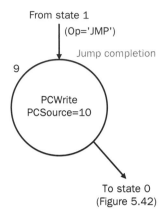

From state 1
(Op='JMP')

Jump completion

9

PCWrite
PCSource=10

To state 0
(Figure 5.42)

FIGURE 5.46 The jump instruction requires a single state that asserts two control signals to write the PC with the lower 26 bits of the Instruction register shifted left two bits.

mentation, and the knowledge that each state requires one clock cycle, we can find the CPI for a typical instruction mix.

Example

Using the control shown in Figure 5.47 and the gcc instruction mix shown in the example starting on page 308, what is the CPI, assuming that each state requires one clock cycle?

Answer

The mix is 22% loads, 11% stores, 49% R-format operations, 16% branches, and 2% jumps. The number of clock cycles for each instruction type is

- Loads: 5,

- Stores: 4,

- R-format instructions: 4,

- Branches: 3, and

- Jumps: 3.

The CPI is given by the following:

$$CPI = \frac{CPU \text{ clock cycles}}{\text{Instruction count}} = \frac{\sum \text{Instruction count}_i \times CPI_i}{\text{Instruction count}}$$

$$= \sum \frac{\text{Instruction count}_i}{\text{Instruction count}} \times CPI_i$$

The ratio

$$\frac{\text{Instruction count}_i}{\text{Instruction count}}$$

is simply the instruction frequency for the instruction class i. We can therefore substitute to obtain

$$CPI = 0.22 \times 5 + 0.11 \times 4 + 0.49 \times 4 + 0.16 \times 3 + 0.02 \times 3$$

$$= 1.1 + 0.44 + 1.96 + 0.48 + 0.06 = 4.04$$

This CPI is considerably better than the worst-case CPI would have been if all the instructions took the same number of clock ticks (5).

A finite state machine can be implemented with a register that holds the current state and a block of combinational logic that determines both the datapath signals to be asserted as well as the next state. Figure 5.48 shows how such an implementation might look. Appendix C describes in detail how the finite state machine is implemented using this structure. In section C.1, the combinational control logic for the finite state machine of Figure 5.47 is implemented both with a ROM (read-only memory) and a PLA (programmable logic array). (Also see Appendix B for a description of these logic elements.) In the next section of this chapter, we consider another way to represent control. Both of these techniques are simply different representations of the same control information.

Elaboration: The style of finite state machine in Figure 5.47 is called a Moore machine, after Edward Moore. Its identifying characteristic is that the output depends only on the current state. An alternative style of machine is a Mealy machine, named after George Mealy. The Mealy machine allows both the input and the current state to be used to determine the output.

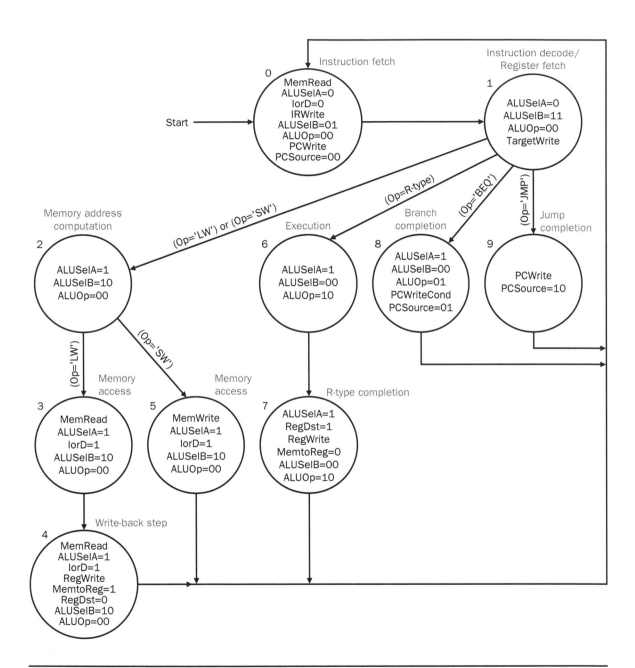

FIGURE 5.47 The complete finite state machine control for the datapath shown in Figure 5.39. The labels on the arcs are conditions that are tested to determine which state is the next state; when the next state is unconditional, no label is given. The labels inside the nodes indicate the output signals asserted during that state; we always specify the setting of a multiplexor control signal if the correct operation requires it. Hence, in some states a multiplexor control will be set to 0. In Appendix C, we will examine how to turn this finite state machine into logic equations and look at how to implement those logic equations.

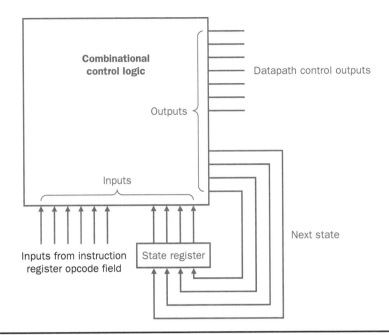

FIGURE 5.48 Finite state machine controllers are typically implemented using a block of combinational logic and a register to hold the current state. The outputs of the combinational logic are the next-state number and the control signals to be asserted for the current state. The inputs to the combinational logic are the current state and any inputs used to determine the next state. In this case, the inputs are the register opcode bits.

5.5 Microprogramming: Simplifying Control Design

For the control of our simple MIPS subset, a graphical representation of the finite state machine, as in Figure 5.47, is certainly adequate. We can draw such a diagram on a single page and translate it into equations (see Appendix C) without generating too many errors. Consider an implementation of the full MIPS instruction set, which contains over 100 instructions (see Appendix A). In one implementation, instructions take from 1 cycle to over 20 cycles. Clearly, the control function will be much more complex. Or consider an instruction set with more instructions of widely varying types: The control unit could easily require thousands of states with hundreds of different sequences. For example, the VAX instruction set has more than 20 addressing mode combinations, each of which can be used for any of up to five operands.

In such cases, specifying the control unit with a graphical representation will be cumbersome, since the finite state machine can contain hundreds to thousands of states and even more arcs! The graphical representation—while useful for a small finite state machine—is hard to fit on a page, let alone understand, when it becomes very large. Programmers know this phenomenon quite well: As programs become large, additional structuring techniques (for example, procedures and modules) are needed to keep the programs comprehensible. Of course, specifying complex control functions directly as equations, without making any mistakes, becomes essentially impossible.

Can we use some of the ideas from programming to help create a method of specifying the control that will make it easier to understand as well as to design? Suppose we think of the set of control signals that must be asserted in a state as an instruction to be executed by the datapath. To avoid confusing the instructions of the MIPS instruction set with these low-level control instructions, the latter are called *microinstructions*. Each microinstruction defines the set of datapath control signals that must be asserted in a given state. Executing a microinstruction has the effect of asserting the control signals specified by the microinstruction.

In addition to defining which control signals must be asserted, we must also specify the sequencing—what microinstruction should be executed next? In the finite state machine shown in Figure 5.47 on page 332, the next state is determined in one of two different ways. Sometimes a single next state follows the current state unconditionally. For example, state 1 always follows state 0, and the only way to reach state 1 is via state 0. In other cases, the choice of the next state depends on the input. This is true in state 1, which has four different successor states. When we write programs, we also have an analogous situation. Sometimes a group of instructions should be executed sequentially, and sometimes we need to branch. In programming, the default is sequential execution, while branching must be indicated explicitly. In describing the control as a program, we will also assume that microinstructions written sequentially are executed in sequence, while branching must be indicated explicitly. The default sequencing mechanism can still be implemented using a structure like the one in Figure 5.48 on page 333; however, it is often more efficient to implement the default sequential state using a counter. We will see how such an implementation looks at the end of this section.

Designing the control as a program that implements the machine instructions in terms of simpler microinstructions is called *microprogramming*. The key idea is to represent the asserted values on the control lines symbolically, so that the microprogram is a representation of the microinstructions, just as assembly language is a representation of the machine instructions. In choosing a syntax for an assembly language, we usually represent the machine instructions as a series of fields (opcode, registers, and offset or immediate field); likewise, we will represent a microinstruction syntactically as a sequence of fields whose functions are related.

Defining a Microinstruction Format

The microprogram is a symbolic representation of the control that will be translated by a program to control logic. In this way, we can choose how many fields a microinstruction should have and what control signals are affected by each field. The format of the microinstruction should be chosen so as to simplify the representation, making it easier to write and understand the microprogram. For example, it is useful to have one field that controls the ALU and a set of three fields that determine the two sources for the ALU operation as well as the destination of the ALU result. In addition to readability, we would also like the microprogram format to make it difficult or impossible to write inconsistent microinstructions. A microinstruction is inconsistent if it requires that a given control signal be set to two different values. We will see an example of how this could happen shortly.

To avoid a format that allows inconsistent microinstructions, we can make each field of the microinstruction responsible for specifying a nonoverlapping set of control signals. To choose how to make this partition of the control signals for this implementation into microinstruction fields, it is useful to re-examine

- Figure 5.37 on page 316, which shows the function of each datapath control signal,

- The control signals that affect the PC (Figure 5.40 on page 324), and

- Figure 5.39 on page 323, which shows all the control signals and how they affect the datapath.

Signals that are never asserted simultaneously may share the same field. Figure 5.49 shows how the microinstruction can be broken into eight fields and defines the general function of each field. The first seven fields of the microinstruction control the datapath, while the Sequencing field (the eighth field) specifies how to select the next microinstruction.

Microinstructions are usually placed in a ROM or a PLA (both described in Appendix B), so we can assign addresses to the microinstructions. The addresses are usually given out sequentially, in the same way that we chose sequential numbers for the states in the finite state machine. Three different methods are available to choose the next microinstruction to be executed:

1. Increment the address of the current microinstruction to obtain the address of the next microinstruction. This is indicated in the micropro-

Field name	Function of field
ALU control	Specify the operation being done by the ALU during this clock.
SRC1	Specify the source for the first ALU operand.
SRC2	Specify the source for the second ALU operand.
ALU destination	Specify a register to be written from the ALU result.
Memory	Specify read or write and the address source.
Memory register	Specify the register destination (for a memory read) or the source of the values (for a memory write).
PCWrite control	Specify the writing of the PC.
Sequencing	Specify how to choose the next microinstruction to be executed.

FIGURE 5.49 Each microinstruction contains these eight fields. The values for each field are shown in Figure 5.50.

gram by putting Seq in the Sequencing field. Since sequential execution of instructions is encountered often, many microprogramming systems make this the default and simply leave the entry blank as the default.

2. Branch to the microinstruction that begins execution of the next MIPS instruction. We will label this initial microinstruction (corresponding to state 0) as Fetch and place the indicator Fetch in the Sequencing field to indicate this action.

3. Choose the next microinstruction based on the control unit input. Choosing the next microinstruction on the basis of some input is called a *dispatch*. Dispatch operations are usually implemented by creating a table containing the addresses of the target microinstructions. This table is indexed by the control unit input and may be implemented in a ROM or in a PLA. There are often multiple dispatch tables; for this implementation, we will need two dispatch tables, one to dispatch from state 1 and one to dispatch from state 2. We indicate that the next microinstruction should be chosen by a dispatch operation by placing Dispatch i, where i is the dispatch table number, in the Sequencing field.

Figure 5.50 gives a description of the values allowed for each field of the microinstruction and the effect of the different field values. Remember that the microprogram is a symbolic representation. This microinstruction format is just one example of many potential formats.

Elaboration: Notice that both the Memory and ALU destination fields can specify a register to be written. However, our datapath will not support this, since it has only a single register file write port. Typically, the microassembler will perform checks on the microinstruction fields to ensure that such inconsistencies are flagged as errors and

Field name	Values for field	Function of field with specific value
ALU control	Add	Cause the ALU to add.
	Func code	Use the instruction's function code to determine ALU control.
	Subt	Cause the ALU to subtract.
SRC1	PC	Use the PC as the first ALU input.
	rs	Register rs is the first ALU input.
SRC2	4	Use 4 for the second ALU input.
	Extend	Use output of the sign-extension unit as the second ALU input.
	Extshft	Use the output of the shift by 2 unit as the second ALU input.
	rt	Register rt is the second ALU input.
ALU destination	Target	ALU output is written into the register Target.
	rd	ALU output is written into register rd.
Memory	Read PC	Read memory using the PC as address.
	Read ALU	Read memory using the ALU output as address.
	Write ALU	Write memory using the ALU output as address.
Memory register	IR	Data read from memory is written into the Instruction register.
	Write rt	Data read from memory is written into register rt.
	Read rt	Data written into memory comes from register rt.
PCWrite control	ALU	Write the output of the ALU into the PC.
	Target-cond	If the Zero output of the ALU is active, write the PC with the contents of the register Target.
	jump address	Write the PC with the jump address from the instruction.
Sequencing	Seq	Choose the next microinstruction sequentially.
	Fetch	Go to the first microinstruction to begin a new instruction.
	Dispatch i	Dispatch using the ROM specified by i (1 or 2).

FIGURE 5.50 Each field of the microinstruction has a number of values that it can take on. The second column gives the possible values that are legal for the field, and the third column defines the effect of that value. Each field value is mapped to a particular setting of the datapath control lines; this mapping is described in Appendix C, section C.3.

corrected. An alternative is to structure the microinstruction format to avoid this. We could achieve this by making the register destination a separate field and describing whether the memory or ALU provided the value to be stored and which instruction field contained the register designator. Of course, this might make the microinstruction harder to read. Most microprogramming systems choose readability and require the microcode assembler to detect such errors.

Creating the Microprogram

Now let's create the microprogram for the control unit. We will label the instructions in the microprogram with symbolic labels, which can be used to specify the contents of the dispatch tables (see Appendix C for a discussion of how the dispatch tables are defined and assembled). In writing the microprogram, there are two situations in which we may want to leave a field of the microinstruction blank. When a field that controls a functional unit or that causes state to be written (such as the Memory field or the ALU dest field) is blank, no control signals should be asserted. When a field *only* specifies the control of a multiplexor that determines the input to a functional unit, such as the SRC1 field, leaving it blank means that we do not care about the input to the functional unit (or the output of the multiplexor).

The easiest way to understand the microprogram is to break it into pieces that deal with each component of instruction execution, just as we did when we designed the finite state machine. The first component of every instruction execution is to fetch the instructions, decode them, and compute both the sequential PC and branch target PC. These actions correspond directly to the first two steps of execution described on pages 317 through 321. The two microinstructions needed for these first two steps are shown below:

Label	ALU control	SRC1	SRC2	ALU destination	Memory	Memory register	PCWrite control	Sequencing
Fetch	Add	PC	4		Read PC	IR	ALU	Seq
	Add	PC	Extshft	Target				Dispatch 1

To understand what each microinstruction does, it is easiest to look at the effect of a group of fields. In the first microinstruction, the fields asserted and their effects are

Fields	Effect
ALU control, SRC1, SRC2	Compute PC + 4.
Memory and memory register	Fetch instruction into IR.
PCWrite control	Causes the output of the ALU to be written into the PC.
Sequencing	Go to the next microinstruction.

For the second microinstruction, the registers will be read using the fields of the instruction register. The other operations controlled by the microinstruction are

Fields	Effect
ALU control, SRC1, SRC2, ALU destination	Store PC + sign-extension (IR[15–0]) << 2 into Target.
Sequencing	Use dispatch table 1 to choose the next microinstruction address.

We can think of the dispatch operation as a *case* statement with the opcode field and the dispatch table 1 used to select one of four different microinstruction sequences (memory reference, R-type instructions, branch, and jump). The microprogram for memory-reference instructions has four microinstructions, as shown below. The first instruction does the memory address calculation. A two-instruction sequence is needed to complete a load (memory read followed by register write), while the store requires only one microinstruction after the memory address calculation:

Label	ALU control	SRC1	SRC2	ALU destination	Memory	Memory register	PCWrite control	Sequencing
LWSW1	Add	rs	Extend					Dispatch 2
LW2	Add	rs	Extend		Read ALU			Seq
	Add	rs	Extend		Read ALU	Write rt		Fetch
SW2	Add	rs	Extend		Write ALU	Read rt		Fetch

Let's look at the fields of the first microinstruction in this sequence:

Fields	Effect
ALU control, SRC1, SRC2	Compute the memory address: Register (rs) + sign-extend (IR[15–0])
Sequencing	Use the second dispatch table to jump to either LW2 or SW2.

The first microinstruction in the sequence specific to `lw` is labeled LW2. This microinstruction has the following effect:

Fields	Effect
ALU control, SRC1, SRC2	The output of the ALU is still the memory address.
Memory	Read memory using the ALU output as the address.
Sequencing	Go to the next microinstruction.

The next microinstruction completes execution with a microinstruction that has the following effects:

Fields	Effect
ALU control, SRC1, SRC2	The output of the ALU is still the memory address.
Memory and memory register	Read memory using the ALU output as the address and write the result into the register designated by rt.
Sequencing	Go to the microinstruction labeled Fetch.

Notice that since the fields of the two microinstructions that complete a load word instruction do not conflict, we could combine these two microinstructions into a single microinstruction of the form:

Label	ALU control	SRC1	SRC2	ALU destination	Memory	Memory register	PCWrite control	Sequencing
LW2	Add	rs	Extend		Read ALU	Write rt		Fetch

This process is often performed by a microcode optimizer to reduce the number of microinstructions. However, if we made this change, it would probably increase the length of the clock cycle, since both the memory access and register write would have to occur in a single microinstruction, and each microinstruction corresponds to a single clock cycle. Thus, when we try to optimize the microcode, either by hand or with a program, we must know what set of datapath actions can fit in the clock cycle that we are designing toward.

The store microinstruction, labeled SW2, operates similarly to the load microinstruction labeled LW2:

Fields	Effect
ALU control, SRC1, SRC2	The output of the ALU is still the memory address.
Memory and Memory register	Write memory using the ALU output as the address and the register designated by rt as the value to write.
Sequencing	Go to the microinstruction labeled Fetch.

The microprogram sequence for R-type instructions consists of two microinstructions: the first performs the ALU operation, while the second writes the result into the register file:

Label	ALU control	SRC1	SRC2	ALU destination	Memory	Memory register	PCWrite control	Sequencing
Rformat1	Func code	rs	rt					Seq
	Func code	rs	rt	rd				Fetch

Like the example of the load instruction above, we could combine these two microinstructions into a single microinstruction. However, this would mean that the ALU and register write back would occur in one clock cycle, possibly leading to a longer clock cycle and a slower machine. The first microinstruction initiates the ALU operation:

Fields	Effect
ALU control, SRC1, SRC2	The ALU operates on the register contents of the rs and rt registers, using the func field to specify the ALU operation.
Sequencing	Go to the next microinstruction.

The second microinstruction causes the ALU output to be written in the register file:

Fields	Effect
ALU control, SRC1, SRC2, ALU destination	The ALU continues the same operation. The ALU dest field specifies that rd is used to choose the destination register.
Sequencing	Go to the microinstruction labeled Fetch.

The microprogram sequence for branch requires one microinstruction:

Label	ALU control	SRC1	SRC2	ALU destination	Memory	Memory register	PCWrite control	Sequencing
BEQ1	Subt	rs	rt				Target–cond	Fetch

The asserted fields of this microinstruction are

Fields	Effect
ALU control, SRC1, SRC2	The ALU subtracts the register operands to generate the Zero output.
PCWrite control	Causes the PC to be written using the value in target, if the Zero output of the ALU is true.
Sequencing	Go to the microinstruction labeled Fetch.

The jump microcode sequence also consists of one microinstruction:

Label	ALU control	SRC1	SRC2	ALU destination	Memory	Memory register	PCWrite control	Sequencing
JUMP1							jump address	Fetch

Only two fields of this microinstruction are asserted:

Fields	Effect
PCWrite control	Causes the PC to be written using the jump field.
Sequencing	Go to the microinstruction labeled Fetch.

The entire microprogram appears in Figure 5.51. It consists of the 10 micro-instructions appearing above. This microprogram matches the 10-state finite state machine we designed earlier, since they were both derived from the same five-step execution sequence for the instructions. In more complex machines the microprogram sequence might consist of hundreds or thousands of micro-instructions.

This microprogram is translated into microinstructions and dispatch tables, which can then be implemented in ROMs or PLAs. This process is directly analogous to the process of translating an assembly language program into machine instructions, or translating the finite state diagram of Figure 5.47 into hardware. The datapath control signals specified in each microinstruction can be implemented using the same logic structures that we used for implementing a finite state machine.

Figure 5.48 on page 333 showed one method for implementing the sequencing. Figure 5.52 shows another type of sequencer that uses an incrementer to choose the next control instruction. In this type of implementation, the

Label	ALU control	SRC1	SRC2	ALU destination	Memory	Memory register	PCWrite control	Sequencing
Fetch	Add	PC	4		Read PC	IR	ALU	Seq
	Add	PC	Extshft	Target				Dispatch 1
LWSW1	Add	rs	Extend					Dispatch 2
LW2	Add	rs	Extend		Read ALU			Seq
	Add	rs	Extend		Read ALU	Write rt		Fetch
SW2	Add	rs	Extend		Write ALU	Read rt		Fetch
Rformat1	Func code	rs	rt					Seq
	Func code	rs	rt	rd				Fetch
BEQ1	Subt	rs	rt				Target–cond.	Fetch
JUMP1							jump address	Fetch

FIGURE 5.51 The microprogram for the control unit. The labels are used to determine the targets for the dispatch operations. Dispatch 1 does a jump based on the IR to a label ending with a 1. The PCWrite control indicates whether the PC should be written conditionally (on the basis of the equal signal from the ALU) by including cond in the specification. There are three possible sources for the value that will be written into the PC: the ALU output, the branch target address register (Target), and the jump address target that comes from combining the lower 26 bits of the instruction and the PC.

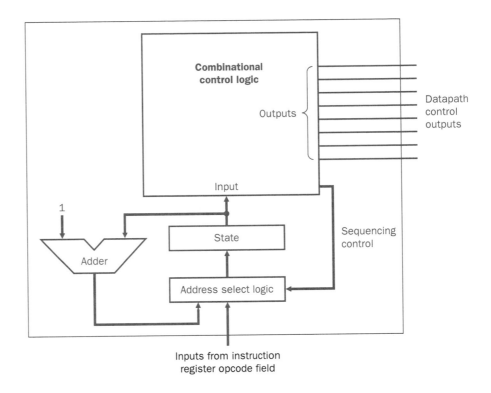

FIGURE 5.52 A typical implementation of a microcode controller would use an explicit incrementer to compute the default sequential next state. A combination logic block would be used to set the datapath control based on the current state and also to determine how the next microinstruction would be chosen. The address select logic would contain the dispatch tables as well as the logic to select from among the alternative next states; the selection of the next microinstruction is controlled by the sequencing control outputs from the control logic. The combination of the current state register, incrementer, dispatch tables, and address select logic forms a sequencer that selects the next microinstruction.

combinational control logic would determine the value of the datapath control lines, as well as how to select the next state. The address select logic would contain the dispatch tables and would, under the control of the address select outputs, determine the next microinstruction to execute. The type of sequencer shown in Figure 5.52 can be used to implement either a finite state or a microprogram control specification, and section C.2 of Appendix C describes how to generate such a sequencer in more detail. Section C.3 describes how a microprogram can be translated to such an implementation. The choice of which way to represent the control and how to implement are independent decisions, affected by both the structure of the control function and the technology used to implement the control. Before we can discuss what factors favor the different implementation mechanisms, we need to talk about one of the hardest aspects of control: exceptions.

5.6 | Exceptions

Control is the most challenging aspect of processor design: it is both the hardest part to get right and the hardest part to make fast. The hardest part of control is implementing *exceptions* and *interrupts*—events other than branches or jumps that change the normal flow of instruction execution. An exception is an unexpected event from within the processor; arithmetic overflow is an example of an exception. An interrupt is an event that also causes an unexpected change in control flow but comes from outside of the processor. Interrupts are used by I/O devices to communicate with the processor, as we will see in Chapter 8. Many architectures and authors do not distinguish between interrupts and exceptions, often using the older name *interrupt* to refer to both types of events. We follow the MIPS convention using the term *exception* to refer to *any* unexpected change in control flow without distinguishing whether the cause is internal and external; we use the term interrupt only when the event is externally caused.

Interrupts were initially created to handle unexpected events like arithmetic overflow and to signal requests for service from I/O devices. The same basic mechanism was extended to handle internally-generated exceptions as well. Here are some examples showing whether the situation is generated internally by the processor or externally generated:

Type of event	From where?	MIPS terminology
I/O device request	External	Interrupt
Invoke the operating system from user program	Internal	Exception
Arithmetic overflow	Internal	Exception
Using an undefined instruction	Internal	Exception
Hardware malfunctions	Either	Exception or interrupt

Many of the requirements to support exceptions come from the specific situation that causes an exception to occur. Accordingly, we will return to this topic in Chapter 7, when we discuss memory hierarchies, and in Chapter 8, when we discuss I/O. In this section, we deal with the control implementation of two types of exceptions that arise from the portions of the instruction set and implementation that we have already discussed.

Detecting exceptional conditions and taking the appropriate action is often on the critical timing path of a machine, which determines the clock cycle time and thus performance. Without proper attention to exceptions during design of the control unit, attempts to add exceptions to a complicated implementation can significantly reduce performance, as well as complicate the task of getting the design correct.

How Are Exceptions Handled?

The two types of exceptions that our current implementation can generate are execution of an undefined instruction and an arithmetic overflow. The basic action that the machine must perform when an exception occurs is to save the address of the offending instruction in the exception program counter (EPC) and then transfer control to the operating system at some specified address. The operating system can then take the appropriate action, which may involve providing some service to the user program, taking some predefined action in response to an overflow, or stopping the execution of the program and reporting an error. After performing whatever action is required due to the exception, the operating system can terminate the program or may continue its execution, using the EPC to determine where to restart the execution of the program. In Chapter 7, we will look more closely at the issue of restarting the execution.

For the operating system to handle the exception, it must know the reason for the exception, in addition to the instruction that caused it. There are two main methods used to communicate the reason for an exception. The method used in the MIPS architecture is to include a Status register (called the *Cause* register), which holds a field that indicates the reason for the exception. A second method is to use *vectored interrupts*. In a vectored interrupt, the address to which control is transferred is determined by the cause of the exception. For example, to accommodate the two exception types listed above, we might define the following:

Exception type	Exception vector address (in binary)
Undefined instruction	$01000000\ 00000000\ 00000000\ 00000000_{two}$
Arithmetic overflow	$01000000\ 00000000\ 00000000\ 01000000_{two}$

The operating system knows the reason for the exception by the address at which it is initiated. The addresses are separated by 32 instructions; thus, the operating system must record the reason for the exception and may perform some limited processing in this sequence. When the exception is not vectored, a single entry point can be used, and the operating system decodes the status register to find the cause. Other key issues in exception handling are related to the memory system and the capabilities of the operating system.

We can perform the processing required for exceptions by adding a few extra registers and control signals to our basic implementation and by slightly extending the finite state machine. Let's assume that we are implementing the exception system used in the MIPS architecture. (Implementing vectored exceptions is no more difficult.) We will need to add two additional registers to the datapath:

- *EPC:* A 32-bit register used to hold the address of the affected instruction.

- *Cause:* A register used to record the cause of the exception. In the MIPS architecture, this register is 32 bits, although some bits are currently unused. Assume that the low-order bit of this register encodes the two possible exception sources mentioned above: undefined instruction=0 and arithmetic overflow=1.

We will need to add two control signals to cause the EPC and Cause registers to be written; call these *EPCWrite* and *CauseWrite*. In addition, we will need a 1-bit control signal to set the low-order bit of the Cause register appropriately; call this signal *IntCause*. Finally, we will need to be able to write the exception address into the PC; let's assume that this address is 01000000 00000000 00000000 00000000_{two}. Currently, the PC is fed from the output of a 3-way multiplexor, which is controlled by the 2-bit signal PCSource (see Figure 5.39 on page 323). We can change this to a 4-way multiplexor, with additional input wired to the constant value 01000000 00000000 00000000 00000000_{two}. Then PCSource is set to 11 (which was previously unused) to select the value 01000000 00000000 00000000 00000000_{two} to be written into the PC.

Because the PC is incremented during the first cycle of every instruction, we cannot just write the value of the PC into the EPC, since the value in the PC will be the instruction address plus 4. However, we can use the ALU to subtract 4 from the PC and write the output into the EPC. This requires no additional control signals or paths, since we can use the ALU to subtract, and the constant 4 is already a selectable ALU input. The data write port of the EPC, therefore, is connected to the ALU output. With these additions, the action to be taken on different types of exceptions can be accomplished by the finite state machine shown in Figure 5.53. To connect this finite state machine to the

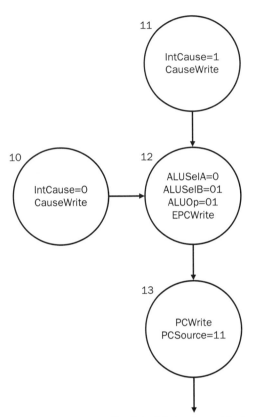

FIGURE 5.53 This four-state machine handles the three aspects of exception processing.
It sets the Cause register (states 10 and 11), gets the address of the offending instruction into the
EPC (state 12), and sets the PC to the exception vector address (state 13). Each of states 10 and 11
represents the starting point for an exception. The function of these states is to set the Cause register input correctly and to cause it to be written. In state 12, we use the ALU to compute PC – 4;
the PC is the first ALU input, and the second is the digit4 (selected by ALUSelB = 01). The ALU
subtracts (since ALUOp = 01), and the result is written into the EPC (EPCWrite). The PC is written with the exception vector address by setting control signals in state 13.

finite state machine of the main control unit, we must determine how to detect
exceptions and add arcs that transfer control from the main execution machine
to this exception-handling finite state machine.

How Control Checks for Exceptions

Now we have to design a method to detect these exceptions and to transfer control to the appropriate state in the exception finite state machine shown in Figure 5.53. Each of the two possible exceptions is detected differently:

- *Undefined Instruction*: This is detected when no next state is defined from state 1 for the op value. We handle this exception by defining the next-state value for all op values other than lw, sw, 0 (R-type), jmp, and beq as state 10. We show this by symbolically using *other* to indicate that the op field does not match any of the opcodes that label arcs out of state 1. A modified finite state diagram is shown in Figure 5.54.

- *Arithmetic overflow*: Chapter 4 included logic in the ALU to detect overflow, and a signal called *Overflow* is provided as an output from the ALU. This signal is used in the modified finite state machine to specify an additional possible next state for state 7, as shown in Figure 5.54.

By combining the finite state machines in Figures 5.53 and 5.54, we can arrive at a complete specification of the control for this MIPS subset with two types of exceptions. Remember that the challenge in designing the control of a real machine is to handle the variety of different interactions between instructions and other exception-causing events in such a way that the control logic remains both small and fast. The complex interactions that are possible are what make the control unit the most challenging aspect of hardware design.

Elaboration: If you examine the finite state machine in Figure 5.54 closely, you can see that some problems could occur in the way the exceptions are handled. For example, in the case of arithmetic overflow, the instruction causing the overflow completes writing its result, because the overflow branch is in the state when the write completes. However, it's possible that the architecture defines the instruction as having no effect if the instruction causes an exception; this is what the MIPS instruction set architecture specifies. In Chapter 7, we will see that certain classes of exceptions require us to prevent the instruction from changing the machine state, and that this aspect of handling exceptions becomes complex and potentially limits performance.

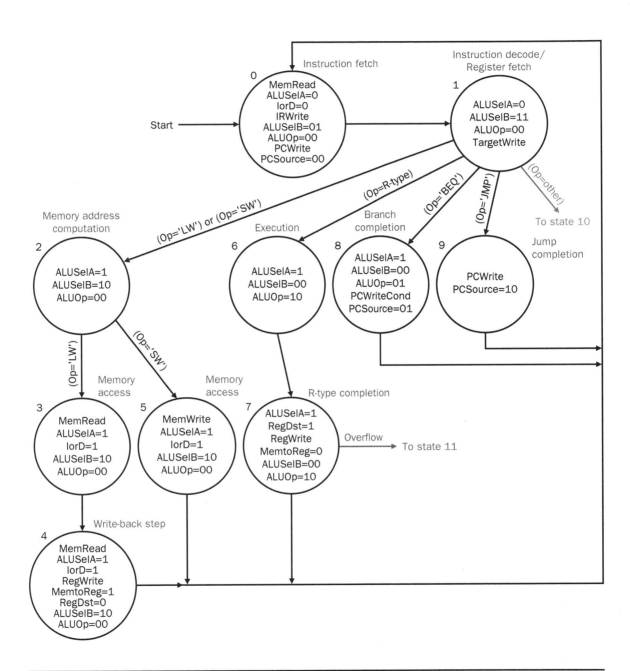

FIGURE 5.54 This shows the finite state machine with the additions to handle exception detection. States 10 and 11 are defined in the exception-handling extension to the base finite state machine appearing in Figure 5.53 on page 347. The branch out of state 1 labeled *(Op=other)* indicates the next state when the input does not match the opcode of any of lw, sw, 0 (R-type), jmp, or beq. The branch out of state 7 labeled Overflow indicates the action to be taken when the ALU signals an overflow.

5.7   Fallacies and Pitfalls

Pitfall: Microcode implementing a complex instruction may not be faster than a sequence using simpler instructions.

Most machines with a large and complex instruction set are implemented using a microcode stored in ROM. Surprisingly, on such machines, sequences of individual simpler instructions are sometimes as fast as or even faster than the custom microcode sequence for a particular instruction. How can this possibly be true? At one time, microcode had the advantage of being fetched from a much faster memory than instructions in the program. Since caches came into use in 1968, microcode no longer has such a consistent edge in fetch time. Microcode does, however, still have the advantage of using internal temporary registers in the computation, which can be helpful on machines with few general-purpose registers. The disadvantage of microcode is that the algorithms must be selected before the machine is announced and can't be changed until the next model of the architecture. The instructions in a program, on the other hand, can utilize improvements in its algorithms at any time during the life of the machine. Along the same lines, the microcode sequence is probably not optimal for all possible combinations of operands.

The VAX Index instruction provides an example of the above phenomenon. This instruction checks to see if the index is between two bounds, one of which is usually 0. The VAX-11/780 microcode uses two compares and two branches to do this, while the standard instructions can perform the same check in one compare and one branch. The program can check the index against the upper limit using *unsigned* comparisons rather than two's complement comparisons. This treats a negative index (less than zero and so failing the comparison) as if it were a very large number, thus exceeding the upper limit. (The algorithm can be used with nonzero lower bounds by first subtracting the lower bound from the index.) Replacing the Index instruction by a sequence of VAX instructions to perform the necessary function always improves performance on the VAX-11/780.

Fallacy: If there is space in control store, new instructions are free of cost.

One of the benefits of a microprogrammed approach is that control store implemented in ROM is not very expensive. Moreover, if we use off-the-shelf parts for the ROM, there may be unused control store available to expand the instruction set. The analogy here is that of building a house and discovering, near completion, that you have enough land and materials left to add a room. This room wouldn't be free, however, since there would be the costs of labor and maintenance for the life of the home. The temptation to add "free" instructions can occur only when the instruction set is not fixed, as is likely to be the case in the first model of a computer. Because upward compatibility of binary programs is a highly desirable feature, all future models of this machine will be forced to include these so-called free instructions, even if space is later at a premium.

The extra instructions may also be costly to implement in future technologies. For example, consider a large instruction set initially implemented with microcode. If a later implementation is done in VLSI, it may be difficult to place all the control store on the same chip as the rest of the processor. Placing the control off-chip is also unattractive, since it requires more pins and may slow down the clock. During the 1980s, VLSI implementations of the VAX encountered exactly this problem and, eventually, some instructions were actually removed from the VAX instruction set; programs that used such instructions generated exceptions that trapped to software to perform these instructions. Lastly, additions to the instruction set may also ignore the cost of a longer development time to test the added instructions, as well as the possibility of costs for repairing bugs in them after the hardware is shipped.

5.8 Concluding Remarks

As we have seen in this chapter, both the datapath and control for a processor can be designed starting with the instruction set architecture and an understanding of the basic characteristics of the technology. In section 5.2, we saw how the datapath for a MIPS processor could be constructed based on the architecture and the decision to build a single-cycle implementation. Of course, the underlying technology also affects many design decisions by dictating what components can be used in the datapath, as well as whether a single-cycle implementation even makes sense. Along the same lines, in the first portion of section 5.4, we saw how the decision to break the clock cycle into a series of steps led to the revised multicycle datapath. In both cases, the top-level organization—a single-cycle or multicycle machine—together with the instruction set, prescribed many characteristics of the datapath design.

Similarly, the control is largely defined by the instruction set architecture, the organization, and the datapath design. In the single-cycle organization, these three aspects essentially define how the control signals must be set. In the multicycle design, the exact decomposition of the instruction execution into cycles, which is based on the instruction set architecture, together with the datapath, define the requirements on the control.

Control is one of the most challenging aspects of computer design. A major reason for this is that designing the control requires an understanding of how all the components in the processor operate. To help meet this challenge, we examined two techniques for specifying control: finite state diagrams and microprogramming. These control representations allow us to abstract the specification of the control from the details of how to implement it. Using abstraction in this fashion is the major method we have to cope with the complexity of computer designs.

Once the control has been specified, we can map it to detailed hardware. The exact details of the control implementation will depend on both the structure of the control and on the underlying technology used to implement it. Abstracting the specification of control is also valuable because the decisions of how to implement the control are technology-dependent and likely to change over time.

In the 1960s and 1970s, microprogramming was one of the most important techniques used in implementing machines. Through most of that period, machines were implemented with discrete components or MSI (medium scale integration—fewer than 1000 gates per chip), and designers had to choose between two types of implementations: *hardwired control* or *microprogrammed control*. Hardwired control was characterized by finite state machines using an explicit next state and implemented primarily with random logic. In this era, microprogrammed control used microcode to specify control that was then implemented with a microprogram sequencer (a counter) and ROMs. Hardwired control received its name because the control was implemented in hardware and could not be easily changed. Microprograms implemented in ROM were also called *firmware*, because they could be changed somewhat more easily than hardware, but not nearly as easily as software.

The reliance on standard parts of low- to medium-level integration made these two design styles radically different. Microprogrammed approaches were attractive because implementing the control with a large collection of low-density gates was extremely costly. Furthermore, the popularity of relatively complex instruction sets demanded a large control unit, making a ROM-based implementation much more efficient. The hardwired implementations were faster, but too costly for most machines. Furthermore, it was very difficult to get the control correct, and changing ROMs was easier than replacing a random logic control unit. Eventually, microprogrammed control was implemented in RAM, to allow changes late in the design cycle, and even in the field after a machine shipped.

As architectures became more complex, so did the control. Designers also took advantage of the relative ease of adding new instruction set features to a microprogrammed machine, and instruction set complexity grew quickly.

Much has changed in the 40 years since Wilkes [1953] wrote the first paper on microprogramming. The most important changes are

- Control units are implemented as integral parts of the processor, often on the same silicon die. They cannot be changed independent of the rest of the processor. Furthermore, given the right computer-aided design tools, the difficulty of implementing a ROM or a PLA is the same.

- ROM, which was used to hold the microinstructions, is no longer faster than RAM, which holds the machine language program. A PLA implementation of a control function is often much smaller than the ROM implementation, which may have many duplicate or unused entries. If the PLA is smaller, it is usually faster.

- Instruction sets have become much simpler than they were in the 1960s and 1970s, leading to reduced complexity in the control.

- Computer-aided design tools have improved so that control can be specified symbolically and, by using much faster computers, thoroughly simulated before hardware is constructed. This makes it plausible to get the control logic correct without the need for fixes later.

These changes have blurred the distinctions among different implementation choices. Certainly, using an abstract specification of control is helpful. How that control is then implemented depends on its size, the underlying technology, and the available CAD tools.

5.9   Historical Perspective and Further Reading

Maurice Wilkes learned computer design in a summer workshop from Eckert and Mauchly and then went on to build the first full-scale, operational, stored-program computer—the EDSAC. From that experience he realized the difficulty of control. He thought of a more centralized control using a diode matrix and, after visiting the Whirlwind computer in the U.S., wrote [Wilkes 1985]:

> *I found that it did indeed have a centralized control based on the use of a matrix of diodes. It was, however, only capable of producing a fixed sequence of eight pulses—a different sequence for each instruction, but nevertheless fixed as far as a particular instruction was concerned. It was not, I think, until I got back to Cambridge that I realized that the solution was to turn the control unit into a computer in miniature by adding a second matrix to determine the flow of control at the microlevel and by providing for conditional micro-instructions.*

The Big Picture

Control may be designed using one of several initial representations. The choice of sequence control, and how logic is represented, can then be determined independently; the control can then be implemented with one of several methods using a structured logic technique. Figure 5.55 shows the variety of methods for specifying the control and moving from the specification to an implementation using some form of structured logic:

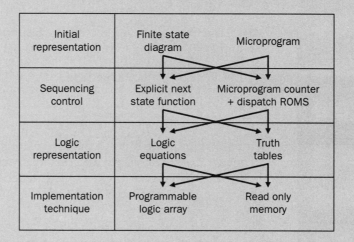

FIGURE 5.55 Alternative methods for specifying and implementing control. The arrows in this figure indicate possible design paths: any path from the initial representation to the final implementation technology is viable. Traditionally, "hardwired control" means that the techniques on the left-hand side are used, and "microprogrammed control" means that the techniques on the right-hand side are used.

Wilkes [1953] was ahead of his time in recognizing that problem. Unfortunately, the solution was also ahead of its time: To provide control, microprogramming relies on fast memory that was not available in the 1950s. Thus, Wilkes's ideas remained primarily academic conjecture for a decade, although he did construct the EDSAC 2 using microprogrammed control in 1958 with ROM made from magnetic cores.

IBM brought microprogramming into the spotlight in 1964 with the IBM 360 family. Before this event, IBM saw itself as a cluster of many small businesses selling different machines with their own price and performance levels, but also with their own instruction sets. (Recall that little programming was done in high-level languages, so that programs written for one IBM machine would not run on another.) Gene Amdahl, one of the chief architects of the IBM 360, said that managers of each subsidiary agreed to the 360 family of computers only because they were convinced that microprogramming made it feasible. To be sure of the viability of microprogramming, the IBM vice president of engineering even visited Wilkes surreptitiously and had a "theoretical" discussion of the pros and cons of microcode. IBM believed that the idea was so important to its plans that it pushed the memory technology inside the company to make microprogramming feasible.

Stewart Tucker of IBM was saddled with the responsibility of porting software from the IBM 7090 to the new IBM 360. Thinking about the possibilities of microcode, he suggested expanding the control store to include simulators, or interpreters, for older machines. Tucker [1967] coined the term *emulation* for this, meaning full simulation at the microprogrammed level. Occasionally, emulation on the 360 was actually faster than on the original hardware.

Once the giant of the industry began using microcode, the rest soon followed. One difficulty in adopting microcode was that the necessary memory technology was not widely available, but that was soon solved by semiconductor ROM and later RAM. The microprocessor industry followed the same history, with the limited resources of the earliest chips forcing hardwired control. But as the resources increased, the advantages of simpler design, ease of change, and the ability to use a wide variety of underlying implementations persuaded many to use microprogramming.

With the increasing popularity of microprogramming came more sophisticated instruction sets. Over the years, most microarchitectures became more and more dedicated to support the intended instruction set, so that reprogramming for a different instruction set failed to offer satisfactory performance. With the passage of time came much larger control stores, and it became possible to consider a machine as elaborate as the VAX with more than 300 different instruction opcodes and more than a dozen memory addressing modes. The use of RAM to store the microcode also made it possible to debug the microcode and even fix some bugs once machines were in the field. The VAX architecture represented the high-water mark for instruction set architectures based on microcode implementations. Typical implementations of the full VAX instruction set required 400 to 500 Kb of control store.

As 1994 begins, the VAX architecture has seen its last days. A new streamlined architecture from Digital, called Alpha, has replaced the VAX. This new architecture is based on the same principles of design used in other RISC architectures, including the MIPS, SPARC, IBM PowerPC, and the HP Precision architecture. With the disappearance of the VAX, traditional microprogramming, in which the control is implemented with one major control store, will largely disappear from new processor designs. Even processors such as the Intel Pentium are employing large amounts of hardwired control, at least for the central core of the processor.

Of course, control unit design will continue to be a major aspect of *all* computers, and the best way to specify and implement the control will vary, just as computers will vary from streamlined RISC architectures with simple control to special-purpose processors with potentially large amounts of more complex and specialized control.

To Probe Further

Kidder, Tracy [1981]. *Soul of a New Machine*, Little, Brown, and Co., New York.

Describes the design of the Data General Eclipse series that replaced the first DG machines such as the Nova. Kidder records the intimate interactions among architects, hardware designers, microcoders, and project management.

Levy, H. M., and R. H. Eckhouse, Jr. [1989]. *Computer Programming and Architecture: The VAX*, 2nd ed., Digital Press, Bedford, Mass.

Good description of the VAX architecture and several different microprogrammed implementations.

Patterson, D. A. [1983]. "Microprogramming," *Scientific American* 248:3 (March) 36–43.

Overview of microprogramming concepts.

Tucker, S. G. [1967]. "Microprogram control for the System/360," *IBM Systems Journal* 6:4, 222–241.

Describes the microprogrammed control for the 360, the first microprogrammed commercial machine.

Wilkes, M. V. [1985]. *Memoirs of a Computer Pioneer*, MIT Press, Cambridge, Mass.

Intriguing biography with many stories about industry pioneers and the trials and successes in building early machines.

Wilkes, M. V., and J. B. Stringer [1953]. "Microprogramming and the design of the control circuits in an electronic digital computer," *Proc. Cambridge Philosophical Society* 49:230–38. Also reprinted in D. P. Siewiorek, C. G. Bell, and A. Newell, *Computer Structures: Principles and Examples* (1982), McGraw-Hill, New York, 158–63, and in "The Genesis of Microprogramming" in *Annals of the History of Computing* 8:116.

These two classic papers describe Wilkes's proposal for microcode.

5.10 Exercises

5.1 [10] <§5.2–5.3> We wish to add the instruction jal (jump and link) to the single-cycle datapath described in this chapter (this instruction is described in Chapter 3, page 119. Add any necessary datapaths and control signals to the single-clock datapath of Figure 5.33 on page 307. You can photocopy the existing datapath (or use Figure 5.22 on page 295, if you prefer) to make it less work to show the additions.

5.2 [5] <§5.3> {ex. 5.1} Show the additions to the table in Figure 5.23 on page 296 needed to set all the control lines that were added in Exercise 5.1for the instruction jal. Remember to add the jump control line if it is needed to implement jal.

5.3 [10] <§5.4> We wish to add the datapath parts and control needed to implement the jal instruction in the multiclock datapath and control. Show the additions to the datapath and control lines of Figure 5.39 on page 323 needed to implement these instructions in the multicycle datapath. You can photocopy the existing datapath to make it less work to show the additions. Again, there are multiple solutions; choose the solution that minimizes the number of clock cycles for this added instruction.

5.4 [5] <§5.4> {ex. 5.3} Show the steps in executing the jal instruction in the multiclock datapath, using the same breakdown of steps as used on pages 317 through 321.

5.5 [5] <§5.4> {ex. 5.3, 5.4} Show the additions to the finite state machine of Figure 5.54 on page 349 to implement the jal instruction.

5.6 [20] <§5.4> Your friends at C^3 (Creative Computer Corporation) have determined that the critical path that sets the clock cycle length of the multi-cycle datapath is memory access for loads and stores (*not* for instructions). This has caused their newest implementation of the MIPS 30000 to run at a clock rate of 500 MHz rather than the target clock rate of 750 MHz. However, Clara at C^3 has a solution. If all the cycles that access memory are broken into two clock cycles, then the machine can run at its target clock rate. Using the gcc mixes shown in Chapter 4 (Figure 4.46 on page 248), determine how much faster the machine with the two-cycle memory accesses is compared with the 500-MHz machine with single-cycle memory access. Assume all jumps and branches take the same number of cycles and that the set instructions and arithmetic immediate instructions are implemented as R-type instructions.

5.7 [15] <§5.1–5.4> For this problem use the gcc data from 4.46 on page 248. Assume there are three machines:

- M1: The multiclock datapath of Chapter 5 with a 50-MHz clock.

- M2: A machine like the multiclock datapath of Chapter 5, except that register updates are done in the same clock as a memory read or ALU operation. Thus, in Figure 5.54 on page 349 states 6 and 7 and states 3 and 4 are combined. This machine has a 40-MHz clock, since the register update increases the length of the critical path.

- M3: A machine like M2, except that effective address calculations are done in the same clock as a memory access. Thus, states 2, 3, and 4 can be combined, as can 2 and 5, as well as 6 and 7. This machine has a 25-MHz clock, because of the long cycle created by combining address calculation and memory access.

Find out which machine is fastest. Are there instruction mixes that would make another machine faster, and if so, what are they?

5.8 [20] <§5.4> Suppose there were a MIPS instruction, called bcp, that copied a block of words from one address to another. Assume that this instruction requires that the starting address of the source block is in register $1 and the destination address is in $2, and the number of words to copy is in $3 (which is ≥ 0). Furthermore, assume that the values of these registers as well as register $4 can be destroyed in executing this instruction (so that the registers can be used as temporaries to execute the instruction).

Write the MIPS assembly language program to implement block copy. How many instructions will be executed to perform a 100-word block copy? Using the CPI of the instructions in the multicycle implementation, how many cycles are needed for the 100-word block copy?

5.9 [30] <§5.5> Microcode has been used to add more powerful instructions to an instruction set; let's explore the potential benefits of this approach. Give a microprogram to implement the bcp instruction. To implement this instruction, we will need to extend the microinstruction format. In the extended format we allow the SRC1 and SRC2 fields to contain either an explicit register designator, and the SRC2 field to contain a small constant (five bits in length). We also allow the ALU destination field to contain an explicit register specifier. Finally, we will need to have microinstructions that can conditionally branch, since implementing bcp will require a loop. Assume the sequencing field is extended to allow a branch based on the 0 bit out of the ALU. The label specifies another microinstruction.

How many microinstructions will be executed to copy a block of 100 words? How does this compare to the number of MIPS instructions required? Assuming each microinstruction takes one cycle, how does the cycle count of the microcode implementation compare the implementation using MIPS instructions in Exercise 5.8. How do you explain the difference?

5.10 [15] <§5.5> {ex. 5.9} To implement the `bcp` instruction in Exercise 5.9, we needed to expand the microinstruction. Assume that each field of the microinstruction is encoded separately and that there will be at most 1024 microinstructions. Find the width of each field in the original and extended microinstruction and the total widths. Remember to include bits that describe fields that can have different types of values (e.g., SRC1 in the extended microinstruction).

5.11 [5] <§5.2–5.3> We wish to add the instruction `addiu` (Add Immediate Unsigned) to the single-cycle datapath described in this chapter. This instruction is described in Chapter 3. Add any necessary datapaths and control signals to the single clock datapath of Figure 5.22 on page 295. You can photocopy the existing datapath to make it faster to show the additions.

5.12 [10] <§5.3> {ex. 5.11} Show the additions to the table in Figure 5.23 on page 296 needed to set the control lines that were added in Exercise 5.11 for the instruction `addiu`.

5.13 5] <§5.4> We wish to add the datapath parts and control needed to implement the `addiu` instruction in the multiclock datapath and control. Show the additions to the datapath and control lines of Figure 5.39 on page 323 needed to implement this instruction in the multicycle datapath.

5.14 [5] <§5.4> {ex. 5.13} Show the steps in executing the `addiu` instruction in the multiclock datapath, using the same breakdown of steps as used in pages 317 through 320.

5.15 [10] <§5.4> {ex. 5.13, 5.14} Show the additions to the finite state machine of Figure 5.47 on page 332 needed to implement the `addiu` instruction.

5.16 [5] <§5.5, 5.8> {ex. 5.13, 5.14, 5.15} Write the microcode sequences for the `addiu` instruction. If you need to make any changes to the microinstruction format or field contents, indicate how the new format and fields will set the control outputs.

5.17 [1 week] <§5.2, 5.3> Using a hardware simulation language such as Verilog, implement a functional simulator for the single-cycle version. Build your simulator using an existing library of parts, if such a library is available. If the parts contain timing information, determine what the cycle time of your implementation will be.

5.18 [1 week] <§5.2, 5.4, 5.5> Using a hardware simulation language such as Verilog, implement a functional simulator for the multicycle version of the design. Build your simulator using an existing library of parts, if such a library is available. If the parts contain timing information, determine what the cycle time of your implementation will be.

5.19 [2–3 months] <§5.1–5.3> Build a machine that implements the single-cycle machine in this chapter using standard parts.

5.20 [2–3 months] <§5.1–5.8> Build a machine that implements the multicycle machine in this chapter using standard parts.

5.21 [Discussion] <§5.5, 5.8, 5.9> Hypothesis: If the first implementation of an architecture uses microprogramming, it affects the instruction set architecture. Why might this be true? Can you find an architecture that will probably always use microcode? Why? Which machines will never use microcode? Why? What control implementation do you think the architect had in mind when designing the instruction set architecture?

5.22 [Discussion] <§5.5, 5.10> Wilkes invented microprogramming in large part to simplify construction of control. Since 1980, there has been an explosion of computer-aided design software whose goal is also to simplify construction of control. This has made control design much easier. Can you find evidence, either based on the tools or real designs, that support or refute this hypothesis?

5.23 [Discussion] <§5.10> The MIPS instructions and the MIPS microinstructions have many similarities. What would make it difficult for a compiler to produce MIPS microcode rather than macrocode? What changes to the microarchitecture would make the microcode more useful for this application?

Enhancing Performance with Pipelining

Thus times do shift,
each thing his turn does hold;
New things succeed,
as former things grow old.

Robert Herrick
Hesperides: Ceremonies for Christmas Eve, 1648

The Five Classic Components of a Computer

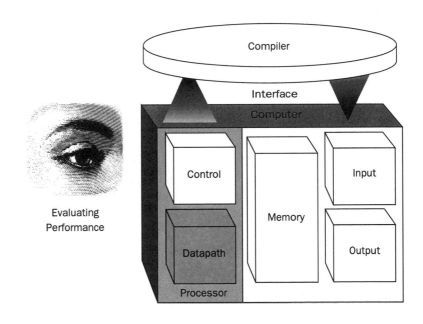

6.1   Introduction

Never waste time.

American Proverb

Pipelining is an implementation technique in which multiple instructions are overlapped in execution. Today, pipelining is key to making processors fast.

A pipeline is like an assembly line: in both, each step completes one piece of the whole job. Workers on a car assembly line perform small tasks, such as installing seat covers. The power of the assembly line comes from many workers performing small tasks to collectively produce many cars per day. On a well-balanced assembly line, a new car exits the line in the time it takes to perform one of the many steps. Note that the assembly line does not reduce the *time* it takes to complete an individual car; it increases the number of cars being built simultaneously and thus the *rate* at which cars are started and completed.

As in a car assembly line, the work to be done in a pipeline for an instruction is broken into small pieces, each of which takes a fraction of the time needed to complete the entire instruction. Each of these steps is called a *pipe stage* or a *pipe segment*. The stages are juxtaposed to form a pipe—instructions enter at one end, are processed through the stages, and exit at the other end. Once again, pipelining does not reduce the time it takes to complete an individual instruction; it increases the number of simultaneously executing instructions and the rate at which instructions are started and completed. In the terms used in Chapter 2, page 50, pipelining improves instruction *throughput* rather than individual instruction *execution time*.

Just as the throughput of a car assembly line is determined by how often a car exits the line, the throughput of an instruction pipeline is determined by how often an instruction exits the pipeline. Because they are hooked together, all the pipe stages must be ready to proceed at the same time; thus, the rate at which instructions exit the pipeline cannot exceed the rate at which they enter the pipeline. The time required to move an instruction one step down the pipeline is ideally one clock cycle. The length of a clock cycle is determined by the time required for the slowest pipe stage, because all stages must proceed at the same rate.

The goal of designers—whether of instruction pipelines or car assembly lines—is to balance the length of each stage; otherwise, there will be idle time during a stage. If the stages are perfectly balanced, then the time between instructions on the pipelined machine—assuming ideal conditions—is equal to

$$\text{Time between instructions}_{\text{pipelined}} = \frac{\text{Time between instructions}_{\text{nonpipelined}}}{\text{Number of pipe stages}}$$

Under ideal conditions, the speedup from pipelining equals the number of pipe stages; a five-stage pipeline is five times faster. Usually, however, the stages are imperfectly balanced. In addition, pipelining involves some overhead. Thus the time per instruction on the pipelined machine will exceed the minimum possible, and speedup will be less than the number of pipeline stages.

To make this discussion concrete, let's create a pipeline using the example components from Chapter 5 from the single-cycle implementation. In this example, and in the rest of this chapter, we limit our attention to seven instructions: load word (lw), store word (sw), add (add), subtract (sub), and (and), or (or), and branch equal (beq). The operation times for the major functional units in the implementation from Chapter 5, page 308 are

- Memory units: 10 ns

- ALU and adders: 10 ns

- Register file (read or write): 5 ns

Assuming that the multiplexors, control unit, PC accesses, and sign-extension unit have no delay, the time required for each of the seven instruction is shown in the table below:

Instruction type	Instruction memory	Register read	ALU operation	Data memory	Register write	Total time
Load word (lw)	10 ns	5 ns	10 ns	10 ns	5 ns	40 ns
Store word (sw)	10 ns	5 ns	10 ns	10 ns		35 ns
R-format (add, sub, and, or)	10 ns	5 ns	10 ns		5 ns	30 ns
Branch (beq)	10 ns	5 ns	10 ns			25 ns

Because the single-cycle design must allow for the worst-case instruction—the slowest instruction in the table above—the time required for every instruction is 40 ns. The execution of a sequence of load instructions would be as shown on the top of the next page:

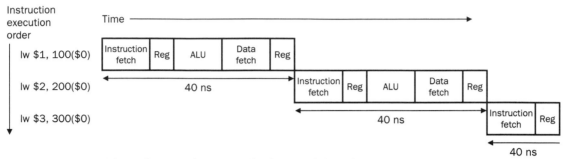

Thus, the time between the first and fourth instructions is 3 × 40 ns or 120 ns.

Instructions were divided into five steps in Chapter 5. This suggests that a five-stage pipeline would be a good starting place. Five stages means we execute five instructions at a time, with one in each pipeline stage. Each pipe stage takes one clock cycle. A sequence of load instructions in the pipelined implementation would then be

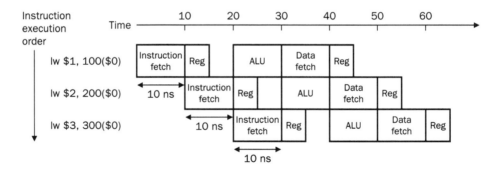

All the stages take a single clock cycle, so the clock cycle must be long enough to accommodate the slowest operation. Just as the single-cycle design must take the worst-case clock cycle of 40 ns even though some instructions can be as fast as 25 ns, the pipelined execution clock cycle must have the worst-case clock cycle of 10 ns even though some stages take only 5 ns. This is still a fourfold improvement. The formula above suggests that a five-stage pipeline could offer a fivefold improvement, or an 8-ns clock cycle; the difference is due to the imbalance in the length of the pipe stages.

Although the example shows a fourfold improvement, the improvement in total execution time for the three instructions is more modest: 70 ns versus 120 ns. To see why total execution time is less important, let's examine what would happen to the execution time if we increased the number of instructions. We start by extending the drawings above to 1003 instructions. We would add 1000 instructions to the left in the pipelined example; each instruction adds 10 ns to the total execution time. The total execution time would be 1000×10 ns + 70 ns, or 10,070 ns. In the nonpipelined example, we would add 1000 instruction, each taking 40 ns, so total execution time would be 1000×40 ns + 120 ns, or 40,120 ns. Under these ideal conditions, the ratio of total execution times for real programs on nonpipelined to pipelined machines is close to the ratio of times between instructions:

$$\frac{40{,}120 \text{ ns}}{10{,}070 \text{ ns}} = 3.98 \approx \frac{40 \text{ns}}{10 \text{ns}}$$

Pipelining improves performance by *increasing instruction throughput, as opposed to decreasing the execution time of an individual instruction*, but instruction throughput is the important metric because real programs execute billions of instructions.

Pipelining is a technique that exploits parallelism among the instructions in a sequential instruction stream. It has the substantial advantage that, unlike some speedup techniques (see Chapter 9), it can be invisible to the programmer. In this chapter, we will first cover the concept of pipelining using the MIPS instruction subset from Chapter 5 (`lw`, `sw`, `add`, `sub`, `and`, `or`, `beq`) and a simplified version of its pipeline. We will then look at the problems that pipelining introduces and the performance attainable under typical situations. Later in the chapter, we will examine advanced techniques that can be used to overcome the difficulties encountered in pipelined machines.

6.2   A Pipelined Datapath

Figure 6.1 shows the single-cycle datapath from Chapter 5. Expanding from the example above, the division of an instruction into five stages means a five-stage pipeline, which in turn means that five instructions will be in execution during any single clock cycle. Thus, we must separate the datapath into five pieces, with each piece named corresponding to a stage of instruction execution:

1. IF: Instruction fetch

2. ID: Instruction decode and register fetch

3. EX: Execution and effective address calculation

4. MEM: Memory access

5. WB: Write back

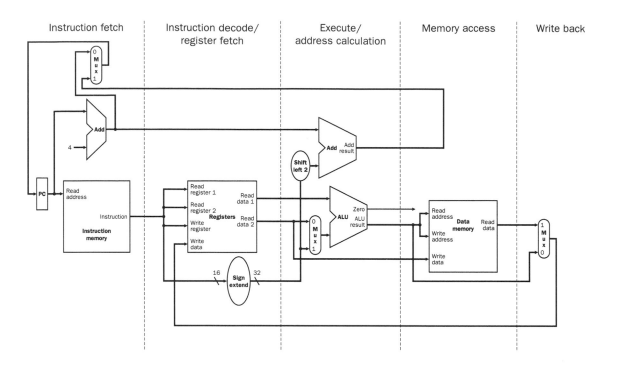

FIGURE 6.1 The single-cycle datapath from Chapter 5 (similar to Figure 5.20 on page 293). Each step of the instruction can be mapped onto the datapath from left to right. The only exceptions are the update of the PC and the write-back step, which sends either the ALU result or the data from memory to the left to be written into the registers.

In Figure 6.1 these five components correspond roughly to the way the datapath is drawn; instructions and data move generally from left to right through the five stages as they complete execution. Going back to our automotive analogy, cars get closer to complete assembly as they move through the line, and they never move backwards through the line.

There are, however, two exceptions to this left-to-right flow of instructions:

■ The write-back stage, which places the result back into the register file in the middle of the datapath.

■ The selection of the next value of the PC, choosing between the incremented PC and the branch address from the MEM stage.

Data flowing from right to left does not affect the current instruction; only later instructions in the pipeline are influenced by these two data movements (see section 6.4).

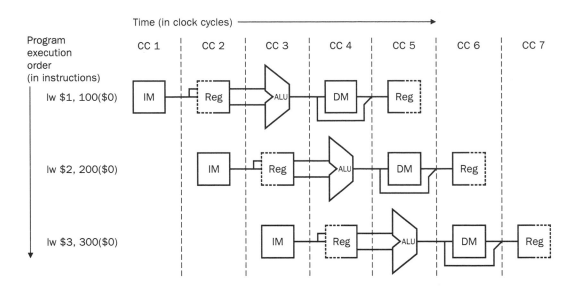

FIGURE 6.2 Instructions being executed in the single-cycle datapath in Figure 6.1, assuming pipelined execution. This figure pretends that each instruction has its own datapath. The five pieces of this stylized datapath correspond to the portions of the datapath in Figure 6.1. IM represents the instruction memory and the PC in the instruction fetch stage, Reg stands for the registers and sign extender in the instruction decode/register fetch phase (ID), and so on. To maintain proper time order, this stylized datapath breaks the register file into two logical halves: registers read during register fetch (ID) and registers write during write back (WB). This dual use is represented by drawing the left half of the registers using dashed lines in the ID stage, when they are not being written, and the right half in dashed lines in the WB stage, when they are not being read. Notice that in pipelined execution the second instruction must read the new instruction from the memory even though the first instruction depends on the instruction memory being stable for the entire instruction. Such conflicts lead to the pipeline registers in Figure 6.3.

One way to show what happens in pipelined execution is to pretend that each instruction has its own datapath, and then to place these datapaths on a timeline to show their relationship. Figure 6.2 shows the execution of the instructions in the example from the previous section by displaying their private datapaths on a common timeline. We use a stylized version of the datapath in Figure 6.1 to show the relationships in Figure 6.2.

Figure 6.2 seems to suggest that three instructions need three datapaths. Recall that in Chapter 5 we added registers to hold data so that portions of the datapath could be shared during instruction execution; we use the same technique here. For example, in Chapter 5 the instruction memory was used only by one instruction at a time for the duration of that instruction execution. With pipelining, as Figure 6.2 shows, the instruction memory is used during only one of the five stages of an instruction, allowing it to be shared by other instructions during the other four stages. To retain the value of an individual in-

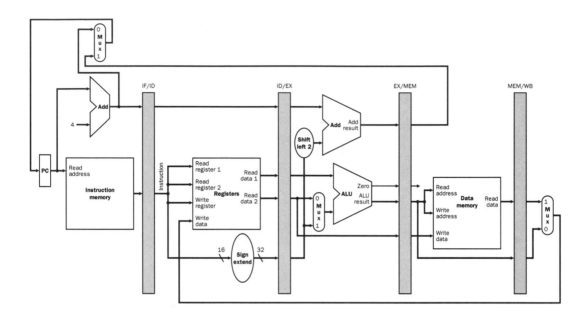

FIGURE 6.3 The pipelined version of the datapath in Figure 6.1. The pipeline registers, in color, separate each pipeline stage. They are labeled by the stages that they separate; for example, the first is labeled "IF/ID" because it separates the instruction fetch and instruction decode stages. The registers must be wide enough to store all the data corresponding to the lines that go through them. For example, the IF/ID register must be 64 bits wide because it must hold both the 32-bit instruction fetched from memory and the incremented 32-bit PC address.

struction for its other four stages, the value read from instruction memory must be saved in a register. Similar arguments apply to every pipeline stage, so we must place registers wherever there are dividing lines between stages in Figure 6.1.

Figure 6.3 shows the pipelined datapath with the pipeline registers highlighted and named for the two stages separated by that register. All instructions advance during each clock cycle from one pipeline register to the next.

Notice that there is no pipeline register separating the write-back stage from the next instruction fetch. All instructions must update some state in the machine, so a separate pipeline register is redundant for the state that is updated. For example, a load instruction will place its result in 1 of the 32 registers, and any later instruction that needs that data will simply read the appropriate register. Sections 6.4 and 6.5 describe what happens when there are dependencies between pipelined instructions; ignore them for now.

To show how the pipelining works, throughout this chapter we show sequences of figures to demonstrate operation over time. These extra pages

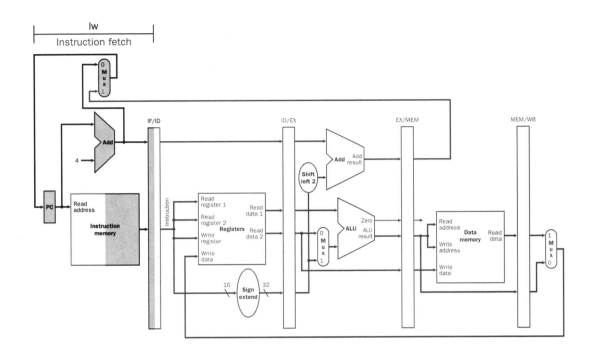

FIGURE 6.4 IF: the first pipe stage of an instruction, with the active portions of the datapath in Figure 6.3 highlighted. Highlighting the right half of a register or memory, such as instruction memory, means it is read in this pipe stage. Highlighting the left half, such as the IF/ID register, means that it is written in this stage. The highlighting of a whole register, such as the PC, means that the register is both read and written in this pipe stage. As in Chapter 5, there is no confusion when reading and writing registers because the contents change only on the clock edge.

would seem to require much more time from the reader. Fear not, for the sequences take much less time to understand because the reader can compare to see what changes in each clock cycle. Figures 6.4 through 6.8, our first sequence, show the active portions of the datapath highlighted as a load instruction goes through the five stages of pipelined execution. We show a load first because it is active in all five stages. We highlight the *right half* of registers or memory when they are being *read* and highlight the *left half* when they are being *written*. We show the instruction abbreviation lw with the name of the pipe stage that is active in each figure. The five stages are

1. *Instruction Fetch:* Figure 6.4 shows the instruction being read from memory using the address in the PC and then placed in the IF/ID pipeline register. (The IF/ID pipeline register is similar to the Instruction register in Figure 5.34 on page 313.) The PC address is incremented by 4 and then loaded back into the PC to be ready for the next clock cycle.

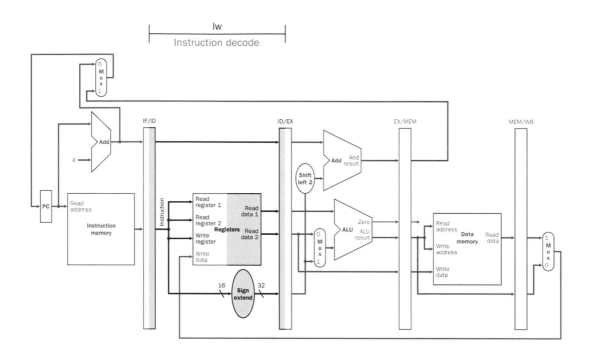

FIGURE 6.5 ID: the second pipe stage of an instruction, with the portions of the datapath in Figure 6.3 highlighted that are used in this pipe stage as in Figure 6.4. Note that although the load will need only the top register, the processor doesn't know what instruction is being loaded, so it both sign-extends the 16-bit constant and reads both registers into the ID/EX pipeline register. The processor doesn't need all three operands for this instruction, but always loading all three can't hurt and makes control simpler.

This incremented address is also saved in the IF/ID pipeline register in case it is needed later for an instruction, such as beq; the computer cannot know which type of instruction is being fetched, so it must prepare for any instruction.

2. *Instruction Decode and Register Read:* Figure 6.5 shows the instruction portion of the IF/ID pipeline register supplying the 16-bit immediate field that is sign-extended to 32 bits and the register numbers to read the two registers. All three values are all stored in the ID/EX pipeline register, along with the incremented PC address. Although, during this clock cycle, we will know the identity of the instruction being decoded and can store only what will be used in later clock cycles, it costs little to save everything. Hence, we again transfer everything that might be needed by any instruction during a later clock cycle.

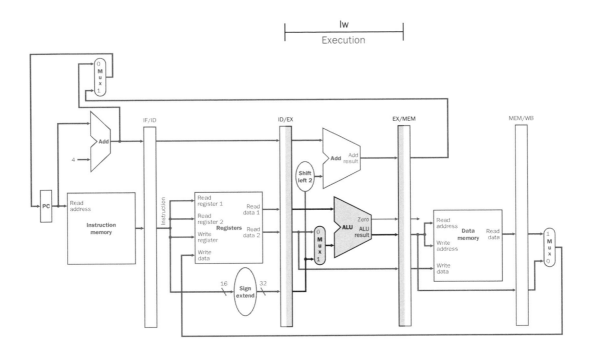

FIGURE 6.6 EX: the third pipe stage of a load instruction, highlighting the portions of the datapath in Figure 6.3 used in this pipe stage. The register is added to the sign-extended immediate, and the sum is placed in the EX/MEM Pipeline Register.

3. *Execute and Effective Address Calculation:* Figure 6.6 shows that the load instruction reads the contents of register 1 and the sign-extended immediate from the ID/EX pipeline register and adds them using the ALU. That sum is placed in the EX/MEM pipeline register.

4. *Memory:* Figure 6.7 shows the load instruction reading the data memory using the address from the EX/MEM pipeline register and loading the data into the MEM/WB pipeline register.

5. *Write Back:* Figure 6.8 shows the final step: reading the data from the MEM/WB pipeline register and writing it into the registers in the middle of the figure.

This walk-through of the load instructions shows that any information needed in the next pipe stage must be passed to that stage via a pipeline register. Walking through a store instruction shows the similarity of instruction execution; moreover, the walk-through emphasizes the need to keep informa-

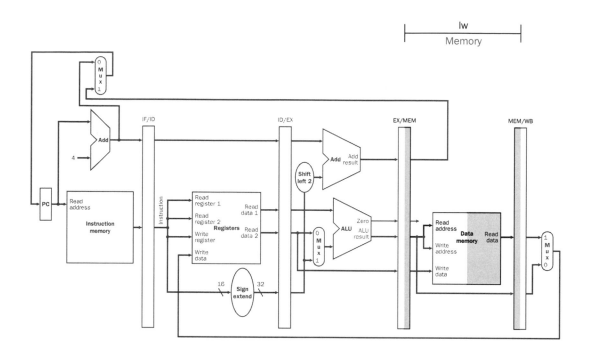

FIGURE 6.7 MEM: the fourth pipe stage of a load instruction, highlighting the portions of the datapath in Figure 6.3 used in this pipe stage. Data memory is read using the address in the EX/MEM pipeline registers, and the data is placed in the MEM/WB pipeline register.

tion used later in the execution of the instruction in the pipeline registers. Here are the five pipe stages of the store instruction:

1. *Instruction Fetch:* The instruction is read from memory using the address in the PC and then is placed in the IF/ID pipeline register. This stage occurs before the instruction is identified, so Figure 6.4 works for store as well as load.

2. *Instruction Decode and Register Read:* The instruction in the IF/ID pipeline register supplies the register numbers for reading two registers and extends the sign of the 16-bit immediate. These three 32-bit values are all stored in the ID/EX pipelining register. Figure 6.5 for load instructions also shows the operations of the second stage for stores. These first two stages are executed by all instructions, since it is too early to know the type of the instruction.

3. *Execute and Effective Address Calculation:* Figure 6.9 shows the third step;

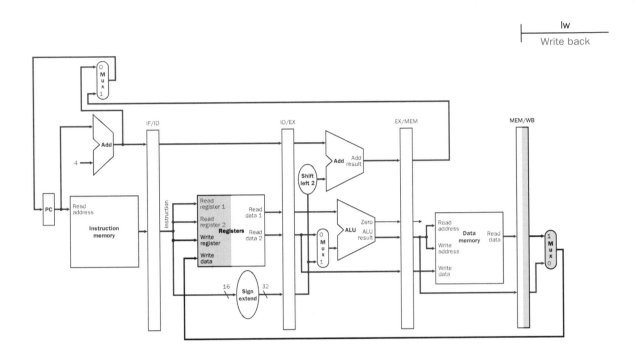

FIGURE 6.8 WB: the final pipe stage of a load instruction, highlighting the portions on the datapath in Figure 6.3 used in this pipe stage. Data is read from the MEM/WB pipeline registers and written into the registers in the middle of the datapath.

the effective address is placed in the EX/MEM pipeline register.

4. *Memory:* Figure 6.10 shows the data being written to memory. Note that the register containing the data to be stored was read in an earlier stage and stored in ID/EX. The only way to make the data available during the MEM stage is to place the data into the EX/MEM pipeline register in the EX stage, just as we stored the effective address into EX/MEM.

5. *Write Back:* Figure 6.11 shows the final step of the store. For this instruction, nothing happens in the write-back stage. Since every instruction behind the store is already in progress, we have no way to accelerate those instructions. Hence an instruction passes through a stage even if there is nothing to do, because later instructions are already progressing at the maximum rate.

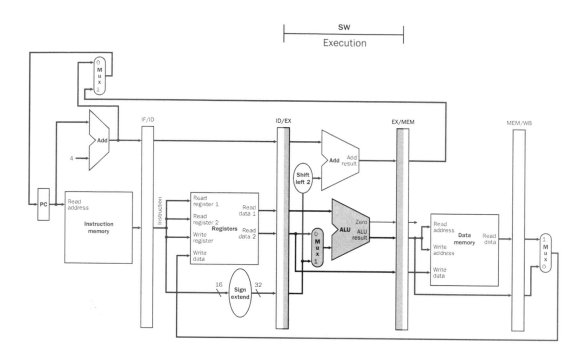

FIGURE 6.9 EX: the third pipe stage of a store instruction. Unlike the third stage of the load instruction in Figure 6.6, the second register value is loaded into the EX/MEM pipeline register to be used in the next stage. Although it wouldn't hurt to always write this second register into the EX/MEM pipeline register, we write the second register only on a store instruction to make the pipeline easier to understand.

The store instruction illustrates that in order to pass something from an early pipe stage to a later pipe stage, the information must be placed in a pipeline register; otherwise the information is lost as the next instruction enters that pipeline stage. For the store instruction we needed to pass one of the registers read in the ID stage to the MEM stage, where it is stored in memory. The data was first placed in the ID/EX pipeline register and then passed to the EX/MEM pipeline register.

Load and store illustrate a second key point: each component of the datapath—such as instruction memory, registers, ALU, and data memory—is used within a *single* pipeline stage. Hence these components, and their control, can be associated with a single pipeline stage.

Now we can uncover a bug in the design of the load instruction. Can you see it? Which register is changed in the final stage of the load? More specifically, which instruction supplies the write register number? The instruction in the

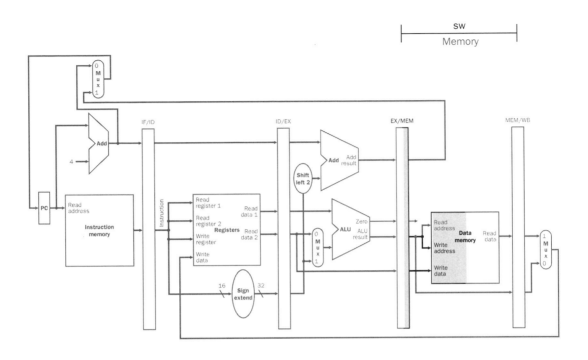

FIGURE 6.10 MEM: the fourth pipe stage of a store instruction. In this stage, the data is written into data memory for the store. Note that the data comes from the EX/MEM pipeline register and that nothing is changed in the MEM/WB pipeline register.

IF/ID pipeline register supplies the write register number, yet this instruction occurs considerably *after* the load instruction!

Hence, we need to preserve the register number in the load instruction. Just as store passed the register *contents* from the ID/EX to the EX/MEM pipeline registers for use in the MEM stage, load must pass the register *number* from the ID/EX through EX/MEM to the MEM/WB pipeline register for use in the WB stage. Another way to think about the passing of the register number is that, in order to share the pipelined datapath, we needed to preserve the instruction read during the ID stage, so each pipeline register contains a portion of the instruction needed for that stage and later stages.

Figure 6.12 shows the correct version of the datapath, passing the write register number first to the ID/EX register, then to the EX/MEM register, and finally to the MEM/WB register. The register number is used during the WB stage to specify the register to be written. Figure 6.13 is a single drawing of the corrected datapath, highlighting all five stages of the load instruction in Fig-

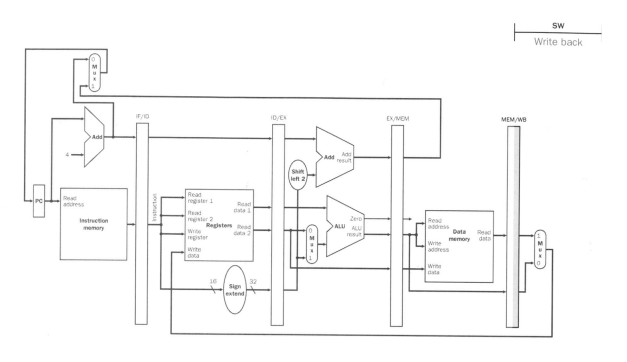

FIGURE 6.11 WB: the final pipe stage of a store instruction. Once the data is written in memory in the previous stage, there is nothing left for the store instruction to do, so nothing happens in this stage.

ures 6.4 to 6.8. (See section 6.7 for an explanation of how to make the branch instruction work as expected.)

Graphically Representing Pipelines

Pipelining can be difficult to understand, since many instructions are simultaneously executing in a single datapath in every clock cycle. To aid understanding there are two basic styles of pipeline figures: multiple-clock-cycle diagrams, such as Figure 6.2 on page 369, and single-clock-cycle diagrams, such as Figures 6.4 through 6.11. Let's try showing a sequence of instructions using both styles of pipeline diagrams for this two-instruction sequence:

```
lw    $10, 9($1)
sub   $11, $2, $3
```

Figure 6.14 shows the multiple-clock-cycle pipeline diagram for these two instructions. Time advances from left to right across the page in these diagrams, and instructions advance from the top to the bottom of the page. A

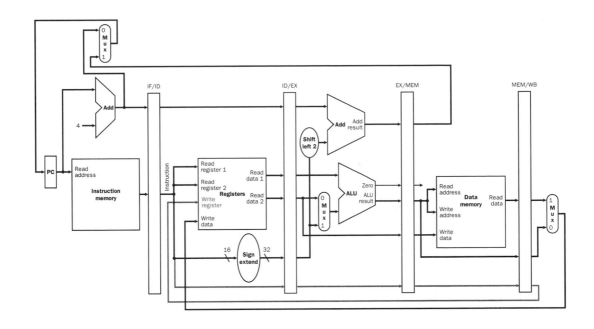

FIGURE 6.12 The corrected pipelined datapath to properly handle the load instruction. The write register number now comes from the MEM/WB pipeline register along with the data. The register number is passed from the ID pipe stage until it reaches the MEM/WB pipeline register. This new path is shown in color.

representation of the pipeline stages is placed in each portion along the instruction axis, occupying the proper clock cycles. These stylized datapaths represent the five stages of our pipeline, but a rectangle naming each pipe stage works just as well. Figure 6.15 shows the more traditional version of the multiple-clock-cycle pipeline diagram. We use multiple-clock-cycle diagrams to give overviews of pipelining situations.

Single-clock drawings show the state of the entire datapath during a single clock cycle, and usually all the instructions in the pipeline are identified by labels above their respective pipeline stages. We use this type of figure to show the details of what is happening within the pipeline during each clock cycle; typically, the drawings appear in groups to show pipeline operation over a sequence of clock cycles for multiple instructions. Figures 6.16 to 6.18 show the single-clock cycle pipeline diagrams for these two instructions.

These two views of the pipeline are equivalent, of course. Taking a single-clock vertical slice from a multiple-clock-cycle diagram shows the state of the pipeline in a single-clock-cycle diagram. One confusing aspect is the order of instructions in the two diagrams: the newest instruction is at the *bottom* of the

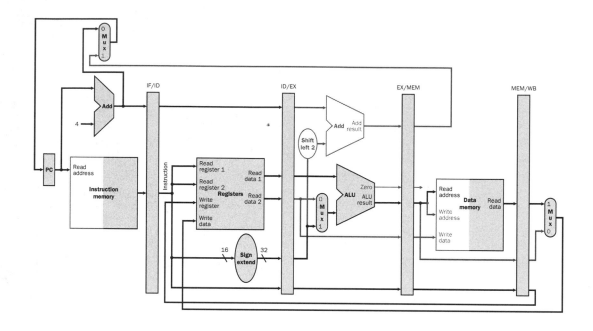

FIGURE 6.13 The portion of the datapath in Figure 6.12 that is used in all five stages of a load instruction.

multiple-clock-cycle diagram, and it is on the *left* in the single-clock-cycle diagram.

Converting from a sequence of single-clock-cycle diagrams to a single multi-clock-cycle diagram is harder: You must rotate each single-clock drawing 90 degrees to make it fit within a clock boundary, and then align the datapaths so that all stages of each instruction occupy a single horizontal line (see Exercise 6.4).

Elaboration: Because the PC communicates information between two instructions, as opposed to within a single instruction, diagrams such as Figure 6.16 show the PC as an explicit register. You could consider it as a pipeline register before the instruction fetch stage, or between the write-back stage of one instruction and the instruction fetch of the next instruction. The PC would then be drawn as an elongated rectangle like the other pipeline registers.

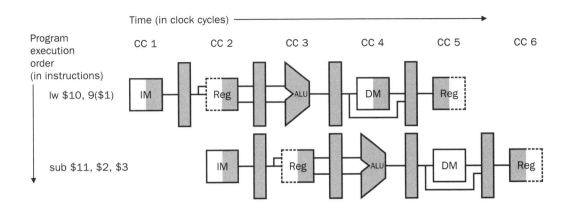

FIGURE 6.14 Multiple-clock-cycle pipeline diagram of two instructions. See Figure 6.15 for the traditional way to draw this diagram, and Figures 6.16 to 6.18 for the single-clock-cycle pipeline diagrams for the same instructions.

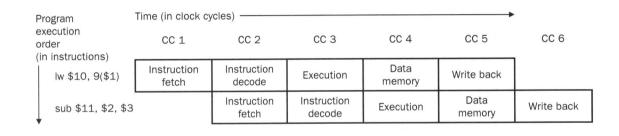

FIGURE 6.15 Traditional multiple-clock-cycle pipeline diagram of two instructions in Figure 6.14.

Pipelined Control

In the 6600 Computer, perhaps even more than in any previous computer, the control system is the difference.

James Thornton, *Design of a Computer: The Control Data 6600*, 1970

Just as we added control to the simple datapath in section 5.2, we now define control for the pipelined datapath. We start with a simple design that views the problem through rose-colored glasses; in sections 6.4 through 6.8, we remove these glasses to reveal complexities of the real world such as branches.

The first step is to label the control lines on the existing datapath. (Figure 6.19 shows those lines.) We borrow as much as we can from the control for the simple datapath in Figure 5.20 on page 293. In particular, we use the same ALU control logic, branch logic, register number multiplexor, and control lines. These functions are defined in Figure 5.15 on page 287, Figure 5.21 on page 294, and Figure 5.23 on page 296. (We reproduce the key information in Figures 6.20 through 6.22 to make the remaining text easier to follow.)

As in Chapter 5, we assume that the PC is written on each clock cycle, so there is no separate write signal for the PC. By the same argument, there are no separate write signals for the pipeline registers (IF/ID, ID/EX, EX/MEM, and MEM/WB), since the pipeline registers are also written during each clock cycle.

To specify control for the pipeline, we need only set the control values during each pipeline stage. Because each control line is associated with a component active in only a single pipeline stage, we can divide the control lines into five groups according to the pipeline stage:

1. *Instruction Fetch:* The control signals to read instruction memory and to write the PC are always asserted, so there is nothing special to control in this pipeline stage.

2. *Instruction Decode/Register Fetch:* As in the previous stage, the same thing happens at every clock cycle, so there are no optional control lines to set.

3. *Execution:* The signals to be set are *RegDst*, *ALUop*, and *ALUSrc* (see Figures 6.20 and 6.22). The signals select the Result register, the ALU operation, and either a register or a sign-extended immediate for the ALU.

4. *Memory Stage:* The control lines set in this stage are *Branch*, *MemRead*, and *MemWrite*. These signals are set by the branch equal, load, and store instructions, respectively.

5. *Write Back*: The two control lines are *MemtoReg*, which decides between sending the ALU result or the memory value to the registers, and *RegWrite*, which writes the chosen value.

Since pipelining the datapath leaves the meaning of the control lines unchanged, we can use the same values per instruction as before. Figure 6.22

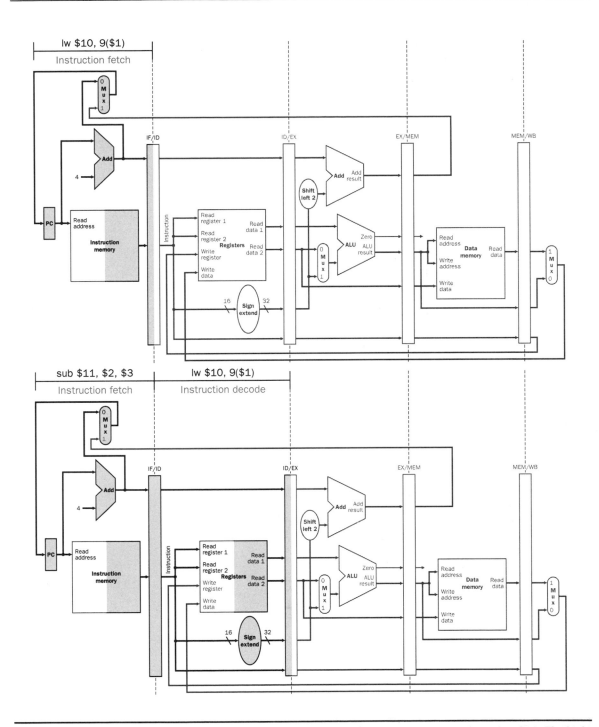

FIGURE 6.16 Single-cycle pipeline diagrams for clock cycles 1 (top diagram) and 2 (bottom diagram). The high-lighted portions of the datapath are active in that clock cycle. The load is fetched in clock cycle 1 and decoded in clock cycle 2, with the subtract fetched in the second clock cycle.

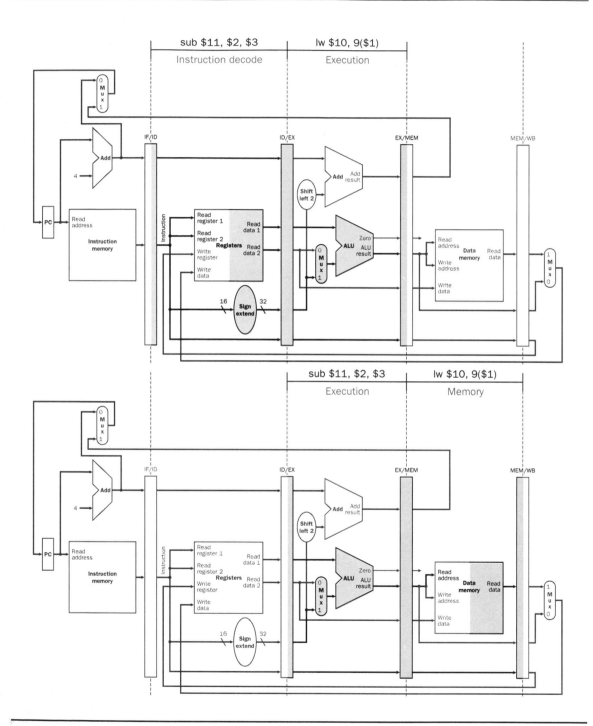

FIGURE 6.17 Single-cycle pipeline diagrams for clock cycles 3 (top diagram) and 4 (bottom diagram). In the third clock cycle in the top diagram, lw enters the EX stage. At the same time, sub enters ID. In the fourth clock cycle (bottom datapath), lw moves into MEM stage, reading memory using the address found in EX/MEM at the beginning of clock cycle 4. At the same time, the ALU subtracts and then places the difference into EX/MEM at the end of the clock cycle.

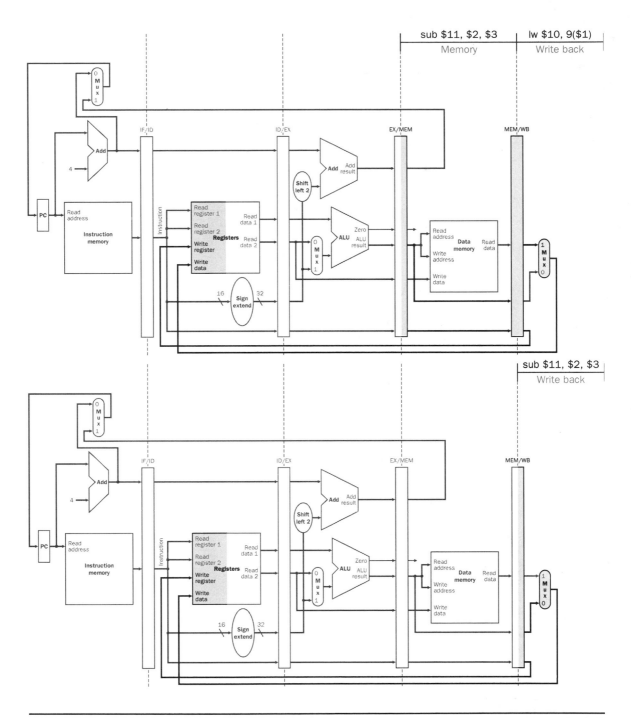

FIGURE 6.18 Single-cycle pipeline diagrams for clock cycles 5 (top diagram) and 6 (bottom diagram). In clock cycle 5, lw completes by writing the data in MEM/WB into register 10 and sub sends the difference in EX/MEM to MEM/WB. In the next clock cycle, sub writes the value in MEM/WB to a register.

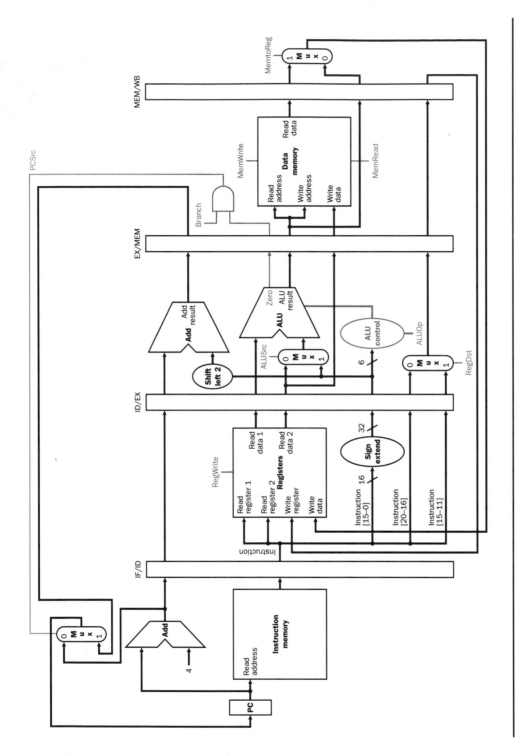

FIGURE 6.19 The pipelined datapath of Figure 6.13 with the control signals identified. This datapath borrows the control logic for PC source, register destination number, and ALU control from Chapter 5. Note that we now need the 6-bit function code of the instruction in the EX stage as input to ALU control, so these bits must also be included in the ID/EX pipeline register. Recall that these 6 bits are also the 6 least significant bits of the immediate field in the instruction, so the ID/EX pipeline register can supply them from the immediate field since sign extension leaves these bits unchanged.

Instruction opcode	ALUOp	Instruction operation	Function code	Desired ALU action	ALU control input
LW	00	load word	XXXXXX	add	010
SW	00	store word	XXXXXX	add	010
Branch equal	01	branch equal	XXXXXX	subtract	110
R-type	10	add	100000	add	010
R-type	10	subtract	100010	subtract	110
R-type	10	AND	100100	and	000
R-type	10	OR	100101	or	001
R-type	10	set-on-less-than	101010	set-on-less-than	111

FIGURE 6.20 A copy of Figure 5.15 from page 287. This figure shows how the ALU control bits are set depending on the ALUOp control bits and the different function codes for the R-type instruction.

Signal name	Effect when deasserted (0)	Effect when asserted (1)
MemRead	None.	Data memory contents at the read address are put on read data output.
MemWrite	None.	Data memory contents at address given by write address are replaced by value on write data input.
ALUSrc	The second ALU operand comes from the second register file output.	The second ALU operand is the sign-extended lower 16 bits of the instruction.
RegDst	The register destination for the register write comes from the rt field.	The register destination number for the register write comes from the rd field.
RegWrite	None.	The register given by write register number input is written into with the value on the write data input.
PCSrc	The PC is replaced by the output of the adder that computes the value of PC + 4.	The PC is replaced by the output of the adder that computes the branch target.
MemtoReg	The value fed to the register write data input comes from the ALU.	The value fed to the register write data input comes from the data memory.

FIGURE 6.21 A copy of Figure 5.21 from page 294. The function of each of seven control signals is defined. The ALU control lines (ALUop) are defined in the leftmost column of Figure 6.20. When a 1-bit control to a two-way multiplexor is asserted, the multiplexor selects the input corresponding to 1. Otherwise, if the control is deasserted, the multiplexor selects the 0 input. Note that PCSrc is controlled by an AND gate in Figure 6.19; if the branch signal and the ALU Zero signal are both set, then PCSrc is 1; otherwise it is 0. Control sets the branch signal only during a beq instruction; otherwise, PCSrc is set to 0.

is the same as Figure 5.23 on page 296, except that the control lines have been grouped by pipeline stage.

Implementing control means setting the nine control lines to these values in each stage for each instruction. The simplest way to do this is to extend the

Instruction	Execution stage control lines				Memory stage control lines			Write back stage control lines	
	Reg Dst	ALU Op1	ALU Op0	ALU Src	Branch	Mem Read	Mem Write	Reg Write	Memto Reg
R-format	1	1	0	0	0	0	0	1	0
lw	0	0	0	1	0	1	0	1	1
sw	X	0	0	1	0	0	1	0	X
beq	X	0	1	0	1	0	0	0	X

FIGURE 6.22 The values of the control lines are the same as in Figure 5.23 on page 296, but they have been shuffled into three groups corresponding to the last three pipeline stages.

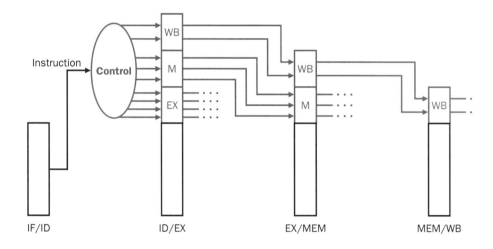

FIGURE 6.23 The control lines for the final three stages. Note that four of the nine control lines are used in the EX phase, with the remaining five control lines passed on to the EX/MEM pipeline register extended to hold the control lines; three are used during the MEM stage; and the last two are passed to MEM/WB for use in the WB stage.

pipeline registers to include control information. Returning to our automotive analogy, imagine a note placed in the car frame saying "Install Corinthian leather interior"; this note would be passed along but ignored until it reached the upholstery stage. The note can be removed once the leather is installed.

Since the optional control lines start with the EX stage, we can create the control information during instruction decode. Figure 6.23 shows that these control signals are then used in the appropriate pipeline stage as the instruction moves down the pipeline, just as the write register number for loads moves down the pipeline in Figure 6.12 on page 379. Figure 6.24 shows the full datapath with the extended pipeline registers and the control lines connected to the proper stage.

Example

Show these five instructions going through the pipeline:

```
lw      $10, 9($1)
sub     $11, $2, $3
and     $12, $4, $5
or      $13, $6, $7
add     $14, $8, $9
```

Label the instructions in the pipeline that precede the lw as before <1>, before <2>, ..., and the instructions after the add as after <1>, after <2>, ...

Answer

Figures 6.25 through 6.29 show these instructions proceeding through the nine clock cycles it takes them to complete execution, highlighting what is active in a stage and identifying the instruction associated with each stage during a clock cycle.

Reviewing these figures carefully will give you insight into how pipelines work. A few items you may notice:

- Although one instruction begins each clock cycle, an individual instruction still takes five clock cycles to complete.

- In Figure 6.27 you can see the sequence of the destination register numbers from left-to-right at the bottom of the Pipeline Registers. The numbers advance to the right during each clock cycle, with the MEM/WB pipeline register supplying the number of the register written during the WB stage.

- Note that it takes four clock cycles before the five-stage pipeline is operating at full efficiency, as shown in Figure 6.27.

- When a stage is inactive, the values of the control lines are deasserted (shown as 0 in the figures), to prevent anything from occurring.

■ In contrast to Chapter 5, where sequencing of control required special hardware, sequencing of control is embedded by the pipeline structure itself. All instructions take the same number of clock cycles, and all control information is computed during instruction decode and then passed along by the pipeline registers.

6.4   Data Hazards

The example in the previous section shows the power of pipelined execution and how the hardware performs the task. It's now time to take off the rose-colored glasses and look at what happens with real programs.

The instructions in Figures 6.25 through 6.29 were independent; none of them used the results calculated by any of the others. Let's look at a sequence with many dependencies, shown in color:

```
sub    $2,$1, $3    # Register $2 written by sub
and    $12,$2, $5    # 1st operand($2) depends on sub
or     $13,$6, $2    # 2st operand($2) depends on sub
add    $14,$2, $2    # 1st($2) & 2nd($2) depend on sub
sw     $15,100($2)   # Index($2) depends on sub
```

The last four instructions are all dependent on the result in register $2 of the first instruction. If register $2 had the value 10 before the subtract instruction and –20 afterwards, the programmer intends that –20 will be used in the instructions that refer to register $2.

How would this sequence perform with our pipeline? Figure 6.30 illustrates the execution of these instructions. Like Figure 6.2 on page 369, a simplified version of the datapath is shown for each instruction, with each datapath aligned to the appropriate clock cycle; program execution goes down the page instruction by instruction and time marches across the page in clock cycles. To demonstrate the execution of this instruction sequence in our current pipeline, the top of Figure 6.30 shows the value of register $2 at the beginning of each clock cycle.

To maintain proper time order, this stylized datapath breaks the register file into two logical halves: registers read during ID and registers write during WB. This split makes sense, because the halves are logically joined only when the same register is being read and written. For now it's helpful to think of the read half and write half as separate resources, but we'll address this factor shortly.

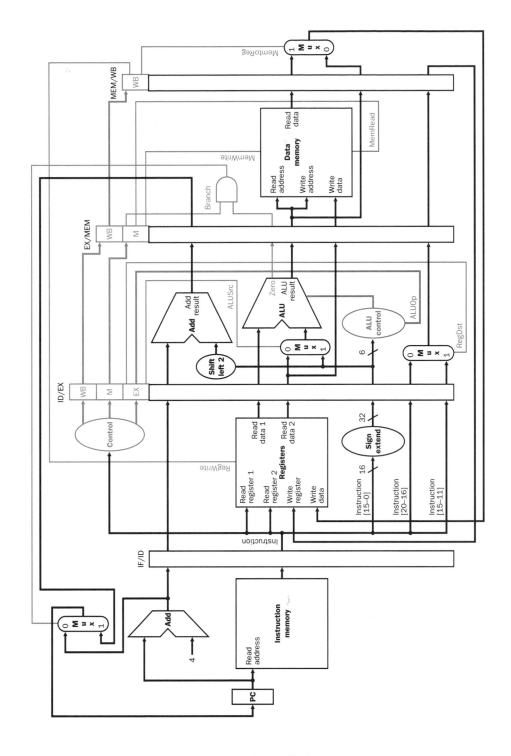

FIGURE 6.24 The pipelined datapath of Figure 6.19, with the control signals connected to the control portions of the pipeline registers. The control values for the last three stages are created during the instruction decode stage and then placed in the ID/EX pipeline register. The control lines for each pipe stage are used, and remaining control lines are then passed to the next pipeline stage.

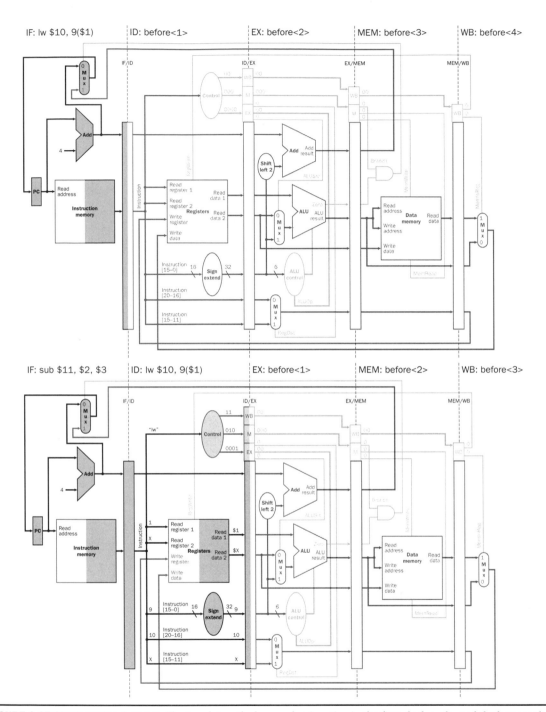

FIGURE 6.25 Clock cycles 1 and 2. The top datapath shows what is active in the first clock cycle, and the bottom shows what is active in the second. The phrase "before<*i*>" means the *i*th instruction before lw. The lw instruction in the top datapath is in the IF stage. At the end of the clock cycle, the lw instruction is in the IF/ID pipeline registers. In the second clock cycle, seen in the bottom datapath, the lw moves to the ID stage and sub enters in the IF stage. Note that the values of the instruction fields and the selected registers are shown in the ID stage. Hence register $1 and the constant 9, the operands of lw, are written into the ID/EX pipeline register. "X" means an unused field in lw. The number 10, representing the destination register number of lw, is also placed in ID/EX. The top of the pipeline register shows the control values for lw to be used in the remaining stages. *(page 392)*

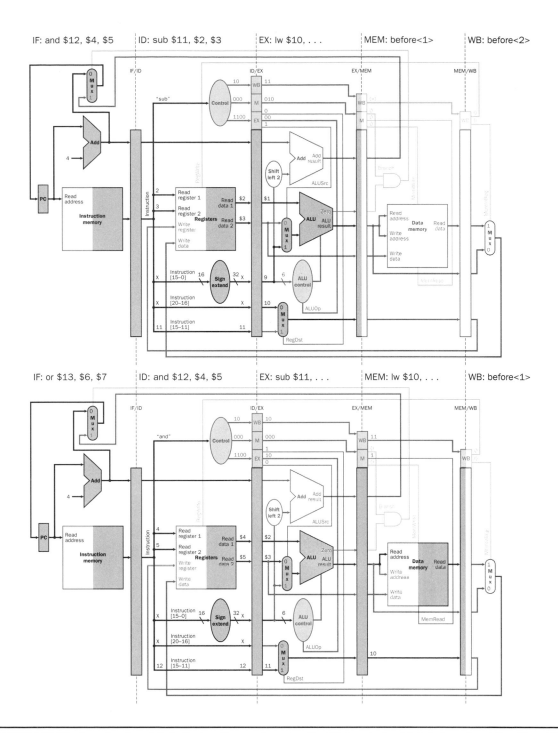

FIGURE 6.26 Clock cycles 3 and 4. In the top diagram, lw enters the EX stage in the third clock cycle, adding $1 and 9 to form the effective address in the EX/MEM pipeline register. At the same time, sub enters ID, reading registers $2 and $3, and the and instruction starts IF. In the fourth clock cycle (bottom datapath), lw moves into MEM stage, reading memory using the value in EX/MEM as the effective address. In the same clock cycle, the ALU subtracts $3 from $2, places the difference into EX/MEM, and reads registers $4 and $5 during ID, and the or instruction enters IF. The two diagrams show the control signals being created in the ID stage and peeled off as they are used in subsequent pipe stages. *(page 393)*

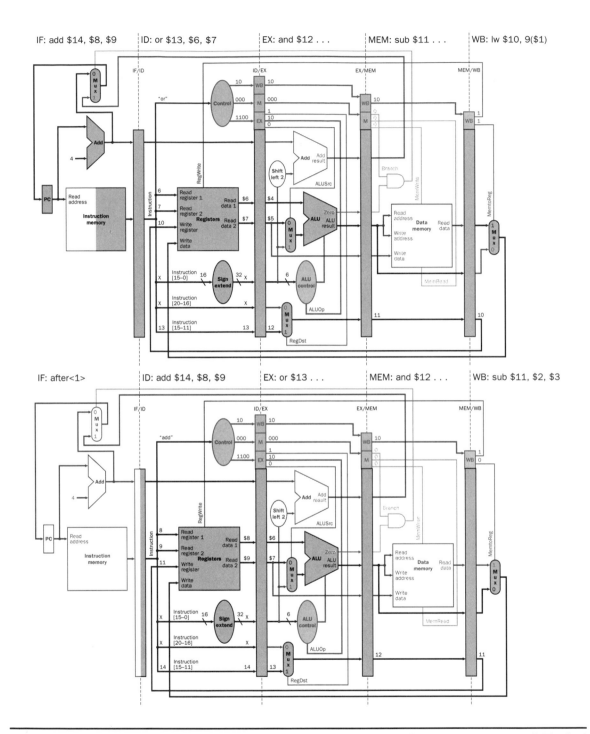

FIGURE 6.27 Clock cycles 5 and 6. With add entering IF in the top datapath, all instructions are engaged. The final instruction in this example, "after<*i*>" means the *i*th instruction after add. By writing the data in MEM/WB into register 10, lw completes; both the data and the register number are in MEM/WB. Then sub sends the difference in EX/MEM to MEM/WB, and the rest of the instructions move forward. In the next clock cycle, sub selects the value in MEM/WB to write to register number 11, again found in MEM/WB. The remaining instructions play follow-the-leader: the ALU calculates the OR of $6 and $7 for the or instruction in the EX stage, and registers $8 and $9 are read in the ID stage for the add instruction. *(page 394)*

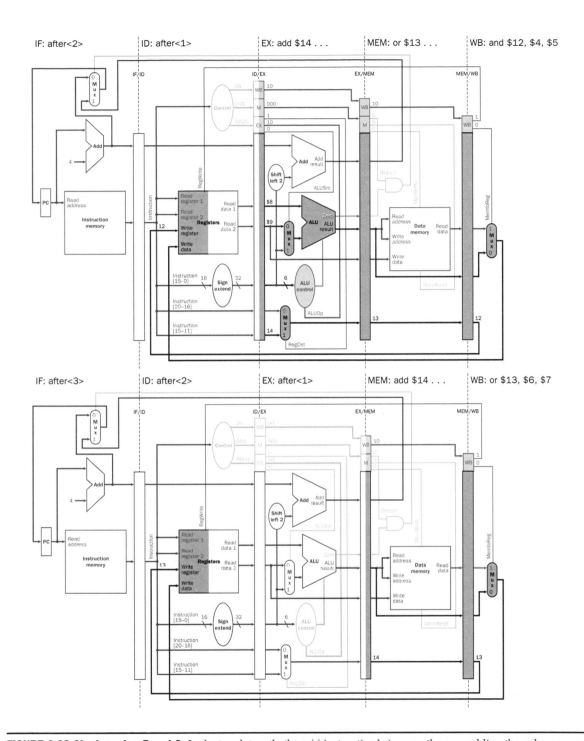

FIGURE 6.28 Clock cycles 7 and 8. In the top datapath, the add instruction brings up the rear, adding the values corresponding to registers $8 and $9 during the EX stage. The result is passed from EX/MEM to MEM/WB in the MEM stage for the or instruction, and the WB stages write the results in MEM/WB to register $12 to finish the and instruction. Note that the control signals are deasserted (set to 0) in the ID stage, since no instruction is being executed. In the following clock cycle (lower drawing), the WB stage writes the result to register $13, thereby completing or, and the MEM stage passes the sum in EX/MEM to MEM/WB. *(page 395)*

IF: after<4>   ID: after<3>   EX: after<2>   MEM: after<1>   WB: add $14, $8, $9

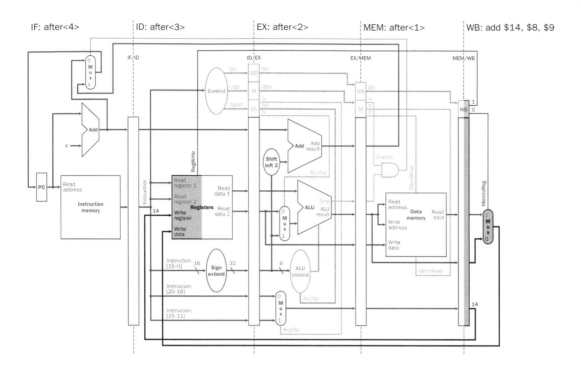

FIGURE 6.29 Clock cycle 9. The WB stage writes the sum in MEM/WB into register $14, completing add and the five-instruction sequence.

Figure 6.30 shows that the values read for register $2 would *not* be the result of the sub instruction unless the read occurred during clock cycle 6 or later. The only instruction that would use the correct value of –20 is the final store instruction; and, or, and add would all use the incorrect value 10. Using this style of drawing, such problems become apparent when a dependence line goes backwards in time. Thus, in Figure 6.30, we see problems with and, or, and add instructions because they are dependent on a value written later.

Such dependencies are called *data hazards*, and they are one reason that high-performance pipelines are hard to design: for hardware, for software, or for both.

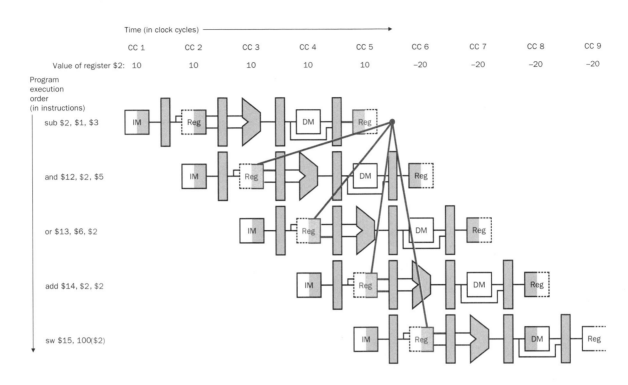

Time (in clock cycles) ⟶

	CC 1	CC 2	CC 3	CC 4	CC 5	CC 6	CC 7	CC 8	CC 9
Value of register $2:	10	10	10	10	10	–20	–20	–20	–20

Program
execution
order
(in instructions)

sub $2, $1, $3

and $12, $2, $5

or $13, $6, $2

add $14, $2, $2

sw $15, 100($2)

FIGURE 6.30 Pipelined dependencies in a five-instruction sequence using simplified datapaths to show the dependencies. All the dependent actions are shown in color, and "CC*i*" at the top of the figure means clock cycle *i*. The first instruction writes into $2, and all the following instructions read $2. This register is written in clock cycle 5, so the proper value is unavailable before clock cycle 6. The colored lines from the top datapath to the lower ones show the dependencies. Those that must go backwards in time are called *pipeline data hazards*. Note that the registers have read and write halves.

Example

For this code from the inner loop of the MIPS sort program, found in Figure 3.20 on page 139, draw a figure like Figure 6.30 showing the data hazards as backwards dependencies:

```
add   $16, $18, $15    # reg $16 = v + j
lw    $24, 0($16)      # reg $24 = v[j]
lw    $25, 4($16)      # reg $25 = v[j+1]
slt   $8, $25, $24     # reg $8 = 0 if $25    $24
beq   $8, $0, exit2    # go to exit2 if $25    $24
```

Answer   Figure 6.31 shows the five data hazards. The first two revolve around the writing of register $16 by add and the reading of it by the two loads. The third is the writing of $24 by the first lw and reading by slt; the fourth is the writing of $25 by the second lw and the reading again by slt; the final data hazard is the writing of $8 by slt and the reading of it by beq.

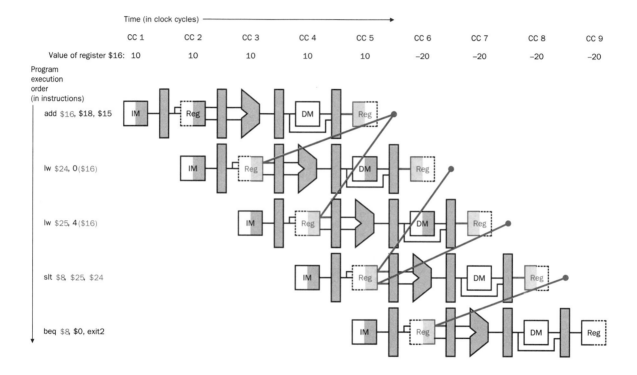

FIGURE 6.31 Pipelined dependencies in another five-instruction sequence. All the dependent actions are shown in color, and "CC*i*" at the top means clock cycle *i*. The first instruction writes into $16, and the next two loads read $16, causing two data hazards. They in turn write $24 and $25 which are read by the slt instruction, causing two more data hazards. The final data hazard is that the slt writes $8 and beq reads $8.

Hardware
Software
Interface

In the next two sections, we'll see hardware schemes for resolving data hazards. One alternative strategy is to legislate data hazards out of existence: the compiler is forbidden to generate sequences such as the five instructions above. For example, the compiler would insert three independent instructions between the sub and the and instructions, thereby making the hazard disappear. When no such instructions can be found, the compiler inserts instructions guaranteed to be independent: nop instructions. The abbreviation stands for "no operation," because nop neither reads a register, modifies data, nor writes a result. The code below uses nop instructions to get the proper result:

```
sub     $2, $1, $3
nop
nop
nop
and     $12, $2, $5
or      $13, $6, $2
add     $14, $2, $2
sw      $15, 100($2)
```

Although this code works properly for this pipeline, these three nop's occupy three clock cycles that do no useful work. Ideally, the compiler will find instructions to perform to help the computation, replacing these idle instructions. Exercise 6.8 is an example of trying to schedule instructions to avoid hazards.

6.5 Control for Data Hazards: Stalls

If at first you don't succeed, redefine success.

A saying

The simplest approach to resolving data hazards in hardware is to stall the instructions in the pipeline until the hazard is resolved. In the example in Figure 6.30, this means stalling the instructions *following* the initial sub instruction until data can be read during clock cycle 6. Computer designers whimsically gave the nickname *bubble* to a stall of instructions in the pipeline, but remember that *bubble* is just a cute name for a pipeline stall.

With this strategy, one first detects a hazard and then stalls instructions in the pipeline (inserts bubbles) until the hazard is resolved. On closer inspection, we see that the hazard occurs exactly when an instruction tries to read a register in its ID stage that an earlier instruction intends to write in its WB stage. A notation that names the fields of the pipeline registers allows for a more precise notation. For example, "IF/ID.ReadRegister1" refers to the number of the register found in the pipeline register IF/ID, that is, the first port of the register file. The first part of the name, to the left of the period, is the name of the pipeline register; the second part is the name of the field in that register. Using this notation, the three pairs of hazard conditions are

1a.	ID/EX.WriteRegister	= IF/ID.ReadRegister1
1b.	ID/EX.WriteRegister	= IF/ID.ReadRegister2
2a.	EX/MEM.WriteRegister	= IF/ID.ReadRegister1
2b.	EX/MEM.WriteRegister	= IF/ID.ReadRegister2
3a.	MEM/WB.WriteRegister	= IF/ID.ReadRegister1
3b.	MEM/WB.WriteRegister	= IF/ID.ReadRegister2

The hazard in the sequence on page 390 is on register $2, between the result of sub $2,$1,$3 and the first read operand of and $12,$2,$5. This hazard is detected when the and instructions in the ID stage and the prior instruction is in the EX stage, so this is hazard 1a:

ID/EX.WriteRegister = IF/ID.ReadRegister1 = $2.

Example

Classify the data hazards in this sequence from page 390:

```
sub    $2,   $1, $3   # Register $2 set by sub
and    $12,  $2, $5   # 1st operand($2) set by sub
or     $13,  $6, $2   # 2st operand($2) set by sub
add    $14,  $2, $2   # 1st($2) & 2nd($2) set by sub
sw     $15,  100($2)  # Index($2) set by sub
```

Answer

As mentioned above, the sub-and hazard is type 1a. The remaining hazards:

■ The sub-or hazard is condition 2b:

```
EX/MEM.WriteRegister = IF/ID.ReadRegister2 = $2;
```

■ The first sub-add hazard is condition 3a:

```
MEM/WB.WriteRegister = IF/ID.ReadRegister1 = $2;
```

■ The second sub-add hazard is condition 3b:

```
MEM/WB.WriteRegister = IF/ID.ReadRegister2 = $2.
```

There is no data hazard between sub and sw because sw reads $2 *after* sub writes $2.

If there is a data hazard, then stalling the dependent instruction in the ID stage until the instruction causing the dependency completes makes the hazard disappear. Figure 6.32 shows how inserting three bubbles before the ID stage of the and instruction removes the problem in Figure 6.30.

Because some instructions do not write registers, this policy is conservative; sometimes there will be unnecessary stalls. One solution is simply to check to see if the RegWrite signal will be active: examining the WB control field of the pipeline register during the ID, EX, and MEM stages determines if RegWrite is asserted. Finally, because the ID/EX register has two WriteRegister fields, we must also use the RegDst signal in the EX stage to select the proper register number for the write port. We'll show this in more detail below.

Now that we can detect hazards, half of the problem is resolved—but we must still stall instructions. If the instruction in the ID stage is stalled, then the instruction in the IF stage must also be stalled; otherwise, we would lose the fetched instruction. Preventing these two instructions from making progress is accomplished simply by changing neither the PC register nor the IF/ID pipeline register. Provided these registers are preserved, the instruction in the

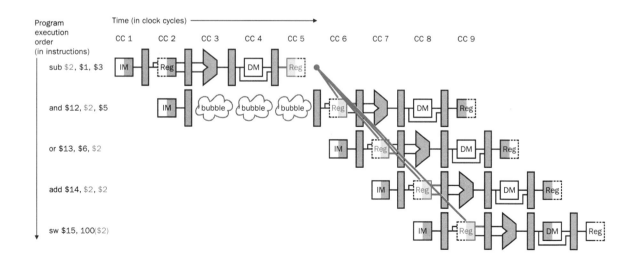

FIGURE 6.32 The pipelined instruction sequence of Figure 6.30 with three bubbles inserted to resolve the data hazard. Note that by resolving the data hazard for the and instruction, the bubbles also resolve hazards for all instructions that *follow* the and instruction.

IF stage will continue to be read using the same PC, and the registers in the ID stage will continue to be read using the same instruction in the IF/ID pipeline register.

To stall the pipeline, we need to get the same effect as inserting nop instructions, as in the Hardware/Software Interface section on page 399, but this time the nop "instructions" begin in the EX pipeline stage. In Figure 6.22 on page 388, we see that deasserting all nine control signals (setting them to 0) in the EX, MEM, and WB stages will create a "do nothing" instruction. Hence, the easiest way to insert a bubble in the pipeline is to change the EX, MEM, and WB control fields of the ID/EX pipeline register to 0. These benign control values are percolated forward at each clock cycle with the proper effect: no registers or memories are written if the control values are all 0. Figure 6.32 is a shorthand representation of what really happens in the hardware. Just like an air bubble in a water pipe, a stall bubble proceeds down the instruction pipe and exits at the far end. The and instruction sits in the IF/ID pipeline register for three cycles and launches three separate bubbles into the pipe, shown in Figure 6.33.

Now that we know how to detect hazards and cause stalls in the pipeline, we can specify the hardware to implement stalls. Figure 6.34 highlights the modified datapath with a new *Hazard Detection Unit* controlling the writing of the PC and IF/ID registers plus the multiplexors that choose between the real control values and all 0s. The Hazard Detection Unit stalls and deasserts the control fields if any of the three hazard tests below are true, relying on a few logic gates to implement these tests:

1. EX hazard:

ID/EX.RegWrite and
((ID/EX.RegDst = 0 and ID/EX.WriteRegisterRt = IF/ID.ReadRegister1) or
(ID/EX.RegDst = 1 and ID/EX.WriteRegisterRd = IF/ID.ReadRegister1) or
(ID/EX.RegDst = 0 and ID/EX.WriteRegisterRt = IF/ID.ReadRegister2) or
(ID/EX.RegDst = 1 and ID/EX.WriteRegisterRd = IF/ID.ReadRegister2))

> The first test is more complicated because we need to know if the operation is a load or an R-format instruction (RegDst = 0 or 1) to select the proper destination register number (load uses WriteRegisterRt and R-format uses WriteRegisterRd).

2. MEM hazard:

> EX/MEM.RegWrite and
> ((EX/MEM.WriteRegister = IF/ID.ReadRegister1) or
> (EX/MEM.WriteRegister = IF/ID.ReadRegister2))

> Here the hazard is between instructions in the ID and MEM stages.

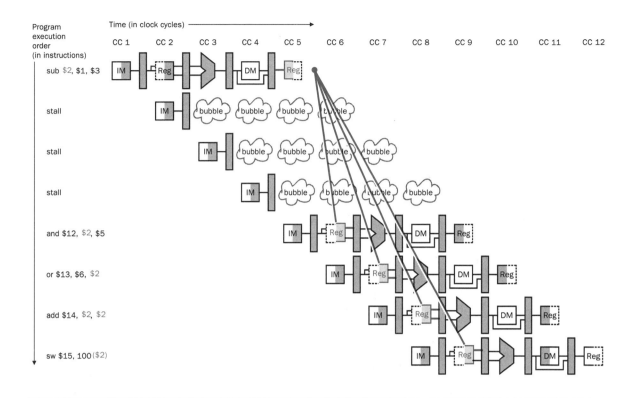

FIGURE 6.33 A version of Figure 6.32, showing the way stalls are really inserted into the pipeline. Since the dependencies go forward in time, there are no data hazards. Note that the three stall clock cycles, shown as bubbles in Figure 6.30, are similar to the nop instructions placed by the compiler in the example on page 399.

3. WB hazard:

MEM/WB.RegWrite and
((MEM/WB.WriteRegister = IF/ID.ReadRegister1) or
(MEM/WB.WriteRegister = IF/ID.ReadRegister2))

This WB hazard can be avoided, depending on what happens when a register is read and written in the same clock cycle: if the read delivers what is written, as is the case for many implementations of register files, the hazard will disappear. We assume it is a hazard in this section.

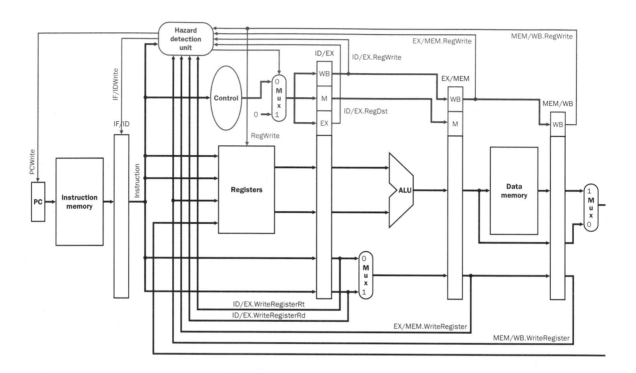

FIGURE 6.34 The Hazard Detection Unit stops the PC and IF/ID pipeline register from being written and selects 0s for the control values in the ID/EX pipeline register if it detects a hazard. It uses the destination register number and write register signals from the last three pipeline registers to determine a hazard, the current instruction in the ID stage, plus the bit from the ID/EX pipeline register that selects the destination register.

Example

Find the hazards and show the stalls in the pipeline as a result of the hazards in this instruction sequence:

```
sub     $2, $1, $3
and     $4, $2, $5
or      $8, $2, $6
add     $9, $4, $2
slt     $1, $6, $7
```

Answer

There are data hazards for register $2 between the first two instructions and for register $4 between the second and fourth instructions. Although there are also dependencies on register $2 between sub and the third and fourth instructions, just as in Figure 6.33 the resolution of the data hazard for the second instruction also removes any hazards on that register for following instructions.

Figures 6.35 through 6.40 show the events in clock cycles 2–13 in the execution of these instructions. In clock cycle 3, the Hazard Detection Unit sees the writing by the sub instruction of register $2 in the EX stage while the and instruction in the ID stage is reading register $2. The HDU stalls the pipeline in clock cycles 4–6, allowing the sub instruction to write its result and the and instruction to read the new value. The next hazard is detected in clock cycle 8, when the write of register $4 by the and instruction in the MEM stage conflicts with the reading of register $4 by the add instruction in the ID stage. After the new value is written (clock cycle 9), the add reads the correct value in clock cycle 10, and the HDU allows the pipeline to continue.

Elaboration: Just as we became less conservative on stalls by checking to see if the first instruction really writes the register, a similar improvement occurs by preventing a match on ReadRegister2 for loads, because loads use only ReadRegister1. For example, this pair of assembly language instructions:

```
add    $8, $1, $2
lw     $8, 1200($5)
```

looks like this in machine language:

op	rs	rt	(rd)	(shamt)	address/funct
0	1	2	8	0	32
35	5	8	1200		

As you can see, the 8 in the rt field of the second instruction would lead to a stall *if* the second instruction was an R-format instruction; since it is a load, and the rt field gives the destination register, this combination should not stall. Hence, we should prevent stalls on matches of ReadRegister2 from loads.

A further enhancement concerns register $0 in the MIPS architecture; $0 can never change from the value 0, so stalls due to writing and reading register $0 should also be prevented.

(Elaboration continues on page 412)

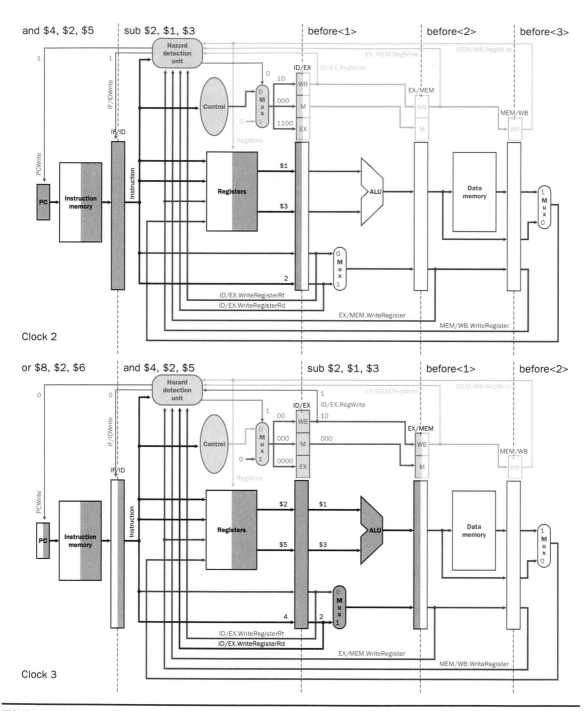

FIGURE 6.35 Clock cycles 2 and 3 of the instruction sequence in the example. The values of the significant control lines, registers, and register numbers are labeled in the figures. The and instruction wants to read the value created by the sub instruction, so the Hazard Detection Unit stalls the and and or instructions in clock cycle 3 until the hazard is resolved in clock cycle 6 (see Figure 6.37).

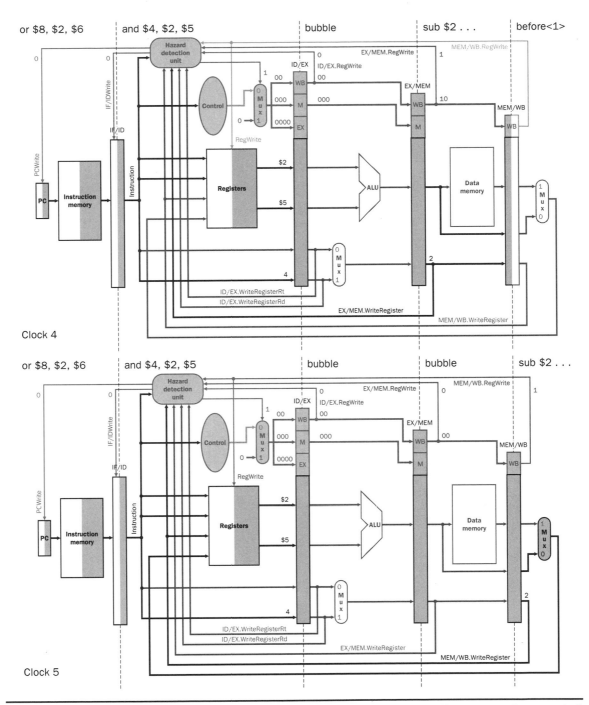

FIGURE 6.36 Clock cycles 4 and 5 of the instruction sequence in the example. The stall continues in these two clock cycles as a result of the hazard. Note that although the correct value for register $2 is written by the end of clock cycle 5, the value read during that clock cycle and loaded into the ID/EX pipeline register is the old value. The pipeline must therefore stall one more clock cycle to allow the correct value to be loaded into the pipeline register.

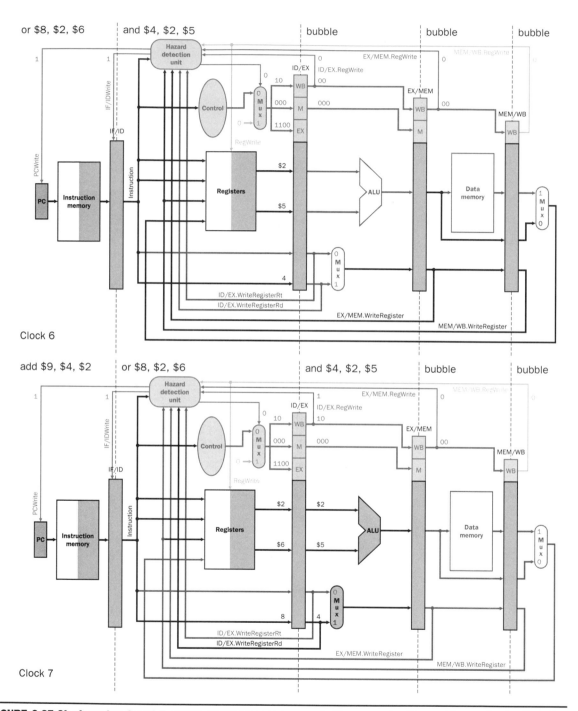

FIGURE 6.37 Clock cycles 6 and 7 of the instruction sequence in the example. The and instruction is allowed to proceed in clock cycle 6, with the rest of the instructions progressing as long as the HDU detects no hazards. Note that there is no instruction in the Datapath writing register $2 any longer, so the or instruction can proceed as well.

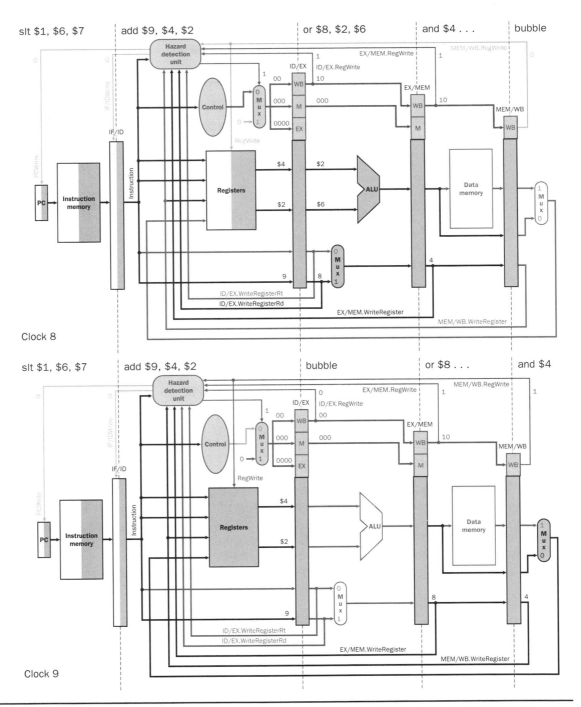

FIGURE 6.38 Clock cycles 8 and 9 of the instruction sequence in the example. In clock cycle 8, Register $4 is a hazard between the and instruction in the MEM stage and add instruction in the EX stage, so the HDU stalls the add and slt instructions in clock cycle 9.

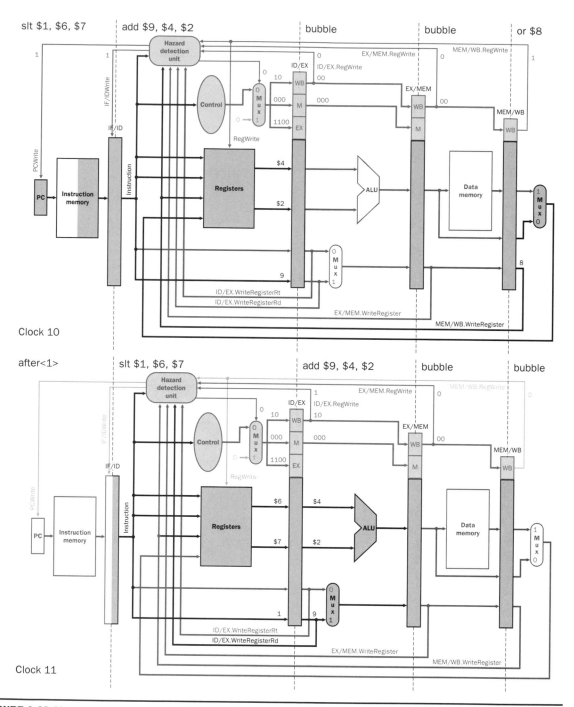

FIGURE 6.39 Clock cycles 10 and 11 of the instruction sequence in the example. The stalled slt and add instructions are allowed to proceed in clock cycle 10.

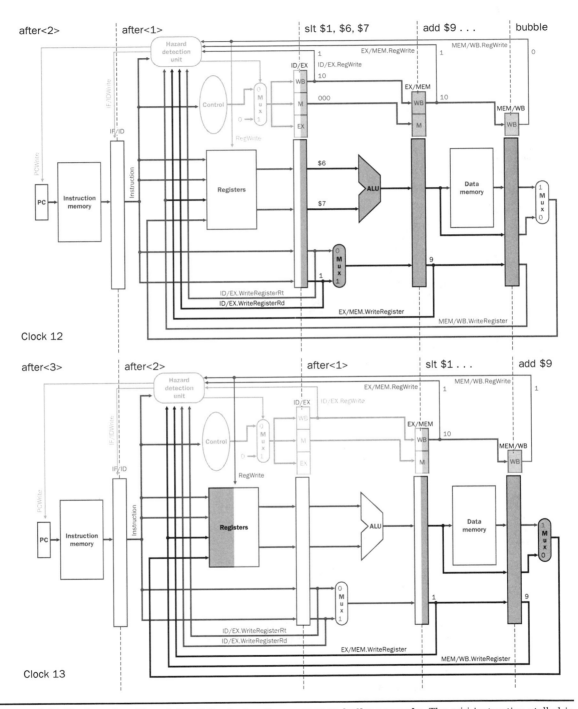

FIGURE 6.40 Clock cycles 12 and 13 of the instruction sequence in the example. The add instruction stalled in Figure 6.39 completes in clock cycle 13.

A final remark is that the hazard checking occurs between the instruction in the ID stage and the instructions in their EX, MEM, and WB stages. This checking occurs in the middle of the clock cycle, and it works as long as the machine knows whether to zero the control lines via the multiplexor by the end of the clock cycle. The first hazard could be simpler if we were willing to look at the opcode bits during the ID stage to determine whether the destination register number was for a load or an R-format instruction.

6.6   Reducing Data Hazards: Forwarding

There is less in this than meets the eye.

Tallulah Bankhead, Remark to Alexander Wollcott, 1922

Stalling the pipeline guarantees correct execution when the compiler generates dependent instructions near each other, but the cost of correctness is lower performance. If we look more carefully at Figure 6.30 on page 397, we see that the value needed by the and instruction as the input to the ALU in clock cycle 4 actually exists in the ALUResult field of the EX/MEM pipeline register of the sub instruction. Similarly, the input to the ALU for the following or instruction can be found in the MEM/WB pipeline register of the sub instruction. If we change the register file so that it will supply the value written if the read and the write are to the same register, the datapath can supply the operand for the add instruction as well. Using the same argument that we don't have to stall as long as there are no backwards dependencies, Figure 6.41 shows the dependencies between the pipeline registers and the inputs to the ALU for the same code sequence as in Figure 6.30. The change is that the dependency begins from a *pipeline* register rather than waiting for the WB stage to write the real registers. The required data exists in the pipeline registers in time to be used by later instructions, suggesting a shortcut that might reduce performance losses from stalling.

If we can take the inputs to the ALU from any pipeline registers rather than just ID/EX, the pipeline can proceed without stalls. This technique, using temporary results instead of waiting for the registers to be written, is called *forwarding* or *bypassing*. By adding multiplexors to the input of the ALU and by supplying control similar to the Hazard Detection Unit, we can run the pipeline at full speed in the presence of these data hazards.

For now, we will assume the only instructions we need to forward are the four R-format instructions: add, sub, and, and or. Figure 6.42 shows a close-up of the ALU and pipeline register before and after adding forwarding.

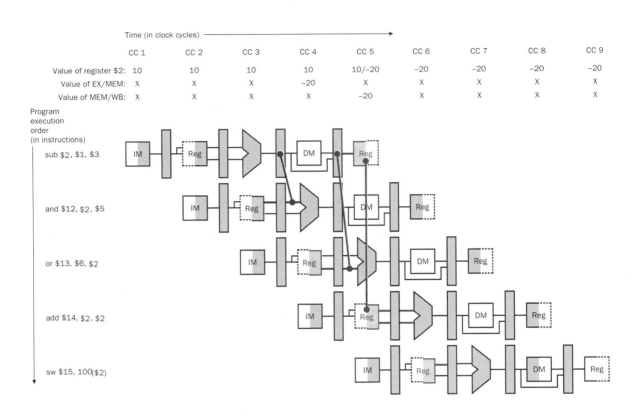

	CC 1	CC 2	CC 3	CC 4	CC 5	CC 6	CC 7	CC 8	CC 9
Value of register $2:	10	10	10	10	10/–20	–20	–20	–20	–20
Value of EX/MEM:	X	X	X	–20	X	X	X	X	X
Value of MEM/WB:	X	X	X	X	–20	X	X	X	X

Time (in clock cycles)

Program
execution
order
(in instructions)

sub $2, $1, $3

and $12, $2, $5

or $13, $6, $2

add $14, $2, $2

sw $15, 100($2)

FIGURE 6.41 The dependencies between the pipeline registers move forward in time, so it is possible to supply the inputs to the ALU needed by the and instruction and or instruction by forwarding the results found in the pipeline registers rather than stall. The values in the pipeline registers show that the desired value is available before it is written into the register. We assume that the register file forwards values that are read and written during the same clock cycle, so the add does not stall, but the values come from the register file instead of a pipeline register. Register file forwarding is why clock cycle 5 shows register $2 having the value 10 at the beginning and –20 at the end of the clock cycle.

Figure 6.43 shows the values of the control lines for the ALU multiplexors that select either the normal register values or one of the forwarded values.

This forwarding control will be in the EX stage, because the ALU forwarding multiplexors are found in that stage. Thus, we must pass the register numbers from the ID stage via the ID/EX pipeline register, to determine whether to forward values. The two conditions for forwarding and the location of the result are as follows:

1. EX hazard:

    if (EX/MEM.RegWrite
    and (EX/MEM.WriteRegister = ID/EX.ReadRegister1)) ALUSelA = 01

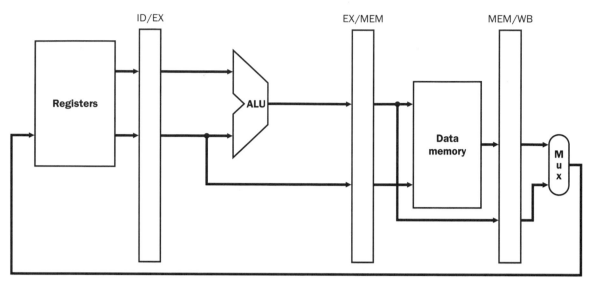

a. No forwarding

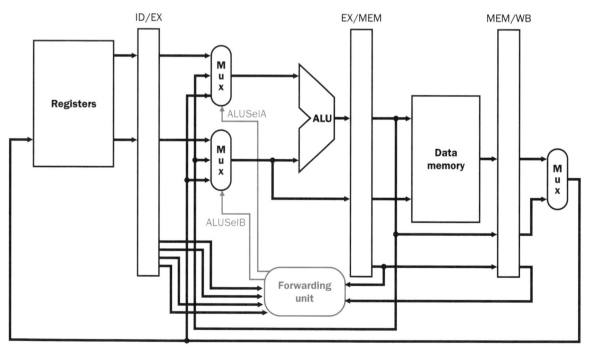

b. With forwarding

FIGURE 6.42 On the top are the ALU and pipeline registers before adding forwarding. On the bottom, the multiplexors have been expanded to add the forwarding paths, and we show the Hazard Forwarding Unit. The new hardware is shown in color.

Mux control	Source	Explanation
ALUSelA = 00	ID/EX	The first ALU operand comes from the normal registers.
ALUSelA = 01	EX/MEM	The first ALU operand is forwarded from the prior ALU result.
ALUSelA = 10	MEM/WB	The first ALU operand is forwarded from data memory or an earlier ALU result.
ALUSelB = 00	ID/EX	The second ALU operand comes from the normal registers.
ALUSelB = 01	EX/MEM	The second ALU operand is forwarded from the prior ALU result.
ALUSelB = 10	MEM/WB	The second ALU operand is forwarded from data memory or an earlier ALU result.

FIGURE 6.43 The control values for the forwarding multiplexors in Figure 6.42. The signed immediate that is another input to the ALU is described in the elaboration at the end of this section.

> if (EX/MEM.RegWrite
> and (EX/MEM.WriteRegister = ID/EX.ReadRegister2)) ALUSelB = 01

This case forwards the result from the previous instruction to either input of the ALU.

2. MEM hazard:

> if (MEM/WB.RegWrite
> and (MEM/WB.WriteRegister = ID/EX.ReadRegister1)) ALUSelA = 10

> if (MEM/WB.RegWrite
> and (MEM/WB.WriteRegister = ID/EX.ReadRegister2)) ALUSelB = 10

This case has the same register number matching, but the forwarded value is determined by whether this instruction depends on an ALU operation (MemtoReg = 0) or a load instruction (MemtoReg = 1).

There is no third hazard, because we assume in this section that the register file supplies the correct result if the instruction in the ID stage reads the same register written by the instruction in the WB stage. This revised register file is another form of forwarding, but it occurs within the register file.

One complication is that hazards can occur in both EX and MEM stages for the same ALU input. For example, when summing a vector of numbers in a single register, a sequence of instructions will all read and write to the same register. In this case, priority goes to the EX hazard, because it is found in the instruction nearest the instruction in the ID stage in the program execution order. Thus, the control for the MEM hazard would be:

> if (MEM/WB.RegWrite
> and (EX/MEM.WriteRegisterRt ≠ ID/EX.ReadRegister1)
> and (MEM/WB.WriteRegister = ID/EX.ReadRegister1)) ALUSelA = 10

if (MEM/WB.RegWrite
and (EX/MEM.WriteRegisterRt ≠ ID/EX.ReadRegister2)
and (MEM/WB.WriteRegister = ID/EX.ReadRegister2)) ALUSelB = 10

Figure 6.44 shows the hardware necessary to support forwarding multiplexors on the inputs to the ALU controlled by the Forwarding Unit.

Example

Show how forwarding works with the instruction sequence from the previous example:

```
sub     $2, $1, $3
and     $4, $2, $5
or      $8, $2, $6
add     $9, $4, $2
slt     $1, $6, $7
```

Answer

Figures 6.45 and 6.46 show the events in clock cycles 3–6 in the execution of these instructions. In clock cycle 4, the Forwarding Unit sees the writing by the sub instruction of register $2 in the MEM stage while the and instruction in the ID stage is reading register $2. The Forwarding Unit selects the EX/MEM pipeline register instead of the ID/EX pipeline register as the upper input to the ALU to get the proper value for register $2. The following or instruction also reads register $2, so the Forwarding Unit selects the MEM/WB pipeline register for the upper input to the ALU in clock cycle 5. The following add instruction reads both register $4, the target of the and instruction, and register $2, still the target of the sub instruction. In clock cycle 6, the Forwarding Unit thus selects the MEM/WB pipeline register for the upper ALU input and the new WB/IF pipeline register for the lower ALU input.

Comparing these figures to Figures 6.35 through 6.40 on pages 406 to 411, we see that forwarding takes 8 clock cycles to complete the add instruction; stalling took 13 clock cycles to complete the same amount of work. This large reduction in clock cycles for the relatively small increase in hardware complexity is the reason why almost all pipelined machines today provide some form of forwarding.

Adding forwarding removes the datapath hazards, because a hazard can be defined only with respect to particular hardware—hence the name Forwarding Unit rather than Hazard Forwarding Unit.

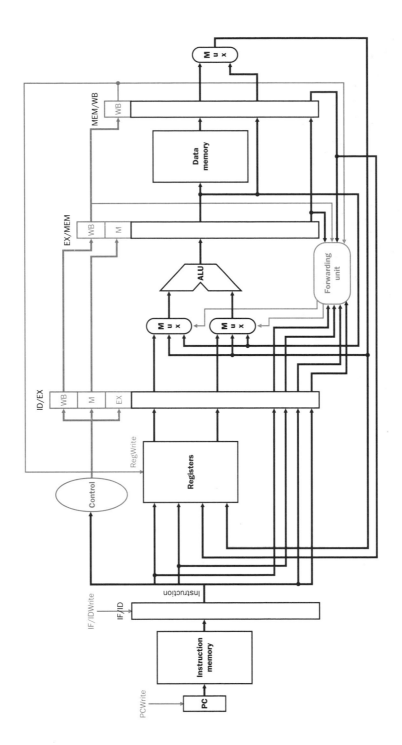

FIGURE 6.44 The datapath modified to resolve hazards via forwarding. Compared with the datapath in Figure 6.34 on page 404, the additions are the multiplexors to the inputs to the ALU. This figure is also a stylized drawing, leaving out details from the full datapath such as the branch hardware and the sign-extension hardware.

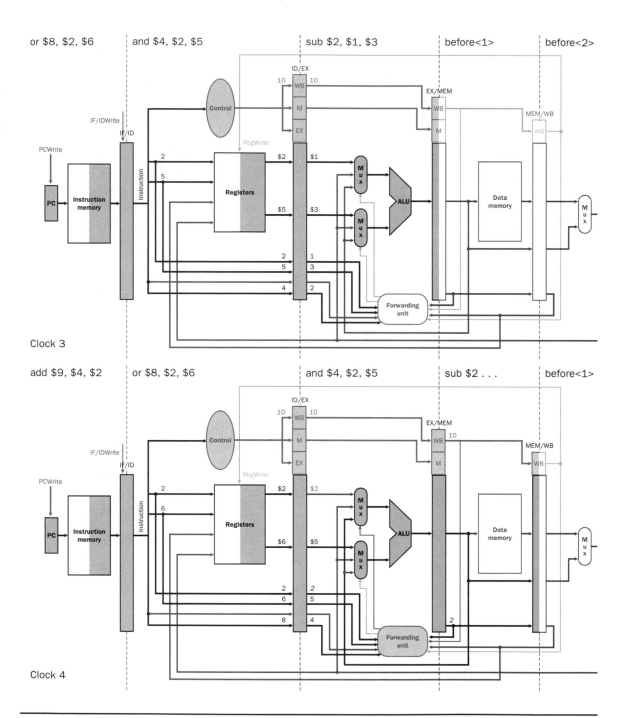

FIGURE 6.45 Clock cycles 3 and 4 of the instruction sequence in the example on page 416. The bold lines show ALU input lines active in a clock cycle, and the italicized register numbers indicate a hazard. The Forwarding Unit is highlighted by shading it when it is forwarding data to the ALU.

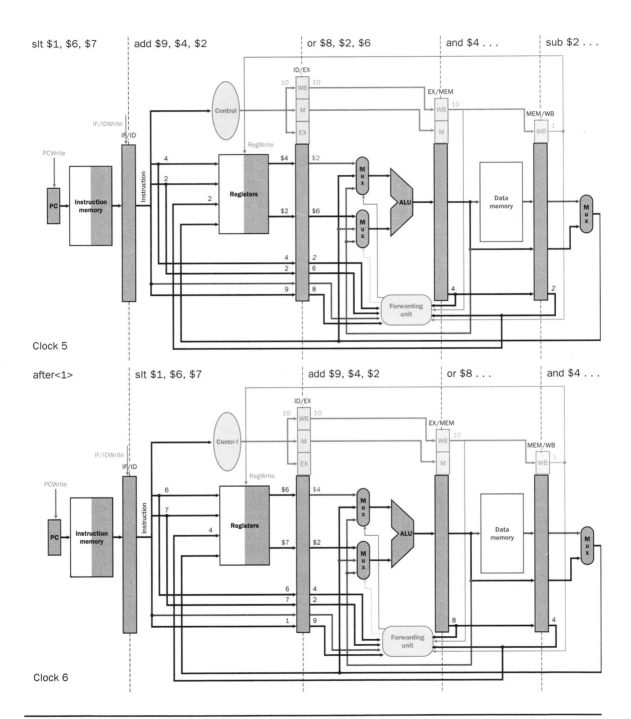

FIGURE 6.46 Clock cycles 5 and 6 of the instruction sequence in the example on page 416. The bold lines show ALU input lines active in a clock cycle, and the italicized register numbers indicate a hazard. The Forwarding Unit is highlighted when it is forwarding data to the ALU. The add completes in two more clock cycles.

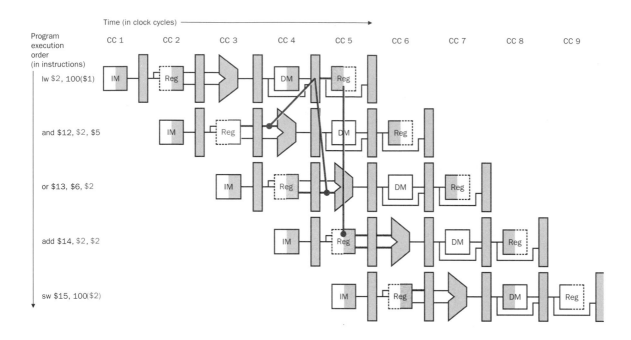

FIGURE 6.47 A pipelined sequence of instructions, this time replacing the "sub" in Figure 6.41 with a load instruction. Since the dependence between the load and the following instruction (and) goes backwards in time, this hazard cannot be solved by forwarding. Hence, this combination must result in a stall by the Hazard Detection Unit.

Elaboration: There is another complication to the conditions for forwarding data. MIPS requires that register $0 never be changed, so every use of $0 *must* supply a 0 as an operand. The conditions above thus work properly as long as ID.EX.ReadRegister1 ≠ 0 and ID.EX.ReadRegister2 ≠ 0.

One alternative to the explanation of forwarding in this section is to determine the control of the multiplexors on the ALU inputs during the ID stage, setting those values in new control fields of the ID/EX pipeline register. The hardware may be faster, because the time to select the ALU inputs is likely to be on the critical path.

Forwarding with Loads and Stores

Alas, there is one case when forwarding cannot save the day—when an instruction tries to read a register following a load instruction that writes the same register. Figure 6.47 illustrates the problem. The data is still being read from memory in clock cycle 4 while the ALU is performing the operation for the following instruction. In this case, something must still stall the pipeline for the combination of load followed by an instruction that reads its result.

Hence, we revive the Hazard Detection Unit. It operates during the ID stage, and it continues to work in the presence of the Forwarding Unit. Checking for load instructions by testing if the control signal ID/EX.RegDst is 0, the Hazard Detection Unit control is now reduced to this single condition:

if (ID/EX.RegWrite and (ID/EX.RegDst = 0) and
  ((ID/EX.WriteRegisterRt = IF/ID.ReadRegister1) or
  (ID/EX.WriteRegisterRt = IF/ID.ReadRegister2)))
    stall the pipeline

Figure 6.48 highlights the pipeline connections for both the Hazard Detection Unit and the Forwarding Unit. As before, the Forwarding Unit controls the ALU multiplexors to replace the value from a general purpose register with the value from the proper pipeline register.

Hardware Software Interface

As another example of the trade-off between compiler and hardware complexity, the original MIPS processors avoided hardware to stall the pipeline by requiring software to follow the load with an instruction independent of that load. In the worst case, nop instructions were placed after loads.

The Big Picture

Although the hardware may or may not rely on the compiler to resolve hazard dependencies to ensure correct execution, the compiler must understand the pipeline to achieve the best performance. Otherwise, unexpected stalls will reduce the performance of the compiled code.

Elaboration: The signed-immediate input to the ALU, needed by loads and stores, is missing from the datapath in Figure 6.48. Since central control decides between register and immediate, and since the Forwarding Unit chooses the pipeline register for a register input to the ALU, the easiest solution is to add a 2:1 multiplexor that chooses between the ALUSelB multiplexor output and the signed immediate. Figure 6.49 shows this addition. Note that this solution differs from what we learned in Chapter 5, where

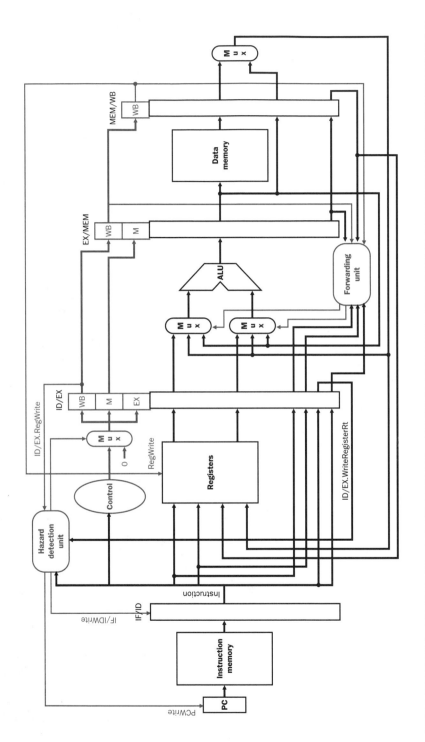

FIGURE 6.48 Pipelined control overview, showing the two multiplexors for forwarding, the hazard Detection Unit, and the Forwarding Unit. Although the ID and EX stages have been simplified—the sign-extended immediate and branch logic are missing—this drawing gives the essence of the forwarding hardware requirements.

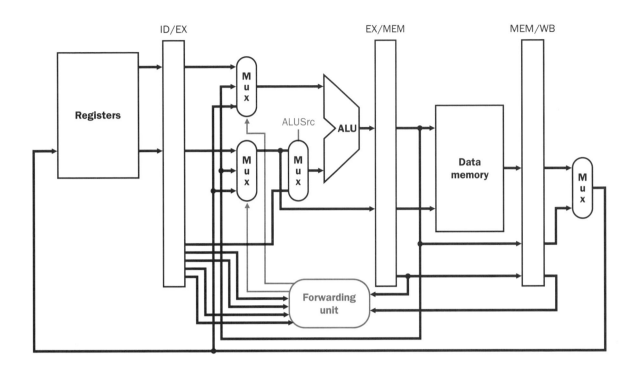

FIGURE 6.49 A close-up of the datapath in Figure 6.42 on page 414 shows a 2:1 multiplexor, which has been added to select the signed immediate as an ALU input.

the multiplexor controlled by line ALUSelB was expanded to include the immediate input.

Forwarding helps with hazards when store instructions are dependent on other instructions. Connecting the ALUSelB output containing store data to the EX/MEM pipeline register forwards the proper value. This added multiplexor for immediates also avoids false matches for the condition mentioned in the elaboration about stalls on page 405.

We can improve the performance of loads followed by stores by adding more forwarding hardware. If we were to redraw Figure 6.47 on page 420, replacing the and instruction that immediately follows lw with an sw, we would see that it is possible to avoid a stall, since the data exists in the MEM/WB register of a load instruction in time for its use in the MEM stage of a store instruction. Exercise 6.17 examines the changes to the datapath necessary to avoid this hazard.

Branch Hazards

There are a thousand hacking at the branches of evil to one who is striking at the root.

Henry David Thoreau, *Walden*, 1854

Thus far we have limited our concern to hazards involving arithmetic operations and data transfers. But another kind of pipeline hazard involves branches. Figure 6.50 shows a sequence of instructions and indicates when the branch would occur in this pipeline. An instruction must be fetched at every clock cycle to sustain the pipeline, yet in our design the decision about whether to branch doesn't occur until the Memory pipeline stage. This delay in determining the proper instruction to fetch is called a *control hazard* or *branch hazard*, in contrast to the *data hazards* we have just examined.

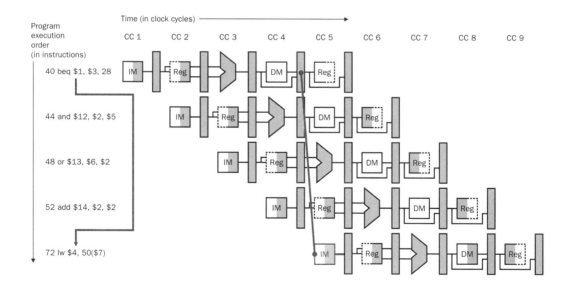

FIGURE 6.50 The impact of the pipeline on the branch instruction. The numbers to the left of the instruction (40, 44, . . .) are the addresses of the instructions. Since the branch instruction decides whether to branch in the MEM stage—clock cycle 4 for the beq instruction above—the three sequential instructions that follow the branch will be fetched and begin execution. Without intervention, those three following instructions will complete before beq branches to lw at location 72.

Returning to our analogy once again, suppose we ran out of Corinthian leather at the upholstery station. We call our suppliers in Spain, but they won't be able to supply the famous material for two months. We then tell the people at the front of the assembly line to stop sending cars needing that option. In the case of computers, this is similar to branching on a condition. The difficulty is that there may be many cars needing Corinthian leather already on the assembly line, and it's too late to stop them; we would set aside those partially completed cars until the new shipment of Corinthian leather arrives. Similarly, we may need to set aside instructions that are fetched before we know the condition of the branch.

This section on control hazards is shorter than previous sections on data hazards. The reasons are that control hazards are relatively simple to understand, they occur much less frequently than data hazards, and there is nothing as effective against control hazards as forwarding for branches, hence we use simpler schemes. We look at two common schemes for resolving control hazards.

Always Stall

One solution is to stall until the branch is complete. This solution, shown in Figure 6.51, will encounter a penalty of several clock cycles for each branch. The drawback is that many times a conditional branch will decide against branching, and the work that would have been accomplished fetching and decoding the following instructions is exactly what will need to happen anyway.

Assume Branch Not Taken

A common improvement over stalling upon fetching a branch is to assume that the branch will not be taken and so will continue execution down the sequential instruction stream. If the branch is taken, the instructions that are being fetched and decoded must be discarded. Execution continues at the branch target. Figure 6.52 shows how this optimization changes the flow in Figure 6.51. If branches are untaken half the time, and it costs little to discard the instructions, this optimization halves the cost of control hazards.

To discard instructions, we merely change the original control values to 0s, much as in the stall approach. The difference is that we must also change the three instructions in the IF, ID, and EX stages when the branch reaches the MEM stage; for stalls, we just changed control to 0 in the ID stage and let them percolate right. Discarding instructions, then, means we must be able to flush instructions in the IF, ID, and EX stages of the pipeline.

To flush instructions in the IF stage, we add a control line, called IF.Flush, that zeros the instruction field of the IF/ID pipeline register to flush the

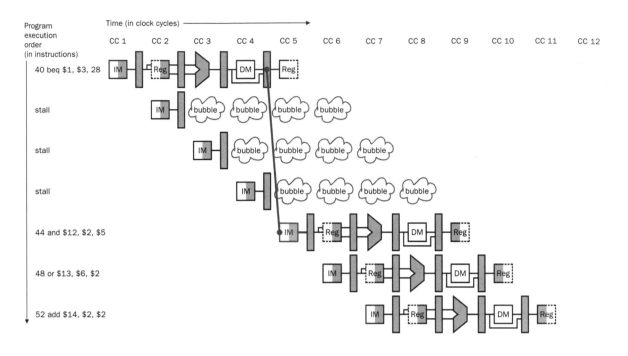

FIGURE 6.51 A branch with stalls to resolve the control hazard. The simplest solution is to stall all instructions that follow the branch until after the decision is clear, and then allow the proper instructions to execute. Stalling essentially increases the cost of a branch from one clock cycle to four clock cycles.

fetched instruction. To flush instructions in the ID stage, we use the multiplexor already in the ID stage that zeros control signals for stalls. A new control signal, called ID.Flush, is ORed with the stall signal from the Hazard Detection Unit to flush during ID. For the EX phase we use a new signal called EX.Flush to cause new multiplexors to zero the EX control lines. Control determines whether to send a flush signal depending on the instruction opcode and the value of the branch condition being tested. Figure 6.53 shows these changes.

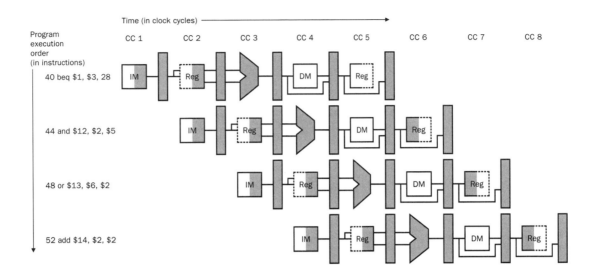

Time (in clock cycles) ⟶

Program execution order (in instructions)

CC 1   CC 2   CC 3   CC 4   CC 5   CC 6   CC 7   CC 8

40 beq $1, $3, 28

44 and $12, $2, $5

48 or $13, $6, $2

52 add $14, $2, $2

FIGURE 6.52 In contrast to Figure 6.51, when the branch is not taken, the instruction takes just one clock cycle. Only when the branch is taken does the instruction take four clock cycles.

Example

Show what happens both when the branch is taken and when it's not taken in this instruction sequence, assuming the optimization on branches not taken:

```
36   sub $10, $4, $8
40   beq  $1, $3, 28 # PC-relative branch to address 72
44   and $12, $2, $5
48   or  $13, $2, $6
52   add $14, $4, $2
56   slt $15, $6, $7
     . . .
72   lw  $4, 50($7)
```

Answer

If the branch in location 40 is untaken, the instructions proceed as in Figure 6.52. Figure 6.54 shows what happens when a branch is taken.

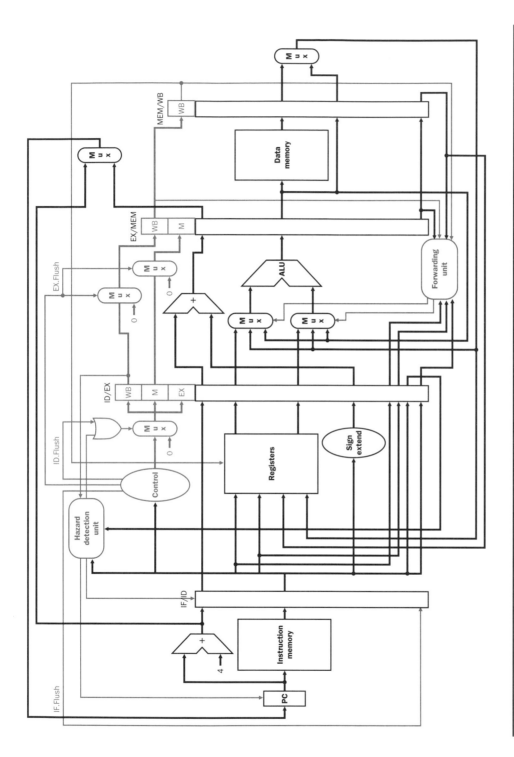

FIGURE 6.53 Datapath for branch, including hardware to flush the instructions that follow branch. Since the branch decision is made in the fourth pipeline stage, three instructions that follow the branch will be in the pipe at that time. The control lines IF.Flush, ID.Flush, and EX.Flush deassert the control lines in the first three stages. Figure 6.52 shows the timing of the operations for a branch. Although the new-PC mux appears in the MEM stage in this figure, the decision between a branch target address from an earlier instruction and PC+4 occurs in the IF stage.

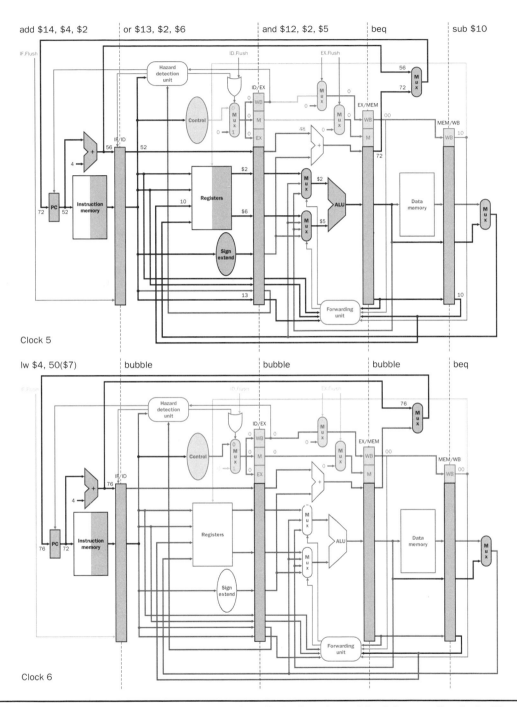

FIGURE 6.54 The MEM stage of clock cycle 5 determines that a branch must be taken, so it selects 72 as the next PC address and zeros the control line values for the next clock cycle. Clock cycle 6 shows the instruction at location 72 being fetched and the three bubbles in the pipeline as a result of the taken branch.

Elaboration: This branch optimization scheme is just one form of *branch prediction*. In this case, we predict that the branch is untaken, flushing the pipeline when we are wrong. With more hardware, it is possible to try other schemes of branch prediction. One approach to predicting when a branch will be taken is to look up the address of the instruction to see if a branch was taken the last time this instruction was executed, and, if so, to begin fetching new instructions from the same place as the last time. Compiler-based approaches are also available; they use a technique called delayed branches. Exercises 6.20 through 6.22 explore this solution to control hazards.

> **The Big Picture**
>
> Pipelining improves throughput but not the time per instruction: the five-stage pipeline still takes five clock cycles for the instruction to complete. Hence data and control dependencies in programs together with instruction latencies offer an upper limit to the benefit of pipelining because the processor must sometimes wait for the full execution time of an instruction for the dependency to be resolved.
>
> This upper limit can be raised, but not eliminated, by reducing control hazards via branch optimizations such as in Figure 6.52, and by reducing data hazards via compiler scheduling.

6.8   Exceptions

To make a computer with automatic program-interruption facilities behave [sequentially] was not an easy matter, because the number of instructions in various stages of processing when an interrupt signal occurs may be large.

Fred Brooks Jr., *Planning a Computer System: Project Stretch*, 1962

Another form of control hazard involves exceptions. For example, suppose the following instruction

```
add    $1,$2,$1
```

has an arithmetic overflow. We need to transfer control to the exception routine immediately after this instruction, because we wouldn't want this invalid value to contaminate other registers or memory locations; the MIPS exception routine is at location 4000 0040$_{hex}$ (see Chapter 5, page 317). Just as we did for the taken branch in the previous section, we must flush the instructions that follow the add instruction from the pipeline and begin fetching instructions from the new address. We will use the same mechanism we used for taken branches, but this time the deasserting of control lines is invoked by the exception. To start fetching instructions from location $4000\ 0040_{hex}$, we simply add a third input to the PC multiplexor that sends $4000\ 0040_{hex}$ to the PC.

This example points out a problem with exceptions: If we do not stop execution in the middle of the instruction, the programmer will not be able to see the original value of register $1 that helped cause the overflow, because it will be clobbered as the destination register of the add instruction. Due to careful planning, the overflow exception is detected during the EX stage, hence we can use the EX.Flush signal to prevent instructions in the EX stage from writing their results in the WB stage.

The final step is to save the address of the offending instruction in the Exception Program Counter (EPC), as we did in Chapter 5. Figure 6.55 shows a stylized version of the datapath, including the branch hardware and necessary accommodations to handle exceptions.

Example

Given this instruction sequence:

```
40hex      sub      $11, $2, $4
44hex      and      $12, $2, $5
48hex      or       $13, $2, $6
4bhex      add       $1, $2, $1
50hex      slt      $15, $6, $7
54hex      lw       $16, 50($7)
. . .
```

Assume the instructions to be invoked on an exception begin like this:

```
40000040hex      sw      $25, 1000($0)
40000044hex      sw      $26, 1004($0)
. . .
```

Show what happens in the pipeline if an overflow exception occurs in the add instruction.

Answer

Figure 6.56 shows the events, starting with the add instruction in the EX stage. The overflow is detected during that phase and $4000\ 0040_{hex}$ is forced into PC. Clock cycle 6 shows that the add and following instructions are flushed, and the first instruction of the exception code is fetched. Note that the address of the instruction *following* the add is saved: $4b_{hex} \times 4 = 50_{hex}$.

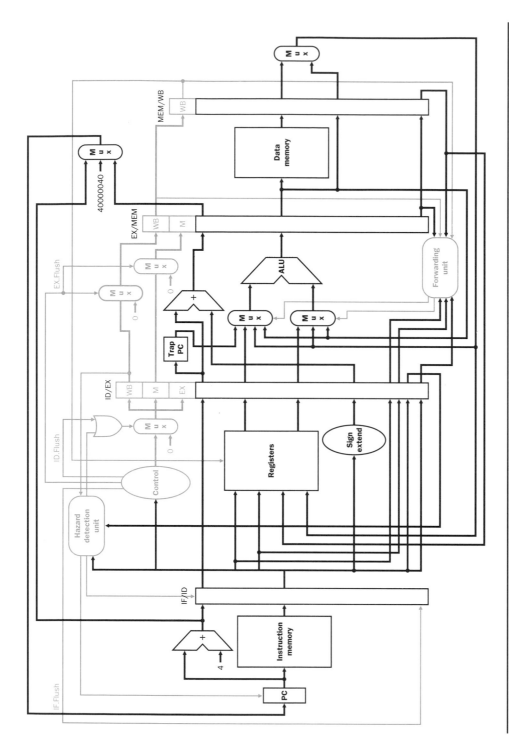

FIGURE 6.55 The datapath with controls to handle exceptions. The changes from Figure 6.53 include a third input, with the value 4000 0040$_{hex}$, in the multiplexor that supplies the new PC value and a Trap PC register to save the address of the instruction that caused the exception. The 4000 0040$_{hex}$ input to the multiplexor is the initial address to begin fetching instructions in the event of an overflow exception. (Trap PC register is just above the ALU multiplexors.)

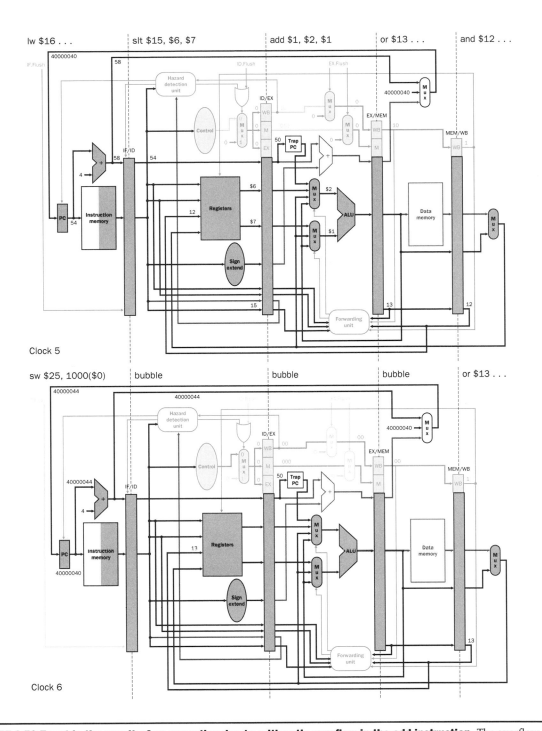

FIGURE 6.56 Event in the result of an exception due to arithmetic overflow in the add instruction. The overflow is detected during the EX stage of Clock 5, saving the address following the add in the TrapPC register ($4b + 4 = 50_{hex}$). Overflow causes all the Flush signals to be set near the end of this clock cycle, deasserting all control values (setting them to 0). Clock cycle 6 shows the instructions converted to bubbles in the pipeline plus the fetching of the first instruction of the exception routine—sw $25,1000($0)—from instruction location 40000040_{hex}. Note that the and and or instructions still complete.

(page 433)

Chapter 5 lists some other causes of exceptions:

- I/O device request
- Invoking an operating system service from a user program
- Using an undefined instruction
- Hardware malfunction

With five instructions active in any clock cycle, the challenge is to associate the exception with the appropriate instruction. The Cause register records all possible exceptions in a clock cycle, and the exception software must match the exception and the instruction. An important clue is knowing in which pipeline stage a type of exception can occur. For example, an undefined instruction is discovered in the ID stage, and invoking the operating system occurs in the EX stage. The hardware will associate the exception with the instruction in the proper stage, allowing earlier instructions to complete and flushing the rest.

The difficulty of always associating the correct exception with the correct instruction in pipelined computers has led some computer designers to relax this requirement in noncritical cases. Such machines are said to have *imprecise interrupts* or *imprecise exceptions*. Hence, a machine with imprecise exceptions might not stop in time, so the EPC might contain 1000, when the offending instruction was really at location 992 or even 1008. Exceptions are precise in MIPS, and the vast majority of machines today support *precise interrupts* or *precise exceptions*.

I/O device requests and hardware malfunctions are not associated with a specific instruction, so the implementation has some flexibility as to when to interrupt the pipeline. The hardware should pick the simplest instruction to associate with the I/O exception, but because the hardware is unstable when a malfunction happens, it may be wise to stop as many instructions as possible.

One complication is that multiple exceptions can occur simultaneously. For example, if an arithmetic overflow was followed by an illegal instruction, we would see the overflow exception and the illegal instruction exception in the same clock cycle. The normal solution is to prioritize the exceptions so that it is easy to determine which is serviced first; this strategy works for pipelined machines as well. In the MIPS R3000, the hardware sorts exceptions so that the earliest instruction is interrupted. In this case it would be the arithmetic overflow. Exceptions are collected in the Cause register, so that the hardware can interrupt based on later exceptions once the earliest one has been serviced.

6.9 Performance of Pipelined Systems

The reason for designing pipelined processors is higher performance, and as we have seen, pipelining reduces the average execution time per instruction. Hazards limit the gains to be made from pipelining, but hardware and software techniques have been devised to circumvent these limits.

The compiler writer must understand the pipeline of the target machine to achieve the best performance; otherwise, unexpected stalls may squander the advantages of pipelined performance.

Example

Find the hazard in this code from the body of the swap procedure in Figure 3.18 on page 136:

```
                          # reg $2 has the address of v[k]
lw      $15, 0($2)        # reg $15 (temp) = v[k]
lw      $16, 4($2)        # reg $16 = v[k+1]
sw      $16, 0($2)        # v[k] = reg $16
sw      $15, 4($2)        # v[k+1] = reg $15 (temp)
```

Reorder the instructions to avoid as many pipeline stalls as possible.

Answer

The hazard occurs on register $16 between the second lw and the first sw. Without forwarding, we would need to find three independent instructions to place between them. Forwarding means that we need find only one, and swapping the second sw is a perfect match:

```
                          # reg $2 has the address of v[k]
lw      $15, 0($2)        # reg $15 (temp) = v[k]
lw      $16, 4($2)        # reg $16 = v[k+1]
sw      $15, 4($2)        # v[k+1] = reg $15 (temp)
sw      $16, 0($2)        # v[k] = reg $16
```

Note that we do not create a new hazard, because there is still one instruction between the write of register $15 by the load and the read of register $15 in the store. Thus, on a machine with forwarding, the reordered sequence takes four clock cycles to start these instructions.

Example

Using the code in the example above, rewrite the code for a machine without forwarding, inserting nop instructions as necessary.

Answer

With comments showing the timing of the load of register $15, the code for the machine without forwarding would look like this:

```
lw   $15, 0($2)  # fetch of lw $15
lw   $16, 4($2)  # decode of lw $15
nop              # lw $15 calculates data address
nop              # lw $15 completes MEM stage
sw   $15, 4($2)  # lw $15 writes reg $15,fetch of sw $15
sw   $16, 0($2)  # read of reg $15 for sw $15, 4($2)
```

The sequence takes six clock cycles on the machine without forwarding compared to four on the machine with forwarding. The benefits of forwarding are so great that even if forwarding reduces the clock rate slightly due to the extra multiplexors, it will still likely lead to a faster machine.

6.10 Fallacies and Pitfalls

Pitfall: Failure to consider instruction set design can adversely impact pipelining.

Many of the difficulties of pipelining arise because of instruction set complications. Here are some examples:

- Variable instruction lengths and running times can lead to imbalance among pipeline stages, causing other stages to back up. They can also severely complicate hazard detection and the maintenance of precise exceptions.

- Sophisticated addressing modes can lead to different sorts of problems. Addressing modes that update registers, such as autoincrement, complicate hazard detection. Other addressing modes that require multiple memory accesses substantially complicate pipeline control and make it difficult to keep the pipeline flowing smoothly.

Perhaps the best recent example is the DEC Alpha and the DEC NVAX. In comparable technology, the new instruction set architecture of the Alpha allowed an implementation whose performance is more than twice as fast as

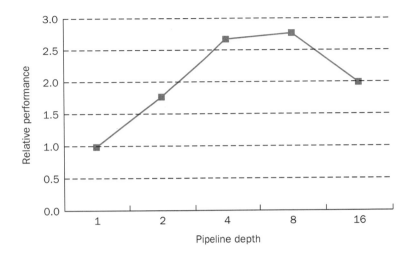

FIGURE 6.57 The depth of pipelining versus the speedup obtained. The x axis shows the number of stages in the EX portion of the floating-point pipeline. A single-stage pipeline corresponds to 32 levels of logic, which might be appropriate for a single FP operation. This data is based on Table 2 in S. R. Kunkel and J. E. Smith, "Optimal pipelining in supercomputers," *Proc. 13th Symposium on Computer Architecture* (June 1986), pages 404–414.

NVAX. In another example, Bhandarkar and Clark [1991] compared the MIPS M/2000 and the VAX 8700 by counting clock cycles of the SPEC benchmarks; they concluded that, although MIPS M/2000 executes more instructions, the VAX on average executes 2.7 times as many clock cycles, so the MIPS is faster (see Figure E.9 on page E-21).

Fallacy: Increasing the depth of pipelining always increases performance.

Three factors combine to limit the performance improvement gained by pipelining. First, data hazards in the code mean that increasing the pipeline depth increases the time per instruction, because a larger percentage of the cycles become stalls. Second, control hazards mean that increasing pipeline depth results in slower branches, thereby increasing the clock cycles for the program. Finally, clock skew and latch overhead combine to limit the decrease in clock period obtained by further pipelining. Figure 6.57 shows the trade-off between pipeline depth and performance for a floating-point pipeline.

Fallacy: Pipelining is easy.

Our books testify to the subtlety of correct pipeline execution. Our first book had a pipeline bug in its first edition, despite its being reviewed by more than 100 people and being class-tested at 18 universities. The bug was uncovered only when someone tried to build the computer in that book. Similarly, the alpha edition of this book had a bug involving forwarding and store instructions, and this bug escaped the scrutiny of many reviewers and students. Beware!

6.11   Concluding Remarks

Nine-tenths of wisdom consists of being wise in time.

American Proverb

Pipelining improves the average execution time per instruction. Depending on whether you start with a single-cycle or multiple-cycle datapath, this reduction can be thought of as decreasing the clock cycle time or as decreasing the number of clock cycles per instruction (CPI). We started with the simple single-cycle datapath, so pipelining was presented as reducing the clock cycle time of the simple datapath. Figure 6.58 shows the effect on CPI and

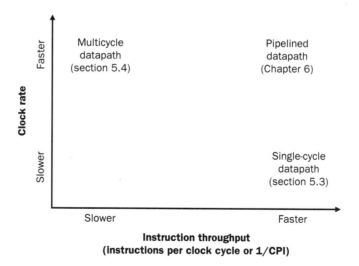

FIGURE 6.58 The performance consequences of simple (single-cycle) datapath and multi-cycle datapath from Chapter 5 and the pipelined execution model in Chapter 6. While the instructions per clock cycle (instruction throughput) is slightly larger than the simple datapath, the pipelined datapath is close and it uses a clock rate as fast as the multicycle datapath.

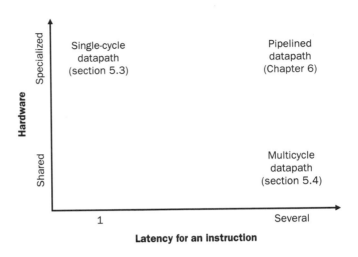

FIGURE 6.59 The basic relationship between the datapaths in Figure 6.58. The pipelined datapath is shown as multiple clock cycles for instruction latency because the execution time of an instruction is not shorter; it's the instruction throughput that is improved.

clock rate for each of the datapaths from Chapters 5 and 6, with pipelining offering both a low CPI *and* a fast clock rate.

Pipelining improves throughput, but not the inherent execution time, or *latency*, of instructions; the latency is similar in length to the multiple-clock cycle approach. Unlike that approach, which uses the same hardware repeatedly during instruction execution, pipelining starts an instruction every clock cycle by having dedicated hardware. Figure 6.59 shows the datapaths from Figure 6.58 placed according to the amount of sharing of hardware and instruction latency.

Latency introduces difficulties due to dependencies in programs, because a dependency means the machine must wait the full instruction latency for the hazard to be resolved. The cost of data dependencies can be reduced through the use of forwarding hardware, and the frequency of control dependencies can be reduced through both branch prediction hardware and compiler scheduling.

While striving for the fastest clock cycle time, hardware designers must also ensure correct execution of all instruction sequences. Compiler writers may or may not be asked to participate by limiting the types of sequences generated, but they *must* understand the pipeline to achieve best performance. Hardware and software techniques cannot completely remove the cost and frequency of hazards; instruction latency and program dependencies bound the benefits of pipelined execution.

Recent Developments

More transistors per chip have meant that techniques formerly limited to mainframe and supercomputers have made their way down to single-chip computers. Functions that are sequential in recent workstations, but are pipelined in supercomputers like the Cray, are being pipelined in the current generation of single-chip computers. These machines are sometimes called *superpipelined* processors, an informal term suggesting a deeper pipeline than the five-stage model discussed in this chapter.

Another method of taking advantage of more transistors is to try to start or *issue* more than one instruction per clock cycle. Multiple issues allow the instruction-execution rate to exceed the clock rate. Machines that issue multiple independent instructions per clock cycle have been called *superscalar machines*. In a superscalar machine, the hardware can issue a small number (say, two to four) of independent instructions in a single clock cycle. If the instructions in the instruction stream are dependent or don't meet certain criteria, however, only the first instruction in sequence is issued. Figure 6.60 compares a superscalar pipeline to a superpipelined pipeline.

The challenges to compiler writers for the two machines are similar. Superscalar machines are sensitive to compilers avoiding pairs of dependent instructions; superpipelined machines depend on compilers scheduling instructions into the longer delays for memory access and until the branch decision stage.

What would a MIPS machine look like as a superscalar implementation? Let's assume that two instructions are issued per clock cycle. One of the instructions could be a load, store, branch, or integer ALU operation, and the other could be any floating-point operation. Issuing two instructions per cycle will require fetching and decoding 64 instruction bits. To keep the decoding simple, we could require that the instructions be paired and aligned on a 64-bit boundary. To make this worthwhile, however, we need either pipelined floating-point units or multiple independent units. Otherwise, floating-point instructions can only be fetched, and not issued, because all the floating-point units will be busy.

Several difficulties may limit the effectiveness of a superscalar pipeline. In our simple MIPS pipeline, loads had a latency of one clock cycle; this prevented one instruction from using the result without stalling. In the superscalar pipeline, the result of a load instruction cannot be used on the same clock cycle or on the next clock cycle. Hence, the next three instructions cannot use the load result without stalling. The consequences of a control hazard also become longer. Effectively exploiting the parallelism available in a superscalar ma-

Instruction fetch	Instruction decode	Execution	Data memory	Write back
Instruction fetch	Instruction decode	Execution	Data memory	Write back

Superscalar

Instr. fetch	Instr. fetch	Instr. dec.	Exec.	Data mem.	Data mem.	Data mem.	Write back

Superpipelined

Instr. fetch	Instr. fetch	Instr. dec.	Exec.	Data mem.	Data mem.	Data mem.	Write back

FIGURE 6.60 A superscalar pipeline vs. a superpipelined pipeline. This two-way superscalar fetches or issues two instructions every clock cycle and follows our traditional five-stage pipeline. The superpipelined model is patterned after the pipeline in the MIPS R4000 and has eight stages. Although the superpipelined model should have a higher clock rate, little else can be said about the relative performance of these two approaches today. The success of superscalar machines is sensitive to compilers avoiding pairs of dependent instructions; the success of super-pipelined machines depends on compilers scheduling instructions into the longer delays for memory accesses and branches.

chine requires more ambitious compiler techniques for scheduling instructions as well as more complex instruction-decoding hardware.

A microprocessor that is both superscalar and superpipelined is the DEC Alpha. This two-way superscalar machine has eight pipeline stages, yielding a clock rate of 200 Mhz. Putting this rate into perspective, the clock rate of the Cray C-90 supercomputer announced in 1991 is just 1.25 times faster than the clock rate of this single chip processor found in single-chip computers announced in 1992. Chapter 2 reminds us that clock rate is only one of three key performance parameters, but this is still an impressive achievement.

6.12   **Historical Perspective and Further Reading**

supercomputer: Any machine still on the drawing board.

Stan Kelly-Bootle, *The Devil's DP Dictionary*, 1981

This section describes some of the major advances in pipelining.

FIGURE 6.61 Photograph of the Stretch computer, one of the first pipelined computers. Photo courtesy of International Business Machines Corporation.

It is generally agreed that one of the first general-purpose pipelined machines was *Stretch*, the IBM 7030 (Figure 6.61). Stretch followed the IBM 704 and had a goal of being 100 times faster than the 704. The goals were a "stretch" of the state of the art at that time—hence the nickname. The plan was to obtain a factor of 1.6 from overlapping fetch, decode, and execute, using a four-stage pipeline. Stretch was also a training ground for both the architects of the IBM 360, Gerrit Blaauw and Fred Brooks Jr., and the architect of the IBM RS/6000, John Cocke.

CDC delivered the first CDC 6600 in 1964 (Figure 6.62). The CDC 6600 was unique in many ways. The interaction between pipelining and instruction set design was understood, and the instruction set was kept simple to promote pipelining. The CDC 6600 also used an advanced packaging technology. Thornton's book [1970] provides an excellent description of the entire machine, from technology to architecture, and includes a foreword by Seymour Cray. (Unfortunately, this book is currently out of print.) The 6600 is considered to be the first supercomputer; the core instructions of Cray's subsequent computers have many similarities to those of the original CDC 6600.

The IBM 360/91 introduced many new concepts, including dynamic detection of memory hazards and generalized forwarding (Figure 6.63). The approach is normally named *Tomasulo's algorithm*, after an engineer who worked on the project. The team that created the 360/91 was led by Michael Flynn,

FIGURE 6.62 Photograph of the CDC-6600, the first supercomputer. Photo courtesy of Charles Babbage Institute, University of Minnesota.

who was given the 1992 ACM Eckert-Mauchly Award, in part for his contributions to the IBM 360/91.

The RISC machines refined the notion of compiler-scheduled pipelines in the early 1980s. The concepts of delayed branches and delayed loads—common in microprogramming—were extended into the high-level architecture. These instructions define away hazards: *delayed loads* mean that the new register value is unavailable for the next instruction, and *delayed branches* mean that the branch occurs *after* the following instruction, not before it (see Exercises 6.20 through 6.22).

An approach that predated superscalar that relies on similar compiler technology is called *long instruction word* (*LIW*) or sometimes *very long instruction word* (*VLIW*). In this approach, several instructions are issued during each clock cycle as in the superscalar case, but in LIW the compiler guarantees that there are no dependencies between instructions that issue at the same time and that there are sufficient hardware resources to execute them, thereby simplifying the instruction decoding and issuing logic. A very practical advantage of superscalar over LIW designs is that superscalar processors can run without changing binary machine programs that run on more traditional architectures; LIW requires the source code for the programs to be available so that the programs can be recompiled. LIW machines are rare today.

FIGURE 6.63 The IBM 360/91 pushed the state-of-the-art in pipelined execution when it was unveiled in 1966. Photo courtesy of International Business Machines Corporation.

A number of papers have explored the trade-offs among alternative pipelining approaches. Jouppi and Wall [1989] examine the performance differences between superpipelined and superscalar systems, concluding that their performance is similar, but that superpipelined machines may require less hardware to achieve the same performance. Recent machines are found in both camps: The MIPS R4000 is superpipelined, the IBM RS/6000 and Sun SuperSPARC are superscalar, and the DEC Alpha is both superpipelined and superscalar.

To Probe Further

Bhandarkar, D., and D. W. Clark [1991]. "Performance from architecture: comparing a RISC and a CISC with similar hardware organizations," *Proc. Fourth Conf. on Architectural Support for Programming Languages and Operating Systems*, IEEE/ACM (April), Palo Alto, 310–19.

A quantitative comparison of RISC and CISC written by scholars who argued for CISCs as well as built them; they conclude that MIPS is between 2 and 4 times faster than a VAX built with similar technology, with a mean of 2.7; Figure E.11 on page E-23 is based on this paper.

Hennessy, J. L., and D. A. Patterson [1990]. *Computer Architecture: A Quantitative Approach*, Morgan Kaufmann Publishers, San Mateo, Calif.

Chapter 6 goes into considerably more detail about pipelined machines, including dynamic hardware scheduling and superpipelined and superscalar machines.

Jouppi, N. P., and D. W. Wall [1989]. "Available instruction-level parallelism for superscalar and superpipelined machines," *Proc. Third Conf. on Architectural Support for Programming Languages and Operating Systems*, IEEE/ACM (April), Boston, 272–82.

A comparison of superpipelined and superscalar systems.

Kogge, P. M. [1981]. *The Architecture of Pipelined Computers*, McGraw-Hill, New York.

A formal text on pipelined control, with emphasis on underlying principles.

Russell, R. M. [1978]. "The CRAY-1 computer system," *Comm. of the ACM* 21:1 (January) 63–72.

A short summary of a classic computer, which uses vectors of operations to remove pipeline stalls.

Smith, A., and J. Lee [1984]. "Branch prediction strategies and branch target buffer design," *Computer* 17:1 (January) 6–22.

An early survey on branch prediction.

Smith, J. E., and A. R. Plezkun [1988]. "Implementing precise interrupts in pipelined processors," *IEEE Trans. on Computers* 37:5 (May) 562–73.

Covers the difficulties in interrupting pipelined computers.

Thornton, J. E. [1970]. *Design of a Computer: The Control Data 6600*, Scott, Foresman, Glenview, Ill.

A classic book describing a classic machine.

6.13 Exercises

6.1 [5] <§6.2> For each pipeline register in Figure 6.3 on page 370, label each portion of the pipeline register by the name of the value that is loaded into the register, as explained on page 402. Also determine the length of each field in bits and the total length of the pipeline register. For example, the lower portion of the IF/ID pipeline register contains an instruction field that is 32 bits wide.

6.2 [5] <§6.3> {ex. 6.1} Following the same procedure as in Exercise 6.1, show the additional widths of the pipeline registers for Figure 6.24 on page 391.

6.3 [20] <§6.3> Figure 6.64 above is similar to Figure 6.27 on page 394, but the instructions are unidentified. Your task is to determine as much as you can of the five instructions in the five pipeline stages. If you cannot fill in a field of an

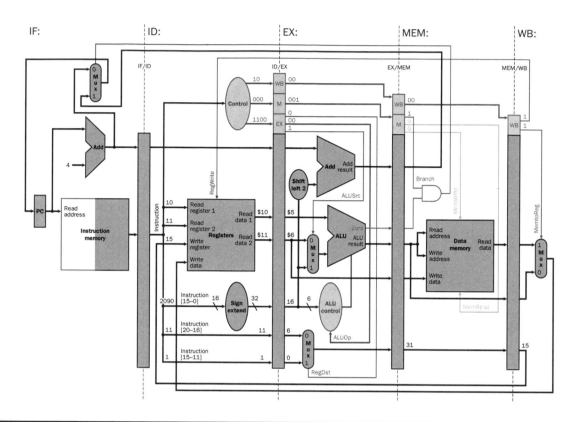

FIGURE 6.64 The pipelined datapath for Exercise 6.3. Use the numeric labels to determine as many fields of each of the five instructions in the pipeline as possible.

instruction, state why. Hint: Try writing as many of the 32 bits of each instruction in binary before writing the instructions in assembly language notation; use the end pages to get the instruction values.

6.4 [40] <§6.3> Using Figure 6.27 on page 394, determine the value of *every* field in the four pipeline registers in clock cycle 5. (These are the values at the beginning of the clock cycle.) Assume that before the instructions are executed the state of the machine was as follows:

- The PC has the value 500$_{ten}$, the address of the `lw` instruction.

- Every register has the initial value 10$_{ten}$ plus the register number (e.g., register $8 has the initial value 18$_{ten}$).

- Every memory word accessed as data has the initial value 1000$_{ten}$ plus the byte address of the word (e.g., Memory[8] has the initial value 1008$_{ten}$).

Determine the value of every field, including those unidentified in the figure and those unnecessary for a specific instruction. If you believe a field value is impossible to determine from the information provided, explain why.

6.5 [10] <§6.2> Using Figures 6.4 through 6.11 on pages 371 through 378 as a guide, use colored pens or markers to show which portions of the datapath are active and which are inactive in each of the five stages of the add instruction. We suggest that you photocopy figures to act as backgrounds to answer this exercise. Be sure to include a legend to explain your color scheme. (We hereby grant the book owner permission to violate the Copyright Protection Act in doing the exercises in Chapters 5 and 6!)

6.6 [15] <§6.3> To be sure you understand the relationship between the two styles of drawing pipelines, draw the information in Figures 6.25 through 6.29 on pages 392 through 396 in the style of Figure 6.30 on page 397. Be sure to highlight the active portions of the datapaths in this simpler figure.

6.7 [10] <§6.4, 6.5, 6.6, 6.9> The example on page 435 shows how to *maximize* performance on our pipelined datapath with forwarding and stalls on a use following a load. Now look at the code in Exercise 3.8 on page 156. Rewrite this code to *minimize* performance on this datapath—that is, reorder the instructions so that this sequence takes the *most* clock cycles to execute while still obtaining the same result. Choose the code in Exercise 3.8 with the bugs intact or with the bugs fixed; the purpose of this exercise is to show the impact of instruction scheduling.

6.8 [20] <§6.4> Programs on pipelined machines often stall without forwarding or compiler help. Start with this simple loop:

```
        mov     $5, $0
 Sum:   lw      $10, 1000($20)
        addu    $5, $5,$10
        addiu   $20, $20,-4
        bne     $20, $0,Sum
```

and assume the pipeline structure of Figure 6.19 on page 386.This datapath neither stalls nor forwards on hazards, so you must add nop instructions. Rewrite the code inserting as few nop instructions as needed for proper execution; reorder the instructions, if possible, to minimize the number of nops while preserving correctness. Write a formula for the number of clock cycles to execute the loop as a function of N, the number of words copied.

6.9 [30] <§6.4> {ex. 6.8} Compilers can help by *unrolling loops* and interleaving the code from different iterations. Making the same assumptions as Exercise 6.8 and using the same initial program, try scheduling instructions to remove nop instructions. Assume that $20 contains $3 \times N$, where N is the number of words to be added together. Show the code and write a formula for the number of clock cycles to execute the optimized loop as a function of *N*. These techniques typically take more registers to get good performance, since formerly sequential computations will be interleaved and registers therefore cannot be reused as quickly. To see if this is true, count the number of registers used in each version of the code. How much faster is this version than Exercise 6.8? Hint: Remember that $20 contains a multiple of 3; try replicating the code within the loop so that each time through the loop you do four loads and four adds.

6.10 [20] <§6.4> This exercise is the same as Exercise 6.8, but replace the code above with this code:

```
Copy: lw      $10, 1000($20)
      sw      $10, 2000($20)
      addiu   $20, $20,-4
      bne     $20, $0,Copy
```

6.11 [30] <§6.4> {ex. 6.10} This exercise is the same as Exercise 6.9, but this time replace the code above with the code found in Exercise 6.10. Assume that $20 contains $3 \times N$, where *N* is the number of words to be copied. Show the code and write a formula for the number of clock cycles to execute the optimized loop as a function of *N*. How much faster is this version than Exercise 6.10?

6.12 [15] <§6.6> Following the suggestion of the elaboration on page 421, one alternative to forwarding control is to determine the control of the multiplexors on the ALU inputs during the *ID stage*, setting those values in new control fields of the ID/EX pipeline register. The hardware may be faster, because the time to select the ALU inputs is likely on the critical path. Redraw Figure 6.48 on page 422 with this change.

6.13 [5] <§6.5>List all of the inputs and outputs of the Hazard Detection Unit in Figure 6.34 on page 404. Give the names and the number of bits for each input and output.

6.14 [15] <§6.5, C> {ex. 6.13} Using Appendix C and the answer to Exercise 6.13, design the hardware to implement the Hazard Detection Unit. Hint: To decide if register numbers are equal, try using an exclusive OR gate (see the Elaboration on page 197 of Chapter 4 or the In More Depth section on page 261 of Chapter 4).

6.15 [15] <§6.6> List all the inputs and outputs of the Forwarding Unit in Figure 6.48 on page 422. Give the names and the number of bits for each input and output.

6.16 [30] <§6.5, C> {ex. 6.15} Using Appendix C and the answer to Exercise 6.15, design the hardware to implement the Forwarding Unit. Hint: To decide if register numbers are equal, try using an exclusive OR gate (see the Elaboration on page 197 of Chapter 4 or the In More Depth section on page 261 of Chapter 4).

6.17 [30] <§6.6, 6.9> The Elaboration that starts on page 421 suggests that we could remove the hazard for a load followed by a store that uses the same register. Show the changes to the datapath in Figure 6.47 on page 420 and change the logic equations starting on page 413 to remove this hazard.

6.18 [20] <§6.6> Let's change the code sequence on page 416 by replacing sub $2,$1,$3 with lw $2,$1,100. Show the state of the pipeline through an instruction sequence as in Figures 6.45 through 6.50 on pages 418 through 424. Assume that the datapath contains both the Forwarding Unit and the Hazard Detection Unit in Figure 6.48 on page 422. You may do much less drawing if you make several photocopies of Figure 6.48 and label the copies appropriately.

6.19 [10] <§6.2, 4.8> In this chapter we used pipelining to improve execution of all instructions. Pipelining can also improve performance of the execution phase of slow instructions. Figure 4.42 on page 235 shows a datapath for floating-point addition. Draw pipeline registers onto that figure, and then the pipeline stages for floating-point addition, starting with instruction fetch.

In More Depth: Delayed Branches

An alternative scheme to branch prediction to reduce the cost of control hazards is called *delayed branch*. In a delayed branch, the execution cycle with a branch delay of length n is

```
branch instruction
sequential successor₁
sequential successor₂
.  .  ..  .  ...
sequential successorₙ
branch target if taken
```

The sequential successors are in the *branch-delay slots*. The job of the software is to make the successor instructions valid and useful. Most machines with delayed branch instructions are limited to a single-branch delay slot.

6.20 [15] <§6.7> Using the example on page 427, rewrite the code to be as fast as possible using a new instruction beqd, which means a branch equal instruction with a single-branch delay slot.

6.21 [10] <§6.7> {ex. 6.20} Using the answer to Exercise 6.20, draw the execution of the instructions as in Figure 6.54 on page 429. Once again, photocopying may save time.

6.22 [30] <§6.7> In which stage must the branch decision be made to reduce the branch delay to a single instruction? Redraw the datapath using new hardware that will reduce the branch delay to one cycle.

6.23 [1 week] <§6.4, 6.5, 6.6> Using the simulator provided with this book, collect statistics on data hazards for a C program (supplied either by the instructor or with the software). You will write a subroutine that is passed the instruction to be executed, and this routine must model the five-stage pipeline in this chapter. Have your program collect the following statistics:

- Number of instructions executed.
- Number of data hazards.
- Number of hazards that result in stalls.
- If the MIPS C compiler that you are using issues nop instructions to avoid hazards, count the number of nop instructions as well.

Assuming that the memory accesses always take one clock cycle, calculate the average number of clock cycles per instruction. Classify nop instructions as stalls inserted by software, then subtract them from the number of instructions executed in the CPI calculation.

6.24 [1 month] <§5.3, 6.3–6.8> If you have access to a simulation system such as Verilog or ViewLogic, first design the single-cycle datapath and control from Chapter 5. Then evolve this design into a pipelined organization, as we did in this chapter. Be sure to run MIPS programs at each step to ensure that your refined design continues to operate correctly.

Large and Fast: Exploiting Memory Hierarchy

. . . the one single development that put computers on their feet was the invention of a reliable form of memory, namely, the core memory . . . . Its cost was reasonable, it was reliable and, because it was reliable, it could in due course be made large.

Maurice Wilkes
Memoirs of a Computer Pioneer, 1985

The Five Classic Components of a Computer

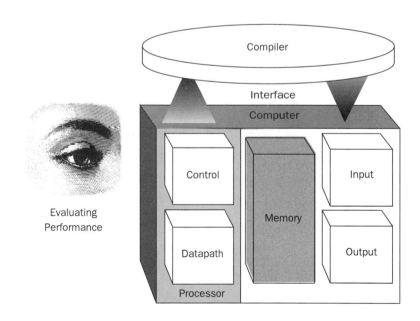

7.1 Introduction

From the earliest days of computing, programmers have wanted unlimited amounts of fast memory. The topics we will look at in this chapter all focus on aiding programmers by creating the illusion of unlimited fast memory. There are many techniques for making this illusion robust and enhancing its performance; accordingly, this chapter has more than its share of elaborations, which you should feel free to skip over. Before we look at how the illusion is actually created, let's consider a simple analogy that illustrates the key principles and mechanisms that we use.

Suppose you were a student writing a term paper on important historical developments in computer hardware. You are sitting at a desk in the engineering or math library with a collection of books that you have pulled from the shelves and are examining. You find that several of the important machines that you need to write about are described in the books you have, but there is nothing about the EDSAC. So, you go back to the shelves and look for an additional book. You find a book on early British computers that covers EDSAC. Once you have a good selection of books on the desk in front of you, there is a good probability that many of the topics you need can be found in them, and you may spend a great deal of time just using the books on the desk without going back to the shelves. Having several books on the desk in front of you saves a lot of time compared to having only one book there and constantly having to go back to the shelves to return it and take out another.

The same principle allows us to create the illusion of a large memory that we can access as fast as a very small memory. Just as you did not need to access all the books in the library at once with equal probability, a program does not access all of its code or data at once with equal probability. Otherwise, it would be impossible to make most memory accesses fast and still have large amounts of memory in machines, just as it would be impossible for you to fit all the library books on your desk and still have a chance of finding what you wanted quickly.

This *principle of locality* underlies both the way in which you did your work in the library and the way that programs operate. The principle of locality states that programs access a relatively small portion of their address space at any instant of time, just as you accessed a very small portion of the library's collection. There are two different types of locality:

- *Temporal locality* (locality in time): If an item is referenced, it will tend to be referenced again soon. If you recently brought a book to your desk to look at, you will probably need to look at it again soon.

■ *Spatial locality* (locality in space): If an item is referenced, items whose addresses are close by will tend to be referenced soon. When you brought out the book on early computers in England to find out about EDSAC, you found that you were also able to use that book to find out about several other early British computers. We'll see how spatial locality is used in memory hierarchies a little later in this chapter.

Just as accesses to books on the desk naturally exhibit locality, locality in programs arises from simple and natural program structures. For example, most programs contain loops, so that instructions and data are likely to be accessed repeatedly, showing high amounts of temporal locality. Since instructions are normally accessed sequentially, programs show high spatial locality. Accesses to data also exhibit a natural spatial locality. For example, accesses to elements of an array or a record will naturally have high degrees of spatial locality.

We take advantage of the principle of locality by implementing the memory of a computer as a *memory hierarchy*. A memory hierarchy consists of multiple levels of memory with different speeds and sizes. The fastest memories are more expensive per bit than the slower memories and thus are usually smaller. Main memory is implemented from DRAM (dynamic random access memory), while levels closer to the CPU (caches) will use SRAM (static random access memory). DRAM is less costly per bit than SRAM, although it is substantially slower. The price difference arises because DRAM uses fewer transistors per bit of memory, and DRAMs thus have larger capacities for the same silicon areas; the speed difference arises from several factors described in section B.5 of Appendix B.

Because of the differences in cost and access time, it is advantageous to build memory as a hierarchy of levels, with the faster memory close to the processor and the slower, less expensive memory below that, as shown in Figure 7.1. The goal is to present the user with as much memory as is available in the cheapest technology, while providing access at the speed offered by the fastest memory. This corresponds directly to what you did in the library: the books on the desk were faster to access, but you didn't have space to keep all the books on the desk. Today, the three major technologies used to construct memory hierarchies are SRAM, DRAM, and disk. The access time and price per bit vary widely among these technologies, as the table below shows, using typical values for 1993:

Memory technology	Typical access time	$ per MByte in 1993
SRAM	8–35 ns	$100–$400
DRAM	90–120 ns	$25–$50
Magnetic disk	10,000,000–20,000,000 ns	$1–$2

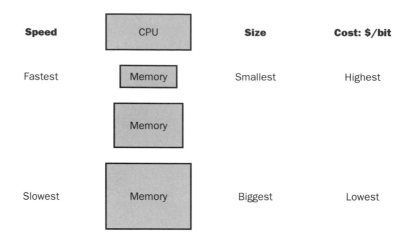

FIGURE 7.1 The basic structure of a memory hierarchy. By implementing the memory system as a hierarchy, the user has the illusion of a memory that is as large as the largest level of the hierarchy, but can be accessed as if it were all built from the fastest memory.

Just as you often found the information in a book on your desk, the principle of temporal locality means that most of the time we will find the data item that we want in the faster memory, since it is likely that the data item was accessed recently. The memory system is organized as a hierarchy: a level closer to the processor is a subset of any level further away, and all the data is stored at the lowest level. By comparison, the books on your desk form a subset of the library you are working in, which is in turn a subset of all the libraries on campus. Furthermore, as we move away from the processor the levels take progressively longer to access, just as we might encounter in a hierarchy of campus libraries.

A memory hierarchy can consist of multiple levels, but data is copied between only two adjacent levels at a time, so we can focus our attention on just two levels. The *upper* level—the one closer to the processor—is smaller and faster (since it uses more expensive technology) than the *lower* level. The minimum unit of information that can be either present or not present in the two-level hierarchy is called a *block*, as shown in Figure 7.2; in our library analogy, a block of information is one book.

If the data requested by the processor appears in some block in the upper level, this is called a *hit* (analogous to your finding the information in one of the books on your desk). If the data is not found in the upper level, the request is called a *miss*. The lower level in the hierarchy is then accessed to retrieve the block containing the requested data. (Continuing our analogy, you get up

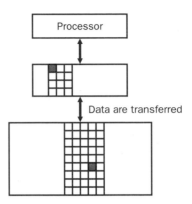

Data are transferred

FIGURE 7.2 Every pair of levels in the memory hierarchy can be thought of as having an upper and lower level. Within each level, the unit of information that is present or not is called a block. Usually we transfer an entire block when we copy something between levels.

from your desk and go over to the shelves to look for the desired information.) The *hit rate*, or hit ratio, is the fraction of memory accesses found in the upper level; it is often used as a measure of the performance of the memory hierarchy. The *miss rate* (1.0 – hit rate) is the fraction of memory accesses not found in the upper level.

Since performance is the major reason for having a memory hierarchy, the speed of hits and misses is important. *Hit time* is the time to access the upper level of the memory hierarchy, which includes the time needed to determine whether the access is a hit or a miss (that is, the time needed to look through the books on the desk). The *miss penalty* is the time to replace a block in the upper level with the corresponding block from the lower level, plus the time to deliver this block to the processor (or, the time to get another book from the shelves and place it on the desk). Because the upper level is smaller and built using faster memory parts, the hit time will be much smaller than the time to access the next level in the hierarchy, which is the major component of the miss penalty. (The time to examine the books on the desk is much smaller than the time to get up and go look for something in a book on the shelves.)

As we will see in this chapter, the concepts used to build memory systems affect many other aspects of a computer, including how the operating system manages memory and I/O, how compilers generate code, and even how applications use the machine. Of course, because all programs spend much of their time accessing memory, the memory system is necessarily a major factor in determining performance. Since memory systems are so critical, there has been a lot of work on them and very sophisticated mechanisms have been developed. In this chapter, we will see the major conceptual ideas, although many simplifications and abstractions have been used to keep the material manageable in length and complexity. We could easily have written hundreds of pages on memory systems, as a number of recent doctoral theses have demonstrated.

The Big Picture

Programs exhibit both temporal locality, the tendency to re-use recently accessed data items, and spatial locality, the tendency to reference data items that are close to other recently accessed items. Memory hierarchies take advantage of *temporal* locality by keeping more recently accessed data items closer to the processor. Memory hierarchies take advantage of *spatial* locality by moving blocks consisting of multiple contiguous words in memory to upper levels of the hierarchy.

A memory hierarchy uses smaller and faster memory technologies close to the processor. Thus accesses that hit in the highest level of the hierarchy can be processed quickly. Accesses that miss go to lower levels of the hierarchy, which are larger but slower. If the hit rate is high enough, the memory hierarchy has an access time close to that of the highest (and fastest) level and a size equal to that of the lowest (and largest) level.

7.2   Caches

Cache: a safe place for hiding or storing things.

Webster's New World Dictionary of the American Language,
Third College Edition (1988)

In our library example, the desk acted as a cache—a safe place to store things (books) that we needed to examine. *Cache* was the name chosen to represent the level of the memory hierarchy between the CPU and main memory in the first commercial machine. Today, although this remains the dominant use of the word *cache*, the term is also used to refer to any storage managed to take advantage of locality of access. Caches first appeared in research machines in

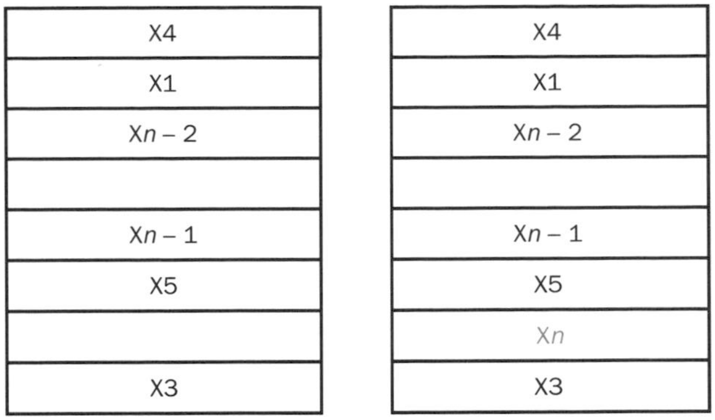

X4	X4
X1	X1
Xn – 2	Xn – 2
Xn – 1	Xn – 1
X5	X5
	Xn
X3	X3

a. Before the reference to Xn.   b. After the reference to Xn.

FIGURE 7.3 The cache just before and just after a reference to a word Xn that is not initially in the cache. This reference causes a miss that forces the cache to fetch Xn from memory and insert it into the cache.

the early 1960s and in production machines later in that same decade; virtually every general-purpose machine built today, from the fastest to the slowest, includes a cache.

In this section, we begin by looking at a very simple cache in which the processor requests are each one word and the blocks also consist of a single word. Figure 7.3 shows such a simple cache, before and after requesting a data item that is not initially in the cache. Before the request, the cache contains a collection of recent references X1, X2, . . . , Xn–1, and the processor requests a word Xn that is not in the cache. This request results in a miss, and the word Xn is brought from memory into cache.

Looking at the scenario in Figure 7.3, we can see that there are two questions we must answer: How do we know if a data item is in the cache? And, if it is, how do we find it? The answers to these two questions are related. If each word can go in exactly one place in the cache, then we will know how to find the word if it is in the cache. The simplest way to assign a location in the cache for each word in memory is to assign the cache location based on the address of the word in memory. This cache structure is called *direct mapped*, since each memory location is mapped to exactly one location in the cache. The typical mapping between addresses and cache locations for a direct mapped cache is usually simple. For example, almost all direct mapped caches use the mapping:

Address of the block *modulo* number of blocks in the cache

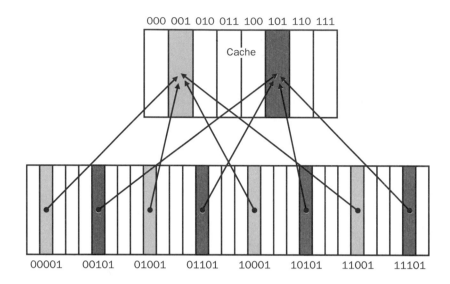

FIGURE 7.4 A direct mapped cache with 8 entries showing the addresses of memory words between 0 and 30 that map to the same cache locations. Because there are 8 words in the cache, an address X maps to the cache word X modulo 8. That is, the low-order $\log_2(8) = 3$ bits are used as the cache index. Thus, addresses 00001_{two}, 01001_{two}, 10001_{two}, and 11001_{two} all map to entry 001_{two} of the cache, while addresses 00101_{two}, 01101_{two}, 10101_{two}, and 11101_{two} all map to entry 101_{two} of the cache.

This mapping is attractive because if the number of entries in the cache is a power of 2, then modulo can be computed simply by using only the low-order $\log_2$ (cache size in blocks) bits of the address; hence the cache may be accessed directly with the low-order bits. For example, Figure 7.4 shows a direct mapped cache of eight words and the memory addresses between 1 (00001_{two}) and 29 (11101_{two}) that map to locations 1 (001_{two}) and 5 (101_{two}) in the cache.

Because each cache location can contain the contents of a number of different memory locations, how do we know whether the data in the cache corresponds to a requested word? That is, how do we know whether a requested word is in the cache or not? We can plan for this by adding a set of *tags* to the cache. The tags contain the information required to identify whether a word in the cache corresponds to the requested word.

We also need a way to recognize that a cache block does not have valid information. For instance, when a processor starts up, the cache will be empty, and the tag fields will be meaningless. Some of the cache entries in Figure 7.3 are empty; we need to know that the tag should be ignored for such entries.

The most common procedure is to add a *valid bit* to indicate whether an entry contains a valid address. If the bit is not set, there cannot be a match on this address.

For the rest of this section, we will focus on explaining how reads work in a cache and how the cache control works for reads. In general, handling reads is a little simpler than handling writes, since reads do not have to change the contents of the cache. After seeing the basics of how reads work and how cache misses can be handled, we'll examine the cache designs for two real machines and detail how these caches handle writes.

Figure 7.5 shows the contents of an eight-word direct mapped cache as it responds to a string of requests from the processor. Since there are eight blocks in the cache, the low-order 3 bits of an address give the block number. Here is the action for each reference:

Decimal address of reference	Binary address of reference	Hit or miss in cache	Assigned cache block (where found or placed)
22	10110_{two}	Miss (7.5b)	(10110_{two} mod 8) = 110_{two}
26	11010_{two}	Miss (7.5c)	(11010_{two} mod 8) = 010_{two}
22	10110_{two}	Hit	(10110_{two} mod 8) = 110_{two}
26	11010_{two}	Hit	(11010_{two} mod 8) = 010_{two}
16	10000_{two}	Miss (7.5d)	(10000_{two} mod 8) = 000_{two}
4	00100_{two}	Miss (7.5e)	(00100_{two} mod 8) = 100_{two}
16	10000_{two}	Hit	(10000_{two} mod 8) = 000_{two}
18	10010_{two}	Miss (7.5f)	(10010_{two} mod 8) = 010_{two}

When the word at address 18 (10010_{two}) is brought into the cache in block 2 (010_{two}), the word at address 26 (11010_{two}), which was in the cache in block 2 (010_{two}), must be replaced by the newly requested data. This behavior allows a cache to take advantage of temporal locality: Recently accessed words replace less-recently referenced words. This is directly analogous to needing a book from the shelves and having no more space on your desk—some book already on your desk must be returned to the shelves. In a direct mapped cache, there is only one place to put the newly requested item and hence only one choice of what to replace.

We know where to look in the cache for each possible address: The low-order bits of an address can be used to find the unique cache entry to which the address could map. Figure 7.6 shows how an address is divided into a cache index, which is used to select the block and a tag field, which is used to compare with the entry in the tag field of the cache. Because a given address can appear in exactly one location, the tag need only correspond to the upper por-

Index	V	Tag	Data
000	N		
001	N		
010	N		
011	N		
100	N		
101	N		
110	N		
111	N		

a. The initial state of the cache after power-on.

Index	V	Tag	Data
000	N		
001	N		
010	N		
011	N		
100	N		
101	N		
110	Y	10_{two}	Memory(10110_{two})
111	N		

b. After handling a miss of address (10110_{two}).

Index	V	Tag	Data
000	N		
001	N		
010	Y	11_{two}	Memory (11010_{two})
011	N		
100	N		
101	N		
110	Y	10_{two}	Memory (10110_{two})
111	N		

c. After handling a miss of address (11010_{two}).

Index	V	Tag	Data
000	Y	10_{two}	Memory (10000_{two})
001	N		
010	Y	11_{two}	Memory (11010_{two})
011	N		
100	N		
101	N		
110	Y	10_{two}	Memory (10110_{two})
111	N		

d. After handling a miss of address (10000_{two}).

Index	V	Tag	Data
000	Y	10_{two}	Memory (10000_{two})
001	N		
010	Y	11_{two}	Memory (11010_{two})
011	N		
100	Y	00_{two}	Memory (00100_{two})
101	N		
110	Y	10_{two}	Memory (10110_{two})
111	N		

e. After handling a miss of address (00100_{two}).

Index	V	Tag	Data
000	Y	10_{two}	Memory (10000_{two})
001	N		
010	Y	10_{two}	Memory (10010_{two})
011	N		
100	Y	00_{two}	Memory (00100_{two})
101	N		
110	Y	10_{two}	Memory (10110_{two})
111	N		

f. After handling a miss of address (10010_{two}).

FIGURE 7.5 The cache contents are shown after each reference request that *misses* with the index and tag fields shown in binary. The cache is initially empty with all valid bits (V entry in cache) turned off (N). The processor requests the following addresses: 10110_{two}(miss), 11010_{two}(miss), 10110_{two}(hit), 11010_{two} (hit), 10000_{two}(miss), 00100_{two}(miss), 10000_{two}(hit), and 10010_{two}(miss). The figures show the cache contents after each miss in the sequence has been handled. When address 10010_{two}(18) is referenced, the entry for address 11010_{two}(26) must be replaced, and a reference to 11010_{two} will cause a subsequent miss. Remember that the tag field will contain only the upper portion of the address. The full address of a word contained in cache block i with tag field j for this cache is $8 \times j + i$, or equivalently the concatenation of the tag field j and the index i. You can see this by looking at the block address in the Data field of any cache entry and the corresponding index and tag. For example, in cache f above, index 010 has tag 10 and corresponds to address 10010.

Address (showing bit positions)

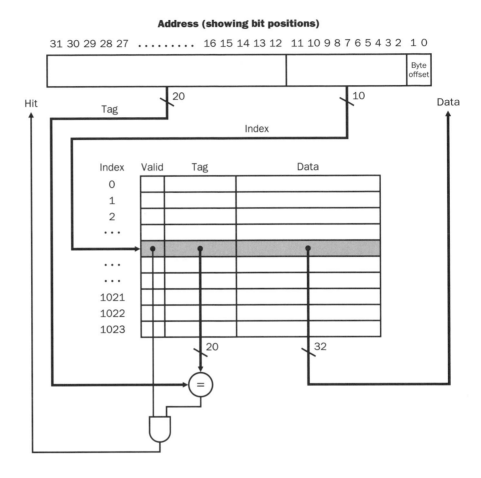

FIGURE 7.6 For this cache, the lower portion of the address is used to select a cache entry consisting of a data word and a tag. The tag from the cache is compared against the upper portion of the address to determine whether the entry in the cache corresponds to the requested address. Because the cache has 2^{10} or 1024 words, and a block size of 1 word, 10 bits are used to index the cache, leaving $32 - 10 - 2 = 20$ bits to be compared against the tag. If the tag and upper 20 bits of the address are equal and the valid bit is on, then the request hits in the cache, and the word is supplied to the processor. Otherwise, a miss occurs.

tion of the address, which is not used to index the cache. Thus, the index of a cache block, together with the tag contents of that block, uniquely specify the memory address of the word contained in the cache block. Because the bits in the index field are used as an address to access the cache, the total number of entries in the cache must be a power of 2. In the MIPS architecture, the least significant 2 bits of every address specify a byte within a word and are not used to select the word in the cache.

The total number of bits needed for a cache is a function of the cache size and the address size, because the cache includes both the storage for the data and for the tags. Assuming the 32-bit byte address of MIPS, a direct mapped cache of size 2^n words with one-word blocks will require a tag field whose width is $32 - (n + 2)$ bits wide, because 2 bits are used for the byte offset and n bits are used for the index. The total number of bits in a direct mapped cache is $2^n \times (\text{block size} + \text{tag size} + \text{valid field size})$. Since the block size is 1 word (32 bits) and the address width is 32-bits, the number of bits in such a cache is: $2^n \times (32 + (32 - n - 2) + 1) = 2^n \times (63 - n)$.

Example   How many total bits are required for a cache with 64 Kbytes of data?

Answer   We know that 64 Kbytes is 16K words, which is 2^{14} words. Thus the total cache size is

$$2^{14} \times (32 + (32 - 14 - 2) + 1) = 2^{14} \times 49 = 784 \times 2^{10} = 784 \, \text{Kbits}$$

or almost 100 KB for a 64 KB cache. For this cache, the total number of bits in the cache is about 1.5 times as many as needed just for the storage of the data.

Handling Cache Misses

Before we look at the cache of a real system, let's see how the control unit deals with cache misses. The control unit must detect a miss and process the miss by fetching the data from memory (or a lower level cache). If the cache reports a hit, the machine continues using the data as if nothing had happened. Consequently, we can use the same basic control that we developed in Chapter 5 and enhanced to accommodate pipelining in Chapter 6. The memories in the datapath used in Chapters 5 and 6 are simply replaced by caches.

Modifying the control to take a hit into account is trivial; misses, however, require some extra work. Let's look at how instruction misses are handled for either the multicycle or pipelined datapath; the same approach can be easily extended to handle data misses. If an instruction access results in a miss, then the contents of the Instruction register are not valid, and the actions that are performed on the next clock cycle (reading the registers) will be useless. Luckily, as we observed in Chapter 5, performing these actions is harmless. Of course, when we do fetch the correct instruction, we will need to reread the registers using the register designators from the actual instruction.

To perform the actions needed for a cache miss on an instruction read, we must be able to instruct the lower level in the memory hierarchy to perform a read. Since the program counter is incremented in the first clock cycle of execution, the address of the instruction that generates the cache miss is equal to the value of the program counter minus 4. We can compute this value using the ALU. Once we have the address, we need to instruct the main memory to perform a read. We wait for the memory to respond (since the access will take multiple cycles), and then write the word into the cache. We can now define the steps to be taken on an instruction cache miss:

1. Compute the value of PC – 4.

2. Instruct the main memory to perform a read and wait for the memory to complete its access.

3. Write the cache entry, putting the data from memory in the data portion of the entry, writing the upper bits of the address (from the ALU) into the tag field, and turning the valid bit on.

4. Restart the instruction execution at the first step, which will re-fetch the instruction, this time finding it in the cache.

The processing of a cache miss creates a *stall*, similar to the pipeline stalls discussed in Chapter 6 but somewhat simpler. For a cache miss we can stall the entire machine while we wait for memory; when memory responds, we simply continue. Pipeline stalls are more complex, because we must continue executing some instructions while we stall others.

The control of the data cache is essentially identical: On a miss, we simply stall the processor until the memory responds with the data. In the rest of this section we describe two different caches from real machines, and we examine how they handle both reads and writes. In section 7.4, we will describe more techniques for handling writes.

Elaboration: To reduce the penalty of cache misses, designers employ two techniques, one which we discuss here and another that we will discuss later. To reduce the number of cycles that a processor is stalled for a cache miss, we can allow a processor to continue executing instructions while the cache miss is handled. This strategy does not help for instruction misses, because we cannot fetch new instructions to execute. In the case of data misses, however, we can allow the machine to continue fetching and executing instructions until the loaded word is required. While this additional effort may save cycles, it will probably not save very many cycles, because the loaded data will likely be needed very shortly.

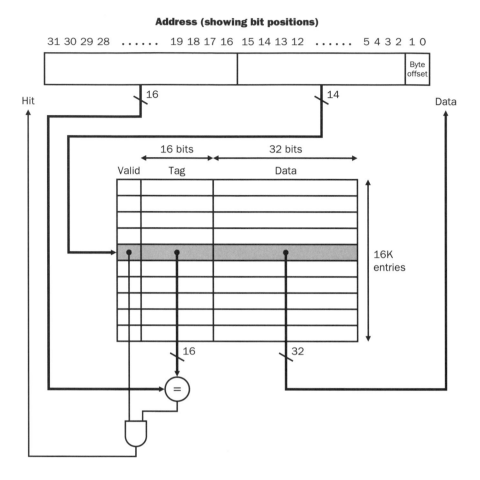

FIGURE 7.7 The caches in the DECStation 3100 each contain 16K blocks with one word per block. This means that the index is 14 bits and that the tag contains 16 bits.

An Example Cache: The DECStation 3100

The DECStation 3100 is a workstation that uses a MIPS R2000 as the processor and a very simple cache implementation. The processor has a pipeline similar to that discussed in Chapter 6. When operating at peak speed, the processor requests both an instruction word and a data word on every clock. To satisfy the demands of the pipeline without stalling, separate instruction and data caches are used. Each cache is 64 KB or 16K words with a one-word block. Figure 7.7 shows the organization of the DS 3100 data cache.

Read requests for the cache are straightforward. Because there are separate data and instruction caches, separate control signals will be needed to read and write each cache. (Remember that we need to write into the instruction cache when a miss occurs.) Thus, the steps for a read request to either cache are as follows:

1. Send the address to the appropriate cache. The address comes either from the PC (for an instruction read) or from the ALU (for a data access).

2. If the cache signals hit, the requested word is available on the data lines. If the cache signals miss, we send the full address to the main memory. When the memory returns with the data, we write it into the cache.

Writes work somewhat differently. Suppose on a store instruction, we wrote the data into only the data cache (without changing main memory); then, after the write into the cache, memory would have a different value from that in the cache. In such a case, the cache and memory are said to be *inconsistent*. The simplest way to keep the main memory and the cache consistent is to always write the data into both the memory and the cache. This scheme, which the DECStation 3100 uses, is called *write-through*. Later in this chapter, we will see another way to handle writes into a cache.

The other key aspect to understand about writes is what occurs on a write miss. Because the data word in the cache is being written by the processor, there is no reason to read a word from memory; it would just be overwritten by the processor. In fact, for this simple cache we can always just write the word into the cache, updating both the tag and data. We do not need to consider whether a write hits or misses in the cache. This leads to the following simple scheme for processing writes, used on the DECStation 3100:

1. Index the cache using bits 15 – 2 of the address.

2. Write both the tag portion (using bits 31 – 16 of the address) and the data portion with the word.

3. Also write the word to main memory using the entire address.

Although this design handles writes very simply, it would not provide very good performance. With a write-through scheme, every write causes the data to be written to main memory. These writes will take a long time and could slow down the machine considerably. In gcc, for example, 11% of the instructions are stores. In the DECStation 3100, the CPI without cache misses for a program like gcc is about 1.2, so spending 10 cycles on every write would lead to a CPI of $1.2 + 10 \times 11\% = 2.3$, reducing performance by a factor of nearly 2.

One solution to this problem is to use a *write buffer*. A write buffer stores the data while it is waiting to be written to memory. After writing the data into the

Program	Instruction miss rate	Data miss rate	Effective combined miss rate
gcc	6.1%	2.1%	5.4%
spice	1.2%	1.3%	1.2%

FIGURE 7.8 Instruction and data miss rates for the DECStation 3100 when executing two different programs. The combined miss rate is the effective miss rate seen. It is obtained by weighting the instruction and data individual miss rates by the frequency of instruction and data references. Remember that data misses include only data reads, because writes cannot miss in the DECStation 3100 cache.

cache and into the write buffer, the processor can continue execution. The write buffer can accommodate a fixed number of words, usually from 1 to less than 10. When a write to main memory completes, the entry in the write buffer is freed up. If the write buffer is full when the processor reaches a write, the processor must stall until there is an empty position in the write buffer. Of course, if the rate at which the memory can complete writes is less than the rate at which the processor is generating writes, no amount of buffering can help, because writes are being generated faster than the memory system can accept them.

The rate at which writes are generated may also be *less* than the rate at which the memory can accept them, and stalls may still occur. This can happen when the writes occur in bursts, even if on average the frequency of stores is low. To reduce the occurrence of such stalls, machines may increase the depth of the write buffer. For example, the DECStation 3100 write buffer is four words deep.

What sort of cache miss rates are attained with a cache like that used by the DECStation 3100? Figure 7.8 shows the miss rates for the instruction and data cache for two programs, which we have seen before. The combined miss rate is the effective rate for each program after accounting for the differing frequency of instruction and data accesses.

Remember that although miss rate is an important characteristic of cache designs, the ultimate measure will be the effect of the memory system on program execution time; we'll see how miss rate and execution time are related shortly. First we must explore how the memory system can take advantage of spatial locality.

Elaboration: A combined cache of the total size equal to the sum of the two split caches will usually have a better hit rate. This is true because the combined cache does not rigidly divide the number of entries that may be used by instructions from those that may be used by data. Nonetheless, many machines use a split instruction and data cache to increase the bandwidth from the cache.

Here are some measurements for the DECStation 3100 for the program gcc, and for a combined cache whose size is equal to the total of the two caches on the 3100:

■ Total cache size: 128 KB

■ Split cache effective miss rate: 5.4%

■ Combined cache miss rate: 4.8%

The miss rate of the split cache is only slightly worse.

For many systems, the advantage of doubling the cache bandwidth, by supplying both an instruction and data word on every cache access, easily overcomes the disadvantage of a slightly increased miss rate. This is another reminder that we cannot use miss rate as the sole measure of cache performance.

Taking Advantage of Spatial Locality

The cache we have described so far, while simple, does nothing to take advantage of spatial locality in requests, since each word is in its own block. As we noted in section 7.1, spatial locality exists naturally in programs. To take advantage of spatial locality, we want to have a cache block that is larger than one word in length. When a miss occurs, we will then fetch multiple words that are adjacent and carry a high probability of being needed shortly. Figure 7.9 shows a cache that holds 64 KB of data, but with blocks of four words (16 bytes) each. Compared with Figure 7.6 on page 463, which shows the same total size cache with a one-word block, an extra block index field occurs in the address of the cache in Figure 7.9. This block index field is used to control the multiplexor (shown at the bottom of the figure), which selects the requested word from the four words in the indexed block. The total number of tags in the cache with a multiword block is smaller, because each tag is used for four words. This improves the efficiency of memory use in the cache.

How do we find the cache block for a particular address? We can use the same mapping that we used for a cache with a one-word block: address of the block modulo number of blocks in the cache. The block address is simply the word address divided by the number of words in the block (or equivalently, the byte address divided by the number of bytes in the block).

Example

Consider a cache with 64 blocks and a block size of 16 bytes. What block number does byte address 1200 map to?

Answer

With 16 bytes per block, byte address 1200 is block address

$$\left\lfloor \frac{1200}{16} \right\rfloor = 75$$

which maps to cache block number (75 modulo 64) = 11. An equivalent way to compute the cache block number is

$$\left(\frac{\text{word address}}{\text{words per block}} \right) \text{ modulo (blocks in cache)}.$$

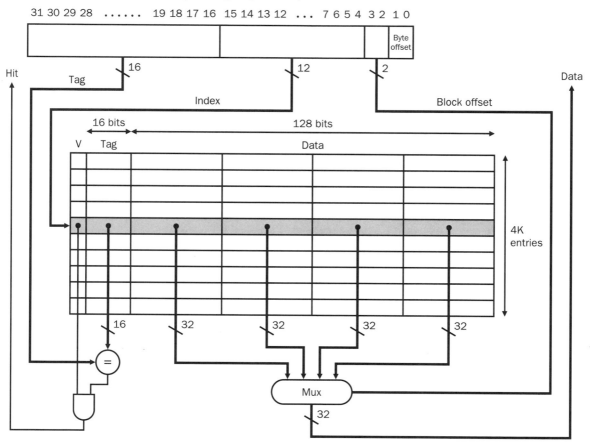

FIGURE 7.9 A 64 KB cache using four-word (16 byte) blocks. The tag field is 16 bits wide and the index field is 12 bits wide, while a 2-bit field (bits 3–2) are used to index the block and select the word from the block using a 4-to-1 multiplexor. In practice, the low-order bits of the address (bits 2 and 3 in this case) are used to enable only those RAMs that contain the desired word. This eliminates the need for the multiplexor. This technique works because the values of the block offset bits are known at the same time as the rest of the address bits.

Program	Block size in words	Instruction miss rate	Data miss rate	Effective combined miss rate
gcc	1	6.1%	2.1%	5.4%
	4	2.0%	1.7%	1.9%
spice	1	1.2%	1.3%	1.2%
	4	0.3%	0.6%	0.4%

FIGURE 7.10 The miss rates for gcc and spice with a cache like that in the DecStation 3100 with a block size of either one word or four words. With the four-word block, we include write misses, which do not incur any penalty for the one-word block and are not included in that case.

Read misses are processed the same way for a multiword block as for a single-word block; a miss always brings back the entire block. Write hits and misses, however, must be handled differently than they were in the DECStation 3100 cache. Because the block contains more than a single word, we cannot just write the tag and data. To see why this is true, assume that there are two memory addresses X and Y, that both map to cache block C, and that C currently contains Y. Now consider writing to address X by simply overwriting the data and tag in cache block C. After the write, block C will have the tag for X, but the data portion of block C will contain one word of X and three words of Y!

We can solve this problem by writing the data while performing a tag comparison, just as if the request were a read. If the tag of the address and the tag in the cache entry are equal, we have a write hit and can continue. If the tags are unequal, we have a write miss and must fetch the block from memory. After the block is fetched and placed into the cache, we can rewrite the word that caused the miss into the cache block. Unlike the case with a one-word block, write misses with a multiword block will require reading from memory.

The reason for increasing the block size was to take advantage of spatial locality to improve performance. So how does a larger block size affect performance? In general, the miss rate falls when we increase the block size. This is easiest to see with an example. Suppose the following byte addresses are requested by a program: 16, . . . , 24, . . . , 20 and none of these addresses is in the cache. Spatial locality tells us that some pattern of this form is highly probable, although the order of the references may vary. If the cache has a four-word block, then the miss to address 16 will cause the block containing addresses 16, 20, 24, and 28 to be loaded into the cache. Only one miss is encountered for the three references, provided that an intervening reference doesn't bump the block out of the cache. With a one-word block, two additional misses are required because each miss brings in only a single word. Figure 7.10 shows the miss rates for the programs gcc and spice with one- and four-word blocks. The

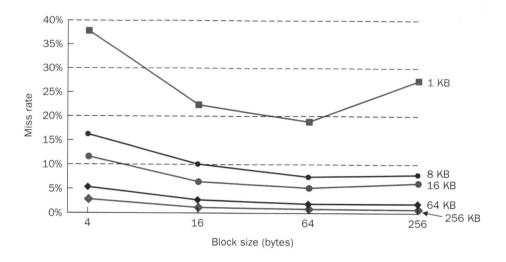

FIGURE 7.11 Miss rate versus block size. For a small 1 KB cache, a large 256-byte block size causes a higher miss rate than the smaller block sizes. This data was collected for a direct mapped cache using traces (SAVE0) collected by Agarwal for the VAX. More details can be found in Agarwal, A. *Analysis of Cache Performance for Operating Systems and Multiprogramming*, Ph.D. Thesis, Stanford Univ., Tech. Rep. No. CSL-TR-87-332 (May 1987).

instruction cache miss rates drop at a rate that is nearly equal to the increase in block size; this is because the instruction references have better spatial locality. The improvement in the data cache miss rate is up to a factor of two.

The miss rate may actually go up, if the block size is made very large, compared with the cache size, because the number of blocks that can be held in the cache will become small, and there will be a great deal of competition for those blocks. As a result, a block will be bumped out of the cache before many of its words are accessed. As Figure 7.11 shows, increasing the block size usually decreases the miss rate. However, the spatial locality among the words in a block decreases with a very large block, consequently, the improvements in the miss rate become smaller—and the miss rate can eventually even increase.

A more serious problem associated with just increasing the block size is that the cost of a miss increases. The miss penalty is determined by the time required to fetch the block from the next lower level of the hierarchy and load it into the cache. The time to fetch the block has two parts: the latency to the first word and the transfer time for the block. Clearly, unless we change the memory system, the transfer time will increase as the block size grows. Since the time to process a miss increases proportionally to the block size, the miss penalty also grows. Furthermore, the improvement in the miss rate starts to decrease as the blocks become larger. The result is that the increase in the miss penalty overwhelms the decrease in the miss rate for large blocks, and cache performance thus decreases. Of course, if we design the memory to transfer larger blocks more efficiently, we can increase the block size and obtain further improvements in cache performance. We discuss this topic in the next section.

Elaboration: The major disadvantage of increasing the block size is that the cache miss penalty increases. Although it is hard to do anything about the latency component of the miss penalty, we may be able to hide some of the transfer time so that the miss penalty is effectively smaller. The simplest method for doing this, called *early restart*, is simply to resume execution as soon as the requested word of the block is returned, rather than wait for the entire block. Many machines use this technique for instruction access, where it works best. Instruction accesses are largely sequential, so if the memory system can deliver a word every clock cycle, the processor may be able to restart operation when the requested word is returned, with the memory system delivering new instruction words just in time. This technique is usually less effective for data caches, because it is likely that the words will be requested from the block in a less predictable way, and the probability that the processor will need another word from a different cache line before the transfer completes is high. If the processor cannot access the data cache because a transfer is ongoing, then it must stall.

An even more sophisticated scheme is to organize the memory so that the requested word is transferred from the memory to the cache first. The remainder of the line is then transferred, starting with the address after the requested word and wrapping around to the beginning of the block. This technique, called *requested word first*, can be slightly faster than early restart, but it is limited by the same properties that limit early restart.

Designing the Memory System to Support Caches

Cache misses are satisfied from main memory, which is constructed from DRAMs. In Chapter 1, we saw that DRAMs are designed with the primary emphasis on density rather than access time. Although it is difficult to reduce the latency to fetch the first word from memory, we can reduce the miss penalty if we increase the bandwidth from the memory to the cache. This allows larger block sizes to be used while still maintaining a low miss penalty, similar to that for a smaller block.

To understand the impact of different organizations for memory, let's define a set of hypothetical memory access times:

- 1 clock cycle to send the address

- 10 clock cycles for each DRAM access initiated

- 1 clock cycle to send a word of data

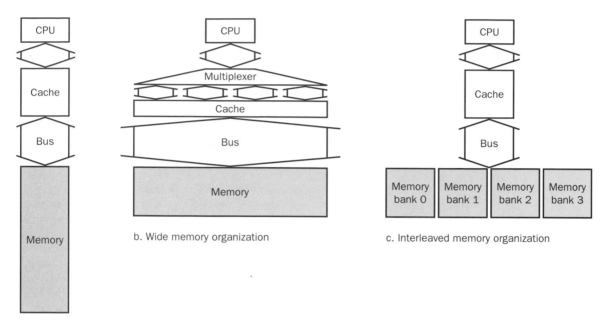

a. One-word-wide memory organization

FIGURE 7.12 The primary method of achieving higher memory bandwidth is to increase the physical or logical width of the memory system. In this figure there are two ways in which the memory bandwidth is improved. The simplest design, (a), uses a memory where all components are one word wide; (b) shows a wider memory, bus, and cache; while (c) shows a narrow bus and cache with an interleaved memory.

If we have a cache block of four words and a one-word-wide bank of DRAMs, the miss penalty would be $1 + 4 \times 10 + 4 \times 1 = 45$ clock cycles. Thus, the number of bytes transferred per clock cycle for a single miss would be

$$\frac{4 \times 4}{45} = 0.36$$

Figure 7.12 shows three options for designing the memory system. The first option follows what we have been assuming so far: memory is one word wide, and all accesses are made sequentially. The second option increases the bandwidth to memory by widening the memory and the buses between the processor and memory; this allows parallel access to all the words of the block. The third option, called *interleaving*, increases the bandwidth by widening the memory but not the interconnection bus. Thus, we still pay a cost to transmit each word, but we can avoid paying the cost of the access latency more than once. Let's look at how much these other two options improve the 45-cycle miss penalty that we would see for option a in Figure 7.12.

Increasing the width of the memory and the bus will increase the memory bandwidth proportionally, decreasing the transfer time portion of the miss penalty. With a main memory width of two words, the miss penalty drops from 45 clock cycles to $1 + 2 \times 10 + 2 \times 1 = 23$ clock cycles. With a four-word-wide memory, the miss penalty is just 12 clock cycles. The bandwidth for a single miss is then 0.6956 (or 0.70) of a byte per clock cycle for a memory that is two words wide, and 1.33 bytes per clock cycle when the memory is four words wide. The major cost of this enhancement is in the wider bus; a secondary cost is in additional buffers at the memory.

Instead of making the entire path between the memory and cache wider, the memory chips can be organized in banks to read or write multiple words in one access time rather than reading and writing a single word each time. Each bank could be one word wide so that the width of the bus and the cache need not change, but sending addresses to several banks permits them all to read simultaneously. This scheme, which is called *interleaving*, retains the advantage of incurring the full memory latency only once. For example, with four banks, the time to get a four-word block would consist of 1 cycle to transmit the address to the banks, 10 cycles for all four banks to access memory, and 4 cycles to send the four words back to the cache. This yields a miss penalty of $1 + 1 \times 10 + 4 \times 1 = 15$ clock cycles. This is an effective bandwidth per miss of just over 1 byte per clock, or about three times the bandwidth for the one-word-wide memory and bus. Banks are also valuable on writes. Each bank can write independently, quadrupling the write bandwidth and leading to fewer stalls in a write-through cache. As we will see, there is an alternative strategy for writes that makes interleaving even more attractive.

Elaboration: As capacity per memory chip increases, there are fewer chips in the same-sized memory system. Memory chips are organized to produce a small number of output bits, usually 1 to 8, with 1 being the most popular. We describe the organization of a RAM as $d \times w$, where d is the number of addressable locations (the depth) and w is the output (or width of each location). Thus, the most popular 4 Mbit DRAMs are 4M x 1. As memory chip densities grow, the width of a memory chip remains constant, but the depth increases (see Appendix B for further discussion of DRAMs). Because of this, multiple banks become much less attractive, because the minimum memory configuration increases quickly. For example, a 16 MB main memory with banks each 32 bits wide takes 128 memory chips of 1 Mb x 1 chips, easily organized into four banks of 32 memory chips. But if 4 Mb x 1-bit memory chips are used for 16 MB, there can be only one bank with a width of 32 bits. This is the main disadvantage of interleaved memory banks.

Another possibility for improving the rate at which we transfer data from the memory to the caches is to take advantage of the structure of DRAMs. DRAMs are organized as

Year introduced	Chip size	$ per MByte	Total access time to a new row/column	Column access time to existing row
1980	64 Kbit	1500	250 ns	150 ns
1983	256 Kbit	500	185 ns	100 ns
1985	1 Mbit	200	135 ns	40 ns
1989	4 Mbit	50	110 ns	40 ns
1992	16 Mbit	15	90 ns	30 ns

FIGURE 7.13 DRAM sizes increase by multiples of four approximately once every three years. The improvements in access time have been slower but continuous, and cost almost tracks density improvements, although cost is often affected by other issues, such as availability and demand. Column access time usually determines the time to perform a page mode access. DRAMs are almost always available in x1 configurations initially (e.g., 4 Mbit x 1). Wider configurations (e.g., 1 Mbit x 4) usually track availability of the x1 configuration by close to a year, and they cost more. Two major reasons for this are that the package for the x1 configuration is cheaper and it is the commodity product.

square arrays, and access time is divided into row access and column access. DRAMs buffer a row of bits inside the DRAM for column access. They also come with optional timing signals that allow repeated accesses to the buffer without a row-access time. One common version of this capability is called *page mode*. In page mode, the buffer acts like a SRAM; by changing column address, random bits can be accessed in the buffer until the next row access or refresh time. This capability changes the access time significantly, since the access time to bits in the row is much lower. Figure 7.13 shows how the density, cost, and access time of DRAMS have changed over the years.

The advantage of these optimizations is that they use the circuitry already on the DRAMs, adding little cost to the system while achieving a significant improvement in bandwidth. (The same is true of interleaving.) Furthermore, these DRAM options allow us to increase the bandwidth without incurring system disadvantages in terms of expandability and minimum memory size that are associated with wider memories or interleaving. The internal architecture of DRAMs and how these optimizations are implemented are described in section B.5 of Appendix B.

Cache Performance

CPU time can be divided into the clock cycles that the CPU spends executing the program and the clock cycles that the CPU spends waiting for the memory system. Normally, we assume that the cost of cache accesses that are hits are part of the normal CPU execution cycles. Thus,

$$\text{CPU time} = (\text{CPU execution clock cycles} + \text{Memory-stall clock cycles}) \times \text{Clock cycle time}$$

The memory-stall clock cycles come primarily from cache misses, and we make that assumption here. We also restrict the discussion to a simplified model of the memory system. In real processors, the stalls generated by reads and writes can be quite complex and accurate performance prediction usually requires very detailed simulations of the processor and memory system.

Memory-stall clock cycles can be defined as the sum of the stall cycles coming from reads plus those coming from writes:

$$\text{Memory-stall clock cycles} = \text{Read-stall cycles} + \text{Write-stall cycles}$$

The read-stall cycles can each be defined in terms of the number of read accesses per program, the miss penalty in clock cycles for a read, and the read miss rate:

$$\text{Read-stall cycles} = \frac{\text{Reads}}{\text{Program}} \times \text{Read miss rate} \times \text{Read miss penalty}$$

Writes are more complicated. For a write-through scheme, we have two sources of stalls: write misses, which require that we fetch the block before continuing the write; and write buffer stalls, which occur when the write buffer is full when a write occurs. Thus, the cycles stalled for writes equals the sum of these two:

$$\text{Write-stall cycles} = \left(\frac{\text{Writes}}{\text{Program}} \times \text{Write miss rate} \times \text{Write miss penalty} \right)$$
$$+ \text{Write buffer stalls}$$

In many cache organizations, the read and write miss penalties are the same (the time to fetch the block from memory). If we assume that the write buffer stalls are negligible (or fold them into the stalls for write cache misses), we can combine the reads and writes by using a single miss rate and the miss penalty:

$$\text{Memory-stall clock cycles} = \frac{\text{Memory accessess}}{\text{Program}} \times \text{Miss rate} \times \text{Miss penalty}$$

We can also write this as

$$\text{Memory-stall clock cycles} = \frac{\text{Instructions}}{\text{Program}} \times \frac{\text{Misses}}{\text{Instruction}} \times \text{Miss penalty}$$

Let's consider a simple example to help us understand the impact of cache performance on machine performance.

Example

Assume an instruction cache miss rate for gcc of 5% and a data cache miss rate of 10%. If a machine has a CPI of 4 without any memory stalls and the miss penalty is 12 cycles for all misses, determine how much faster a machine would run with a perfect cache that never missed. Use the instruction frequencies for gcc from Chapter 4, Figure 4.46 on page 248.

Answer

The number of memory miss cycles for instructions in terms of the Instruction count (IC) is

$$\text{Instruction miss cycles} = \text{IC} \times 5\% \times 12 = 0.6 \times \text{IC}$$

We know that the frequency of loads and stores is 33%. Therefore, we can find the number of memory miss cycles for data references:

$$\text{Data miss cycles} = \text{IC} \times 33\% \times 10\% \times 12 = 0.4 \times \text{IC}$$

Thus, the total number of memory stall cycles is 0.6 IC + 0.4 IC = 1.0 IC. This is one cycle of memory stall per instruction. Accordingly, the CPI with memory stalls is 4 + 1 = 5. Since there is no change in instruction count or clock rate, the ratio of the CPU execution times is

$$\frac{\text{CPU time with stalls}}{\text{CPU time with perfect cache}} = \frac{\text{IC} \times \text{CPI}_{\text{stall}} \times \text{Clock Cycle}}{\text{IC} \times \text{CPI}_{\text{perfect}} \times \text{Clock cycle}}$$

$$= \frac{\text{CPI}_{\text{stall}}}{\text{CPI}_{\text{perfect}}} = \frac{5}{4}$$

The performance with the perfect cache is better by $\frac{5}{4} = 1.25$.

What happens if the processor is made faster, but the memory system stays the same? The amount of time spent on memory stalls will take up an increasing fraction of the execution time; Amdahl's Law, which we examined in Chapter 2, reminds us of this fact. A few simple examples show how serious this problem can be. Suppose we speed up the machine in the previous example by reducing its CPI from 4 to 2 without changing the clock rate. The system with cache misses would then have a CPI of 2 + 1 = 3, and the system with the perfect cache would be

$$\frac{3}{2} = 1.5 \text{ times faster.}$$

The amount of execution time spent on memory stalls would have risen from

$$\frac{1}{5} = 20\% \text{ to } \frac{1}{3} = 33\%.$$

Similarly, increasing the clock rate without changing the memory system also increases the performance lost due to cache misses, as the next example shows.

Example   Suppose we increase the performance of the machine in the previous example by doubling its clock rate. Since the main memory speed is unlikely to change, assume that the absolute time to handle a cache miss does not change. How much faster will the machine be with the faster clock, assuming the same miss rate as the previous example?

Answer   Measured in the faster clock cycles, the new miss penalty will be twice as long, or 24 clock cycles. Hence:

$$\text{Total miss cycles per instruction} = (5\% \times 24) + 33\% \times (10\% \times 24) = 2.0$$

This means that the faster machine with cache misses will have a CPI of 4 + 2 = 6, compared to a CPI with cache misses of 5 for the slower machine.

Using the formula for CPU time from the previous example, we can compute the relative performance as:

$$\frac{\text{Performance with fast clock}}{\text{Performance with slow clock}} = \frac{\text{Execution time with slow clock}}{\text{Execution time with fast clock}}$$

$$= \frac{\text{IC} \times \text{CPI} \times \text{Clock cycle}}{\text{IC} \times \text{CPI} \times \dfrac{\text{Clock cycle}}{2}}$$

$$= \frac{5}{6 \times \dfrac{1}{2}} = \frac{5}{3}$$

This means the machine with the faster clock is 1.67 times faster rather than 2 times faster, which it would have been without the increased effect of cache misses.

As these examples illustrate, cache behavior penalties increase as a machine becomes faster. Furthermore, if a machine improves both clock rate and CPI, it suffers a double hit:

1. The lower the CPI, the more pronounced the impact of stall cycles.

2. The main memory system is unlikely to improve as fast as processor cycle time. When calculating CPI, the cache miss penalty is measured in *CPU clock cycles* needed for a miss. Therefore, a higher CPU clock rate leads to a larger miss penalty, if the main memories of two machines have the same absolute access times.

Thus, the importance of cache performance for CPUs with low CPI and high clock rates is greater; and, consequently, the danger of neglecting cache behavior in assessing the performance of such machines is greater.

The previous examples and equations assume that the hit time is not a factor in determining cache performance. Although, clearly, if the hit time increases, the total time to access a word from the memory system will increase, possibly causing an increase in the processor cycle time. Although we will see additional examples of this shortly, one example is increasing the cache size. A larger cache could clearly have a longer access time, just as if your desk in the library was very large (say 10' by 10'), it would take longer to locate a book on the desk. At some point, the increase in hit time for a larger cache could dominate the improvement in hit rate, leading to a decrease in processor performance. An example of this behavior is shown in the Fallacies and Pitfalls in section 7.1.

Summary: The Basics of Caches

In this section, we started by examining the simplest of caches: a direct mapped cache with a one-word block. In such a cache, both hits and misses are simple, since a word can go in exactly one location and there is a separate tag for every word. To keep the cache and memory consistent, a write-through scheme can be used, so that every write into the cache also causes memory to be updated.

To take advantage of spatial locality, a cache must have a block size larger than one word. The use of a larger block decreases the miss rate and improves the efficiency of the cache by reducing the amount of tag storage relative to the amount of data storage in the cache. Although a larger block size decreases the miss rate, it can also increase the miss penalty. If the miss penalty increased linearly with the block size, larger blocks could easily lead to lower performance. To avoid this, the bandwidth of main memory is increased to transfer cache blocks more efficiently. The two common methods for doing this are making the memory wider and interleaving. In both cases, we reduce the time to fetch the block by minimizing the number of times we must start a new memory access to fetch a block. These schemes may also reduce the transfer time to move the block from the memory to the cache.

The last part of the section examined cache performance. Since the total number of cycles spent on a program is the sum of the processor cycles and the memory stall cycles, the memory system can have a significant effect on program execution time. In fact, as processors get faster (either by lowering CPI or increasing the clock rate), the relative effect of the memory stall cycles increases, making a good memory system critical to achieving high performance. The number of memory stall cycles depends on both the miss rate and the miss penalty. The challenge, as we will see in section 7.4, is to reduce one of these factors without significantly affecting other critical factors in the memory hierarchy.

7.3 Virtual Memory

. . . a system has been devised to make the core drum combination appear to the programmer as a single level store, the requisite transfers taking place automatically.

Kilburn et al., *One-level storage system*, 1962

In the previous section, we saw how caches served as a method for providing fast access to recently used portions of a program's code and data. Similarly, the main memory can act as a "cache" for the secondary storage, usually implemented with magnetic disks. This technique is called *virtual memory*. There are two major motivations for virtual memory: to allow efficient sharing of memory among multiple programs and to remove the programming burdens of a small, limited amount of main memory.

Consider a collection of programs running at once on a machine. The total memory required by all the programs may be much larger than the amount of physical memory available on the machine, but only a fraction of this memory is actively being used at any point in time. Main memory need contain only the active portions of the programs, just as a cache contains only the active portion of one program. This allows us to efficiently share the processor as well as the main memory.

A second motivation is to allow user programs to exceed the size of primary memory. Formerly, if a program became too large for physical memory, it was up to the programmer to make it fit. Programmers divided programs into pieces and then identified the pieces that were mutually exclusive. These *overlays* were loaded or unloaded under user program control during execution, with the programmer ensuring that the program never tried to access an overlay that was not loaded and that the overlays loaded never exceeded the total size of the memory. As one can well imagine, this responsibility was a substantial burden on programmers. *Virtual memory*, which was invented to relieve programmers of this difficulty, automatically manages the two levels of the memory hierarchy represented by main memory and secondary storage.

Of course, we cannot know which programs will share the physical memory with other programs when we compile them. In fact, the programs sharing the physical memory can even change dynamically while the programs are running. Because of this, we would like to compile each program into its own *address space*, that is, a separate range of memory locations accessible only to this program. Because multiple user programs share a single physical memo-

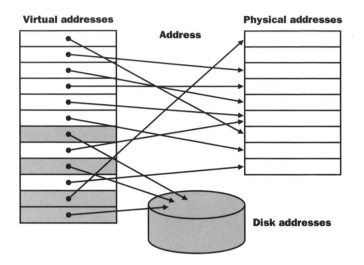

FIGURE 7.14 In virtual memory, pages are mapped from one set of addresses, called virtual addresses, to another set called physical addresses. The processor generates virtual addresses while the memory is accessed using physical addresses. Both the virtual memory and the physical memory are broken into pages, so that a virtual page is really mapped to a physical page. Of course, it is also possible for a virtual page to be absent from physical memory and not be mapped to a physical address as soon, residing instead on disk. Physical pages can be shared by having two virtual addresses point to the same physical address. This capability is used to allow two different programs to share data or code.

ry, which the operating system must also share, we must be able to protect the programs from one another. Both the translation of each program's address space and the protection of the address space from other programs are provided by virtual memory.

Although the concepts at work in virtual memory and in caches are the same, their differing historical roots have led to the use of different terminology. A virtual memory block is called a *page*, and a virtual memory miss is called a *page fault*. With virtual memory, the CPU produces a *virtual address*, which is translated by a combination of hardware and software to a *physical address*, which in turn can be used to access main memory. Figure 7.14 shows the virtual addressed memory with pages mapped to physical memory. This process is called *memory mapping* or *address translation*. Today, the two memory hierarchy levels controlled by virtual memory are DRAMs and magnetic disks. If we return to our library analogy, we can think of a virtual address as the title of a book and a physical address as the location of that book in the library (which might be given by the Library of Congress number).

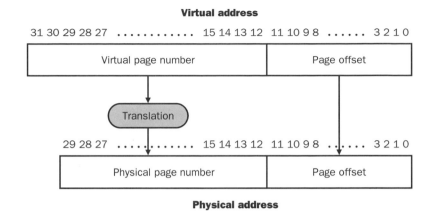

FIGURE 7.15 Mapping from a virtual to a physical address. The page size is $2^{12} = 4$ KB. The number of physical pages allowed in memory is 2^{18}, since the physical page number has 18 bits in it. This means that main memory can have at most 1 gigabyte, while the virtual address space is 4GB.

Virtual memory also simplifies loading the program for execution. Virtual memory provides *relocation*, because the virtual addresses used by a program are mapped to different physical addresses before they are used to access memory. This mapping allows us to load the program into any location in physical memory. Furthermore, all virtual memory systems in use today relocate the program as a set of fixed-size blocks (pages), thereby eliminating the need to find a contiguous block of memory to allocate to a program; instead, the operating system need only find sufficient pages in physical memory. Formerly, relocation and allocation problems required special hardware and special support in the operating system; today, virtual memory also provides this function.

In virtual memory, the address is broken into a *virtual page number* and a *page offset*. Figure 7.15 shows the translation of the virtual page number to a *physical page number*. The physical page number constitutes the upper portion of the physical address, while the page offset, which is not changed, constitutes the lower portion. The number of bits in the page offset field determines the page size. The number of pages addressable with the virtual address need not match the number of pages addressable with the physical address.

Many design choices in virtual memory systems are motivated by the high cost of a miss. A page fault will take hundreds of thousands of cycles to process. (The table on page 455 shows the relative speeds of main memory and disk.). This enormous miss penalty, dominated by the time to get the first word for typical page sizes, leads to several key decisions in designing virtual memory systems:

- Pages should be large enough to amortize the high access time. Sizes from 4 KB to 16 KB are typical, and designers are considering sizes as large as 64 KB.

- Organizations that reduce the page fault rate are attractive. The primary technique used here is to allow flexible placement of pages.

- Misses in a virtual memory system can be handled in software, because the overhead will be small compared to the access time to disk. Furthermore, the software can afford to use clever algorithms for choosing how to place pages, because even small reductions in the miss rate will pay for the cost of such algorithms.

- Using write-through to manage writes in virtual memory will not work, since writes take too long. Instead, we need a scheme that reduces the number of disk writes.

The next few sections address these factors in virtual memory design.

Elaboration: The discussion of virtual memory in this book focuses on *paging*, which uses fixed-size blocks. There is also a variable-size block scheme called *segmentation*. In segmentation, an address consists of two parts: a segment number and a segment offset. The segment register is mapped to a physical address, and the offset is *added* to find the actual physical address. Because the segment can vary in size, a check is also needed to make sure that the offset is within the segment. The major use of segmentation is to support more powerful methods of protection and sharing in an address space. Most operating system textbooks contain extensive discussions of segmentation compared to paging and of the use of segmentation to logically share the address space. The major disadvantage of segmentation is that it splits the address space into logically separate pieces that must be manipulated as a two-part address: the segment number and the offset. Paging, in contrast, makes the boundary between page number and offset invisible to programmers and compilers.

Segments have also been used as a method to extend the address space, without changing the word size of the machine. Such attempts have been unsuccessful because of the awkwardness and performance penalties inherent in a two-part address of which programmers and compilers must be aware.

Many architectures divide the address space into large fixed-size blocks that simplify protection between the operating system and user programs and increase the efficiency of implementing paging. Although these divisions are often called segments, this mechanism is much simpler than variable-block segmentation and is not visible to user programs; we discuss it in more detail shortly.

Placing a Page and Finding It Again

Because of the incredibly high penalty for a miss, designers would like to reduce the number of misses by optimizing the page placement. If we allow a virtual page to be mapped to any physical page, the operating system can then choose to replace any page it wants when a page fault occurs. For example, the operating system can use a sophisticated algorithm to try to choose a page that will not be needed for a long time. Thus, virtual memory systems allow a virtual page to be mapped to any physical page. This mapping is called *fully associative*, since any page (or block) can be *associated* with any location in the physical memory (or cache). Correspondingly, our task in the library is much easier if we can place a book anywhere on the desk than if each book could go in only one location, since the set of books we can have on the desk is more flexible.

If a page can reside anywhere, we need a mechanism to find it. This mechanism is a structure called a *page table*. A page table, which resides in memory, is indexed with the page number from the virtual address and contains the corresponding physical page number. Each program has its own page table, which maps the virtual address space of the program to physical memory. In our library analogy, the page table corresponds to a mapping between book titles and library locations. Just as the card catalog may contain entries for books in another library on campus rather than the local branch library, we will see that the page table may contain entries for pages not present in memory. To indicate the location of the page table in memory, the hardware includes a register that points to the start of the page table; we call this the *page table register*. Assume (for now) that the page table is in a fixed and contiguous area of memory.

Figure 7.16 uses the page table register, the virtual address, and the indicated page table to show how the hardware can form a physical address. A valid bit is used in each page table entry, just as we did in a cache. If the bit is off, the page is not present in physical memory and a page fault occurs. If the bit is on, the page is valid and the entry contains the physical page number. Because the page table contains a mapping for every possible virtual page, no tags are required.

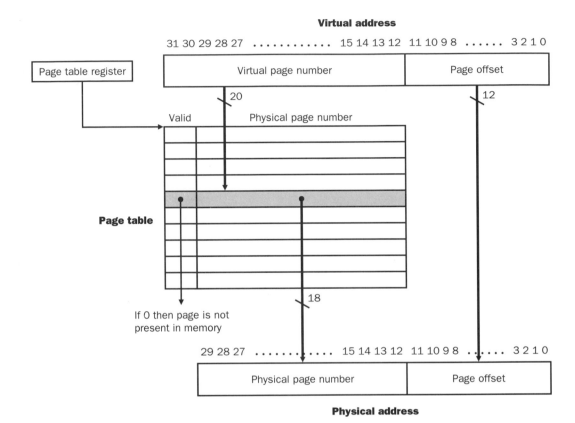

FIGURE 7.16 The page table is indexed with the virtual page number to obtain the corresponding portion of the physical address. The starting address of the page table is given by the page table pointer. In this figure, the page size is 2^{12} bytes = 4 KB. The virtual address space is 2^{32} or 4 GigaBytes, and the physical address space is 2^{30} bytes, which allows main memory of up to 1 GigaByte. The number of entries in the page table will be 2^{20} or 1 million entries. The valid bit for each entry indicates whether the mapping is legal. If it is off, then the page is not present in memory.

> **Hardware Software Interface**
>
> The page table, together with the program counter and the registers, specifies the state of a program. If we want to allow another program to use the CPU, we must save this state. Later, after restoring this state, the program can continue execution. We often refer to this state as a *process*. The process is considered *active* when it is in possession of the CPU and; otherwise, it is considered *inactive*. The operating system can make a process active by loading the process's state, including the program counter, which will initiate execution at the value of the saved program counter. The process's address space, and hence all the data it can access in memory, is defined by its page table, which resides in memory. Rather than save the entire page table, the operating system simply loads the page table register to point to the page table of the process it wants to make active.

Page Faults

If the valid bit for a virtual page is off, a page fault occurs. The operating system must be given control. This is done with the exception mechanism, the details of which we discuss later in this section. Once the operating system gets control, it must find the page in the next level of the hierarchy (usually magnetic disk) and decide where to place the requested page in physical memory. The virtual address alone does not immediately tell us where the page is on disk. Returning to our library analogy, we cannot find the location of a library book on the shelves just by knowing its title. Instead, we go to the catalog and look up the book, obtaining an address for the location on the shelves (for example, the Library of Congress number). Likewise, in a virtual memory system, we must keep track of the location on disk of each page in the virtual address space. Because we do not know ahead of time when a page will be chosen to be replaced, the operating system usually creates the space on disk for all the pages of a process when it creates the process. At that time, it also creates a data structure to record where each virtual page is stored on disk. This data structure may be part of the page table, or may be an auxiliary data structure indexed in the same way as the page table. Figure 7.17 shows the organization when a single table holds either the physical page number or the disk address.

Assuming that all the pages in physical memory are in use, the operating system must choose a page to replace. Because we want to minimize the number of page faults, most operating systems try to choose a page that they hy-

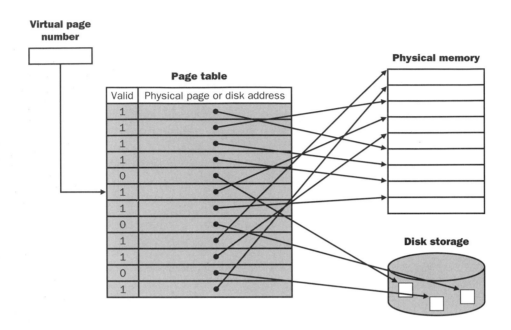

FIGURE 7.17 The page table maps each page in virtual memory to either a page in physical memory or a page stored on disk, which is the next level in the hierarchy. The virtual page number is used to index the page table. If the valid bit is on, the page table supplies the physical page number (i.e., the starting address of the page in memory) corresponding to the virtual page. If the valid bit is off, the page currently resides only on disk, at a specified address. In many systems, the table of physical page addresses and disk page addresses, while logically one table, are stored in two separate data structures. Dual tables are justified in part because we must keep the disk addresses of all the pages, even if they are currently in main memory.

pothesize will not be needed in the near future. Relying on the principle of temporal locality, the operating system can search for the *least recently used* (LRU) page, making the assumption that a page that has not been used in a long time is less likely to be needed than a more recently accessed page.

For example, suppose the most recent page references (in order) were 10, 12, 9, 7, 11, 10, and then we referenced page 8, which was not present in memory. The LRU page is page 12; in LRU replacement, we would replace page 12 in physical memory with page 8. If the next reference also generated a page fault, we would replace page 9, since it would be the LRU among the pages present in memory.

Hardware Software Interface

To help the operating system estimate the LRU pages, some machines provide a *use bit* or *reference bit*, which is set whenever a page is accessed. The operating system periodically clears the use bits and later records them so it can determine which pages were touched during a particular time period. By keeping track in this way, the operating system can select a page that is among the least recently referenced. If this bit is not provided by the hardware, the operating system must find another way to estimate which pages have been accessed.

Elaboration: With a 32-bit virtual address, 4 KB pages, and 4 bytes per page table entry, the total page table size is

$$\frac{2^{32}}{2^{12}} = 2^{20} \text{ pages} \times 2^2 \frac{\text{bytes}}{\text{page}} = 4 \text{ MB}$$

That is, we would need to use 4 MB of memory for each program in execution at any time. On a machine with tens to hundreds of active programs and a fixed-size page table, most or all of the memory would be tied up in page tables! To reduce the size of the page table, two different techniques are used. Both techniques try to reduce the amount of page table storage needed to map the amount of physical memory in use.

The simplest technique is to keep a bounds register that limits the size of the page table for a given process. If the virtual page number becomes larger than the contents of the limit register, entries must be added to the page table. This allows the page table to grow as a process consumes more space. Thus, the page table will only be large if the process is using many pages of virtual address space. This technique requires that the address space expand in only one direction.

Allowing growth in only one direction is not sufficient, since most languages require two areas whose size is expandable. One area holds the stack and the other area holds the heap. Because of this, it is convenient to divide the page table and let it grow from the highest address down, as well as from the lowest address up. This means that there will be two separate page tables and two separate limits. The use of two page tables breaks the address space into two segments. The high-order bit of an address determines the segment and thus which page table to use for that address. Since the segment is specified by the high-order address bit, each segment can be as large as one-half of the address space. A limit register for each segment specifies the current size of the segment, which grows in units of pages. This type of segmentation is used by many architectures, including the MIPS architecture. Unlike the type of segmentation discussed in the Elaboration on page 484, this form of segmentation is invisible to the applications program, although not to the operating system.

Another approach to reducing the page table size is to apply a hashing function to the virtual address so that the page table data structure need be only the size of the number of *physical* pages in main memory. Such a structure is called an *inverted page table*. Of course, the look-up process is slightly more complex with an inverted page table, because we can no longer just index the page table.

Lastly, most modern systems also allow the page tables to be paged. Although this sounds tricky, it works by using the same basic ideas of virtual memory and simply allowing the page tables to reside in the virtual address space. In addition, there are some small but critical problems, such as a never-ending series of page faults, that must be avoided. How these problems are overcome is both very detailed and typically highly machine specific; these topics are covered in many operating system textbooks.

What About Writes?

In a cache, the difference between the access time to the cache and main memory is tens of cycles, and write-through schemes can be used, although we need a write buffer to hide the latency of the write from the processor. In a virtual memory system, writes to the next level of the hierarchy (disk) take hundreds of thousands of cycles; therefore, building a write buffer to allow the system to write-through to disk would be completely impractical. The alternative strategy is called *write back*. In a write-back scheme, individual writes are accumulated into a page. When the page is replaced in the memory, it is copied back into the next level of the memory hierarchy, hence, the other name for this scheme, *copy back*.

Hardware Software Interface

A write-back scheme has another major advantage in a virtual memory system. Because the disk transfer time is small compared with its access time, copying back an entire page is much more efficient than writing individual words back to the disk. A write-back operation, while more efficient than transferring individual words, is still costly. Thus, we would like to know whether a page needs to be copied back when we choose to replace it. To track whether a page has been written since it was read into the memory, a *dirty bit* is added to the page table. The dirty bit is set when the page is first written. If the operating system chooses to replace the page, the dirty bit indicates whether the page needs to be written out before its location in memory can be given to another page.

Making Address Translation Fast: The TLB

Page tables are so large that they must be stored in main memory. This means that every memory access takes at least twice as long: one memory access to obtain the physical address and a second access to get the data. The key to improving access performance is to rely on locality of reference to the page table. When a translation for a virtual page number is used, it will probably be needed again in the near future, because the references to the words on that page have both temporal and spatial locality. Accordingly, modern machines include a special cache that keeps track of recently used translations. As mentioned earlier, this special address translation cache is referred to as a translation-lookaside buffer, or TLB. The TLB corresponds to that little piece of paper we typically use to record the location of a set of books we look up in the card catalog; rather than continually searching the entire catalog, we record the location of several books and use the scrap of paper as a cache.

A TLB is a cache that holds only page table mappings. Thus, each tag entry in the TLB holds a portion of the virtual page number, and each data entry of the TLB holds a physical page number. Because we will no longer access the page table on every reference, instead accessing the TLB, the TLB will need to include other bits, such as the reference bit and the dirty bit. Figure 7.18 shows how the TLB acts as a cache for the page table references.

On every reference, we look up the virtual page number in the TLB. If we get a hit, the physical page number is used to form the address, and the corresponding reference bit is turned on. If the processor is performing a write, the dirty bit is also turned on. If a miss in the TLB occurs, we must determine whether it is a page fault or merely a TLB miss. Because the TLB has many fewer entries than the number of pages in physical memory, TLB misses will be much more frequent than true page faults. On a TLB miss, if the page exists in memory, the translation can be loaded from the page table into the TLB and the reference can be tried again. If the page is not present in memory, a page fault has occurred and the operating system must be notified with an exception. TLB misses can be handled either in hardware or software. In practice, there is little performance difference between the two approaches, because the basic operations that must be performed are the same in either case.

When a TLB miss occurs and the missing translation has been retrieved from the page table, we will need to select a TLB entry to replace. Because the use and dirty bits are contained in the TLB entry, we need to copy these bits back to the page table entry when we replace an entry. These bits are the only portion of the TLB entry that can be changed. Using a write-back strategy (that is, copying these entries back at miss time rather than whenever they are written) is very efficient, since we expect the TLB miss rate to be small. Some systems use other techniques to approximate the use and dirty bits, eliminating

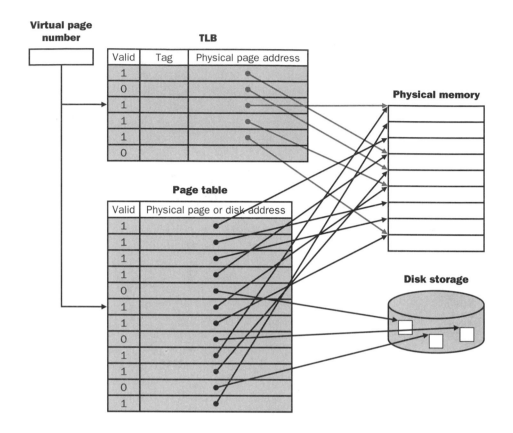

FIGURE 7.18 The TLB acts as a cache on the page table for the entries that map to physical pages only. The TLB contains a subset of the virtual-to-physical page mappings that are in the page table. (The TLB mappings are shown in color.) Because the TLB is a cache, it must have a tag field. If there is no matching entry in the TLB for a page, the page table must be examined. The page table either supplies a physical page number for the page (which can then be used to build a TLB entry) or indicates that the page resides on disk, in which case a page fault occurs. Since the page table has an entry for every virtual page (it is *not* a cache, in other words), no tag field is needed.

the need to write into the TLB except to load a new map entry on a miss; the MIPS R2000 and R3000 use such a scheme, as we will see shortly.

Some typical values for a TLB might be

Block size	1–2 page-table entries (typically 4–8 bytes each)
Hit time	1/2 to 1 clock cycle
Miss penalty	10–30 clock cycles
Miss rate	0.01%–1%
TLB size	32–1,024 entries

In addition to these parameters, the mapping of translations to entries in the TLB varies widely. Many systems use fully associative TLBs because a fully associative mapping has a lower miss rate; furthermore, since the TLB is small, the cost of a fully associative mapping is not too high (we'll return to this topic in section 7.4). With a fully associative mapping, choosing the entry to replace becomes tricky. Since TLB misses are much more frequent than page faults and must be handled more cheaply, we cannot afford an expensive software algorithm, as we can for page faults. Some TLB designs maintain support for LRU in the hardware, but the cost of LRU support increases with the size of a fully associative TLB. As a result, many systems provide some support for randomly choosing an entry to replace. We'll examine such replacement schemes in section 7.4.

Now let's take a closer look at the TLB in the DECStation 3100, and then look at all the steps involved in satisfying a memory request. The processor in the DECStation 3100 is a MIPS R2000, which includes the TLB on the microprocessor. The processor uses 4 KB pages; thus the virtual page number is 20 bits long, as shown in Figure 7.16 on page 486. The physical address is the same size as the virtual address. The TLB contains 64 entries, is fully associative, and is shared between the instruction and data references. Each entry is 64 bits wide and contains a 20-bit tag (which is the virtual page number for that TLB entry), the corresponding physical page number (also 20 bits), a valid bit, a dirty bit, and several other bookkeeping bits. When a TLB miss occurs, the hardware saves the page number of the reference and the matching TLB entry (if such an entry exists) in a pair of special registers. These registers help the operating system efficiently handle the TLB miss in software, using a few special instructions that can access and update the TLB. A miss can take as few as 10 cycles, but on average takes about 16 cycles. The hardware maintains an index that indicates the recommended entry to replace; the recommended entry is chosen randomly. Figure 7.19 shows the TLB and one of the caches, while Figure 7.20 shows the steps in processing a read or write request.

Elaboration: There are several different ways to combine address translation and cache access. In Figure 7.19, the virtual address must first go through the TLB to form a physical address that is used to access the cache. As a result, the amount of time to access memory must accommodate both a TLB access and a cache access; of course, these accesses can be pipelined. Alternatively, the machine can index the cache with an address that is completely or partially virtual (called a *virtually addressed cache*). When the cache is accessed with such an address and pages are shared between programs (which may access them with different virtual addresses), there is the possibility of *aliasing*. Aliasing occurs when the same object has two names—in this case, two virtual addresses for the same page. This creates a problem in that a word on such a page may be cached in two different locations, each corresponding to different virtual

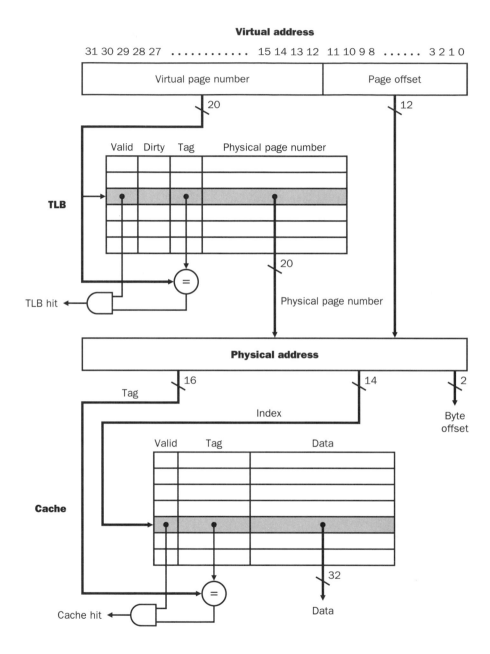

FIGURE 7.19 The TLB and cache implement the process of going from a virtual address to a data item in the Dec-Station 3100. This figure shows the organization of the TLB and one of the caches in the DECStation 3100. This diagram focuses on a read; Figure 7.20 describes how to handle writes. While the cache is direct mapped, the TLB is fully associative. Implementing a fully associative TLB requires that every TLB tag be compared against the index value, since the entry of interest can be anywhere in the TLB. We return to this topic in section 7.4

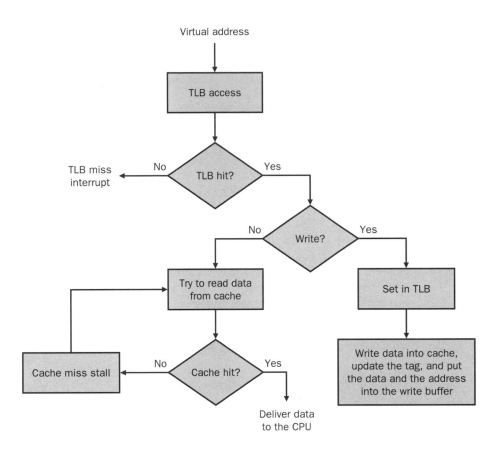

FIGURE 7.20 Processing a read or a write through the DECStation 3100 TLB and cache. If the TLB generates a hit, the cache can be accessed with the resulting physical address. If the operation is a write, the cache entry is overwritten and the data is sent to the write buffer; remember, though, that a cache write miss cannot occur for the DECStation 3100 cache, which uses one-word blocks and a write-through cache. For a read, the cache generates a hit or miss and supplies the data or causes a stall while the data is brought from memory. In actuality, the TLB does not contain a true dirty bit; instead, it uses the write protection bit to detect the first write. How this works will be explained in the next section. Notice that a TLB hit and a cache hit are independent events; this is examined further in the exercises at the end of this chapter.

addresses. This would allow one program to write the data without the other program being aware that the data had changed. Virtually addressed caches introduce either design limitations on the cache and TLB to avoid aliases or require the operating system to take steps to ensure that aliases do not occur.

Implementing Protection with Virtual Memory

Although each process has its own virtual address space, the physical memory is shared among multiple user processes and also with the operating system. Nevertheless, we do not want a renegade process to be able to write into the address space of another user process or into the operating system. For example, if the program that maintains student grades is running on a machine at the same time as the programs of the students in the first programming course, we wouldn't want the errant program of a beginner to write over someone's grades. We also want to prevent one process from reading the data of another process. For example, we wouldn't want one student program to read the grades while they were in the processor's memory. Once we begin sharing physical memory, we must provide the ability for a process to protect its data both from reading and writing by another process.

Remember that each process has its own virtual address space. Thus, if the operating system keeps the page tables organized so that the independent virtual pages map to disjoint physical pages, one process will not be able to access another's data. Of course, this also requires that a user process not be able to change the page table mapping. The operating system can assure this if it prevents the user process from modifying its own page tables. Yet the operating system must be able to modify the page tables.

Hardware Software Interface

To enable the operating system to implement protection in the virtual memory system, the hardware must provide at least the three basic capabilities summarized below.

1. Support at least two modes that indicate whether the running process is a user process or an operating system process, variously called a *kernel* process, a *supervisor* process, or an *executive* process.

2. Provide a portion of the CPU state that a user process can read but not write. This includes the user/supervisor mode bit(s) and the page table pointer.

3. Provide mechanisms whereby the CPU can go from user mode to supervisor mode, and vice versa. The first direction is typically accomplished by a *system call* exception, implemented as a special instruction (*syscall* in the MIPS instruction set) that transfers control to a dedicated location in supervisor code space. As with any other exception, the program counter from the point of the system call is saved, and the CPU is placed in supervisor mode. The return to user mode from the exception will restore the state of the process that generated the exception.

With these mechanisms the operating system can change the page tables as well as prevent a user process from changing them, ensuring that a user process can access only the storage provided to it by the operating system.

Processes may want to share information in a limited way. For example, the operating system may want to allow the user process to read some information about the process, such as running time, but may not want the user program to modify this data. Similarly, two user programs may want to share data for reading but not for writing. Accordingly, most systems provide the ability to distinguish between reading and writing a page, protecting them separately. This is usually done with a write protection bit, or separate read and write bits. This bit is included in each page table entry and is checked on every access.

Hardware Software Interface

To allow another process, say P1, to read a page owned by process P2, P2 would ask the operating system to create a page table entry for a virtual page in P1's address space that points to the same physical page that P2 wants to share. The operating system could use the write protection bit to prevent P1 from writing the data, if that was P2's wish. Any bits that determine the access rights for a page must be included in both the page table and TLB, because the page table is accessed only on a TLB miss.

Elaboration: When the operating system decides to change from running process P1 to running process P2 (called a *context switch* or *process switch*), it must ensure that P2 cannot get access to the page tables of P1, because that would compromise protection. If there is no TLB, it suffices to change the page table register to point to P2's page table (rather than to P1's); with a TLB, we must clear the TLB entries that belong to P1—both to protect the data of P1 and to force the TLB to load the entries for P2. If the process switch rate were high, this could be quite inefficient. For example, P2 might load only a few TLB entries before the operating system switched back to P1. Unfortunately, P1 would then find that all its TLB entries were gone and would have to go through TLB misses to reload them. This problem arises because the virtual addresses used by P1 and P2 are the same, and we must clear out the TLB to avoid confusing these addresses. A common alternative is to extend the virtual address space by adding a *process identifier* or *task identifier*. This small field identifies the currently running process; it is kept in a register loaded by the operating system when it switches processes. The process identifier is added to the tag portion of the TLB, so that a TLB hit occurs only if both the page number and the process identifier match. This eliminates the need to clear the TLB except on rare occasions.

Handling Page Faults and TLB Misses

While the translation of virtual to physical addresses with a TLB is straight-forward when we get a TLB hit, handling TLB misses and page faults is more complex. A TLB miss occurs when no entry in the TLB matches a virtual address. A TLB miss can indicate one of two possibilities:

1. The page is present in memory, and we need only create the missing TLB entry.

2. The page is not present in memory, and we need to transfer control to the operating system to deal with a page fault.

How do we know which of these two circumstances has occurred? When we process the TLB miss we will look for a page table entry to bring into the TLB; if the matching page table entry has a valid bit that is turned off, then the corresponding page is not in memory and we have a page fault, rather than just a TLB miss. If the valid bit is on, we can simply retrieve the physical page number from the page table entry and use it to create the TLB entry. A TLB miss can be handled in software or hardware, because it will require only a short sequence of operations to copy a valid page table entry from memory into the TLB.

Handling a page fault requires using the exception mechanism to interrupt the active process, transferring control to the operating system, and later resuming execution of the interrupted process. A page fault will be recognized sometime during the clock cycle used to access memory. To restart the instruction after the page fault is handled, the program counter of the instruction that caused the page fault must be saved. Just as in Chapters 5 and 6, the exception program counter (EPC) is used to hold this value. In addition, the page fault exception must be asserted early enough to change the state immediately following the clock cycle when the memory access occurs. If the page fault was not recognized until later, a load instruction could overwrite a register, and this could be disastrous when we try to restart the instruction. For example, for the instruction lw $1,0($1), the machine must be able to prevent the write back from occurring; otherwise, it could not properly restart the instruction, since the contents of $1 would have been destroyed. A similar complication arises on stores. We must prevent the write into memory from actually completing when there is a page fault; this is usually done by deasserting the write control line to the memory.

Once the process that generated the page fault has been interrupted and the operating system has control, it uses the Exception cause register to diagnose the cause of the exception. Because the exception is a page fault, the operating system knows that extensive processing will be required. Thus, it saves the entire state of the active process. This includes all the general-purpose and floating-point registers, the page table address register, the EPC, and the exception cause register. The virtual address that caused the fault depends on whether the fault was an instruction or data fault. The address of the instruction that generated the fault is in the EPC. If it was an instruction page fault, the EPC contains the virtual address of the faulting page; otherwise, the faulting virtual address can be computed by examining the instruction (whose address is in the EPC) to find the base register and offset field.

Once the operating system knows the virtual address that caused the page fault, it must complete three steps:

1. Look up the page table entry using the virtual address and find the location of the referenced page on disk.

2. Choose a physical page to replace; if the chosen page is dirty, it must be written out to disk first.

3. Start a read to bring the referenced page in from disk into the chosen physical page.

Of course, this last step will take hundreds of thousands of cycles (so will the second if the replaced page is dirty); accordingly, the operating system will usually select another process to execute in the CPU until the disk access completes. Because the operating system has saved the state of the process, it can freely give control of the processor to another process.

When the read of the page from disk is complete, the operating system can restore the state of the process that originally caused the page fault and execute an instruction that returns from the exception. This instruction will reset the processor from kernel to user mode, as well as restore the program counter. The user process then re-executes the instruction that faulted, accesses the requested page successfully, and continues execution.

Hardware Software Interface

Between the time we begin executing the exception handler in the operating system and the time that the operating system has saved all the state of the process, the operating system is particularly vulnerable. For example, if another exception occurred when we were processing the first exception in the operating system, the control unit would overwrite the exception program counter, making it impossible to return to the instruction that caused the page fault! We can avoid this by providing the ability to both mask out and enable exceptions. When an exception first occurs, we set a bit that masks all other exceptions; this could happen at the same time we set the supervisor mode bit. The operating system will then save just enough state to allow it to recover if another exception occurs (namely, the exception program counter and Cause register). The operating system can then re-enable exceptions. These steps make sure that exceptions will not cause the processor to lose any state and thereby be unable to restart execution of the interrupting instruction.

Page fault exceptions are difficult to implement due to a combination of three characteristics: They occur in the middle of instructions; the instruction cannot be completed before handling the exception; and, after handling the exception, the instruction must be restarted as if nothing had occurred.

Making instructions *restartable*, so that the exception can be handled and the instruction later continued, is relatively easy in an architecture like the MIPS. Because each instruction writes only one data item and this write occurs at the end of the instruction cycle, we can simply prevent the instruction from completing (by not performing the write) and restart the instruction at the beginning.

For machines with much more complex instructions that may touch many memory locations and write many data items, making instructions restartable is much harder. Processing one instruction may generate several page faults in the middle of the instruction. For example, some machines have block move instructions that touch thousands of data words. In such machines instructions often cannot be restarted from the beginning, as we do for MIPS instructions. Instead, the instruction must be interrupted and later continued midstream in its execution. Resuming an instruction in the middle of its execution usually requires saving some special state, processing the exception, and restoring that special state. Making this work properly requires careful and detailed coordination between the exception handling code in the operating system and the hardware.

Because the TLB is the subset of the page map that is accessed on every cycle, protection violations are also seen as TLB exceptions. The operating system can handle these with the same basic hardware that it uses to deal with TLB misses and page faults. A special set of values in the Cause register may be used to indicate protection violations, as opposed to a TLB miss. The operating system can access the TLB or page table entry that matched the virtual page so that it can examine the process's access rights and report the appropriate error.

Elaboration: Handling TLB misses in software is analogous to handling page faults: Both a TLB miss and a page fault are signaled by the same event. To speed up processing of a simple TLB miss that will be much more frequent than a true page fault, two different values for the Cause register are generated by a TLB miss. One setting indicates that there was no matching TLB entry, while another setting indicates that the TLB entry exists but that the page is not present in memory (the TLB valid bit really contains the page table valid bit). On a MIPS R2000/3000 processor, these two events are distinguished. Because the exception for TLB entry missing is much more frequent, the operating system loads the TLB from the page map without examining the entry and restarts the instruction when such an exception occurs. If the entry is invalid, another exception occurs, and the operating system recognizes that a page fault has occurred. This method makes the frequent case of a TLB miss fast, at a slight performance penalty for the infrequent case of a page fault.

Summary: Virtual Memory

Virtual memory is the name for the level of memory hierarchy that manages caching between the main memory and disk. Because the misses, called page faults, are so expensive, several techniques are used to reduce the miss rate:

1. Blocks, called pages, are made large to take advantage of spatial locality and to reduce the miss rate.

2. The mapping between virtual addresses and physical addresses, which is implemented with a page table, is made fully associative so that a virtual page can be placed anywhere in physical memory.

3. The operating system uses techniques, such as LRU and a reference bit, to choose which pages to replace.

Writes to disk are also expensive, so virtual memory uses a write-back scheme and also tracks whether a page is unchanged (with a dirty bit) to avoid writing unchanged pages back to disk.

Because virtual memory creates another address space (the virtual address space), it allows the virtual memory to be larger than the physical memory. In addition, because the physical memory is shared by multiple processes, the virtual memory system must also implement protection, so that processes can only access their own pages. By restricting access to the page table, so that only the operating system can change the mapping, we can safely share the memory and CPU among processes.

If a CPU had to access a page table resident in memory to translate every access, virtual memory would have too much overhead. Instead, a TLB caches the translations from the page table. Each address is then translated from a virtual address to a physical address using the translations in the TLB.

Caches, virtual memory, and TLBs all rely on a common set of principles and policies, as the next section shows.

7.4 | A Common Framework for Memory Hierarchies

By now, you've recognized that the different types of memory hierarchies share a great deal in common. Although many of the aspects of memory hierarchies differ quantitatively, many of the policies and features that determine how a hierarchy functions qualitatively are similar. Figure 7.21 shows how

Feature	Typical values for caches	Typical values for paged memory	Typical values for a TLB
Total size in blocks	250–10,000	2,000–250,000	32–1024
Total size in bytes	4 KB–4 MB	8 MB–1 GB	128–8000
Block size in bytes	4–256	4 KB–16 KB	4–16
Miss penalty in clocks	10–100	100,000–1,000,000	10–50
Miss rates	0.1%–20%	0.00001%–0.0001%	0.01%–1%

FIGURE 7.21 The key quantitative design parameters that characterize the three major memory hierarchies in a machine. These are typical values for these levels as of 1993. Although the range of values is wide, this is partially because many of the values that have shifted over time are related; for example, as caches become larger to overcome larger miss penalties, block sizes also grow.

some of the quantitative characteristics of memory hierarchies can differ. In the rest of this section, we will discuss the common operational aspects of memory hierarchies and how these determine their behavior. We will examine these policies as a series of four questions that apply between any two levels of a memory hierarchy, athough for simplicity we will primarily use terminology for caches.

Question 1: Where Can a Block Be Placed?

When we looked at the cache hierarchy, we saw the simplest placement scheme: A block could go in exactly one place in the upper level of the hierarchy. This placement scheme is called *direct mapped*. In a virtual memory system, we saw that a page could be placed anywhere in the physical memory, a scheme called *fully associative*. In fact, there is really a spectrum of design points from direct mapped to fully associative.

The middle range of designs is called *set associative*. In a set associative cache, there are a fixed number of locations (at least two) where each block can be placed; a set associative cache with n locations for a block is called an n-way set associative cache. An n-way set associative cache consists of a number of sets, each of which consists of n blocks. Each block in the memory maps to a unique *set* in the cache given by the index field, and a block can be placed in *any* element of that set. Given this, a set associative placement combines direct mapped placement and fully associative placement: A block is directly mapped into a set, and then all the blocks in the set are searched for a match.

Remember that in a direct mapped cache, the position of a block is given by

Block number modulo number of blocks in the cache

In a set associative cache, the *set* containing a block is given by

Block number modulo number of *sets* in the cache

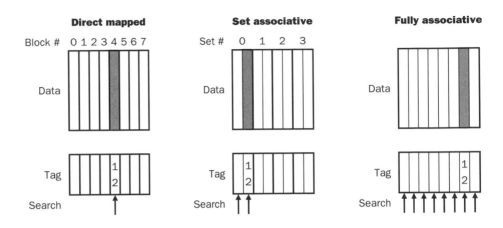

FIGURE 7.22 Placement of a block whose address is 12 varies for direct mapped, set associative, and fully associative caches. In direct mapped placement, there is only one cache block where memory block 12 can be found and that block is given by (12 modulo 8) = 4. In a two-way set associative cache, there would be four sets, and memory block 12 must be in set (12 mod 4) = 0; the memory block could be in either element of the set. In a fully associative placement, the block for block address 12 can appear in any of the eight blocks.

Since the block may be placed in any element of the set, all the elements of the set must be searched. In a fully associative cache, the block can go anywhere and all the blocks in the cache must be searched. Figure 7.22 shows where block 12 can be placed in a cache with eight blocks total, according to the block placement policy for a direct mapped, two-way set associative, and fully associative cache. Although we discuss the use of set associativity with caches, TLBs often use set associative placement.

We can think of every block placement strategy as a variation on set associativity. A direct mapped cache is simply a one-way set associative cache: Each cache entry holds one block and forms a set with one element. A fully associative cache with m entries is simply an m-way set associative cache; it has one set with m blocks and an entry can reside in any block within that set. Figure 7.23 shows the possible associativity structures for an eight-block cache.

The advantage of increasing the degree of associativity is that it usually decreases the miss rate, as the next example shows.

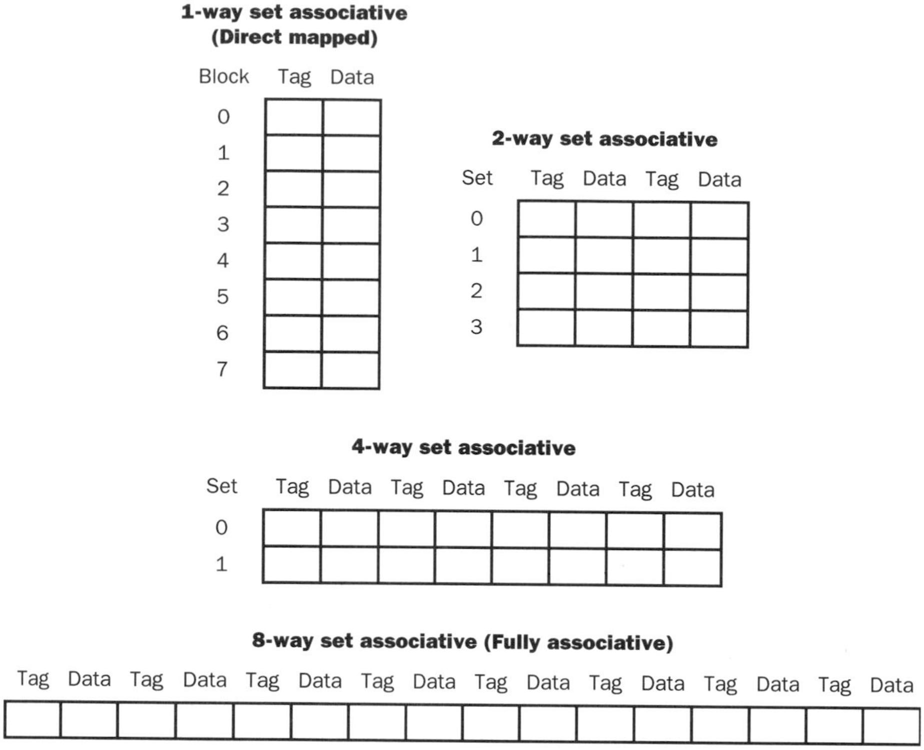

**1-way set associative
(Direct mapped)**

Block   Tag   Data

0
1
2
3
4
5
6
7

2-way set associative

Set   Tag   Data   Tag   Data

0
1
2
3

4-way set associative

Set   Tag   Data   Tag   Data   Tag   Data   Tag   Data

0
1

8-way set associative (Fully associative)

Tag   Data   Tag   Data   Tag   Data   Tag   Data   Tag   Data   Tag   Data   Tag   Data   Tag   Data

FIGURE 7.23 An eight-block cache configured as direct mapped, two-way set associative, four-way set associative, and fully associative. The total size of the cache in blocks is equal to the number of sets times the associativity (or set size). Thus, for a fixed cache size, increasing the associativity decreases the number of sets, while the number of elements per set increases. With eight blocks, an eight-way set associative cache is the same as a fully associative cache, although for realistically sized caches, these two organizations would usually look rather different.

Example

There are three small caches, each consisting of four one-word blocks. One cache is fully associative, a second is two-way set associative, and the third is direct mapped. Assuming that the replacement policy used is least recently used, find the number of misses for each cache organization given the following sequence of block addresses: 0, 8, 0, 6, 8.

Answer

The direct mapped case is easiest. First, let's determine to which cache block each block address maps.

Block address	Cache block
0	(0 modulo 4) = 0
4	(4 modulo 4) = 0
6	(6 modulo 4) = 2
8	(8 modulo 4) = 0

Now we can fill in the cache contents after each reference, using a blank entry to mean that the block is invalid:

Address of memory block accessed	Hit or miss	Contents of cache blocks after reference			
		0	1	2	3
0	Miss	Memory[0]			
8	Miss	Memory[8]			
0	Miss	Memory[0]			
6	Miss	Memory[0]		Memory[6]	
8	Miss	Memory[8]			

The direct mapped cache generates five misses.

The set associative cache has two sets (with indices 0 and 1) with two elements per set. Let's first determine to which set each block address maps.

Block address	Cache block
0	(0 modulo 2) = 0
4	(4 modulo 2) = 0
6	(6 modulo 2) = 0
8	(8 modulo 2) = 0

Because we have a choice of which entry in a set to replace on a miss, we need a replacement rule. Set associative caches usually employ LRU replacement, which we used when we examined virtual memory. Thus, the contents of the set associative cache after each reference look like

Address of memory block accessed	Hit or miss	Contents of cache blocks after reference			
		Set 0	Set 0	Set 1	Set 1
0	Miss	Memory[0]			
8	Miss	Memory[0]	Memory[8]		
0	Hit	Memory[0]	Memory[8]		
6	Miss	Memory[0]	Memory[6]		
8	Miss	Memory[0]	Memory[8]		

The two-way set associative cache has a total of four misses, one less than the direct mapped cache.

The fully associative cache has four cache blocks (in a single set); any memory block can be stored in any cache block. Its performance is best:

Address of memory block accessed	Hit or miss	Contents of cache blocks after reference			
		Set 0	Set 0	Set 1	Set 1
0	Miss	Memory[0]			
8	Miss	Memory[0]	Memory[8]		
0	Hit	Memory[0]	Memory[8]		
6	Miss	Memory[0]	Memory[8]	Memory[6]	
8	Hit	Memory[0]	Memory[8]	Memory[6]	

The fully associative cache clearly has the best performance, with only three misses. For this string of references, this is the best we can do because three unique addresses are accessed. Notice that if we had eight blocks in the cache, there would be no replacements in the two-way set associative cache (check this for yourself) and it would have the same number of misses as the fully associative cache. Similarly, if we had 16 blocks all three caches would have the same number of misses. This shows us that cache size and associativity are not independent in determining cache performance.

If this example used a cache with multiword blocks and the memory addresses were given in words, we could use the same function to compute the cache block after converting the memory addresses to block addresses by simply dividing the memory word address by the number of words in the block.

How much of a reduction in the miss rate is achieved by associativity? Figure 7.24 shows the improvement for the programs gcc and spice with a pair of 64 KB caches (split instruction and data) with a four-word block, and associativity ranging from direct-mapped to four-way. On gcc, going from one-way to two-way associativity improves the effective combined miss rate by about 20%, but there is no further improvement in going to four-way associa-

Program	Associativity	Instruction miss rate	Data miss rate	Effective combined miss rate
gcc	1	2.0%	1.7%	1.9%
gcc	2	1.6%	1.4%	1.5%
gcc	4	1.6%	1.4%	1.5%
spice	1	0.3%	0.6%	0.4%
spice	2	0.3%	0.6%	0.4%
spice	4	0.3%	0.6%	0.4%

FIGURE 7.24 The miss rates for gcc and spice with a cache like that in the DecStation 3100 but with a block size of four words and associativity varying from one-way to four-way.

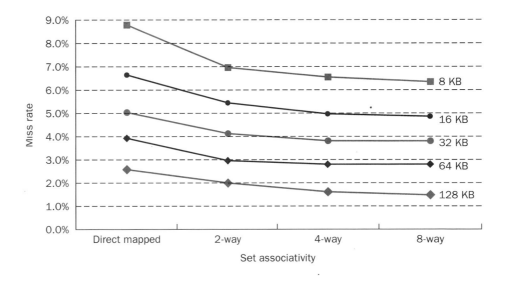

FIGURE 7.25 The miss rates for each of five cache sizes improve as the associativity increases. While the benefit of going from one-way (direct mapped) to two-way set associative is significant, the benefits of further associativity shrink. There is little improvement in going from four-way to eight-way set associative. This data was generated from traces of the VAX running the Ultrix operating system and a multiprogrammed workload. It uses 32-byte blocks and LRU replacement.

tivity. The low miss rates for spice leave little opportunity for improvement by associativity.

The advantage of set associativity in improving the miss rate gets smaller as the cache (or other level in the hierarchy) gets larger. Figure 7.25 shows the miss rate for caches from one-way to eight-way set associative for five differ-

Tag	Index	Block Offset

FIGURE 7.26 The three portions of an address in a set associative or direct mapped cache. The tag is used to check all the blocks in the set, and the index is used to select the set by comparing against the blocks. The block offset is the address of the desired data within the block.

ent size caches. The incremental benefit of each additional degree of associativity shrinks. A fully associative cache would have a miss rate only slightly better than that of the eight-way set associative design. The advantage of associativity is clearly an improved miss rate. The potential disadvantages are increased cost and slower access time, as we will see in the next section.

Question 2: How Is a Block Found?

We have seen how to find a block in a virtual memory system: We simply index the page table. Similarly, in a direct mapped cache, we index the cache to find the one block of interest. Let's consider the task of finding a block in a cache that is set associative. Each block in the cache includes an address tag that gives the block address. The tag of every cache block that might contain the desired information is checked to see if it matches the block address from the CPU. Figure 7.26 shows how the address is decomposed. The index value is used to select the set containing the address of interest, and the tags of all the blocks in the set must be searched. Because speed is of the essence, all the tags in the selected set are searched in parallel. A serial search would make the hit time of a set associative cache too slow.

If the total size is kept the same, increasing the associativity increases the number of blocks per set, which is the number of simultaneous compares needed to perform the search in parallel: Each increase by a factor of two in associativity doubles the number of blocks per set and halves the number of sets. Accordingly, each factor of two increase in associativity decreases the size of the index by 1 bit and increases the size of the tag by 1 bit. In a fully associative cache, there is effectively only 1 set, and all the blocks must be checked in parallel. Thus, there is no index, and the entire address, excluding the block offset, is compared against the tag of every block. In other words, we search the entire cache without any indexing.

In a direct mapped cache, such as that shown in Figure 7.4 on page 460, only a single comparator is needed, because the entry can be in only one block, and we access the cache simply by indexing. In a four-way set associative cache, shown in Figure 7.27, four comparators are needed, together with a 4-to-1 multiplexor to choose among the four potential members of the selected set. The cache access consists of indexing the appropriate set and then searching the elements of the set. The costs of an associative cache are the extra compar-

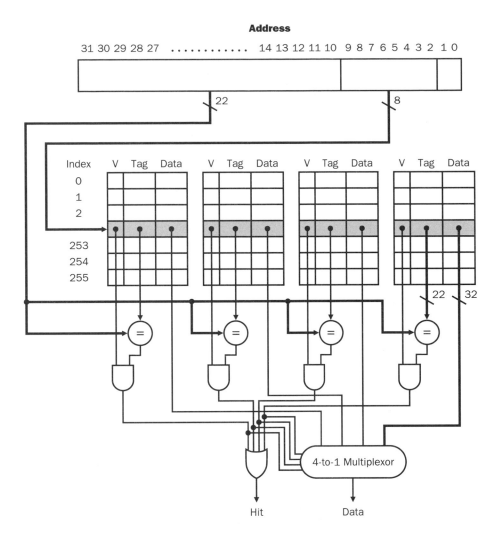

FIGURE 7.27 The implementation of a four-way set associative cache requires four comparators and a 4-to-1 multiplexor. The comparators determine which element of the selected set (if any) matches the tag. The output of the comparators is used to select the data from one of the four indexed sets, using a multiplexor. In some implementations, the output enable signals on the data portions of the cache RAMs can be used to select the entry in the set that drives the output. The output enable signal comes from the comparators, causing the element that matches to drive the data outputs. This eliminates the need for the multiplexor.

ators and any delay imposed by having to do the compare and select from among the elements of the set.

The choice among direct mapped, set associative, or fully associative mapping in any memory hierarchy will depend on the cost of a miss versus the cost of implementing associativity, both in time and in extra parts. In virtual memory systems, three facts are important in making the choice:

1. Miss rates are crucial since the miss penalty is so high.

2. The mapping is implemented in software with no cycle time impact.

3. The large page size means the page table size overhead is small.

Therefore, virtual memory systems always use fully associative placement. Set associative placement is often used for caches and TLBs, where the access combines indexing and the search of a small set. Many recent systems have used direct mapped caches because of their advantage in access time and simplicity. The advantage in access time occurs because finding the requested block does not depend on a comparison. Large caches never use fully associative placement, because of the cost and hit time penalties, coupled with the small performance advantage over a set associative cache. The use of a full map, like a page table for virtual memory, is not practical for a cache, because the map would be very large (with considerably more entries than a page table), and could not be accessed quickly.

Question 3: Which Block Should Be Replaced on a Cache Miss?

When a miss occurs in an associative cache, we must decide which block to replace. In a fully associative cache, all blocks are candidates for replacement. If the cache is set associative, we must choose among the blocks in the set. Of course, replacement is easy in a direct mapped cache, because there is only one candidate.

There are two primary strategies employed for selecting which block to replace:

■ *Random:* Candidate blocks are randomly selected, possibly using some hardware assistance.

■ *Least recently used (LRU):* The block replaced is the one that has been unused for the longest time.

A virtue of random selection is that it is simple to build in hardware. As the number of blocks to keep track of increases, LRU becomes increasingly expensive and, in practice, is only approximated. In a two-way set associative cache, random replacement has a miss rate about 1.1 times higher than LRU replacement. As the caches become larger, the miss rate for both replacement strategies falls, and the absolute difference becomes small. LRU replacement shows a wider advantage with larger degrees of associativity, but it is also harder to implement. In virtual memory, some form of LRU is always approximated since even a tiny reduction in the miss rate can be important when the cost of a miss is enormous.

Question 4: What Happens on a Write?

A key characteristic of any memory hierarchy is how it deals with writes. We have already seen the two basic options:

- *Write through*: The information is written to both the block in the cache *and* to the block in the lower level of the memory hierarchy (main memory for a cache). The caches in section 7.2 used this scheme.

- *Write back* (also called *copy back*): The information is written only to the block in the cache. The modified block is written to the lower level of the hierarchy only when it is replaced. Virtual memory systems always use write back, for the reasons discussed in section 7.3.

Both write back and write through have their advantages. The key advantages of write back are

- Individual words can be written by the processor at the rate the cache, rather than the memory, can accept them.

- Multiple writes within a block require only one write to the lower level in the hierarchy.

- When blocks are written back, the system can make effective use of a wide lower level, since the entire block is written. We also want to widen this interface to improve the handling of read misses.

With write through, the advantages are

- Read misses are cheaper, because they never require writes to the lower level.

- Write through is easier to implement than write back, although to be practical in a high-speed system, a write-through cache will need to use a write buffer.

In virtual memory systems, only a write-back policy is practical because of the long latency of a write to the lower level of the hierarchy (disk). As CPUs continue to increase in performance at a faster rate than DRAM-based main memory, the rate at which writes are generated by a processor will exceed the rate at which the memory system can process them, even allowing for physically and logically wider memories. As a consequence, it is likely that more and more caches will use a write-back strategy in the future

The Big Picture

While caches, TLBs, and virtual memory may initially look very different, they rely on the same two principles of locality and can be understood by looking at how they deal with four questions:

Question 1: Where can a block be placed?
Answer 1: One place (direct mapped), a few places (set associative), or any place (fully associative).

Question 2: How is a block found?
Answer 2: There are three methods: indexing (as in a direct mapped cache), limited search (as in a set associative cache), and full search (as in a fully associative cache). Note that a page table is indexed, but provides fully associative placement. This is possible because a page table is a full map—every possible index is included in the page table.

Question 3: What block is replaced on a miss?
Answer 3: Typically, either the least recently used or a random block.

Question 4: How are writes handled?
Answer 4: Each level in the hierarchy can use either write through or write back.

Elaboration: Actually implementing stores efficiently in a cache that uses a write-back strategy is more complex than in a write-through cache. In a write-back cache, we must write the block back to memory if the data in the cache is dirty and we have a cache miss. If we simply overwrote the block on a store before we knew whether the store had hit in the cache (as we would for a write-through cache), we would destroy the contents of the block, which is not backed up in memory.

This means that stores in a write-back cache either require two cycles (a cycle to check for a hit followed by a cycle to actually perform the write) or require an extra buffer, called a *store buffer*, to hold that data—effectively allowing the store to take only one cycle by pipelining it.

The Three C's: An Intuitive Model for Understanding the Behavior of Memory Hierarchies

In this section, we look at a model that provides good insight into the sources of misses in a memory hierarchy and how the misses will be affected by changes in the hierarchy. We will explain the ideas in terms of caches, although the ideas carry over directly to any other level in the hierarchy. In this model, all misses are classified into one of three categories:

- *Compulsory misses*: The first access to a block is not in the cache, so the block must be brought into the cache. These are also called *cold start misses*.

- *Capacity misses*: If the cache cannot contain all the blocks needed during execution of a program, capacity misses will occur due to blocks being discarded and later retrieved.

- *Conflict misses*: If the block-placement strategy is set associative or direct mapped, conflict misses (in addition to compulsory and capacity misses) will occur, because a block can be discarded and later retrieved if too many blocks map to its set. These are also called *collision misses*.

Figure 7.28 shows how the miss rate divides into the three sources. These sources of misses can be directly attacked by changing some aspect of the cache design. Since conflict misses arise directly from contention for the same cache block, a fully associative placement avoids all conflict misses. Associativity, however, may slow access time (as we will see shortly), leading to lower overall performance.

Capacity misses can easily be reduced by enlarging the cache; indeed, caches have been growing steadily larger for many years. Of course, when we make the cache larger we must also be careful about increasing the access time, which could lead to slower overall performance.

Because compulsory misses are generated by the first reference to a block, the primary way for the cache system to reduce the number of compulsory misses is to increase the block size. This will reduce the number of references required to touch each block of the program once, because the program will consist of fewer cache blocks. Increasing the block size too much can have a negative effect on performance, because of the increase in the miss penalty.

The decomposition of misses into the three C's is a useful qualitative model. In real cache designs, many of the design choices interact and changing one cache characteristic will often affect several components of the miss rate. Despite such shortcomings, this model is a useful way to gain insight into the performance of cache designs.

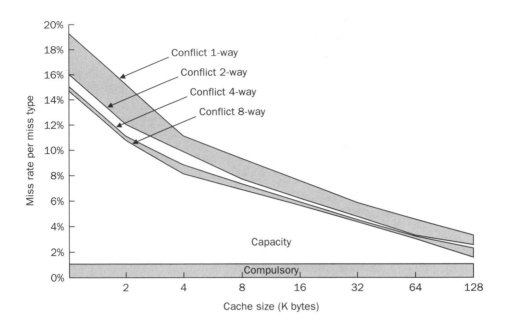

FIGURE 7.28 The miss rate can be broken into the three sources of misses. The total miss rate and source compared to cache size are shown. The conflict portion is shown for associativities from one-way to eight-way.

The Big Picture

The challenge in designing memory hierarchies is that every change that potentially improves the miss rate can also negatively affect overall performance as the table below summarizes. This combination of the positive and negative effects of each design parameter is what makes the design of memory hierarchy challenging.

Design change	Effect on miss rate	Possible negative performance effect
Increase size	Decreases capacity misses	May increase access time
Increase associativity	Decreases miss rate due to conflict misses	May increase access time
Increase block size	Decreases miss rate for a wide range of block sizes	May increase miss penalty

7.5 Fallacies and Pitfalls

As one of the most naturally quantitative aspects of the computer architecture, memory hierarchy would seem to be less vulnerable to fallacies and pitfalls. Not only have there been many fallacies propagated and pitfalls encountered, but some have led to major negative outcomes. We start with a pitfall that often traps students in exercises and exams.

Pitfall: Forgetting to account for byte addressing or the cache block size in simulating a cache.

When simulating a cache (by hand or machine), we need to make sure we account for the effect of byte addressing or multiword blocks in determining which cache block a given address maps into. For example, if we have a cache with a size of 32 bytes and a block size of 4 bytes, the byte address 36 maps into block 1 of the cache, since byte address 36 is block address 9 and (9 modulo 8) = 1. On the other hand, if address 36 is a word address, then it maps into block (36 mod 8) = 4. Make sure the problem clearly states the base of the address.

In like fashion, we must account for the block size. Suppose we have a cache with 256 bytes and a block size of 32 bytes: Which block does the byte address 300 fall into? Byte address 300 is block address

$$\left\lfloor \frac{300}{32} \right\rfloor = 9.$$

The number of blocks in the cache is

$$\left\lfloor \frac{256}{32} \right\rfloor = 8,$$

Block number 9 falls into cache block number (9 modulo 8) = 1.

This mistake catches many people, including authors (in earlier drafts) and instructors who forget whether they intended the addresses to be in words, bytes, or block numbers. Remember this pitfall when you tackle the exercises.

Pitfall: Selecting too small an address space.

Just five years after DEC designed the new PDP-11 computer family, it was apparent that its creation had a major flaw—the size of its addresses. Address size limits the program length, since the size of a program and the amount of data needed by the program must be less than $2^{\text{address size}}$. The reason the address size is so hard to change is that it determines the minimum width of anything that can contain an address: PC, register, memory word, and effective-address arithmetic. If there is no plan to expand the address from the start, the chances of successfully changing address size are so slim that it normally means the end of that computer family. Bell and Strecker put it like this:

> There is only one mistake that can be made in computer design that is difficult to recover from—not having enough address bits for memory addressing and memory management. The PDP-11 followed the unbroken tradition of nearly every known computer. [Bell, C. G., and W. D. Strecker. "Computer structures: What have we learned from the PDP-11?," *Proc. Third Annual Symposium on Computer Architecture* (January 1976), Pittsburgh, Penn., 1–14]

The IBM 360 series was announced six years prior to the PDP-11 and continues to sell well with only minor extensions. The reason is that the 360 had a 24-bit address space, and it was possible to extend its address space to 32 bits, the natural word size for the machine. Similarly, the VAX, introduced as a 32-bit replacement for the PDP-11, has survived longer, selling over 100,000 units.

A partial list of successful general-purpose machines that eventually starved to death for lack of address bits includes the PDP-8, PDP-10, PDP-11, Intel 8086, Intel 80186, Intel 80286 (although the 80386 provided a 16-bit backward compatibility mode), AMI 6502, Zilog Z80, Cray-1, and Cray X-MP. In fact, as this book was being written, Digital announced a new architecture offering a 64-bit address space that will replace the VAX. The consensus is that 32 bits of address space is rapidly becoming too little: The R4000 implements a 64-bit version of the MIPS architecture, and 64-bit versions of the SPARC architecture and the IBM Power architecture are under development.

Pitfall: Using miss rate as the only metric for evaluating a memory hierarchy.

As we just discussed, miss rate can be a misleading metric when other cache parameters are ignored. Let's consider a specific example. Suppose that we were running the workload used for the measurements in Figure 7.25 on page 507. Increasing the direct mapped cache size from 32 KB to 64 KB reduces the miss rate from 5.0% to about 4.0%. Suppose the machine with the larger cache has a clock cycle time of 20 ns, while the machine with the smaller cache has a clock cycle time of 17 ns, and we assume that the CPI without memory stalls is the same. If the miss penalty is 200 ns and there are 1.5 memory references per instruction, the machine with the larger cache is actually slower, despite its superior cache hit rate. To see this, use the following equation:

$$\text{CPU time } = \text{ (CPU execution clock cycles + Memory-stall clock cycles)}$$
$$\times \text{ Clock cycle time}$$

where the memory stall cycles are given using the equation from page 477:

$$\text{Memory-stall clock cycles} = \frac{\text{Instructions}}{\text{Program}} \times \frac{\text{Misses}}{\text{Instruction}} \times \text{Miss penalty}$$

The term *misses per instruction* combines the instruction and data miss rates into a single term:

$$\frac{\text{Misses}}{\text{Instruction}} = \text{Instruction miss rate} + \left(\text{Data miss rate} \times \frac{\text{Data references}}{\text{Instruction}} \right)$$

For the smaller cache (using IC to stand for *instruction per program*):

$$\text{Memory-stall clock cycles} = \text{IC} \times (0.05 + (0.05 \times 0.5))$$
$$\times \left\lceil \frac{\text{Absolute miss penalty}}{\text{Clock cycle time}} \right\rceil$$
$$\text{Memory-stall clock cycles} = \text{IC} \times 0.075 \times \left\lceil \frac{200}{17} \right\rceil = 0.9 \times \text{IC}$$

For the machine with the larger cache:

$$\text{Memory-stall clock cycles} = \text{IC} \times (0.04 + (0.04 \times 0.5))$$
$$\times \left\lceil \frac{\text{Absolute miss penalty}}{\text{Clock cycle time}} \right\rceil$$
$$\text{Memory-stall clock cycles} = \text{IC} \times 0.06 \times \left\lceil \frac{200}{20} \right\rceil = 0.6 \times \text{IC}$$

Now we can put these pieces into the CPU time equation. Let the CPI without memory stalls be C. Then the number of CPU clock cycles is $C \times IC$. This leads to the following CPU execution time for the machine with the smaller cache:

$$\text{CPU time} = (\text{CPU execution clock cycles} + \text{Memory-stall clock cycles})$$
$$\times \text{Clock cycle time}$$

$$\text{CPU time} = ((C \times IC) + (0.9 \times IC)) \times 17 \text{ ns}$$
$$= 17 \times C \times IC + 15 \times IC = (17C + 15) IC$$

Now, for the larger cache we obtain:

$$\text{CPU time} = (C \times IC + 0.6 \times IC) \times 20 \text{ ns}$$
$$= 20 \times C \times IC + 18 \times IC = (20C + 18) IC$$

Thus, the machine with the larger cache has a longer execution time and is actually slower. The next fallacy discusses a common misconception that follows similar lines.

Pitfall: Choosing a set associative cache over a direct mapped cache solely because the set associative cache has a better miss rate.

As we just saw, the cache access time strongly influences the CPU clock rate. If the impact on clock rate to implement set associativity exceeds the performance improvement from the lower miss rate, the set associative cache will have worse performance than a direct mapped cache. The data in Figures 7.10 and 7.25 clearly show that this can occur.

In the mid-1980s, many designers recognized this danger and selected direct mapped placement. The advantages of direct mapped caches include lower costs, faster hit times, and therefore smaller average access times for large, direct mapped caches. Of course, this choice is highly dependent on the implementation technology, and the best choice may change from design to design or over time. In the early 1990s, the migration of first-level caches onto the processor chip has reduced the overhead required to implement set associativity and has led some designers to choose set associativity for these small, on-chip caches.

Pitfall: Extending an address space by adding segments on top of a flat address space.

During the 1970s, many programs grew so large that not all the code and data could be addressed with just a 16-bit address. Machines were then revised to offer 32-bit addresses, either through a flat 32-bit address space or by adding 16 bits of segment to the existing 16-bit address. From a marketing point of view, adding segments that were programmer-visible and that forced the programmer and compiler to decompose programs into segments could solve the addressing problem. Unfortunately, there is trouble any time a programming language wants an address that is larger than one segment, such as indices for large arrays, unrestricted pointers, or reference parameters. Moreover, adding segments can turn every address into two words—one for the segment number and one for the segment offset—causing problems in the use of addresses in registers. As this book is being completed, the limits of 32-bit addresses are being reached. Some architectures, such as the MIPS R4000, DEC Alpha, and SUN SPARC, have chosen to support 64-bit flat address spaces. Others, such as HP PA-RISC are providing an extended address space via segmentation, although this may change in the near future. Still other architectures, such as the VAX, will come to an end rather than try to make the leap to a larger address space.

7.6 Concluding Remarks

The difficulty of building a memory system to keep pace with faster CPUs is underscored by the fact that the raw material for main memory, DRAMs, is essentially the same in the fastest computers as it is in the slowest (and cheapest). It is the principle of locality that gives us a chance to overcome the long latency of memory access—and the soundness of this strategy is demonstrated at all levels of the memory hierarchy. Although these levels of the hierarchy look quite different in quantitative terms, they follow similar strategies in their operation and exploit the same properties of locality.

Because CPU speeds continue to increase faster than either DRAM access times or disk access times, memory will increasingly be a factor that limits performance. Processors continue to increase in performance at a spectacular rate, and DRAMs show every sign of continuing their fourfold improvement in density every three years. The *access time* of DRAMs, however, is improving at a much slower rate—about 7% per year. Figure 7.29 plots optimistic and pes-

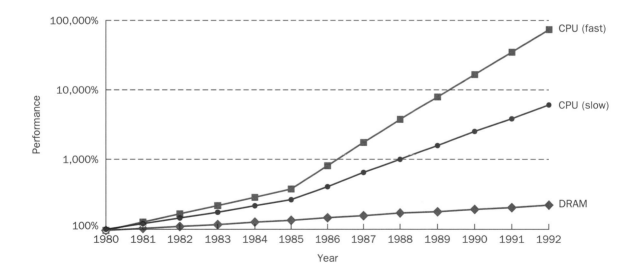

FIGURE 7.29 Using their 1980 performance as a baseline, the performance of DRAMs and processors is plotted over time. The DRAM baseline is 64 KB in 1980, with three years to the next generation. The slow processor line assumes a 19% improvement per year until 1985 and a 50% improvement thereafter. The fast processor line assumes a 26% performance improvement between 1980 and 1985 and 100% per year thereafter. Note that the vertical axis must be on a logarithmic scale to record the size of the processor-DRAM performance gap.

simistic processor performance projections against the steady 7% annual performance improvement in DRAM speeds. The processor-DRAM performance gap is clearly becoming a problem.

Recent Trends

The challenge in designing memory hierarchies to close this growing gap, as we noted in The Big Picture on page 514, is that all the hardware design choices for memory hierarchies have both a positive and negative effect on performance. This means that for each level of the hierarchy there is an optimal performance point, which must include some misses. If this is the case, how can we overcome the growing gap between CPU speeds and lower levels of the hierarchy? This question is currently the topic of much research. One possible answer is to increase the number of levels in the hierarchy, using *multilevel caches*. For example, a two-level cache would add another cache between the first-level cache and the main memory. We can then design each cache to satisfy different criteria. For example, the first-level cache can be small enough to match the clock cycle time of a fast processor, while the second-level cache can be large enough to achieve very high hit rates. This flexibility has led to the adoption of two-level caches in a number of machines announced since 1990. Many recent high-end workstations and microprocessor-based servers now use two-level caches, with the first-level cache being on the processor chip.

The parameters of second-level caches may be quite different from those of first-level caches. The foremost difference between the two levels is that the speed of the first-level cache usually affects the clock rate of the processor, while the speed of the second-level cache affects only the miss penalty of the first-level cache. We can consider, therefore, many alternatives in the second-level cache that would be inappropriate for the first-level cache. Size is one example. Second-level caches are usually much larger than primary caches. For example, the Silicon Graphics Crimson workstation uses a 1 MB secondary cache, which is as large as the main memory of many workstations from the 1980s!

Another attempt to reduce the processor–DRAM performance gap is to reassess the interface on the DRAM chips. Several efforts are under way to redesign that interface to offer much higher bandwidth than standard DRAMs, in part by supplying a clock to DRAM chips to synchronize transfers and in part by increasing the number of pins on the DRAMS. In the next several years, we will know if computer designers will pay the higher costs of specialized DRAMs to get the higher performance of new interfaces.

Another possible direction is to seek software help. Efficiently managing the memory hierarchy using a variety of program transformation and hardware facilities is a major focus of research in compilers. Two different ideas are being explored. One idea is to reorganize the program to enhance its spatial and temporal locality. This approach focuses on loop-oriented programs that use large arrays as the major data structure; large linear algebra problems are a typical example. By restructuring the loops that access the arrays, substantially improved locality—and, therefore, cache performance—can be obtained. Another direction is to try to use compiler-directed *prefetching*. In prefetching, a block of data is brought into the cache before it is actually referenced. The compiler tries to identify data blocks needed in the future and, using special instructions, tells the memory hierarchy to move the blocks into the cache. When the block is actually referenced it is found in the cache, rather than causing a cache miss.

As we will see in Chapter 9, memory systems are also a central design issue for parallel processors. The growing importance of the memory hierarchy in determining system performance in both uniprocessor and multiprocessor systems means that this important area will continue to be a focus of both designers and researchers for some years to come.

7.7 Historical Perspective and Further Reading

Ideally one would desire an indefinitely large memory capacity such that any particular. . . word would be immediately available. . . . We are . . . forced to recognize the possibility of constructing a hierarchy of memories, each of which has greater capacity than the preceding but which is less quickly accessible.

A. W. Burks, H. H. Goldstine, and J. von Neumann,
*Preliminary Discussion of the Logical Design
of an Electronic Computing Instrument,* 1946

The developments of most of the concepts in this chapter have been driven by revolutionary advances in the technology we use for memory. Before we discuss how memory hierarchies were developed, let's take a brief tour of the development of memory technology. In this section, we focus on the technologies for building main memory and caches; Chapter 8 will provide some of the history of developments in disk technology.

The ENIAC had only a small number of registers (about 20) for its storage and implemented these with the same basic vacuum tube technology that it used for building logic circuitry. However, the vacuum tube technology was far too expensive to be used to build a larger memory capacity. Eckert came up with the idea of developing a new technology based on mercury delay lines. In this technology, electrical signals were converted into vibrations that were sent down a tube of mercury, reaching the other end where they were read out

FIGURE 7.30 The mercury delay lines in the EDSAC. This technology made it possible to build the first stored program computer. The young engineer in this photograph is none other than Maurice Wilkes, the lead architect of the EDSAC. Photo courtesy of The Computer Museum, Boston.

and recirculated. One mercury delay line could store about 0.5K bits. Although these bits were accessed serially, the mercury delay line was about a hundred times more cost-effective than vacuum tube memory. The first known working mercury delay lines were developed at Cambridge for the EDSAC. Figure 7.30 shows the mercury delay lines of the EDSAC, which had 32 tanks and a total of 512 36-bit words.

Despite the tremendous advance offered by the mercury delay lines, they were terribly unreliable and still rather expensive. The breakthrough came with the invention of core memory by J. Forrester at MIT as part of the Whirlwind project, in the early 1950s. Core memory uses a ferrite core, which can be magnetized, and once magnetized, acts as a store (just as a magnetic recording tape stores information). A set of wires running through the center of the core make it possible to read the value stored on any ferrite core. The Whirlwind

FIGURE 7.31 A core memory plane from the Whirlwind containing 256 cores arranged in a 16x16 array. Core memory was invented for the Whirlwind, which was used for air defense problems, and is now on display at the Smithsonian. (Incidentally, Ken Olsen, the founder and president of Digital for 20 years, built the machine that tested these core memories; it was his first computer.) Photo courtesy of The Computer Museum, Boston.

eventually included a core memory with 2048 16-bit words, or a total of 32 K bits. Core memory was a tremendous advance: It was cheaper, faster, much more reliable, and had higher density.

Core memory was so much better than the alternatives that it became the dominant memory technology only a few years after its invention and remained so for nearly 20 years. The technology that replaced core memory was the same one that we now use both for logic and memory: the integrated circuit. While registers were built out of transistorized memory in the 1960s, and IBM machines used transistorized memory for microcode store and caches in 1970, building main memory out of transistors remained prohibitive until the development of the integrated circuit. With the integrated circuit, it became possible to build a DRAM (dynamic random access memory—see Appendix B for a description). The first DRAMS were built at Intel in 1970, and the machines using DRAM memories (as a high-speed option to core) came shortly thereafter; they used 1K-bit DRAMs. Figure 7.32 shows an early DRAM board. By the late 1970s, core memory became a historical curiosity. Just as core memory technology had allowed a tremendous expansion in memory size, DRAM technology allowed a comparable expansion. In the 1990s, many personal

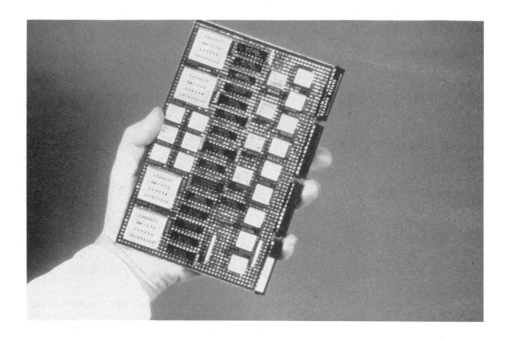

FIGURE 7.32 An early DRAM board. This board uses 18 Kbit chips. Photo courtesy of International Business Machines Corporation.

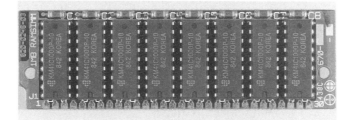

FIGURE 7.33 A modern 1 MB SIMM, using 1 Mbit chips. This SIMM, used in a Macintosh, sells for about $25/MB. Photo courtesy of MIPS Technology, Inc.

computers have as much memory as the largest machines using core memory ever had.

Modern DRAMs are often packaged with multiple chips on a little board (called SIMMs). The SIMM shown in Figure 7.33 contains a total of 1 MB and sells for about $25 in 1993. While DRAMs will remain the dominant memory technology for some time to come, dramatic innovations in the packaging of DRAMs to provide both higher bandwidth and greater density are ongoing.

The Development of Memory Hierarchies

Although the pioneers of computing foresaw the need for a memory hierarchy and coined the term, the automatic management of two levels was first proposed by Kilburn and his colleagues and demonstrated at the University of Manchester with the Atlas computer, which implemented virtual memory. This was the year *before* the IBM 360 was announced. IBM planned to include virtual memory with the next generation (System/370), but the operating system wasn't up to the challenge in 1970. Virtual memory was announced for the 370 family in 1972, and it was for this machine that the term *translation-lookaside buffer* was coined. The only computers today without virtual memory are a few supercomputers, and even they may add this feature in the near future.

The problems of inadequate address space have plagued designers repeatedly. The architects of the PDP-11 identified a small address space as the only architectural mistake that is difficult to recover from. When the PDP-11 was designed, core memory densities were increasing at a very slow rate, and the competition from 100 other minicomputer companies meant that DEC might not have a cost-competitive product if every address had to go through the 16-bit datapath twice. Hence the decision to add just four more address bits than the predecessor of the PDP-11. The architects of the IBM 360 were aware of the importance of address size and planned for the architecture to extend to 32 bits of address. Only 24 bits were used in the IBM 360, however, because the low-end 360 models would have been even slower with the larger addresses. Unfortunately, the expansion effort was greatly complicated by programmers who stored extra information in the upper eight "unused" address bits.

Many of the early ideas in memory hierarchies originated in England. Just a few years after the Atlas paper, Wilkes [1965] published the first paper describing the concept of a cache, calling it a *slave*:

> The use is discussed of a fast core memory of, say, 32,000 words as slave to a slower core memory of, say, one million words in such a way that in practical cases the effective access time is nearer that of the fast memory than that of the slow memory.

This two-page paper describes a direct mapped cache. While this was the first publication on caches, the first implementation was probably a direct mapped instruction cache built at the University of Cambridge by Scarrott and described at the 1965 IFIP Congress. It was based on tunnel diode memory, the fastest form of memory available at the time.

Subsequent to that publication, IBM started a project that led to the first commercial machine with a cache, the IBM 360/85. Gibson at IBM recognized that memory-accessing behavior would have a significant impact on performance. He described how to measure program behavior and cache behavior and showed that the miss rate varies between programs. Using a sample of 20 programs (each with 3 million references—an incredible number for that time), Gibson analyzed the effectiveness of caches using average memory-access time as the metric. Conti, Gibson, and Pitkowsky described the resulting performance of the 360/85 in the first paper to use the term *cache*. Since this early work, it has become clear that caches are one of the most important ideas not only in computer architecture, but in software systems as well. The idea of caching has found applications in operating systems, networking systems, databases, and compilers, to name a few. There are thousands of papers on the topic of caching, and it continues to be an important area of research.

Protection Mechanisms

Architectural support for protection has varied greatly over the past 20 years. In early machines, before virtual memory, protection was very simple at best. In the 1970s, more elaborate mechanisms that supported different protection levels (called *rings*) were invented. In the late 1970s and early 1980s, very elaborate mechanisms for protection were devised and later built; these mechanisms supported a variety of powerful protection schemes that allowed controlled instances of sharing, in such a way that a process could share data while controlling exactly what was done to the data. The most powerful method, called *capabilities*, created a data object that described the access rights to some portion of memory. These capabilities could then be passed to other processes, thus granting access to the object described by the capability. Supporting this sophisticated protection mechanism was both complex and costly, because creation, copying, and manipulation of capabilities required a combination of operating system and hardware support. Recent machines all support a simpler protection scheme based on virtual memory, similar to that discussed in section 7.3.

To Probe Further

Conti, C., D. H. Gibson, and S. H. Pitowsky [1968]. "Structural aspects of the System/360 Model 85, part I: General organization," *IBM Systems* J. 7:1, 2–14.

Describes the first commercial machine to use a cache and its resulting performance.

Hennessy, J., and D. Patterson [1990]. *Computer Architecture: A Quantitative Approach*, Morgan Kaufmann Publishers, San Mateo, Calif., Chapter 8.

For more in-depth coverage of a variety of topics including protection, register windows, improving write performance, virtually addressed caches, multilevel caches, and cache coherency.

Kilburn, T., D. B. G. Edwards, M. J. Lanigan, F. H. Sumner [1962]. "One-level storage system," *IRE Transactions on Electronic Computers* EC-11 (April) 223–35. Also appears in D. P. Siewiorek, C. G. Bell, and A. Newell, *Computer Structures: Principles and Examples*, McGraw-Hill, New York, 135–48, 1982.

This classical paper is the first proposal for virtual memory.

Przybylski, S. A. [1990]. *Cache and Memory Hierarchy Design: A Performance-Directed Approach*, Morgan Kaufmann Publishers, San Mateo, Calif.

A thorough exploration of multi-level memory hierarchies and their performance.

Smith, A. J. [1982]. "Cache memories," *Computing Surveys* 14:3 (September) 473–530.

The classic survey paper on caches. This paper defined the terminology for the field and has served as a reference for many computer designers.

Tanenbaum, A. [1991]. *Operating Systems Principles*, Addison-Wesley, Reading, Mass.

An operating system textbook with a good discussion of virtual memory.

Wilkes, M. [1965]. "Slave memories and dynamic storage allocation," *IEEE Trans. Electronic Computers* EC-14:2 (April) 270–71.

The first, classic, paper on caches.

7.8 Exercises

7.1 [10] <§7.2> Here is a string of address references given as word addresses: 1, 4, 8, 5, 20, 17, 19, 56, 9, 11, 4, 43, 5, 6, 9, 17. Assuming a direct mapped cache with 16 one-word blocks that is initially empty, label each reference in the list as a hit or miss and show the final contents of the cache.

7.2 [10] <§7.2> Using the reference string listed in Exercise 7.1, show the hits and misses and final cache contents for a direct mapped cache with four-word blocks and a *total size* of 16 words.

7.3 [10] <§7.2, 7.4> Using the reference string listed in Exercise 7.1, show the hits and misses and final cache contents for a two-way set associative cache with one-word blocks and a *total size* of 16 words. Assume LRU replacement.

7.4 [10] <§7.2, 7.4> Using the reference string listed in Exercise 7.1, show the hits and misses and final cache contents for a fully associative cache with one-word blocks and a *total size* of 16 words. Assume LRU replacement.

7.5 [10] <§7.2, 7.4> Using the reference string listed in Exercise 7.1, show the hits and misses and final cache contents for a fully associative cache with four-word blocks and a *total size* of 16 words. Assume LRU replacement.

7.6 [15] <§7.2> Cache C1 is direct mapped with 16 one-word blocks. Cache C2 is direct mapped with 4 four-word blocks. Assume that the miss penalty for

C1 is 8 clock cycles and the miss penalty for C2 is 11 clock cycles. Assuming that the caches are initially empty, find a reference string for which C2 has a lower miss rate but spends more cycles on cache misses than C1. Use word addresses.

7.7 [15] <§7.2> For the caches in Exercise 7.6, find a reference string for which C2 has more misses than C1. Use word addresses.

7.8 [10] <§7.2> Compute the number of bytes in the cache in Figure 7.9.

7.9 [15] <§7.3> Consider a virtual memory system with the following properties:

- 40-bit virtual address
- 16 KB pages
- 36-bit physical address

What is the total size of the page table for each process on this machine, assuming that the valid, protection, dirty, and use bits take a total of 4 bits and that all the virtual pages are in use. Assume that disk addresses are not stored in the page table.

7.10 [15] <§7.3> Assume that the virtual memory system of Exercise 7.9 is implemented with a two-way set associative TLB with a total of 256 TLB entries. Show the virtual to physical mapping with a figure like the top half of Figure 7.19 on page 494. Make sure to label the width of all fields and signals.

7.11 [15] <§7.2, 7.4> Assume that the cache for the system described in Exercise 7.9 is two-way set associative and has eight-word blocks and a total size of 16 KB. Show the cache organization and access using the same format as Figure 7.27 on page 509.

7.12 [10] <§7.2> Find a method to eliminate the AND gate on the valid bit in Figure 7.6 on page 463. Hint: you need to change the comparison.

7.13 [20] <§7.2, 7.4> Consider three machines with different cache configurations:

1. *Cache 1:* Direct mapped with one-word blocks.
2. *Cache 2:* Direct mapped with four-word blocks.
3. *Cache 3:* 2-way set associative with four-word blocks.

The following miss rate measurements have been made:

1. *Cache 1:* Instruction miss rate is 4%; data miss rate 8%.
2. *Cache 2:* Instruction miss rate is 2%; data miss rate 5%.

3. *Cache 3:* Instruction miss rate is 2%; data miss rate 4%.

For these machine, one-half of the instructions contain a data reference. Assume that the cache miss penalty is $6 +$ Block size in words . The CPI for this workload was measured on a machine with cache 1 and was found to be 2.0.

Determine which machine spends the most cycles on cache misses.

7.14 [5] <§7.2> {ex. 7.13} The clock rates for the machines in Exercise 7.13 are 10 ns for the first and second machine and 12 ns for the third machine. Determine which machine is the fastest and which is the slowest.

7.15 [10] <§7.2> Consider a memory hierarchy using one of the three organizations for main memory shown in Figure 7.12 on page 474. Assume that the cache block size is 16 words, that the width of organization b of the figure is four words, and the number of banks in organization c is four. If the main memory latency for a new access is 10 cycles and the transfer time is one cycle, what are the miss penalties for each of these organizations?

7.16 [10] <§7.2> {ex. 7.15} Suppose a processor with a 16-word block size has an effective miss rate per instruction of 0.5%. Assume the CPI without cache misses is 1.2. How much faster is this processor when using the wide memory described in Exercise 7.15 compared to the narrow or interleaved memories described in the exercise?

7.17 [20] <§7.2–7.4> In a memory hierarchy like that of Figure 7.19 that includes a TLB and a cache organized as shown, a memory reference can encounter three different types of misses: a cache miss, a TLB miss, and a page fault. Consider all the combinations of these three events with one or more occurring (seven possibilities). For each possibility, state whether this event can actually occur and under what circumstances.

7.18 [3 hours] <§7.2–7.4> Use a cache simulator to simulate several different cache organizations for the first 1 million references in a trace of gcc. Both dinero (a cache simulator) and the gcc traces are available—see the preface. Assume an instruction cache of 32 KB and a data cache of 32 KB using the same organization. You should choose at least two kinds for associativity and two block sizes. Draw a diagram like that in Figure 7.27 showing the data cache organization with the best hit rate.

7.19 [4 hours] <§7.2–7.4> We want to use a cache simulator to simulate several different TLB and virtual memory organizations. Use the first 1 million references of gcc for this evaluation. We want to know the TLB miss rate for each of the following TLBs and page sizes:

1. 64-entry TLB with full associativity and 4 KB pages
2. 32-entry TLB with full associativity and 8 KB pages
3. 64-entry TLB with 8-way associativity and 4 KB pages
4. 128-entry TLB with 4-way associativity and 4 KB pages

In More Depth

To capture the fact that the time to access data for both hits and misses affects performance, designers often use average memory access time (AMAT) as a way to examine alternative cache designs. Average memory access time is the average time to access memory considering both hits and misses and the frequency of different accesses; it is equal to the following:

$$\text{AMAT} = \text{Time for a hit} + \text{Miss rate} \times \text{Miss penalty}$$

AMAT is useful as a figure of merit for different cache systems.

7.20 [10] <§7.2> Find the AMAT for a machine with a 10-ns clock, a miss penalty of 20 clock cycles, a miss rate of 0.05 misses per instruction, and a cache access time including hit detection of 1 clock cycle. Assume that the read and write miss penalties are the same and ignore other write stalls.

7.21 [10] <§7.2> Suppose we can improve the miss rate to 0.03 misses per reference by doubling the cache size. This causes the cache access time to increase to 1.2 clock cycles. Using the AMAT as a metric, determine if this is a good trade-off.

7.22 [10] <§7.2> If the cache access time determines the processor's clock cycle time, which is often the case, AMAT may not correctly indicate whether one cache organization is better than another. If the machine's clock cycle time must be changed to match that of a cache, is this a good trade-off? Assume the machines are identical except for the clock rate and number of cache miss cycles; assume 1.5 references per instruction and a CPI without cache misses of 2. The miss penalty is 20 cycles for both machines.

7.23 [1 day] <§7.2, 7.4> You are commissioned to design a cache for a MIPS R3000 system. It has a 32-bit physical byte address and requires separate instruction and data caches. The RAMs have an access time of 15 ns, and a size of 32 K × 8 bits, and you have a total of 16 RAMs to use. The miss penalty for the memory system is $8 + 2 \times \text{Block size in words}$. Using set associativity adds 2 ns to the cache access time. Using the first 1 million references of gcc, find the best I and D cache organizations, given the available RAMs.

Interfacing Processors and Peripherals

I/O certainly has been lagging in the last decade.

Seymour Cray
Public lecture, 1976

The Five Classic Components of a Computer

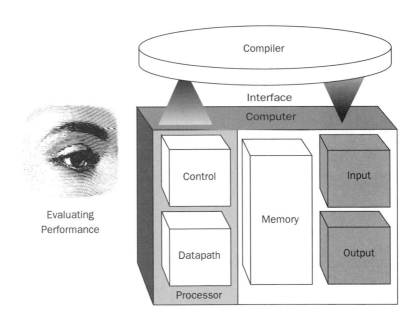

8.1   Introduction

As in processors, many of the characteristics of *input/output* (I/O) systems are driven by technology. For example, the properties of disk drives affect how the disks should be connected to the processor, as well as how the operating system interacts with the disks. I/O systems, however, differ from processors in several important ways. Although processor designers often focus primarily on performance, designers of I/O systems must consider issues such as expandability and resilience in the face of failure as much as they consider performance. Second, performance in an I/O system is a more complex measurement than for a processor. For example, with some devices we may care primarily about access latency, while with others throughput is crucial. Furthermore, performance depends on many aspects of the system: the device characteristics, the connection between the device and the rest of the system, the memory hierarchy, and the operating system. Figure 8.1 shows the struc-

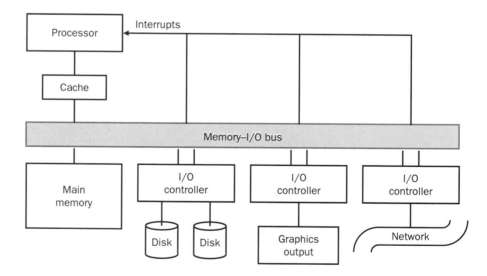

FIGURE 8.1 Typical collection of I/O devices. The connections between the I/O devices, processor, and memory are usually called *buses*. Communication among the devices and the processor use both protocols on the bus and interrupts, as we will see in this chapter.

ture of a system with its I/O. All of the components from the individual I/O devices to the processor to the system software will affect the performance of tasks that include I/O.

The difficulties in assessing and designing I/O systems have often relegated I/O to second-class status. Research focuses on processor design; companies present performance using primarily processor-oriented measures; courses in every aspect of computing, from programming to computer architecture, often ignore I/O or give it scanty coverage; and textbooks leave the subject to near the end, making it easier for students and instructors to skip it!

This situation doesn't make sense: imagine how you'd like to use a computer without I/O! Furthermore, in an era when machines from low-end PCs to the fastest mainframes and even supercomputers are being built from the same basic microprocessor technology, I/O capability is often one of the most distinctive features of the machines. Many of the recent developments in the computer industry are exciting as much for their new I/O capabilities as for their processor power. This is because machines interact with people through I/O.

If these concerns are still not convincing, our discussion of Amdahl's Law in Chapter 2 should remind us that ignoring I/O is dangerous. A simple example demonstrates this.

Example

Suppose we have a benchmark that executes in 100 seconds of elapsed time, where 90 seconds is CPU time and the rest is I/O time. If CPU time improves by 50% per year for the next five years but I/O time doesn't improve, how much faster will our program run at the end of five years?

Answer

We know that

$$\text{Elapsed time} = \text{CPU time} + \text{I/O time}$$

$$100 = 90 + \text{I/O time}$$

$$\text{I/O time} = 10 \text{ seconds}$$

The new CPU times and the resulting elapsed times are computed in the following table:

After n years	CPU time	I/O time	Elapsed time	% I/O time
0	90 seconds	10 seconds	100 seconds	10%
1	$\dfrac{90}{1.5} = 60$ seconds	10 seconds	70 seconds	14%
2	$\dfrac{60}{1.5} = 40$ seconds	10 seconds	50 seconds	20%
3	$\dfrac{40}{1.5} = 27$ seconds	10 seconds	37 seconds	27%
4	$\dfrac{27}{1.5} = 18$ seconds	10 seconds	28 seconds	36%
5	$\dfrac{18}{1.5} = 12$ seconds	10 seconds	22 seconds	45%

The improvement in CPU performance over five years is

$$\frac{90}{12} = 7.5$$

However, the improvement in elapsed time is only

$$\frac{100}{22} = 4.5$$

and the I/O time has increased from 10% to 45% of the elapsed time.

How we should assess I/O performance often depends on the application. In some environments, we may care primarily about system throughput. In these cases, I/O bandwidth will be most important. Even I/O bandwidth can be measured in two different ways:

1. How much data can we move through the system in a certain time?

2. How many I/O operations can we do per unit time?

Which measurement is best may depend on the environment. For example, in many supercomputer applications, most I/O requests are for long streams of data, and transfer bandwidth is the important characteristic. In another environment, we may wish to process a large number of small, unrelated accesses to an I/O device. An example of such an environment might be a tax-processing office of the National Income Tax Service (NITS). NITS mostly cares about processing a large number of forms in a given time; each tax form is stored separately and is fairly small. A system oriented toward large file transfer may be satisfactory, but an I/O system that can support the simulta neous transfer of many small files may be cheaper and faster for processing millions of tax forms.

In other applications, we care primarily about response time, which you will recall is the total elapsed time to accomplish a particular task. If the I/O requests are extremely large, response time will depend heavily on bandwidth, but in many environments most accesses will be small, and the I/O system with the lowest latency per access will deliver the best response time. On single-user machines such as workstations and personal computers, response time is the key performance characteristic.

A large number of applications, especially in the vast commercial market for computing, require both high throughput and short response times. Examples include automatic teller machines (ATMs), airline reservation systems, order entry and inventory tracking systems, file servers, and machines for timesharing. In such environments, we care about both how long each task takes *and* how many tasks we can process in a second. The number of ATM requests you can process per hour doesn't matter if each one takes 15 minutes—you won't have any customers left! Similarly, if you can process each ATM request quickly, but only handle a small number of requests at once, you won't be able to support many ATMs or the cost of the computer per ATM will be very high.

If I/O is truly important, how should we compare I/O systems? This is a complex question, because I/O performance depends on many aspects of the system and different applications stress different aspects of the I/O system. Furthermore, a design can trade response time for throughput, or vice versa, making it impossible to measure just one aspect in isolation. For example, response time is generally minimized by handling a request as early as possible, while greater throughput can be achieved if we try to handle related requests together. Accordingly, we may increase throughput on a disk by grouping requests that access locations that are close together. Such a policy will increase the response time for some requests. As a result, throughput may improve, but average response time will probably increase.

Before discussing the aspects of I/O devices and how they are connected, let's look briefly at some performance measures for I/O systems.

8.2 | I/O Performance Measures: Some Examples from Disk and File Systems

Assessment of an I/O system must take into account a variety of factors. Performance is one of these, and in this section, we give some examples of measurements proposed for determining the performance of disk systems. These benchmarks are affected by a variety of system features, including the disk technology, how disks are connected, the memory system, the processor, and the file system provided by the operating system. Overall, the state of benchmarking on the I/O side of computer systems remains quite primitive compared with the extensive activity lately seen in benchmarking processor systems. Perhaps this situation will change as designers realize the importance of I/O and the inadequacy of our techniques to evaluate it.

Supercomputer I/O Benchmarks

Supercomputer I/O is dominated by accesses to large files on magnetic disks. Many supercomputer installations run batch jobs, each of which may last for hours. In these situations, I/O consists of one large read followed by writes to snapshot the state of the computation should the computer crash. As a result, supercomputer I/O in many cases consists more of output than input. The overriding supercomputer I/O measure is data throughput: the number of bytes per second that can be transferred between a supercomputer's main memory and disks during large transfers.

Transaction Processing I/O Benchmarks

Transaction processing (TP) applications involve both a response time requirement and a performance measurement based on throughput. Furthermore, most of the I/O accesses are small. Because of this, TP applications are chiefly concerned with *I/O rate*, measured as the number of disk accesses per second, as opposed to *data rate*, measured as bytes of data per second. TP applications generally involve changes to a large data base with the system meeting some response time requirements as well as gracefully handling certain types of failures. These applications are extremely critical and cost-sensitive. For example, banks normally use TP systems because they are concerned about a range of characteristics. These include making sure transactions aren't lost, handling transactions quickly, and minimizing the cost of processing each transaction. Although reliability in the face of failure is an absolute requirement in such systems, both response time and throughput are critical to building cost-effective systems.

A number of transaction processing benchmarks have been developed. The best known benchmark, called TPC-B, has a number of variations. The basic benchmark simulates a transaction system such as a network of ATMs. Performance is rated as throughput with the additional requirement that only transactions serviced within a predetermined, constant response time count toward the service rate. The throughput measure is transactions per second or TPS; in 1993, the TPS for high-end, one-processor machines is about 300.

Depending on how cleverly the transaction processing system is designed, each transaction results in between 2 and 10 disk I/Os and takes between 5,000 and 20,000 CPU instructions per disk I/O. What makes this benchmark particularly challenging is that the size of the database is scaled up as the TPS rate increases. This reflects how real systems operate and prevents the database from becoming totally memory resident on very large machines. The following table shows how the number of ATMs and the database size scale with the target TPS rate:

TPS	Number of ATMs	Account-file size
10	1000	0.1 GB
100	10,000	1.0 GB
1000	100,000	10.0 GB
10,000	1,000,000	100.0 GB

File System I/O Benchmarks

File systems, which are stored on disks, have a different access pattern. For example, measurements of UNIX file systems in an engineering environment have found that 80% of accesses are to files of less than 10 KB and that 90% of all file accesses are to data with sequential addresses on the disk. Furthermore, 67% of the accesses were reads, 27% were writes, and 6% were read-write accesses. Such measurements have led to the creation of synthetic file-system benchmarks. One of the most popular of such benchmarks has five phases, using 70 files with a total size of 200 KB:

- *MakeDir*: Constructs a directory subtree that is identical in structure to the given directory subtree.

- *Copy*: Copies every file from the source subtree to the target subtree.

- *ScanDir*: Recursively traverses a directory subtree and examines the status of every file in it.

- *ReadAll*: Scans every byte of every file in a subtree once.

- *Make*: Compiles and links all the files in a subtree.

8.3 Types and Characteristics of I/O Devices

I/O devices are incredibly diverse. Three characteristics are useful in organizing this wide variety:

- *Behavior*: Input (read once), output (write only, cannot be read), or storage (can be reread and usually rewritten).

- *Partner*: Either a human or a machine is at the other end of the I/O device, either feeding data on input or reading data on output.

Device	Behavior	Partner	Data rate (KB/sec)
Keyboard	Input	Human	0.01
Mouse	Input	Human	0.02
Voice input	Input	Human	0.02
Scanner	Input	Human	200.00
Voice output	Output	Human	0.60
Line printer	Output	Human	1.00
Laser printer	Output	Human	100.00
Graphics display	Output	Human	30,000.00
Network-terminal	Input or output	Machine	0.05
Network-LAN	Input or output	Machine	200.00
Floppy disk	Storage	Machine	50.00
Optical disk	Storage	Machine	500.00
Magnetic tape	Storage	Machine	2000.00
Magnetic disk	Storage	Machine	2000.00

FIGURE 8.2 The diversity of I/O devices. I/O devices can be distinguished by whether they serve as input, output, or storage devices, their communication partner (people or other computers), and their peak communication rates. The data rates span six orders of magnitude. Note that a network can be an input or an output device, but cannot be used for storage. For historical reasons, disk and memory sizes as well as transfer rates are always quoted in base two, so that 1 KB = 1024 bytes. Networks, on the other hand, specify transfer rates in decimal, so that 10 Mb = 10 million bits per second.

■ *Data rate*: The peak rate at which data can be transferred between the I/O device and the main memory or processor. It is useful to know what maximum demand the device may generate.

For example, a keyboard is an *input* device used by a *human* with a *peak data rate* of about 10 bytes per second. Figure 8.2 shows some of the I/O devices connected to computers.

In Chapter 1, we briefly discussed four important and characteristic I/O devices: mice, graphics displays, disks, and networks. We use mice, disks, and networks as examples to illustrate how I/O devices interface to processors and memories, but before we do that it will be useful to discuss these devices in more detail than in Chapter 1.

Mouse

The interface between a mouse and a system can take one of two forms: the mouse either generates a series of pulses when it is moved (using the LED and detector described in Chapter 1 to generate the pulses), or it increments

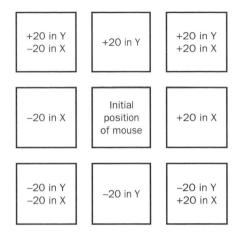

FIGURE 8.3 Moving the mouse in the horizontal direction or vertical direction causes the X or Y counter, respectively, to increment or decrement. Moving it along a diagonal causes both counters to change. Since the ball doesn't move when the mouse is not contacting the surface, it may be picked up and moved without changing the counters. When the mouse uses pulses to communicate its movement, there are four types of pulses: +X, –X, +Y, and –Y. Rather than generate a change in the counter value, the mouse generates the appropriate number of pulses on each of the four pulse signal lines. The value 20 is an arbitrary count that measures how far the mouse has moved.

and decrements counters. Figure 8.3 shows how the counters change when the mouse is moved and describes how the interface would operate if it generated pulses instead. The processor can periodically read these counters, or count up the pulses, and determine how far the mouse has moved since it was last examined. The system then moves the cursor on the screen appropriately. This motion appears smooth because the rate at which you can move the mouse is slow compared with the rate at which the processor can read the mouse status and move the cursor on the screen.

Most mice also include one or more buttons, and the system must be able to detect when a button is depressed. By monitoring the status of the button, the system can also differentiate between clicking the button and holding it down. Of course, the mapping between the counters and the button position and what happens on the screen is totally controlled by software. That's why, for example, the rate at which the mouse moves across the screen and the rate at which single and double clicks are recognized can usually be set by the user. Similarly, software interpretation of the mouse position means that the cursor doesn't jump completely off the screen when the mouse is moved a long distance in one direction. This method of having the system monitor the status of the mouse by reading signals from it is a common way to interface lower performance devices to machines; it is called *polling*, and we'll revisit it in section 8.5.

Magnetic Disks

As mentioned in Chapter 1, there are two major types of magnetic disks: floppy disks and hard disks. Both types of disks rely on a rotating platter coated with a magnetic surface and use a moveable read/write head to access the disk. Disk storage is nonvolatile, meaning that the data remains even when power is removed. Because the platters in a hard disk are metal (or, recently, glass), they have several significant advantages over floppy disks:

- The hard disk can be larger, because it is rigid.

- The hard disk has higher density, because it can be controlled more precisely.

- The hard disk has a higher data rate, because it spins faster.

- Hard disks can incorporate more than one platter.

For the rest of this section we will focus on hard disks, and we use the term *magnetic disk* to mean hard disk.

A magnetic disk consists of a collection of platters (2 to 20), each of which has two recordable disk surfaces, as shown in Figure 8.4. The stack of platters is rotated at 3600 to 5400 RPM and has a diameter of from just over an inch to just over 10 inches. Each disk surface is divided into concentric circles, called *tracks*. There are typically 500 to 2000 tracks per surface. Each track is in turn divided into *sectors* that contain the information; each track may have 32 to 128 sectors, and the sector is the smallest unit that can be read or written. The sequence recorded on the magnetic media is a sector number, a gap, the information for that sector including error correction code (see Appendix B, page B-33), a gap, the sector number of the next sector, and so on. Traditionally, all tracks have the same number of sectors and hence the same number of bits. The wider disks have usually offered the best performance and the smaller diameter disks have the best cost per megabyte.

As we saw in Chapter 1, to read and write information the read/write heads must be moved so that they are over the correct location. The disk arms for each surface are connected together and move in conjunction, so that every arm is over the same track of every surface. The term *cylinder* is used to refer to all the tracks under the arms at a given point on all surfaces.

To access data, the operating system must direct the disk through a three-stage process. The first step is to position the arm over the proper track. This operation is called a *seek*, and the time to move the arm to the desired track is

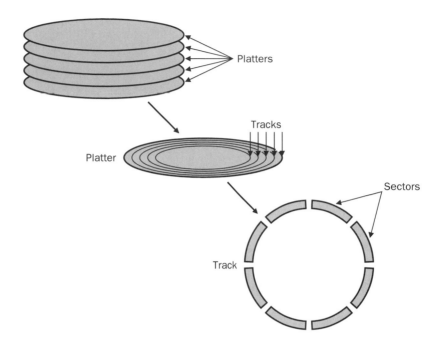

FIGURE 8.4 Disks are organized into platters, tracks, and sectors. Both sides of a platter are coated so that information can be stored on both surfaces. Floppy disks have the same organization, but consist of only one platter.

called *seek time*. Disk manufacturers report minimum seek time, maximum seek time, and average seek time in their manuals. The first two are easy to measure, but the average is open to wide interpretation because it depends on the seek distance. The industry has decided to calculate average seek time as the sum of the time for all possible seeks divided by the number of possible seeks. Average seek times are usually advertised as 12 ms to 20 ms, but, depending on the application and scheduling of disk requests, the actual average seek time may be only 25% to 33% of the advertised number, due to locality of disk references. This locality arises both because of successive access to the same file and because the operating system tries to schedule such access together.

Once the head has reached the correct track, we must wait for the desired sector to rotate under the read/write head. This time is called the *rotation latency* or *rotational delay*. The average latency to the desired information is halfway around the disk. Because the disks rotate at 3600 RPM to 5400 RPM, the average rotation time is between

$$\text{Average rotational latency} = \frac{0.5 \text{ rotation}}{3600 \text{ RPM}} = \frac{0.5 \text{ rotation}}{3600 \text{ RPM} / (60 \frac{\text{seconds}}{\text{minute}})}$$

$$= 0.0083 \text{ sec} = 8.3 \text{ ms}$$

and

$$\text{Average rotational latency} = \frac{0.5 \text{ rotation}}{5400 \text{ RPM}} = \frac{0.5 \text{ rotation}}{5400 \text{ RPM} / (60 \frac{\text{seconds}}{\text{minute}})}$$

$$= 0.0056 \text{ sec} = 5.6 \text{ ms}$$

Smaller diameter disks are attractive because they can spin at higher rates without excessive power consumption, thereby reducing rotational latency.

The last component of a disk access, *transfer time*, is the time to transfer a block of bits, typically a sector. This is a function of the transfer size, the rotation speed, and the recording density of a track. Transfer rates in 1992 are typically 2 to 4 MB per second.

The detailed control of the disk and the transfer between the disk and the memory is usually handled by a *disk controller*. The controller adds the final component of disk-access time, *the controller time*, which is the overhead the controller imposes in performing an I/O access. The average time to perform an I/O operation will consist of these four times plus any wait time incurred because other processes are using the disk.

Example   What is the average time to read or write a 512-byte sector for a typical disk rotating at 4500 RPM? The advertised average seek time is 20 ms, the transfer rate is 2 MB/sec, and the controller overhead is 2 ms. Assume that the disk is idle so that there is no waiting time.

Answer   Average disk access is equal to average seek time + average rotational delay + transfer time + controller overhead. Using the advertised average seek time, the answer is

$$20 \text{ ms} + 6.7 \text{ ms} + \frac{0.5 \text{ KB}}{2.0 \text{ MB/sec}} + 2 \text{ ms} = 20 + 6.7 + 0.2 + 2 = 28.9 \text{ ms}$$

If the measured average seek time is 25% of the advertised average time, the answer is

$$5 \text{ ms} + 6.7 \text{ ms} + 0.2 \text{ ms} + 2 \text{ ms} = 13.9 \text{ ms}$$

Notice that when we consider average measured seek time, as opposed to average advertised seek time, the rotational latency can be the largest component of the access time.

Disk densities have continued to increase for more than 30 years. The impact of this compounded improvement in density and the reduction in physical size of a disk drive has been amazing, as Figure 8.5 shows. The aims of different disk designers have led to a wide variety of drives being available at any particular time. Figure 8.6 shows the characteristics of five different magnetic disks from three manufacturers. Large-diameter drives have many more megabytes to amortize the cost of electronics, so the traditional wisdom was that they had the lowest cost per megabyte. But this advantage is offset for the small drives by the much higher sales volume, which lowers manufacturing costs: In 1993, disks cost between $1.00 and $2.00 per megabyte, almost independent of width. The small drives also have advantages in power and volume.

FIGURE 8.5 Six magnetic disks, varying in diameter from 14 inches down to 1.8 inches. These disks were introduced over more than a decade ago and hence are not intended to be representative of the best 1993 capacity of disks of these diameters. This photograph does, however, accurately portray their relative physical sizes. The widest disk is the DEC R81, containing four 14-inch diameter platters and storing 456 MB. It was manufactured in 1985. The 8-inch diameter disk comes from Fujitsu, and this 1984 disk stores 130 MB on six platters. The Micropolis RD53 has five 5.25-inch platters and stores 85 MB. The IBM 0361 also has five platters, but these are just 3.5 inches in diameter. This 1988 disk holds 320 MB. The Conner CP 2045 has two 2.5-inch platters containing 40 MB, and was made in 1990. The smallest and newest disk is the Integral 1820. This single 1.8-inch platter contains 20 MB and was made in 1992. (Photographed by Peg Skorpinski.)

Characteristics	IBM 3090	Seagate ST4160	IBM 0663	IBM WDA260	Integral 1820
Disk diameter (inches)	10.88	5.25	3.50	2.50	1.80
Formatted data capacity (MB)	22,700	1350	1000	63	21
MTTF (hours)	50,000	250,000	400,000	45,000	100,000
Number of arms/box	12	1	1	1	1
Maximum I/Os/second/arm	50	55	55	35	35
Maximum I/Os/second/box	600	55	55	35	35
Rotation speed (RPM)	3600	3600	4318	3600	3600
Transfer rate (MB/sec)	4.2	3–4.2	4	2.3	1.9
Power/box (watts)	2900	37	12	3	2
MB/watt	8	37	102	21	10.5
Volume (cu. ft.)	97	1	0.13	0.08	0.02
MB/cu. ft.	234	1350	7692	1050	1050

FIGURE 8.6 Characteristics of five magnetic disks. There is a dramatic variation from the enormous capacity of the large IBM 3090, intended for mainframes, to the tiny Integral disk, suitable for portable computers. Although the capacity and I/O rates of the large-diameter disks are much greater, and the smallest disks take much less space, the IBM 0663 (in the middle) offers the best storage density per watt and per cubic foot. The entry MTTF is the *mean time to failure*, which is a common measure of reliability.

Elaboration: Each track has the same number of bits, and the outer tracks are longer. The outer tracks thus record information at a lower density per inch of track than do tracks closer to the center of the disk. Recording more sectors on the outer tracks than on the inner tracks, called *constant bit density*, is becoming more widespread with the advent of intelligent interface standards such as SCSI (see section 8.4). The rate at which an inch of track moves under the head varies: it is faster on the outer tracks. Accordingly, if the number of bits per inch is constant, the rate at which bits must be read or written varies, and the electronics must accommodate this factor when constant bit density is used.

Networks

Networks are the major medium used to communicate between computers. The table below shows key characteristics of typical networks:

Distance	0.01 to 10,000 kilometers
Speed	0.001 MB/sec to 100 MB/sec
Topology	Bus, ring, star, tree
Shared lines	None (point-to-point) or shared (multidrop)

We'll illustrate these characteristics with three examples.

The *RS232* standard provides a 0.3- to 19.2-Kbit-per-second *terminal network*. A central computer connects to many terminals over slow but cheap dedicated wires. These point-to-point connections form a star from the central computer, with each terminal ranging from 10 to 100 meters in distance from the computer.

The *local area network*, or LAN, is what is commonly meant today when people mention a network, and *Ethernet* is what most people mean when they mention a LAN. (Ethernet has in fact become such a common term that it is often used as a generic term for LAN.) The Ethernet is essentially a 10,000 Kbit-per-second, one-wire bus that has no central control. Messages, or *packets*, are sent over the Ethernet in blocks that vary from 64 bytes to 1518 bytes and take 0.1 ms and 1.5 ms to send, respectively. An Ethernet is essentially a bus with multiple masters and a scheme for determining who gets bus control; we'll discuss how the distributed control is implemented in the Exercises. Because the Ethernet is a bus, only one sender can be transmitting at any time; this limits the bandwidth. In practice, this is not usually a problem because the utilization is fairly low. Of course, some LANs become overloaded through poor capacity planning, and response time and throughput can degrade rapidly at higher utilization.

Long-haul networks cover distances of 10 to 10,000 kilometers. The first and most famous long-haul network was the ARPANET (named after its funding agency, the Advanced Research Projects Agency of the U.S. government). It transferred data at 56 Kbits per second and used point-to-point dedicated lines leased from telephone companies. The host computer talked to an *interface message processor* (IMP), which communicated over the telephone lines. The IMP took information and broke it into 1-Kbit packets, which could take separate paths to the destination node. At each hop a packet was stored (for recovery in case of failure) and then forwarded to the proper IMP according to the address in the packet. The destination IMP reassembled the packets into a message and then gave it to the host. Most networks today use this *packet-switched* approach, in which packets are individually routed from source to destination.

The bandwidths of networks are probably growing faster than the bandwidth of any other type of device at present. High-speed networks using copper and coaxial cable offer 100 Megabit/second bandwidths, while optical fiber offers bandwidths up to 1 Gigabit/second. The challenge in putting these networks into use lies primarily in building systems that can efficiently interface to these media and sustain these bandwidths between two programs that want to communicate. Accomplishing this requires that all the pieces of the I/O system, from the operating system to the memory system to the bus to the device interface, be able to accommodate these bandwidths. This is truly a top-to-bottom systems challenge.

8.4 Buses: Connecting I/O Devices to Processor and Memory

In a computer system, the various subsystems must have interfaces to one another. For example, the memory and processor need to communicate, as do the processor and the I/O devices. This is commonly done with a *bus*. A bus is a shared communication link, which uses one set of wires to connect multiple subsystems. The two major advantages of the bus organization are versatility and low cost. By defining a single connection scheme, new devices can easily be added, and peripherals can even be moved between computer systems that use the same kind of bus. Furthermore, buses are cost effective, because a single set of wires is shared in multiple ways.

The major disadvantage of a bus is that it creates a communication bottleneck, possibly limiting the maximum I/O throughput. When I/O must pass through a single bus, the bandwidth of that bus limits the maximum I/O throughput. In commercial systems, where I/O is very frequent, and in supercomputers, where the I/O rates must be very high because the processor performance is high, designing a bus system capable of meeting the demands of the processor as well as connecting large numbers of I/O devices to the machine presents a major challenge.

One reason bus design is so difficult is that the maximum bus speed is largely limited by physical factors: the length of the bus and the number of devices. These physical limits prevent us from running the bus arbitrarily fast. Within these limits, there are a variety of techniques we can use to increase the performance of the bus; however, these techniques may adversely affect other performance metrics. For example, to obtain fast response time for I/O operations, we must minimize the bus latency by streamlining the communication path. On the other hand, to sustain high I/O data rates, we must maximize the bus bandwidth. The bus bandwidth can be increased by using more buffering and by communicating larger blocks of data, both of which increase the bus latency! Clearly, these two goals, low latency and high bandwidth, can lead to conflicting design requirements. Finally, the need to support a range of devices with widely varying latencies and data transfer rates also makes bus design challenging.

A bus generally contains a set of control lines and a set of data lines. The control lines are used to signal requests and acknowledgments, and to indicate what type of information is on the data lines. The data lines of the bus carry information between the source and the destination. This information may consist of data, complex commands, or addresses. For example, if a disk wants to write some data into memory from a disk sector, the data lines will be used to indicate the address in memory in which to place the data as well as to carry the actual data from the disk. The control lines will be used to indicate what type of information is contained on the data lines of the bus at each point in the transfer. Some buses have two sets of signal lines to separately communicate both data and address in a single bus transmission. In either case, the control lines are used to indicate what the bus contains and to implement the bus protocol. And because the bus is shared, we also need a protocol to decide who uses it next; we will discuss this problem shortly.

Let's consider a typical *bus transaction*. A bus transaction includes two parts: sending the address and receiving or sending the data. Bus transactions are typically defined by what they do to memory. A *read* transaction transfers data *from* memory (to either the processor or an I/O device), and a *write* transaction writes data to the memory. Clearly, this terminology is confusing. To avoid this, we'll try to use the terms *input* and *output*, which are always defined from the perspective of the processor. Figure 8.7 shows the steps in a typical output operation, in which data will be read from memory and sent to the device. Figure 8.8 shows the steps in an input operation where data is read from the device and written to memory. In both figures, the active portions of the bus and memory are shown in color, and a read or write is shown by shading the unit, as we did in Chapter 6.

Types of Buses

Buses are traditionally classified as one of three types: *processor-memory buses*, *I/O buses*, or *backplane buses*. Processor-memory buses are short, generally high speed, and matched to the memory system so as to maximize memory-processor bandwidth. I/O buses, by contrast, can be lengthy, can have many types of devices connected to them, and often have a wide range in the data bandwidth of the devices connected to them. I/O buses do not typically interface directly to the memory, but use either a processor-memory or a backplane bus to connect to memory. Backplane buses are designed to allow processors, memory, and I/O devices to coexist on a single bus; they balance the demands of processor-memory communication with the demands of I/O device-memory communication. Backplane buses received their name because they were often built into the *backplane*, an interconnection structure within the chassis; processor, memory, and I/O boards would then plug into the backplane using the bus for communication.

Processor-memory buses are often design-specific, while both I/O buses and backplane buses are frequently re-used in different machines. In fact, backplane and I/O buses are often *standard buses* that are used by many different computers manufactured by different companies. By comparison, processor-memory buses are often proprietary, although in many recent machines

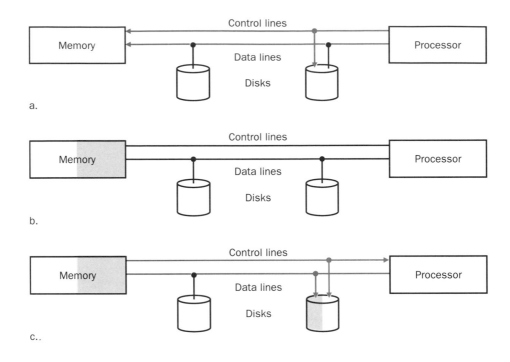

FIGURE 8.7 The three steps of an output operation. In each step the active participants in the communication are shown in color. Notice that the data lines of the bus can carry both an address (as in step a) and data (as in step c). (a) First step in an output operation that reads from memory. The control lines indicate a read request, while the data lines contain the address. (b) Second step in an output operation. The memory is accessing the data. (c) Third and final step in an output operation. The memory transfers the data using the data lines of the bus, signaling that the data is available with the control lines. The device stores the data as it appears on the bus.

they may be the backplane bus, and the standard or I/O buses plug into the processor-memory bus. In many recent machines, the distinction among these bus types, especially between backplane buses and processor-memory buses, may be very minor.

During the design phase, the designer of a processor-memory bus knows all the types of devices that must connect to the bus, while the I/O or backplane bus designer must design the bus to handle unknown devices that vary in latency and bandwidth characteristics. Normally, an I/O bus presents a fairly simple and low-level interface to a device, requiring minimal additional electronics to interface to the bus. A backplane bus usually requires additional logic to interface between the bus and a device or between the backplane bus and a lower level I/O bus. A backplane bus offers the cost advantage of a

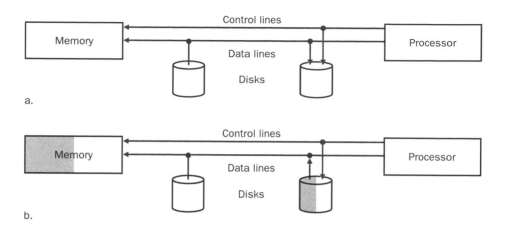

FIGURE 8.8 An input operation takes less active time because the device does not need to wait for memory to access data. In the steps shown, we assume that the device did wait for memory to indicate its readiness, but even this will not be true in some systems. As in the previous figures, the active participants in each step in the communication are shown in color. The shading on the memory in step (b) indicates that it is writing. (a) First step in an input operation. The control lines indicate a write request for memory, while the data lines contain the address. (b) When the memory is ready, it signals the device, which then transfers the data. Typically, the memory will store the data as it receives it. The device need not wait for the store to be completed.

single bus. Figure 8.9 shows a system using a single backplane bus, a system using a processor-memory bus with attached I/O buses, and a system using all three types of buses. Machines with a separate processor-memory bus normally use a bus adapter to connect the I/O bus to the processor-memory bus. Some high-performance, expandable systems use an organization that combines the three buses: the processor-memory bus has one or more bus adaptors that interface a standard backplane bus to the processor-memory bus. I/O buses, as well as device controllers, can plug into the backplane bus. The IBM RS/6000 and Silicon Graphics multiprocessors use this type of organization. This organization offers the advantage that the processor-memory bus can be made much faster than a backplane or I/O bus and that the I/O system can be expanded by plugging many I/O controllers or buses into the backplane bus, which will not affect the speed of the processor-memory bus.

Synchronous and Asynchronous Buses

The substantial differences between the circumstances under which a processor-memory bus and an I/O bus or backplane bus are designed lead to two

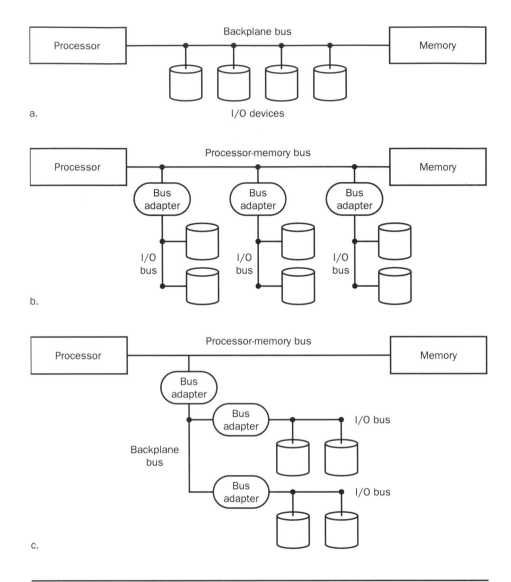

FIGURE 8.9 Many machines use a single backplane bus for both processor–memory and I/O traffic. Some high-performance machines use a separate processor–memory bus that I/O buses "plug" into. Some systems make use of all three types of buses, organized in a hierarchy. (a) A single bus used for processor to memory communication, as well as communication between I/O devices and memory. The bus used in an IBM PC has this structure. (b) A separate bus is used for processor–memory traffic. To communicate data between memory and I/O devices, the I/O buses interface to the processor–memory bus, using a bus adapter. The bus adapter provides speed-matching between the buses. In an Apple Macintosh-II, the processor memory bus is a NuBus (a backplane bus) that has I/O devices that interface directly as well as an I/O bus that plugs into the NuBus; the latter is a SCSI bus. (c) A separate bus is used for processor-memory traffic. A small number of backplane buses tap into the processor–memory bus. The processor–memory buses interface to the lower level I/O bus. This is usually done with a single-chip controller, such as a SCSI bus controller. An advantage of this organization is the small number of taps into the high-speed processor–memory bus. *(page 552)*

different schemes for communication on the bus: *synchronous* and *asynchronous*. If a bus is synchronous, it includes a clock in the control lines and a fixed protocol for communicating that is relative to the clock. For example, for a processor-memory bus performing a read from memory, we might have a protocol that transmits the address and read commands on the first clock cycle, using the address lines to indicate the type of request. The memory might then be required to respond with the data word on the fifth clock. This type of protocol can be implemented easily in a small finite state machine. Because the protocol is predetermined and involves little logic, the bus can run very fast and the interface logic will be small. Synchronous buses have two major disadvantages, however. First, every device on the bus must run at the same clock rate. Second, because of clock-skew problems, synchronous buses cannot be long if they are fast (see Appendix B for a discussion of clock skew). Processor-memory buses are often synchronous because the devices communicating are close, small in number, and prepared to operate at high clock rates.

An asynchronous bus is not clocked. Because it is not clocked, an asynchronous bus can accommodate a wide variety of devices, and the bus can be lengthened without worrying about clock skew or synchronization problems. To coordinate the transmission of data between sender and receiver, an asynchronous bus uses a *handshaking protocol*. A handshaking protocol consists of a series of steps in which the sender and receiver proceed to the next step only when both parties agree. The protocol is implemented with an additional set of control lines.

A simple example will illustrate how asynchronous buses work. Let's consider a device requesting a word of data from the memory system. Assume that there are three control lines:

1. *ReadReq*: Used to indicate a read request for memory. The address is put on the data lines at the same time.

2. *DataRdy*: Used to indicate that the data word is now ready on the data lines. In an output transaction, the memory will assert this signal since it is providing the data. In an input transaction, an I/O device would assert this signal, since it would provide data. In either case, the data is placed on the data lines at the same time.

3. *Ack*: Used to acknowledge the ReadReq or the DataRdy signal of the other party.

In an asynchronous protocol, the control signals ReadReq and DataRdy are asserted until the other party (the memory or the device) indicates that the control lines have been seen and the data lines have been read; this indication is made by asserting the Ack line. This complete process is called *handshaking*.

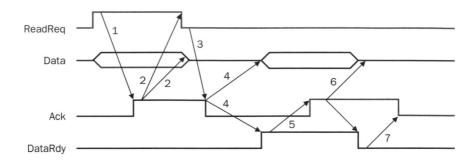

The steps in the protocol begin immediately after the device signals a request by raising ReadReq and putting the address on the Data lines:

1. When Memory sees the ReadReq line, it reads the address from the data bus and raises Ack to indicate it has been seen.
2. I/O device sees the Ack line high and releases the ReadReq and data lines.
3. Memory sees that ReadReq is low and drops the Ack line to acknowledge the Readreq signal.
4. This step starts when the memory has the data ready. It places the data from the read request on the data lines and raises DataRdy.
5. The I/O device sees DataRdy, reads the data from the bus, and signals that it has the data by raising Ack.
6. The memory sees the Ack signal, drops DataRdy, and releases the data lines.
7. Finally, the I/O device, seeing DataRdy go low, drops the Ack line, which indicates that the transmission is completed.

A new bus transaction can now begin.

FIGURE 8.10 The asynchronous handshaking protocol consists of seven steps to read a word from memory and receive it in an I/O device. The signals in color are those asserted by the I/O device, while the memory asserts the signals shown in black. The arrows label the seven steps and the event that triggers each step. The symbol showing two lines (high and low) at the same time on the data lines indicates that the data lines have valid data at this point. (The symbol indicates that the data is valid, but the value is not known.)

Figure 8.10 shows how such a protocol operates by depicting the steps in the communication.

An asynchronous bus protocol works like a pair of finite state machines that are communicating in such a way that a machine does not proceed until it knows that another machine has reached a certain state; thus, the two machines are coordinated.

The handshaking protocol does not solve all the problems of communicating between a sender and receiver that have different clocks. An additional problem arises when we sample an asynchronous signal (such as ReadReq). This problem, called a synchronization failure, can lead to unpredictable behavior; it can be overcome with devices called *synchronizers*, which are described in Appendix B.

Example

Show how the control for an input transaction from an I/O device to memory (as in Figure 8.8) can be implemented as a pair of finite state machines.

Answer

Figure 8.11 shows the two finite state machine controllers that implement the handshaking protocol of Figure 8.10.

If a synchronous bus can be used, it is usually faster than an asynchronous bus because of the overhead required to perform the handshaking. An example demonstrates this.

Example

We want to compare the maximum bandwidth for a synchronous and an asynchronous bus. The synchronous bus has a clock cycle time of 50 ns, and each bus transmission takes 1 clock cycle. The asynchronous bus requires 40 ns per handshake. The data portion of both buses is 32 bits wide. Find the bandwidth for each bus when performing one-word reads from a 200-ns memory.

Answer

First, the synchronous bus, which has 50-ns bus cycles. The steps and times required for the synchronous bus are as follows:

1. Send the address to memory: 50 ns.

2. Read the memory: 200 ns.

3. Send the data to the device: 50 ns.

Thus, the total time is 300 ns. This yields a maximum bus bandwidth of 4 bytes every 300 ns, or

$$\frac{4 \text{ bytes}}{300 \text{ ns}} = \frac{4 \text{ MB}}{0.3 \text{ seconds}} = 13.3 \frac{\text{MB}}{\text{second}}$$

At first glance, it might appear that the asynchronous bus will be *much* slower, since it will take seven steps, each at least 40 ns, and the step corresponding to the memory access will take 200 ns. If we look carefully at Figure 8.10, we realize that several of the steps can be overlapped with the memory access time. In particular, the memory receives the address at the end of step 1 and does not need to put the data on the bus until the beginning of step 5; steps 2, 3, and 4 can overlap with the memory access time. This leads to the following timing:

Step 1: 40 ns

Steps 2, 3, 4: maximum (3 x 40 ns, 200 ns) = 200 ns

Steps 5, 6, 7: 3 x 40 ns = 120 ns

Thus, the total time to perform the transfer is 360 ns, and the maximum bandwidth is

$$\frac{4 \text{ bytes}}{360 \text{ ns}} = \frac{4 \text{ MB}}{0.36} = 11.1 \frac{\text{MB}}{\text{second}}$$

Accordingly, the synchronous bus is only about 20% faster. Of course, to sustain these rates, the device and memory system on the asynchronous bus will need to be fairly fast to accomplish each handshaking step in 40 ns.

Even though a synchronous bus may be faster, the choice between a synchronous and an asynchronous bus has implications not only for data bandwidth but also for an I/O system's capacity in terms of physical distance and the number of devices that can be connected to the bus. Asynchronous buses scale better with technology changes and can support a wider variety of device response speeds. It is for these reasons that I/O buses are often asynchronous, despite the increased overhead.

Increasing the Bus Bandwidth

Although much of the bandwidth of a bus is decided by the choice of a synchronous or asynchronous protocol and the timing characteristics of the bus, several other factors affect the bandwidth that can be attained by a single transfer. The most important of these are

1. *Data bus width*: By increasing the width of the data bus, transfers of multiple words require fewer bus cycles.

2. *Separate versus multiplexed address and data lines*: Our example in Figure 8.8 used the same wires for address and data; including separate lines for addresses will make the performance of writes faster, because the address and data can be transmitted in one bus cycle.

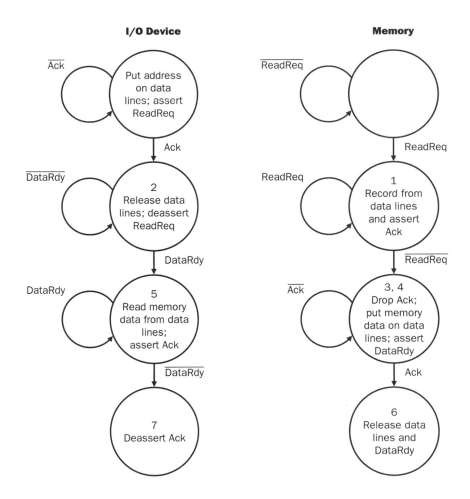

FIGURE 8.11 These finite state machines implement the control for the handshaking protocol illustrated in Figure 8.10. The numbers in each state correspond to the steps shown in Figure 8.10. The first state of the I/O device (upper left corner) starts the protocol, just as in Figure 8.10. Each state in the finite state machine effectively records the state of both the device and memory. This is how they stay synchronized during the transaction.

3. *Block transfers*: Allowing the bus to transfer multiple words in back-to-back bus cycles without sending an address or releasing the bus will reduce the time needed to transfer a large block.

Each of these design alternatives will increase the bus performance for a single bus transfer. The cost of implementing one of these enhancements is one or more of the following: more bus lines, increased complexity, or increased response time for requests that may need to wait while a long block transfer occurs.

Elaboration: Another method for increasing the effective bus bandwidth when multiple parties want to communicate on the bus is to release the bus when it is not being used for transmitting information. Consider the example of a memory read that we examined in Figure 8.10. What happens to the bus while the memory access is occurring? In this simple protocol, the device and memory continue to hold the bus during the memory access time when no actual transfer is taking place. An alternative protocol, which releases the bus, would operate like this:

1. The device signals the memory and transmits the request and address.

2. After the memory acknowledges the request, both the memory and device release all control lines.

3. The memory access occurs, and the bus is free for other uses during this period.

4. The memory signals the device on the bus to indicate that the data is available.

5. The device receives the data via the bus and signals that it has the data, so the memory system can release the bus.

For the synchronous bus in the example above, such a scheme would occupy the bus for only 100 of the 300 ns required for the complete bus transaction.

This type of protocol is called a *split transaction protocol*. The advantage of such a protocol is that, by freeing the bus during the time data is not being transmitted, the protocol allows another requestor to use the bus. This can improve the effective bus bandwidth for the entire system, if the memory is sophisticated enough to handle multiple, overlapping transactions.

With a split transaction, however, the time to complete one transfer is probably increased because the bus must be acquired twice. Split transaction protocols are also more expensive to implement, primarily because of the need to keep track of the other party in a communication. In a split transaction protocol, the memory system must contact the requestor to initiate the reply portion of the bus transaction, so the identity of the requestor must be transmitted and retained by the memory system.

Obtaining Access to the Bus

Now that we have reviewed some of the many design options for buses, we can deal with one of the most important issues in bus design: How is the bus reserved by a device that wishes to use it to communicate? We touched on this question in several of the above discussions, and it is crucial in designing large I/O systems that allow I/O to occur without the processor's continuous and low-level involvement.

Why is a scheme needed for controlling bus access? Without any control, multiple devices desiring to communicate could each try to assert the control and data lines for different transfers! Just as chaos reigns in a classroom when everyone tries to talk at once, multiple devices trying to use the bus simultaneously would result in confusion.

Chaos is avoided by introducing one or more *bus masters* into the system. A bus master controls access to the bus: it must initiate and control all bus requests. The processor must be able to initiate a bus request for memory and thus is always a bus master. The memory is usually a *slave*—since it will respond to read and write requests but never generate its own requests.

The simplest system possible has a single bus master: the processor. Having a single bus master is similar to what normally happens in a classroom—all communication requires the permission of the instructor. In a single master system, all bus requests must be controlled by the processor. The steps involved in a bus transaction with a single master bus are shown in Figure 8.12. The major drawback of this approach is that the processor must be involved in every bus transaction. A single sector read from a disk may require the processor to get involved hundreds to thousands of times, depending on the size of each transfer. Because devices have become faster and capable of transferring at much higher bandwidths, involving the processor in every bus transaction has become less and less attractive.

The alternative scheme is to have multiple bus masters, each of which can initiate a transfer. If we want to allow several people in a classroom to talk without the instructor having to recognize each one, we must have a protocol for deciding who gets to talk next. Similarly, with multiple bus masters, we must provide a mechanism for arbitrating access to the bus so that it is used in a cooperative rather than a chaotic way.

Bus Arbitration

Deciding which bus master gets to use the bus next is called *bus arbitration*. There are a wide variety of schemes for bus arbitration; these may involve special hardware or extremely sophisticated bus protocols. In a bus arbitration scheme, a device (or the processor) wanting to use the bus signals a *bus request* and is later *granted* the bus. After a grant, the device can use the bus, later signaling to the arbiter that the bus is no longer required. The arbiter can then grant the bus to another device. Most multiple-master buses have a set of bus lines for performing requests and grants. A bus release line is also needed if each device does not have its own request line. Sometimes the signals used for bus arbitration have physically separate lines, while in other systems the data lines of the bus are used for this function (though this prevents overlapping of arbitration with transfer).

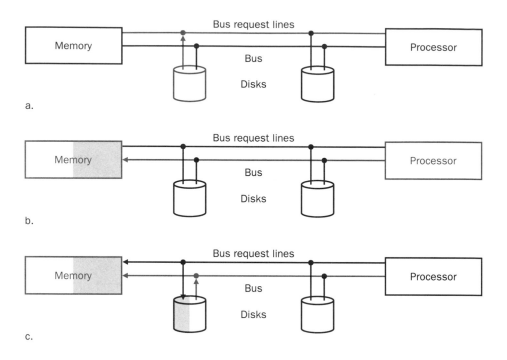

FIGURE 8.12 The initial steps in a bus transaction with a single master (the processor). A set of bus request lines is used by the device to communicate with the processor, which then initiates the bus cycle on behalf of the requesting device. The active lines and units are shown in color in each step. Shading is used to indicate the source of a read (memory) or destination of a write (the disk). After step c, the bus cycle continues like a normal read transaction, as in Figure 8.7. (a) First, the device generates a bus request to indicate to the processor that the device wants to use the bus. (b) The processor responds and generates appropriate bus control signals. For example, if the device wants to perform output from memory, the processor asserts the read request lines to memory. (c) The processor also notifies the device that its bus request is being processed; as a result, the device knows it can use the bus and places the address for the request on the bus.

Arbitration schemes usually try to balance two factors in choosing which device to grant the bus. First, each device has a *bus priority*, and the highest priority device should be serviced first. Second, we would prefer that any device, even one with low priority, never be completely locked out from the bus. This property, called *fairness*, ensures that every device that wants to use the bus is guaranteed to get it eventually. In addition to these factors, more sophisticated schemes aim at reducing the time needed to arbitrate for the bus. Because arbitration time is overhead and increases latency, it should be reduced and overlapped with bus transfers whenever possible.

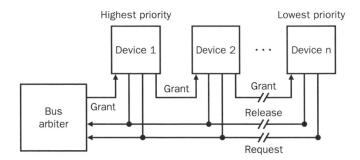

FIGURE 8.13 A daisy chain bus uses a bus grant line that chains through each device from highest to lowest priority. If the device has requested bus access, it uses the grant line to determine access has been given to it. Because the grant line is passed on only if a device does not want access, priority is built into the scheme. The name daisy chain arises from the structure of the grant line that chains from device to device. The detailed protocol used by a daisy chain is described in an elaboration on page 562.

Bus arbitration schemes can be divided into four broad classes:

- *Daisy chain arbitration*: In this scheme, the bus grant line is run through the devices from highest priority to lowest (the priorities are determined by the position on the bus). A high-priority device that desires bus access simply intercepts the bus grant signal, not allowing a lower priority device to see the signal. Figure 8.13 shows how a daisy chain bus is organized. The advantage of a daisy chain bus is simplicity; the disadvantages are that it cannot assure fairness—a low-priority request may be locked out indefinitely—and the use of the daisy chain grant signal also limits the bus speed. The *VME* bus, a standard backplane bus, uses multiple daisy chains for arbitration.

- *Centralized, parallel arbitration*: These schemes use multiple request lines, and the devices independently request the bus. A centralized arbiter chooses from among the devices requesting bus access and notifies the selected device that it is now bus master. The disadvantage of this scheme is that it requires a central arbiter, which may become the bottleneck for bus usage.

- *Distributed arbitration by self-selection*: These schemes also use multiple request lines, but the devices requesting bus access determine who will be granted access. Each device wanting bus access places a code indicating its identity on the bus. By examining the bus, the devices can determine the highest priority device that has made a request. There is no need for a central arbiter; each device determines independently whether it is the high-priority requestor. This scheme, however, does require more lines for request signals. The NuBus, which is the backplane bus in Apple Macintosh IIs, uses this scheme.

- *Distributed arbitration by collision detection*: In this scheme, each device independently requests the bus. Multiple simultaneous requests result in a *collision*. The collision is detected and a scheme for selecting among the colliding parties is used. Ethernets, which use this scheme, are further described in Exercise 8.20 on page 591.

The suitability of different arbitration schemes is determined by a variety of factors including how expandable the bus must be both in terms of the number of I/O devices and the bus length, how fast the arbitration should be, and what degree of fairness is needed.

Elaboration: The protocol followed by a device on a daisy chain bus is

1. Signal the request line.

2. Wait for a transition on the grant line from low to high, indicating that the bus is being reassigned. Intercept the grant signal, and do not allow lower priority devices to see it. Drop the winning device's request.

3. Use the bus.

4. Signal that the bus is no longer required by asserting the release line.

By watching for a transition on the grant line, rather than just a level, we prevent the device from taking the bus away from a lower priority device that believes it has been granted bus access. To improve fairness in a daisy chain scheme, we can simply make the rule that a device that has just used the bus cannot reacquire the bus until it sees the bus request line go low. Since a device will not release the request line until its request is satisfied, all devices will have an opportunity to use the bus before any single device uses it twice. Some bus systems—VME, for example—use multiple daisy chains with a separate set of request and grant lines for each daisy chain and a priority encoder to select from among the multiple requests.

Bus Standards

Most computers allow users to add additional and even new types of peripherals. The I/O bus serves as a way of expanding the machine and connecting new peripherals. To make this easier, the computer industry has developed several bus standards. The standards serve as a specification for the computer manufacturer and for the peripheral manufacturer. A bus standard ensures the computer designer that peripherals will be available for a new machine, and it ensures the peripheral builder that users will be able to hook up their new equipment.

The Big Picture

The different bus characteristics allow the creation of buses optimized for a wide range of different devices, number of devices, and bandwidth demands.

Figure 8.14 shows some of the design alternatives we have discussed and what choices might be made in low-cost versus high-performance systems. In general, higher cost systems use wider and faster buses with more sophisticated protocols—typically a synchronous bus for the reasons we saw in the example on page 555. In contrast, a low-cost system favors a bus that is narrower and does not require intelligence among the devices (hence a single master), and is asynchronous so that low-speed devices can interface inexpensively.

Option	High performance	Low cost
Bus width	Separate address and data lines	Multiplex address and data lines
Data width	Wider is faster (e.g., 32 bits)	Narrower is cheaper (e.g., 8 bits)
Transfer size	Multiple words require less bus overhead	Single-word transfer is simpler
Bus masters	Multiple masters (requires arbitration)	Single master (no arbitration)
Clocking	Synchronous	Asynchronous

FIGURE 8.14 The I/O bus characteristics determine the performance of I/O transfers, the number of I/O buses that can be connected, and the cost of connecting devices. Shorter buses can be faster, but will not be as expandable. Similarly, wider buses can have higher bandwidth but will be more expensive. Split transaction buses are another way to increase bandwidth at the expense of cost (see the Elaboration on page 558).

Machines sometimes become so popular that their I/O buses become de facto standards, as is the case with the IBM PC-AT bus. Once a bus standard is heavily used by peripheral designers, other computer manufacturers incorporate that bus and offer a wide range of peripherals. Sometimes standards are created by groups that are trying to address a common problem. The *intelligent peripheral interface* (IPI), *small computer system interface* (SCSI), and Ethernet are examples of standards that arose from the cooperation of manufacturers. Sanctioning bodies like ANSI or IEEE also create and approve standards. The Futurebus standard was created by an IEEE standards committee.

Characteristic	VME Bus	NuBus	FutureBus	IPI	SCSI
Bus type	Backplane	Backplane	Backplane	I/O	I/O
Bus width (signals)	128	96	96	16	8
Address/data multiplexed?	Not multiplexed	Multiplexed	Multiplexed	N/A	N/A
Data width (primary)	16–32 bits	32 bits	32 bits	16 bits	8 bits
Number of bus masters	Multiple	Multiple	Multiple	Single	Multiple
Arbitration	Multiple daisy chain	Distributed self-selection	Distributed self-selection	NA	Self-selection
Clocking	Asynchronous	Synchronous	Asynchronous	Asynchronous	Either
Bandwidth, 150-ns memory, single word	12.9 MB/sec	13.2 MB/sec	15.5 MB/sec	25.0 MB/sec	5.0 MB/sec or 1.5 MB/sec
Bandwidth, 150-ns memory, multiple words (infinite length)	13.6 MB/sec	26.4 MB/sec	20.8 MB/sec	25.0 MB/sec	5.0 MB/sec or 1.5 MB/sec
Maximum number of devices	21	16	20	8	7
Maximum bus length	0.5 meter	0.5 meter	0.5 meter	50 meters	25 meters
Standard name	IEEE 1014	pending	IEEE 896.1	ANSI X3.129	ANSI X3.131

FIGURE 8.15 Key characteristics of five different bus standards. The first three buses are backplane buses and the last two are I/O buses. For the backplane buses, the bandwidth calculations assume a fully loaded bus and are given for both single-word transfers and block transfers of unlimited length; measurements are shown assuming 150 ns access time. All these buses can perform single-word or multiword transfers. The bandwidth for the I/O buses is given as their maximum data transfer rate. The SCSI standard offers either asynchronous or synchronous I/O; the asynchronous version transfers at 1.5 MB/sec and the synchronous at 5 MB/sec.

Figure 8.15 summarizes the key characteristics of several bus standards. Two different types of buses are included in this figure. The first three (VME, NuBus, and FutureBus) are general-purpose, backplane buses designed for interconnecting processors, memory, and I/O devices. The last two (IPI and SCSI) are I/O buses. Connecting these buses to memory requires a controller that interfaces the devices on the I/O bus to a processor-memory bus. The controller coordinates transfers from a device on the I/O bus to the memory via the processor-memory bus.

Bus bandwidth for a general-purpose bus containing memory is not simply a single number. Because of bus overhead, the size of the transfer affects bandwidth significantly. Since the bus usually transfers to or from memory, the speed of the memory also affects the bandwidth.

Buses provide the electrical interconnect among I/O devices, processors, and memory, and also define the lowest level protocol for communication. Above this basic level, we must define hardware and software protocols for controlling data transfers between I/O devices and memory, and for the processor to specify commands to the I/O devices. These topics are covered in the next section.

Interfacing I/O Devices to the Memory, Processor, and Operating System

A bus protocol defines how a word or block of data should be communicated on a set of wires. This still leaves several other tasks that must be performed to actually cause data to be transferred from a device and into the memory address space of some user program. This section focuses on these tasks and will answer such questions as:

- How is a user I/O request transformed into a device command and communicated to the device?
- How are data actually transferred to or from a memory location?
- What is the role of the operating system?

As we will see when we answer these questions, the operating system plays a major role in handling I/O, acting as the interface between the hardware and the program that requests I/O.

The responsibilities of the operating system arise from three characteristics of I/O systems:

1. The I/O system is shared by multiple programs using the processor.

2. I/O systems often use interrupts (externally generated exceptions) to communicate information about I/O operations. Because interrupts cause a transfer to kernel or supervisor mode, they must be handled by the operating system (OS).

3. The low-level control of an I/O device is complex because it requires managing a set of concurrent events and because the requirements for correct device control are often very detailed.

Hardware Software Interface

The three characteristics of I/O systems above lead to several different functions the OS must provide:

- The OS guarantees that a user's program accesses only the portions of an I/O device to which the user has rights. For example, the OS must not allow a program to read or write a file on disk if the owner of the file has not granted access to this program. In a system with shared I/O devices, protection could not be provided if user programs could perform I/O directly.

- The OS provides abstractions for accessing devices by supplying routines that handle low-level device operations.

- The OS handles the interrupts generated by I/O devices, just as it handles the exceptions generated by a program.

- The OS tries to provide equitable access to the shared I/O resources, as well as schedule accesses in order to enhance system throughput.

To perform these functions on behalf of user programs, the operating system must be able to communicate with the I/O devices and to prevent the user program from communicating with the I/O devices directly. Three types of communication are required:

1. The OS must be able to give commands to the I/O devices. These commands include not only operations like read and write, but other operations to be done on the device, such as a disk seek.

2. The device must be able to notify the OS when the I/O device has completed an operation or has encountered an error. For example, when a disk has completed a seek, it will notify the OS.

3. Data must be transferred between memory and an I/O device. For example, the block being read on a disk read must be moved from disk to memory.

In the next few sections, we will see how these communications are performed.

Giving Commands to I/O Devices

To give a command to an I/O device, the processor must be able to address the device and to supply one or more command words. Two methods are used to address the device: *memory-mapped* I/O and special I/O instructions. In memory-mapped I/O, portions of the address space are assigned to I/O devices. Reads and writes to those addresses are interpreted as commands to the I/O device.

For example, a write operation can be used to send data to an I/O device where the data will be interpreted as a command. When the processor places the address and data on the memory bus, the memory system ignores the operation, because the address indicates a portion of the memory space used for I/O. The device controller, however, sees the operation, records the data, and transmits it to the device as a command. User programs are prevented from issuing I/O operations directly, because the OS does not provide access to the address space assigned to the I/O devices and thus the addresses are protected by the address translation. Memory-mapped I/O can also be used to transmit data by writing or reading to select addresses. The device uses the address to determine the type of command and the data may be provided by a write or obtained by a read. In any event, the address accessed by the instructions encodes both the device identity and the type of transmission between processor and device.

Actually performing a read or write of data to fulfill a program request usually requires several separate I/O operations. Furthermore, the processor may have to interrogate the status of the device between individual commands to determine whether the command completed successfully. For example, the DEC LP11 line printer has two I/O device registers—one for status information and one for data to be printed. The Status register contains a *done bit*, set by the printer when it has printed a character, and an *error bit*, indicating that the printer is jammed or out of paper. Each byte of data to be printed is put into the Data register. The processor must then wait until the printer sets the done bit before it can place another character in the buffer. The processor must also check the error bit to determine if a problem has occurred. Each of these operations requires a separate I/O device access.

Elaboration: The alternative to memory-mapped I/O is to use dedicated I/O instructions in the processor. These I/O instructions can specify both the device number and the command word (or the location of the command word in memory). The processor communicates the device address via a set of wires normally included as part of the I/O bus. The actual command can be transmitted over the data lines in the bus. Examples of computers with I/O instructions are the Intel 80x86 and the IBM 370 computers. By making the I/O instructions illegal to execute when not in kernel or supervisor mode, user programs can be prevented from accessing the devices directly.

Communicating with the Processor

The process of periodically checking status bits to see if it is time for the next I/O operation, as in the previous example, is called *polling*. Polling is the simplest way for an I/O device to communicate with the processor. The I/O device simply puts the information in a Status register, and the processor must come and get the information. The processor is totally in control and does all the work. A mouse is an input-only device that is usually accessed by polling.

The disadvantage of polling is that it can waste a lot of processor time because processors are so much faster than I/O devices. The processor may read the Status register many times, only to find that the device has not yet completed a comparatively slow I/O operation, or that the mouse has not budged since the last time it was polled. When the device has completed an operation, we must still read the status to determine whether it was successful.

Example

Let's determine the impact of polling overhead for three different devices. Assume that the number of clock cycles for a polling operation is 100 and that the processor executes with a 50-MHz clock.

Determine the fraction of CPU time consumed for the following three cases, assuming that you poll often enough so that no data is ever lost:

1. The mouse must be polled 30 times per second to ensure that we do not miss any movement made by the user.

2. The floppy disk transfers data to the processor in 16-bit units and has a data rate of 50 KB/second. No data transfer can be missed.

3. The hard disk transfers data in one-word chunks and can transfer at 2 MB/second. Again, no transfer can be missed.

Answer

First the mouse:

$$\text{Clock cycles per second for polling } = 30 \times 100 = 3000 \text{ cycles per second}$$

$$\text{Fraction of the processor clock cycles consumed } = \frac{3000}{50 \times 10^6} = 0.006\%$$

Polling can clearly be used for the mouse without much performance impact on the processor.

For the floppy disk, the rate at which we must poll is

$$\frac{50 \dfrac{\text{KB}}{\text{second}}}{2 \dfrac{\text{bytes}}{\text{polling access}}} = 25\text{K} \frac{\text{polling accesses}}{\text{second}} = 25 \times 2^{10} \frac{\text{polling accesses}}{\text{second}}$$

Thus, we can compute the number of cycles (converting from K to 1024, as well):

$$\text{Cycles per second for polling } = 25 \times 2^{10} \times 100$$

$$= 25.6 \times 10^5 \text{ clock cycles per second}$$

$$\text{Fraction of the processor consumed } = \frac{25.6 \times 10^5}{50 \times 10^6} = 5\%$$

This amount of overhead is substantial, but might be tolerable in a low-end system with only a few I/O devices like this floppy disk.

In the case of the hard disk, we must poll at a rate equal to the data rate in words, which is 500K times per second (2 MB per second/4 bytes per transfer). Thus,

$$\text{Cycles per second for polling} = 500 \times 2^{10} \times 100$$

$$= 51.2 \times 10^6 \text{cycles per second}$$

$$\text{Fraction of the processor consumed} = \frac{51.2 \times 10^6}{50 \times 10^6} = 100\%$$

Thus the processor is totally consumed by polling the disk. Clearly, polling will not be acceptable for a hard disk on this machine.

The overhead in a polling interface was recognized long ago, leading to the invention of interrupts to notify the processor when an I/O device requires attention from the processor. *Interrupt-driven* I/O, which is used by almost all systems for at least some devices, employs I/O interrupts to indicate to the processor that an I/O device needs attention. When a device wants to notify the processor that it has completed some operation or needs attention, it causes the processor to be interrupted.

An I/O interrupt is just like the exceptions we saw in Chapters 5, 6, and 7, with two important exceptions:

1. An I/O interrupt is asynchronous with respect to the instruction execution. That is, the interrupt is not associated with any instruction and does not prevent the instruction completion. This is very different from either page fault exceptions or exceptions such as arithmetic overflow. Our control unit need only check for a pending I/O interrupt at the time it starts a new instruction.

2. In addition to the fact that an I/O interrupt has occurred, we would like to convey further information such as the identity of the device generating the interrupt. Furthermore, the interrupts represent devices that may have different priorities and whose interrupt requests have different urgencies associated with them.

To communicate information to the processor, such as the identity of the device raising the interrupt, a system can use either vectored interrupts or an exception Cause register. When the interrupt is recognized by the processor, the device can send either the vector address or a status field to place in the Cause register. As a result, when the OS gets control it knows the identity of the device that caused the interrupt and can immediately interrogate the device. An interrupt mechanism eliminates the need for the processor to poll the device and instead allows the processor to focus on executing programs.

Elaboration: To deal with the different priorities of the I/O devices, most interrupt mechanisms have several levels of priority. These priorities indicate the order in which the processor should process them. Both internally generated exceptions and I/O interrupts have priorities; typically, I/O interrupts have lower priority than internal exceptions. There may be multiple I/O interrupt priorities, with high-speed devices associated with the higher priorities. If the exception mechanism is vectored (see Chapter 5, section 5.6), the vector address for a fast device will correspond to the higher priority interrupt. If a Cause register is used, then the register contents for a faster device are set for the higher priority interrupt.

Transferring the Data between a Device and Memory

We have seen two different methods that enable a device to communicate with the processor. These two techniques, polling and I/O interrupts, form the basis for two methods of implementing the transfer of data between the I/O device and memory. Both these techniques work best with lower bandwidth devices, where we are more interested in reducing the cost of the device controller and interface than in a providing a high-bandwidth transfer. Both polling and interrupt-driven transfers put the burden of moving data and managing the transfer on the processor. After looking at these two schemes, we will examine a scheme more suitable for higher performance devices or collections of devices.

We can use the processor to transfer data between a device and memory based on polling. Consider our mouse example. The processor can periodically read the mouse counter values and the position of the mouse buttons. If the position of the mouse or one of its buttons has changed, the operating system can notify the program associated with interpreting the mouse changes.

An alternative mechanism is to make the transfer of data *interrupt driven*. In this case, the OS would still transfer data in small numbers of bytes from or to the device. But because the I/O operation is interrupt driven, the OS simply works on other tasks while data is being read from or written to the device. When the OS recognizes an interrupt from the device, it reads the status to check for errors. If there are none, the OS can supply the next piece of data, for example, by a sequence of memory-mapped writes. When the last byte of an I/O request has been transmitted and the I/O operation is completed, the OS can inform the program. The processor and OS do all the work in this process, accessing the device and memory for each data item transferred. Let's see how an interrupt-driven I/O interface might work for the floppy disk.

Example

Suppose we have the same floppy disk and processor we used in the example on page 568. Assume that it wants to transfer 16-bit quantities at a rate of 50 KB per second. The overhead for each transfer, including the interrupt, is 100 clock cycles. Find the fraction of the processor consumed when the floppy disk is active.

Answer

The rate at which we must interrupt the processor when the disk is transferring:

$$\frac{50\,\dfrac{\text{KB}}{\text{second}}}{2\,\dfrac{\text{bytes}}{\text{polling access}}} = 25\text{K}\,\frac{\text{polling accesses}}{\text{second}} = 25 \times 2^{10}\,\frac{\text{polling accesses}}{\text{second}}$$

Thus,

$$\text{Cycles per second for floppy} = 25 \times 2^{10} \times 100$$

$$= 25.6 \times 10^5 \text{ cycles per second}$$

Fraction of the processor consumed during a transfer

$$= \frac{25.6 \times 10^5}{50 \times 10^6} = 5\%$$

Of course, the floppy disk is not busy 100% of the time, and the processor is undisturbed when the disk is idle, since no polling is required. For example, if the floppy disk is actively transferring only 10% of the time, the overhead is only 0.5%. This absence of overhead when the I/O is inactive is the major advantage of an interrupt-driven interface versus polling.

Interrupt-driven I/O relieves the processor from having to wait for every I/O event, although if we used this method for transferring data from or to a hard disk, the overhead could still be intolerable, since it would consume 100% of the processor when the disk was transferring. For high-bandwidth devices like hard disks, the transfers consist primarily of relatively large blocks of data (hundreds to thousands of bytes). So computer designers invented a mechanism for off-loading the processor and having the device controller transfer data directly to or from the memory without involving the processor. This mechanism is called *direct memory access* (DMA). The interrupt mechanism is still used by the device to communicate with the processor, but only on completion of the I/O transfer or when an error occurs.

DMA is implemented with a specialized controller that transfers data between an I/O device and memory independent of the processor. The DMA controller becomes the bus master and directs the reads or writes between itself and memory. There are three steps in a DMA transfer:

1. The processor sets up the DMA by supplying the identity of the device, the operation to perform on the device, the memory address that is the source or destination of the data to be transferred, and the number of bytes to transfer.

2. The DMA starts the operation on the device and arbitrates for the bus. When the data is available (from the device or memory), it transfers the data. The DMA device supplies the memory address for the read or write. If the request requires more than one transfer on the bus, the DMA unit generates the next memory address and initiates the next transfer. Using this mechanism, a DMA unit can transfer an entire disk sector that may be thousands of bytes in length without bothering the processor. Many DMA controllers contain some buffering to allow them to deal flexibly with delays either in transfer or those incurred while waiting to become bus master.

3. Once the DMA transfer is complete, the controller interrupts the processor, which can then determine by interrogating the DMA device or examining memory whether the entire operation completed successfully.

There may be multiple DMA devices in a computer system. For example, in a system with a single processor-memory bus and multiple I/O buses, each I/O bus controller will often contain a DMA processor that handles any transfers between a device on the I/O bus and the memory. Let's see how much of the processor is consumed using DMA to handle our hard disk example.

Example

Suppose we have the same processor and hard disk as our earlier example on page 568. Assume that the initial set-up of a DMA transfer takes 1000 clock cycles for the processor, and assume the handling of the interrupt at DMA completion requires 500 clock cycles for the processor. The hard disk has a transfer rate of 2 MB/second and uses DMA. If the average transfer from the disk is 4KB, what fraction of the 50-MHz processor is consumed if the disk is actively transferring 100% of the time? Ignore any impact from bus contention between the processor and DMA controller.

Answer

Each DMA transfer takes

$$\frac{4\ \text{KB}}{2\dfrac{\text{MB}}{\text{second}}} = 2 \times 10^{-3}\,\text{seconds}$$

So if the disk is constantly transferring, it requires

$$\frac{1000 + 500\dfrac{\text{cycles}}{\text{transfer}}}{2 \times 10^{-3}\dfrac{\text{seconds}}{\text{transfer}}} = 750 \times 10^3\,\frac{\text{clock cycles}}{\text{second}}$$

Since the processor runs at 50 MHz:

$$\text{Fraction of processor consumed} = \frac{750 \times 10^3}{50 \times 10^6} = 15 \times 10^{-3} = 1.5\%$$

Unlike either polling or interrupt-driven I/O, DMA can be used to interface a hard disk without consuming all the processor cycles for a single I/O. In addition, the disk will not be actively transferring data most of the time, and this number will be considerably lower. Of course, if the processor is also contending for memory, it will be delayed when the memory is busy doing a DMA transfer. By using caches, the processor can avoid having to access memory most of the time, thereby leaving most of the memory bandwidth free for use by I/O devices.

Elaboration: To further reduce the need to interrupt the processor and occupy it in handling an I/O request that may involve doing several actual operations, the I/O controller can be made more intelligent. Intelligent controllers are often called *I/O processors* (as well as *I/O controllers* or *channel controllers*). These specialized processors basically execute a series of I/O operations, called an *I/O program*. The program may be stored in the I/O processor, or it may be stored in memory and fetched by the I/O processor. When using an I/O processor, the operating system typically sets up an I/O program that indicates the I/O operations to be done as well as the size and transfer address for any reads or writes. The I/O processor then takes the operations from the I/O program and interrupts the processor only when the entire program is completed. DMA processors are essentially special-purpose processors (usually single-chip and nonprogrammable), while I/O processors are often implemented with general-purpose microprocessors, which run a specialized I/O program.

Direct Memory Access and the Memory System

When DMA is incorporated into an I/O system, the relationship between the memory system and processor changes. Without DMA, all accesses to the memory system come from the processor and thus proceed through address translation and cache access as if the processor generated the references. With DMA, there is another path to the memory system—one that does not go through the address translation mechanism or the cache hierarchy. This difference generates some problems in both virtual memory systems and systems with caches. These problems are usually solved with a combination of hardware techniques and software support.

Hardware Software Interface
In a system with virtual memory, should DMA work with virtual addresses or physical addresses? The obvious problem with virtual addresses is that the DMA unit will need to translate the virtual addresses to physical addresses. The major problem with DMA in regard to physical addresses is that a transfer cannot easily cross a page boundary. If an I/O request crossed a page boundary, then the memory locations to which it was being transferred would not be contiguous in the physical memory. This is because the memory locations would correspond to multiple virtual pages, each of which could be mapped to any physical page. Consequently, if we use physical addresses, we must constrain all DMA transfers to stay within one page.

One method to allow the system to initiate DMA transfers that cross page boundaries is to make the DMA work on virtual addresses. In such a system, the DMA unit has a small number of map entries that provide virtual-to-physical mapping for a transfer. The operating system provides the mapping when the I/O is initiated. By using this mapping, the DMA unit need not worry about the location of the virtual pages involved in the transfer.

Another technique is for the operating system to break the DMA transfer into a series of transfers, each confined within a single physical page. The transfers are then *chained* together and handed to an I/O processor or intelligent DMA unit that executes the entire sequence of transfers; alternatively, the operating system can individually request the transfers.

Whichever method is used, the operating system must still cooperate by not moving pages around while a DMA transfer involving that page is in progress.

The difficulties in having DMA in a virtual memory system arise because pages have both a physical and a virtual address. DMA also creates problems for systems with caches because there can be two copies of a data item: one in the cache and one in memory. Because the DMA processor issues memory requests directly to the memory rather than through the cache, the value of a memory location seen by the DMA unit and the processor may differ. Consider a read from disk that the DMA unit places directly into memory. If some of the locations into which the DMA writes are in the cache, the processor will receive the old value when it does a read. Similarly, if the cache is write-back, the DMA may read a value directly from memory when a newer value is in the cache, and the value has not been written back. This is called the *stale data problem* or *coherency problem*.

Hardware Software Interface

This problem is avoided by using one of three major techniques. One approach is to route the I/O activity through the cache. This ensures that reads see the latest value while writes update any data in the cache. Routing all I/O through the cache is expensive and potentially has a large negative performance impact on the processor, since the I/O data is rarely used immediately and may displace useful data that a running program needs. A second choice is to have the OS selectively invalidate the cache for an I/O read or force write-backs to occur for an I/O write (often called cache *flushing*). This approach has no hardware drawbacks and is probably more efficient if the software can perform the function easily and efficiently. Because this flushing of large parts of the cache need only happen on DMA block accesses, it will be relatively infrequent. The third approach is to provide a hardware mechanism for selectively flushing (or invalidating) cache entries. Hardware invalidation to ensure cache coherence is typical in multiprocessor systems, and the same technique can be used for I/O; we discuss this topic in detail in Chapter 9.

We have looked at three different methods for transferring data between an I/O device and memory. In moving from polling to an interrupt-driven to a DMA interface, we shift the burden for managing an I/O operation from the processor to a progressively more intelligent I/O controller. These methods have the advantage of freeing up processor cycles. Their disadvantage is that they increase the cost of the I/O system. Because of this, a given computer system can choose which point along this spectrum is appropriate for the I/O devices connected to it.

8.6   Fallacies and Pitfalls

Pitfall: Using the peak transfer rate of a portion of the I/O system to make performance projections or performance comparisons.

Many of the components of an I/O system, from the devices to the controllers to buses, are specified using their peak bandwidths. In practice, these peak bandwidth measurements are often based on unrealistic assumptions about the system or are unattainable due to other system limitations. For example, in quoting bus performance, the peak transfer rate is often specified using a memory system that is impossible to build. A VME bus has a peak bandwidth of about 28 MB/second with an impossible 0 access time memory and 13.6 MB/second with a 150-ns memory. Similarly, if we compared the transfer rate of Futurebus to VME with 0-ns access time memories, we would conclude that Futurebus has almost four times the bandwidth of VME. But with 150-ns memories, Futurebus has only 1.5 times the bandwidth. In addition to these gaps between peak and actual performance, Amdahl's Law reminds us that the throughput of an I/O system will be limited by the lowest performance component in the I/O path.

Fallacy: Magnetic storage is on its last legs and will be replaced shortly.

This is both a fallacy and a pitfall. Such claims have been made constantly for the past 20 years, though the string of failed alternatives in recent years seems to have reduced the level of claims for the death of magnetic storage. Among the unsuccessful candidates proposed to replace magnetic storage have been magnetic bubble memories, optical storage, and photographic storage. None of these systems has matched the combination of characteristics that favor magnetic disks: nonvolatility, low cost, reasonable access time, and high reliability. Magnetic storage technology continues to improve at the same pace it has sustained over the past 25 years.

Possibly the biggest challenge for magnetic storage will come from semiconductor memory. Because semiconductor memory continues to decrease in price faster than magnetic storage and because it is much faster, it is likely that semiconductor memory will play an even larger role in future machines. Nonvolatile forms of semiconductor memory (flash memories, for example) are also likely to grow in importance.

Pitfall: Moving functions from the CPU to the I/O processor expecting to improve performance without a careful analysis.

There are many examples of this pitfall trapping people, although I/O processors, when properly used, can certainly enhance performance. A frequent instance of this fallacy is the use of intelligent I/O interfaces, which, because of the higher overhead to set up an I/O, can turn out to have worse latency than a processor-directed I/O activity (although if the processor is freed up sufficiently, system throughput may still increase). Frequently, performance falls when the I/O processor has much lower performance than the main processor. Consequently, a small amount of main processor time is replaced with a larger amount of peripheral processor time. Workstation designers have seen both these phenomena repeatedly.

A more serious problem can occur when the migration of an I/O feature changes the instruction set architecture or system architecture in a programmer-visible way. This forces all future machines to have to live with a decision that made sense in the past. If CPUs improve in cost/performance more rapidly than the I/O processor (and this will likely be the case), then moving the function may result in a slower machine in the next computer.

The most telling example comes from the IBM 360. It was decided that the performance of the ISAM system, an early database system, would improve if some of the record searching occurred in the disk controller itself. A key field was associated with each record, and the device searched each key as the disk rotated until it found a match. It would then transfer the desired record. This technique requires an extra large gap between records when a key is present.

The speed at which a track can be searched is limited by the speed of the disk and of the number of keys that can be packed on a track. On an IBM 3330 disk, the key is typically 10 characters; the gap is equivalent to 191 characters if there is a key, and 135 characters when no key is present. If we assume that the data is also 10 characters and that the track has nothing else on it, a 13,165-byte track can contain

$$\frac{13{,}165}{191 + 10 + 10} = 62 \text{ key-data records}$$

The time per key search is

$$\frac{16.7 \text{ ms (1 revolution)}}{62} = 0.27 \text{ ms/key search}$$

In place of this scheme, we could put several key-data pairs in a single block and have smaller inter-record gaps. Assuming that there are 15 key-data pairs per block and that the track has nothing else on it, then

$$\frac{13165}{135 + 15 \times (10 + 10)} = \frac{13165}{135 + 300} = 30 \text{ blocks of key-data pairs}$$

The revised performance is then

$$\frac{16.7 \text{ ms (1 revolution)}}{30 \times 15} \approx 0.04 \text{ ms/key search}$$

Of course, the disk-based search would look better if the keys were much longer.

As processors got faster, the CPU time for a search became trivial, while the time for a search using the hardware facility improved very little. While the strategy made early machines faster, programs that use the search-key operation in the I/O processor run up to six times slower on today's machines!

8.7   Concluding Remarks

I/O systems are evaluated on several different characteristics: the variety of I/O devices supported; the maximum number of I/O devices; cost; and performance, measured both in latency and in throughput. These goals lead to widely varying schemes for interfacing I/O devices. In the low end, schemes like buffering and even DMA can be avoided to minimize cost. In midrange systems, buffered DMA is likely to be the dominant transfer mechanism. In the high end, latency and bandwidth may both be important, and cost may be secondary. Multiple paths to I/O devices with limited buffering often characterize high-end I/O systems. Increasing the bandwidth with both more and wider connections eliminates the need for buffering at an increase in cost. Typically, being able to access the data on an I/O device at any time (high availability) becomes more important as systems grow. As a result, redundancy and error correction mechanisms become more and more prevalent as we enlarge the system.

The design of I/O systems is complicated because the limiting factor in I/O system performance can be any of several critical resources in the I/O path, from the operating system to the device. Furthermore, independent requests from different programs interact in the I/O system, making the performance of an I/O request dependent on other activity that occurs at the same time. Lastly, design techniques that improve bandwidth often negatively impact latency, and vice versa. For example, adding buffering usually increases the system cost and also the system bandwidth. But it also increases latency by placing additional hardware between the device and memory. It is this combination of factors, including some that are unpredictable, that makes designing I/O systems and improving their performance challenging not only for architect, but also for OS designers, and even applications programmers building I/O-intensive applications.

Future Directions in I/O Systems

What does the future hold for I/O systems? The rapidly increasing performance of processors strains I/O systems, whose physical components cannot

> **The Big Picture**
>
> The performance of an I/O system, whether measured by bandwidth or latency, depends on all the elements in the path between the device and memory, including the operating system that generates the I/O commands. The bandwidth of the buses, the memory, and the device determine the maximum transfer rate from or to the device. Similarly, the latency depends on the device latency, together with any latency imposed by the memory system or buses. The effective bandwidth and response latency also depend on other I/O requests that may cause contention for some resource in the path. Finally, the operating system is a bottleneck. In some cases, the OS takes a long time to deliver an I/O request from a user program to an I/O device, leading to high latency. In other cases, the operating system effectively limits the I/O bandwidth because of limitations in the number of concurrent I/O operations it can support. In some cases, the memory system and operating system, rather than the device, are the major bottlenecks.

improve in performance as fast as processors. To hide the growing gap between the speed of processors and the access time to secondary storage (primarily disks), main memory is used as a cache for secondary storage. These *file caches*, which rely on spatial and temporal locality in access to secondary storage, are maintained by the operating system. The use of file caches allows many file accesses to be handled from memory rather than from disk.

Magnetic disks are increasing in capacity quickly, but access time is improving only slowly. One reason for this is that the opportunities for magnetic disks are growing faster in the low end of the market than in the high end, and the low end is driven primarily by the demand for lower cost per megabyte. This market has helped shrink the size of the disk from the 14-inch platters of the mainframe disk to the 1.3-inch disks developed for laptop and palmtop computers.

One future candidate for optimizing storage is not a new technology, but a new organization of disk storage—arrays of small and inexpensive disks. The argument for arrays is that since price per megabyte is independent of disk size, potential throughput can be increased by having many disk drives and, hence, many disk arms. Simply spreading data over multiple disks automatically forces accesses to several disks. (While arrays improve throughput, latency is not necessarily reduced.) Adding redundant disks to the array offers the opportunity for the array to discover a failed disk and automatically recover the lost information. Arrays may thus enhance the reliability of a computer system as well as performance. This redundancy has inspired the acronym *RAID* for these arrays: *redundant arrays of inexpensive disks.*

The next level of the storage hierarchy below magnetic disks promises to offer extraordinary increases in capacity in the next several years. The driving force may well be the *helical scan tape.* Found in 8-mm video cameras and 4-mm digital audio tapes, helical scan tape records at an angle to the tape rather than parallel, as in longitudinally recorded tapes. The tape still moves at the same speed, but the fast-spinning tape head records bits much more densely—a factor of about 50 to 100 denser than longitudinally recorded tapes. And because the medium was created for consumer products, the improvement in cost per bit over time has been even greater than for traditional magnetic tapes used solely by the computer industry.

Advances in tape capacity are being enhanced by advances on two other fronts: compression and robots. Faster processors have enabled systems to begin using compression to multiply storage capacity. Factors of 2 to 3 are common, with compression of 20:1 possible for certain types of data such as images. The second enhancement is inexpensive robots to automatically load and store tapes, offering a new level in the hierarchy between *on-line* magnetic disks and *off-line* magnetic disks on shelves. This "*robo-line*" storage means access to terabytes of information at the delay of tens of seconds, without the intervention of a human operator. Figure 8.16 is a photograph of a tape "robot."

Computer networks are also making great strides, mainly by taking advantage of the properties of optical fibers to send information. Optical fiber will be the foundation of the National Research and Educational Network (NREN), which will be installed in the middle of the 1990s. This nationwide network will transfer data at 1 gigabit per second, or a factor of 20 faster than the current Internet. This opens the possibility of nationwide networks operating at speeds formerly associated with the backplanes within a single cabinet.

Such advances offer "computing science fiction" scenarios that would have seemed absurd just a few years ago. For example, if all the books the Library of Congress were converted to ASCII they would occupy just 10 terabytes (although the pictures might take even more, depending on their number and resolution). Helical scan tapes, tape robots, compression, and high-speed networks could be the building blocks of an electronic library. All the information on all the books in the world available at your fingertips for the cost of a large minicomputer. And parallel processing, discussed in the next chapter, will allow this information to be indexed so that all books could be searched by content rather than by title. Electronic libraries would change the lives of anyone with a library card, and the technology to create them is within our grasp.

FIGURE 8.16 The Exabyte EXB-120 holds 116 8-mm helical scan tapes. Each tape holds 10 gigabytes, yielding a total capacity of over a terabyte. The EXB-120 costs about as much as two to four workstations. Photo courtesy of the Exabyte Corporation.

8.8 Historical Perspective and Further Reading

The history of I/O systems is a fascinating one. Many of the most interesting artifacts of early computers are their I/O devices. The sealed Winchester disk, which today completely dominates disk technology, is a relatively new invention. Prior to that, most hard disks were removable. In fact, the earliest rotating storage devices were drums and fixed-head disks. A drum had a cylindrical surface coated with a magnetic film. It used a large number of read/write heads positioned over each track on the drum. Drums were relatively high-speed I/O devices often used for virtual memory paging or for creating a file cache to slower speed devices. Large (2 to 3 feet in diameter) fixed-head disks were also in use in the 1960s. Moving-head disks became the dominant high-speed magnetic storage in the 1970s, though their high cost meant that magnetic tape continued to be used extensively until later in the decade. Winchester disks grew rapidly in popularity in the 1980s, completely replacing removable disks by the middle of the decade.

The 1970s saw the invention of a number of remarkable I/O devices. Perhaps one of the most unusual was a film storage device that stored data optically on small strips of photographic film. These film storage devices could not only read and write film, but actually kept the filmstrips stored in the device (which was about 5 feet by 4 feet by 3 feet), retrieving them mechanically.

The early IBM 360s pioneered many of the ideas that we use in I/O systems today. The 360 was the first machine to make heavy use of DMA, and it introduced the notion of I/O programs that could be interpreted by the device. Chaining of I/O programs was a key feature. The concept of channels introduced in the 360 corresponds to the I/O bus of today.

The trend for high-end machines has been toward use of programmable I/O processors. The original machine to use this concept was the CDC 6600, which used I/O processors called *peripheral processors*.

The forerunner of today's workstations as well as the Macintosh and other systems using windows was the Alto, developed at Xerox Palo Alto Research Center in 1973 [Thacker et al. 1982]. This machine integrated the needs of the I/O functions into the microcode of the processor. This included support for the bit-mapped graphics display, the disk, and the network. The network for the Alto was the first Ethernet [Metcalfe and Boggs 1976]. The Alto also supported the first laser printer, configured as a print server accessible over the Ethernet. Similarly, disk servers were also built. The mouse, invented earlier by Doug Engelbart of SRI, was a key part of the Alto. The 16-bit processor used a writable control store, which enabled researchers to program in support for the I/O devices. The single microprogrammed engine drove the graphics display, mouse, disks, network, and, when there was nothing else to do, ran the user's program.

While today we associate microprocessors with the personal computer revolution, they were originally developed to meet the demand for special-purpose controllers. Since the invention of the microprocessor, designers have developed many I/O controllers that adapt a microprocessor to a specific task. These include everything from DMA controllers to SCSI controllers to complete Ethernet controllers on a single chip.

The first multivendor bus may have been the PDP-11 Unibus in 1970. DEC encouraged other companies to build devices that would plug into its bus, and many companies did. A more recent example is SCSI, which stands for *small computer systems interface*. This bus, originally called SASI, was invented by

Shugart and was later standardized by the IEEE. This open system approach to buses contrasts with proprietary buses using patented interfaces, which companies adopt to forestall competition from plug-compatible vendors. The use of proprietary buses also raises the costs and lowers the availability of I/O devices that plug into proprietary buses, because such devices must have an interface designed exclusively for that bus.

Ongoing development in the areas of tape robots, head-mounted displays, gloves for complete tactile feedback, and computer screens that you write on with pens are indications that the incredible developments in I/O technology are likely to continue in the future.

To Probe Further

Bashe, C. J., L. R. Johnson, J. H. Palmer, and E. W. Pugh [1986]. *IBM's Early Computers*, MIT Press, Cambridge, Mass.

Describes the I/O system architecture and devices in IBM's early computers.

Borrill, P. L. [1986]. "32-bit buses: An objective comparison," *Proc. Buscon 1986 West,* San Jose, Calif., 138–45.

A comparison of various 32-bit bus standards.

Gray, J. and Reuter, A. [1993]. *Transaction Processing: Concepts and Techniques*, Morgan Kaufmann, San Mateo, CA.

A description of transaction processing, including discussions of benchmarking and performance evaluation.

Kahn, R. E. [1972]. "Resource-sharing computer communication networks," *Proc. IEEE* 60:11 (November) 1397–1407.

A classic paper that describes the ARPANet.

Katz, R. H., D. A. Patterson, and G. A. Gibson [1989]. "Disk system architectures for high performance computing," *Proc. IEEE* 78:2 (December).

Introduces disk arrays and discusses the advantages of adopting such an organization.

Levy, J. V. [1978]. "Buses: The skeleton of computer structures," in *Computer Engineering: A DEC View of Hardware Systems Design*, C. G. Bell, J. C. Mudge, and J. E. McNamara, eds., Digital Press, Bedford, Mass.

This is a good overview of key concepts in bus design with some examples from DEC machines.

Metcalfe, R. M., and D. R. Boggs [1976]. "Ethernet: Distributed packet switching for local computer networks," *Comm. ACM* 19:7 (July) 395–404.

Describes the Ethernet network.

Smotherman, M. [1989]. "A sequencing-based taxonomy of I/O systems and review of historical machines," *Computer Architecture News* 17:5 (September) 5–15.

Describes the development of important ideas in I/O.

Thacker, C. P., E. M. McCreight, B. W. Lampson, R. F. Sproull, and D. R. Boggs [1982]. "Alto: A personal computer," in *Computer Structures: Principles and Examples*, D. P. Siewiorek, C. G. Bell, and A. Newell, eds., McGraw-Hill, New York, 549–572.

Describes the Alto—forerunner of workstations as well as the Apple Macintosh.

8.9   Exercises

8.1 [10] <§8.1–8.2> Here are two different I/O systems intended for use in transaction processing:

- System A can support 1000 I/O operations per second.

- System B can support 750 I/O operations per second.

The systems use the same processor that executes 50 million instructions per second. Assume that each transaction requires 5 I/O operations and that each I/O operation requires 10,000 instructions. Ignoring response time and assuming transactions may be arbitrarily overlapped, what is the maximum transaction per second rate that each machine can sustain?

8.2 [15] <§8.1–8.2> {ex. 8.1} The latency of an I/O operation for the two systems in Exercise 8.1 differs. The latency for an I/O on System A is equal to 20 ms, while for System B the latency is 18 ms for the first 500 I/Os per second and 25 ms per I/O for each I/O between 500 and 750 I/O per second. In the workload, every tenth transaction depends on the immediately preceding transaction and must wait for its completion. What is the maximum transaction rate that still allows every transaction to complete in 1 second and does not exceed the I/O bandwidth of the machine? For simplicity, assume all transaction requests arrive at the beginning of a 1-second interval.

8.3 [10] <§8.4> Suppose we have a memory system that uses a 50-MHz clock. The memory transmits 8-word requests at the rate of 1 word per cycle. For reads from memory, the accesses occur as follows:

1. 1 cycle to accept the address,

2. 3 cycles of latency, and

3. 8 clock cycles to transmit the 8 words.

For writes to memory, accesses occur as follows:

1. 1 cycle to accept the address,

2. 2 cycles of latency,

3. 8 clock cycles to transmit the 8 words, and

4. 3 cycles to recover and write the error correction code.

Find the maximum bandwidth in megabytes per second for an access pattern consisting of

a. All reads from memory.

b. All writes to memory.

c. A mix of 65% reads from memory and 35% writes to memory.

8.4 [15] <§8.4> {ex. 8.3} The memory system and bus system of Exercise 8.3 were originally designed to support a processor with 8-word cache blocks. A new processor is designed that has 16-word cache blocks. There are two alternative organizations for the memory and bus:

1. Use the 8-word organization described in Exercise 8.3 and perform two separate 8-word accesses for each miss.

2. Convert the memory system to provide 16 words by initiating two separate 8-word accesses. For reads, the system transmits the first 8 words while fetching the second 8. For writes, the transmission of the second 8 words can begin immediately after receipt of the first 8 words.

Using the access steps from Exercise 8.3, find the maximum bandwidth sustainable for each of these mechanisms assuming that reads and writes occur with equal frequency.

8.5 [15] <§8.4> Consider two different bus systems:

- Bus 1 is a 64-bit-wide multiplexed address and data bus. Transmitting an address or a 64-bit data item takes one bus cycle. Reads or writes to the memory incur a three-cycle latency. Starting with the fourth cycle, the memory system can accept or deliver up to 8 words at a rate of 2 words every bus cycle.

- Bus 2 is a bus with separate 32-bit address and 32-bit data. Each transmission takes one bus cycle. A read to the memory incurs a three-cycle latency, then, starting with the fourth cycle, the memory system can deliver up to 8 words at a rate of 1 word every bus cycle. For a write, the first word is transmitted with the address; after a three-cycle latency up to 7 additional words may be transmitted at the rate of 1 word every bus cycle.

Evaluate these buses assuming only 1 word requests where 60% of the requests are reads and 40% are writes. Find the maximum bandwidth that each bus and memory system can provide in words per bus cycle.

8.6 [15] <§8.4> Assume that the memory requests in Exercise 8.5 are all 8 words long. Find the maximum bandwidth that each bus and memory system can provide to the processor in words per bus cycle.

8.7 [20] <§8.4> Assume the bus and memory systems in Exercise 8.5 are used to handle disk access, where 75% of the accesses are input operations (memory writes) and 25% are output operations (memory reads). The disks transfer data at 2 MB per second and have 8 word buffers, so that data can be transferred 8 words at a time. Find the maximum number of simultaneous disk transfers that can be sustained for each bus system if the bus is clocked at 50 MHz and I/O is allowed to consume 100% of the bus and memory bandwidth.

8.8 [15] <§8.4> We need to interface an I/O device with the memory system described in Exercise 8.3 using an asynchronous bus. Assume the same type of handshaking protocol as Figure 8.10 on page 554 uses. Show the steps in the asynchronous protocol for reading a block of 8 words from memory. Assume as in Exercise 8.3 that the memory latency is incurred only once.

8.9 [15] <§8.4> {ex. 8.8} Let's determine the maximum bandwidth that can be sustained for the asynchronous bus and memory system of Exercise 8.8. Assume each handshaking step takes 20 ns and memory access takes 60 ns. Allow the maximum overlap among memory access and handshaking, as in the example on page 555. Assume the memory lines are buffered so that the access for the next word can start immediately. Find the maximum bandwidth for 8-word reads from memory to the device. How does this compare to the rates that could be sustained with a synchronous interface?

8.10 [20] <§8.3–8.5> Here are a variety of building blocks used in an I/O system that has a synchronous processor-memory bus running at 50 MHz, and one or more I/O adapters that interface I/O buses to the processor-memory bus.

- *Memory system:* The memory system has a 32-bit interface and handles four word transfers. For writes to memory, the memory system accepts a word every clock cycle for four clock cycles and then takes an additional four clock cycles before the words have been stored and it can accept another transaction.

- *DMA interfaces:* The I/O adapters use DMA to transfer the data between the I/O buses and the processor-memory bus. The DMA unit arbitrates for the processor-memory bus and sends/receives four word blocks from/to the memory system. The DMA controller can accommodate up to 8 disks. Initiating a new I/O operation (including the seek and access) takes 2 ms during which another I/O cannot be initiated by this controller (but outstanding operations can be handled).

■ *The I/O bus:* The I/O bus is a synchronous bus with a sustainable bandwidth of 4 MB per second; each transfer is one word long.

■ *The disks:* The disks have a measured average seek plus rotational latency of 20 ms. The disks have a read/write bandwidth of 2 MB per second, when they are transferring.

Find the time required to read a 16 KB sector from a disk to memory, assuming this is the only activity on the bus.

8.11 [15] <§8.3–8.5> {ex. 8.10} For the I/O system described in Exercise 8.10, find the maximum instantaneous bandwidth at which data can be transferred from disk to memory using as many disks as needed; how many disks and I/O buses (the minimum of each) do you need to achieve the bandwidth? Since you need only achieve this bandwidth for an instant, latencies need not be considered.

8.12 [20] <§8.3–8.5> {ex. 8.10, 8.11} Assume all accesses in the I/O system described in Exercise 8.10 are 4 KB block reads. If there are a total of 6 I/O buses (and DMA controllers), find the maximum number of I/Os the system can sustain in steady state assuming the reads are uniformly distributed to the disks. What is the sustained I/O bandwidth?

8.13 [15] <§8.3–8.5> {ex. 8.10, 8.11, 8.12} Find the size for I/O block reads that will allow the organization in Exercise 8.12 to saturate the I/O buses (the size should be a power of 2). How many I/O operations per second can the system perform and what is the I/O bandwidth?

8.14 [15] <§8.4–8.5, 7.2, 7.4> Consider a 50-MHz processor that uses the memory system of Exercise 8.3 to handle cache misses. Assume the processor has a write-back cache and the following measurements have been made:

■ The cache miss rate is 0.05 misses per instruction.

■ Forty percent of the misses require a write-back operation, while the other 60% require only a read.

Assuming the processor is stalled for the duration of a miss (including the write-back time if a write-back is needed), find the number of cycles per instruction spent handling cache misses.

8.15 [15] <§7.4, 8.4> We are considering changing the block size of the cache in the processor of Exercise 8.14 to 16 words. We would like to use one of the two memory and bus systems described in Exercise 8.4. With a 16-word block, the miss rate is reduced to 0.03 misses per instruction. The fraction of write-back operations will not be affected. The processor will still be stalled for the duration of a miss. Find the cycles per instruction spent handling cache misses for the 16-word block size using the two different bus systems.

8.16 [2 days to 1 week] <§8.5, Appendix A> This assignment uses SPIM to build a simple set of I/O routines that will perform I/O to the terminal using polling. First, you need to build two I/O routines, whose C declarations and descriptions are shown below:

```
void print (char *string);
```

`print` takes a single argument, which is the address of a NULL-terminated ASCII string. All of the characters of the string except the null terminating character should be output by `print` . It should print the characters one at a time, waiting for each character to be output before sending the next one. It should not return until all the characters have been output. The procedure `print` should work for strings of any length. This version of `print` should not use interrupts; just test the "ready" bit of the transmitter control register continuously until the device is ready.

```
char getchar();
```

The procedure `getchar` takes no arguments and returns a character result. If `getchar` waits until a character has been typed on the terminal, then it should return the character's value in $2 (the result register). Do not use interrupts; simply test the ready bit continuously until a character has arrived.

Write a main program that uses these two procedures to read a line from the terminal, which will be terminated by a carriage return. Then print the entire line to the terminal including a carriage return and line feed. All your code should obey the conventions in Appendix A for procedure calling, stack usage, and register usage.

8.17 [3 days–1 week] <§8.5, Appendix A> Your assignment is to build an interrupt-driven mechanism for buffered I/O to and from the terminal. This exercise handles output only, but the next one handles input.

For the output only portion, there are three parts to the program:

1. A main program, which repeatedly calls procedure `print` to print the string "I know what I am doing."

2. The procedure `print`, which stores the output characters in a buffer shared by it and the interrupt routine.

3. The interrupt routine, which copies characters from the output buffer to the transmitter.

You need to write all three routines. The routine `print` and the interrupt routine should communicate by using a shared circular buffer with space for 32 characters. The `print` procedure should take a string as argument and add the characters of the string to the output buffer one at a time, advancing as soon as there is space in the buffer. Keep in mind that `print` should not manipulate the terminal device registers directly except to make sure that transmitter interrupts are enabled. Furthermore, `print` should contain additional code to deal with a full output buffer. The main program generates characters much faster than they can be output, so the buffer will quickly fill up. In a real system, if the output buffer fills up, the operating system will stop running the current user's process and switch to a different process. Your program doesn't need to support multiple users, so `print` can take a simpler approach: it just checks the buffer over and over again until eventually it isn't full anymore. The buffer is full when the next position in which `print` wants to insert a character has not been emptied by the interrupt routine.

After writing print, write the interrupt routine called by `print`. Here is a list of things the interrupt routine must do:

1. If the transmitter is not ready, then the interrupt routine should not do anything. (You shouldn't have gotten an interrupt in the first place if the transmitter isn't ready, but it's a good idea to check anyway.)

2. If the output buffer isn't empty, copy the next character from the output buffer to the Transmitter Data register and adjust the buffer pointers.

3. If the output buffer is empty, turn off the interrupt-enable bit in the Transmitter Control register. Otherwise continuous interrupts will occur. Each time it deposits a character in the buffer, `print` will need to turn this bit on.

4. Don't forget that you must save and restore any registers that you use in the interrupt routine, even temporary registers like register $8 and register $9. This is necessary because interrupts can occur at any time and those registers could have been in use at the time of the interrupt. You must save the registers on the stack. The only exceptions to this rule are registers $26 and $27, which are reserved for use by interrupt routines; these registers need not be saved and restored. One of these registers can be used to return from the interrupt routine back to the code that was interrupted.

Test your code by writing the routine main that calls `print` to print the string. It should output lines continuously, with each line containing the characters "`I know what I am doing.`".

8.18 [3 days–1 week] <§8.5, Appendix A> {ex. 8.17} Extend the code you've already written to handle interrupt-driven input. This program should do input in the same way as the previous program did output: by using a buffer to communicate between the routine `getchar` and the interrupt routine. Be aware that `getchar` returns a character from the buffer, waiting in a loop if no characters are present. Similarly, the interrupt routine will add characters as they are typed, discarding characters if the buffer is full when they arrive. In this an 8-entry buffer should work well.

Use these two routines to read characters from the terminal and output them to the terminal. Try typing characters rapidly to make sure your program can handle the output or the input buffer filling up. For example, if you type two or three characters rapidly, the output buffer may fill up. However, no output should be lost: the print procedure will simply have to spin for a bit, during which time additional input characters will be buffered in the input buffer. If you type eight or ten characters very rapidly, then the input buffer will probably fill up. When this happens, your interrupt routine will have to discard characters: the program should continue to function, but there won't be any output of the discarded input characters you typed. Once the output catches up with the input, your program should accept input again just as if the input buffer had never filled up.

8.19 [1 day to 1 week] <§8.2–8.4> Take your favorite computer and write programs that achieve the following:

1. Maximum bandwidth from and to a single disk.

2. Maximum bandwidth from and to multiple disks.

3. The maximum number of 512-byte transactions from and to a single disk.

4. The maximum number of 512-byte transactions from and to multiple disks.

What is the percentage of the bandwidth that you achieve compared to what the I/O device manufacturer claims? Also, record processor utilization in each case for the programs running separately. Next, run all four together and see what percentage of the maximum rates you can achieve. From this, can you determine where the system bottlenecks lie?

In More Depth: Ethernet

An Ethernet is essentially a standard bus with multiple masters (each computer can be a master) and a distributed arbitration scheme using collision detection. Most Ethernets are implemented using coaxial cable as the medium. When a particular node wants to use the bus, it first checks to see whether some other node is using the bus; if not, it places a carrier signal on the bus, and then proceeds to transmit. A complication can arise because the control is distributed and the devices may be physically far apart. As a result, two nodes can both check the Ethernet, find it idle, and begin transmitting at once; this is called a *collision*. A node detects collisions also by listening to the network when transmitting, to see whether a collision has occurred. A collision is detected when the node finds that what it hears on the Ethernet differs from what it transmitted. When collisions occur, both nodes stop transmitting and delay a random time interval before trying to resume using the network—just as two polite people do when they both start talking at the same time! Consequently, the number of nodes on the network is limited—if too many collisions occur, the performance will be poor. In addition, constraints imposed by the requirement that collisions be detected by all nodes limit the length of the Ethernet and the number of connections to the network. Although this idea sounds like it might not work, it actually works amazingly well and has been central to the enormous growth in the use of local area networks.

8.20 [3 days to 1 week] <§8.3–8.4> Write a program that simulates an Ethernet. Assume the following network system characteristics:

- A transmission bandwidth of 10 Mbits per second.
- A latency for a signal to travel the entire length of the network and return to its origin of 15 microseconds. This is also the time to detect a collision.

Make the following assumptions about the 100 hosts on the network:

- The packet size is 1000 bytes.
- Each host tries to send a packet after T seconds of computation, where T is exponentially distributed with mean M. Note that the host begins its T seconds of computation only after successfully transmitting a packet.
- If a collision is detected, the host waits a random amount of time chosen from an exponential distribution with a mean of 60 microseconds.

Simulate and plot the sustained bandwidth of the network compared to the mean time between transmission attempts (M). Also, plot the average wait time between trying to initiate a transmission and succeeding in initiating it (compared to M).

Ethernets actually use an exponential back-off algorithm that increases the mean of the back-off time on successive collisions. Assume that the mean of the distribution from which the host chooses how much to delay is doubled on successive collisions. How well does this work? Is the bandwidth higher than when a single distribution is used? Can the initial mean be lower?

In More Depth: Disk Arrays

As mentioned in section 8.7, one direction for future disk systems is to use arrays of smaller disks that provide more bandwidth through parallel access. In most disk arrays, all the spindles are synchronized—sector 0 in every disk rotates under the head at the exact same time—and the arms on all the disks are always over the same track. Furthermore, the data is "striped" across the disks in the array, so that consecutive sectors can be read in parallel. Let's explore how such a system might work.

8.21 <§8.3–8.5> [20] Assume that we have the following two magnetic-disk configurations: a single disk and an array of four disks. Each disk has 16 sectors/track, each sector holds 1K bytes, and it revolves at 3600 RPM. Assume the seek time is 10 ms. The delay of the disk controller is 2 ms per transaction, either for a single disk or for the array. Assume the performance of the I/O system is limited only by the disks and controller. Remember that the consecutive sectors on the single disk system will be spread one sector per disk in the array. Compare the performance in I/Os per second of these two disk organizations, assuming the requests are random reads, half of which are 4KB and half of which are 16KB of data from sequential sectors. The sectors may be read in any order; for simplicity, assume that the rotational latency is one-half the revolution time for the single disk read of four sectors and the disk array read of 16 sectors. Challenge: Can you work out the actual average rotational latency in these two cases?

8.22 <§8.3–8.5> [10] {ex. 8.21} Using the same disk systems as Exercise 8.21, with the same access patterns, determine the performance in megabytes per second for each system.

Parallel
Processors

*There are finer fish in the sea than
have ever been caught.*

Irish Proverb

*The future belongs to those who
prepare for it.*

American Proverb

The Five Classic Components of a Computer

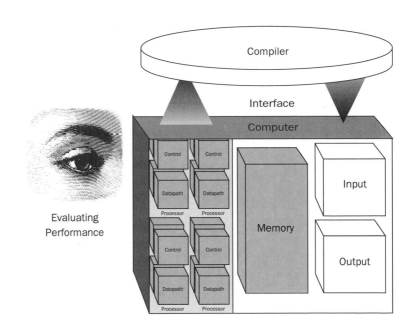

9.1   Introduction

Future computers of all sizes will embrace parallelism even more than they do today. We believe that the exploitation of parallel machines will provide an exciting opportunity in this decade. Those who understand applications, algorithms, and architecture will be prepared for this opportunity.

As parallelism can appear at many levels, it is useful to categorize the alternatives. In 1966, Flynn proposed a simple model of categorizing computers that is still useful today. Scrutinizing the most constrained component of the machine, he counted the number of parallel instruction and data streams and then labeled the computer with this count:

1. *Single instruction stream, single data stream* (SISD, the uniprocessor)

2. *Single instruction stream, multiple data streams* (SIMD)

3. *Multiple instruction streams, single data stream* (MISD)

4. *Multiple instruction streams, multiple data streams* (MIMD)

Some machines are hybrids of these categories, of course, but we stick with this classic model because it is simple, easy to understand, and gives a good first approximation. It is also—perhaps because of its understandability—the most widely used scheme.

Your first question about the model should be, "Single or multiple compared with what?" A machine that adds a 32-bit number in one clock cycle would seem to have multiple data streams when compared with a bit-serial computer that takes 32 clock cycles to add. Flynn chose computers popular during that time, the IBM 704 and IBM 7090, as the model of SISD; today, the MIPS implementations in Chapters 5 and 6 would be fine reference points.

Having established the reference point for SISD, we move to the next class: SIMD.

9.2   SIMD Computers—Single Instruction Stream, Multiple Data Streams

The cost of a general multiprocessor is, however, very high and further design options were considered which would decrease the cost without seriously degrading the power or efficiency of the system. The options consist of recentralizing one of the three major components . . . Centralizing the [control unit] gives rise to the basic organization of [an] . . . array processor such as the Illiac IV.

Bouknight et al., "The Illiac IV system," Proc. IEEE 60:4, 369–379, 1972

SIMD computers operate on vectors of data. For example, when a single SIMD instruction adds 64 numbers, the SIMD hardware sends 64 data streams to 64 ALUs to form 64 sums within a single clock cycle.

The virtues of SIMD are that all the parallel execution units are synchronized and they all respond to a single instruction that emanates from a single program counter (PC). From a programmer's perspective, this is close to the already familiar SISD. Although every unit will be executing the same instruction, each execution unit has its own address registers, and so each unit can have different data addresses.

The original motivation behind SIMD was to amortize the cost of the control unit over dozens of execution units. Another advantage is the reduced size of program memory—SIMD needs only one copy of the code that is being simultaneously executed, while MIMD may need a copy in every processor. Virtual memory and increasing capacity of DRAM chips have reduced the importance of this advantage.

Real SIMD computers have a mixture of SISD and SIMD instructions. There is typically a SISD host computer to perform sequential operations such as branches or address calculations. The SIMD instructions are broadcast to all the execution units, each with its own set of registers and memory. Execution units rely on interconnection networks to exchange data.

SIMD works best when dealing with arrays in *for* loops. Hence, for massive parallelism to work in SIMD, there must be massive data, or *data parallelism.* SIMD is at its weakest in *case* or *switch* statements, where each execution unit must perform a different operation on its data, depending on what data it has. Execution units with the wrong data are disabled so that units with proper data may continue. Such situations essentially run at $1/n$th performance, where n is the number of cases.

Example

Let's sketch an SIMD program to better understand this style of architecture. Suppose we want to sum 100,000 numbers on a SIMD computer with 100 execution units.

Answer

The first step is to split 100,000 numbers into 100 subsets, one subset per execution unit. The front end processor places each subset of numbers into the local memory of each of the execution units. If the 100,000 numbers are in the array A in the host, then let's call the name of the local array A1.

The next step is to get the sum of each subset. This step, the first piece of SIMD code, is simply a loop that every execution unit follows; read a word from local memory and add it to a local variable:

```
sum = 0;
for (i = 0; i < 1000; i = i + 1) /* loop over each array */
   sum = sum + A1[i]; /* sum the local arrays */
```

The last step is adding these 100 partial sums. The hard part is that each partial sum is located in a different execution unit. Hence, we must use the interconnection network to send partial sums for the final summing. Rather than sending all the partial sums to a single processor, which would result in sequentially adding the partial sums, we divide to conquer. First, half of the execution units send their partial sums to the other half of the execution units, where two partial sums are added together. Then one quarter of the execution units (half of the half) send this new partial sum to the other quarter of the execution units (the remaining half of the half) for the next round of sums. This halving, sending, and receiving continues until there is a single sum of all numbers. Let Pn represent the number of the execution unit, send(x,y) be a routine that sends over the interconnection network to execution unit number x the value y, and receive() be a function that accepts a value from the network for this execution unit.

The SIMD code for summing the distributed partial sums is then:

```
limit = 100;
half = 100;/* 100 execution units in SIMD*/
repeat
   half = half/2; /* send vs. receive dividing line*/
   if (Pn >= half && Pn < limit) send(Pn % half,sum);
   if (Pn < half) sum = sum + receive();
   limit = half; /* upper limit of senders */
until (half == 1); /* exit with final sum */
```

This loop divides the execution units into senders and receivers, with the senders passing their sums to the execution unit whose number is the sender's execution unit number modulo half the number of units.

The complete SIMD program consists of the two code segments above.

A basic trade-off in SIMD machines is processor performance versus

Institution	Name	Maximum no. of proc.	Bits/ proc.	Proc. clock rate	Number of FPUs	Maximum memory size/system (MB)	Communi- cations BW/system (MB/sec)	Year
U. Illinois	Illiac IV	64	64	5 MHz	64	0.125	2,560	1972
ICL	DAP	4,096	1	5 MHz	0	2	2,560	1980
Goodyear	MPP	16,384	1	10 MHz	0	2	20,480	1982
Thinking Machines	CM-2	65,536	1	7 MHz	2048 (optional)	512	16,384	1987
Maspar	MP-1216	16,384	4	25 MHz	0	256 or 1024	23,000	1989

FIGURE 9.1 Characteristics of four SIMD computers. Number of FPUs means number of floating-point units.

number of processors. The machines in the marketplace today emphasize a high degree of parallelism over performance of the individual processors. The Connection Machine 2 (CM-2), for example, offers 65,536 single-bit-wide processors, while the Illiac IV had 64 64-bit processors. Figure 9.1 lists the characteristics of some well-known SIMD computers.

The Connection Machine 2 from Thinking Machines

The Connection Machine 2 (CM-2) consists of up to 65,536 processors, with each processor having a single-bit ALU, four 1-bit registers, 64K bits of memory, and a connection to a network that allows any processor to talk to any other. Figure 9.2 is a photograph of the CM-2. An additional floating-point accelerator (FPA) is optional, and it is shared by 32 of the 1-bit processors, resulting in 2048 FPAs in a CM-2. Since floating point is so much faster using the FPA, it is more accurate for floating-point problems to think of the CM-2 as having 2048 powerful processors, rather than 65,536 weak ones. There are only four types of chips in the CM-2: a custom chip containing 16 of the 1-bit processors, commercial DRAMs, a custom chip to act as the interface to the FPA, and an off-the-shelf FPA chip. Thus, a full system has 4096 custom processor chips which include the communication interface to other processors, 22,528 DRAM chips (including extra memory for error correction), 2048 custom FPA interface chips, and 2048 standard FPA chips.

The basic CM-2 operation reads 2 bits from the local memory and one from a register, computes two separate 1-bit results, and stores one back to local memory and one to a register. The CM-2 stores the result conditionally, depending on the value of a third 1-bit register. The clock cycle is determined by the time to read memory. Arithmetic is performed 1 bit at a time, with the program for a 32-bit add taking about 21 microseconds.

Putting this in perspective, the MIPS R2000 of the same time period took just 0.066 microseconds to perform a 32-bit add when the operands are all reg-

FIGURE 9.2 Photograph of the CM-2. Photo courtesy of Thinking Machines Corporation.

isters; if the operands were in the cache an add would take on average about 0.198 microseconds. Although R2000 could perform a single 32-bit add about 100 times (21/0.198) to 300 times (21/0.066) faster, the CM-2 performs 65,536 additions at once. Thus, the CM-2 can perform about 200 (65,536/300) to 600 (65,536/100) times as many 32-bit adds per second as the R2000.

With 16 processors per chip, the network connecting the processors together has two logical pieces: within chips and between chips. Within the chip, every processor has a dedicated link to each of the other processors. The network that connects the chips together is called a *Boolean n-cube*; with 4096 or 2^{12}, chips, it is a 12-cube. Section 9.6 describes this network in more detail, but small versions of this topology are easy to imagine: a 2-cube is simply a square with processors at the four corners and a 3-cube is simply a cube with processors at the eight corners.

At the time the machine was announced, the clock rate was 7 MHz, the memory per node was 64K bits, and the FPA was 32 bits wide internally and ran at 7 MHz. Later versions tracked technology with increases in the processor clock rate, the memory capacity, and the width and clock rate of the FPA.

Figure 9.3 shows the organization of the CM-2. The CM-2 is connected to a traditional SISD machine, called a *front end*, via a *sequencer*. The front end exe-

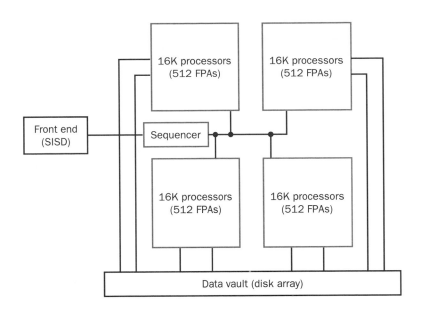

FIGURE 9.3 Organization of the CM-2. The CM-2 can have multiple front-end computers and data vaults.

cutes the program, sending SIMD instructions to the sequencer when they are encountered. The sequencer is something like the microprogram controller of Chapter 5, except that instead of sending the microinstruction to a single data-path as in Chapter 5, the CM-2 sequencer broadcasts its instructions to all 65,536 processors and 2048 FPAs.

The CM-2 also has an I/O channel for every 8096 processors. This can be connected to a custom frame buffer or to a disk array to offer high I/O bandwidth as an alternative to going through the front end.

Elaboration: Although MISD fills out Flynn's classification, it is difficult to envision. A single instruction stream is simpler than multiple instruction streams, but multiple instruction streams with multiple data streams (MIMD) are easier to imagine than multiple instructions with a single data stream (MISD).

MIMD Computers—Multiple Instruction Streams, Multiple Data Streams

Multis are a new class of computers based on multiple microprocessors. The small size, low cost, and high performance of microprocessors allow design and construction of computer structures that offer significant advantages in manufacture, price-performance ratio, and reliability over traditional computer families… Multis are likely to be the basis for the next, the fifth, generation of computers.

C. G. Bell, "Multis: A new class of multiprocessor computers,"
Science 228 (April 26, 1985), p.463

Computer architects have always sought the El Dorado of computer design: To create powerful computers simply by connecting many existing smaller ones. This is the idea behind MIMDs. The user orders as many processors as the budget allows and receives a commensurate amount of performance. MIMDs are also scalable: the hardware and software are designed to be sold with a variable number of processors, with current machines varying by a factor of more than 20. Since software is scalable, some MIMDs can support operation in the presence of broken hardware; that is, if a single processor fails in a MIMD with n processors, the system provides continued service with $n - 1$ processors. Finally, MIMDs may have the highest absolute performance—faster than the fastest uniprocessor.

The good news is that MIMD has established a beachhead. While the microprocessor has improved dramatically in performance, making it the most cost-effective uniprocessor, it is generally agreed that if you can't handle a time-shared workload on a single-chip SISD, then a MIMD composed of many single-chip SISDs is probably more effective than building a high-performance SISD from a more exotic technology.

Small companies like Sequent offer low-end MIMDs; large companies like IBM, DEC, and Cray Research deliver the high-end MIMDs. Moreover, virtually all current file servers can be ordered with multiple processors. Consequently, multiprocessors now embody a significant market, responsible for a majority of mainframes, virtually all supercomputers, and an increasing fraction of file servers.

MIMDs define high performance as high throughput for independent tasks. This is in contrast to running a single task on multiple processors. We use the term *parallel processing program* to refer to a single program that runs on multiple processors simultaneously. Although parallel processing programs may not yet be important commercially for more than a small percentage of users, we can expect that the percentage will increase in the future.

Here are two key questions that drive the designs of MIMDs:

■ How do parallel processors share data?

■ How do parallel processors coordinate?

The answers to the first question fall in two main camps. Processors with a *single address space*, sometimes called *shared-memory* processors, offer the programmer a single memory address space that all processors share. Processors communicate through shared variables in memory, with loads and stores capable of accessing any memory location. As processors operating in parallel normally will share data, they also need to coordinate when operating on shared data; otherwise, one processor could start working on data before another is finished with it. This coordination is called *synchronization*. When sharing is supported with a single address space, there must be a separate mechanism for synchronization. One approach uses a *lock*: only one processor at a time can acquire the lock, and other processors interested in shared data must wait until the original processor unlocks the variable. Locking is described in section 9.5.

An alternative model for communicating data uses *message sending* for communicating among processors. As an extreme example, processors on different workstations communicate by sending messages over a local area network. Provided the system has routines to send and receive messages, coordination is built-in with message sending since one processor knows when it sends a message and the receiving processor knows when the message arrives. The receiving processor can then send a message back to the sender saying the message has arrived, if the sender needs that confirmation.

MIMDs are constructed in two basic styles: processors connected by a single bus, and processors connected by a network. We will examine these two styles in detail in following sections, but first let's look at the general issues in programming MIMDs.

9.4 Programming MIMDs

I don't know what the programming language of the future will look like, but I know it will be called Fortran.

Anonymous

The bad news is that it remains to be seen how many important applications will run faster on MIMDs via parallel processing. The obstacle is not the price of the SISD used to compose MIMDs, the flaws in topologies of interconnection networks, nor the unavailability of appropriate programming languages;

the difficulty has been that too few important application programs have been rewritten to complete tasks sooner on parallel processors. Because it is even harder to find applications that can take advantage of many processors, the challenge is greater for large-scale MIMDs.

But why is this so? Why should parallel processing programs be so much harder to develop than sequential programs? One reason is that it is difficult to write MIMD programs that are fast, especially as the number of processors increases. As an analogy, think of the communication overhead for a task done by one person compared to the overhead for a task done by a committee, especially as the size of the committee increases. Although n people may have the potential to finish any task n times faster, the communication overhead for the group may prevent it; n-fold speedup becomes especially unlikely as n increases. (Imagine the change in communication overhead if a committee grows from 10 people to 1000 people to 1,000,000.)

Another reason why it is difficult to write parallel processing programs is that the programmer must know a good deal about the hardware. On a uniprocessor, the high-level language programmer writes the program largely ignoring the underlying machine organization—that's the job of the compiler. But, so far at least, the parallel processing programmer had better know the underlying organization to write programs that are fast and capable of running with a variable number of processors. Moreover, such parallel programs are not portable to other MIMDs.

Although this second obstacle is beginning to lessen, our discussion in Chapter 2 reveals a third obstacle: Amdahl's Law. It reminds us that even small parts of a program must be parallelized to reach their full potential; thus, coming close to linear speedup involves discovering new algorithms that are inherently parallel.

Example

Suppose you want to achieve linear speedup with 100 processors. What fraction of the original computation can be sequential?

Answer

Amdahl's Law (page 71) says

$$\text{Execution time after improvement} =$$

$$\frac{\text{Execution time affected by improvement}}{\text{Amount of improvement}} + \text{Execution time unaffected}$$

Substituting for the goal of linear speedup with 100 processors means the execution time is reduced by 100:

$$\frac{\text{Execution time after improvement}}{100} =$$

$$\frac{\text{Execution time affected by improvement}}{100} + \text{Execution time unaffected}$$

Solving for the unaffected execution time:

$$\text{Execution time unaffected} = \frac{\text{Execution time after improvement}}{100}$$

$$- \frac{\text{Execution time affected by improvement}}{100} = 0$$

Accordingly, to achieve linear speedup with 100 processors, *none* of the original computation can be sequential. Put another way, to get a speedup of 99 from 100 processors means the percentage of the original program that was sequential would have to be 0.01% or less.

Yet there are applications with substantial parallelism.

Example

Suppose you want to perform two sums: one is a sum of two scalar variables and one is a matrix sum of a pair of two-dimensional arrays, size 1000 by 1000. What speedup do you get with 1000 processors?

Answer

If we assume performance is a function of the time for an addition t, then there is 1 addition that does not benefit from parallel processors and 1,000,000 additions that do. If the time before is $1,000,001\,t$,

$$\text{Execution time after improvement} =$$

$$\frac{\text{Execution time affected by improvement}}{\text{Amount of improvement}} + \text{Execution time unaffected}$$

$$\text{Execution time after improvement} = \frac{1,000,000t}{1000} + 1t$$

$$= 1001$$

Speedup is then

$$\text{Speedup} = \frac{1,000,001}{1001} = 999$$

Even if there were 100 sums of scalar variables to one sum of a pair of 1000 by 1000 arrays, the speedup would still be 909.

Massive Parallelism

The term *massively parallel* is widely used but rarely defined, but no one would define a computer with less than 100 processors as massively parallel. Even with such a conservative dividing line, parallel processing using more than 100 processors is not yet important in everyday computing. Ideally, we should have a simple model that allows programmers to more easily create portable programs that achieve good performance on real parallel processors *and* to enable researchers to invent new algorithms that will work well on many parallel processors. Unfortunately, traditional theoretical models for parallel computation do not accurately predict performance of current commercial parallel processors.

The need for new portable algorithms for massively parallel machines underlines our belief that parallel machines offer an exciting challenge for the future, predicated on a clear understanding of applications, algorithms, and architecture.

Single Program Multiple Data

While the search for algorithms and models continues, progress has been made on the general approach to programming; we are converging on a *Single Program Multiple Data* (*SPMD*). It was conceivable to write 1000 different programs for 1000 different processors in an MIMD machine, but in practice this proved to be impossible. Today MIMD programmers write a single source program and think of the same program running on all processors.

The SIMD and MIMD camps realized that synchronization simplified programming, but MIMD advocates feared that they gave up too much by requiring every instruction on every processor to be synchronized. Given independent memories, however, processors interact only during communication. Thus, if processors operate in MIMD-style when not communicating, and in SIMD-style when communicating, then this compromise eliminates weaknesses of SIMD while maintaining its simplified programming model. Of course, not all communications need to be synchronized, but this generalization is the essence of the insight. SPMD offers the programming advantages of

SIMD without suffering either the inflexibility of the problem domain or the inability to utilize off-the-shelf processors.

In addition to a standard style of programming, scientific programmers seem to be headed for agreement on a programming language. The choice appears to be a version of Fortran that supports array operators and allows hints to the compiler on memory allocation to try to keep the data near the processor. Alas, for non-scientific programs, the language of choice remains unclear. The current popular languages are versions of C or C++ extended with communication procedures and a preprocessor to support parallel constructs, but there is no consensus yet, as there is in the Fortran community, of the features to be included in such a language.

9.5 | MIMDs Connected by a Single Bus

The high performance and low cost of the microprocessor inspired renewed interest in multiprocessors in the 1980s. Figure 9.4 lists the characteristics of some commercial single-bus computers. Several microprocessors can usefully be placed on a common bus because:

- Each microprocessor is much smaller than a multichip processor, so busses can be shorter.

- Caches can lower bus traffic.

- Mechanisms were invented to keep caches and memory consistent for multiprocessors, just as caches and memory are kept consistent for I/O.

Traffic per processor and the bus bandwidth determine the useful number of processors in such a multiprocessor. Figure 9.5 is a drawing of a generic single-bus multiprocessor. The caches replicate data in their faster memories both to reduce the latency to the data *and* to reduce the memory traffic on the bus.

Institution	Name	Maximum number proc.	Bits proc.	Proc. clock rate	Number of FPUs	Maximum memory size/ system (MB)	Communi- cations BW/ system (MB/sec)	Year
Sequent	Symmetry	30	32	16 MHz	30	240	53	1988
Silicon Graphics	4/360	16	32	40 MHz	16	512	320	1990
Sun	4/640	4	32	40 MHz	4	768	320	1991

FIGURE 9.4 Characteristics of four MIMD computers connected by a single backplane bus. Number of FPUs means number of floating-point units. Communications bandwidth for these machines is the bus bandwidth.

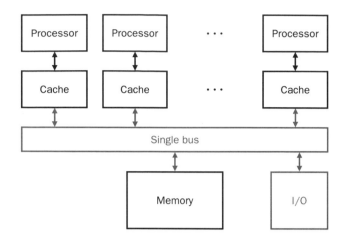

FIGURE 9.5 A single-bus multiprocessor. Typical size is between 2 and 32 processors.

Recall from Chapter 8 that I/O can experience inconsistencies in the value of data between the version in memory and the version in the cache. This *cache-coherency* problem applies to multiprocessors as well as I/O.

Example	Let's consider the parallel summing program we sketched in the example on page 597, but this time for a single-bus MIMD computer; let's assume we have 10 processors to sum the 100,000 numbers.

Answer	The first step again would be to split the set of numbers into subsets of the same size. This time we do not allocate the subsets to a different memory, since there is a single memory for this machine; we just give different starting addresses to each processor. Pn is the number of the processor, between 0 and 9. All processors start the program by running the loop that sums their subset of numbers:

```
sum[Pn] = 0;
for (i = 10000*Pn; i < 10000*(Pn+1); i = i + 1)
    sum[Pn] = sum[Pn] + A[i]; /* sum the assigned areas*/
```

This loop uses load instructions to bring the correct subset of numbers to the caches of each processor from the common main memory.

The next step is again to add these many partial sums, and once again we divide to conquer. Half of the processors add pairs of partial sums, then a quarter add pairs of the new partial sums, and so on until we have the final sum.

There are two important differences in this second step from the SIMD program. First, the partial sums are not sent and received; the requesting processor just loads from the address to get a copy of the partial sum. The hardware guarantees that the correct value will be supplied. The second difference is that the cooperating processors must synchronize to be sure the result is ready. With SIMD, each instruction is issued in lock step to all units, so there is no need to synchronize before sending and receiving results; with MIMD processors, there is no such implicit coordination, so there must be explicit synchronization at key points in the program. In this example, the two processors must synchronize before the "consumer" processor tries to read the result from the memory location written by the "producer" processor; otherwise, the consumer may read the old value of the data. Here is the code:

```
half = 10; /* 10 processors in single-bus MIMD*/
repeat
    synch(); /* wait for completion of partial sums */
    half = half/2; /* dividing line on who sums */
    if (Pn < half) sum[Pn] = sum[Pn] + sum[2*Pn];
until (half == 1); /* exit with final sum in Sum[0] */
```

We have used what is called a *barrier synchronization* primitive; processors wait at the barrier until every processor has reached it. Then they proceed. Barrier synchronization allows all processors to rapidly synchronize. This function can be implemented either in software with the lock synchronization primitive, described on pages 614 to 616, or with special hardware that combines each processor "ready" signal into a single global signal that all processors can test.

Unlike I/O, which rarely uses multiple data copies (a situation to be avoided whenever possible), as this example suggests, multiple processors require copies of the same data in multiple caches. Alternatively, accesses to shared data could be forced always to go around the cache to memory, but that would be too slow and it would require too much bus bandwidth; performance of a multiprocessor program depends on the performance of the system when sharing data. The protocols to maintain coherency for multiple processors are called *cache-coherency protocols*. The next few subsections explain cache-

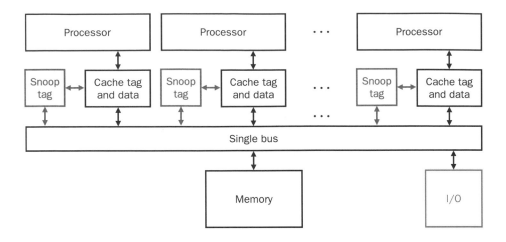

FIGURE 9.6 A single-bus multiprocessor using snooping cache coherency. The extra set of tags, shown in color, are used to handle snoop requests. The tags are duplicated to reduce the demands of snooping on the caches.

coherency protocols, methods of synchronizing processors using cache coherency, and the Sequent Symmetry multiprocessor as an example of a single-bus MIMD.

Multiprocessor Cache Coherency

The most popular protocol to maintain cache coherency is called *snooping*: Figure 9.6 shows how caches access memory over a common bus. All cache controllers monitor or *snoop* on the bus to determine whether or not they have a copy of the shared block.

Snooping became popular with machines of the 1980s, which used single buses to main memory. These uniprocessors were extended by adding multiple processors on that bus to give easy access to the shared memory. Caches were then added to improve the performance of each processor, leading to schemes to keep the caches up-to-date by snooping on the information over that shared bus.

Maintaining coherency has two components: reads and writes. Multiple copies are not a problem when reading, but a processor must have exclusive access to write a word. Processors must also have the most recent copy when reading an object, so all processors must get new values after a write. Thus, snooping protocols must locate all the caches that share an object to be written.

The consequence of a write to shared data is either to invalidate all other copies or to update the shared copies with the value being written.

The status bits already in a cache block are expanded for snooping protocols, and that information is used in monitoring bus activities. On a read miss, all caches check to see if they have a copy of the requested block and then take the appropriate action, such as supplying the data to the cache that missed. Similarly, on a write, all caches check to see if they have a copy and then act, either invalidating or updating their copy to the new value.

Since every bus transaction checks cache-address tags, one might assume that it interferes with the processor. It would interfere if not for duplicating the address-tag portion of the cache (not the whole cache) to get an extra read port for snooping; see Figure 9.6. This way, snooping rarely interferes with the processor's access to the cache. When there is interference, the processor will likely stall because the cache is unavailable.

Snooping protocols are of two types, depending on what happens on a write:

■ *Write-invalidate*: The writing processor causes all copies in other caches to be invalidated before changing its local copy; it is then free to update the *local* data until another processor asks for it. The writing processor issues an invalidation signal over the bus, and all caches check to see if they have a copy; if so, they must invalidate the block containing the word. Thus, this scheme allows multiple readers but only a single writer.

■ *Write-update*: Rather than invalidate every block that is shared, the writing processor broadcasts the new data over the bus; all copies are then updated with the new value. This scheme, also called *write broadcast*, continuously broadcasts writes to shared data while write invalidate deletes all other copies so that there is only one local copy for subsequent writes.

Write-update is like write-through because all writes go over the bus to update copies of the shared data. Write invalidate uses the bus only on the *first* write to invalidate the other copies, and hence subsequent writes do not result in bus activity. Consequently, write-invalidate has similar benefits to write-back in terms of reducing demands on bus bandwidth, while write-update has the advantage of making the new values appear in caches sooner, which can reduce latency.

Commercial cache-based multiprocessors use write-back caches because write-back reduces bus traffic and thereby allows more processors on a single bus. To preserve that precious communications bandwidth, all commercial machines also use write-invalidate as the standard protocol.

> **Hardware Software Interface**
>
> One insight is that block size plays an important role in cache coherency. For example, take the case of snooping on a cache with a block size of eight words, with a single word alternatively written and read by two processors. The protocol that only broadcasts or sends one word has an advantage over a scheme that transfers the full block.
>
> Large blocks can also cause what is called *false sharing*: When two unrelated shared variables are located in the same cache block, the full block is exchanged between processors even though the processors are accessing different variables (see Exercises 9.3 and 9.4). Compiler research is underway to reduce cache miss rates by allocating highly correlated data to the same cache block. Success in this effort could increase the desirability of large blocks for multiprocessors.

Measurements to date indicate that shared data has lower spatial and temporal locality than other types of data. Thus, shared data misses often dominate cache behavior even though they may be just 10% to 40% of the data references.

Elaboration: In a multiprocessor using cache coherency over a single bus, what happens if two processors try to write to the same shared data word in the same clock cycle? The bus arbiter decides which processor gets the bus first, and this processor will invalidate or update the other processor's copy depending on the protocol. The second processor then does its write. This sequential operation makes writes to different words in the same block work correctly.

An Example of a Cache-Coherency Protocol

To illustrate the intricacies of a cache-coherency protocol, Figure 9.7 shows a finite state transition diagram for a write-invalidation protocol based on a write-back policy. Each cache block is in one of three states:

1. *Read only*: This cache block is clean (not written) and may be shared.

2. *Read/Write*: This cache block is dirty (written) and is not shared.

3. *Invalid*: This cache block does not have valid data.

The three states of the protocol are duplicated in the figure to show transitions based on processor actions as opposed to transitions based on bus oper-

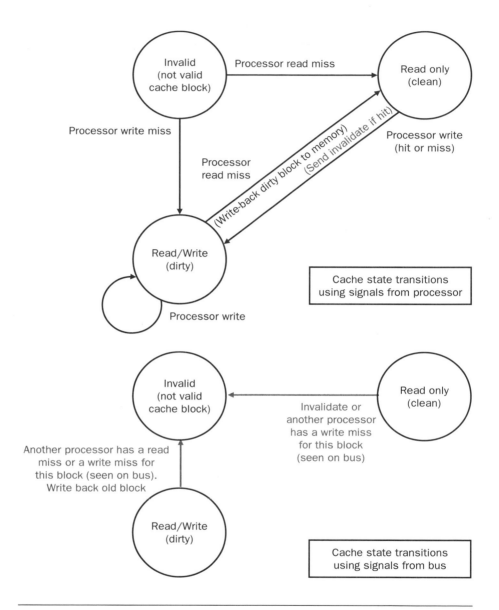

FIGURE 9.7 A write-invalidate, cache-coherency protocol. The upper part of the diagram shows state transitions based on actions of the processor associated with this cache; the lower part shows transitions based on actions of other processors seen as operations on the bus. There is only one state machine in a cache, although there are two represented here to clarify when a transition occurs. The black arrows and actions specified in black text would be found in caches without coherency, with the colored arrows and actions added to achieve cache coherency. In contrast to what is shown here, some protocols call writes to clean data a write miss, so that there is no separate signal for invalidation.

ations. This is done only for purposes of illustration; there is really only one finite state machine per cache, with stimuli coming either from the attached processor or from the bus.

Transitions in the state of a cache block happen on read misses, write misses, or write hits; read hits do not change cache state. Let's start with a read miss. When the processor has a read miss that maps onto a block, it will change the state of that block to Read Only and write back the old block if the block was in the Read/Write state (dirty). All the caches in the other processors monitor the read miss to see if this block is in their cache. If one has a copy and it is in the Read/Write state, then the block is written to memory and, in this protocol, that block is changed to the Invalid state. (Some protocols would change the state to Read Only.) The read miss is then satisfied by reading from memory.

Now let's try writes. To write a block, the processor acquires the bus, sends an invalidate signal, writes into that block and places it in the Read/Write state. Because other caches monitor the bus, all caches check to see if they have a copy of that block; if they do, they invalidate it.

As you might imagine, there are many variations on cache coherency that are much more complicated than this simple model. The variations include whether or not the other caches try to supply the block if they have a copy, whether or not the block must be invalidated on a read miss, as well as whether writes invalidate or update the results as discussed earlier.

Synchronization Using Coherency

One of the major requirements of a single-bus multiprocessor is to be able to coordinate processes that are working on a common task. Typically, a programmer will use *lock variables* to coordinate or synchronize the processes. The challenge for the architect of a multiprocessor is to provide a mechanism to decide which processor gets the lock and to provide the operation that locks a variable. Arbitration is easy for single-bus multiprocessors, since the bus is the only path to memory: the processor that gets the bus locks out all other processors from memory. If the processor and bus provide an *atomic swap operation*, programmers can create locks with the proper semantics. The adjective *atomic* is key, for it means that a processor can both read a location *and* set it to the locked value in the same bus operation, preventing any other processor from reading or writing memory.

Figure 9.8 shows a typical procedure for locking a variable using an atomic swap instruction. Assume that 0 means unlocked ("go") and 1 means locked ("stop"). A processor first reads the lock variable to test its state. A processor keeps reading and testing until the value indicates that the lock is unlocked. The processor then races against all other processors that were similarly *spin waiting* to see who can lock the variable first. All processors use an atomic

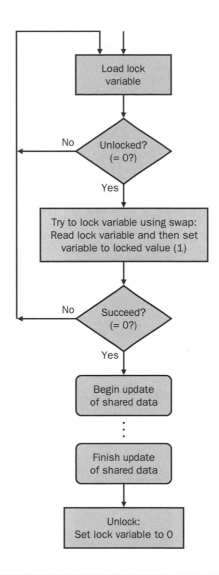

FIGURE 9.8 Steps to acquire a lock to synchronize processes and then to release the lock on exit from the key section of code.

swap instruction that reads the old value and stores a 1 ("stop") into the lock variable. The single winner will see the 0 ("go"), and the losers will see a 1 that was placed there by the winner. (The losers will continue to write the variable with the locked value of 1, but that doesn't change its value.) The winning pro-

Step	Processor P0	Processor P1	Processor P2	Bus activity
1	Has lock	Spins, testing if lock = 0	Spins, testing if lock = 0	None
2	Sets lock to 0 and 0 sent over bus	Spins, testing if lock = 0	Spins, testing if lock = 0	Write-invalidate of lock variable from P0
3		Cache miss	Cache miss	Bus decides to service P2 cache miss
4		(Waits while bus busy)	Lock = 0	Cache miss for P2 satisfied
5		Lock = 0	Swap: reads lock and sets to 1	Cache miss for P1 satisfied
6		Swap: reads lock and sets to 1	Value from swap = 0 and 1 sent over bus	Write-invalidate of lock variable from P2
7		Value from swap = 1 and 1 sent over bus	Owns the lock, so can update shared data	Write-invalidate of lock variable from P1
8		Spins, testing if lock = 0		None

FIGURE 9.9 Cache-coherency steps and bus traffic for three processors, P0, P1, and P2. This figure assumes write-invalidate coherency. P0 starts with the lock (step 1). P0 exits and unlocks the lock (step 2). P1 and P2 race to see which reads the unlocked value during the swap (steps 3–5). P2 wins and enters the critical section (steps 6 and 7), while P1 spins and waits (steps 7 and 8).

cessor then executes the code that updates the shared data. When the winner exits, it stores a 0 ("go") into the lock variable, thereby starting the race all over again.

Let's examine how the spin lock scheme of Figure 9.8 works with bus-based cache coherency. One advantage of this algorithm is that it allows processors to spin wait on a local copy of the lock in their caches. This reduces the amount of bus traffic; Figure 9.9 shows the bus and cache operations for multiple processors trying to lock a variable. Once the processor with the lock stores a 0 into the lock, all other caches see that store and invalidate their copy of the lock variable. Then they try to get the new value for the lock of 0. (With write-update cache coherency, the caches would update their copy rather than first invalidate and then load from memory.) This new value starts the race to see who can set the lock first. The winner gets the bus and stores a 1 into the lock; the other caches replace their copy of the lock variable containing 0 with a 1. They read that the variable is already locked and must return to testing and spinning.

This scheme has difficulty scaling up to many processors because of the communication traffic generated when the lock is released.

The Sequent Symmetry Multiprocessor

Several research projects and companies investigated the single-bus multiprocessors in the 1980s. One example is Sequent Computer Systems, Inc.,

FIGURE 9.10 Photograph of the Sequent Symmetry. Photo courtesy of Sequent Computer Systems, Inc.

founded to build multiprocessors based on standard microprocessors and the UNIX operating system. In 1986, Sequent began to design the Symmetry multiprocessor, assuming a microprocessor four to five times faster than the processor in an earlier system. Figure 9.10 is a photograph of the Sequent Symmetry. The goal was to support as many processors as possible using the I/O controllers developed for the earlier system. This meant the bus had to remain compatible, although the new memory and bus system had to deliver roughly four to five times more bandwidth than the older system. Figure 9.11 shows the organization of the machine.

The goal of higher memory-system bandwidth with a similar bus was attacked on four levels. First, the cache was increased to 64 KB, increasing the hit rate and therefore the effective memory bandwidth as seen by the processor. Second, the cache policy was changed from write-through to write-back to reduce the number of write operations on the shared bus. To maintain cache coherency with write-back, Symmetry used a write-invalidate scheme. The third change was to double the bus width to 64 bits, thereby doubling the bus bandwidth to 53 MB/sec. The final change was to have each memory controller interleave memory as two banks, allowing the memory system to match the bandwidth of the wider bus. The memory system can have up to six controllers with up to 240 MB of main memory.

One experiment evaluated the Symmetry as a timeshared (multiprogrammed) multiprocessor running ten independent programs, comparing

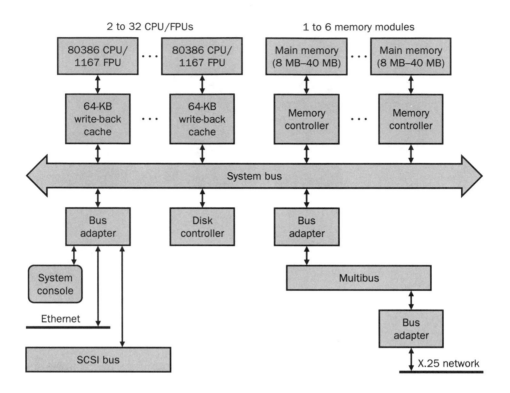

FIGURE 9.11 The Sequent Symmetry multiprocessor has up to 30 microprocessors, each with 64 KB of two-way set associative, write-back caches connected over the shared system bus. Up to six memory controllers also talk to this 64-bit-wide bus, plus some interfaces for I/O. In addition to a special-purpose disk controller, there is an interface for the system console, Ethernet network, and SCSI I/O bus (see Chapter 8), as well as another interface for Multibus. I/O devices can be attached either to SCSI or to Multibus, as the customer desires. (Although all interfaces are labeled "Bus adapter," each is a unique design.) For more details on cache behavior of this machine, see T. Lovett and S. Thakkar, "The Symmetry multiprocessor system," in *Proc. 1988 International Conference on Parallel Processing*, 303–310.

write-through and write-back cache policies. The experiment ran *n* copies of the program on *n* processors. This study found that with write-through, about half the programs started to stray from linearly increasing throughput at 6 to 8 processors, yet with write-back, all but one of the ten programs stayed near linear for up to 28 processors. (The single failure was caused by hot spots in the operating system rather than by the write-back coherency protocol.)

Notice that in this style of parallel processor, memory access times are uniform: for all processors, the time of a memory access is equally fast (in the local cache) or slow (in main memory). This is in contrast to the network-connected machines discussed in the next section. Hence, the label *uniform memory access* is applied to machines in which the time for a memory access is uniform; *nonuniform memory access* applies to other machines. In the next section, we will discuss examples of nonuniform access computers.

9.6 MIMDs Connected by a Network

Single-bus designs are attractive, but limited because the three desirable bus characteristics are incompatible: high bandwidth, low latency, and unlimited length. There is also a limit to the bandwidth of a single memory module attached to a bus. Thus, a single bus imposes practical constraints on the number of processors that can be connected to it; to date, the largest number of processors connected to a single bus in a commercial computer is 30.

If the goal is to connect many more processors together, then the computer designer needs to use more than a single bus. Figure 9.12 shows how this can be organized. Note that in Figure 9.5 on page 608, the connection medium—the bus—is between the processors and memory, whereas in Figure 9.12, memory is attached to each processor and the connection medium—the network—is between these combined nodes. For single-bus systems the medium is used on every memory access, while in the latter case it is used only for interprocessor communication.

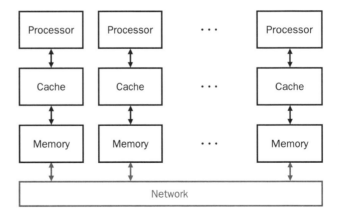

FIGURE 9.12 The organization of a network-connected multiprocessor. Typical size is between 32 and 1024 processors. Note that, in contrast to Figure 9.5, the multiprocessor connection is no longer between memory and the processor. MIMDs have also been built with the network between the processors and memory; the Cray XMP and YMP multiprocessors are perhaps the best known examples, but this placement is currently out of favor.

This brings us to a debate about the organization of memory in large-scale parallel processors. The debate unfortunately often centers on a false dichotomy: *shared memory* versus *distributed memory*. Shared memory really means a single address space, implying implicit communication with loads and stores. The real opposite of a single address is *multiple private address spaces*, implying explicit communication with sends and receives. Distributed memory refers to the physical location of the memory. If physical memory is divided into modules, with some placed near each processor, as in Figure 9.12, then physical memory is distributed. The real opposite of distributed memory is *centralized memory*, where access time to a physical memory location is the same for all processors because every access goes over the interconnect, as in Figure 9.5. This style of machine is sometimes called *dance hall*, with the processors all on one side and the memories all on the other, invoking the image of a school dance with the boys on one side of the floor and the girls on the other.

Single address space versus multiple address spaces and distributed memory versus centralized memory are orthogonal issues: MIMDs can have a single address space and a distributed physical memory or multiple private address spaces and a centralized physical memory. The proper debates concern the pros and cons of a single address space, of explicit communication, and of distributed physical memory.

For large-scale parallel machines, the argument about distribution of physical memory was recently resolved; every large-scale machine distributes physical memory, as the cost/performance advantage of keeping some memory near each processor is too great to ignore. Another argument is that it is much easier to construct a machine that can scale by a factor of 100 if the memory and the processor are on the same unit being replicated. In such organizations, the local memory is much faster than nonlocal memory, varying from 3 to 10 times faster with hardware support; it is even slower if messages are sent. Programmers of large-scale parallel machines try to minimize accesses to non-local memory. These parallel processors are called *nonuniform memory access machines*.

In machines without a single global address, communication is explicit; the programmer or the compiler must send messages to ship data to another node and must receive messages to accept data from another node.

Example   Let's try our summing example again for a network-connected MIMD with 100 processors using multiple address spaces.

Answer

Since this computer has multiple address spaces just like a SIMD, the code might be similar to that version. Like the SIMD code and in contrast to the single-bus MIMD code, the first step is distributing the 100 subsets to each of the local memories. The processor containing the 100,000 numbers sends the subsets to each of the 100 processor-memory nodes.

Now let's examine the SIMD code to see what changes need to be made to run on the network-connected MIMD:

```
sum = 0;
for (i = 0; i < 1000; i = i + 1) /* loop over each array */
  sum = sum + A1[i]; /* sum the local arrays */
limit = 100;
half = 100;/* 100 processors in this network-MIMD*/
repeat
  half = half/2; /* send vs. receive dividing line*/
  if (Pn >= half && Pn < limit) send(Pn % half,sum);
  if (Pn < half) sum = sum + receive();
  limit = half; /* upper limit of senders */
until (half == 1); /* exit with final sum */
```

The first three lines sum the subset of numbers in each node. This code works fine as is. The last seven lines perform the sum of the partial sums from multiple address spaces. The only potential problem with the code above is synchronization; in SIMD, each instruction is executed in all units at the same time, but there is no such lockstep operation in MIMD. This code divides all processors into senders or receivers and each receiving processor gets only one message, so we can presume that a receiving processor will stall until it receives a message. Thus, send and receive can be used as primitives for synchronization as well as for communication, as the processors are aware of the transmission of data. With these assumptions, this SIMD code works without modification on the network-connected MIMD.

Figure 9.13 shows the characteristics of several network-connected MIMDs. Since the number of pins per chip is limited, not all processors can be connected directly. This restriction has inspired a whole zoo of topologies for consideration in the design of the network. In the next subsection, we'll look at the characteristics of some of the key alternatives of network designs.

Network Topologies

The straightforward way to connect processor-memory nodes is to have a dedicated communication link between every node. Between the high cost/performance of this *fully connected* network and the low cost/performance of a bus are a set of networks that constitute a wide range of trade-offs

Institution	Name	No. proc.	Bits proc.	Proc. clock rate MHz	No. of FPUs	Memory size/ system (MB)	Communications BW (MB/sec)		Year
							Peak	Bisection	
Intel	iPSC/2	128	16	16 MHz	128	512 MB	896	345	1988
nCube	nCube/ten	1024	32	10 MHz	1024	512 MB	10,240	640	1987
Intel	Delta	540	32	40 MHz	540	17,280 MB	21,600	640	1991
Thinking Machines	CM-5	1024	32	33 MHz	4096	32,768 MB	5120	5120	1991

FIGURE 9.13 Characteristics of four MIMD computers connected by a network. Number of FPUs means number of floating-point units. All these machines have distributed physical memory and multiple private address spaces.

in cost/performance. Network costs include the number of switches, the number of links on a switch to connect to the network, the width (number of bits) per link, and length of the links when the network is mapped into a physical machine. For example, on a machine that scales between tens and thousands of processors, some links may be metal rectangles within a chip that are a few millimeters long, and others may be cables that must stretch several meters from one cabinet to another. Network performance is multifaceted as well. It includes the latency on an unloaded network to send and receive a message, the throughput in terms of the maximum number of messages that can be transmitted in a given time period, delays caused by contention for a portion of the network, and variable performance depending on the pattern of communication. Another obligation of the network may be fault tolerance, for very large systems may be required to operate in the presence of broken components.

Networks are normally drawn as graphs, with each arc of the graph representing a link of the communication network. The processor-memory node is shown as the black square and the switch is shown as a colored circle. In this section, all links are *bidirectional*; that is, information can flow in either direction. All networks consist of *switches* whose links go to processor-memory nodes and to other switches. The first improvement over a bus is a network that connects a sequence of nodes together:

This topology is called a *ring*. Since some nodes are not directly connected, some messages will have to hop along intermediate nodes until they arrive at the final destination.

Unlike a bus, a ring is capable of many simultaneous transfers. Because there are numerous topologies to chose from, performance metrics are needed to distinguish these designs. Two are popular. The first is *total network bandwidth*, which is the bandwidth out each link multiplied by the number of links. This represents the very best case. For the ring network above with P processors, the total network bandwidth would be P times the bandwidth of one link; the total network bandwidth of a bus is just the bandwidth of that bus, or 1 times the bandwidth of that link.

To balance this best case, we include another metric which is closer to the worst case: the *bisection bandwidth*. This is calculated by dividing the machine into two parts, each with half the nodes. Then you sum the bandwidth of the links that cross that imaginary dividing line. The bisection bandwidth of a ring is 2 times the link bandwidth and it is 1 time the link bandwidth for the bus. If a single link is as fast as the bus, the ring is only twice as fast as a bus in the worst case, but it is P times faster in the best case.

Since some network topologies are not symmetric, the question arises of where to draw the imaginary line when bisecting the machine. This is a worst-case metric, so the answer is to choose the division that yields the most pessimistic network performance; stated alternatively, calculate all possible bisection bandwidths and pick the smallest.

At the other extreme from a ring is a *fully connected network*, where every processor has a bidirectional link to every other processor. For fully connected networks, the total network bandwidth is $(P \times P{-}1)/2$ and the bisection bandwidth is $(P/2)^2$.

The tremendous improvement in performance of fully connected networks is offset by the tremendous increase in cost. This inspires engineers to invent new topologies that are between the cost of rings and the performance of fully connected networks. The evaluation of success depends in large part on the nature of the communication in the workload of parallel programs run on the machine.

The number of different topologies that have been discussed in publications would be difficult to count, but the number that have been used in commercial parallel processors is just a handful. Figure 9.14 illustrates two of the popular topologies. Real machines frequently add extra links to these simple topologies to improve performance and reliability. Figure 9.15 summarizes these different topologies using the two metrics of this section for 64 nodes.

An alternative to placing a processor at every node in a network is to leave only the switch at some of these nodes. The switches are smaller than processor-memory-switch nodes, and thus may be packed more densely, thereby lessening distance and increasing performance. Such networks are frequently called *multistage networks* to reflect the multiple steps that a message may travel. Types of multistage networks are as numerous as single-stage networks;

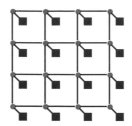
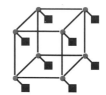

a. 2D grid or mesh of 16 nodes   b. N-cube tree of 8 nodes ($8 = 2^3$ so n = 3)

FIGURE 9.14 Network topologies that have appeared in commercial parallel processors. The colored circles represent switches and the black squares represent processor-memory nodes. Even though a switch has many links, generally only one goes to the processor. The Boolean n-cube topology is an n-dimensional interconnect with 2^n nodes, requiring n links per switch (plus one for the processor) and thus n nearest neighbor nodes. Frequently these basic topologies have been supplemented with extra arcs to improve performance and reliability. For example, the switches in the left and right columns of the 2D grid could be connected through the unused ports on each switch, making four horizontal rings.

Evaluation category		Bus	Ring	2D grid	6-cube	Fully connected
Performance	Total network bandwidth	1	64	112	192	2016
	Bisection bandwidth	1	2	8	32	1024
Cost	Ports per switch	n.a.	3	5	7	64
	Total number of links	1	128	176	256	2080

FIGURE 9.15 Relative cost and performance of several interconnects for 64 nodes. Note that any network topology that scales the bisection bandwidth linearly must scale the number of network links faster than linearly. Figure 9.16a is an example of a fully connected network.

Figure 9.16 illustrates two of the popular multistage organizations. A *fully connected* or *crossbar network* allows any node to communicate with any other node in one pass through the network. An *Omega network* uses less hardware than the crossbar network ($2n \log_2 n$ vs. n^2 switches), but contention can occur between messages, depending on the pattern of communication. For example, the Omega network in Figure 9.16 cannot send a message from P0 to P6 at the same time it sends a message from P1 to P7.

Implementing Network Topologies

This simple analysis of all the networks in this section ignores important practical considerations in the construction of a network. The distance of each link affects the cost of communicating at a high clock rate—generally, the

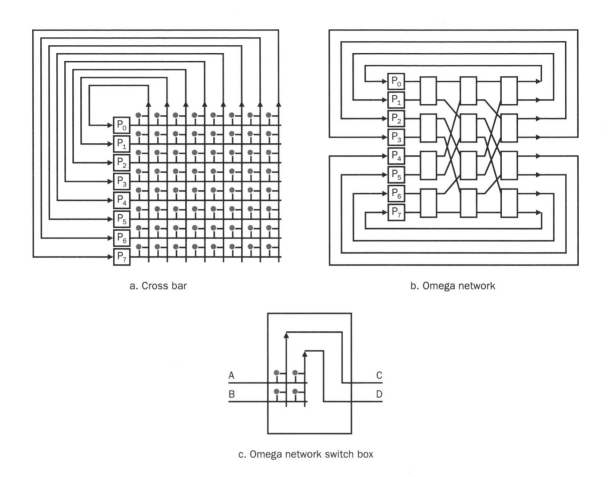

a. Cross bar

b. Omega network

c. Omega network switch box

FIGURE 9.16 Popular multistage network topologies for 8 nodes. The switches in these drawings are simpler than in earlier drawings because the links are unidirectional; data comes in at the bottom and exits out the right link. The switch box in (c) can pass A to C and B to D or B to C and A to D. The crossbar uses n^2 switches, where n is the number of processors while the Omega network uses $n/2 \log_2 n$ of the large switch boxes, each of which is logically composed of 4 of the smaller switches. In this case the crossbar uses 64 switches versus 12 switch boxes or 48 switches in the Omega network. The crossbar, however, can support any combination of messages between processors while the Omega network cannot.

longer the distance, the more expensive it is to run at a high clock rate. Shorter distances also make it easier to assign more wires to the link, as the power to drive many wires from a chip is less if the wires are short. Shorter wires are also cheaper than long wires. A final practical limitation is that the three-dimensional drawings must be mapped onto chips and boards which are essentially two-dimensional media. The bottom line is that topologies that

Institution	Name	Number of nodes	Basic topology	Bits/ link	Network clock rate	BW/Link (MB/sec)	BW/System (MB/sec)	Bisection (MB/sec)	Year
U. Illinois	Illiac IV	64	2D grid	64	5 MHz	40	2560	320	1972
ICL	DAP	4096	2D grid	1	5 MHz	0.6	2560	40	1980
Goodyear	MPP	16,384	2D grid	1	10 MHz	1.2	20,480	160	1982
Thinking Machines	CM-2	1024 to 4096	12-cube	1	7 MHz	1	65,536	1024	1987
nCube	nCube/ten	1 to 1024	10-cube	1	10 MHz	1.2	10,240	640	1987
Intel	iPSC/2	16 to 128	7-cube	1	16 MHz	2	896	345	1988
Maspar	MP-1216	32 to 512	2D grid + multistage Omega	1	25 MHz	3	23,000	1300	1989
Intel	Delta	540	2D grid	16	40 MHz	40	21,600	640	1991
Thinking Machines	CM-5	32 to 1024	Multistage fat tree	4	40 MHz	20	20,480	5120	1991

FIGURE 9.17 Characteristics of networks of some parallel processors mentioned in this chapter. The Maspar machine packs 32 4-bit processors per node chip, and the CM-2 packs 16 1-bit processors per node chip. The 2D grid of the Intel Delta is 16 rows by 35 columns.

appear elegant when sketched on the blackboard may look awkward when constructed from chips, cables, boards, and boxes. To put this section in perspective, Figure 9.17 lists the networks used in the parallel processors used in this book. Note that this figure includes SIMDs as well as MIMDs. In the following subsection, we describe a network-connected MIMD in more detail.

The Connection Machine 5 from Thinking Machines

One system design goal of the CM-5, which was introduced by Thinking Machines Corporation in 1991, was to scale to 1 teraFLOPs—one million megaFLOPS—which would require thousands of processors, given the available technologies. As a result, the design emphasizes the scalability of all aspects of the system, particularly the data network. The CM-5 attaches both processing nodes and I/O devices to the data network, allowing both computation and I/O bandwidth to scale as required by the customer. Thus, users could have a machine with 1024 processors and connections for 32 disk systems, or 32 processors and 1024 disk systems. Initial orders for the machine varied between 32 and 1024 processors.

The CM-5 bridges traditional SIMD and MIMD architectures by supplementing the traditional data network with a second network, called the *control network*, which directly supports SIMD communication operations. This allows the CM-5 to take advantage of the SIMD software technology developed for the CM-2, as well as supporting other MIMD programming styles.

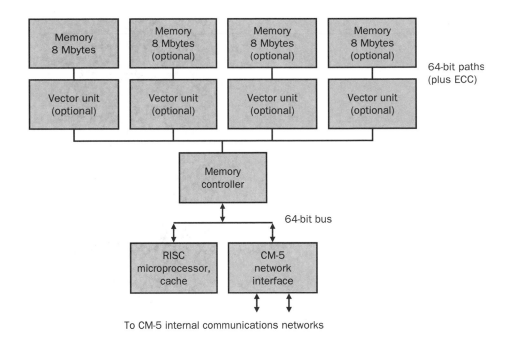

FIGURE 9.18 The CM-5 processing node. The base configuration has between 8 and 32 MB of memory, while the vector units only come with 32 MB. The RISC microprocessor chosen is SPARC.

Because of the desire to build very large systems, the CM-5 designers included a number of features to enhance the overall system reliability. First, the CM-5 is designed to operate in the presence of processor or network failures, minimizing the performance effects of hardware failures. Second, the CM-5 includes a third network, called the *diagnostics network*, which is capable of running manufacturing quality tests on the components while they are in the system. Finally, the CM-5 includes many mechanisms to detect runtime failures in a timely manner. These include error correcting codes on data stored in processor memory, and checks on the sanity of network messages as they pass through each switch.

The CM-5 computation node consists of a SPARC microprocessor with an optional vector execution unit, up to 32 MB of memory, and a network interface. Figure 9.18 illustrates the node. The SPARC processor controls the node and makes use of the slave vector units for operations on large floating-point or integer arrays. A vector unit executes SIMD-like instructions of a single operation on a collection of data. Instead of using multiple execution units as in

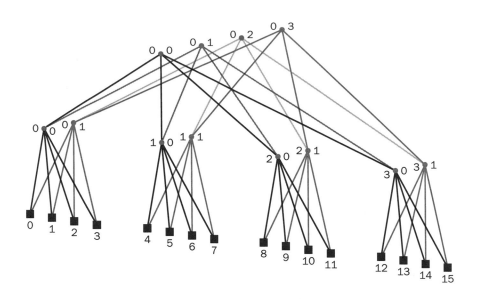

FIGURE 9.19 The CM-5 data network fat-tree topology for 16 nodes or I/O devices. The colored circles in are switches and the squares at the bottom are processor-memory nodes. Some lines are in color to make the fat tree easier to understand. In this fat-tree implementation, the switches have four downward connections and two or four upward connections; in this figure, switches have two upward connections. This three-dimensional view shows the increase in bandwidth over a simple tree as you move up from the nodes at the bottom.

SIMD, vector processors use a single unit that is heavily pipelined. All other computations are performed by the SPARC processor itself. The node memory is addressable by both the vector units and the SPARC processor.

The vector units are optimized for streaming 64-bit data from their memory bank through their internal IEEE floating-point and integer ALUs. The vector units include internal registers for storage of temporary variables, and are capable of generating their own independent memory addresses. Each vector unit is capable of a peak rate of 32 megaflops, giving the CM-5 computation node an aggregate peak rate of 128 megaflops.

The network interface attaches the node to both the data network and control network, and allows direct user access to both networks without being encumbered by the operating system overhead. The elaboration at the end of this section gives the details on how the CM-5 does this.

The CM-5 data network is a tree-based topology, but has bandwidth added higher in the tree to match the requirements of common communications patterns. This topology, commonly called a *fat tree*, is shown in Figure 9.19. Data travels between nodes in messages which can hold 1 to 4 data words. The

FIGURE 9.20 The Thinking Machines' CM-5, announced in 1991, scales from 32 processors up to 16,384 processors. The machine in the photograph has 768 processors. The largest initial order was for 1024 processors. If someone has $100,000,000 in 1993, Thinking Machines will build a machine with a peak performance of over one teraFLOPS. Photo courtesy of Thinking Machines Corporation.

nodes are numbered starting at 0, and nodes address messages to other nodes by this numeric address. The fat-tree topology provides many different paths between a given pair of nodes. The switches in the tree use randomization techniques to evenly spread the message load across the possible paths, and use switching strategies which avoid message deadlock and guarantee equal access to the network to all nodes.

Figure 9.20 is a photograph of the CM-5.

Elaboration: Giving users the ability to send and receive messages without invoking the operating system would seem to defeat protection mechanisms necessary in a multiuser system. This is not the case in the CM-5 because of several mechanisms. First, messages for the operating system are tagged so that they cause an interrupt upon arrival at the destination, thereby invoking the operating system kernel in each node. Thus the user cannot subvert messages for the operating system. Second, the

CM-5 operating system schedules all the processors in a particular section of the machine to be running the same program, and the CM-5 hardware and operating system prevent messages from leaving a section, called a *partition*. Moreover, the complete state of the network in a partition can be saved and restored when a processor is swapped in and out. Because of this, a user program cannot send or receive messages intended for other programs. Finally, portions of the network interface that support these mechanisms are protected from the user, so a user program is limited to sending and receiving user messages.

9.7 | Future Directions for Parallel Processors

Uniprocessor performance is improving at an unprecedented rate, with microprocessors leading the way. Figure 1.19 on page 27 shows that the fastest microprocessors have increased in performance by 50% per year every year since 1987. This rapid rate of change does not come free: estimates of the cost of development of the recent MIPS R4000 include 30 engineers for three years, requiring about $30 million to develop the chip, another $10 million to fabricate it, and 50,000 hours on machines rated at 20 MIPS to simulate the chip. The effort needed to reach such high levels of performance, combined with the relatively low cost of purchasing such microprocessors, led Cray Research, Intel, and Thinking Machines to use off-the-shelf microprocessors in their new large-scale parallel processors.

Memory capacity has improved at a high rate for a considerably longer time than for processors. Figure 1.14 on page 22 shows that DRAMs have increased their capacity fourfold every three years. Once again, the tremendous development investment, combined with the low cost of purchasing DRAMs, has led almost all computer manufacturers, including parallel processor companies, to build their memories from DRAMs.

A final technology is the interconnection network. The bandwidth of the interconnection network has improved because of improvements in the speed of logic, improvements in the packaging of parallel processors, and simply by increasing the number of wires in the links that make up the interconnection network. For example, Intel improved its peak bandwidth per link from 0.5 MB/second in the iPSC in 1986 to 40 MB/second in the Delta in 1991, in part by increasing the number of bits per link from 1 to 16.

Thus, the three technologies available to parallel processor designers are fast microprocessors, high-capacity DRAMs, and increasing network bandwidth; interestingly, are all improving at comparable rates.

Facts of Life for Large-Scale Parallel Processors

These exciting opportunities are constrained by some "facts of life" for the parallel processor designer. The first fact of life is that because the nodes are very similar to the core of a workstation, the cost of a large-scale parallel processor node is comparable to the cost of a workstation. As the most expensive supercomputer costs less than $25,000,000 for processor and memory and as the price of workstations has remained between $5000 and $10,000, even if such machines could match workstation prices the largest parallel processors will have between 2500 and 5000 nodes. This does not include the cost of the interconnection network, leading to even fewer nodes. Furthermore, many computers are purchased for scientific applications at a much lower price; thus, these machines have far fewer nodes than the practical maximum. For example, Los Alamos National Labs purchased a CM-5 with 1024 nodes, the Army High Performance Computer Research Center purchased a CM-5 with 512 nodes, and both the University of California and the University of Wisconsin have parallel processors with 128 nodes. Accordingly, while a practical limit of the number of processors is 1000 to 10,000 in the 1990s, for many customers and applications, 100 to 1000 processors will be sufficient.

While this number is smaller than many researchers assumed it would be, it is still large enough to give pause to the parallel processor designer, who must be very sensitive to the cost of a node. An extra $1000 per node, when multiplied by 1000, costs the designer's company $1,000,000, with the increased price to the customer on the order of $4,000,000.

The topology of the interconnection network is important in the construction of a machine that can scale from 100 to 10,000 nodes, and the best topology for 100 to 500 nodes may not be the choice for 1000 to 10,000 nodes. Thus, the topology may vary with the maximum number of nodes and the packaging choices for that machine. The good news is that there are many good interconnection network topologies to choose from; the bad news is that, given these fine alternatives and the importance of the topology to the cost of the machine, there is unlikely to be a single topology that all parallel processor companies will follow. For example, the nCube/2 uses a hypercube topology, the Intel Delta uses a two-dimensional grid, and the TMC CM-5 uses a fat tree (Figure 9.19).

**Hardware
Software
Interface**

The lack of a standard topology is less of an obstacle to portable parallel processor programs than one might first suspect. One reason is that the software overhead to send a message is so large that it masks the effects of the topology. In other words, these costs are so high that the time to send a message to the nearest neighbor node is similar to the time to send to the furthest neighbor. Figure 9.21 shows the overhead cost to send a message for several parallel processors. The overhead is high in some cases because the protocols are designed to send large messages, so that sometimes by pipelining them, the latency is seen only once. Such pipelined routing is called *wormhole routing*. Other reasons for the high overhead are invoking the operating system on sending or receiving a message and a slow interface between the processor and the network.

The second reason for the lesser importance of topologies is that cost-effective fault tolerance is incompatible with topology-dependent algorithms, because by definition a broken link or node means that sometimes messages will follow different paths than the programmer would expect from the network topology. Fault tolerance is critical because a machine with 10,000 nodes, each similar to a workstation, should have a mean time between failures that is 10,000 times worse than a workstation. Thus, with large parallel processors, the question is not *whether* anything is broken at any point in time, but rather *how many* components are broken. Parallel processors must work in the presence of broken network links and broken nodes; hence large parallel proces-

Machine	Message overhead in processor clock cycles	Clock cycle rate	Year
nCube	6400	40 MHz	1987
nCube, optimized software	1000	40 MHz	1987
Intel iPSC/860	1500	33 MHz	1990
CM-5	3600	40 MHz	1991
CM-5, optimized software	132	40 MHz	1991

FIGURE 9.21 Measured message overhead on several parallel processors. This does not include the latency of the network; just the time to launch a message. The optimized software uses active messages which operate at the kernel level in most machines, while the unoptimized software is what came from the manufacturer (T. von Eicken et al., *Active Messages: A Mechanism for Integrated Communication and Computation*, 19th Annual Symposium on Computer Architecture, Gold Coast, Australia, May 1992, 256–266). While we can expect the overhead to drop, it is likely to remain significant.

sors are not amenable to topology-specific algorithms even if the overhead of communication is reduced.

Taken in combination, these elements deflate the value of topology-specific algorithms:

- The lack of a standard topology combined with the importance of portable parallel processor programs to the success of the industry;

- the high overhead of communication, making the latency virtually the same for messages independent of the distance between nodes; and

- operation in the presence of broken links and broken nodes.

Two other facts of life for the parallel processor designer are summarized more quickly. As we saw in Figure 7.13 on page 476 in Chapter 7, DRAMs are getting bigger but not faster, so caches are very important to bridging the gap between DRAM speed and processor speed; virtually all new microprocessors come with caches on the chip. For this reason, locality of reference will be important to get the best performance per node, just as it is for workstations. The second point is that floating-point performance is critical for the parallel processors. Floating-point applications created a need for vector supercomputers, and they sustained the vector supercomputer industry which in turn led to more of these applications. Hence the natural software applications for parallel processors are floating-point intensive applications.

A Common Building Block

There was considerably more diversity in the parallel processors of the 1980s, but the technological opportunities and facts of life of the 1990s are driving commercial parallel processors toward a common hardware organization. Figure 9.22 shows the four components of this organization: DRAM-based main memory, microprocessors, an interconnection network, and network interfaces between the processor-memory pairs and the interconnection network. We believe this organization will dominate commercial parallel processors at least for the rest of this decade, for the reasons discussed above. Current examples of this popular organization include the Cray Research T3D, Intel Delta and Paragon, nCube parallel processors, Thinking Machines' CM-5, and the Transputer-based parallel processors. These companies and machines dominate today's large-scale parallel processor industry.

For all these reasons, we believe designers of the massively parallel processors of the 1990s are much more likely to limit the largest machine to thousands of 64-bit processors rather than to millions of 1-bit processors.

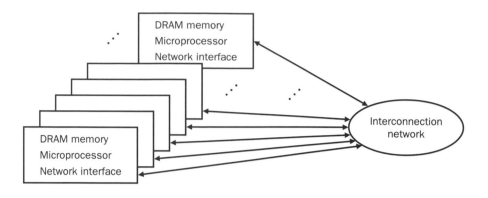

FIGURE 9.22 The common organization of parallel processors for the 1990s. This organization characterizes most parallel processors. For example, it covers the Cray Research MPPP, Intel Paragon, nCube, Thinking Machines CM-5, and Transputer-based parallel processors, such as the Meiko Computing Surface or the Parsytec GC.

> ### The Big Picture
>
> A key characteristic of programs for parallel machines is frequency of synchronization and communication. Large-scale parallel machines have distributed physical memory; the higher bandwidth and lower overhead of local memory compared to nonlocal memory strongly rewards parallel processing programmers who utilize locality.

Addressing in Large-Scale Parallel Processors

With widespread agreement on distributed memory, the next question facing future machines is communication. For the hardware designer the simplest solution is to offer only send and receive instead of the implicit communication that is possible as part of any load or store. Send and receive also have the advantage of making it easier for the programmer to optimize communication: It's simpler to overlap computation with communication by using explicit sends and receives rather than implicit loads and stores.

On the other hand, loads and stores normally have much lower communication overhead than do sends and receives. And some applications will have references to remote information that is only occasionally and unpredictably accessed, so it is much more efficient to use an address to remote data rather than to retrieve it in case it might be used. Adding a single address space to sends and receives so that communication is possible as part of any load or store is harder, although it is comparable to the virtual memory system already found in most processors (see Chapter 7). A uniprocessor uses page tables to decide if an address points to data in local memory or on a disk; this translation system might be modified to decide if the address points to local data, to data in another processors's memory, or to disk.

Caches are important to performance no matter how communication is performed, so we want to allow the shared data to appear in the cache of the processor that owns the data as well as in the processor that requests the data. Thus, the single global address resurrects cache coherency, since there are multiple copies of the same data with the same address in different processors. Clearly the bus-snooping protocols of section 9.5 won't work here, as there is no single bus on which all memory references are broadcast.

An alternative to bus snooping is *directories*. In directory-based protocols there is logically a single directory that keeps the state of every block in main memory. Information in the directory can include which caches have copies of the block, whether it is dirty, and so on. Of course, directory entries can be distributed so that different requests can go to different memories, thereby reducing contention and allowing a scalable design. Directories retain the characteristic that the sharing status of a block is always in a single known location, making a large-scale parallel processor plausible.

Designers of snooping caches and directories face similar issues; the only difference is the mechanism that detects when there is a write to shared data. Instead of watching the bus to see if there are requests that require that the local cache be updated or invalidated, the directory controller sends explicit commands to each processor that has a copy of the data. Such messages can then be sent over the network.

Hardware Software Interface

Note that with a single address space, the data could be placed arbitrarily in memories of different processors. This has two negative performance consequences. The first is that the miss penalty would be much longer because the request must go over the network. The second is that the network bandwidth would be consumed moving data to the proper processors. For programs that have low miss rates, this may not be significant. On the other hand, programs with high miss rates will have much lower performance when data is assigned randomly. If the programmer or the compiler allocates data to the processor that is likely to use it, then this performance pitfall is removed. Unlike private memory organizations, this allocation only needs to be good, since missing data can still be fetched. Such leniency simplifies the allocation problem.

Another possible solution is to add a second level of coherence to the *main memory* for every processor. This directory would allow blocks of main memory to migrate, relieving the programmer or the compiler of memory allocation. As long as main memory blocks are not frequently shipped back and forth repeatedly, this scheme may achieve the performance of intelligent allocation of memory at the cost of considerably more hardware complexity. This scheme is called *cache only* memory and is used by the Kendall Square Research KSR-1.

Figure 9.23 summarizes the coherency options for a single address space.

"Superclusters"

The similarity of the parallel processing nodes and workstations suggests that parallel processing of the future may use off-the-shelf computers. If high-speed local area networks connect desktop computers through a high-bandwidth central switch and the message sending overhead can be reduced on workstations, then the distinction between parallel processors and clusters of workstations may vanish later in the decade. Parallel processing in the year 2000 may simply be software that uses idle workstations on the network.

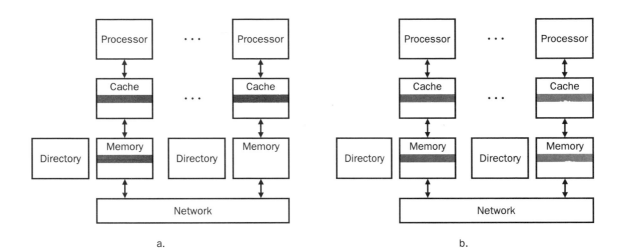

FIGURE 9.23 Options for a single address space in a large-scale parallel processor. The colored rectangles represent the replicated data. (a) Coherence at cache level using directories in a network-connected parallel processor. The original data is in memory and the copies are replicated only in the caches. (b) Coherence at memory level using directories in a network connected parallel processor. The copies are replicated in remote memory *and* in the caches. The scheme in (b) is similar to the scheme used in the Kendall Square Research parallel processor, the KSR-1. As long as memory is coherent, the data can be safely cached. If the data in a memory is invalidated, then corresponding blocks in the cache must be invalidated as well.

9.8 Fallacies and Pitfalls

> *Number 9: Quote performance in terms of processor utilization, parallel speedups or MFLOPS per dollar.*
>
> David H. Bailey, "Twelve ways to fool the masses when giving performance results on parallel supercomputers," *Supercomputing Review*, 1991

The many assaults on parallel processing have uncovered numerous fallacies and pitfalls. We cover three here.

Pitfall: Measuring performance of parallel processors by linear speedup versus execution time.

"Mortar shot" graphs—plotting performance compared to the number of processors showing linear speedup, a plateau, and then a falling-off—have long been used to judge the success of parallel processors. Although scalability is one facet of a parallel program, it is an indirect measure of performance. The primary question to be asked concerns the power of the processors being scaled: a program that linearly improves performance to equal 100 Intel 8086s may be slower than the sequential version on a workstation. Be especially careful of floating-point-intensive programs, as processing elements without floating-point hardware assist may scale wonderfully but have poor collective performance.

Measuring results using linear speedup compared to the execution time can mislead the programmer as well as those hearing the performance claims of the programmer. Many programs with poor speedup are faster than programs which show excellent speedup as the number of processors increases.

Comparing execution times is fair only if you are comparing the best algorithms on each machine. (Of course, you can't subtract time for idle processors when evaluating a parallel processor, so CPU time is an inappropriate metric for parallel processors.) Comparing the identical code on two machines may seem fair, but it is not; the parallel program may be slower on a uniprocessor than a sequential version. Sometimes, developing a parallel program will lead to algorithmic improvements, so that comparing the previously best-known sequential program with the parallel code—which seems fair—compares inappropriate algorithms. To reflect this issue, sometimes the terms *relative speedup* (same program) and *true speedup* (best programs) are used.

Fallacy: Amdahl's Law doesn't apply to parallel computers.

In 1987 the head of a research organization claimed that Amdahl's Law had been broken by a MIMD machine. To try to understand the basis of the media reports, let's see the quote that gave us Amdahl's Law [1967, p. 483]:

> A fairly obvious conclusion which can be drawn at this point is that the effort expended on achieving high parallel processing rates is wasted unless it is accompanied by achievements in sequential processing rates of very nearly the same magnitude.

This statement must still be true; the neglected portion of the program must limit performance. One interpretation of the law leads to the following lemma: portions of every program must be sequential, so there must be an economic upper bound to the number of processors—say 100. By showing linear speedup with 1000 processors, this lemma is disproved and hence the claim that Amdahl's Law was broken.

The approach of the researchers was to change the input to the benchmark: Rather than going 1000 times faster, they computed 1000 times more work in comparable time. For their algorithm, the sequential portion of the program was constant, independent of the size of the input, and the rest

Machine	Peak MFLOPS rating	Harmonic mean MFLOPS of the Perfect Club benchmarks	Percent of peak MFLOPS
Cray X-MP/416	940	14.8	1%
IBM 3090-600S	800	8.3	1%
NEC SX/2	1300	16.6	1%

FIGURE 9.24 Peak performance and harmonic mean of actual performance for the 12 Perfect Club Benchmarks. These results are for the programs run unmodified. When tuned by hand, performance of the three machines moves to 24.4, 11.3, and 18.3 MFLOPS, respectively. This is still 2% or less of peak performance.

was fully parallel—hence, linear speedup with 1000 processors. Simply scaling the size of applications, without also scaling floating-point accuracy, the number of iterations, the I/O requirements, and the way applications deal with error may be naive. Many applications will not calculate the correct result if the problem size is increased unwittingly.

We see no reason why Amdahl's Law doesn't apply to parallel processors. What this research does point out is the importance of having benchmarks that can grow large enough to demonstrate performance of large-scale parallel processors.

Fallacy: Peak performance tracks observed performance.

One definition of peak performance is "performance that a machine is guaranteed not to exceed." Alas, the supercomputer industry uses this metric in marketing, and its fallacy is being exacerbated with parallel machines. Not only are industry marketers using the nearly unattainable peak performance of a uniprocessor node (Figure 9.24), but they are then multiplying it by the total number of processors, assuming perfect speedup! Amdahl's Law suggests how difficult it is to reach either peak; multiplying the two together also multiplies the sins. Figure 9.25 compares the peak to sustained performance on two benchmarks; the 128 processor iPSC achieves only 3% to 9% of peak performance. Clearly peak performance does not track observed performance. (The iPSC cost one-tenth of the Cray, so it is has better cost/performance.)

Such performance claims can confuse the manufacturer as well as the user of the machine. The danger is that the manufacturer will develop software libraries with success judged as percentage of peak performance measured in megaflops compared to less time, or that hardware will be added that increases peak node performance but is difficult to use.

	Cray YMP (8 Procs)		Intel iPSC/860 (128 Procs)	
	MFLOPS	**% Peak**	**MFLOPS**	**% Peak**
Peak	2666	100%	7680	100%
3D FFT PDE	1795	67%	696	9%
LU Pseudo App	1705	64%	224	3%

FIGURE 9.25 Peak versus observed performance for Cray YMP and Intel iPSC/860. The prices are estimated at $25,000,000 for the Cray versus $2,500,000 for the iPSC, so the iPSC has better price/performance. This table was derived from the talk, "Performance Results for the NAS Parallel Benchmarks" given by David H. Bailey at Supercomputing '91 in Albuquerque, New Mexico, on November 14, 1991.

9.9   Concluding Remarks—Evolution versus Revolution in Computer Architecture

The stumbling way in which even the ablest of the scientists in every generation have had to fight through thickets of erroneous observations, misleading generalizations, inadequate formulations, and unconscious prejudice is rarely appreciated by those who obtain their scientific knowledge from textbooks.

James B. Conant, *Science and Common Sense*, 1951

Reading conference and journal articles from the last 25 years can leave one discouraged; so much effort has been expended with so little impact. Optimistically speaking, these papers act as gravel and, when placed logically together, form the foundation for the next generation of computers. From a more pessimistic point of view, if 90% of the ideas disappeared, no one would notice.

One reason for this predicament is what could be called the "von Neumann syndrome." By hoping to invent a new model of computation that will revolutionize computing, researchers are striving to become the von Neumann of the 21st century. Another reason is taste: researchers often select problems that no one else cares about. Even if important problems are selected, there is frequently a lack of experimental evidence to demonstrate convincingly the value of the solution. Moreover, when important problems are selected and the solutions are demonstrated, the proposed solutions may be too expensive relative to their benefit. Sometimes this expense is measured as straightforward cost/performance—the performance enhancement does not merit the added cost. More often the expense of innovation comes from being too disruptive to computer users. Figure 9.26 shows what we mean by the *evolution-revolution spectrum* of computer architecture innovation. To the left are ideas that are in-

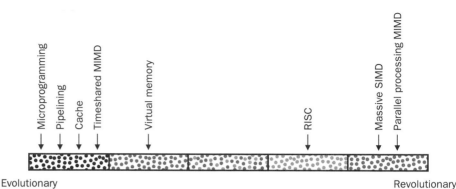

FIGURE 9.26 The evolution-revolution spectrum of computer architecture. The first four columns are distinguished from the last column in that applications and operating systems may be ported from other computers rather than written from scratch. For example, RISC is listed in the closer to the spectrum because user compatibility is only at the level of high-level languages (HLLs), while microprogramming allows binary compatibility, and parallel processing MIMDs require changes to algorithms and extending HLLs. Timeshared MIMD means MIMDs justified by running many independent programs at once, while parallel processing MIMD means MIMDs intended to run a single program faster.

visible to the user (presumably except better cost, better performance, or both); this is the evolutionary end of the spectrum. At the other end are revolutionary architecture ideas. These are the ideas that require new applications from programmers who must learn new programming languages and models of computation, and must invent new data structures and algorithms.

Revolutionary ideas are easier to publish than evolutionary ideas, but to be adopted they must have a much higher payoff. Caches are an example of an evolutionary improvement. Within five years after the first publication about caches, almost every computer company was designing a machine with a cache. The Reduced Instruction Set Computer (RISC) ideas were nearer to the middle of the spectrum, for it took closer to ten years for most companies to have a RISC product. An example of a revolutionary computer architecture is the Connection Machine-1. Every program that runs efficiently on that machine was either substantially modified or written especially for it, and programmers need to learn a new style of programming for it. Thinking Machines was founded in 1983, but only a few companies offer machines like the CM-1, and that company has significantly evolved away from the original architecture. Note that Thinking Machines is older than most RISC companies, and yet the RISC technology is practically universal.

Projects that the computer industry ignores may be valuable if they document the lessons learned for future efforts. The sin is not in having a novel architecture that is commercially unsuccessful, but in neglecting to quantitatively evaluate the strengths and weaknesses of the novel ideas. Failures of past research projects do not mean that the ideas are dead forever. Changes in technology may rejuvenate an idea that previously had the wrong trade-offs or rejuvenate an idea that was ahead of the technology.

When contemplating the future—and inventing your own contributions to the field—remember the evolution-revolution spectrum. Acceptance of hardware ideas means acceptance by software people; therefore, hardware people must learn more about software. And if software people want good machines, they must learn more about hardware to be able to communicate with and thereby influence hardware designers. Also, keep in mind the principles of computer organization found in this book; these will surely guide computers of the future, just as they have guided computers of the past.

9.10 Historical Perspective and Further Reading

For over a decade prophets have voiced the contention that the organization of a single computer has reached its limits and that truly significant advances can be made only by interconnection of a multiplicity of computers in such a manner as to permit cooperative solution . . . . Demonstration is made of the continued validity of the single processor approach . . .

Gene Amdahl, "Validity of the single processor approach to achieving large scale computing capabilities," Spring Joint Computer Conference, 1967

The earliest ideas on SIMD predate the Illiac IV (seen in Figure 9.27), perhaps the most infamous of the supercomputer projects. Although successful in pushing several technologies useful in later projects, the Illiac IV failed as a computer. Costs escalated from the $8 million estimated in 1966 to $31 million by 1972, despite the construction of only a quarter of the planned machine. Actual performance was at best 15 MFLOPS compared to initial predictions of 1000 MFLOPS for the full system (see Falk [1976]). Delivered to NASA's Ames Research in 1972, the computer took three more years of engineering before it was operational. For better or worse, computer architects are not easily discouraged; SIMD successors of the Illiac IV include the ICL DAP, Goodyear MPP (Figure 9.28), Thinking Machines CM-1 and CM-2, and Maspar MP-1 and MP-2.

It is difficult to distinguish the first parallel processor. The first computer from the Eckert-Mauchly Corporation, for example, had duplicate units to im-

FIGURE 9.27 The Illiac IV control unit followed by its 64 processing elements. It was perhaps the most infamous of supercomputers. The project started in 1965 and ran its first real application in 1976. The 64 processors used a 13-MHz clock, and their combined main memory size was 1 megabyte: $64 \times 16\text{KB}$. The Illiac IV was the first machine to teach us that software for parallel machines dominates hardware issues. Photo courtesy of NASA Ames Research Center.

prove reliability. After several laboratory attempts at parallel processors, the first successful commercial parallel processors appeared in the 1980s. Bell [1985] suggests the key to success was that the smaller size of the microprocessor allowed the memory bus to replace the interconnection network hardware, and that portable operating systems meant that parallel processor projects no longer required the invention of a new operating system. He distinguishes parallel processors with multiple private address by calling them *multicomputers*, reserving the term *multiprocessor* for machines with a single address space.

There is a vast amount of information on parallel processors: conferences, journal papers, and even books seem to be appearing faster than any single person can absorb the ideas. One good source is the Supercomputing conference, held annually since 1988. The papers cover applications, algorithms, and architecture, a mix that we think bodes well for the future. Textbooks on par-

FIGURE 9.28 The Goodyear MPP with 16,384 processors. It was delivered May 2, 1983 to NASA Goddard Space Center and was operational the next day. It was decommissioned on March 1, 1991.

allel computing have been written by Almasi and Gottlieb [1989], Hockney and Jesshope [1988], and Hwang [1993].

It is hard to predict the future, yet Gordon Bell has made two predictions for 1995. The first is that a computer capable of sustaining a TeraFLOPS (TFLOPS)—one million MFLOPS—will be constructed by 1995, using either a MIMD with 4K to 32K nodes or a SIMD with several million processing elements [Bell 1989]. To put this prediction in perspective, each year the Gordon Bell Prize acknowledges advances in parallelism, including the fastest real program (highest MFLOPS). Figure 9.29 shows the winners of the prize. Machines and programs will have to improve by a factor of 3 each year for the fastest program to achieve 1 TFLOPS in 1995. So far they are on track. In 1991 Thinking Machines announced the CM-5, a computer that can scale to 1 TFLOPS—provided someone is willing to pay well in excess of $100,000,000 to buy one.

The second Bell prediction concerns the number of data streams in supercomputers shipped in 1995. Danny Hillis of Thinking Machines believes that while supercomputers with a small number of data streams may be best-sellers, the biggest machines will have many data streams, and these will perform

Year	Rate (MFLOPS)	Machine	Number of processors	Number of floating-point units
1988	400	Cray X-MP	4	8
1989	1680	Cray Y-MP	8	16
1990	5600	CM-2	65,536	2048
1991	14,200	CM-2	65,536	2048

FIGURE 9.29 Winners of Gordon Bell Prize for highest floating-point performance for a real application program. The 1991 example is for 32-bit floating-point operations, while the others are for 64-bit floating-point operations.

the bulk of the computations. Bell bet Hillis that in the last quarter of 1995, more sustained MFLOPS will be shipped in machines using few data streams (≤ 100) as opposed to many data streams (≥ 1000). This bet concerns only super-computers, defined as machines costing more than $1,000,000 and used for scientific applications. Sustained MFLOPS is defined for this bet as the number of floating-point operations per month, so the availability of machines affects their rating. The loser must write and publish an article explaining why his prediction failed; your authors will act as judge and jury.

To Probe Further

Almasi, G. S., and A. Gottlieb [1989]. *Highly Parallel Computing,* Benjamin/Cummings, Redwood City, Calif.

A textbook covering parallel computers.

Amdahl, G. M., [1967]. "Validity of the single processor approach to achieving large scale computing capabilities," *Proc. AFIPS Spring Joint Computer Conf.* 30, Atlantic City, N. J. (April) 483–485.

Written in response to the claims of the Illiac IV, this three-page article describes Amdahl's Law and gives the classic reply to arguments for abandoning the current form of computing.

Bell, C. G. [1989]. "The future of high performance computers in science and engineering," *Comm. ACM* 32:9 (September) 1091–1101.

Reviews the trends in computing and speculates on the future of SIMD and MIMD.

Falk, H. [1976]. "Reaching for the Gigaflop," *IEEE Spectrum* 13:10 (October) 65-70.

Chronicles the sad story of the Illiac IV: four times the cost and less than one-tenth the performance of original goals.

Flynn, M. J. [1966]. "Very high-speed computing systems," *Proc. IEEE* 54:12 (December) 1901–1909.

Classic article showing SISD/SIMD/MISD/MIMD classifications.

Hockney, R. W., and C. R. Jesshope [1988]. *Parallel Computers-2, Architectures, Programming and Algorithms*, Adam Hilger Ltd., Bristol, England, and Philadelphia.

Another textbook covering parallel computers.

Hord, R. M. [1982]. *The Illiac-IV, the First Supercomputer*, Computer Science Press, Rockville, Md.

A historical accounting of the Illiac IV project.

Hwang, K. [1993]. *Advanced Computer Architecture with Parallel Programming*, McGraw-Hill, New York.

Another textbook covering parallel computers.

Moldovan, D. I. [1993]. *Parallel Processing from Applications to Systems*, Morgan Kaufmann Publishers, San Mateo, Calif.

An introduction to multiprocessor architectures, including the structure of parallel processors and parallel algorithms.

Seitz, C. [1985]. "The Cosmic Cube," *Comm. ACM* 28:1 (January) 22–31.

A tutorial article on a parallel processor connected via a hypertree. The Cosmic Cube is the ancestor of the Intel supercomputers.

Slotnick, D. L. [1982]. "The conception and development of parallel processors—A personal memoir," *Annals of the History of Computing*, 4:1 (January) 20-30.

Recollections of the beginnings of parallel processing by the architect of the Illiac IV.

9.11   Exercises

9.1 [15] <§9.2, 9.3> What trends favor MIMD over SIMD, and vice versa? Consider synchronization and utilization of memory and processors.

9.2 [15] <§9.7> Figure 9.21 shows how communication in a large-scale parallel processor can take hundreds of clock cycles. What hardware and software techniques might reduce this time? How can you change the architecture or the programming model to make a computer more immune to such delays?

9.3 [5] <§9.5> Count the number of transactions on the bus for the following sequence of activities involving shared data. Assume that both processors use write-back caches and write-update cache coherency and use a block size of one word. Assume that all the words in both caches are clean.

Step	Processor	Memory activity	Memory address
1	Processor 1	Write	100
2	Processor 2	Write	104
3	Processor 1	Read	100
4	Processor 2	Read	104

9.4 [10] <§9.5> False sharing can lead to unnecessary bus traffic and delays. Follow the directions for Exercise 9.3, except change the block size to four words.

9.5 [15] <§9.6> Another possible network topology is a three-dimensional grid. Draw the topology as in Figure 9.14 for 64 nodes. What is the bisection bandwidth of this topology?

9.6 [10] <§9.6> The fat tree used in the CM-5 has four children instead of two as in the binary tree. Recall that the processors are only on the leaves of the tree with the parents only being switches. Compare the worst-case latency for a machine with 1024 *processors* for a binary tree and a fat tree.

9.7 [15] <§9.10> Construct a scenario whereby a truly revolutionary architecture—pick your favorite candidate—will play a significant role. Significant is defined as 10% of the computers sold, 10% of the users, 10% of the money spent on computers, or 10% of some other figure of merit.

9.8 [2 hours] <§9.2> The CM-2 uses 64K 1-bit processors in SIMD mode. Bit-serial operations may easily be simulated 32 bits per operation by a 32-bit-wide SISD, at least for logical operations. The CM-2 takes about 500 ns for such operations. If you have access to a fast SISD, calculate how long add and AND take on 64K 1-bit numbers. Find a way to make them run fast on the SISD.

9.9 [2 hours] <§9.2> A popular use of the CM-2 is to operate on 32-bit data using multiple steps with the 64K 1-bit processors. The CM-2 takes about 21 microseconds for a 32-bit AND or add. Simulate this activity on a fast SISD; calculate how long it takes to add and AND 64K *32-bit* numbers.

9.10 [1 week] <§9.8> *Super-linear* performance improvement means a program on *n* processors is more than *n* times faster than the equivalent uniprocessor. One argument for super-linear speedup is that time spent servicing interrupts or switching contexts is reduced when you have many processors, because only one needs service interrupts and there are more processors to be shared by users. Measure the time spent on a workload in handling interrupts or context switching on a uniprocessor versus a parallel processor. This workload may be a mix of independent jobs for a multiprogramming environment or a single large job. Does the argument hold?

9.11 [1 week] <§9.5, 9.6> A parallel processor is typically marketed using programs that can scale performance linearly with the number of processors. Port programs written for one parallel processor to the other and measure their absolute performance and how it changes as you change the number of processors. What changes must be made to improve performance of the ported programs on each machine? What is performance according to each program?

9.12 [1 week] <§9.5, 9.6> Instead of trying to create fair benchmarks, invent programs that make one parallel processor look terrible compared with the others, and also programs that always make one look better than others. What are the key performance characteristics of each program and machine?

9.13 [1 week] <§9.5, 9.6> Parallel processors usually show performance increases as you increase the number of processors, with the ideal being n times speedup for n processors. The goal of this exercise is to create a biased benchmark that gets worse performance as you add processors. For example, this means that 1 processor on the parallel processor would run the program fastest, 2 would be slower, 4 would be slower than 2, and so on. What are the key performance characteristics for each organization that give inverse linear speedup?

9.14 [1 week] <§9.6, 9.7> Networked workstations may be considered parallel processors, albeit with slow communication relative to computation. Port parallel processor benchmarks to a network using remote procedure calls for communication. How well do the benchmarks scale on the network versus the parallel processor? What are the practical differences between networked workstations and a commercial parallel processor?

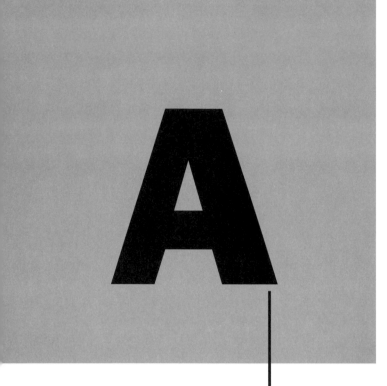

Assemblers, Linkers, and the SPIM Simulator

James R. Larus
Computer Sciences Department
University of Wisconsin—Madison

Fear of serious injury cannot alone justify suppression of free speech and assembly.

Louis Brandeis,
Whitney v. California, 1927

A.1   Introduction

Encoding instructions as binary numbers is natural and efficient for computers. Humans, however, have a great deal of difficulty understanding and manipulating these numbers. People read and write symbols (words) much better than long sequences of digits. Chapter 3 showed that we need not choose between numbers and words because computer instructions can be represented in many ways. Humans can write and read symbols and computers can execute the equivalent binary numbers. This appendix describes the process by which a human-readable program is translated into a form that a computer can execute, provides a few hints about writing assembly programs, and explains how to run these programs on SPIM, a simulator that executes MIPS programs.

Assembly language is the symbolic representation of a computer's binary encoding—*machine language*. Assembly language is more readable than machine language because it uses symbols instead of bits. The symbols in assembly language name commonly occurring bit patterns, such as opcodes and register specifiers, so people can read and remember them. In addition, assembly language permits programmers to use *labels* to identify and name particular memory words that hold instructions or data.

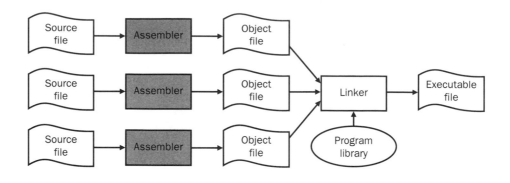

FIGURE A.1 The process that produces an executable file. An assembler translates a file of assembly language into an object file, which is linked with other files and libraries into an executable file.

A tool called an *assembler* translates assembly language into binary instructions. Assemblers provide a friendlier representation than a computer's zeros and ones that simplifies writing and reading programs. Symbolic names for operations and locations are one facet of this representation. Another facet is programming facilities that increase a program's clarity. For example, *macros*, discussed in section A.2, enable a programmer to extend the assembly language by defining new operations.

An assembler reads a single assembly language *source file* and produces an *object file* containing machine instructions and bookkeeping information that helps combine several object files into a program. Figure A.1 illustrates how a program is built from modules. Most programs consist of several files—also called *modules*—that are written, compiled, and assembled independently. A program may also use prewritten routines supplied in a *program library*. A module typically contains *references* to subroutines and data defined in other modules and in libraries. The code in a module cannot be executed when it contains *unresolved references* to labels in other object files or libraries. Another tool called a *linker* combines a collection of object and library files into an *executable file*, which a computer can run.

To see the advantage of assembly language, consider the following sequence of figures, all of which contain a short subroutine that computes and prints the sum of the squares of integers from 0 to 100. Figure A.2 shows the machine language that a MIPS computer executes. With considerable effort, you could use the opcode and instruction format tables in Chapters 3 and 4 to translate the instructions into a symbolic program similar to Figure A.3. This form of the routine is much easier to read because operations and operands are

```
00100111101111011111111111100000
10101111101111110000000000010100
10101111101001000000000000100000
10101111101001010000000000100100
10101111101000000000000000011000
10101111101000000000000000011100
10001111101011100000000000011100
10001111101110000000000000011000
00000001110011100000000000011001
00100101110010000000000000000001
00101001000000010000000001100101
10101111101010000000000000011100
00000000000000000111100000010010
00000011000011111100100000100001
00010100001000001111111111110111
10101111101110010000000000011000
00111100000000100000100000000000
10001111101001010000000000011000
00001100000100000000000011101100
00100100100001000000010000110000
10001111101111110000000000010100
00100111101111010000000000100000
00000011111000000000000000001000
00000000000000000001000000100001
```

FIGURE A.2 MIPS machine language code for a routine to compute and print the sum of the squares of integers between 0 and 100.

written with symbols, rather than with bit patterns. However, this assembly language is still difficult to follow because memory locations are named by their address, rather than by a symbolic label.

Figure A.4 shows assembly language that labels memory addresses with mnemonic names. Most programmers prefer to read and write this form. Names that begin with a period, for example .data and .globl, are *assembler directives* that tell the assembler how to translate a program but do not produce machine instructions. Names followed by a colon, such as str or main, are labels that name the next memory location. This program is as readable as most assembly language programs (except for a glaring lack of comments), but it is still difficult to follow because many simple operations are required to accomplish simple tasks and because assembly language's flat structure and lack of control-flow constructs provide few hints about the program's operation. By contrast, the C routine in Figure A.5 is both shorter and clearer since variables have mnemonic names and the loop is explicit rather than constructed with branches. (Readers unfamiliar with C should look at Appendix D.) In fact, the C routine is the only one that the author wrote. The other forms of the program were produced by a C compiler and assembler.

```
addiu       $29, $29, -32
sw          $31, 20($29)
sw          $4, 32($29)
sw          $5, 36($29)
sw          $0, 24($29)
sw          $0, 28($29)
lw          $14, 28($29)
lw          $24, 24($29)
multu       $14, $14
addiu       $8, $14, 1
slti        $1, $8, 101
sw          $8, 28($29)
mflo        $15
addu        $25, $24, $15
bne         $1, $0, -9
sw          $25, 24($29)
lui         $4, 4096
lw          $5, 24($29)
jal         1048812
addiu       $4, $4, 1072
lw          $31, 20($29)
addiu       $29, $29, 32
jr          $31
move        $2, $0
```

FIGURE A.3 The same routine written in assembly language. However, the code for the routine does not label memory locations nor include comments.

In general, assembly language plays two roles (see Figure A.6). The first role is the output language of compilers. A *compiler* translate a program written in a *high-level language* (such as C or Pascal) into an equivalent program in machine or assembly language. The high-level language is called the *source language* and the compiler's output is its *target language*.

Assembly language's other role is as a language in which to write programs. This role used to be the dominant one. Today, however, because of larger main memories and better compilers, most programmers write in a high-level language and rarely, if ever, see the instructions that a computer executes. Nevertheless, assembly language is still important to write programs in which speed or size are critical or to exploit hardware features that have no analogues in high-level languages.

Elaboration: Compilers can produce machine language directly instead of relying on an assembler. These compilers typically execute much faster than those that invoke an assembler as part of compilation. However, a compiler that generates machine language must perform many tasks that an assembler normally handles, such as resolv-

```
                .text
                .align    2
                .globl    main
        main:
                subu      $29, $sp, 32
                sw        $31, 20($29)
                sd        $4, 32($29)
                sw        $0, 24($29)
                sw        $0, 28($29)
        loop:
                lw        $14, 28($29)
                mul       $15, $14, $14
                lw        $24, 24($29)
                addu      $25, $24, $15
                sw        $25, 24($29)
                addu      $8, $14, 1
                sw        $8, 28($29)
                ble       $8, 100, loop
                la        $4, str
                lw        $5, 24($29)
                jal       printf
                move      $2, $0
                lw        $31, 20($29)
                addu      $29, $29, 32
                j         $31


                .data
                .align    0
        str:
                .asciiz   "The sum from 0 .. 100 is %d\n"
```

FIGURE A.4 The same routine written in assembly language with labels, but no comments. The commands that start with periods are assembler directives (see pages A-48–A-50). .text indicates that succeeding lines contain instructions. .data indicates that they contain data. .align n indicates that the items on the succeeding lines should be aligned on a 2^n byte boundary. Hence, .align 2 means the next item should be on a word boundary. .globl main declares that main is a global symbol that should be visible to code stored in other files. Finally, .asciiz stores a null-terminated string in memory.

ing addresses and encoding instructions as binary numbers. The trade-off is between compilation speed and compiler simplicity.

Although this appendix focuses on MIPS assembly language, assembly programming on most other machines is very similar. The additional instructions and address modes in CISC machines, such as the VAX (see Appendix E), can make assembly programs shorter but do not change the pro-

```
#include <stdio.h>

int
main (int argc, char *argv[])
{
     int i;
     int sum = 0;

     for (i = 0; i <= 100; i = i + 1) sum = sum + i * i;
     printf ("The sum from 0 .. 100 is %d\n", sum);
}
```

FIGURE A.5 The routine written in the C programming language.

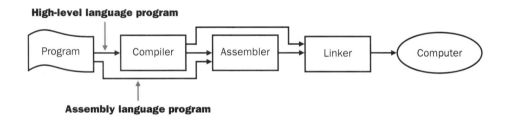

FIGURE A.6 Assembly language is either written by a programmer or is the output of a compiler.

cess of assembling a program or provide assembly language with the advantages of high-level languages such as type-checking and structured control flow.

When to Use Assembly Language

The primary reason to program in assembly language, as opposed to an available high-level language, is that the speed or size of a program is critically important. For example, consider a computer that controls a piece of machinery such as a car's brakes. A computer that is incorporated in another device, such as a car, is called an *embedded computer*. This type of computer needs to respond rapidly and predictably to events in the outside world. Because a compiler introduces uncertainty about the time cost of operations, programmers may find it difficult to ensure that a high-level language program responds within a definite time interval—say, 1 millisecond after a sensor detects that a tire is skidding. An assembly language programmer, on the other hand, has tight control over which instructions execute. In addition, in embedded applications, reducing a program's size, so that it fits in fewer memory chips, reduces the cost of the embedded computer.

Elaboration: Despite these considerations, some embedded applications are written in a high-level language. Many of these applications are large and complex programs that must be extremely reliable. Assembly language programs are longer and more difficult to write and read than high-level language programs. This greatly increases the cost of writing an assembly language program and make it extremely difficult to verify the correctness of this type of program. In fact, these considerations led the Department of Defense, which pays for many complex embedded systems, to develop Ada, a new high-level language for writing embedded systems.

A hybrid approach, in which most of a program is written in a high-level language and time-critical sections are written in assembly language, builds on the strengths of both languages. Programs typically spend most of their time executing a small fraction of the program's source code. This observation is just the principle of locality that underlies caches (see section 7.2 in Chapter 7). Program profiling measures where a program spends its time and can find the time-critical parts of a program. In many cases, this portion of the program can be made faster with better data structures or algorithms. Sometimes, however, significant performance improvements only come from recoding a critical portion of a program in assembly language.

This improvement is not necessarily an indication that the high-level language's compiler has failed. Compilers typically are better than programmers at producing uniformly high-quality machine code across an entire program. Programmers, however, understand a program's algorithms and behavior at a deeper level than a compiler and can expend considerable effort and ingenuity improving small sections of the program. In particular, programmers often consider several procedures simultaneously while writing their code. Compilers typically compile each procedure in isolation and must follow strict conventions governing the use of registers at procedure boundaries. By retaining commonly used values in registers, even across procedure boundaries, programmers can make a program run faster. Another major advantage of assembly language is the ability to exploit specialized instructions, for example, string copy or pattern-matching instructions. Compilers, in most cases, cannot determine that a program loop can be replaced by a single instruction. However, the programmer who wrote the loop can replace it easily with a single instruction.

In the future, a programmer's advantage over a compiler is likely to become increasingly difficult to maintain as compilation techniques improve and machines' pipelines increase in complexity (see section 3.10 in Chapter 3).

The final reason to use assembly language is that no high-level language is available on a particular computer. Many older or specialized computers do not have a compiler, so a programmer's only alternative is assembly language.

Drawbacks of Assembly Language

Assembly language has many disadvantages that strongly argue against its widespread use. Perhaps its major disadvantage is that programs written in assembly language are inherently machine-specific and must be totally rewritten to run on another computer architecture. The rapid evolution of computers discussed in Chapter 1 means that architectures become obsolete. An assembly language program remains tightly bound to its original architecture, even after the computer is eclipsed by new, faster, and more cost-effective machines.

Another disadvantage is that assembly language programs are longer than the equivalent programs written in a high-level language. For example, the C program in Figure A.4 is 11 lines long, while the assembly program in Figure A.4 is 31 lines long. In more complex programs, the ratio of assembly to high-level language (its *expansion factor*) can be much larger than the factor of three in this example. Unfortunately, empirical studies have shown that programmers write roughly the same number of lines of code per day in assembly as in high-level languages. This means that programmers are roughly x times more productive in a high-level language, where x is the assembly language expansion factor.

To compound the problem, longer programs are more difficult to read and understand and they contain more bugs. Assembly language exacerbates the problem because of its complete lack of structure. Common programming idioms, such as *if-then* statements and loops, must be built from branches and jumps. The resulting programs are hard to read because the reader must reconstruct every higher-level construct from its pieces and each instance of a statement may be slightly different. For example, look at Figure A.4 and answer these questions: What type of loop is used? What are its lower and upper bounds?

A.2   Assemblers

An assembler translates a file of assembly language statements into a file of binary machine instructions and binary data. The translation process has two major parts. The first step is to find memory locations with labels so the relationship between symbolic names and addresses is known when instructions are translated. The second step is to translate each assembly statement by combining the numeric equivalents of opcodes, register specifiers, and labels into a legal instruction. As shown in Figure A.1, the assembler produces an output file, called an object file, which contains the machine instructions, data, and bookkeeping information.

An object file typically cannot be executed because it references procedures or data in other files. A label is *external* (also called *global*) if the labeled object can be referenced from files other than the one in which it is defined. A label is *local* if the object can be used only within the file in which it is defined. In most assemblers, labels are local by default and must be explicitly declared global. Subroutines and global variables require external labels since they are referenced from many files in a program. Local labels hide names that should not be visible to other modules—for example, static functions in C, which can only be called by other functions in the same file. In addition, compiler-generated names—for example, a name for the instruction at the beginning of a loop—are local so the compiler need not produce unique names in every file.

Example   Consider the program in Figure A.4 on page A-7. The subroutine has an external (global) label `main`. It also contains two local labels—`loop` and `str`—that are only visible with this assembly language file. Finally, the routine also contains an unresolved reference to an external label `printf`, which is the library routine that prints values. What are the local and global labels in Figure A.4?

Answer   The local labels are `loop` and `str` and the global label is `main`.

Since the assembler processes each file in a program individually and in isolation, it only knows the addresses of local labels. The assembler depends on another tool, the linker, to combine a collection of object files and libraries into an executable file by resolving external labels. The assembler assists the linker by providing lists of labels and unresolved references.

However, even local labels present an interesting challenge to an assembler. Unlike names in most high-level languages, assembly labels may be used before they are defined. In the example, in Figure A.4, the label `str` is used by the `la` instruction before it is defined. The possibility of a *forward reference*, like this one, forces an assembler to translate a program in two steps: first find all labels and then produce instructions. In the example, when the assembler sees the `la` instruction, it does not know where the word labeled `str` is located or even whether `str` labels an instruction or datum.

An assembler's first pass reads each line of an assembly file and breaks it into its component pieces. These pieces, which are called *lexemes*, are individual words, numbers, and punctuation characters. For example, the line:

```
ble     $8, 100, loop
```

contains 6 lexemes: the opcode `ble`, the register specifier `$8`, a comma, the number 100, a comma, and the symbol `loop`.

If a line begins with a label, the assembler records in its *symbol table* the name of the label and the address of the memory word that the instruction occupies. The assembler then calculates how many words of memory the instruction on the current line will occupy. By keeping track of the instructions' sizes, the assembler can determine where the next instruction goes. To compute the size of a variable-length instruction, like those on the VAX, an assembler has to examine it in detail. On the other hand, fixed-length instructions, like those on MIPS, only require a cursory examination. The assembler performs a similar calculation to compute the space required for data statements. When the assembler reaches the end of an assembly file, the symbol table records the location of each label defined in the file.

The assembly uses the information in the symbol table during a second pass over the file, which actually produces machine code. The assembler again examines each line in the file. If the line contains an instruction, the assembler combines the binary representations of its opcode and operands (register specifiers or memory address) into a legal instruction. The process is similar to the one used in section 3.4 in Chapter 3. Instructions and data words that reference an external symbol defined in another file cannot be completely assembled (they are unresolved) since the symbol's address is not in the symbol table. An assembler does not complain about unresolved references since the corresponding label is likely to be defined in another file.

Elaboration: If an assembler's speed is important, this two-step process can be done in one pass over the assembly file with a technique known as *backpatching*. In its pass over the file, the assembler builds a (possibly incomplete) binary representation of every instruction. If the instruction references a label that has not yet been defined, the assembler records the label and instruction in a table. When a label is defined, the assembler consults this table to find all instructions that contain a forward reference to the label. The assembler goes back and corrects their binary representation to incorporate the address of the label. Backpatching speeds assembly, because the assembler only reads its input once. However, it requires an assembler to hold the entire binary representation of a program in memory so instructions can be backpatched. This requirement can limit the size of programs that can be assembled.

The Big Picture

Assembly language is a programming language. Its principal difference from high-level languages such as BASIC, Pascal, and C is that assembly language provides only a few, simple types of data and control flow. Assembly language programs do not specify the type of value held in a variable. Instead, a programmer must apply the appropriate operations (e.g., integer or floating-point addition) to a value. In addition, in assembly language programs must implement all control flow with goto's. Both factors make assembly language programming for any machine—MIPS or VAX (see Appendix E)—more difficult and error-prone than writing in a high-level language.

Object File Format

Assemblers produce object files. An object file on Unix contains six distinct sections (see Figure A.7):

- The *object file header* describes the size and position of the other pieces of the file.

- The *text segment* contains the machine language code for routines in the source file. These routines may be unexecutable because of unresolved references.

- The *data segment* contains a binary representation of the data in the source file. The data also may be incomplete because of unresolved references to labels in other files.

- The *relocation information* identifies instructions and data words that depend on absolute addresses. These references must change if portions of the program are moved in memory.

- The *symbol table* associates addresses with external labels in the source file and lists unresolved references.

Object file header	Text segment	Data segment	Relocation information	Symbol table	Debugging information

FIGURE A.7 Object File. A Unix assembler produces an object file with six distinct sections.

■ The *debugging information* contains a concise description of the way in which the program was compiled, so a debugger can find which instruction addresses correspond to lines in a source file and print the data structures in readable form.

The assembler produces an object file that contains a binary representation of the program and data and additional information to help link pieces of a program. This relocation information is necessary because the assembler does not know which memory locations a procedure or piece of data will occupy after it is linked with the rest of the program. Procedures and data from a file are stored in a contiguous piece of memory, but the assembler does not know where this memory will be located. The assembler also passes some symbol table entries to the linker. In particular, the assembler must record which external symbols are defined in a file and what unresolved references occur in a file.

Elaboration: For convenience, assemblers assume each file starts at the same address (for example, location 0) with the expectation that the linker will *relocate* the code and data when they are assigned locations in memory. The assembler produces *relocation information*, which contains an entry describing each instruction or data word in the file that references an absolute address. On MIPS, only the subroutine call, load, and store instructions reference absolute addresses. Instructions that use PC-relative addressing, such as branches, need not be relocated.

Additional Facilities

Assemblers provide a variety of convenience features that help make assembler programs short and easier to write, but do not fundamentally change assembly language. For example, *data layout directives* allow a programmer to describe data in a more concise and natural manner than its binary representation.

Example

In Figure A.4, the directive

```
.asciiz "The sum from 0 .. 100 is %d\n"
```

stores characters from the string in memory. Contrast this line with the alternative of writing each character as its ASCII value (Figure 3.26 in Chapter 3 describes the ASCII encoding for characters):

```
.byte 84, 104, 101, 32, 115, 117, 109, 32
.byte 102, 114, 111, 109, 32, 48, 32, 46
.byte 46, 32, 49, 48, 48, 32, 105, 115
.byte 32, 37, 100, 10, 0
```

The .asciiz directive is easier to read because it represents characters as letters, not binary numbers. An assembler can translate characters to their binary representation much faster and more accurately than a human. Data layout directives specify data in a human-readable form that the assembler translates to binary. Other layout directives are described in section A.10 on pages A-48–A-50. Define the sequence of bytes produced by this directive:

```
.asciiz "The quick brown fox jumps over the lazy dog"
```

Answer

```
.byte 84, 104, 101, 32, 113, 117, 105, 99
.byte 107, 32, 98, 114, 111, 119, 110, 32
.byte 102, 111, 120, 32, 106, 117, 109, 112
.byte 115, 32, 111, 118, 101, 114, 32, 116
.byte 104, 101, 32, 108, 97, 122, 121, 32
.byte 100, 111, 103, 0
```

Macros are a pattern-matching and replacement facility that provide a simple mechanism to name a frequently used sequence of instructions. Instead of repeatedly typing the same instructions every time they are used, a programmer invokes the macro and the assembler replaces the macro call with the corresponding sequence of instructions. Macros, like subroutines, permit a programmer to create and name a new abstraction for a common operation. Unlike subroutines, however, macros do not cause a subroutine call and return when the program runs since a macro call is replaced by the macro's body when the program is assembled. After this replacement, the resulting assembly is indistinguishable from the equivalent program written without macros.

Example

As an example, suppose that a programmer needs to print many numbers. The library routine printf accepts a format string and one or more values to print as its arguments. A programmer could print the integer in register $7 with the following instructions:

```
          .data
int_str:  .asciiz"%d"
          .text
          la  $4, int_str    # Load string address
                             # into first arg (4)
          mov $5, $7         # Load value into
                             # second arg (5)
          jal printf         # Call the printf routine
```

The .data directive tells the assembler to store the string in the program's data segment and the .text directive tells the assembler to store the instructions in its text segment.

However, printing many numbers in this fashion is tedious and produces a verbose program that is difficult to understand. An alternative is to introduce a macro, print_int, to print an integer:

```
        .data
int_str: .asciiz "%d"
        .text
        .macro print_int($arg)
        la   $4, int_str   # Load string address into
                           # first arg (4)
        mov $5, $arg       # Load macro's parameter
                           # ($arg) into second arg (5)
        jal  printf        # Call the printf routine
        .end_macro

    print_int($7)
```

The macro has a *formal parameter*, $arg, that names the argument to macro. When the macro is expanded, the argument from a call is substituted for the formal parameter throughout the macro's body. Then the assembler replaces the call with the macro's newly expanded body. In the first call on print_int, the argument is $7, so the macro expands to the code:

```
la $4, int_str
mov $5, $7
jal printf
```

In a second call on print_int, say print_int($8), the argument is $8, so the macro expands to:

```
la $4, int_str
mov $5, $8
jal printf
```

What does the call print_int($4) expand to?

Answer

```
la $4, int_str
mov $5, $4
jal printf
```

This example illustrates one drawback of macros. A programmer who uses this macro must be aware that `print_int` uses register $4 and so cannot correctly print the value in that register.

Elaboration: Assemblers *conditionally assemble* pieces of code, which permits a programmer to include or exclude groups of instructions when a program is assembled. This feature is particularly useful when several versions of a program differ by a small amount. Rather than keep these programs in separate files—which greatly complicates fixing bugs in the common code—programmers typically merge the versions into a single file. Code particular to one version is conditionally assembled, so it can be excluded when other versions of the program are assembled.

If macros and conditional assembly are useful, why do assemblers for Unix systems rarely, if ever, provide them? One reason is that most programmers on these systems write programs in higher-level languages like C. Most of the assembly code is produced by compilers, which find it more convenient to repeat code rather than define macros. Another reason is that other tools on Unix—such as `cpp`, the C preprocessor, or `m4`, a general macro processor—can provide macros and conditional assembly for assembly language programs.

Hardware Software Interface

Some assemblers also implement *pseudoinstructions*, which are instructions provided by an assembler, but not implemented in hardware. Chapter 3 contains many examples of how the MIPS assembler synthesizes pseudoinstructions and addressing modes from the spartan MIPS hardware instruction set. For example, section 3.5 in Chapter 3 describes how the assembler synthesizes the `blt` instruction from two other instructions: `slt` and `bne`. By extending the instruction set, the MIPS assembler makes assembly language programming easier without complicating the hardware. Many pseudoinstructions could also be simulated with macros, but the MIPS assembler can generate better code for these instructions because it can use a dedicated register ($1) and is able to optimize the generated code.

A.3 Linkers

Separate compilation permits a program to be split into pieces that are stored in different files. Each file contains a logically related collection of subroutines and data structures that form a *module* in a larger program. A file can be compiled and assembled independently of other files, so changes to one module do not require recompiling the entire program. As we discussed above, separate compilation necessitates the additional step of linking to combine object files from separate modules and fix their unresolved references.

The tool that merges these files is the *linker*. It performs three tasks:

- Searches the program libraries to find library routines used by the program.

- Determines the memory locations that code from each module will occupy and relocates its instructions by adjusting absolute references.

- Resolves references among files.

A linker's first task is to ensure that a program contains no undefined labels. The linker matches the external symbols and unresolved references from a program's files. An external symbol in one file resolves a reference from another file if both refer to a label with the same name. Unmatched references mean a symbol was used, but not defined anywhere in the program.

Unresolved references at this stage in the linking process do not necessarily mean a programmer made a mistake. The program could have referenced a library routine whose code was not in the object files passed to the linker. After matching symbols in the program, the linker searches the system's program libraries to find predefined subroutines and data structures that the program references. The basic libraries contain routines that read and write data, allocate and deallocate memory, and perform numeric operations. Other libraries contain routines to access a database or manipulate terminal windows. A program that references an unresolved symbol that is not in any library is erroneous and cannot be linked. When the program uses a library routine, the linker extracts the routine's code from the library and incorporates it into the program text segment. This new routine, in turn, may depend on other library routines, so the linker continues to fetch other library routines until no external references are unresolved or a routine cannot be found.

If all external references are resolved, the linker next determines the memory locations that each module will occupy. Since the files were assembled in isolation, the assembler could not know where a module's instructions or data will be placed relative to other modules. When the linker places a module in memory, all absolute references must be *relocated* to reflect its true location. Since the linker has relocation information that identifies all relocatable references, it can efficiently find and backpatch these references.

The linker produces an executable file that can run on a computer. Typically, this file has the same format as an object file, except that it contains no unresolved references or relocation information.

Loading

A program that links without an error can be run. Before being run, the program resides in a file on secondary storage, such as a disk. On Unix systems, the operating system kernel brings a program into memory and starts it running. To start a program, the operating system performs the following steps:

1. Reads the executable file's header to determine the size of the text and data segments.

2. Creates a new address space for the program. This address space is large enough to hold the text and data segments, along with a stack segment (see section A.5).

3. Copies instructions and data from the executable file into the new address space.

4. Copies arguments passed to the program onto the stack.

5. Initializes the machine registers. In general, most registers are cleared, but the stack pointer must be assigned the address of the first free stack location (see section A.5).

6. Jumps to a start-up routine that copies the program's arguments from the stack to registers and calls the program's `main` routine. If the `main` routine returns, the start-up routine terminates the program with the exit system call.

Memory Usage

The next few sections elaborate the description of the MIPS architecture presented earlier in the book. Earlier chapters focused primarily on hardware and its relationship with low-level software. These sections focus primarily on how assembly language programmers use MIPS hardware. These sections describe a set of conventions followed on many MIPS systems. For the most part, the hardware does not impose these conventions. Instead, they represent an agreement among programmers to follow the same set of rules so that software written by different people can work together and make effective use of MIPS hardware.

Systems based on MIPS processors typically divide memory into three parts (see Figure A.8). The first part, near the bottom of the address space

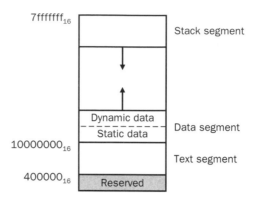

FIGURE A.8 Layout of memory.

(starting at address 400000_{hex}), is the *text segment*, which holds the program's instructions.

The second part, above the text segment is the *data segment*, which is further divided into two parts. *Static data* (starting at address 10000000_{hex}) contains objects whose size is known to the compiler and whose lifetime—the interval during which a program can access them—is the program's entire execution. For example, in C, global variables are statically allocated since they can be referenced anytime during a program's execution. The linker both assigns static objects to locations in the data segment and resolves references to these objects.

Immediately above static data is *dynamic data*. This data, as its name implies, is allocated by the program as it executes. In C programs, the malloc library routine finds and returns a new block of memory. Since a compiler cannot predict how much memory a program will allocate, the operating system expands the dynamic data area to meet demand. As the upward arrow in the figure indicates, malloc expands the dynamic area with the sbrk system call, which causes the operating system to add more pages to the program's virtual address space (see section 7.3 in Chapter 7) immediately above the dynamic data segment.

The third part, the program *stack segment*, resides at the top of the virtual address space (staring at address $7fffffff_{hex}$). Like dynamic data, the maximum size of a program's stack is not known in advance. As the program pushes values on the stack, the operating system expands the stack segment down, towards the data segment.

This three-part division of memory is not the only possible one. However, it has two important characteristics: the two dynamically-expandable segments are as far apart as possible, and they can grow to use a program's entire address space.

Hardware Software Interface

Because the data segment begins far above the program at address 1000000_{hex}, load and store instructions cannot directly reference data objects with their 16-bit offset fields (see section 3.4 in Chapter 3). For example, to load the word in the data segment at address 10008000_{hex} into register $2 requires two instructions:

```
lui  $16, 0x1000     # 0x1000 means 1000 base 16 or 4096 base 10
lw   $2, 0x8000($16) # 0x10000000 + 0x8000 = 0x10008000
```

(The 0x before a number means that it is a hexadecimal value. For example, 0x8000 is 8000_{hex} or 32768.)

To avoid repeating the lui instruction at every load and store, MIPS systems typically dedicate a register ($28) as a *global pointer* to the static data segment. This register contains address 10008000_{hex}, so load and store instructions can use their signed 16-bit offset fields to access the first 64KB of the static data segment. With this global pointer, we can rewrite the example as a single instruction:

```
lw $2, 0($28)
```

Of course, the global pointer register makes addresses 10000000_{hex}–10010000_{hex} faster to access than other heap locations. The MIPS compiler usually stores global variables in this area because these variables are more frequently accessed than other global data.

A.6 Procedure Call Convention

Conventions governing the use of registers are necessary when procedures in a program are compiled separately. To compile a particular procedure, a compiler must know which registers it may use and which registers are reserved for other procedures. Rules for using registers are called *register-use* or *procedure call conventions*. As the name implies, these rules are, for the most part, conventions followed by software rather than rules enforced by hardware.

However, most compilers and programmers try very hard to follow these conventions, because violating them causes insidious bugs.

The calling convention described in this section is the one used by gcc compiler. The native MIPS compiler uses a more complex convention that is slightly faster.

The MIPS CPU contains 32 general purpose registers that are numbered 0–31. Register $0 always contains the hardwired value 0.

- Registers $at (1), $k0 (26), and $k1 (27) are reserved for the assembler and operating system and should not be used by user programs or compilers.

- Registers $a0–$a3 (4–7) are used to pass the first four arguments to routines (remaining arguments are passed on the stack). Registers $v0 and $v1 (2, 3) are used to return values from functions.

- Registers $t0–$t9 (8–15, 24, 25) are caller-saved registers that are used to hold temporary quantities that need not be preserved across calls (see section 3.6 in Chapter 3).

- Registers $s0–$s7 (16–23) are callee-saved registers that hold long-lived values that should be preserved across calls.

- Register $gp (28) is a global pointer that points to the middle of a 64K block of memory in the static data segment.

- Register $sp (29) is the stack pointer, which points to the first free location on the stack. Register $fp (30) is the frame pointer. The jal instruction writes register $ra (31), the return address from a procedure call. These two registers are explained in the next section.

The two-letter abbreviations and names for these registers—for example $sp for the stack pointer—reflect the registers' intended uses in the procedure call convention. In describing this convention, we will use the names instead of register numbers. The table in Figure A.9 lists the registers and describes their intended uses.

Procedure Calls

This section describes the steps that occur when one procedure (the *caller*) invokes another procedure (the *callee*). Programmers who write in a high-level language (like C or Pascal) never see the details of how one procedure calls another because the compiler takes care of this low-level bookkeeping. However, assembly language programmers must explicitly implement every procedure call and return.

Register name	Number	Usage
zero	0	Constant 0
at	1	Reserved for assembler
v0	2	Expression evaluation and results of a function
v1	3	Expression evaluation and results of a function
a0	4	Argument 1
a1	5	Argument 2
a2	6	Argument 3
a3	7	Argument 4
t0	8	Temporary (not preserved across call)
t1	9	Temporary (not preserved across call)
t2	10	Temporary (not preserved across call)
t3	11	Temporary (not preserved across call)
t4	12	Temporary (not preserved across call)
t5	13	Temporary (not preserved across call)
t6	14	Temporary (not preserved across call)
t7	15	Temporary (not preserved across call)
s0	16	Saved temporary (preserved across call)
s1	17	Saved temporary (preserved across call)
s2	18	Saved temporary (preserved across call)
s3	19	Saved temporary (preserved across call)
s4	20	Saved temporary (preserved across call)
s5	21	Saved temporary (preserved across call)
s6	22	Saved temporary (preserved across call)
s7	23	Saved temporary (preserved across call)
t8	24	Temporary (not preserved across call)
t9	25	Temporary (not preserved across call)
k0	26	Reserved for OS kernel
k1	27	Reserved for OS kernel
gp	28	Pointer to global area
sp	29	Stack pointer
fp	30	Frame pointer
ra	31	Return address (used by function call)

FIGURE A.9 MIPS registers and usage convention.

Most of the bookkeeping associated with a call is centered around a block of memory called a *procedure call frame*. This memory is used for a variety of purposes:

- To hold values passed to a procedure as arguments.
- To save registers that a procedure may modify, but which the procedure's caller does not want changed.
- To provide space for variables local to a procedure.

In most programming languages, procedure calls and returns follow a strict last-in, first-out (LIFO) order so this memory can be allocated and deallocated on a stack, which is why these blocks of memory are sometimes called *stack frames*.

Elaboration: A programming language that does not permit recursive procedures—procedures that call themselves either directly or indirectly through a chain of calls—need not allocate frames on a stack. In a nonrecursive language, each procedure's frame may be statically allocated since only one invocation of a procedure can be active at a time. Older versions of Fortran prohibited recursion because statically-allocated frames produced faster code on some older machines. However, on load-store architectures like MIPS, stack frames may be just as fast because a frame pointer register points directly to the active stack frame, which permits a single load or store instruction to access values in the frame. In addition, recursion is a valuable programming technique.

Figure A.10 shows a typical stack frame. The frame consists of the memory between the frame pointer ($fp), which points to the first word of the frame, and the stack pointer ($sp), which points to the first stack word after the frame. The stack grows down from higher memory addresses, so the frame pointer points above the stack pointer. The executing procedure uses the frame pointer to quickly access values in its stack frame. For example, an argument in the stack frame can be loaded into register $2 with the instruction:

```
lw $2, 0($fp)
```

A stack frame may be built in many different ways; however, the caller and callee must agree on the sequence of steps. The steps below describe the calling convention used on most MIPS machines. This convention comes into play at three points during a procedure call: immediately before the caller invokes the callee, just as the callee starts executing, and immediately before the callee

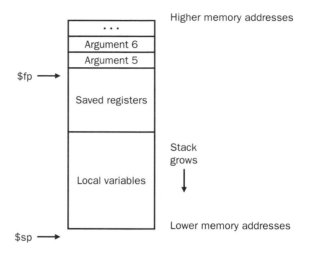

FIGURE A.10 Layout of a stack frame. The frame pointer ($fp) points to the first word in the currently executing procedure's stack frame. The stack pointer ($sp) points to the first free word on the stack after the frame. The first four arguments are passed in registers, so the fifth argument is the first one stored on the stack.

returns to the caller. In the first part, the caller puts the procedure call arguments in standard places and invokes the callee to:

1. Pass arguments. By convention, the first four arguments are passed in registers $a0–$a3. Any remaining arguments are pushed on the stack and appear at the beginning of the called procedure's stack frame.

2. Save caller-saved registers. The called procedure can use these registers ($a0– $a3 and $t0–$t9) without first saving their value. If the caller expects to use one of these registers after a call, it must save its value before the call.

3. Execute a jal instruction (see section 3.6 of Chapter 3), which jumps to the callee's first instruction and saves the return address in register $ra.

Before a called routine starts running, it must take the following steps to set up its stack frame:

1. Allocate memory for the frame by subtracting the frame's size from the stack pointer.

2. Save callee-saved registers in the frame. A callee must save the values in these registers ($s0–$s7, $fp, and $ra) before altering them since the

caller expects to find these registers unchanged after the call. Register $fp is saved by every procedure that allocates a new stack frame. However, register $ra only needs to be saved if the callee itself makes a call. The other callee-saved registers that are used also must be saved.

3. Establish the frame pointer by adding the stack frame's size to $sp and storing the sum in register $fp.

Hardware Software Interface

The MIPS register-use convention provides callee- and caller-saved registers because both types of registers are advantageous in different circumstances. Callee-saved registers are better used to hold long-lived values, such as variables from a user's program. These registers are only saved during a procedure call if the callee expects to use the register. On the other hand, caller-saved registers are better used to hold short-lived quantities that do not persist across a call, such as immediate values in an address calculation. During a call, the callee can also use these registers for short-lived temporaries.

Finally, the callee returns to the caller by executing the following steps:

1. If the callee is a function that returns a value, it places the returned value in register $v0.

2. Restore all callee-saved registers that were saved upon procedure entry.

3. Pop the stack frame by subtracting the frame size from $sp.

4. Return by jumping to the address in register $ra.

Procedure Call Example

As an example, consider the C routine:

```
main ()
{
    printf ("The factorial of 10 is %d\n", fact (10));
}

int fact (int n)
{
    if (n < 1)
            return (1);
```

```
    else
            return (n * fact (n - 1));
}
```

which computes and prints 10! (the factorial of 10, $10! = 10 \times 9 \times \ldots \times 1$). fact is a recursive routine that computes $n!$ by multiplying n times $(n-1)$. The assembly code for this routine illustrates how programs manipulate stack frames.

Upon entry, the routine main creates its stack frame and saves the two callee-saved registers it will modify: $fp and $ra (for unimportant reasons, the minimum size of a stack frame is 32 bytes, so the frame is larger than required for these two registers):

```
        .text
        .globl main
main:
        subu    $sp,$sp,32      # Stack frame is 32 bytes long
        sw      $ra,20($sp)     # Save return address
        sw      $fp,16($sp)     # Save old frame pointer
        addu    $fp,$sp,32      # Set up frame pointer
```

The routine main then calls the factorial routine and passes it the single argument 10. After fact returns, main calls the library routine printf and passes it both a format string and the result returned from fact:

```
        li      $a0,10          # Put argument (10) in $a0
        jal     fact            # Call factorial function

        la      $a0,$LC         # Put format string in $a0
        move    $a1,$v0         # Move fact result to $a1
        jal     printf          # Call the print function
```

Finally, after printing the factorial, main returns. But first, it must restore the registers it saved and pop its stack frame:

```
        lw      $ra,20($sp)     # Restore return address
        lw      $fp,16($sp)     # Restore frame pointer
        addu    $sp,$sp,32      # Pop stack frame
        jr      $ra             # Return to caller

        .rdata
$LC0:
        .ascii  "The factorial of 10 is %d\n\000"
```

The factorial routine is similar in structure to `main`. First, it creates a stack frame and saves the callee-saved registers it will use. In addition to saving `$ra` and `$fp`, `fact` also saves its argument (`$a0`), which it will use for the recursive call:

```
        .text
fact:
        subu    $sp,$sp,32      # Stack frame is 32 bytes long
        sw      $ra,20($sp)     # Save return address
        sw      $fp,16($sp)     # Save frame pointer
        addu    $fp,$sp,32      # Set up frame pointer

        sw      $a0,0($fp)      # Save argument (n)
```

The heart of the `fact` routine performs the computation from the C program. It tests if the argument is greater than zero. If not, the routine returns the value 1. If the argument is greater than zero, the routine recursively calls itself to compute `fact(n-1)` and multiplies that value times n:

```
        lw      $2,0($fp)       # Load n
        bgtz    $2,$L2          # Branch if n > 0
        li      $2,1            # Return 1
        j       $L1             # Jump to code to return

$L2:
        lw      $3,0($fp)       # Load n
        subu    $2,$3,1         # Compute n - 1
        move    $a0,$2          # Move value to $a0
        jal     fact            # Call factorial function

        lw      $3,0($fp)       # Load n
        mul     $2,$2,$3        # Compute fact(n-1) * n
```

Finally, the factorial routine restores the callee-saved registers and returns the value in register `$2`:

```
$L1:                            # Result is in $2
        lw      $ra, 20($sp)    # Restore $ra
        lw      $fp, 16($sp)    # Restore $fp
        addu    $sp, $sp, 32    # Pop stack
        j       $ra             # Return to caller
```

Example

Figure A.11 shows the stack at the call: `fact(7)`. `main` runs first, so its frame is deepest on the stack. `main` calls `fact(10)`, whose stack frame is next on the stack. Each invocation recursively invokes `fact` to compute the next-lowest factorial. The stack frames parallel the LIFO order of these calls. What does the stack look like when the call to `fact(6)` returns?

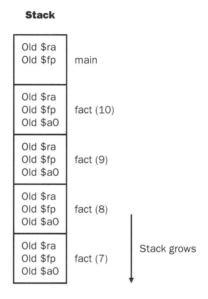

FIGURE A.11 Stack frames during the call of fact(7).

Answer

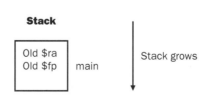

Elaboration: The difference between the MIPS compiler and the gcc compiler is that the MIPS compiler usually does not use a frame pointer, so this register is available as another callee-saved register $s8. This change saves a couple of instructions in the procedure call and return sequence. However, it complicates code generation because a procedure must access its stack frame with $sp, whose value changes during the procedure's execution as values are pushed on the stack.

A.7   Exceptions and Interrupts

Section 5.6 of Chapter 5 describes the MIPS exception facility, which responds both to exceptions caused by errors during an instruction's execution and to external interrupts caused by I/O devices. This section describes exception and interrupt handling in more detail. In MIPS processors, a part of the CPU called *coprocessor 0* records the information the software needs to handle exceptions and interrupts. The MIPS simulator SPIM does not implement all of coprocessor 0's registers, since many are not useful in a simulator or are part of the memory system, which SPIM does not implement. However, SPIM does provide the following coprocessor 0 registers:

Register name	Register number	Usage
BadVAddr	8	Register containing the memory address at which memory reference occurred
Status	12	Interrupt mask and enable bits
Cause	13	Exception type and pending interrupt bits
EPC	14	Register containing address of instruction that caused exception

These four registers are part of coprocessor 0's register set and are accessed by the lwc0, mfc0, mtc0, and swc0 instructions. After an exception, register EPC contains the address of the instruction that was executing when the exception occurred. If the instruction made a memory access that caused the exception, register BadVAddr contains the referenced memory location's address. The two other registers contain many fields and are described below.

Figure A.12 shows the Status register fields implemented by the MIPS simulator SPIM. The interrupt mask field contains a bit for each of the five hardware and three software possible interrupt levels. A bit that is 1 allows interrupts at that level. A bit that is 0 disables interrupts at that level. The low 6 bits of the Status register implement a three-deep stack for the kernel/user and interrupt enable bits. The kernel/user bit is 0 if a program was in the

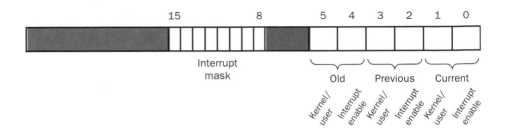

FIGURE A.12 The Status register.

kernel when an exception occurred and 1 if it was running in user mode. If the `interrupt enable` bit is 1, interrupts are allowed. If it is 0, they are disabled. When an interrupt occurs, these six bits are shifted left by two bits, so the current bits become the previous bits and the previous bits become the old bits (the old bits are discarded). The current bits are both set to 0 so the interrupt handler runs in the kernel interrupts disabled.

Figure A.13 shows the Cause register fields implemented by SPIM. The five `pending interrupt` bits correspond to the five interrupt levels. A bit becomes 1 when an interrupt at its level has occurred but has not been serviced. The Exception code register describes the cause of an exception with the following codes:

Number	Name	Description
0	INT	External interrupt
4	ADDRL	Address error exception (load or instruction fetch)
5	ADDRS	Address error exception (store)
6	IBUS	Bus error on instruction fetch
7	DBUS	Bus error on data load or store
8	SYSCALL	Syscall exception
9	BKPT	Breakpoint exception
10	RI	Reserved instruction exception
12	OVF	Arithmetic overflow exception

Exceptions and interrupts cause a MIPS processor to jump to a piece of code, at address 80000080_{hex} (in the kernel, not user address space), called an

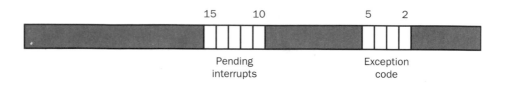

FIGURE A.13 The Cause register.

interrupt handler. This code examines the exception's cause and jumps to an appropriate point in the operating system. The operating system responds to an exception either by terminating the process that caused the exception or by performing some action. A process that causes an error, such as executing an unimplemented instruction, is killed by the operating system. On the other hand, exceptions such as page-faults are requests from a process to the operating system to perform a service, such as bringing in a page from disk. The operating system processes these requests and resumes the process. The final type of exceptions are interrupts from external devices. These generally cause the operating system to move data to or from an I/O device and resume the interrupted process. The code in the example below is a simple interrupt handler, which invokes a routine to print a message at each exception (but not interrupts). This code is similar to the interrupt handler used by the SPIM simulator described in the Example that follows.

Example

The interrupt handler first saves registers $a0 and $a1, which it later uses to pass arguments. The interrupt handler cannot store the old values from these registers on the stack, as would an ordinary routine, because the cause of the interrupt might have been a memory reference that used a bad value (such as 0) in the stack pointer. Instead the interrupt handler stores these registers in two memory locations: (save0 and save1). If the interrupt routine itself could be interrupted, two locations would not be enough since the second interrupt would overwrite values saved during the first interrupt. However, this simple interrupt handler finishes running before it enables interrupts, so the problem does not arise.

```
.ktext 0x80000080
sw $a0 save0     # Handler is not re-entrent and can't use
sw $a1 save1     # stack to save $a0, $a1
                 # Don't need to save $k0/$k1
```

The interrupt handler then moves the `Cause` and `EPC` registers into CPU registers. The `Cause` and `EPC` registers are not part of the CPU register set. Instead, they are registers in coprocessor 0, which is the part of the CPU that handles interrupts. The instruction `mfc0 $k0, $13` moves coprocessor 0's register 13 (the Cause register) into CPU register `$k0`. Note that the interrupt handler need not save registers `$k0` and `$k1` because user programs are not supposed to use these registers. The interrupt handler uses the value from the Cause register to test if the exception was caused by an interrupt (see the preceding table). If so, the exception is ignored. If the exception was not an interrupt, the handler calls `print_excp` to print a warning message.

```
mfc0    $k0 $13         # Move Cause into $k0
mfc0    $k1 $14         # Move EPC into $k1

sgt     $v0 $k0 0x44    # Ignore interrupts
bgtz    $v0 done

mov     $a0, $k0        # Move Cause into $a0
mov     $a1, $k1        # Move EPC into $a0
jal     print_excp      # Print exception error message
```

Before returning, the interrupt handler restores registers `$a0` and `$a1`. It then executes the `rfe` (return from exception) instruction, which restores the previous interrupt mask and kernel/user bits in the Status register. This switches the processor state back to what it was before the exception and prepares to resume program execution. The interrupt handler then returns to the program by jumping to the instruction following the one that caused the exception.

```
done:
        lw      $a0 save0
        lw      $a1 save1
        addiu   $k1 $k1 4       # Do not reexecute
                                # faulting instruction
        rfe                     # Restore interrupt state
        jr      $k1

        .kdata
save0:  .word 0
save1:  .word 0
```

Elaboration: On real MIPS processors, the return from an interrupt handler is more complex. The `rfe` instruction must execute in the delay slot of the `jr` instruction that returns to the user program so that no interrupt-handler instruction executes with the user program's interrupt mask and kernel/user bits. In addition, the interrupt handler cannot always jump to the instruction following EPC. For example, if the instruction that caused the exception was in a branch instruction's delay slot (see Chapter 6), the next instruction may not be the following instruction in memory.

A.8 Input and Output

SPIM simulates one I/O device: a memory-mapped terminal. When a program is running, SPIM connects its own terminal (or a separate console window in the X-window version xspim) to the processor. A MIPS program running on SPIM can read the characters that you type. In addition, if the MIPS program writes characters to the terminal, they appear on SPIM's terminal or console window. One exception to this rule is control-C: this character is not passed to the program, but instead causes SPIM to stop and return to command mode. When the program stops running (for example, because you typed control-C or because the program hit a breakpoint), the terminal is reconnected to spim so you can type SPIM commands. To use memory-mapped I/O (see below), spim or xspim must be started with the -mapped_io flag.

The terminal device consists of two independent units: a *receiver* and a *transmitter*. The receiver reads characters from the keyboard. The transmitter writes characters to the display. The two units are completely independent. This means, for example, that characters typed at the keyboard are not automatically "echoed" on the display. Instead, a program must explicitly echo a character by reading it from the receiver and writing it to the transmitter.

A program controls the terminal with four memory-mapped device registers, as shown in Figure A.14. "Memory-mapped" means that each register appears as a special memory location. The *Receiver Control register* is at location ffff0000$_{hex}$. Only two of its bits are actually used. Bit 0 is called "ready": if it is 1, it means that a character has arrived from the keyboard but has not yet been read from the Receiver Data register. The ready bit is read-only: writes to it are ignored. The ready bit changes from 0 to 1 when a character is typed at the keyboard, and it changes from 1 to 0 when the character is read from the Receiver Data register.

Bit 1 of the Receiver Control register is the keyboard "interrupt enable." This bit may be both read and written by a program. The interrupt enable is initially 0. If it is set to 1 by a program, the terminal requests an interrupt at level 0 whenever the ready bit is 1. However, for the interrupt to affect the processor, interrupts must also be enabled in the Status register (see section A.7). All other bits of the Receiver Control register are unused.

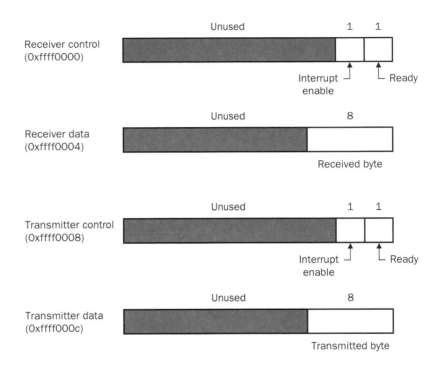

FIGURE A.14 The terminal is controlled by four device registers, each of which appears as a memory location at the given address. Only a few bits of these registers are actually used. The others always read as 0s and are ignored on writes.

The second terminal device register is the *Receiver Data register* (at address ffff0004$_{hex}$). The low-order eight bits of this register contain the last character typed at the keyboard. All other bits contain 0s. This register is read-only and changes only when a new character is typed at the keyboard. Reading the Receiver Data register resets the ready bit in the Receiver Control register to 0.

The third terminal device register is the *Transmitter Control register* (at address ffff0008$_{hex}$). Only the low-order two bits of this register are used. They behave much like the corresponding bits of the Receiver Control register. Bit 0 is called "ready" and is read-only. If this bit is 1, the transmitter is ready to accept a new character for output. If it is 0, the transmitter is still busy writing the previous character. Bit 1 is "interrupt enable" and is readable and writable. If this bit is set to 1, then the terminal requests an interrupt on level one whenever the ready bit is 1.

The final device register is the *Transmitter Data register* (at address ffff000c$_{hex}$). When a value is written into this location, its low-order eight bits (i.e., an ASCII character as in Figure 3.27 in Chapter 3) are sent to the console. When the Transmitter Data register is written, the ready bit in the Transmitter Control register is reset to 0. This bit stays 0 until enough time has elapsed to transmit the character to the terminal; then the ready bit becomes 1 again. The Transmitter Data register should only be written when the ready bit of the Transmitter Control register is 1. If the transmitter is not ready, writes to the Transmitter Data register are ignored (the write appears to succeed but the character is not output).

Real computers require time to send characters over the serial lines that connect terminals to computers. These time lags are simulated by SPIM. For example, after the transmitter starts to write a character, the transmitter's ready bit becomes 0 for a while. SPIM measures time in instructions executed, not in real clock time. This means that the transmitter does not become ready again until the processor executes a certain number of instructions. If you stop the machine and look at the ready bit, it will not change. However, if you let the machine run, the bit eventually changes back to 1.

A.9   SPIM

SPIM is a software simulator that runs programs written for MIPS R2000/R3000 processors. SPIM's name is just MIPS spelled backwards. SPIM can read and immediately execute assembly language files or (on some systems) MIPS executable files. SPIM is a self-contained system for running MIPS programs. It contains a debugger and provides a few operating system-like services. SPIM is much slower than a real computer (100 or more times). However, its low cost and wide availability cannot be matched by real hardware!

An obvious question is, Why use a simulator when many people have workstations that contain MIPS chips that are significantly faster than SPIM? One reason is that these workstations are not universally available. Another reason is rapid progress towards new and faster computers renders these machines obsolete (see Chapter 1). The current trend is to make computers faster by executing several instructions concurrently. This makes architectures more difficult to understand and program. The MIPS architecture may be the epitome of a simple, clean RISC machine.

In addition, simulators can provide a better environment for programming than an actual machine because they can detect more errors and provide more features than an actual computer. For example, SPIM has an X-window interface that works better than most debuggers on the actual machines.

Finally, simulators are a useful tool in studying computers and the programs that run on them. Because they are implemented in software, not silicon, simulators can be easily modified to add new instructions, build new systems such as multiprocessors, or simply to collect data.

Simulation of a Virtual Machine

The MIPS architecture, like that of many RISC computers, is difficult to program directly because of delayed branches, delayed loads, and restricted address modes. This difficulty is tolerable since these computers were designed to be programmed in high-level languages and present an interface appropriate for compilers rather than assembly language programmers. A good part of the programming complexity results from delayed instructions. A *delayed branch* requires two cycles to execute (see section 6.7 of Chapter 6). In the second cycle, the instruction immediately following the branch executes. This instruction can perform useful work that normally would have been done before the branch. It can also be a nop (no operation). Similarly, *delayed loads* require two cycles so the instruction immediately following a load cannot use the value loaded from memory (see section 6.2 of Chapter 6).

MIPS wisely chose to hide this complexity by having its assembler implement a *virtual machine*. This virtual computer appears to have nondelayed branches and loads and a richer instruction set than the actual hardware. The assembler *reorganizes* (rearranges) instructions to fill the delay slots. It also simulates the additional, *pseudoinstructions* with short sequences of actual instructions.

By default, SPIM simulates the richer virtual machine. However, it can also simulate the bare hardware. Below, we describe the virtual machine and only mention in passing features that do not belong to the actual hardware. In doing so, we follow the convention of MIPS assembly language programmers (and compilers), who routinely use the extended machine. (For a description of the real machines, see Gerry Kane and Joe Heinrich, *MIPS RISC Architecture*, Prentice Hall, 1992.)

Getting Started with SPIM

The rest of this appendix contains a complete and rather detailed description of SPIM. Many details should never concern you; however, the sheer volume of information can obscure the fact that SPIM is a simple, easy-to-use program. This section contains a quick tutorial on SPIM that should enable you to load, debug, and run simple MIPS programs.

SPIM comes in two versions. The plain version is called spim. It runs on any type of terminal. It operates like most programs of this type: you type a line of text, hit the return key, and spim executes your command.

The fancier version of SPIM is called xspim. It uses the X-window system, so you must have a bit-mapped display to run it. xspim, however, is a much easier program to learn and use because its commands are always visible on the screen and because it continually displays the machine's registers.

Since most people use and prefer xspim, this section only discusses that program. If you plan to use spim, do not skip this section. Read it first and then look at the SPIM Command-Line Options (starting on page A-41) to see how to accomplish the same thing with spim commands.

To start xspim, type xspim in response to your system's prompt ('%'):

```
% xspim
```

On your system, xspim may be kept in an unusual place and you may need to execute a command first to add that place to your search path. Your instructor should tell you how to do this.

When xspim starts up, it pops up a large window on your screen. Figure A.15 shows a picture of this window. The window is divided into five panes:

■ The top pane is called the *register display*. It shows the values of all registers in the MIPS CPU and FPU. This display is updated whenever your program stops running.

■ The pane below contains the *control buttons* to operate xspim. These buttons are discussed below, so we can skip the details for now.

■ The next pane, called the *text segments*, displays instructions both from your program and the system code that is loaded automatically when xspim starts running. Each instruction is displayed on a line that looks like

```
[0x00400000] 0x8fa40000 lw $4, 0($29)  ; 89: lw $a0, 0($sp)
```

The first number on the line, in square brackets, is the hexadecimal memory address of the instruction. The second number is the instruction's numerical encoding, again displayed as a hexadecimal number. The third item is the instruction's mnemonic description. Everything following the semicolon is the actual line from your assembly file that produced the instruction. The number 89 is the line number in that file. Sometimes nothing is on the line after the semicolon. This means that the instruction was produced by SPIM as part of translating a pseudoinstruction. Look down a line or two to find the pseudoinstruction that you wrote.

■ The next pane, called the *data segments*, displays the data loaded into your program's memory and the data on the program's stack.

■ The bottom pane is the *SPIM messages* that xspim uses to write messages. This is where error messages appear.

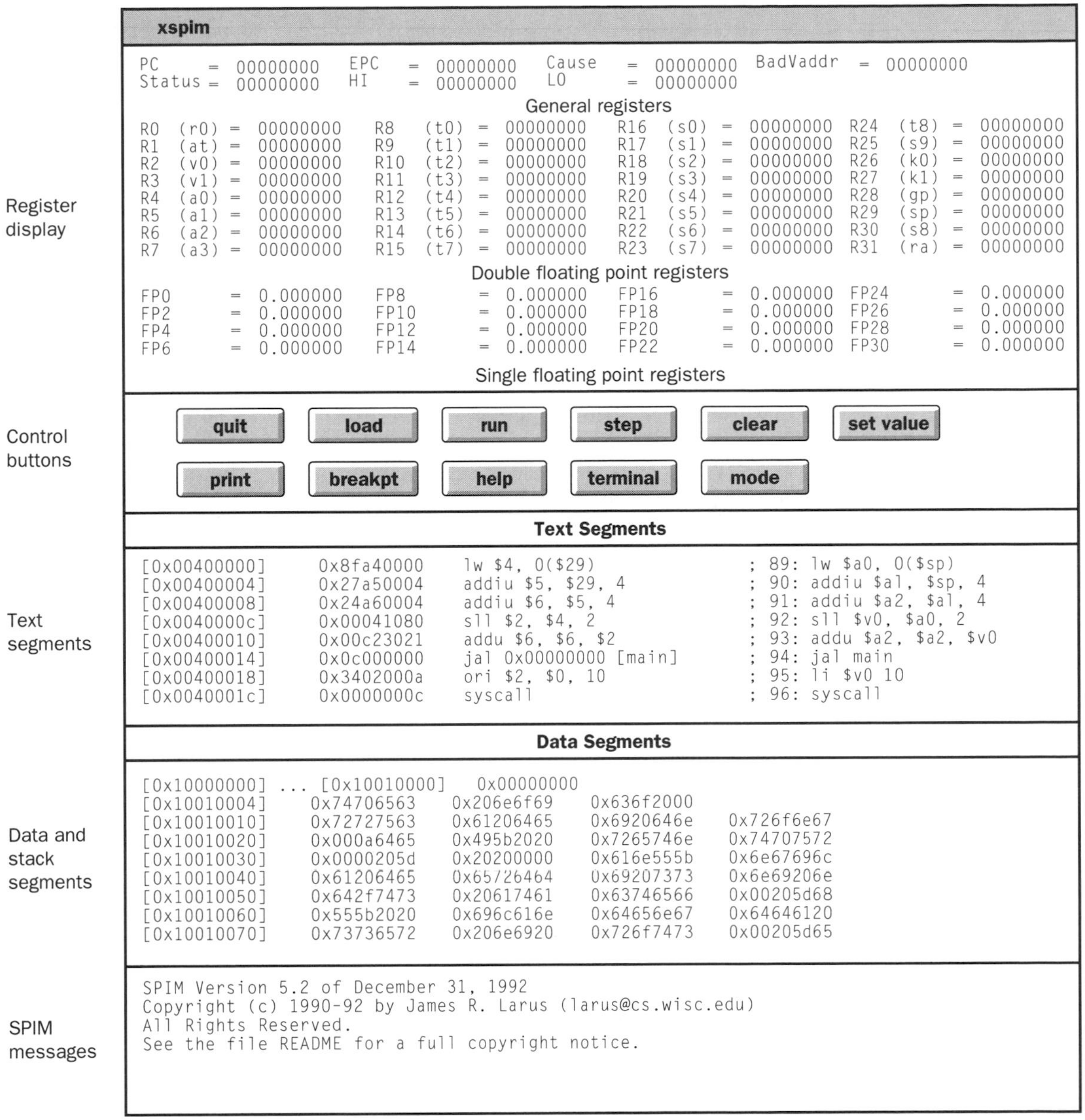

Register display

Control buttons

Text segments

Data and stack segments

SPIM messages

```
xspim

PC     = 00000000   EPC  = 00000000   Cause  = 00000000   BadVaddr = 00000000
Status = 00000000   HI   = 00000000   LO     = 00000000
                                General registers
R0   (r0) = 00000000   R8   (t0) = 00000000   R16  (s0) = 00000000   R24  (t8) = 00000000
R1   (at) = 00000000   R9   (t1) = 00000000   R17  (s1) = 00000000   R25  (s9) = 00000000
R2   (v0) = 00000000   R10  (t2) = 00000000   R18  (s2) = 00000000   R26  (k0) = 00000000
R3   (v1) = 00000000   R11  (t3) = 00000000   R19  (s3) = 00000000   R27  (k1) = 00000000
R4   (a0) = 00000000   R12  (t4) = 00000000   R20  (s4) = 00000000   R28  (gp) = 00000000
R5   (a1) = 00000000   R13  (t5) = 00000000   R21  (s5) = 00000000   R29  (sp) = 00000000
R6   (a2) = 00000000   R14  (t6) = 00000000   R22  (s6) = 00000000   R30  (s8) = 00000000
R7   (a3) = 00000000   R15  (t7) = 00000000   R23  (s7) = 00000000   R31  (ra) = 00000000
                            Double floating point registers
FP0    = 0.000000   FP8    = 0.000000   FP16   = 0.000000   FP24   = 0.000000
FP2    = 0.000000   FP10   = 0.000000   FP18   = 0.000000   FP26   = 0.000000
FP4    = 0.000000   FP12   = 0.000000   FP20   = 0.000000   FP28   = 0.000000
FP6    = 0.000000   FP14   = 0.000000   FP22   = 0.000000   FP30   = 0.000000
                            Single floating point registers

  [ quit ]    [ load ]    [ run ]    [ step ]    [ clear ]    [ set value ]

  [ print ]   [ breakpt ] [ help ]   [ terminal ] [ mode ]

                                  Text Segments

[0x00400000]    0x8fa40000    lw $4, 0($29)        ; 89: lw $a0, 0($sp)
[0x00400004]    0x27a50004    addiu $5, $29, 4     ; 90: addiu $a1, $sp, 4
[0x00400008]    0x24a60004    addiu $6, $5, 4      ; 91: addiu $a2, $a1, 4
[0x0040000c]    0x00041080    sll $2, $4, 2        ; 92: sll $v0, $a0, 2
[0x00400010]    0x00c23021    addu $6, $6, $2      ; 93: addu $a2, $a2, $v0
[0x00400014]    0x0c000000    jal 0x00000000 [main] ; 94: jal main
[0x00400018]    0x3402000a    ori $2, $0, 10       ; 95: li $v0 10
[0x0040001c]    0x0000000c    syscall              ; 96: syscall

                                  Data Segments

[0x10000000] ... [0x10010000]    0x00000000
[0x10010004]    0x74706563    0x206e6f69    0x636f2000
[0x10010010]    0x72727563    0x61206465    0x6920646e    0x726f6e67
[0x10010020]    0x000a6465    0x495b2020    0x7265746e    0x74707472
[0x10010030]    0x0000205d    0x20200000    0x616e555b    0x6e67696c
[0x10010040]    0x61206465    0x65726464    0x69207373    0x6e69206e
[0x10010050]    0x642f7473    0x20617461    0x63746566    0x00205d68
[0x10010060]    0x555b2020    0x696c616e    0x64656e67    0x64646120
[0x10010070]    0x73736572    0x206e6920    0x726f7473    0x00205d65

SPIM Version 5.2 of December 31, 1992
Copyright (c) 1990-92 by James R. Larus (larus@cs.wisc.edu)
All Rights Reserved.
See the file README for a full copyright notice.
```

FIGURE A.15 SPIM's X-window interface: xspim.

Let's see how to load and run a program. The first thing to do is to click on the LOAD button (the second one in the first row of buttons) with the left mouse key. Your click tells xspim to pop up a small prompt window that contains a box and two or three buttons. Move your mouse so the cursor is over the box and type the name of your file of assembly code. Then click on the button labeled ASSEMBLY FILE. If you change your mind, click on the button labeled ABORT COMMAND and xspim gets rid of prompt window. When you click on ASSEMBLY FILE, xspim gets rid of the prompt window, then loads your program and redraws the screen to display its instructions and data. Now move the mouse to put the cursor over the scrollbar to the left of the *text segments* and click the left mouse button on the white part of this scrollbar. A click scrolls the text pane down so you can find all instructions in your program.

To run your program, click on the RUN button in xspim's control button pane. It pops up a prompt window with two boxes and two buttons. Most of the time, these boxes contain the correct values to run your program, so you can ignore them and just click on OK. This button tells xspim to run your program. Notice that when your program is running, xspim blanks out the *register display* pane because the registers are continually changing. You can always tell whether xspim is running by looking at this pane. If you want to stop your program, make sure the mouse cursor is somewhere over xspim's window and type control-C. This causes xspim to pop up a prompt window with two buttons. Before doing anything with this prompt window, you can look at registers and memory to find out what your program was doing. When you understand what happened, you can either continue the program by clicking on CONTINUE or stop your program by clicking on ABORT COMMAND.

If your program reads or writes from the terminal, xspim pops up another window called the *console*. All characters that your program writes appear on the console and everything that you type as input to your program should be typed in this window.

Suppose your program does not do what you expect. What can you do? SPIM has two features that help debug your program. The first, and perhaps the most useful, is single-stepping, which allows you to run your program an instruction at a time. Click on the button labeled step and another prompt pops up. This prompt contains two boxes and three buttons. The first box asks for the number of instructions to step every time you click the mouse. Most of the time, the default value of 1 is a good choice. The other box asks for arguments to pass to the program when it starts running. Again, most of the time you can ignore this box because it contains an appropriate value. The button labeled STEP runs your program for the number of instructions in the top box. If that number is 1, xspim executes the next instruction in your program, updates the display, and returns control to you. The button labeled CONTINUE stops single-stepping and continues running your program. Finally, ABORT COMMAND stops single-stepping and leaves your program stopped.

What do you do if your program runs for a long time before the bug arises? You could single-step until you get to the bug, but that can take a long time and it is easy to get so bored and inattentive that you step past the problem. A better alternative is to use a *breakpoint*, which tells xspim to stop your program immediately before it executes a particular instruction. Click on the button in the second row of buttons marked BREAKPOINTS. The xspim program pops up a prompt window with one box and many buttons. Type in this box the address of the instruction at which you want to stop. Or, if the instruction has a global label, you can just type the name of the label. This is a particularly convenient way to stop at the first instruction of a procedure. To actually set the breakpoint, click on ADD. You can then run your program. When SPIM is about to execute the breakpointed instruction, xspim pops up a prompt with the instruction's address and two buttons. The CONTINUE button continues running your program and ABORT COMMAND stops your program. If you want to delete a breakpoint, type in its address and click on DELETE. Finally, LIST tells xspim to print (in the bottom pane) a list of all breakpoints that are set.

Single-stepping and setting breakpoints will probably help you find a bug in your program quickly. How do you fix it? Go back to the editor that you used to create your program and change it. To run the program again, you need a fresh copy of SPIM, which you get in two ways. Either you can exit from xspim by clicking on the QUIT button, or you can clear xspim and reload your program. If you reload your program, you *must* clear out the memory so remnants of your previous program do not interfere with your new program. To do this, click on the button labeled CLEAR. Hold the left mouse key down and a two-item menu will pop up. Move the mouse so the cursor is over the item labeled MEMORY & REGISTERS and release the key. This causes xspim to clear its memory and registers and return the processor to the state it was in when xspim first started. You can now load and run your new program.

The other buttons in xspim perform functions that are occasionally useful. When you are more comfortable with xspim, you should look at the description below to see what they do and how they can save you time and effort.

SPIM Command-Line Options

Both versions of SPIM—spim, the terminal version, and xspim, the X version—accept the following command-line options:

-bare   Simulate a bare MIPS machine without pseudoinstructions or the additional addressing modes provided by the assembler. Implies -quiet.

-asm   Simulate the virtual MIPS machine provided by the assembler. This is the default.

-notrap   Do not load the standard exception handler and start-up code. This exception handler handles exceptions. When an exception occurs, SPIM jumps to location 80000080$_{hex}$, which must contain code to service the exception. In addition, this file contains start-up code that invokes the routine main. Without the start-up routine, SPIM begins execution at the instruction labeled __start.

-trap   Load the standard exception handler and start-up code. This is the default.

-noquiet   Print a message when an exception occurs. This is the default.

-quiet   Do not print a message at exceptions.

-nomapped_io   Disable the memory-mapped I/O facility (see section A.8). This is the default.

-mapped_io   Enable the memory-mapped I/O facility (see section A.8). Programs that use SPIM syscalls (see section on System Calls, page A-45) to read from the terminal *cannot* also use memory-mapped I/O.

-file   Load and execute the assembly code in the file.

-execute   Load and execute the code in the MIPS executable file *a.out*. This command is only available when SPIM runs on a system containing a MIPS processor.

-s seg size   Sets the initial size of memory segment *seg* to be *size* bytes. The memory segments are named: text, data, stack, ktext, and kdata. The text segment contains instructions from a program. The data segment holds the program's data. The stack segment holds its runtime stack. In addition to running a program, SPIM also executes system code that handles interrupts and exceptions. This code resides in a separate part of the address space called the *kernel*. The ktext segment holds this code's instructions and kdata holds its data. There is no kstack segment since the system code uses the same stack as the program. For example, the pair of arguments -sdata 2000000 starts the user data segment at 2,000,000 bytes.

-lseg size   Sets the limit on how large memory segment *seg* can grow to be *size* bytes. The memory segments that can grow are data, stack, and kdata.

Terminal Interface (spim)

The simpler version of SPIM is called spim. It does not require a bitmapped display and can be run from any terminal. Although spim may be more difficult to learn, it operates just like xspim and provides the same functionality.

The spim terminal interface provides the following commands:

exit   Exit the simulator.

read "file"   Read *file* of assembly language into SPIM. If the file has already been read into SPIM, the system must be cleared (see reinitialize, below) or global symbols will be multiply defined.

load "file"   Synonym for read.

execute "a.out"   Read the MIPS executable file *a.out* into SPIM. This command is only available when SPIM runs on a system containing a MIPS processor.

run <addr>   Start running a program. If the optional address *addr* is provided, the program starts at that address. Otherwise, the program starts at the global symbol __start, which is usually the default startup code that calls the routine at the global symbol main.

step <N>   Step the program for *N* (default: 1) instructions. Print instructions as they execute.

continue   Continue program execution without stepping.

print $N   Print register *N*.

print $fN   Print floating point register *N*.

print addr   Print the contents of memory at address *addr*.

print_sym   Print the symbol table, i.e., the addresses of the global (but not local) symbols.

reinitialize   Clear the memory and registers.

breakpoint addr   Set a breakpoint at address *addr*. *addr* can be either a memory address or symbolic label.

delete addr   Delete all breakpoints at address *addr*.

list   List all breakpoints.

.   Rest of line is an assembly instruction that is stored in memory.

<nl>   A newline re-executes previous command.

?   Print a help message.

Most commands can be abbreviated to their unique prefix, e.g., ex, re, l, ru, s, p. More dangerous commands, such as reinitialize, require a longer prefix.

X-Window Interface (xspim)

The tutorial, "Getting Started with SPIM" (page A-37), explains the most common xspim commands. However, xspim has other commands that are occasionally useful. This section provides a complete list of the commands.

The X version of SPIM, xspim, looks different but operates in the same manner as spim. The X window has five panes (see Figure A.4). The top pane displays the registers. These values are continually updated, except while a program is running.

The next pane contains buttons that control the simulator:

quit   Exit from the simulator.

load   Read a source or executable file into SPIM.

run   Start the program running.

step   Single-step a program.

clear   Reinitialize registers or memory.

set value   Set the value in a register or memory location.

print   Print the value in a register or memory location.

breakpoint   Set or delete a breakpoint or list all breakpoints.

help   Print a help message.

terminal   Raise or hide the console window.

mode   Set SPIM operating modes.

The next two panes display the memory. The top one shows instructions from the user and kernel text segments. (These instructions are real—not pseudo—MIPS instructions. SPIM translates assembler pseudoinstructions to 1–3 MIPS instructions. Each source instruction appears as a comment on the first instruction to which it is translated.) The first few instructions in the text segment are the default start-up code (__start) that loads argc and argv into registers and invokes the main routine. The lower of these two panes displays the data and stack segments. Both panes are updated as a program executes.

The bottom pane is used to display SPIM messages. It does not display output from a program. When a program reads or writes, its I/O appears in a separate window, called the Console, which pops up when needed.

Surprising Features

Although SPIM faithfully simulates the MIPS computer, SPIM is a simulator and certain things are not identical to an actual computer. The most obvious differences are that instruction timing and the memory systems are not identical. SPIM does not simulate caches or memory latency, nor does it accurately reflect floating-point operation or multiply and divide instruction delays.

Another surprise (which occurs on the real machine as well) is that a pseudoinstruction expands to several machine instructions. When you single-step or examine memory, the instructions that you see are different from the source program. The correspondence between the two sets of instructions is fairly simple since SPIM does not reorganize instructions to fill delay slots.

Byte Order

Processors can number bytes within a word so the byte with the lowest number is either the leftmost or rightmost one. The convention used by a machine is its *byte order*. MIPS processors can operate with either *big-endian* byte order:

Byte #			
0	1	2	3

or *little-endian* byte order:

Byte #			
3	2	1	0

SPIM operates with both byte orders. SPIM's byte order is the same as the byte order of the underlying machine that runs the simulator. For example, on a DECstation 3100, SPIM is little-endian, while on a Macintosh, HP Bobcat, or Sun SPARC, SPIM is big-endian.

System Calls

SPIM provides a small set of operating system-like services through the system call (syscall) instruction. To request a service, a program loads the system call code (see Figure A.16) into register $v0 and arguments into registers $a0 ... $a3 (or $f12 for floating-point values). System calls that return values put their results in register $v0 (or $f0 for floating-point results). For example, the following code prints "the answer = 5":

Service	System call code	Arguments	Result
print_int	1	$a0 = integer	
print_float	2	$f12 = float	
print_double	3	$f12 = double	
print_string	4	$a0 = string	
read_int	5		integer (in $v0)
read_float	6		float (in $f0)
read_double	7		double (in $f0)
read_string	8	$a0 = buffer, $a1 = length	
sbrk	9	$a0 = amount	address (in $v0)
exit	10		

FIGURE A.16 System services.

```
        .data
str:
        .asciiz  "the answer = "
        .text
        li      $v0, 4      # system call code for print_str
        la      $a0, str    # address of string to print
        syscall             # print the string

        li      $v0, 1      # system call code for print_int
        li      $a0, 5      # integer to print
        syscall             # print it
```

The print_int system call is passed an integer and prints it on the console. print_float prints a single floating-point number; print_double prints a double precision number; and print_string is passed a pointer to a null-terminated string, which it writes to the console.

The system calls read_int, read_float, and read_double read an entire line of input up to and including the newline. Characters following the number are ignored. read_string has the same semantics as the Unix library routine fgets. It reads up to $n - 1$ characters into a buffer and terminates the string with a null byte. If fewer than $n - 1$ characters are on the current line, read_int reads up to and including the newline and again null-terminates the string. *Warning:* Programs that use these syscalls to read from the terminal should not use memory-mapped I/O (see section A.8).

Finally, sbrk returns a pointer to a block of memory containing n additional bytes, and exit stops a program from running.

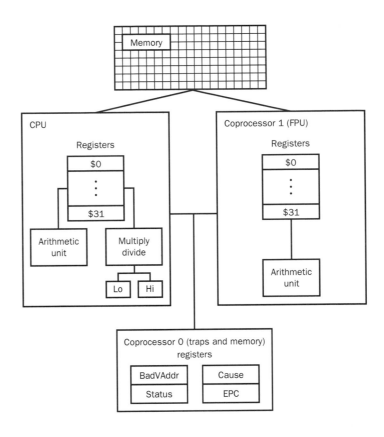

FIGURE A.17 MIPS R2000 CPU and FPU.

A.10 MIPS R2000 Assembly Language

A MIPS processor consists of an integer processing unit (the CPU) and a collection of coprocessors that perform ancillary tasks or operate on other types of data such as floating-point numbers (see Figure A.17). SPIM simulates two coprocessors. Coprocessor 0 handles exceptions, interrupts, and the virtual memory system. SPIM simulates most of the first two and entirely omits details of the memory system. Coprocessor 1 is the floating-point unit. SPIM simulates most aspects of this unit.

Addressing Modes

MIPS is a load/store architecture, which means that only load and store instructions access memory. Computation instructions operate only on values in registers. The bare machine provides only one memory-addressing mode: c(rx), which uses the sum of the immediate c and register rx as the address. The virtual machine provides the following addressing modes for load and store instructions:

Format	Address computation
(register)	contents of register
imm	immediate
imm (register)	immediate + contents of register
symbol	address of symbol
symbol imm	address of symbol + or – immediate
symbol imm (register)	address of symbol + or – (immediate + contents of register)

Most load and store instructions operate only on aligned data. A quantity is *aligned* if its memory address is a multiple of its size in bytes. Therefore, a halfword object must be stored at even addresses and a full word object must be stored at addresses that are a multiple of 4. However, MIPS provides some instructions to manipulate unaligned data (lwl, lwr, swl, and swr).

Assembler Syntax

Comments in assembler files begin with a sharp sign (#). Everything from the sharp sign to the end of the line is ignored.

Identifiers are a sequence of alphanumeric characters, underbars (_), and dots (.) that do not begin with a number. Instructions opcodes are reserved words that *cannot* be used as identifiers. Labels are declared by putting them at the beginning of a line followed by a colon, for example:

```
        .data
item:   .word 1
        .text
        .globl main              # Must be global
main:   lw   $t0, item
```

Numbers are base 10 by default. If they are preceded by 0x, they are interpreted as hexadecimal. Hence, 256 and 0x100 denote the same value.

Strings are enclosed in double-quotes ("). Special characters in strings follow the C convention:

- newline   \n
- tab   \t
- quote   \"

SPIM supports a subset of the assembler directives of the MIPS assembler directives:

.align n   Align the next datum on a 2^n byte boundary. For example,

.align 2 aligns the next value on a word boundary. .align 0 turns off automatic alignment of .half, .word, .float, and .double directives until the next .data or .kdata directive.

.ascii str   Store the string str in memory, but do not null-terminate it.

.asciiz str   Store the string str in memory and null-terminate it.

.byte b1, ..., bn   Store the n values in successive bytes of memory.

.data <addr>   Subsequent items are stored in the data segment. If the optional argument *addr* is present, subsequent items are stored starting at address *addr*.

.double d1, ..., dn   Store the n floating-point double precision numbers in successive memory locations.

.extern sym size   Declare that the datum stored at sym is size bytes large and is a global symbol. This directive enables the assembler to store the datum in a portion of the data segment that is efficiently accessed via register $gp.

.float f1, ..., fn   Store the n floating-point single precision numbers in successive memory locations.

.globl sym   Declare that symbol sym is global and can be referenced from other files.

.half h1, ..., hn   Store the n 16-bit quantities in successive memory halfwords.

.kdata <addr>   Subsequent data items are stored in the kernel data segment. If the optional argument *addr* is present, subsequent items are stored starting at address *addr*.

.ktext <addr>   Subsequent items are put in the kernel text segment. In SPIM, these items may only be instructions or words (see the .word directive below). If the optional argument *addr* is present, subsequent items are stored starting at address *addr*.

.set noat .set at   The first directive prevents SPIM from complaining about subsequent instructions that use register $1. The second directive reenables the warning. Since pseudoinstructions expand into code that uses register $1, programmers must be very careful about leaving values in this register.

.space n   Allocate *n* bytes of space in the current segment (which must be the data segment in SPIM).

.text <addr>   Subsequent items are put in the user text segment. In SPIM, these items may only be instructions or words (see the .word directive below). If the optional argument *addr* is present, subsequent items are stored starting at address *addr*.

.word w1, ..., wn   Store the *n* 32-bit quantities in successive memory words.

SPIM does not distinguish various parts of the data segment (.data, .rdata, and .sdata).

Encoding MIPS Instructions

Figure A.18 explains how a MIPS instruction is encoded in a binary number. Each column contains instruction encodings for a field (a contiguous group of bits) from an instruction. The numbers at the left margin are values for a field. For example, the j opcode has a value of 2 in the opcode field. The text at the top of a column names a field and specifies which bits it occupies in an instruction. For example, the op field is contained in bits 26 to 31 of an instruction. This field encodes most instructions. However, some groups of instructions use additional fields to distinguish related instructions. For example, the different floating-point instructions are specified by bits 0 to 5. The arrows from the first column show which opcodes use these additional fields.

Instruction Format

The rest of this appendix describes both the instructions implemented by actual MIPS hardware and the pseudoinstructions provided by the MIPS assembler. The two types of instructions are easily distinguished. Actual instructions depict the fields in their binary representation. For example, in:

the add instruction consists of six fields. Each field's size in bits is the small number below the field. This instruction begins with 6 bits of zeros. Register

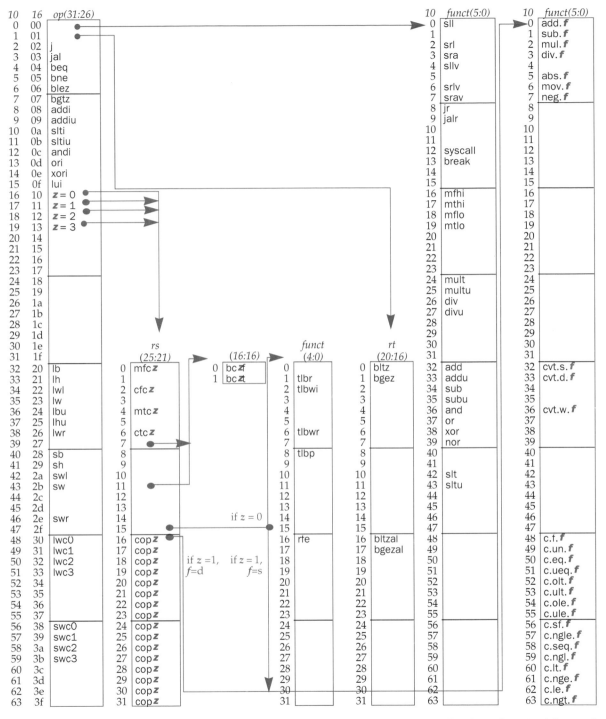

FIGURE A.18 MIPS opcode map. The values of each field are shown to its left. The first column shows the values in base 10 and the second shows base 16 for the op field (bits 31 to 26) in the third column. This op field completely specifies the MIPS operation except for 6 op values: 0, 1, 16, 17, 18, and 19. These operations are determined by other fields, identified by pointers. The last field (funct) uses "f" to mean "s" if rs = 16 and op = 17 or "d" if rs = 17 and op = 17. The second field (rs) uses "z" to mean "0", "1", "2", or "3" if op = 16, 17, 18, or 19, respectively. If rs = 16, the operation is specified elsewhere: if z = 0, the operations are specified in the fourth field (bits 4 to 0); if z = 1, then the operations are in the last field with f = s. If rs = 17 and z = 1, then the operations are in the last field with f = d.   (page A-51)

specifiers begin with a capital "R," so the next field is a 5-bit register specifier called Rs. This is the same register that is the second argument in the symbolic assembly at the left of this line. Another common field is Imm$_{16}$, which is a 16-bit immediate number.

Pseudoinstructions follow roughly the same conventions, but omit instruction encoding information. In these instructions, Rdest and Rsrc are registers and Src2 is either a register or an immediate value.

In general, the assembler and SPIM translate a more general form of an instruction (e.g., add $3, $4, 0x55) to a specialized form (e.g., addi $3, $4, 0x55).

Arithmetic and Logical Instructions

abs Rdest, Rsrc   Absolute value

Put the absolute value of register Rsrc in register Rdest.

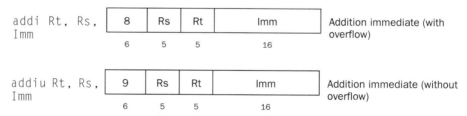

add Rd, Rs, Rt

0	Rs	Rt	Rd	0	0x20
6	5	5	5	5	6

Addition (with overflow)

addu Rd, Rs, Rt

0	Rs	Rt	Rd	0	0x21
6	5	5	5	5	6

Addition (without overflow)

Put the sum of registers Rs and Rt into register Rd.

addi Rt, Rs, Imm

8	Rs	Rt	Imm
6	5	5	16

Addition immediate (with overflow)

addiu Rt, Rs, Imm

9	Rs	Rt	Imm
6	5	5	16

Addition immediate (without overflow)

Put the sum of register Rs and the sign-extended immediate into register Rd.

and Rd, Rs, Rt

0	Rs	Rt	Rd	0	0x24
6	5	5	5	5	6

AND

Put the logical AND of registers Rs and Rt into register Rd.

```
andi  Rt, Rs,      | 0xc | Rs | Rt |    Imm    |   AND immediate
Imm                    6     5    5       16
```

Put the logical AND of register Rs and the zero-extended immediate into register Rd.

```
div  Rs, Rt        | 0 | Rs | Rt |   0   | 0x1a |   Divide (with overflow)
                     6    5    5     10      6
```

```
divu  Rs, Rt       | 0 | Rs | Rt | 0 | 0x1b |   Divide (without overflow)
                     6    5    5   10    6
```

Divide register Rs by register Rt. Leave the quotient in register lo and the remainder in register hi. Note that if an operand is negative, the remainder is unspecified by the MIPS architecture and depends on the convention of the machine on which SPIM is run.

```
div Rdest, Rsrc1,                          Divide (with overflow)
Src2
```

```
divu Rdest, Rsrc1,                         Divide (without overflow)
Src2
```

Put the quotient of register Rsrc1 and Src2 into register Rdest.

```
mul Rdest, Rsrc1,                          Multiply (without overflow)
Src2
```

```
mulo Rdest, Rsrc1,                         Multiply (with overflow)
Src2
```

```
mulou Rdest, Rsrc1, Src2                   Unsigned multiply (with
                                           overflow)
```

Put the product of register `Rsrc1` and `Src2` into register `Rdest`.

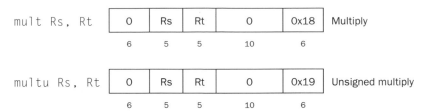

`mult Rs, Rt`	0	Rs	Rt	0	0x18	Multiply
	6	5	5	10	6	

`multu Rs, Rt`	0	Rs	Rt	0	0x19	Unsigned multiply
	6	5	5	10	6	

Multiply registers `Rs` and `Rt`. Leave the low-order word of the product in register `lo` and the high-order word in register `hi`.

`neg Rdest, Rsrc`   Negate value (with overflow)

`negu Rdest, Rsrc`   Negate value (without overflow)

Put the negative of register `Rsrc` into register `Rdest`.

`nor Rd, Rs, Rt`	0	Rs	Rt	Rd	0	0x27	NOR
	6	5	5	5	5	6	

Put the logical NOR of registers `Rs` and `Rt` into register `Rd`.

`not Rdest, Rsrc`   NOT

Put the bitwise logical negation of register `Rsrc` into register `Rdest`.

`or Rd, Rs, Rt`	0	Rs	Rt	Rd	0	0x25	OR
	6	5	5	5	5	6	

Put the logical OR of registers `Rs` and `Imm` into register `Rt`.

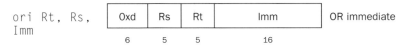

`ori Rt, Rs, Imm`	0xd	Rs	Rt	Imm	OR immediate
	6	5	5	16	

Put the logical OR of register Rs and the zero-extended immediate into register Rd.

rem Rdest, Rsrc1, Rsrc2	Remainder
remu Rdest, Rsrc1, Rsrc2	Unsigned remainder

Put the remainder of register Rsrc1 divided by register Src2 into register Rdest. Note that if an operand is negative, the remainder is unspecified by the MIPS architecture and depends on the convention of the machine on which SPIM is run.

rol Rdest, Rsrc1, Rsrc2	Rotate left
ror Rdest, Rsrc1, Rsrc2	Rotate right

Rotate register Rsrc1 left (right) by the distance indicated by Src2 and put the result in register Rdest.

sll Rd, Rt, Sa

0	Rs	Rt	Rd	Sa	0	Shift left logical
6	5	5	5	5	6	

sllv Rd, Rt, Rs

0	Rs	Rt	Rd	0	4	Shift left logical variable
6	5	5	5	5	6	

sra Rd, Rt, Sa

0	Rs	Rt	Rd	Sa	3	Shift right arithmetic
6	5	5	5	5	6	

srav Rd, Rt, Rs

0	Rs	Rt	Rd	0	7	Shift right arithmetic variable
6	5	5	5	5	6	

srl Rd, Rt, Sa

0	Rs	Rt	Rd	Sa	2	Shift right logical
6	5	5	5	5	6	

`srlv Rd, Rt, Rs`

0	Rs	Rt	Rd	0	6
6	5	5	5	5	6

Shift right logical variable

Shift register `Rt` left (right) by the distance indicated by immediate `Sa` (`Rs`) and put the result in register `Rd`.

`sub Rd, Rs, Rt`

0	Rs	Rt	Rd	0	0x22
6	5	5	5	5	6

Subtract (with overflow)

`subu Rd, Rs, Rt`

0	Rs	Rt	Rd	0	0x23
6	5	5	5	5	6

Subtract (without overflow)

Put the difference of registers `Rs` and `Rt` into register `Rd`.

`xor Rd, Rs, Rt`

0	Rs	Rt	Rd	0	0x26
6	5	5	5	5	6

XOR

Put the logical XOR of registers `Rs` and `Rt` into register `Rd`.

`xori Rt, Rs, Imm`

0xe	Rs	Rt	Imm
6	5	5	16

XOR immediate

Put the logical XOR of register `Rs` and the zero-extended immediate into register `Rd`.

Constant-Manipulating Instructions

`li Rdest, imm`   load immediate

Move the immediate `imm` into register `Rdest`.

`lui Rt, Imm`

0xf	Rs	Rt	Imm
6	5	5	16

Load upper immediate

Load the lower halfword of the immediate `imm` into the upper halfword of register `Rt`. The lower bits of the register are set to 0.

Comparison Instructions

seq Rdest, Rsrc1, Rsrc2   Set equal

Set register Rdest to 1 if register Rsrc1 equals Src2 and to 0 otherwise.

sge Rdest, Rsrc1, Rsrc2   Set greater than equal

sgeu Rdest, Rsrc1, Rsrc2   Set greater than equal
                                                          unsigned

 Set register Rdest to 1 if register Rsrc1 is greater than or equal to Src2 and to
0 otherwise.

sgt Rdest, Rsrc1, Rsrc2   Set greater than

sgtu Rdest, Rsrc1, Rsrc2   Set greater than unsigned

Set register Rdest to 1 if register Rsrc1 is greater than Src2 and to 0 otherwise.

sle Rdest, Rsrc1, Rsrc2   Set less than equal

sleu Rdest, Rsrc1, Rsrc2   Set less than equal unsigned

Set register Rdest to 1 if register Rsrc1 is less than or equal to Src2 and to 0
otherwise.

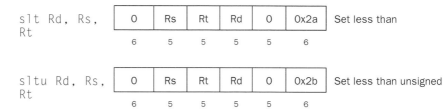

slt Rd, Rs, Rt

0	Rs	Rt	Rd	0	0x2a
6	5	5	5	5	6

Set less than

sltu Rd, Rs, Rt

0	Rs	Rt	Rd	0	0x2b
6	5	5	5	5	6

Set less than unsigned

Set register `Rd` to 1 if register `Rs` is less than `Rt` and to 0 otherwise.

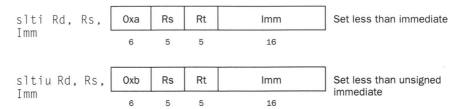

Set register `Rd` to 1 if register `Rs` is less than the sign-extended immediate and to 0 otherwise.

`sne Rdest, Rsrc1, Rsrc2`   Set not equal

Set register `Rdest` to 1 if register `Rsrc1` is not equal to `Src2` and to 0 otherwise.

Branch and Jump Instructions

Branch instructions use a signed 16-bit instruction offset field; hence they can jump $2^{15} - 1$ *instructions* (not bytes) forward or 2^{15} instructions backwards. The *jump* instruction contains a 26-bit address field.

In the descriptions below, the offsets are not specified. Instead, the instructions branch to a label. This is the form used in most assembly language programs because the distance between instructions is difficult to calculate when pseudoinstructions expand into several real instructions.

`b label`   Branch instruction

Unconditionally branch to the instruction at the label.

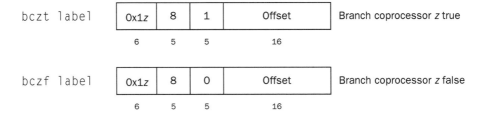

Conditionally branch the number of instructions specified by the offset if z's condition flag is true (false).

beq Rs, Rt, label

4	Rs	Rt	Offset	Branch on equal
6	5	5	16	

Conditionally branch the number of instructions specified by the offset if register Rs equals Rt. z is 0, 1, 2, or 3.

beqz Rsrc, label   Branch on equal zero

Conditionally branch to the instruction at the label if Rsrc equals 0.

bge Rsrc,Src2, label   Branch on greater than equal

bgeu Rsrc, Src2, label   Branch on greater than equal
                                                                    unsigned

Conditionally branch to the instruction at the label if register Rsrc1 is greater than or equal to Src2.

bgez Rs,label

1	Rs	1	Offset	Branch on greater than equal
---	----	---	--------	zero
6	5	5	16	

Conditionally branch the number of instructions specified by the offset if register Rs is greater than or equal to 0.

bgezal Rs,label

1	Rs	0x11	Offset	Branch on greater than equal
---	----	------	--------	zero and link
6	5	5	16	

Conditionally branch the number of instructions specified by the offset if register Rsrc is greater than or equal to 0. Save the address of the next instruction in register 31.

bgt Rsrc1, Src2, label   Branch on greater than

bgtu Rsrc1, Src2, label   Branch on greater than
                                                                   unsigned

Conditionally branch to the instruction at the label if register Rsrc1 is greater than Src2.

bgtz Rs,label	7	Rs	0	Offset	Branch on greater than zero

bgtz Rs,label

7	Rs	0	Offset
6	5	5	16

Branch on greater than zero

Conditionally branch the number of instructions specified by the offset if register Rs is greater than 0.

ble Rsrc1, Src2, label   Branch on less than equal

bleu Rsrc1, Src2, label   Branch on less than equal unsigned

Conditionally branch to the instruction at the label if register Rsrc1 is less than or equal to Src2.

blez Rs,label

6	Rs	0	Offset
6	5	5	16

Branch on less than equal zero

Conditionally branch the number of instructions specified by the offset if register Rs is less than or equal to 0.

bgezal
Rs,label

1	Rs	0x11	Offset
6	5	5	16

Branch on greater than equal zero and link

bltzal
Rs,label

1	Rs	0x10	Offset
6	5	5	16

Branch on less than and link

Conditionally branch the number of instructions specified by the offset if register Rs is greater than or equal to 0 or less than 0, respectively. Save the address of the next instruction in register 31.

blt Rsrc1, Src2, label   Branch on less than

bltu Rsrc1, Src2, label   Branch on less than unsigned

Conditionally branch to the instruction at the label if register Rsrc1 is less than Src2.

bltz Rs,label — Branch on less than zero

Conditionally branch the number of instructions specified by the offset if register Rs is less than 0.

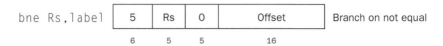

bne Rs,label — Branch on not equal

Conditionally branch the number of instructions specified by the offset if register Rs is not equal to Rt.

bnez Rsrc, label — Branch on not equal zero

Conditionally branch to the instruction at the label if register Rsrc is not equal to 0.

j label — Jump

Unconditionally jump to the instruction at Target.

jal label — Jump and link

Unconditionally jump to the instruction at Target. Save the address of the next instruction in register Rd. ($31)

jalr Rs — Jump and link register

Unconditionally jump to the instruction whose address is in register Rs. Save
the address of the next instruction in register Rd (which defaults to 31).

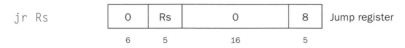

jr Rs

0	Rs	0	8	Jump register
6	5	16	5	

Unconditionally jump to the instruction whose address is in register Rsrc.

Load Instructions

la Rdest, address   Load address

Load computed *address*—not the contents of the location—into register
R-dest.

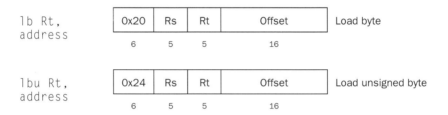

lb Rt,
address

0x20	Rs	Rt	Offset	Load byte
6	5	5	16	

lbu Rt,
address

0x24	Rs	Rt	Offset	Load unsigned byte
6	5	5	16	

Load the byte at *address* into register Rt. The byte is sign-extended by lb, but
not by lbu.

ld Rdest, address   Load double-word

Load the 64-bit quantity at *address* into registers Rdest and Rdest + 1.

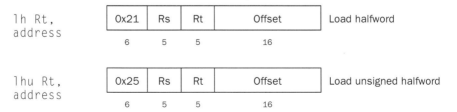

lh Rt,
address

0x21	Rs	Rt	Offset	Load halfword
6	5	5	16	

lhu Rt,
address

0x25	Rs	Rt	Offset	Load unsigned halfword
6	5	5	16	

Load the 16-bit quantity (halfword) at *address* into register Rdt. The halfword is sign-extended by lh, but not by lhu.

lw Rt,
address

0x23	Rs	Rt	Offset	Load word
6	5	5	16	

(offset (Rs))   *Opcode Rs, Rt, offset*

Load the 32-bit quantity (word) at *address* into register Rt.

lwc*z* Rt,
address

0x3*Z*	Rs	Rt	Offset	Load word coprocessor
6	5	5	16	

Load the word at *address* into register Rt of coprocessor *z* (0–3).

lwl Rt,
address

0x22	Rs	Rt	Offset	Load word left
6	5	5	16	

lwr Rt,
address

0x23	Rs	Rt	Offset	Load word right
6	5	5	16	

Load the left (right) bytes from the word at the possibly unaligned *address* into register Rt.

ulh Rdest, address   Unaligned load halfword

ulhu Rdest, address   Unaligned load halfword
                                                          unsigned

Load the 16-bit quantity (halfword) at the possibly unaligned *address* into register Rdest. The halfword is sign-extended by the ulh, but not the ulhu, instruction

ulw Rdest, address   Unaligned load word

Load the 32-bit quantity (word) at the possibly unaligned *address* into register Rdest.

Store Instructions

`sb Rt,`
`address`

0x28	Rs	Rt	Offset
6	5	5	16

Store byte

Store the low byte from register `Rt` at *address*.

`sd Rsrc, address`   Store double-word

Store the 64-bit quantity in registers `Rsrc` and `Rsrc + 1` at *address*.

`sh Rt,`
`address`

0x29	Rs	Rt	Offset
6	5	5	16

Store halfword

Store the low halfword from register `Rt` at *address*.

`sw Rt,`
`address`

0x2b	Rs	Rt	Offset
6	5	5	16

Store word

offset (Rs)

Store the word from register `Rt` at *address*.   *opcode Rs Rt offset*

`swcz Rt,`
`address`

0x3(1-Z)	Rs	Rt	Offset
6	5	5	16

Store word coprocessor

Store the word from register `Rt` of coprocessor *z* at *address*.

`swl Rt,`
`address`

0x2a	Rs	Rt	Offset
6	5	5	16

Store word left

`swr Rt,`
`address`

0x2e	Rs	Rt	Offset
6	5	5	16

Store word right

Store the left (right) bytes from register `Rt` at the possibly unaligned *address*.

`ush Rsrc, address`   Unaligned store halfword

Store the low halfword from register Rsrc at the possibly unaligned *address*.

usw Rsrc, address   Unaligned store word

Store the word from register Rsrc at the possibly unaligned *address*.

Data Movement Instructions

move Rdest, Rsrc   Move

Move register Rsrc to Rdest.

The multiply and divide unit produces its result in two additional registers, hi and lo. These instructions move values to and from these registers. The multiply, divide, and remainder pseudoinstructions that make this unit appear to operate on the general registers move the result after the computation finishes.

mfhi Rd

0	0	Rd	0	0x10	Move from hi
6	10	5	5	6	

mfloi Rd

0	0	Rd	0	0x12	Move from hi
6	10	5	5	6	

Move the hi (lo) register to register Rd.

mthi

0	Rs	0	0x11	Move to hi
6	5	15	6	

mtlo

0	Rs	0	0x13	Move to lo
6	5	15	6	

Move register Rs to the hi (lo) register.

Coprocessors have their own register sets. These instructions move values between these registers and the CPU's registers.

mfc*z* Rdest,
CPsrc

Move from coprocessor *Z*

Move coprocessor *z*'s register CPsrc to CPU register Rdest.

mfc1.d Rdest, FRsrc1   Move double from
                                                      coprocessor 1

Move floating-point registers FRsrc1 and FRsrc1 + 1 to CPU registers Rdest and Rdest + 1.

mtc*z* Rdest,
CPsrc

Move to coprocessor *Z*

Move CPU register Rsrc to coprocessor *z*'s register CPdest.

Floating-Point Instructions

The MIPS has a floating-point coprocessor (numbered 1) that operates on single precision (32-bit) and double precision (64-bit) floating-point numbers. This coprocessor has its own registers, which are numbered $f0–$f31. Because these registers are only 32-bits wide, two of them are required to hold doubles. To simplify matters, floating-point operations, even single precision operations, only use even-numbered registers.

Values are moved in or out of these registers one word (32-bits) at a time by lwc1, swc1, mtc1, and mfc1 instructions described above or by the l.s, l.d, s.s, and s.d pseudoinstructions described below. The flag set by floating-point comparison operations is read by the CPU with its bc1t and bc1f instructions.

In the actual instructions below, *fmt* is 0 for single precision and 1 for double precision. In the pseudoinstructions below, FRdest is a floating-point register (e.g., $f2).

abs.d Fd, Fs

0x11	1	0	Fs	Fd	5
6	5	5	5	5	6

Floating-point absolute value double

abs.s Fd, Fs

0x11	0	0	Fs	Fd	5
6	5	5	5	5	6

Floating-point absolute value single

Compute the absolute value of the floating-point double (single) in register Fs and put it in register Fd.

add.d Fd, Fs, Ft

0x11	1	Ft	Fs	Fd	0
6	5	5	5	5	6

Floating-point addition double

add.s Fd, Fs, Ft

0x11	0	Ft	Fs	Fd	0
6	5	5	5	5	6

Floating-point addition single

Compute the sum of the floating-point doubles (singles) in registers Fs and Ft and put it in register Fd.

c.eq.d Fs, Ft

0x11	1	Ft	Fs	Fd	FC	2
6	5	5	5	5	2	4

Compare equal double

c.eq.s Fs, Ft

0x11	0	Ft	Fs	Fd	FC	2

Compare equal single

Compare the floating-point double in register Fs against the one in Ft and set the floating-point condition flag true if they are equal.

c.le.d Fs, Ft

0x11	1	Ft	Fs	0	FC	2
6	5	5	5	5	2	4

Compare less than equal double

c.le.s Fs, Ft

0x11	0	Ft	Fs	0	FC	2
6	5	5	5	5	2	4

Compare less than equal single

Compare the floating-point double in register Fs against the one in Ft and set the floating-point condition flag true if the first is less than or equal to the second.

c.lt.d Fs, Ft

0x11	1	Ft	Fs	0	FC	0xc
6	5	5	5	5	2	4

Compare less than equal double

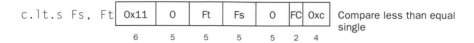

`c.lt.s Fs, Ft`

0x11	0	Ft	Fs	0	FC	0xc
6	5	5	5	5	2	4

Compare less than equal single

Compare the floating-point double in register `Fs` against the one in `Ft` and set the condition flag true if the first is less than the second.

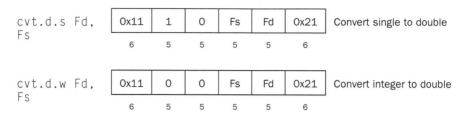

`cvt.d.s Fd, Fs`

0x11	1	0	Fs	Fd	0x21
6	5	5	5	5	6

Convert single to double

`cvt.d.w Fd, Fs`

0x11	0	0	Fs	Fd	0x21
6	5	5	5	5	6

Convert integer to double

Convert the single precision floating-point number or integer in register `Fs` to a double precision number and put it in register `Fd`.

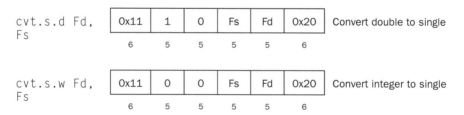

`cvt.s.d Fd, Fs`

0x11	1	0	Fs	Fd	0x20
6	5	5	5	5	6

Convert double to single

`cvt.s.w Fd, Fs`

0x11	0	0	Fs	Fd	0x20
6	5	5	5	5	6

Convert integer to single

Convert the double precision floating-point number or integer in register `Fs` to a single precision number and put it in register `Fd`.

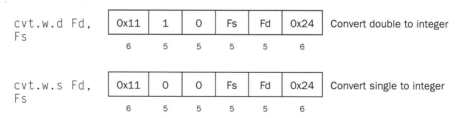

`cvt.w.d Fd, Fs`

0x11	1	0	Fs	Fd	0x24
6	5	5	5	5	6

Convert double to integer

`cvt.w.s Fd, Fs`

0x11	0	0	Fs	Fd	0x24
6	5	5	5	5	6

Convert single to integer

Convert the double or single precision floating-point number in register `Fs` to an integer and put it in register `Fd`.

`div.d Fd, Fs, Ft`

0x11	1	Ft	Fs	Fd	3
6	5	5	5	5	6

Floating-point divide double

```
div.s Fd, Fs,
Ft
```

0x11	0	Ft	Fs	Fd	3
6	5	5	5	5	6

Floating-point divide single

Compute the quotient of the floating-point doubles (singles) in registers Fs and Ft and put it in register Fd.

```
l.d Fdest, address
```

Load floating-point double

```
l.s Fdest, address
```

Load floating-point single

Load the floating-point double (single) at address into register Fdest.

```
mov.d Fd, Fs
```

0x11	1	0	Fs	Fd	6
6	5	5	5	5	6

Move floating-point double

```
mov.s Fd, Fs
```

0x11	0	0	Fs	Fd	6
6	5	5	5	5	6

Move floating-point single

Move the floating-point double (single) from register Fs to register Fd.

```
mul.d Fd, Fs,
Ft
```

0x11	1	Ft	Fs	Fd	2
6	5	5	5	5	6

Floating-point multiply double

```
mul.s Fd, Fs,
Ft
```

0x11	0	Ft	Fs	Fd	2
6	5	5	5	5	6

Floating-point multiply single

Compute the product of the floating-point doubles (singles) in registers Fs and Ft and put it in register Fd.

```
neg.d Fd, Fs,
Ft
```

0x11	1	Ft	Fs	Fd	7
6	5	5	5	5	6

negate double

```
neg.s Fd, Fs,
Ft
```

0x11	0	Ft	Fs	Fd	7
6	5	5	5	5	6

negate single

Negate the floating-point double (single) in register Fs and put it in register Fd.

s.d Fdest, address   Store floating-point double

s.s Fdest, address   Store floating-point single

Store the floating-point double (single) in register Fdest at address.

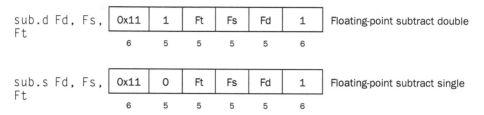

sub.d Fd, Fs, Ft

| 0x11 | 1 | Ft | Fs | Fd | 1 | Floating-point subtract double |
| 6 | 5 | 5 | 5 | 5 | 6 | |

sub.s Fd, Fs, Ft

| 0x11 | 0 | Ft | Fs | Fd | 1 | Floating-point subtract single |
| 6 | 5 | 5 | 5 | 5 | 6 | |

Compute the difference of the floating-point doubles (singles) in registers Fs and Ft and put it in register Fd.

Exception and Interrupt Instructions

rfe

| 0x10 | 1 | 0 | 0x20 | Return from exception |
| 6 | 1 | 19 | 6 | |

Restore the Status register.

syscall

| 0 | 0 | 0xc | System call |
| 6 | 20 | 6 | |

Register $v0 contains the number of the system call (see Figure A.16) provided by SPIM.

break

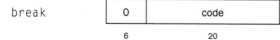

| 0 | code | 0xd | Break |
| 6 | 20 | 6 | |

Cause exception *code*. Exception 1 is reserved for the debugger.

nop

0	0	0	0	0	0	No operation
6	5	5	5	5	6	

Do nothing.

A.11   Concluding Remarks

Programming in assembly language requires a programmer to trade off helpful features of high-level languages—such as data structures, type checking, and control constructs—for complete control over the instructions that a computer executes. External constraints on some applications, such as response time or program size, require a programmer to pay close attention to every instruction. However, the cost of this level of attention is assembly language programs that are longer, more time-consuming to write, and more difficult to maintain than high-level language programs.

Moreover, three trends are reducing the need to write programs in assembly language. The first trend is toward the improvement of compilers. Modern compilers produce code that is typically comparable to the best handwritten code and is sometimes better. The second trend is the introduction of new processors that are not only faster, but in the case of processors that execute multiple instructions simultaneously, also more difficult to program by hand. In addition, the rapid evolution of the modern computer favors high-level language programs that are not tied to a single architecture. Finally, we witness a trend toward increasingly complex applications—characterized by complex graphic interfaces and many more features than their predecessors. Large applications are written by teams of programmers and require the modularity and semantic checking features provided by high-level languages.

To Probe Further

Kane, G., and Heinrich, J. [1992]. *MIPS RISC Architecture*, Prentice Hall, Englewood Cliffs, N.J.

The last word on the MIPS instruction set and assembly language programming on these machines.

Aho, A., Sethi, R., and Ullman, J. [1985]. *Compilers: Principles, Techniques, and Tools*, Addison-Wesley, Reading, Mass.

Slightly dated and lacking in coverage of modern architectures, but still the standard reference on compilers.

A.12 Exercises

A.1 [5] <§A.5> Section A.5 described how memory is partitioned on most MIPS systems. Propose another way of dividing memory that meets the same goals.

A.2 [10] <§A.6> Write and test a MIPS assembly language program to compute and print the first 100 prime numbers. A number n is prime if no numbers except 1 and n divide it evenly. You should implement two routines:

- test_prime (n)   Return 1 if n is prime and 0 if n is not prime.
- main ()   Iterate over the integers, testing if each is prime. Print the first 100 numbers that are prime.

Test your programs by running them on SPIM.

A.3 [5] <§A.6> Rewrite the code for fact to use fewer instructions.

A.4 [5] <§A.7> Is it ever safe for a user program to use registers k0 or k1?

A.5 [15] <§A.7> Section A.7 contains code for a very simple exception handler. One serious problem with this handler is that it disables interrupts for a long time. This means that interrupts from a fast I/O device may be lost. Write a better exception handler that is interruptable and enables interrupts as quickly as possible.

A.6 [15] <§A.7> The simple exception handler always jumps back to the instruction following the exception. Write a better handler that uses the EPC register to determine which instruction should be executed after the exception.

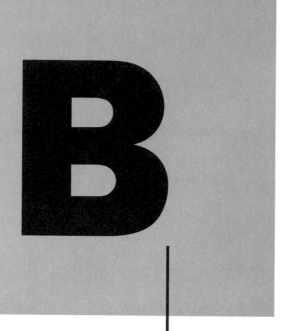

B

The Basics of Logic Design

I always loved that word, Boolean.

Claude Shannon
IEEE Spectrum, April 1992, p. 72
(Shannon's master's thesis showed that the algebra
invented by George Boole in the 1800s could represent the
workings of electrical switches.)

B.1   Introduction

This appendix provides a brief discussion of the basics of logic design. It does not replace a course in logic design nor does it enable the reader to design significant working logic systems. For readers with little or no exposure to logic design, however, this appendix will provide sufficient background to understand all the material in this book. In addition, for those looking to understand some of the motivation behind how computers are implemented, this material will serve as a useful introduction. For readers whose curiosity is aroused and not sated by this appendix, the references at the end provide several additional sources of information.

Section B.2 introduces the basic building blocks of logic, namely *gates*. Section B.3 uses these building blocks to construct simple *combinational* logic systems, which contain no memory. Readers with some exposure to logic or digital systems will probably be familiar with the material in these first two sections. Section B.4 is a short introduction to the topic of clocking, which is necessary to discuss how memory elements work. Section B.5 introduces memory elements; it describes both the characteristics that are important to understanding how they are used in Chapters 5 and 6, and the background that motivates many of the aspects of memory hierarchy design in Chapter 7. Section B.6 describes the design and use of finite state machines, which are sequential logic blocks. Readers who intend to read Appendix C should thoroughly understand the material in Sections B.2 through B.6, while those who intend to read only the material on control in Chapters 5 and 6 can skim the appendices, but should have some familiarity with all the material except Section B.7. Section B.7 is intended for the reader who wants a deeper understanding of clocking methodologies and timing. It explains the basics of how edge-triggered clocking works, introduces another clocking scheme, and briefly describes the problem of synchronizing asynchronous inputs.

B.2   Gates, Truth Tables, and Logic Equations

The electronics inside a modern computer are *digital*. Digital electronics operate with only two voltage levels of interest: a high voltage and a low voltage. All other voltage values are temporary and occur while transitioning between the values. As mentioned in Chapter 3, this is a key reason why computers use binary numbers, since a binary system matches the underlying abstraction inherent in the electronics. In various logic families, the values and relationships between the two voltage values differ. Thus, rather than refer to the voltage levels, we talk about signals that are (logically) true, or are 1, or are *asserted*; or signals that are (logically) false, or 0, or *deasserted*. The values 0 and 1 are called *complements* or *inverses* of one another.

Logic blocks are categorized as one of two types, depending on whether they contain memory. Blocks without memory are called *combinational*; the output of a combinational block depends only on the current input. In blocks with memory, the outputs can depend on both the inputs and the value stored in memory, which is called the *state* of the logic block. In this section and the next, we will focus only on combinational logic. After introducing different memory elements in section B.5, we will describe how *sequential* logic, which is logic including state, is designed.

Truth Tables

Because a combinational logic block contains no memory, it can be completely specified by defining the values of the outputs for each possible set of input values. Such a description is normally given as a *truth table*. For a logic block with n inputs, there are 2^n entries in the truth table, since there are that many possible combinations of input values. Each entry specifies the value of all the outputs for that particular input combination.

Example

Consider a logic function with three inputs, A, B, and C and three outputs, D, E, and F. The function is defined as follows: D is true if at least one input is true, E is true if exactly two inputs are true, and F is true only if all three inputs are true. Show the truth table for this function.

Answer

The truth table will contain $2^3 = 8$ entries. Here it is:

Inputs			Outputs		
A	**B**	**C**	**D**	**E**	**F**
0	0	0	0	0	0
0	0	1	1	0	0
0	1	0	1	0	0
0	1	1	1	1	0
1	0	0	1	0	0
1	0	1	1	1	0
1	1	0	1	1	0
1	1	1	1	0	1

Truth tables can completely describe any combinational logic function; however, they grow in size quickly and may not be easy to understand. Sometimes we want to construct a logic function that will be 0 for many input combinations, and we use a shorthand of specifying only the truth table entries for the nonzero outputs. This approach is used in Chapter 5 and Appendix C.

Boolean Algebra

Another approach is to express the logic function with logic equations. This is done with the use of *Boolean algebra* (named after Boole, a 19th-century mathematician). In Boolean algebra, all the variables have the values 0 or 1 and, in typical formulations, there are three operators.

- The OR operator is written as +, as in $A + B$. The result of an OR operator is 1 if either of the variables is 1. The OR operation is also called a *logical sum*, since its result is 1 if either operand is 1.

- The AND operator is written as $\cdot$, as in $A \cdot B$. The result of an AND operator is 1 only if both inputs are 1. The AND operator is also called *logical product*, since its result is 1 only if both operands are 1.

- The unary operator NOT, written as $\overline{A}$. The result of a NOT operator is 1 only if the input is zero. Applying the operator NOT to a logical value results in an inversion or negation of the value (i.e., if the input is 0 the output is 1, and vice versa).

There are several laws of Boolean algebra that are helpful in manipulating logic equations.

- Identity law: $A + 0 = A$ and $A \cdot 1 = A$.

- Zero and One laws: $A + 1 = 1$ and $A \cdot 0 = 0$.

- Inverse laws: $A + \overline{A} = 1$ and $A \cdot \overline{A} = 0$.

- Commutative laws: $A + B = B + A$ and $A \cdot B = B \cdot A$.

- Associative laws: $A + (B + C) = (A + B) + C$ and $A \cdot (B \cdot C) = (A \cdot B) \cdot C$.

- Distributive laws: $A \cdot (B + C) = (A \cdot B) + (A \cdot C)$ and $A + (B \cdot C) = (A + B) \cdot (A + C)$.

In addition, there are two other useful laws, called DeMorgan's Laws, that are the subject of Exercise B.6.

Any logic function can be written as a series of equations with an output on the left-hand side of each equation and a formula consisting of variables and the three operators above on the right-hand side.

Example

Show the logic equations for the logic function described in the previous example.

Answer

Here's the equation for D:

$$D = A + B + C$$

F is equally simple:

$$F = A \cdot B \cdot C$$

E is a little tricky. Think of it in two parts: what must be true for E to be true (two of the three inputs must be true), and what cannot be true (all three cannot be true). Thus we can write E as

$$E = ((A \cdot B) + (A \cdot C) + (B \cdot C)) \cdot (\overline{A \cdot B \cdot C})$$

We can also derive E by realizing that E is true only if exactly two of the inputs are true. Then we can write E as an OR of the three possible terms that has two true inputs and one false input:

$$E = (A \cdot B \cdot \overline{C}) + (A \cdot C \cdot \overline{B}) + (B \cdot C \cdot \overline{A})$$

Proving that these two expressions are equivalent is the task of Exercise B.7.

Gates

Logic blocks are built from *gates* that implement basic logic functions. For example, an AND gate implements the AND function and an OR gate implements the OR function. Since both AND and OR are commutative and associative, an AND or an OR gate can have multiple inputs, with the output equal to the AND or OR of all the inputs. The logical function NOT is implemented with an inverter that always has a single input. The standard representation of these three logic building blocks is shown in Figure B.1.

Rather than draw inverters explicitly, a common practice is to add "bubbles" to the inputs or output of a gate to cause the logic value on that input line or output line to be inverted. For example, Figure B.2 shows the logic diagram

FIGURE B.1 Standard drawing for an AND gate, OR gate, and an inverter, shown from left to right. The signals to the left of each symbol are the inputs, while the output appears on the right. The AND and OR gates both have two inputs. Inverters have a single input.

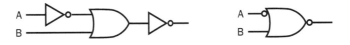

FIGURE B.2 Logic gate implementation of $\overline{A + B}$ **using explicit inverts on the left and using bubbled inputs and output on the right.** This logic function can be simplified to $A \cdot \overline{B}$.

for the function $\overline{A} + B$, using explicit inverters on the left and using bubbled inputs and outputs on the right.

Any logical function can be constructed using AND gates, OR gates, and inversion; Exercises B.2 through B.5 give you the opportunity to try implementing some common logic functions with gates. In the next section we'll see how an implementation of any logic function can be constructed using this knowledge.

In fact, all logic functions can be constructed with only a single gate type, if that gate is inverting. The two common inverting gates are called NOR and NAND and correspond to inverted OR and AND gates, respectively. NOR and NAND gates are called *universal*, since any logic function can be built using this one gate type. Exercises B.10 and B.11 ask you to prove this fact.

B.3   Combinational Logic

In this section we look at a couple of basic logic building blocks that we use heavily, and we discuss the design of structured logic that can be automatically implemented from a logic equation or truth table by a translation program. Lastly, we discuss the notion of an array of logic blocks.

Multiplexors

One basic logic function that we saw quite often in Chapters 4, 5, and 6 is the *multiplexor*. A multiplexor might more properly be called a *selector*, since its output is one of the inputs that is selected by a control. Consider the two-input multiplexor. As shown on the left side of Figure B.3, this multiplexor has three inputs: two data values and a selector (or control) value. The

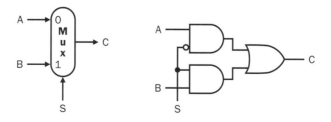

FIGURE B.3 A two-input multiplexor, on the left, and its implementation with gates, on the right. The multiplexor has two data inputs (A and B), which are labeled 0 and 1, and one selector input (S), as well as an output C.

Inputs			Outputs							
I2	I1	I0	Out7	Out6	Out5	Out4	Out3	Out2	Out1	Out0
0	0	0	0	0	0	0	0	0	0	1
0	0	1	0	0	0	0	0	0	1	0
0	1	0	0	0	0	0	0	1	0	0
0	1	1	0	0	0	0	1	0	0	0
1	0	0	0	0	0	1	0	0	0	0
1	0	1	0	0	1	0	0	0	0	0
1	1	0	0	1	0	0	0	0	0	0
1	1	1	1	0	0	0	0	0	0	0

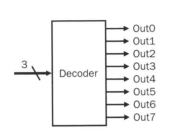

a. A 3-bit decoder.

b. The truth table.

FIGURE B.4 A 3-bit decoder has 3 inputs, called I2, I1, and I0, and 2^3 = 8 outputs, called Out0 to Out7. Only the output corresponding to the binary value of the input is true, as shown in the truth table. The label 3 on the input to the decoder says that the input signal is 3 bits wide.

selector value determines which of the inputs becomes the output. We can represent the logic function computed by a two-input multiplexor as $C = (A \cdot \overline{S}) + (B \cdot S)$, which is shown in gate form on the right side of Figure B.3. Multiplexors can be created with an arbitrary number of data inputs. If there are n data inputs there will need to be $\lceil \log_2 n \rceil$ selector inputs. To associate the inputs with selector values, we often label the data inputs numerically (i.e., $0, 1, 2, 3, \ldots, n–1$) and interpret the data selector inputs as a binary number. When there are only two inputs, the selector is a single signal that selects one of the inputs if it is true (1) and the other if it is false (0).

Decoders

Another logic block that we will use in building larger components is a *decoder*. The most common type of decoder has an n-bit input and 2^n outputs where only one output is asserted for each input combination. This decoder translates the n-bit input into a signal that corresponds to the binary value of the n-bit input. The outputs are thus usually numbered, say Out0, Out1, $\ldots$, Outm. If the value of the input is i, then Out$i$ will be true and all other outputs will be false. Figure B.4 shows a 3-bit decoder and the truth table. This decoder is called a *3-to-8 decoder* since there are 3 inputs and 8 (2^3) outputs. There is also a logic element called an *encoder* that performs the inverse function of a decoder, taking 2^n inputs and producing an n-bit output.

Two-level Logic and PLAs

As pointed out in the previous section, any logic function can be implemented with only AND, OR, and NOT functions. In fact, a much stronger result is true. Any logic function can be written in a canonical form, where every input is either a true or complemented variable and there are only two levels of gates—one being AND and the other OR—with a possible inversion on the final output. Such a representation is called a *two-level representation* and there are two forms, called *sum-of-products* and *product-of-sums*. A sum of products representation is a logical sum (OR) of products (terms using the AND operator); whereas, a product of sums is just the opposite. In our earlier example we had two equations for the output E:

$$E = ((A \cdot B) + (A \cdot C) + (B \cdot C)) \cdot (\overline{A \cdot B \cdot C})$$

and

$$E = (A \cdot B \cdot \overline{C}) + (A \cdot C \cdot \overline{B}) + (B \cdot C \cdot \overline{A})$$

This second equation is in a sum-of-products form: it has two levels of logic and the only inversions are on individual variables. The first equation has three levels of logic.

Elaboration: We can also write E as a product of sums:

$$E = \overline{(\overline{A} + \overline{B} + C) \cdot (\overline{A} + \overline{C} + B) \cdot (\overline{B} + \overline{C} + A)}$$

To derive this form, you need to use *DeMorgan's theorems*, which are discussed in Exercise B.6. Exercise B.8 asks you to derive the product of sums representation from the sum of products using DeMorgan's theorems.

In this text, we use the more common sum-of-products form. It is easy to see that any logic function can be represented as a sum of products by constructing such a representation from the truth table for the function. Each truth table entry for which the function is true corresponds to a product term. The product term consists of a logical product of all the inputs or the complements of the inputs, depending on whether the entry in the truth table has a 0 or 1 corresponding to this variable. The logic function is the logical sum of the products term where the function is true. This is more easily seen with an example.

Example   Show the sum-of-products representation for the following truth table.

Inputs			Output
A	B	C	D
0	0	0	0
0	0	1	1
0	1	0	1
0	1	1	0
1	0	0	1
1	0	1	0
1	1	0	0
1	1	1	1

Answer   There are four product terms, since the function is true (1) for four different input combinations. These are

$$\overline{A} \cdot \overline{B} \cdot C$$

$$\overline{A} \cdot B \cdot \overline{C}$$

$$A \cdot \overline{B} \cdot \overline{C}$$

$$A \cdot B \cdot C$$

Thus, we can write the function for D as the sum of these terms:

$$D = (\overline{A} \cdot \overline{B} \cdot C) + (\overline{A} \cdot B \cdot \overline{C}) + (A \cdot \overline{B} \cdot \overline{C}) + (A \cdot B \cdot C)$$

Note that only those truth table entries for which the function is true generate terms in the equation.

We can use this relationship between a truth table and a two-level representation to generate a gate-level implementation of any set of logic functions. A set of logic functions corresponds to a truth table with multiple output columns, as we saw in the example on page B-5. Each output column represents a different logic function, which may be directly constructed from the truth table.

The sum-of-products representation corresponds to a common structured-logic implementation called a *programmable logic array* (or *PLA*). A PLA has a set of inputs and corresponding input complements (which can be implemented with a set of inverters), and two stages of logic. The first stage is an array of

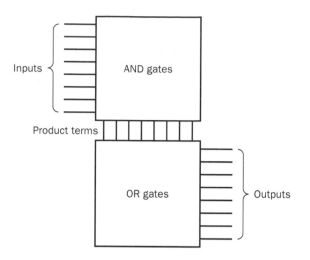

FIGURE B.5 The basic form of a PLA consists of an array of AND gates followed by an array of OR gates. Each entry in the AND gate array is a product term consisting of any number of inputs or inverted inputs. Each entry in the OR gate array is a sum term consisting of any number of these product terms.

AND gates that form a set of product terms (sometimes called *minterms*); each product term can consist of any of the inputs or their complements. The second stage is an array of OR gates, each of which forms a logical sum of any number of the product terms. Figure B.5 shows the basic form of a PLA.

A PLA can directly implement the truth table of a set of logic functions with multiple inputs and outputs. Since each entry where the truth table is true requires a product term, there will be a corresponding row in the PLA. Each output corresponds to a potential row of OR gates in the second stage. The number of OR gates corresponds to the number of truth table entries for which the output is true. The total size of a PLA, such as that shown in Figure B.5, is equal to the sum of the size of the AND gate array (called the *AND plane*) and the size of the OR gate array (called the *OR plane*). Looking at Figure B.5, we can see that the size of the AND gate array is equal to the number of inputs times the number of different product terms, and the size of the OR gate array is the number of outputs times the number of product terms.

A PLA has two characteristics that help make it an efficient way to implement a set of logic functions. One, only the truth table entries that produce a true value for at least one output have any logic gates associated with them. Two, each different product term will have only one entry in the PLA, even if the product term is used in multiple outputs. Let's look at an example.

Example

Consider the set of logic functions defined in the example on page B-5. Show a PLA implementation of this example.

Answer

Here is the truth table we constructed earlier:

Inputs			Outputs		
A	**B**	**C**	**D**	**E**	**F**
0	0	0	0	0	0
0	0	1	1	0	0
0	1	0	1	0	0
0	1	1	1	1	0
1	0	0	1	0	0
1	0	1	1	1	0
1	1	0	1	1	0
1	1	1	1	0	1

Since there are seven unique product terms with at least one true value in the output section, there will be seven columns in the AND plane. The number of rows in the AND plane is three (since there are three inputs), and there are also three rows in the OR plane (since there are three outputs). Figure B.6 shows the resulting PLA with the product terms corresponding to the truth table entries from top to bottom.

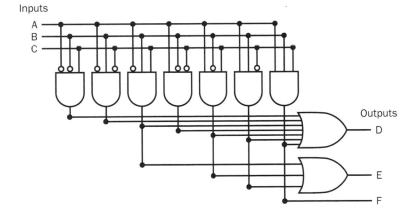

FIGURE B.6 The PLA for implementing the logic function described above.

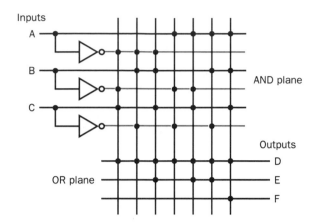

FIGURE B.7 A PLA drawn using dots to indicate the components of the product terms and sum terms in the array. Rather than use inverters on the gates, usually all the inputs are run the width of the AND plane in both true and complement forms. A dot in the AND plane indicates that the input, or its inverse, occurs in the product term. A dot in the OR plane indicates that the corresponding product term appears in the corresponding output.

Rather than drawing all the gates, as we did in Figure B.6, designers often show just the position of AND gates and OR gates. Dots are used on the intersection of a product term signal line and an input line or an output line when a corresponding AND gate or OR gate is required. Figure B.7 shows how the PLA of Figure B.6 would look when drawn in this way. The contents of a PLA are fixed when the PLA is created, although there are also forms of PLA-like structures, called *PALs*, that can be programmed electronically when a designer is ready to use them.

ROMs

Another form of structured logic that can be used to implement a set of logic functions is a *read-only memory*, commonly called a *ROM*. A ROM is called a memory because it has a set of locations that can be read; however, the contents of these locations are fixed, usually at the time the ROM is created. There are also *programmable ROMs* (*PROMs*) that can be programmed electrically, when a designer knows their contents. There are also erasable PROMs; these devices require a slow erasure process using ultraviolet light, and thus are used as read-only memories, except during the design and debugging process.

A ROM has a set of input address lines and a set of outputs. The number of addressable entries in the ROM determines the number of address lines: if the ROM contains 2^n addressable entries, called the *height*, then there are n input lines. The number of bits in each addressable entry is equal to the number of output bits and is sometimes called the *width* of the ROM. The total number of bits in the ROM is equal to the height times the width. The height and width are sometimes collectively referred to as the *shape* of the ROM.

A ROM can encode a collection of logic functions directly from the truth table. For example, if there are n functions with m inputs, we need a ROM with m address lines (and 2^m entries), with each entry being n bits wide. The entries in the input portion of the truth table represent the addresses of the entries in the ROM, while the contents of the output portion of the truth table constitute the contents of the ROM. If the truth table is organized so that the sequence of entries in the input portion constitute a sequence of binary numbers (as have all the truth tables we have shown so far), then the output portion gives the ROM contents in order as well. In the previous example starting on page B-13, there were three inputs and three outputs. This leads to a ROM with $2^3 = 8$ entries, each 3 bits wide. The contents of those entries in increasing order by address are directly given by the output portion of the truth table that appears on page B-13.

ROMs and PLAs are closely related. A ROM is fully decoded: it contains a full output word for every possible input combination. A PLA is only partially decoded. This means that a ROM will always contain more entries. For the earlier truth table on page B-13, the ROM contains entries for all eight possible inputs, whereas the PLA contains only the seven active product terms. As the number of inputs grows, the number of entries in the ROM grows exponentially. In contrast, for most real logic functions the number of product terms grows much more slowly (see the examples in Appendix C). This difference makes PLAs generally more efficient for implementing combinational logic functions. ROMs have the advantage of being able to implement any logic function with the matching number of inputs and outputs. This advantage makes it easier to change the ROM contents if the logic function changes, since the size of the ROM need not change.

Don't Cares

Often in implementing some combinational logic, there are situations where we do not care what the value of some output is, either because another output is true or because a subset of the input combinations determine the values of the outputs. Such situations are referred to as *don't cares*. Don't cares are important because they make it easier to optimize the implementation of a logic function.

There are two types of don't cares: output don't cares and input don't cares, both of which can be represented in a truth table. *Output don't cares* arise when we don't care about the value of an output for some input combination. They appear as X's in the output portion of a truth table. When an output is a don't care for some input combination, the designer or logic optimization program is free to make the output true or false for that input combination. Input don't cares arise when an output depends on only some of the inputs, and they are also shown as X's, though in the input portion of the truth table.

Example

Consider a logic function with inputs A, B, and C defined as follows.

- If A or C is true, then output D is true, whatever the value of B.

- If A or B is true, then output E is true, whatever the value of C.

- Output F is true if exactly one of the inputs is true, although we don't care about the value of F, whenever D and E are both true.

Show the full truth table for this function and the truth table using don't cares. How many product terms are required in a PLA for each of these?

Answer

Here's the full truth table, without don't cares:

Inputs			Outputs		
A	B	C	D	E	F
0	0	0	0	0	0
0	0	1	1	0	1
0	1	0	0	1	1
0	1	1	1	1	0
1	0	0	1	1	1
1	0	1	1	1	0
1	1	0	1	1	0
1	1	1	1	1	1

This requires seven product terms without optimization. The truth table written with output don't cares looks like:

Inputs			Outputs		
A	B	C	D	E	F
0	0	0	0	0	0
0	0	1	1	0	1
0	1	0	0	1	1
0	1	1	1	1	X
1	0	0	1	1	X
1	0	1	1	1	X
1	1	0	1	1	X
1	1	1	1	1	X

This truth table can be further simplified to yield:

Inputs			Outputs		
A	B	C	D	E	F
0	0	0	0	0	0
0	0	1	1	0	1
0	1	0	0	1	1
X	1	1	1	1	X
1	X	X	1	1	X

This simplified truth table requires a PLA with four minterms, or it can be implemented in discrete gates with one two-input AND gate and three OR gates (two with three inputs and one with two inputs). This compares to the original truth table that had seven minterms and would require four AND gates.

Logic minimization is critical to achieving efficient implementations. One tool useful for hand minimization of random logic is *Karnaugh maps*. Karnaugh maps represent the truth table graphically so that product terms that may be combined are easily seen. Nevertheless, hand optimization of significant logic functions using Karnaugh maps is impractical, due both to the size of the maps and their complexity. Fortunately, the process of logic minimization is highly mechanical and can be performed by design tools. In the process of minimization the tools take advantage of the don't cares, so specifying them is important. The textbook references at the end of this appendix provide further discussion on logic minimization, Karnaugh maps, and the theory behind such minimization algorithms.

Arrays of Logic Elements

Many of the combinational operations to be performed on data have to be done to an entire word (32-bits) of data. Thus we often want to build an array of logic elements, which we can represent simply by showing that a given operation will happen to an entire collection of inputs. For example, we saw on page B-8 what a one-bit multiplexor looked like, but inside a machine, much of the time we want to select between a pair of *buses*. A bus is a collection of data lines that is treated together as a single logical signal. (The term *bus* is also used to indicate a shared collection of lines with multiple sources and uses, especially in Chapter 8, where I/O buses were discussed.)

For example, in the MIPS instruction set the result of an instruction that is written into a register can come from one of two sources. A multiplexor is used to choose which of the two buses (each 32 bits wide) will be written into the Result register. The one-bit multiplexor, which we showed earlier, will need to be replicated 32 times. We indicate that a signal is a bus rather than a single one-bit line by showing it with a thicker line in a figure. Most buses are 32 bits wide; those that are not are explicitly labeled with their width. When we show a logic unit whose inputs and outputs are buses, this means that the unit must be replicated a sufficient number of times to accommodate the width of the input. Figure B.8 shows how we draw a multiplexor that selects between a pair of 32-bit buses and how this expands in terms of 1-bit-wide multiplexors. Sometimes we need to construct an array of logic elements, where the inputs for some elements in the array are outputs from earlier elements. For example, this is how a multibit wide ALU is constructed. In such cases, we must explicitly show how to create wider arrays, since the individual elements of the array are no longer independent, as they are in the case of a 32-bit-wide multiplexor.

B.4   Clocks

Before we discuss memory elements and sequential logic, it is useful to discuss briefly the topic of clocks. This short section introduces the topic and is similar to the discussion found at the beginning of Chapter 5. More details on clocking and timing methodologies are presented in section B.7.

Clocks are needed in sequential logic to decide when an element that contains state should be updated. A clock is simply a free-running signal with a fixed *cycle time*; the *clock frequency* is simply the inverse of the cycle time. As shown in Figure B.9, the *clock cycle time* or *clock period* is divided into two portions: when the clock is high and when the clock is low. In this text, we use only *edge-triggered clocking*. This means that all state changes occur on a clock edge. We use an edge-triggered methodology because it is simpler to explain. Depending on the technology, it may or may not be the best choice for a clocking methodology.

In an edge-triggered methodology, either the rising edge or the falling edge of the clock is *active* and causes state changes to occur. As we will see in

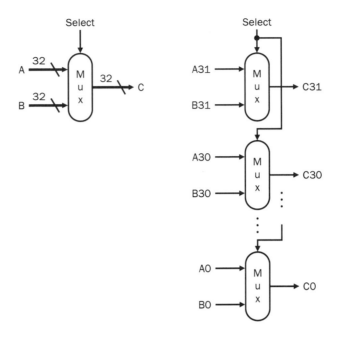

a. A 32-bit wide 2-to-1 multiplexor.

b. The 32-bit wide multiplexor is actually an array of 32 1-bit multiplexors.

FIGURE B.8 A multiplexor is arrayed 32 times to perform a selection between two 32-bit inputs. Note that there is still only one data selection signal used for all 32-bit multiplexors.

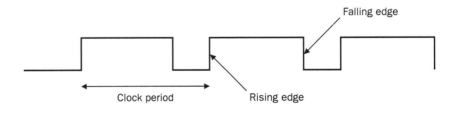

FIGURE B.9 A clock signal oscillates between high and low values. The clock period is the time for one full cycle. In an edge-triggered design, either the rising or falling edge of the clock is active and causes state to be changed.

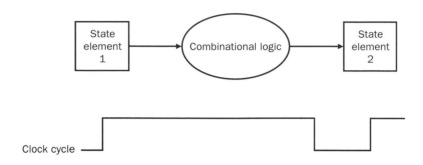

FIGURE B.10 The inputs to a combinational logic block come from a state element, and the outputs are written into a state element. The clock edge determines when the contents of the state elements are updated.

the next section, the state elements in an edge-triggered design are implemented so that the contents of the state elements only change on the active clock edge. The choice of which edge is active is influenced by the implementation technology and does not affect the concepts involved in designing the logic.

The major constraint in a clocked system, also called a *synchronous system*, is that the signals that are written into state elements must be *valid* when the active clock edge occurs. A signal is valid if it is stable (i.e., not changing) and the value will not change again until the inputs change. Since combinational circuits cannot have feedback, if the inputs to a combinational logic unit are not changed, the outputs will eventually become valid. Figure B.10 shows the relationship among the state elements and the combinational logic blocks in a synchronous, sequential logic design. The state elements, whose outputs change only on the clock edge, provide valid inputs to the combinational logic block. To ensure that the values written into the state elements on the active clock edge are valid, the clock must have a long enough period so that all the signals in the combinational logic block stabilize. This constraint sets a lower bound on the length of the clock period. In the rest of this appendix, as well as in Chapters 5 and 6, we usually omit the clock signal, since we are assuming that all state elements are updated on the same clock edge. Some state elements will be written on every clock edge, while others will be written only under certain conditions (such as a register being updated). In such cases, we will have an explicit write signal for that state element. The write signal must still be gated with the clock so that the update occurs only on the clock edge if the write signal is active. We will see how this is done and used in the next section.

One other advantage of an edge-triggered methodology is that it is possible to have a state element that is used as both an input and output to the same

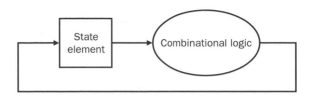

FIGURE B.11 An edge-triggered methodology allows a state element to be read and written in the same clock cycle without creating a race that could lead to undermined data values. Of course, the clock cycle must still be long enough so that the input values are stable when the active clock edge occurs.

combinational logic block, as shown in Figure B.11. In practice, care must be taken to prevent races in such situations and to ensure that the clock period is long enough; this topic is discussed further in section B.7.

Now that we have discussed how clocking is used to update state elements, we can discuss how to construct the state elements.

B.5 Memory Elements

In this section we discuss the basic principles behind memory elements, starting with flip-flops and latches, moving on to registers files, and finally to memories. All memory elements store state: the output from any memory element depends both on the inputs and on the value that has been stored inside the memory element. Thus, all logic blocks containing a memory element contain state and are sequential.

The simplest type of memory elements are *unclocked*; that is, they do not have any clock input. Although we only use clocked memory elements in this text, an unclocked latch is the simplest memory element, so let's look at this circuit first. Figure B.12 shows an *S-R latch* (set-reset latch), built from a pair of NOR gates (OR gates with inverted outputs). The outputs Q and $\overline{Q}$ represent the value of the stored state and its complement. When neither S nor R are asserted, the cross-coupled NOR gates act as inverters and store the previous values of Q and $\overline{Q}$. For example, if the output, Q, is true, then the bottom inverter produces a false output (which is $\overline{Q}$), which becomes the input to the top inverter, which produces a true output, which is Q, and so on. If S is asserted then the output Q will be asserted and $\overline{Q}$ will be deasserted, while if R is asserted, then the output $\overline{Q}$ will be asserted and Q will be deasserted. When S and R are both deasserted the last values of Q and $\overline{Q}$ will continue to be stored in the cross-coupled structure. Asserting S and R simultaneously can lead to

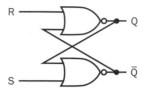

FIGURE B.12 A pair of cross-coupled NOR gates can store an internal value. The value stored on the output Q is recycled by inverting it to obtain $\overline{Q}$ and then inverting $\overline{Q}$ to obtain Q. If either R or $\overline{Q}$ are asserted Q will be deasserted and vice-versa.

---

incorrect operation: Depending on how S and R are deasserted, the latch may oscillate or become metastable (this is described in more detail in section B.7).

This cross-coupled structure is the basis for more complex memory elements that allow us to store data signals. These elements contain additional gates used to store signal values and to cause the state to be updated only in conjunction with a clock. The next section shows how these elements are built.

Flip-Flops and Latches

Flip-flops and *latches* are the simplest memory elements. In both flip-flops and latches the output is equal to the value of the stored state inside the element. Furthermore, unlike the S-R latch described above, all the latches and flip-flops we will use from this point on are clocked, which means they have a clock input and the change of state is triggered by that clock. The difference between a flip-flop and a latch is the point at which the clock causes the state to actually change. In a clocked latch the state is changed whenever the appropriate inputs change and the clock is asserted, whereas in a flip-flop, the state is changed only on a clock edge. Since throughout this text we use an edge-triggered timing methodology where state is only updated on clock edges, we need only use flip-flops. Flip-flops are often built from latches, so we start by describing the operation of a simple clocked latch and then discuss the operation of a flip-flop constructed from that latch.

For computer applications, the function of both flip-flops and latches is to store a signal. A *D latch* or *D flip-flop* stores the value of its data input signal in the internal memory. Although there are many other types of latches and flip-flops, the D type is the only basic building block that we will need. A D latch has two inputs and two outputs. The inputs are the data value to be stored (called D) and a clock signal (called C) that indicates when the latch should read the value on the D input and store it. The outputs are simply the value of the internal state (Q) and its complement ($\overline{Q}$). When the clock input C is asserted, the latch is said to be *open*, and the value of the output (Q) becomes the val-

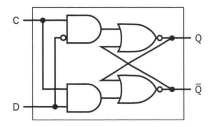

FIGURE B.13 A D latch implemented with NOR gates. A NOR gate acts as an inverter, if the other input is zero. Thus, the cross-coupled pair of NOR gates acts to store the state value unless the clock input, C, is asserted, in which case the value of input D replaces the value of Q and is stored. The value of input D must be stable when the clock signal C changes from asserted to deasserted.

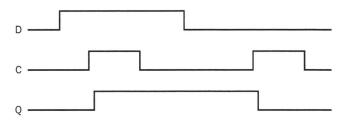

FIGURE B.14 Operation of a D latch assuming the output is initially deasserted. When the clock, C, is asserted, the latch is open and the Q output immediately assumes the value of the D input.

ue of the input D. When the clock input C is deasserted, the latch is said to be *closed*, and the value of the output (Q) is whatever value was stored the last time the latch was open.

Figure B.13 shows how a D latch can be implemented with two additional gates added to the cross-coupled NOR gates. Since when the latch is open the value of Q changes as D changes, this structure is sometimes called a *transparent latch*. Figure B.14 shows how this D latch works, assuming that the output Q is initially false and that D changes first.

As mentioned earlier, we use flip-flops as the basic building block rather than latches. Flip-flops are not transparent: their outputs change only on the clock edge. A flip-flop can be built so that it triggers on either the rising (positive) or falling (negative) clock edge; for our designs we can use either type. Figure B.15 shows how a falling-edge D flip-flop is constructed from a pair of

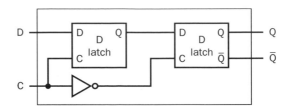

FIGURE B.15 A D flip-flop with a falling-edge trigger. The first latch, called the master, is open and follows the input *D* when the clock input, *C*, is asserted. When the clock input, *C*, falls, the first latch is closed, but the second latch, called the slave, is open and gets its input from the output of the master latch.

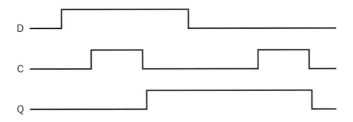

FIGURE B.16 Operation of a D flip-flop with a falling-edge trigger, assuming the output is initially deasserted. When the clock input (*C*) changes from asserted to deasserted, the *Q* output stores the value of the *D* input.

D latches. In a D flip-flop, the output is stored when the clock edge occurs. Figure B.16 shows how this flip-flop operates.

Because the D input is sampled on the clock edge, it must be valid for a period of time immediately before and immediately after the clock edge. The minimum time that the input must be valid before the clock edge is called the *set-up time*; the minimum time during which it must be valid after the clock edge is called the *hold time*. Thus the inputs to any flip-flop (or anything built using flip-flops) must be valid during a window that begins at time t_{set-up} before the clock edge and ends at t_{hold} after the clock edge, as shown in Figure B.17. Section B.7 talks about clocking and timing constraints in more detail.

We can use an array of D flip-flops to build a register that can hold a multibit datum, such as a byte or word. We used registers throughout our datapaths in Chapters 5 and 6.

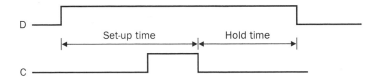

FIGURE B.17 Set-up and hold time requirements for a D flip-flop with a falling-edge trigger. The input must be stable a period of time before the clock edge, as well as after the clock edge. The minimum time the signal must be stable before the clock edge is called the set-up time, while the minimum time the signal must be stable after clock is called the hold time. Failure to meet these minimum requirements can result in a situation where the output of the flip-flop may not even be predictable, as described in section B.7. Hold times are usually either 0 or very small and thus not a cause of worry.

Register Files

One structure that is central to our datapath is a *register file*. A register file consists of a set of registers that can be read and written by supplying a register number to be accessed. A register file can be implemented with a decoder for each read or write port and an array of registers built from D flip-flops. Because reading a register does not change any state, we need only supply a register number as an input, and the only output will be the data contained in that register. For writing a register we will need three inputs: a register number, the data to write, and a clock that controls the writing into the register. In Chapters 5 and 6, we used a register file that has two read ports and one write port. This register file is drawn as shown in Figure B.18. The read ports can be implemented with a pair of multiplexors, each of which is as wide as the number of bits in the register file. Figure B.19 shows the implementation of two register read ports for a 32-bit-wide register file.

Implementing the write port is slightly more complex since we can only change the contents of the designated register. We can do this by using a decoder to generate a signal that can be used to determine which register to write. Figure B.20 shows how to implement the write port for a register file. It is important to remember that the flip-flop changes state only on the clock edge. In Chapters 5 and 6, we hooked up write signals for the register file explicitly and assume the clock shown in Figure B.20 is attached implicitly.

What happens if the same register is read and written during a clock cycle? Because the write of the register file occurs on the clock edge, the register will be valid during the time it is read, as we saw earlier in Figure B.10. The value returned will be the value written in an earlier clock cycle. If we want a read to return the value currently being written, additional logic in the register file or outside of it is needed. Chapter 6 makes extensive use of such logic.

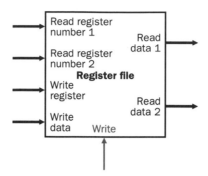

FIGURE B.18 A register file with 2 read ports and 1 write port has 5 inputs and 2 outputs. The control input Write is shown in color.

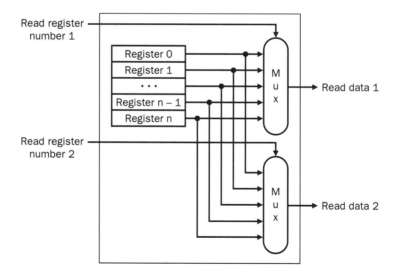

FIGURE B.19 The implementation of two read ports for a register file with *n* registers can be done with a pair of *n*-to-1 multiplexors each 32 bits wide. The register read number signal is used as the multiplexor selector signal. Figure B.20 shows how the write port is implemented.

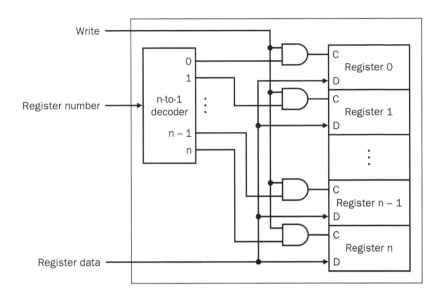

FIGURE B.20 The write port for a register file is implemented with a decoder that is used with the write signal to generate the C input to the registers. All three inputs (the register number, the data, and the write signal) will have set-up and hold-time constraints that ensure that the correct data is written into the register file.

SRAMs

Registers and register files provide the basic building block for small memories, but larger amounts of memory are built using either *SRAMs* (static random access memories) or *DRAMs* (dynamic random access memories). In this section, we discuss SRAMs, which are somewhat simpler, while the next section discusses DRAMs. SRAMs are simply integrated circuits that are memory arrays with (usually) a single access port that can provide either a read or a write. SRAMs have a fixed access time to any datum, though the read and write access characteristics often differ.

A SRAM chip has a specific configuration in terms of the number of addressable locations, as well as the width of each addressable location. For example, a 256Kx1 SRAM provides 256K entries, each of which is 1 bit wide. Thus, it will have 18 address lines (since $256K = 2^{18}$), a single data output line, and a single data input line. A 32Kx8 SRAM has the same total number of bits, but will have 15 address lines to address 32K entries each of which holds an 8-bit wide datum; thus there are 8 data output and 8 data input lines. As with ROMs, the number of addressable locations is often called the *height*, with the number of bits per unit called the *width*. For a variety of technical reasons, the

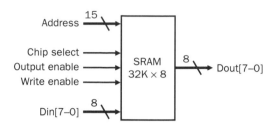

FIGURE B.21 A 32Kx8 SRAM showing the 15 address (32K = 2^{15}) and 8 data inputs, the three control lines, and the 8 data outputs.

newest and fastest SRAMs are typically available in narrow configurations: x1 and x4. Figure B.21 shows the input and output signals for a 32Kx8 SRAM.

To initiate a read or write access, the Chip select signal must be made active. For reads, we must also activate the Output enable signal that controls whether or not the datum selected by the address is actually driven on the pins. The Output enable is useful for connecting multiple memories to a single-output bus and using Output enable to determine which memory drives the bus. The SRAM read access time is usually specified as the delay from the time that Output enable is true and the address lines are valid until the time that the data is on the output lines. Typical read access times for SRAMs in 1993 vary from about 8 ns for the fastest CMOS parts to 35 ns parts, which, while slower, are usually cheaper and often denser. The largest SRAMs available in 1993 have over 1 million bits of data.

For writes, we must supply the data to be written and the address, as well as signals to cause the write to occur. When both the Write enable and Chip select are true, the data on the data input lines is written into the cell specified by the address. There are set-up-time and hold-time requirements for the address and data lines, just as there were for D flip-flops and latches. In addition, the Write enable signal is not a clock edge but a pulse with a minimum width requirement. The time to complete a write is specified by the combination of the set-up times, the hold times, and the Write enable pulse width.

Large SRAMs cannot be built in the same way we build a register file, because unlike a register file where a 32-to-1 multiplexor might be practical, the 64K to 1 multiplexor that would be needed for a 64Kx1 SRAM is totally impractical. Rather than use a giant multiplexor, large memories are implemented with a shared output line, called a *bit line*, which multiple memory cells in the memory array can assert. To allow multiple sources to drive a single line, a *three-state buffer* (or *tri-state buffer*) is used. A three-state buffer has two inputs: a data signal and an Output enable. The single output from a three-

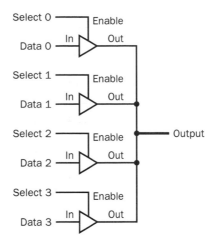

FIGURE B.22 Four three-state buffers are used to form a multiplexor. Only one of the four Select inputs can be asserted. A three-state buffer with a deasserted Output enable, has a high-impedance output that allows a three-state buffer whose Output enable is asserted to drive the shared output line.

state buffer is equal to the asserted or deasserted input signal if the Output enable is asserted, and is otherwise in a *high-impedance state* that allows another three-state buffer whose Output enable is asserted to determine the value of a shared output. Figure B.22 shows a set of three-state buffers wired to form a multiplexor with a decoded input. It is critical that the Output enable of at most one of the three-state buffers be asserted; otherwise, the three-state buffers may try to set the output line differently. By using three-state buffers in the individual cells of the SRAM, each cell that corresponds to a particular output can share the same output line. The use of a set of distributed three-state buffers is a more efficient implementation than a large centralized multiplexor. The three-state buffers are incorporated into the flip-flops that form the basic cells of the SRAM. Figure B.23 shows how a small 4x2 SRAM might be built, using D latches with an input called Enable that controls the three-state output.

The design in Figure B.23 eliminates the need for an enormous multiplexor; however, it still requires a very large decoder and a correspondingly large number of word lines. For example, in a 16Kx8 SRAM, we would need a 14-to-16K decoder and 16K word lines (which are the lines used to enable the individual flip-flops)! To circumvent this problem, large memories are organized as rectangular arrays and use a two-step decoding process. Figure B.24 shows

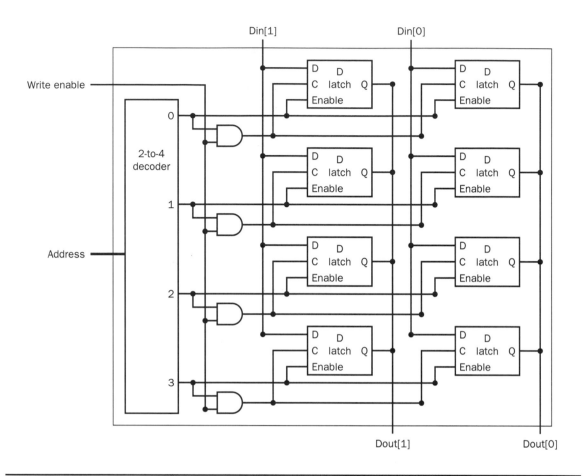

FIGURE B.23 The basic structure of a 4x2 SRAM consists of a decoder that selects which pair of cells to activate. The activated cells use a three-state output connected to the vertical bit lines that supply the requested data. The address that selects the cell is sent on one of a set of vertical address lines, called the word lines. For simplicity, the Output Enable and Chip Select signals have been omitted, but they could easily be added with a few AND gates.

how a 32Kx8 SRAM might be organized using a two-step decode. As we will see, the two-level decoding process is quite important in understanding how DRAMs operate.

DRAMs

In a Static RAM (SRAM) the value stored in a cell is kept on a pair of inverting gates, and as long as power is applied the value can be kept indefinitely. In a Dynamic RAM (DRAM), the value kept in a cell is stored as a charge in a

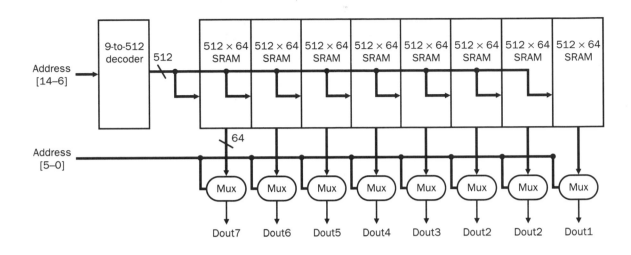

FIGURE B.24 Typical organization of a 32Kx8 SRAM as an array of 512x64 arrays. The first decoder generates the addresses for 8 512x64 arrays; then a set of multiplexors is used to select one bit from each 64-bit-wide array. This is a much easier design than a single-level decode that would need either an enormous decoder (15 to 32K) or a gigantic multiplexor (32K to 1).

capacitor. A single transistor is then used to access this stored charge, either to read the value or to overwrite the charge stored there. Because DRAMs use only a single transistor per bit of storage, they are much denser and cheaper per bit. By comparison, SRAMs require four to six transistors per bit. In DRAMs, the charge is stored on a capacitor, so it cannot be kept indefinitely and must periodically be *refreshed*. That is why this memory structure is called *dynamic*, as opposed to the static storage in an SRAM cell. To refresh the cell, we merely read its contents and write it back. The charge can be kept for several milliseconds, which might correspond to close to a million clock cycles. Today, single-chip memory controllers often handle the refresh function independently of the processor. If every bit had to be read out of the DRAM and then be written back individually, with large DRAMs containing multiple megabytes, we would constantly be refreshing the DRAM, leaving no time for accessing it. Fortunately, DRAMs also use a two-level decoding structure and this allows us to refresh an entire row (which shares a word line) with a read cycle followed immediately by a write cycle. Typically, refresh operations consume 1 to 2% of the active cycles of the DRAM, leaving the remaining 98% to 99% of the cycles available for reading and writing data.

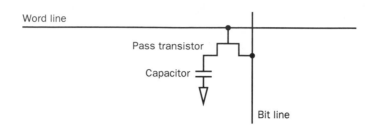

FIGURE B.25 A 1-transistor DRAM cell contains a capacitor that stores the cell contents and a transistor used to access the cell.

Elaboration: How does a DRAM read and write the signal stored in a cell? The transistor inside the cell is a switch, called a *pass transistor*, that allows the value stored on the capacitor to be accessed either for reading or writing. Figure B.25 shows how the single-transistor cell looks. The pass transistor acts like a switch: when the signal on the word line is asserted, the switch is open, connecting the capacitor to the bit line. If the operation is a write, then the value to be written is placed on the bit line. If the value is a 1, the capacitor will be charged. If the value is a 0, then the capacitor will be discharged. Reading is slightly more complex, since the DRAM must detect a very small charge stored in the capacitor. Before activating the word line for a read, the bit line is charged to the voltage that is halfway between the low and high voltage. Then, by activating the word line, the charge on the capacitor is read out onto the bit line. This causes the bit line to move slightly towards the high or low direction, and this change is detected with a sense amplifier, which can detect small changes in voltage.

DRAMs use a two-level decoder, as shown in Figure B.26, consisting of a *row access,* followed by a *column access.* The row access chooses one of a number of rows and activates the corresponding word line. The contents of all the columns in the active row are then stored in a set of latches. The column access then selects the data from the column latches. To save pins and reduce the package cost, the same address lines are used for both the row and column address; a pair of signals called RAS (Row Access Strobe) and CAS (Column Access Strobe) are used to signal the DRAM that either a row or column address is being supplied. Refresh is performed by simply reading the columns into the column latches and then writing the same values back. Thus an entire row is refreshed in one cycle. The two-level addressing scheme, combined with the internal circuitry, make DRAM access times much longer (by a factor of 5 to 10) than SRAM access times. In 1993, typical DRAM access times range from 70 to 120 ns. The much lower cost per bit makes DRAM the choice for main memory, while the faster access time makes SRAM the choice for caches.

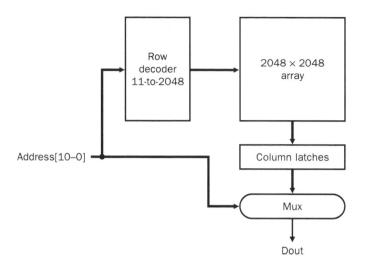

FIGURE B.26 A 4Mx1 DRAM is built with a 2048x2048 array. The row access uses 11 bits to select a row, which is then latched in 2048 1-bit latches. A multiplexor chooses the output bit from these 2048 latches. The RAS and CAS signals control whether the address lines are sent to the row decoder or column multiplexor.

You might observe that a 4M×1 DRAM actually accesses 2048 bits on every row access and then throws away 2047 of those during a column access. DRAM designers have used the internal structure of the DRAM as a way to provide higher bandwidth out of a DRAM. This is done by allowing the column address to change without changing the row address, resulting in an access to other bits in the column latches. *Page-mode* and *static-column-mode* RAMs both provide the ability to change access multiple bits out of a row by changing the column address only. (The difference is whether CAS must also be reasserted or not.) *Nibble-mode* RAMs internally generate the next three column addresses, thus providing four bits (called a *nibble*) for every row access. As we demonstrated in Chapter 7, these modes can be used to boost the bandwidth available out of main memory to match the needs of the processor and caches.

Error Correction

Because of the potential for data corruption in large memories, most computer systems use some sort of error-checking code to detect possible corruption of data. One simple code that is heavily used is a *parity code*. In a parity code the number of 1s in a word is counted; the word has odd parity if the number of 1s is odd and even otherwise. When a word is written into memory, the parity bit is also written (1 for odd, 0 for even). Then, when the word is read out, the parity bit is read and checked. If the parity of the memory word and the stored parity bit do not match, an error has occurred. A one-bit parity scheme can detect at most one bit of error in a data item; if there are two bits of error, then a 1-bit parity scheme will not detect any errors, since the parity will match the data with two errors. (Actually, a 1-bit parity scheme can detect any odd number of errors; however, the probability of having three errors is much lower than the probability of having two, so, in practice, a 1-bit parity code is limited to detecting a single bit of error.) Of course, a parity code cannot tell which bit in a data item is in error.

A 1-bit parity scheme is an error-detecting code; there are also *error-correcting codes* (*ECC*) that will detect and allow correction of an error. For large main memories, many systems use a code that allows the detection of up to 2 bits of error and the correction of a single bit of error. These codes work by using more bits to encode the data; for example, the typical codes used for main memories require 7 or 8 bits for every 128 bits of data.

Elaboration: A 1-bit parity code is a *distance-2 code*, which means that if we look at the data plus the parity bit, no 1-bit change is sufficient to generate another legal combination of the data plus parity. For example, if we change a bit in the data, the parity will be wrong, and vice versa. Of course, if we change 2 bits (any two data bits or one data bit and the parity bit), the parity will match the data and the error cannot be detected. Hence, there is a distance of two between legal combinations of parity and data.

To detect more than one error or correct an error we need a *distance-3 code*, which has the property that any legal combination of the bits in the error correction code and the data have at least 3 bits differing from any other combination. Suppose we have such a code and we have one error in the data. In that case the code plus data will be 1 bit away from a legal combination and we can correct the data to that legal combination. If we have two errors, we can recognize that there is an error, but we cannot correct the errors. Let's look at an example. Here are the data words and a distance-3 error correction code for a 4-bit data item.

Data	Code bits	Data	Code bits
0000	000	1000	111
0001	011	1001	100
0010	101	1010	010
0011	110	1011	001
0100	110	1100	001
0101	101	1101	010
0110	011	1110	100
0111	000	1111	111

To see how this works, let's choose a data word, say 0110, whose error correction code is 011. Here are the four 1-bit error possibilities for this data: 1110, 0010, 0100, and 0111. Now look at the data item with the same code (011), which is the entry with the value 0001. If the error correction decoder received one of the four possible data words with an error, it would have to choose between correcting to 0110 or 0001. While these four words with error have only 1 bit changed from the correct pattern of 0110, they each have 2 bits that are different from the alternate correction of 0001. Hence the error correction mechanism can easily choose to correct to 0110, since a single error is much lower probability. To see that two errors can be detected, simply notice that all the combinations with 2 bits changed have a different code. The one re-use of the same code is with 3 bits different, but if we correct a 2-bit error, we will correct to the wrong value, since the decoder will assume that only a single error has occurred. If we want to correct 1-bit errors and detect, but not erroneously correct, 2-bit errors, we need a distance-4 code.

Although we distinguished between the code and data in our explanation, in truth, an error correction code treats the combination of code and data as a single word in a larger code (7 bits in this example). Thus it deals with errors in the code bits in the same fashion as errors in the data bits.

While the above example requires $n-1$ bits for n bits of data, the number of bits required grows slowly, so that for a distance-3 code, a 64-bit word needs 7 bits and a 128-bit word needs 8. This type of code is called a *Hamming code*, after R. Hamming, who described a method for creating such codes.

B.6   Finite State Machines

As we saw earlier, digital logic systems can be classified as combinational or sequential. Sequential systems contain state stored in memory elements internal to the system. Their behavior depends both on the set of inputs supplied and on the contents of the internal memory, or state of the system. Thus a sequential system cannot be described with a truth table. Instead, a sequential system is described as a *finite state machine* (or often just *state machine*). A finite state machine has a set of states and two functions called the *next-state function* and the *output function*. The set of states correspond to all the possible values of the internal storage. Thus, if there are n bits of storage, there are 2^n states. The next-state function is a combinational function that, given the inputs and the current state, determines the next state of the system. The output function produces a set of outputs from the current state and the inputs. Figure B.27 shows this diagrammatically.

The state machines we discuss here and in Chapter 5 are *synchronous*. This means that the state changes together with the clock cycle and a new state is computed once every clock. Thus, the state elements are updated only on the

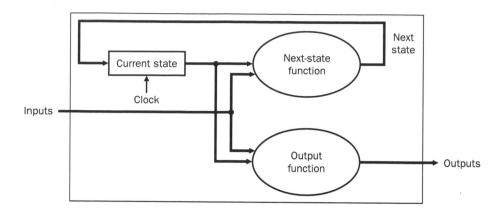

FIGURE B.27 A state machine consists of internal storage that contains the state and two combinational functions: the next-state function and the output function. Often, the output function is restricted to take only the current state as its input; this does not change the capability of a sequential machine, but does affect its internals.

clock edge. We use this methodology in this section and throughout Chapters 5 and 6, and we do not usually show the clock explicitly. We use state machines throughout Chapters 5 and 6 to control the execution of the processor and the actions of the datapath.

To illustrate how a finite state machine operates and is designed, let's look at a simple and classic example: controlling a traffic light. (Chapters 5 and 6 contain more detailed examples of using finite state machines to control processor execution.) When a finite state machine is used as a controller, the output function is often restricted to depend on just the current state. Such a finite state machine is called a *Moore machine*. This is the type of finite state machine we use throughout this book. If the output function can depend on both the next state and the current input, the machine is called a *Mealy machine*. These two machines are equivalent in their capabilities and one can be turned into the other mechanically.

Our example concerns the control of a traffic light at an intersection of a north-south bound route and an east-west route. For simplicity, we will consider only the green and red lights; adding the yellow light is left for an exercise. We want the lights to cycle no faster than 30 seconds in each direction, so we will use a 0.033-Hz clock so that the machine cycles between states at no faster than once every 30 seconds. There are two output signals.

- *NSlite:* When this signal is asserted, the light on the north-south road is green; when this signal is deasserted the light on the north-south road is red.

■ *EWlite:* When this signal is asserted, the light on the east-west road is green; when this signal is deasserted the light on the east-west road is red.

In addition, there are two inputs: NScar and EWcar.

■ *NScar:* Indicates that a car is over the detector placed in the roadbed in front of the light on the north-south road (going north or south).

■ *EWcar:* Indicates that a car is over the detector placed in the roadbed in front of the light on the east-west road (going east or west).

The traffic light should change from one direction to the other only if a car is waiting to go in the other direction; otherwise, the light should continue to show green in the same direction as the last car that crossed the intersection.

To implement this simple traffic light we need two states.

■ *NSgreen:* the traffic light is green in the north-south direction.

■ *EWgreen:* the traffic light is green in the east-west direction.

We also need to create the next-state function, which can be specified with a table.

Current state	Inputs		Next state
	NScar	EWcar	
NSgreen	0	0	NSgreen
NSgreen	0	1	EWgreen
NSgreen	1	0	NSgreen
NSgreen	1	1	EWgreen
EWgreen	0	0	EWgreen
EWgreen	0	1	EWgreen
EWgreen	1	0	NSgreen
EWgreen	1	1	NSgreen

Notice that we didn't specify in the algorithm what happens when a car approaches from both directions. In this case, the next-state function given above changes the state to ensure that a steady stream of cars from one direction cannot lock out a car in the other direction.

The finite state machine is completed by specifying the output function.

Current state	Outputs	
	NSlite	EWlite
NSgreen	1	0
EWgreen	0	1

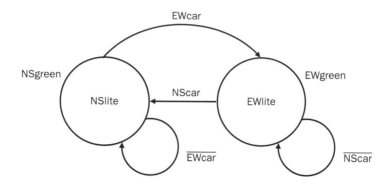

FIGURE B.28 The graphical representation of the two-state traffic light controller. We simplified the logic functions on the state transitions. For example, the transition from NSgreen to EWgreen in the next state table is $(\overline{\text{NScar}} \cdot \text{EWcar}) + (\text{NScar} \cdot \text{EWcar})$, which is equivalent to EWcar.

Before we examine how to implement this finite state machine, lets look at a graphical representation, which is often used for finite state machines. In this representation, nodes are used to indicate states. Inside the node we place a list of the outputs that are active for that state. Directed arcs are used to show the next-state function, with labels on the arcs specifying the input condition as logic functions. The graphical representation for this finite state machine is shown in Figure B.28.

A finite state machine can be implemented, with a register to hold the current state and a block of combinational logic that computes the next-state function and the output function. Figure B.29 shows how a finite state machine with four bits of state and, thus, up to 16 states, might look. To implement the finite state machine in this way, we must first assign state numbers to the states. This process is called *state assignment*. For example, we could assign NSgreen to state 0 and EWgreen to state 1. The state register would contain a single bit. The next-state function would be given as

$$\text{NextState} = (\overline{\text{CurrentState} \cdot \text{EWcar}}) + (\text{CurrentState} \cdot \overline{\text{NScar}})$$

where CurrentState is the contents of the state register (0 or 1) and NextState is the output of the next-state function that will be written into the state register at the end of the clock cycle. The output function is also simple:

$$\text{NSlite} = \overline{\text{CurrentState}}$$

$$\text{EWlite} = \text{CurrentState}$$

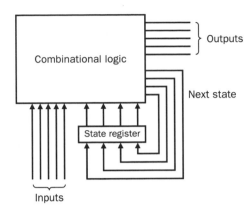

FIGURE B.29 A finite state machine is implemented with a state register that holds the current state and a combinational logic block to compute the next state and output functions. The latter two functions are often split apart and implemented with two separate blocks of logic, which may require fewer gates.

The combinational logic block is often implemented using structured logic, such as a PLA. A PLA can be constructed automatically from the next-state and output-function tables. In fact, there are computer-aided-design (CAD) programs that take either a graphical or textual representation of a finite state machine and produce an optimized implementation automatically. In Chapters 5 and 6, finite state machines were used to control processor execution. Appendix C will discuss the detailed implementation of these controllers with both PLAs and ROMs.

B.7 Timing Methodologies

Throughout this appendix and in the rest of the text we use an edge-triggered timing methodology. This timing methodology has the advantage that it is simpler to explain and understand than a level-triggered methodology. In this section we explain this timing methodology in a little more detail and also introduce level-sensitive clocking. We conclude this section by briefly discussing the issue of asynchronous signals and synchronizers, an important problem for digital designers.

The purpose of this section is to introduce the major concepts in clocking methodology. The section makes some important simplifying assumptions;

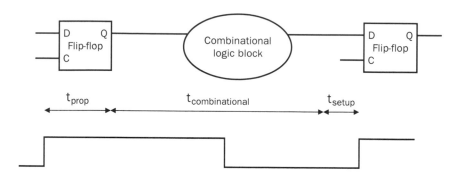

FIGURE B.30 In an edge-triggered design the clock must be long enough to allow signals to be valid for the required set-up time before the next clock edge. The time for a flip-flop input to propagate to the flip-flip outputs is t_{prop}; the signal then takes $t_{combinational}$ to travel through the combinational logic and must be valid t_{setup} before the next clock edge.

the reader interested in understanding timing methodology in more detail should look at one of the references listed at the end of this appendix.

We use an edge-triggered timing methodology because it is simpler to explain and has fewer rules required for correctness. In particular, if we assume that all clocks arrive at the same time, we are guaranteed that a system with edge-triggered registers between blocks of combinational logic can operate correctly without races, if we simply make the clock long enough. A *race* occurs when the contents of a state element depend on the relative speed of different logic elements. In an edge-triggered design, the clock cycle must be long enough to accommodate the path from one flip-flop through the combinational logic to another flip-flop where it must satisfy the set-up time requirement. Figure B.30 shows this requirement for a system using rising-edge triggered flip-flops. In such a system the clock period (or cycle time) must be at least as large as

$$t_{prop} + t_{combinatorial} + t_{setup}$$

for the worst case values of these three delays. The simplifying assumption is that the hold-time requirements are satisfied. Satisfying the hold-time requirements in most designs is not a problem, since the propagation time (t_{prop}) is always larger than the hold time for a flip-flop.

One additional complication that must be considered in edge-triggered designs is *clock skew*. Clock skew is the difference in absolute time between when two state elements see a clock edge. Clock skew arises because the clock signal will often use two different paths, with slightly different delays, to reach two

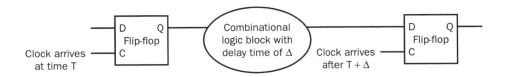

FIGURE B.31 Illustration of how clock skew can cause a race, leading to incorrect operation. Because of the difference in when the two flip-flops see the clock, the signal that is stored into the first flip-flop can race forward and change the input to the second flip-flop before the clock arrives at the second flip-flop.

different state elements. If the clock skew is large enough, it may be possible for a state element to change and cause the input to another flip-flop to change before the clock edge is seen by the second flip-flop. Figure B.31 illustrates this problem, ignoring set-up time and flip-flop propagation delay. To avoid incorrect operation the clock period is increased to allow for the maximum clock skew. Thus, the clock period must be longer than

$$t_{\text{prop}} + t_{\text{combinatorial}} + t_{\text{setup}} + t_{\text{skew}}.$$

With this constraint on the clock period, the two clocks can also arrive in the opposite order, with the second clock arriving t_{skew} earlier, and the circuit will work correctly. Designers reduce clock skew problems by carefully routing the clock signal to minimize the difference in arrival times. In addition, smart designers also provide some margin by making the clock a little longer than the minimum; this allows for variation in components as well in the power supply. Since clock skew can also affect the hold-time requirements, minimizing the size of the clock skew is important.

Edge-triggered designs have two drawbacks: they require extra logic and they may sometimes be slower. Just looking at the D flip-flop versus the level-sensitive latch that we used to construct the flip-flop shows that edge-triggered design requires more logic. An alternative is to use *level-sensitive clocking*. Because state changes in a level-sensitive methodology are not instantaneous, a level-sensitive scheme is slightly more complex and requires additional care to make it operate correctly.

Level-Sensitive Timing

In a level-sensitive timing methodology, the state changes occur at either high or low levels, but they are not instantaneous as they are in an edge-triggered methodology. Because of the noninstantaneous change in state, races can easily occur. To ensure that a level-sensitive design will also work correctly if the clock is slow enough, designers use *two-phase clocking*, which makes use of

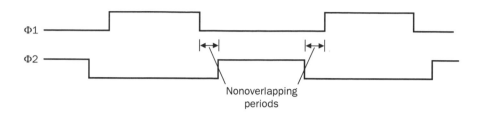

FIGURE B.32 A two-phase clocking scheme showing the cycle of each clock and the nonoverlapping periods.

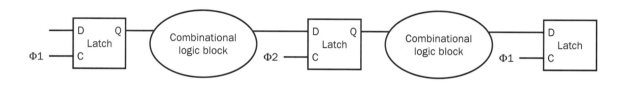

FIGURE B.33 A two-phase timing scheme with alternating latches showing how the system operates on both clock phases. The output of a latch is stable on the opposite phase from its C input. Thus, the first block of combinational inputs has a stable input during ϕ_2 and its output is latched by ϕ_2. The second (rightmost) combinational block operates in just the opposite fashion with stable inputs during ϕ_2. Thus the delays through the combinational blocks determine the minimum time that the respective clocks must be asserted. The size of the nonoverlapping period is determined by the maximum clock skew and the minimum delay of any logic block.

two nonoverlapping clocks. The clocks, typically called ϕ_1 and ϕ_2, are constructed so that at most one of the clock signals is high at any given time, as shown in Figure B.32. We can use these two clocks to build a system that has level sensitive latches and is free from any race conditions, just as the edge-triggered designs were.

One simple way to design such a system is to alternate the use of latches that are open on ϕ_1 with latches that are open on ϕ_2. Because both clocks are not asserted at the same time, a race cannot occur. If the input to a combinational block is a ϕ_1 clock, then its output is latched by a ϕ_2 clock, which is open only during ϕ_2 when the input latch is closed and hence has a valid output. Figure B.33 shows how a system with two-phase timing and alternating latches operates. As in an edge-triggered design, we must pay attention to clock skew, particularly between the two clock phases. By increasing the amount of nonoverlap between the two phases, we can reduce the potential margin of error. Thus the system is guaranteed to operate correctly if each phase is long enough and there is large enough nonoverlap between the phases.

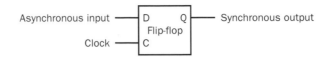

FIGURE B.34 A synchronizer build from a D flip-flop is used to sample an asynchronous signal to produce an output that is synchronous with the clock. This "synchronizer" will *not* work properly!

Asynchronous Inputs and Synchronizers

By using a single clock or a two-phase clock, we can eliminate race conditions, if clock skew problems are avoided. Unfortunately, it is impractical to make an entire system function with a single clock and still keep the clock skew small. While the CPU may use a single clock, I/O devices will probably have their own clock. In Chapter 8, we showed how an asynchronous device may communicate with the CPU through a series of handshaking steps. To translate the asynchronous input to a synchronous signal that can be used to change the state of a system, we need to use a *synchronizer*, whose inputs are the asynchronous signal and a clock and whose output is a signal synchronous with the input clock.

Our first attempt to build a synchronizer uses an edge-triggered D flip-flop, whose D input is the asynchronous signal, as shown in Figure B.34. Because we communicate with a handshaking protocol (as we will see in Chapter 8), it does not matter whether we detect the asserted state of the asynchronous signal on one clock or the next, since the signal will be held asserted until it is acknowledged. Thus, you might think that this simple structure is enough to sample the signal accurately, which would be the case except for one small problem.

The problem is a situation called *metastability*. Suppose the asynchronous signal is transitioning between high and low when the clock edge arrives. Clearly, it is not possible to know whether the signal will be latched as high or low. That problem we could live with. Unfortunately, the situation is worse: when the signal that is sampled is not stable for the required set-up and hold times, the flip-flop may go into a *metastable* state. In such a state, the output will not have a legitimate high or low value, but will be in the indeterminate region between them. Furthermore, the flip-flop is not guaranteed to exit this state in any bounded amount of time. Some logic blocks that look at the output of the flip-flop may see its output as 0, while other may see it as 1. This situation is called a *synchronizer failure*. In a purely synchronous system, synchronizer failure can be avoided by ensuring that the set-up and hold times for a flip-flop or latch are always met, but this is impossible when the input is asynchronous. Instead, the only solution possible is to wait long enough before looking at the output of the flip-flop to ensure that its output is stable, and

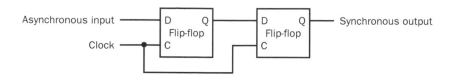

FIGURE B.35 This synchronizer will work correctly if the period of metastability that we wish to guard against is less than the clock period. Although the output of the first flip-flop will may be metastable, it will not be seen by any other logic element until the second clock, when the second D flip-flop samples the signal, which by that time should no longer be in a metastable state.

that it has exited the metastable state, if it ever entered it. How long is long enough? Well, the probability that the flip-flop will stay in the metastable state decreases exponentially, so after a very short time the probability that the flip-flop is in the metastable state is very low; however, the probability never reaches 0! So designers wait long enough that the probability of a synchronizer failure is very low, and the time between such failures will be years or even thousands of years. For most flip-flop designs, waiting for a period that is several times longer than the set-up time makes the probability of synchronization failure very low. If the clock rate is longer than the potential metastability period (which is likely), then a safe synchronizer can be built with two D flip-flops, as shown in Figure B.35. The reader interested in reading more about these problems should look into the references.

To Probe Further

There are a number of good texts on logic design. Here are some you might like to look into.

Katz, Randy H. [1993]. *Modern Logic Design.* Benjamin/Cummings, Redwood City.

A general text on logic design.

McCluskey, E. J. [1986]. *Logic Design Principles.* Prentice Hall, Englewood Cliffs, New Jersey.

Contains extensive discussions of hazards, optimization principles, and testability.

Mead, C., and L. Conway [1980]. *Introduction toVLSI Ssystems.* Addison-Wesley, New York.

Discusses the design of VLSI systems using nMOS technology.

Proser, F. P., and D. E. Winkel [1987]. *The Art of Digital Design.* 2nd edition. Prentice Hall, Englewood Cliffs, New Jersey.

A general text on logic design.

Wakerly, J. F. [1990]. *Digital Design: Principles and Practices.* Prentice Hall, Englewood Cliffs, New Jersey.

A general text on logic design.

B.8 Exercises

B.1 [10] <§B.2> Show that there are 2^n entries in a truth table for a function with n inputs.

B.2 [10] <§B.2> One logic function that is used for a variety of purposes (including within adders and to compute parity) is *exclusive-or*. The output of a two-input exclusive-or function is true only if exactly one of the inputs is true. Show the truth table for a two-input exclusive OR function and implement this function using AND gates, OR gates, and inverters.

B.3 [10] <§B.2, B.5> Construct the truth table for a four-input even-parity function (see page B-33 for a description of parity).

B.4 [10] <§B.2, B.5> Implement the four-input even-parity function with AND and OR gates using bubbled inputs and outputs.

B.5 [10] <§B.2, B.3, B.5> Implement the four-input even-parity function with a PLA.

In More Depth

In addition to the basic laws we discussed on pages B-5 and B-6, there are two important theorems, called DeMorgan's theorems, which are

$$\overline{A + B} = \overline{A} \cdot \overline{B} \quad \text{and} \quad \overline{A \cdot B} = \overline{A} + \overline{B}$$

B.6 [10] <§B.2> Prove DeMorgan's theorems with a truth table of the form:

A	B	$\overline{A}$	$\overline{B}$	$\overline{A} \cdot \overline{B}$	$\overline{A} + \overline{B}$	$\overline{A + B}$	$\overline{A \cdot B}$
0	0						
0	1						
1	0						
1	1						

B.7 [15] <§B.2> Prove that the two equations for E in the example starting on B-6 are equivalent by using DeMorgan's theorems and the axioms shown on page B-6.

B.8 [15] <§B.2–B.3> Derive the product of sums representation for E shown on B-10 starting with the sum-of-products representation. You will need to use DeMorgan's theorems.

B.9 [30] <§B.2–B.3> Give an algorithm for constructing the sum-of-products representation for an arbitrary logic equation consisting of AND, OR, and

NOT. The algorithm should be recursive and should not construct the truth table in the process.

B.10 [15] <§B.2> Prove that the NOR gate is universal by showing how to build the AND, OR, and NOT functions using a two-input NOR gate.

B.11 [15] <§B.2> Prove that the NAND gate is universal by showing how to build the AND, OR, and NOT functions using a two-input NAND gate.

B.12 [15] <§B.2, B.3> Prove that a two-input multiplexor is also universal by showing how to build the AND, OR, and NOT functions using a multiplexor.

B.13 [15] <§B.2, B.5> Construct a 3-bit counter using three D flip-flops and a selection of gates. The inputs should consist of a signal that resets the counter to 0, called *reset*, and a signal to increment the counter, called *inc*. The outputs should be the value of the counter. When the counter has value 7 and is incremented, it should wrap around and become 0.

B.14 [20] <§B.3, B.5> A *Gray code* is a sequence of binary numbers with the property that no more than one bit changes in going from one element of the sequence to another. For example, here is a 3-bit binary Gray code: 000, 001, 011, 010, 110, 111, 101, and 100. Using three D flip-flops and a PLA, construct a 3-bit Gray code counter that has two inputs: *reset*, which sets the counter to 000, and *inc*, which makes the counter go to the next value in the sequence. Note that the code is cyclic, so that the value after 100 in the sequence is 000.

B.15 [25] <§B.2, B.6> We wish to add a yellow light to our traffic light example. We will do this by changing the clock to run at 0.25 Hz (a four-second clock cycle time), which is the duration of a yellow light. To prevent the green and red lights from cycling too fast, we add a 30-second timer. The timer has a single input called *TimerReset*, which restarts the timer, and a single output, called *TimerSignal* that indicates that the 30-second period has expired. Also, we must redefine the traffic signals to include yellow. We do this by defining two output signals for each light: green and yellow. If the output NSgreen is asserted, the green light is on; if the output NSyellow is asserted, the yellow light is on. If both signals are off, the red light is on. Do *not* assert both the green and yellow signals at the same time, since American drivers will certainly be confused, even if the European drivers understand what this means! Draw the graphical representation for the finite state machine for this improved controller. Choose names for the states that are *different* from the names of the outputs!

B.16 [15] <§B.6> Write down the next-state and output-function tables for the traffic light controller described in Exercise B.15.

B.17 [15] <§B.2, B.6> Assign state numbers to the states in the traffic light example and use the tables of Exercise B.16 to write a set of logic equations for each of the outputs, including the next-state outputs.

B.18 [15] <§B.3, B.6> Implement the logic equations of Exercise B.17 as a PLA.

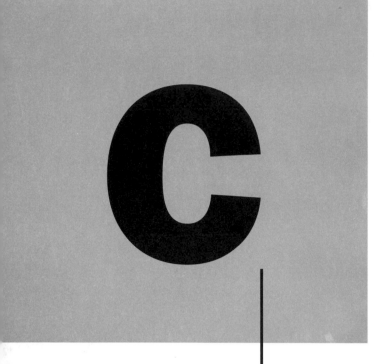

Mapping Control to Hardware

A custom format such as this is slave to the architecture of the hardware and the instruction set it serves. The format must strike a proper compromise between ROM size, ROM-output decoding, circuitry size, and machine execution rate.

Jim McKevit et. al.
8086 Design Report, Internal Memorandum, 1977

C.1   Introduction

There are several different techniques for implementing the control unit. The usefulness of these techniques depends on the complexity of the control, characteristics such as the average number of next states for any given state, and the implementation technology.

The most straightforward way to implement the control function is with a block of logic that takes as inputs the current state and the opcode field of the Instruction register and produces as outputs the datapath-control signals and the value of the next state. The initial representation may be either a finite state diagram or a microprogram. In the latter case, each microinstruction represents a state. In an implementation using a finite-state controller, the next-state function will be computed with logic. Section C.2 constructs such an implementation both for a ROM and a PLA.

An alternative method of implementation computes the next-state function by using a counter that increments the current state to determine the next state. When the next state doesn't follow sequentially, other logic is used to determine the state. Section C.3 explores this type of implementation and shows how it can be used for the finite-state control created in Chapter 5.

In Section C.4, we show how a microprogram representation of the control is translated to control logic.

C.2   Implementing Finite State Machine Control

To implement the control as a finite state machine, we must first assign a number to each of the 10 states; any state could use any number, but we will use the sequential numbering for simplicity as we did in Chapter 5. (Figure C.1 is a copy of the finite state diagram from Figure 5.47 on page 332, reproduced for ease of access.) With 10 states we will need 4 bits to encode the state number, and we call these state bits: S3, S2, S1, S0. The current-state number will be stored in a state register, as shown in Figure C.2. If the states are assigned sequentially, state i is encoded using the state bits as the binary number i. For example, state 6 is encoded as 0110_{two} or S3 = 0, S2 = 1, S1 = 1, S0 = 0, which can also be written as

$$\overline{S3} \cdot S2 \cdot S1 \cdot \overline{S0}.$$

The control unit has outputs that specify the next state. These are written into the state register on the clock edge and become the new state at the beginning of the next clock cycle following the active clock edge. We name these outputs NS3, NS2, NS1, NS0. Once we have determined the number of inputs, states, and outputs, we know what the basic outline of the control unit will look like, as we show in Figure C.2.

The block labeled "control logic" in Figure C.2 is combinational logic. We can think of it as a big table giving the value of the outputs in terms of the inputs. The logic in this block implements the two different parts of the finite state machine. One part is the logic that determines the setting of the datapath-control outputs, which depend only on the state bits. The other part of the control logic implements the next-state function; these equations determine the values of the next-state bits based on the current-state bits and the other inputs (the 6-bit opcode).

Figure C.3 shows the logic equations: the top portion showing the outputs, and the bottom portion showing the next-state function. The values in this table were determined from the state diagram in Figure C.1. For each state in which a control line is active an entry in the second column is made. Likewise, the next state entries are made whenever one state is a successor to another. In this table we use the abbreviation stateN to stand for current state N. Thus, stateN is replaced by the term that encodes the state number N. We use NextStateN to stand for the setting of the next-state outputs to N. This output is implemented using the next-state outputs (NS). When NextStateN is active, the bits NS[3–0] are set corresponding to the binary version of the value N. Of course, since a given next-state bit is activated in multiple next states, the equation for each state bit will be the OR of the terms that activate that signal. Likewise, when we use a term such as (Op='lw'), this corresponds to an AND of the opcode inputs that specifies the encoding of the opcode lw in 6 bits, just as

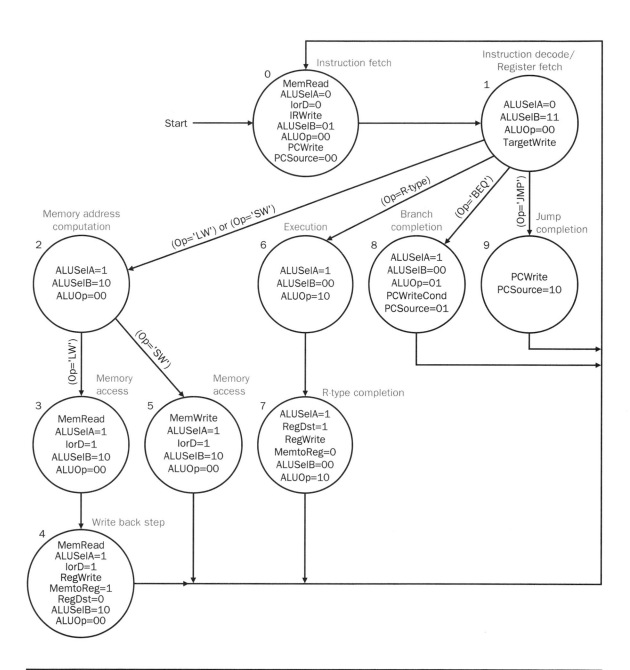

FIGURE C.1 The finite state diagram that was developed in Chapter 5.

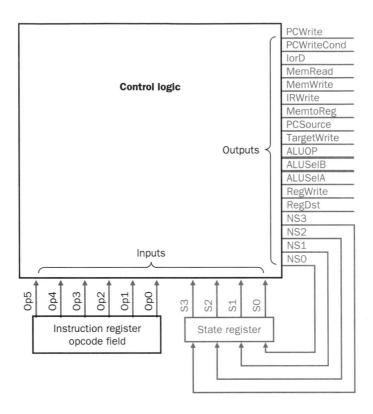

FIGURE C.2 The control unit for MIPS will consist of some control logic and a register to hold the state. The state register is written at the active clock edge and is stable during the clock cycle.

we did for the simple control unit in Chapter 5 (see Figures 5.23 on page 296 and 5.30 on page 304). Translating the entries in Figure C.3 into logic equations for the outputs is straightforward.

Output	Current states	Op
PCWrite	state0+state9	
PCWriteCond	state8	
IorD	state3+state4+state5	
MemRead	state0+state3+state4	
MemWrite	state5	
IRWrite	state0	
MemtoReg	state4	
PCSource1	state9	
PCSource0	state8	
TargetWrite	state1	
ALUOp1	state6+state7	
ALUOp0	state8	
ALUSelB1	state1+state2+state3+state4+state5	
ALUSelB0	state0+state1	
ALUSelA	state2+state3+state4+state5+state6+state7+state8	
RegWrite	state4+state7	
RegDst	state7	
NextState0	state4+state5+state7+state8+state9	
NextState1	state0	
NextState2	state1	(Op='lw') + (Op='sw')
NextState3	state2	(Op='lw')
NextState4	state3	
NextState5	state2	(Op='sw')
NextState6	state1	(Op='R-type')
NextState7	state6	
NextState8	state1	(Op='beq')
NextState9	state1	(Op='jmp')

FIGURE C.3 The logic equations for the control unit shown in a shorthand form. Remember that "+" stands for OR in logic equations. The state inputs and NextState entries outputs must be expanded by using the state encoding. Any blank entry is a don't care.

Example   Give the logic equation for the low-order next-state bit, NS0.

Answer

The next-state bit NS0 should be active whenever the next state has NS0 = 1 in the state encoding. This is true for NextState1, NextState3, NextState5, NextState7, and NextState9. The entries for these states in Figure C.3 supply the conditions when these next-state values should be active. The equation for each of these next states is given below. The first equation states that the next state is 1, if the current state is 0; the current state is 0 if each of the state input bits is 0, which is what the rightmost product term indicates.

$$
\begin{aligned}
\text{NextState1} &= \text{State 0} = \overline{S3} \cdot \overline{S2} \cdot \overline{S1} \cdot \overline{S0} \\
\text{NextState3} &= \text{State2} \cdot (\text{Op[5-0]} = \text{'LW'}) \\
&= \overline{S3} \cdot \overline{S2} \cdot S1 \cdot \overline{S0} \cdot \text{Op5} \cdot \overline{\text{Op4}} \cdot \overline{\text{Op3}} \cdot \overline{\text{Op2}} \cdot \text{Op1} \cdot \text{Op0} \\
\text{NextState5} &= \text{State2} \cdot (\text{Op[5-0]} = \text{'SW'}) \\
&= \overline{S3} \cdot \overline{S2} \cdot S1 \cdot \overline{S0} \cdot \text{Op5} \cdot \overline{\text{Op4}} \cdot \text{Op3} \cdot \overline{\text{Op2}} \cdot \text{Op1} \cdot \text{Op0} \\
\text{NextState7} &= \text{State6} = \overline{S3} \cdot S2 \cdot S1 \cdot \overline{S0} \\
\text{NextState9} &= \text{State1} \cdot (\text{Op[5-0]} = \text{'MP'}) \\
&= \overline{S3} \cdot \overline{S2} \cdot \overline{S1} \cdot S0 \cdot \overline{\text{Op5}} \cdot \overline{\text{Op4}} \cdot \overline{\text{Op3}} \cdot \overline{\text{Op2}} \cdot \text{Op1} \cdot \overline{\text{Op0}}
\end{aligned}
$$

NS0 is the logical sum of all these terms.

As we have seen, the control function can be expressed as a logic equation for each output. This set of logic equations can be implemented in two ways: corresponding to a complete truth table, or corresponding to a two-level logic structure that allows a sparse encoding of the truth table. Before we look at these implementations, let's look at the truth table for the complete control function.

It is simplest if we break the control function defined in Figure C.3 into two parts: the next-state outputs, which may depend on all the inputs, and the control signal outputs, which depend only on the current-state bits. Figure C.4 shows the truth tables for all the datapath-control signals. Because these signals actually depend only on the state bits, each of the entries in a table in Figure C.4 actually represents 64 entries, with the 6 bits named Op having all possible values; that is, the Op bits are don't-care bits in determining the datapath-control outputs. Figure C.5 shows the truth table for the next-state bits NS[3–0], which depend on the state input bits and the instruction bits, which supply the opcode.

s3	s2	s1	s0
0	0	0	0
1	0	0	1

a. Truth table for PCWrite.

s3	s2	s1	s0
1	0	0	0

b. Truth table for PCWriteCond.

s3	s2	s1	s0
0	0	1	1
0	1	0	0
0	1	0	1
0	0	1	1

c. Truth table for IorD.

s3	s2	s1	s0
0	0	0	0
0	0	1	1
0	1	0	0

d. Truth table for MemRead.

s3	s2	s1	s0
0	1	0	1

e. Truth table for MemWrite.

s3	s2	s1	s0
0	0	0	0

f. Truth table for IRWrite.

s3	s2	s1	s0
0	1	0	0

g. Truth table for MemtoReg.

s3	s2	s1	s0
1	0	0	1

h. Truth table for PCSource1.

s3	s2	s1	s0
1	0	0	0

i. Truth table for PCSource0.

s3	s2	s1	s0
0	0	0	1

j. Truth table for TargetWrite.

s3	s2	s1	s0
0	1	1	0
0	1	1	1

k. Truth table for ALUOp1.

s3	s2	s1	s0
1	0	0	0

l. Truth table for ALUOp0.

s3	s2	s1	s0
0	0	0	1
0	0	1	0
0	0	1	1
0	1	0	0
0	1	0	1

m. Truth table for ALUSelB1.

s3	s2	s1	s0
0	0	0	0
0	0	0	1

n. Truth table for ALUSelB0.

s3	s2	s1	s0
0	0	1	0
0	0	1	1
0	1	0	0
0	1	0	1
0	1	1	0
0	1	1	1
1	0	0	0

o. Truth table for ALUSelA.

s3	s2	s1	s0
0	1	0	0
0	1	1	1

p. Truth table for RegWrite.

s3	s2	s1	s0
0	1	1	1

q. Truth table for RegDst.

FIGURE C.4 The truth tables are shown for the 17 datapath-control signals that depend only on the current-state input bits, which are shown for each table. Each truth table row corresponds to 64 entries: one for each possible value of the six Op bits. Notice that some of the outputs are active under nearly the same circumstances. For example, in the case of ALUSelB0 and IRWrite, these signals are both active only in state 0 (see tables b and l). These two signals could be replaced by one signal. The same applies to PCWriteCond and ALUOp0. There are other opportunities for reducing the logic needed to implement the control function by taking advantage of further similarities in the truth tables.

A ROM Implementation

Probably the simplest way to implement the control function is to encode the truth tables in a Read-Only Memory (ROM). The number of entries in the memory for the truth tables of Figures C.4 and C.5 is equal to all possible values of the inputs (the 6 opcode bits plus the 4 state bits), which is $2^{\text{\# inputs}} = 2^{10} = 1024$. The inputs to the control unit become the address lines for the ROM, which implements the control logic block that was shown in Figure C.2 on page C-6. The width of each entry (or word in the memory) is 21 bits since there are 17 datapath-control outputs and 4 next-state bits. This means the total size of the ROM is $2^{10} \times 21 = 21\,\text{Kbits}$.

The setting of the bits in a word in the ROM depends on which outputs are active in that word. Before we look at the control words, we need to order the bits within the control input (the address) and output words (the contents), respectively. We will number the bits using the order in Figure C.2 on page C-6, with the next-state bits being the low-order bits of the control *word* and the current-state input bits being the low-order bits of the *address*. This means that the PCWrite output will be the high-order bit (bit 20) of each memory word and NS0 will be the low-order bit. The high-order *address* bit will be given by Op5, which is the first bit of the instruction, and the low-order address bit will be given by S0.

We can construct the ROM contents by building the entire truth table in a form where each row corresponds to one of the 2^n unique input combinations, and a set of columns indicate which outputs are active for that input combination. We don't have the space here to show all 1024 entries in the truth table. However, by separating the datapath-control and next-state outputs we do, since the datapath-control outputs depend only on the current state. The truth table for the datapath-control outputs is shown in Figure C.6. We include only the encodings of the state inputs that are in use (that is, values 0 through 9 corresponding to the 10 states of the state machine)

The truth table in Figure C.6 directly gives the contents of the upper 17 bits of each word in the ROM. The 4-bit input field gives the low-order four address bits of each word and the column gives the contents of the word at that address.

The datapath-control signals depend only on the state input bits—the opcode inputs do not affect these outputs. If we did show a full truth table for the datapath-control bits with both the state number and the opcode bits as inputs, the opcode inputs would all be don't cares. When we construct the ROM, we cannot have any don't cares, since the addresses into the ROM must be complete. Thus, the same datapath-control outputs will occur many times in the ROM, since this part of the ROM is the same whenever the state bits are identical, independent of the value of the opcode inputs.

Op5	Op4	Op3	Op2	Op1	Op0	S3	S2	S1	S0
0	0	0	0	1	0	0	0	0	1
0	0	0	1	0	0	0	0	0	1

a. The truth table for the NS3 output, active when the next state is 8 or 9. This signal is activated from state 1.

Op5	Op4	Op3	Op2	Op1	Op0	S3	S2	S1	S0
0	0	0	0	0	0	0	0	0	1
1	0	1	0	1	1	0	0	1	0
X	X	X	X	X	X	0	0	1	1
X	X	X	X	X	X	0	1	1	0

b. The truth table for the NS2 output, which is active when the next state is 4, 5, 6, or 7. This situation occurs when the current state is one of 1, 2, 3, or 6.

Op5	Op4	Op3	Op2	Op1	Op0	S3	S2	S1	S0
0	0	0	0	0	0	0	0	0	1
1	0	0	0	1	1	0	0	0	1
1	0	1	0	1	1	0	0	0	1
1	0	0	0	1	1	0	0	1	0
X	X	X	X	X	X	0	1	1	0

c. The truth table for the NS1 output, which is active when the next state is 2, 3, 6, or 7. The next state is one of 2, 3, 6, or 7 only if the current state is one of 1, 2, or 6.

Op5	Op4	Op3	Op2	Op1	Op0	S3	S2	S1	S0
X	X	X	X	X	X	0	0	0	0
1	0	0	0	1	1	0	0	1	0
1	0	1	0	1	1	0	0	1	0
X	X	X	X	X	X	0	1	1	0
0	0	0	0	1	0	0	0	0	1

d. The truth table for the NS0 output, which is active when the next state is 1, 3, 5, 7, or 9. This happens only if the current state is one of 0, 1, 2, or 6.

FIGURE C.5 The four truth tables for the four next-state output bits (NS[3–0]). The next-state outputs depend on the value of Op[5–0], which is the opcode field, and the current state, given by S[3–0]. The entries with 'X' are don't care terms. Each entry with a don't care term corresponds to two entries, one with that input at 0 and one with that input at 1. Thus an entry with n don't care terms actually corresponds to 2^n truth table entries.

Outputs	Input values (S[3–0])									
	0000	0001	0010	0011	0100	0101	0110	0111	1000	1001
PCWrite	1	0	0	0	0	0	0	0	0	1
PCWriteCond	0	0	0	0	0	0	0	0	1	0
IorD	0	0	0	1	1	1	0	0	0	0
MemRead	1	0	0	1	1	0	0	0	0	0
MemWrite	0	0	0	0	0	1	0	0	0	0
IRWrite	1	0	0	0	0	0	0	0	0	0
MemtoReg	0	0	0	0	1	0	0	0	0	0
PCSource1	0	0	0	0	0	0	0	0	0	1
PCSource0	0	0	0	0	0	0	0	0	1	0
TargetWrite	0	1	0	0	0	0	0	0	0	0
ALUOp1	0	0	0	0	0	0	1	1	0	0
ALUOp0	0	0	0	0	0	0	0	0	1	0
ALUSelB1	0	1	1	1	1	1	0	0	0	0
ALUSelB0	1	1	0	0	0	0	0	0	0	0
ALUSelA	0	0	1	1	1	1	1	1	1	0
RegWrite	0	0	0	0	1	0	0	1	0	0
RegDst	0	0	0	0	0	0	0	1	0	0

FIGURE C.6 The truth table for the 17 datapath-control outputs, which depend only on the state inputs. The values are determined from Figure C.4. Although there are 16 possible values for the 4-bit state field, only 10 of these are used and are shown here. The 10 possible values are shown at the top; each column shows the setting of the datapath-control outputs for the state input value that appears at top of the column. For example, when the state inputs are 0011 (state 3), the active datapath-control outputs are IorD, MemRead, ALUSelB1, and ALUSelA.

Example

For what ROM addresses will the bit corresponding to PCWrite, the high bit of the control word, be 1?

Answer

PCWrite is high in states 0 and 9, this corresponds to addresses with the low 4-order bits being either 0000 or 1001. The bit will be high in the memory word independent of the inputs Op[5–0], so the addresses with the bit high are 000000000, 0000001001, 0000010000, 0000011001,..., 1111110000, 1111111001. The general form of this is XXXXXX0000 or XXXXXX1001, where XXXXXX is any combination of bits, and correspond to the 6-bit opcode on which this output does not depend.

Lower 4 bits of the address	Bits 20–4 of the word
0000	10010100000001000
0001	00000000010011000
0010	00000000000010100
0011	00110000000010100
0100	00110010000010110
0101	00101000000010100
0110	00000000001000100
0111	00000000001000111
1000	01000000100100100
1001	10000001000000000

FIGURE C.7 The contents of the upper 17 bits of the ROM depend only on the state inputs. These values are the same as those in Figure C.6, simply rotated 90°. This set of control words would be duplicated 64 times for every possible value of the upper 6 bits of the address.

We will show the entire contents of the ROM in two parts to make it easier to show. Figure C.7 shows the upper 17 bits of the control word; this comes directly from Figure C.6. These datapath-control outputs depend only on the state inputs, and this set of words would be duplicated 64 times in the full ROM, as we discussed above. The entries corresponding to input values 1010 through 1111 are not used and we do not care what they contain.

Figure C.8 shows the lower 4 bits of the control word corresponding to the next-state outputs. The last column of the table in Figure C.8 corresponds to all the possible values of the opcode that do not match the specified opcodes. In state 0 the next state is always state 1, since the instruction was still being fetched. After state 1, the opcode field must be valid. The table indicates this by the entries marked illegal; we discuss how to deal with these illegal opcodes in section 5.6.

Not only is this representation as two separate tables a more compact way to show the ROM contents, it is also a more efficient way to implement the ROM. The majority of the outputs (17 of 21 bits) depend only on 4 of the 10 inputs. The number of bits in total when the control is implemented as two separate ROMs is $2^4 \times 17 + 2^{10} \times 4 = 272 + 4096 = 4.3$ Kbits, which is about one-fifth of the size of a single ROM, which requires $2^{10} \times 21 = 21$ Kbits. There is some overhead associated with any structured-logic block, but in this case the additional overhead of an extra ROM would be much smaller than the savings.

Although this ROM encoding of the control function is simple, it is very wasteful, even when divided into two pieces. For example, the values of the Instruction register inputs are often not needed to determine the next state. Thus the next-state ROM has many entries that are either duplicated or are

	Op [5–0]					
Current state S[3–0]	000000 (R format)	000010 (jmp)	000100 (beq)	100011 (lw)	101011 (sw)	Any other value
0000	0001	0001	0001	0001	0001	0001
0001	0110	1001	1000	0010	0010	illegal
0010	XXXX	XXXX	XXXX	0011	0101	illegal
0011	0100	0100	0100	0100	0100	illegal
0100	0000	0000	0000	0000	0000	illegal
0101	0000	0000	0000	0000	0000	illegal
0110	0111	0111	0111	0111	0111	illegal
0111	0000	0000	0000	0000	0000	illegal
1000	0000	0000	0000	0000	0000	illegal
1001	0000	0000	0000	0000	0000	illegal

FIGURE C.8 This table contains the lower 4 bits of the control word (the NS outputs), which depend on both the state inputs, S[3–0], and the opcode, Op [5–0], which correspond to the instruction opcode. These values can be determined from Figure C.5. The opcode name is shown under the encoding in the heading. The 4 bits of the control word whose address is given by the current-state bits and Op bits are shown in each entry. For example, when the state-input bits are 0000, the output is always 0001, independent of the other inputs; when the state is 2, the next state is don't care for three of the inputs, 3 for lw, and 5 for sw. Together with the entries in Figure C.7, this table specifies the contents of the control unit ROM. For example, the word at address 1000110001 is obtained by finding the upper 17 bits in the table in Figure C.7 using only the state input bits (0001) and concatenating the lower 4 bits found by using the entire address (0001 to find the row and 100011 to find the column). The entry from Figure C.7 yields 00000000010010000, while the appropriate entry in the table immediately above is 0010. Thus, the control word at address 1000110001 is 000000000100100000010. The column labeled "any other value" applies only when the Op bits do match one of the specified opcodes.

don't care. Consider the case when the machine is in state 0: There are 2^6 entries in the ROM (since the opcode field can have any value), and these entries will all have the same contents (namely, the control word 10010100000001000). The reason that so much of the ROM is wasted is that the ROM implements the complete truth table providing the opportunity to have a different output for every combination of the inputs. But most combinations of the inputs either never happen or are redundant!

A PLA Implementation

We can reduce the amount of control storage required at the cost of using more complex address decoding for the control inputs, which will encode only the input combinations that are needed. The logic structure most often used to do this is a *programmed logic array* (PLA), which we briefly mentioned earlier and illustrated in Figure 5.31 on page 305. In a PLA, each output is the logical OR of one or more of minterms. A *minterm*, also called a *product term*, is simply a logical AND of one or more inputs. The inputs can be thought of as the address for indexing the PLA, while the minterms select which of all possible address combinations are interesting. A minterm corresponds to a single entry in a truth table, such as those in Figure C.4 on page C-9, including possible don't care terms. Each output consists of an OR of these minterms, which exactly corresponds to a complete truth table. However, unlike a ROM, only those truth table entries that produce an active output are needed, and only one copy of each minterm is required, even if the minterm contains don't cares. Figure C.9 shows the PLA that implements this control function.

As we can see from the PLA in Figure C.9, there are 18 unique minterms—10 that depend only on the current state and 8 others that depend on a combination of the Op field and the current-state bits. The total size of the PLA is proportional to (#inputs × #product terms) + (#outputs × #product terms), as we can see symbolically from the figure. This means the total size of the PLA in Figure C.9 is proportional to $(10 \times 18) + (21 \times 18) = 558$. By comparison, the size of a single ROM is proportional to 21Kbits, and even the two-part ROM has a total of 4.3Kbits. Because the size of a PLA cell will be only slightly larger than the size of a bit in a ROM, a PLA will be a much more efficient implementation for this control unit. Of course, just as we split the ROM in two, we could split the PLA in two. This would yield one PLA whose size is proportional to $(4 \times 10) + (10 \times 17) = 210$, and another PLA whose size is proportional to $(10 \times 8) + (4 \times 8) = 112$. This would yield a total size proportional to 312 PLA cells, about 55% of the size of a single PLA. This will be considerably smaller than a two ROM implementation. The interested reader should see Appendix B for more details on PLAs and their implementation.

C.3 Implementing the Next-State Function with a Sequencer

Let's look carefully at the control unit we built in the last section. If you examine the ROMs that implement the control in Figures C.7 and C.8, you can see that much of the logic is used to specify the next-state function. In fact, for the implementation using two separate ROMs, 4096 out of the 4368 bits (94%) correspond to the next-state function! Furthermore, imagine what the control logic would look like if the instruction set had many more different instruction types, some of which required many clocks to implement. There would be many more states in the finite state machine. In some states, we might be branching to a large number of different states depending on the instruction type (as we did in state 1 of the finite state machine in Figure C.1 on page C-5). However, many of the states would proceed in a sequential fashion, just as states 3 and 4 do in Figure C.1. For example, if we included

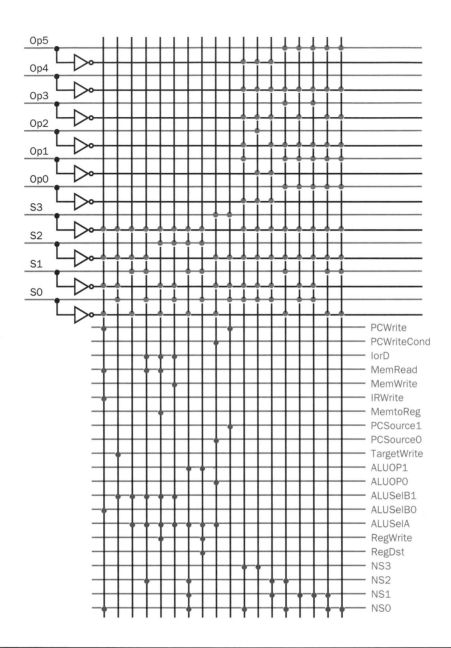

FIGURE C.9 This PLA implements the control function logic for the multicycle implementation. The inputs to the control appear on the left and the outputs on the right. The top half of the figure is the AND plane that computes all the minterms. The minterms are carried to the OR plane on the vertical lines. Each colored dot corresponds to a signal that makes up the minterm carried on that line. The sum terms are computed from these minterms with each grey dot representing the presence of the intersecting minterm in that sum term. Each output consists of a single sum term.

floating point, we would see a sequence of many states in a row that implement a multistep floating-point instruction. Alternatively, consider how the control might look for a machine that can have multiple memory operands per instruction. It would require many more states to fetch multiple memory operands. The result of this would be that the control logic will be dominated by the encoding of the next-state function. Furthermore, much of the logic will be devoted to sequences of states with only one path through them that look like states 2 through 4 in Figure C.1. With more instructions, these sequences will consist of many more sequentially numbered states than for our simple subset.

To encode these more complex control functions efficiently, we can use a control unit that has a counter to supply the sequential next state. This often eliminates the need to encode the next-state function explicitly in the control unit. As shown in Figure C.10, an adder is used to increment the state, essentially turning it into a counter. The incremented state is always the state that follows in numerical order. However, the finite state machine sometimes "branches." For example, in state 1 of the finite state machine (see Figure C.1 on page C-5), there are four possible next states, only one of which is the sequential next state. Thus, we need to be able to choose between the incremented state and a new state based on the inputs from the Instruction register and the current state. Each control word will include control lines that will determine how the next state is chosen.

Since each state in the finite state machine corresponds to a control word in ROM or PLA, we can translate the finite state machine of Figure C.1 into a sequence of control words. It is easy to implement the control output signal portion of the control word, since, if we use the same state numbers, this portion of the control word will look exactly like the ROM contents shown in Figure C.7 on page C-13. However, the method for selecting the next state differs from the next-state function in the finite state machine.

With an explicit counter providing the sequential next state, the control unit logic need only specify how to choose the state when it is not the sequentially following state. There are two methods for doing this. The first is a method we have already seen, namely, the control unit explicitly encodes the next-state function. The difference is that the control unit need only set the next state lines when the designated next state is not the state that the counter indicates. If the number of states is large and the next-state function that we need to encode is mostly empty, this may not be a good choice, since the resulting control unit will have lots of empty or redundant space. An alternative approach is to use separate external logic to specify the next state, when the counter does not specify the state. Many control units, especially those that implement large instruction sets, use this approach, and we will focus on specifying the control externally.

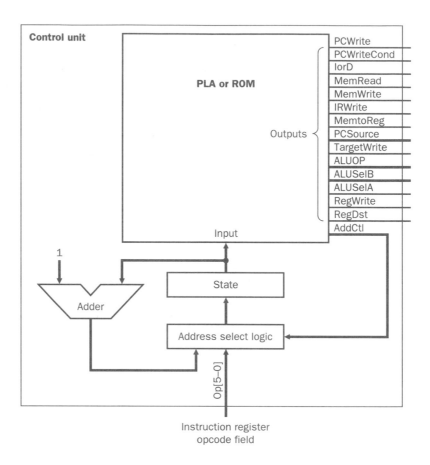

FIGURE C.10 The control unit using an explicit counter to compute the next state. In this control unit, the next state is computed using a counter (at least in some states). By comparison, Figure C.2 on page C-6 encodes the next state in the control logic for every state. In this control unit, the signals labeled AddrCtl control how the next state is determined.

Although the nonsequential next state will come from an external table, the control unit needs to specify when this should occur and how to find that next state. There are two kinds of "branching" that we must implement in the address select logic. First, we must be able to jump to one of a number of states based on the opcode portion of the Instruction register. This operation, called a *dispatch*, is usually implemented by using a set of special ROMS or PLAs included as part of the address selection logic. An additional set of control outputs, which we call AddrCtl, indicates when a dispatch should be done.

Looking at the finite state diagram (Figure C.1 on page C-5), we see that there are two states in which we do a branch based on a portion of the opcode. Thus, we will need two small dispatch tables. (Alternatively, we could also use a single dispatch table and a control output to choose which portion of the dispatch table to select the address from.)

The second type of branching that we must implement consists of branching back to state 0, which initiates the execution of the next MIPS instruction. Thus there are four possible ways to choose the next state (three types of branches, plus incrementing the current-state number), which can be encoded in two bits. Let's assume that the encoding is as follows:

AddrCtl value	Action
0	Set state to 0
1	Dispatch with ROM 1
2	Dispatch with ROM 2
3	Use the incremented state

If we use this encoding, the address select logic for this control unit can be implemented as shown in Figure C.11.

To complete the control unit, we need only specify the contents of the dispatch ROMs, and the values of the address-control lines for each state. We have already specified the datapath-control portion of the control word using the ROM contents of Figure C.7 on page C-13 (or the corresponding portions of the PLA in Figure C.9 on page C-16). The next state counter and dispatch ROMs take the place of the portion of the control unit that was computing the next state, which was shown in Figure C.8 on page C-14. We are only implementing a portion of the instruction set, so the dispatch ROMs will be largely empty. Figure C.12 shows the entries that must be assigned for this subset. Section 5.6 of Chapter 5 discusses what to do with the entries in the dispatch ROMs that do not correspond to any instruction.

Now we can determine the setting of the address selection lines (AddrCtl) in each control word. The table in Figure C.13 shows how the address control must be set for every state. This information will be used to specify the setting of the AddrCtl field in the control word associated with that state.

The contents of the entire control ROM are shown in Figure C.14. The total storage required for the control is quite small. There are ten control words each 19 bits wide for a total of 190 bits. In addition, the two dispatch tables are 4 bits wide and each has 64 entries, for a total of 512 additional bits. This total of 702 bits beats the implementation that uses two ROMs with the next-state function encoded in the ROMs (which requires 4.3K bits).

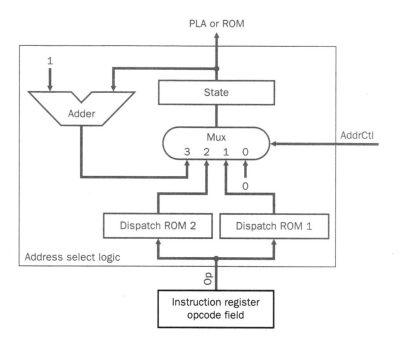

FIGURE C.11 This is the address select logic for the control unit of Figure C.10. A decoder is used to change the two-bit address-control signal into one of four values. This selects which of the four possible sources will supply the new state number.

Of course, the dispatch tables are sparse and could be more efficiently implemented with two small PLAs. The control ROM could also be replaced with a PLA.

Optimizing the Control Implementation

We can further reduce the amount of logic in the control unit by two different techniques. The first is *logic minimization*, which uses the structure of the logic equations, including the don't-care terms, to reduce the amount of hardware required. The success of this process depends on how many entries exist in the truth table, and how those entries are related. For example, in this subset, only the lw and sw opcodes have an active value for the signal Op5, so we can replace the two truth table entries that test whether the input is lw or sw, by a single test on this bit; similarly we can eliminate several bits used to index the dispatch ROM, because this single bit can be used to find lw and sw in the first dispatch ROM. Of course, if the opcode space were less sparse, opportunities

Dispatch ROM 1		
Op	Opcode name	Value
000000	R format	0110
000010	jmp	1001
000100	beq	1000
100011	lw	0010
101011	sw	0010

Dispatch ROM 2		
Op	Opcode name	Value
100011	lw	0011
101011	sw	0101

FIGURE C.12 The dispatch ROMs each have 2^6 = 64 entries that are 4 bits wide, since that is the number of bits in the state encoding. This figure only shows the entries in the ROM that are of interest for this subset. The first column in each table indicates the value of Op, which is the address used to access the dispatch ROM. The second column shows the symbolic name, which is the opcode. The third column indicates the value at that address in the ROM.

State number	Address-control action	Value of AddrCtl
0	Use incremented state	3
1	Use dispatch ROM 1	1
2	Use dispatch ROM 2	2
3	Use incremented state	3
4	Replace state number by 0	0
5	Replace state number by 0	0
6	Use incremented state	3
7	Replace state number by 0	0
8	Replace state number by 0	0
9	Replace state number by 0	0

FIGURE C.13 The values of the address-control lines are set in the control word that corresponds to each state.

for this optimization would be more difficult to locate. However, in choosing the opcodes the architect can provide additional opportunities by choosing related opcodes for instructions that are likely to share states in the control.

A different sort of optimization can be done by assigning the state numbers in a finite state or microcode implementation to minimize the logic. This optimization, called *state assignment*, tries to choose the state numbers such that the resulting logic equations contain more redundancy and can thus be simplified. Let's consider the case of a finite state machine with an encoded next-state control first, since it allows states to be assigned arbitrarily. For example, notice

State number	Control word bits 18–2	Control word bits 1–0
0	10010100000001000	11
1	00000000010011000	01
2	00000000000010100	10
3	00110000000010100	11
4	00110010000010110	00
5	00101000000010100	00
6	00000000001000100	11
7	00000000001000111	00
8	01000000100100100	00
9	10000001000000000	00

FIGURE C.14 The contents of the control memory for an implementation using an explicit counter. The first column shows the state, while the second shows the datapath-control bits, and the last column shows the address-control bits in each control word. Bits 18–2 are identical to those in Figure C.7.

that in the finite state machine the signal RegWrite is active only in states 4 and 7. If we encoded those states as 8 and 9, rather than 4 and 7, we could rewrite the equation for RegWrite as simply a test on bit S3 (which is only on for states 8 and 9). This allows us to combine the two truth table entries in part p of Figure C.4 on page C-9 and replace them with a single entry, eliminating one term in the control unit. Of course, we would have to renumber the existing states 8 and 9, perhaps as 4 and 7. The same optimization can be applied in an implementation that uses an explicit program counter, though we are more restricted. Because the next-state number is often computed by incrementing the current-state number, we cannot arbitrarily assign the states. However, if we keep the states where the incremented state is used as the next state in the same order, we can reassign the consecutive states as a block. In an implementation with an explicit next state counter, state assignment may allow us to simplify the contents of the dispatch ROMs.

If we look again at the control unit in Figure C.10 on page C-18 it looks remarkably like a computer in its own right. The ROM or PLA can be thought of as memory supplying instructions for the datapath. The state can be thought of as an instruction address. Hence the origin of the name *microcode* or *microprogrammed* control. The control words are thought of as *microinstructions* that control the datapath, and the State register is called the microprogram counter. Figure C.15 shows a view of the control unit as *microcode*. The next section describes how we map from a microprogram to microcode.

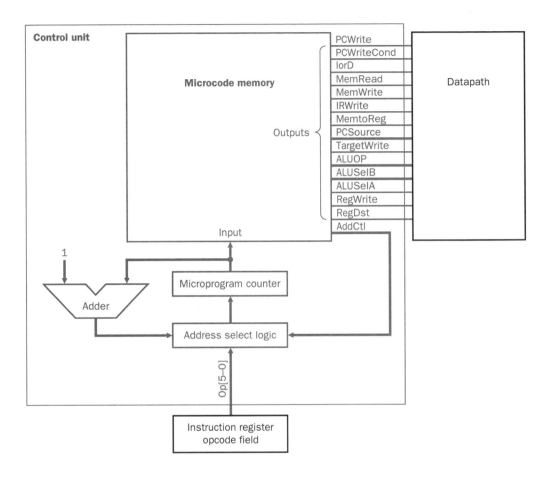

FIGURE C.15 The control unit as a microcode. The use of the word "micro" serves to distinguish between the program counter in the datapath and the microprogram counter, and between the microcode memory and the instruction memory.

C.4   Translating a Microprogram to Hardware

To translate the microprogram of section 5.5 into actual hardware, we need to specify how each field translates into control signals. We can implement the microprogram with either finite-state control or a microcode implementation with an explicit sequencer. If we choose a finite state machine, we need to construct the next-state function from the microprogram. Once this function is known, we can map a set of truth table entries for the next-state outputs. In this section, we will show how to translate the microprogram assuming that the next state is specified by a sequencer. From the truth tables we will construct, it would be straightforward to build the next-state function for a finite state machine.

Assuming an explicit sequencer, we need to do two additional tasks to translate the microprogram: assign addresses to the microinstructions and fill in the contents of the dispatch ROMs. This process is essentially the same as the process of translating an assembly language program into machine instructions: the fields of the assembly language or microprogram instruction are translated and labels on the instructions must be resolved to addresses.

Figure C.16 shows the various values for each microinstruction field that controls the datapath and how these fields are encoded as control signals. If the field corresponding to a signal that affects a unit with state (i.e., Memory, Memory Register, ALU destination, or PCWriteControl) is blank, then no control signal should be active. If a field corresponding to a multiplexor control signal or the ALU operation control (i.e., ALUOp, SRC1, or SRC2) is blank, the output is unused so the associated signals may be set as don't care.

The sequencing field can have four values: Fetch (meaning go to the Fetch state), dispatch 1, dispatch 2, and seq. These four values are encoded to set the 2-bit address control just as they were in Figure C.17 on page C-26: Fetch = 0, Dispatch 1 = 1. Dispatch 2 = 2, Seq = 3. Finally, we need to specify the contents of the dispatch tables to relate the dispatch entries of the sequence field to the symbolic labels in the microprogram. We specify these in Figure C.12.

A microcode assembler would use the encoding of the sequencing field, the contents of the symbolic dispatch tables in Figure C.17, the specification in Figure C.16, and the actual microprogram in Figure 5.51 on page 342 to generate the microinstructions.

Since the microprogram is an abstract representation of the control, there is a great deal of flexibility in how the microprogram is translated. For example, the address assigned to many of the microinstructions can be chosen arbitrarily, the only restrictions are those imposed by the fact that certain microinstructions must occur in sequential order (so that incrementing the State register generates the address of the next instruction). Thus the microcode assembler may reduce the complexity of the control by assigning the microinstructions cleverly.

Organizing the Control to Reduce the Logic

For a machine with complex control, there may be a great deal of logic in the control unit. The control ROM or PLA may be very costly. Although our simple implementation had only a 21-bit microinstruction, there have been machines with microinstructions that are hundreds of bits wide. Clearly, one would like to reduce the number of microinstructions and the width. The

Field name	Value	Signals active	Comment
ALU control	Add	ALUOp=00	ALU adds.
	Func. code	ALUOp=10	ALU uses function code.
	Subtract	ALUOp=01	ALU does subtract.
SRC1	PC	ALUSelA=0	PC is the first operand.
	rs	ALUSelA=1	Register rs is source.
SRC2	1	ALUSelB=01	Use 1 as the second ALU input.
	Extend	ALUSelB=10	Use the sign extend (IR[15–0]) as second input operand.
	Extshft	ALUSelB=11	Use the sign-extended, shifted offset as second input.
	rt	ALUSelB=00.	Register rt is the second ALU input.
ALU destination	Target	TargetWrite	Write the ALUoutput to the register Target.
	rd	RegWrite, RegDst=1, MemtoReg=0.	Write the ALU output to the register number rd.
Memory	Read PC	MemRead, IorD=0.	Read from memory; address is in PC.
	Read ALU	MemRead, IorD=1	Read from memory; address is the ALU output.
	Write ALU	MemWrite, IorD=1	Write to memory; address is the ALU output.
Memory register	IR	IRWrite	Causes the IR to be written from memory.
	Read rt		No signals needed since rt is always source for a store.
	Write rt	RegWrite, MemtoReg=1 RegDst=0	Causes the result from memory to be written in the register given the rt field.
PC write control	ALU	PCSource=00, PCWrite	Write the ALU output into the PC.
	Target–cond.	PCWriteCond, PCSource=01	If ALU Zero output is active, then write the value in Target into the PC.
	Jump address	PCWrite, PCSource=10	Write the jump target address into the PC.
Sequencing	seq	AddrCtl=11	The next microinstruction follows sequentially.
	fetch	AddrCtl=00	The next microinstruction is the one labeled Fetch.
	dispatch 1	AddrCtl=01	Use dispatch ROM 1 to choose next microinstruction.
	dispatch 2	AddrCtl=10	Use dispatch ROM 2 to choose next microinstruction.

FIGURE C.16 Each microcode field translates to a set (possibly empty) of control signals to be set. These 23 different values of the fields specify all the required combinations of the 19 control lines. Control lines that are not set which correspond to actions are 0 by default. Multiplexor control lines are set to 0 if the output matters. If a multiplexor control line is not explicitly set, its output is a don't care and is not used.

Microcode dispatch table 1		
Opcode field	Opcode name	Value
000000	R format	Rformat1
000010	jmp	Jump1
000100	beq	BEQ1
100011	lw	LWSW1
101011	sw	LWSW1

Microcode dispatch table 2		
Opcode field	Opcode name	Value
100011	lw	LW2
101011	sw	SW2

FIGURE C.17 The two microcode dispatch ROMs showing the contents in symbolic form and using the labels in the microprogram.

ideal approach to reducing control store is to first write the complete micro-program in a symbolic notation and then measure how control lines are set in each microinstruction. By taking measurements we are able to recognize control bits that can be encoded into a smaller field. For example, if more than one of 8 lines is set simultaneously in the same microinstruction, then they can be encoded into a 3-bit field ($\log_2 8 = 3$). This change saves 5 bits in every microinstruction and does not hurt CPI, though it does mean the extra hardware cost of a 3-to-8 decoder needed to generate the 8 control lines when they are required at the datapath. It may also have some small clock cycle impact, since the decoder is in the signal path. However, shaving 5 bits off control-store width will usually overcome the cost of the decoder, and the cycle time impact will probably be small or nonexistent. This technique can be applied to the microinstructions in this machine, since only 1 bit of the first 3 bits of the control word is ever active (see Figure C.14 on page C-22).

This technique of reducing field width is called *encoding*. To further save space, control lines may be encoded together if they are only occasionally set in the same microinstruction; two microinstructions instead of one are then required when both must be set. As long as this doesn't happen in critical routines, the narrower microinstruction may justify a few extra words of control store.

Microinstructions can be made narrower still if they are broken into different formats and given an opcode or *format field* to distinguish them. The format field gives all the unspecified control lines their default values, so as not to change anything else in the machine, and is similar to the opcode of an instruction in a more powerful instruction set. For example, we could use a different format for microinstructions that did memory accesses from those that did register-register ALU operations, taking advantage of the fact that the memory access control lines are not needed in microinstructions controlling ALU operations.

Reducing hardware costs by using format fields usually has an additional performance cost beyond the requirement for more decoders. A microprogram using a single microinstruction format can specify any combination of operations in a datapath and can take fewer clock cycles than a microprogram made up of restricted microinstructions that cannot perform any combination of operations in a single microinstruction. However, if the full capability of the wider microprogram word is not heavily used, then much of the control store will be wasted and the machine could be made smaller and faster by restricting the microinstruction capability.

The narrow, but usually longer, approach is often called *vertical microcode,* while the wide but short approach is called *horizontal microcode.* It should be noted that the terms "vertical microcode" and "horizontal microcode" have no universal definition—the designers of the 8086 considered its 21-bit microinstruction to be more horizontal than other single-chip computers of the time. The related terms, *maximally encoded* and *minimally encoded*, are probably better than vertical and horizontal.

C.5   Concluding Remarks

We began this chapter by looking at how to translate a finite state diagram to an implementation using a finite state machine. We then looked at explicit sequencers that use a different technique for realizing the next-state function. Although large microprograms are often targeted at implementations using this explicit next state approach, we can also implement a microprogram with a finite state machine. As we saw, both ROM and PLA implementations of the logic functions are possible. The advantages of explicit versus encoded next state and ROM versus PLA implementation are summarized below.

The Big Picture

Independent of whether the control is represented as a finite state diagram or as a microprogram, translation to a hardware control implementation is similar. Each state or microinstruction asserts a set of control outputs and specifies how to choose the next state.

The next-state function may be implemented by either encoding it in a finite state machine or by using an explicit sequencer. The explicit sequencer is more efficient if the number of states is large and there are many sequences of consecutive states without branching.

The control logic may be implemented with either ROMS or PLAs (or even a mix). PLAs are more efficient unless the control function is very dense. ROMs may be appropriate if the control is stored in a separate memory, as opposed to within the same chip as the datapath.

Exercises

C.1 [5] <§C.2> {ex. 5.1, 5.2} How many product terms are required in a PLA that implements the single-cycle datapath for jal assuming the control additions described in Exercises 5.1–5.2 on page 357?

C.2 [10] <§C.2> {ex. 5.5} Determine the number of product terms in a PLA that implements the finite state machine for jal constructed in Exercise 5.5 on page 357. The easiest method to do this is to construct the truth tables for any new outputs or any outputs affected by the addition.

C.3 [5] <§C.2> {ex. 5.12} How many product terms are required in a PLA that implements the single-cycle datapath and control for addiu assuming the control additions you needed were found in Exercise 5.12 on page 359.

C.4 [10] <§C.2> {ex. 5.15} Determine the number of product terms in a PLA that implements the finite state machine for addiu in Exercise 5.15 on page 359. The easiest way to do this is to construct the additions to the truth tables for addiu.

C.5 [20] <§C.3> {ex. 5.15} Implement the finite state machine of Exercise 5.15 using an explicit counter to determine the next state. Fill in the new entries for the additions to the Figure C.14 on page C-22. Also, add any entries needed to the dispatch ROMs of Figure C.12 on page C-21.

C.6 [15] <§C.2–C.5> {ex. C.5} Determine the size of the PLAs needed to implement the multicycle machine assuming that the next-state function using a counter. Implement the dispatch tables of Figure C.12 on page C-21 using two PLAs, and the contents of the main control unit in Figure C.14 on page C-22 using another PLA. How does the total size of this solution compare to the single PLA solution with the next state encoded? What if the main PLAs for both approaches are split into two separate PLAs, by factoring out the next state or address select signals?

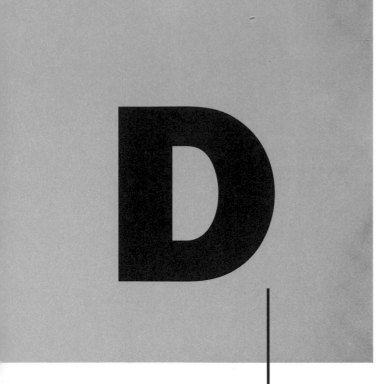

A P P E N D I X

Introducing C
to Pascal
Programmers

*C is not a "very high level" language . . . and is
not specialized to any particular area of application. But its absence of restrictions and its generality
make it more convenient and effective for many
tasks than supposedly more powerful languages.*

Brian W. Kernighan and Dennis M. Ritchie
The C Programming Language, Preface, 1978

*A primary motivation for . . . Pascal was
the need for a powerful and flexible language
that could be reasonably efficiently implemented on most computers.*

Kathleen Jensen and Niklaus Wirth
Pascal User Manual and Report, pp. 165, 197

D.1 Introduction

This Appendix is meant for readers familiar with Pascal but not C. It is not intended as a tutorial on how to write C programs, but as a way of allowing the reader familiar with Pascal to better understand the small amount of C code that appears in this book. Given the level of examples in this book, these differences are primarily syntactic.

D.2 Variable Declarations

There is no standard Pascal type for unsigned integers or double precision floating point. Also, Pascal ignores capitalization in variable names while capitalization counts in C. For example, `Apple` and `apple` are different variables in C. Here are the corresponding standard types:

Type	C declaration	Pascal declaration
Integer	`int`	`integer`
Single precision floating point	`float`	`real`
Unsigned integer	`unsigned int`	?
Double precision floating point	`double`	?

D.3   Assignment Statements

The primary difference is that C uses the "=" while Pascal uses ":=" to indicate an assignment. Here are C examples from the book with their equivalents in Pascal.

Examples in C	Corresponding Pascal code
`a = b + c;`	`a := b + c;`
`d = a - e;`	`d := a - e;`
`f = (g + h) - (i + j);`	`f := (g + h) - (i + j);`
`g = h + P[i];`	`g := h + P[i];`
`P[i] = h + P[i];`	`P[i] := h + P[i];`

In addition to standard arithmetic operators (+,-,*,/), C has some logical operators sometimes found as library routines in other languages.

Logical operations	C operator
Shift Left	`<<`
Shift Right	`>>`
AND	`&`
OR	`|`
XOR	`^`
NOT	`~`

Operators << and >> are logical operations only on unsigned integers in C.

D.4 Relational Expressions and Conditional Statements

There is more difference in the *if* statements of the two programming languages, both in the statements themselves and in the expressions that commonly occur. C leaves off the keyword "then" in the traditional *if* statement, and since "=" is used to mean assignment, new symbols are used to mean relational equality. The table below shows the mapping of the relational operators in both languages:

Operation	C	Pascal
Equal	==	=
Not equal	!=	<>
Less than	<	<
Less than or equal	<=	<=
Greater than	>	>
Greater than or equal	>=	>=

Here are two examples of *if* statements.

C	Pascal
`if (i == j) f = g + h;` `    else f = g - h;`	`if i = j then f := g + h` `    else f := g - h;`

`if (i == j) goto L1;`
`f = g + h;`
`L1: f = f - i;`
	`if i = j then goto 1;`
	`f := g + h;`
	`1:  f := f - i;`

C replaces the `begin end` of Pascal's compound statements with { }.

The *case* statement in Pascal is quite similar to the *switch* statement in C. Each switching alternative in C starts with the keyword "case" and ends with the keyword "break." Here are equivalent statements:

C	Pascal
| ```
switch (k) {
    case 0: f = i + j; break;
    case 1: f = g + h; break;
    case 2: f = g - h; break;
    case 3: f = i - j; break;
};
``` | ```
case k of
    0: f := i + j;
    1: f := g + h;
    2: f := g - h;
    3: f := i - j;
end;
``` |

D.5   Loops

The *while* loops are almost identical in the two languages. Here is an example:

C	Pascal
| ```
while (save[i] == k)
    i = i + j;
``` | ```
while save[i] = k do
    i := i + j;
``` |

Of course, *while* loops can be constructed from `gotos`:

C	Pascal
| ```
Loop:   g = g + P[i];
        i = i + j;
        if (i != h) goto Loop;
``` | ```
2:   g := g + P[i];
     i := i + j;
     if i <> h then goto 2;
``` |

The *for* statement may be the most unusual. In keeping with the philosophy of no restrictions, the initialization, exit test, and per loop operation can be any statements. They appear in three pieces in that order in the *for* statement:

C	Pascal
| ```
for (i = 0; i < n; i = i + 1)
    {...}
``` | ```
for i := 0 to n - 1 do
    begin ... end
``` |

In addition to the relational operators, there are logical relational operators to connect conditions. Here they are in the two languages:

Operation	C	Pascal
And	&&	and
Or	||	or
Not	!	not

This example shows some of the power of the *for* statement; the compound exit test requires nested statements in Pascal.

C	Pascal

``
for (j = i - 1; j >= 0
    && v[j] > v[j + 1]; j = j - 1)
    { ... }
``
	``
	    for j := i - 1 downto 0 do
	        if v[j] > v[j + 1] then
	            begin ... end
	        else goto 3;
	3: ...
	``

D.6   Examples to Put it All Together

Procedures in C and Pascal are quite similar. The primary difference is that arrays are normally declared as types, with the type name used to declare array variables:

C	Pascal

``
 	
swap (int v[], int k)
 	
{
    int temp;
 	
    temp   = v[k];
    v[k]   = v[k + 1];
    v[k + 1] = temp;
};
``
	``
	type
	names = array [0..19] of integer;
	...
	procedure swap (var v: names;
	                k: integer);
	    var
	     temp: integer;
	begin
	    temp := v[k];
	    v[k] := v[k + 1];
	    v[k + 1] := temp
	end;
	``

Here is a longer example::

C	Pascal

``
sort (int v[], int n)
 	
{
  int i, j;
 	
  for (i = 0; i < n; i = i + 1)
    for (j = i-1; j >= 0 &&
        v[j] > v[j + 1]; j = j - 1)
      swap(v,j);
 	
};
``
	``
	procedure sort (var v: names;
	                      n: integer);
	  var
	    i, j: integer;
	  begin
	    for i := 0 to n - 1 do
	      for j := i-1 downto 0 do
	        if v[j] > v[j + 1] then
	            swap(v,j)
	        else goto 4;
	    4: ;
	  end;
	``

To Probe Further

Kernighan, Brian W. and Dennis M. Ritchie [1988]. *The C Programming Language*, 2nd edition, Prentice Hall, Englewood Cliffs, N.J.

This classic text is so widely used it's known as "K&R"; be sure to get the second edition. The first section, which is a tutorial, is a good introduction to C for someone who knows how to program.

Tondo, Clovis L. and Scott E. Gimpel [1989]. *The C Answer Book: Solutions to the Exercises in The C Programming Language*, 2nd edition, Prentice Hall, Englewood Cliffs, N.J.

The second edition of this book has the answers to the exercises in the second edition of K&R.

D.7   Exercises

D.1 [5] Write a Pascal version of the C program for summing shown in Appendix A, Figure A.5 on page A-8.

D.2 [5] Write a Pascal version of the first C procedure to set an array to zero, Clear1, shown in Chapter 3, Figure 3.22 on page 145.

D.3 [10] Write a Pascal version of the second C procedure to set an array to zero, Clear2, shown in Chapter 3, Figure 3.22 on page 145.

A P P E N D I X

Another Approach to Instruction Set Architecture—VAX

In principle, there is no great challenge in designing a large virtual address minicomputer system . . . . The real challenge lies in two areas: compatibility—very tangible and important; and simplicity—intangible but nonetheless important.

William Strecker
"VAX-11/780—A Virtual Address Extension to the PDP-11 Family,"
AFIPS Proc., National Computer Conference, 1978.

Entities should not be multiplied unnecessarily.

William of Occam
Quodlibeta Septem, 1320
(This quote is known as "Occam's Razor.")

E.1 Introduction

The purpose of this appendix is to give you insight into an alternative to the *Reduced Instruction Set Computer* (*RISC*) used in this book. To enhance your understanding of instruction set architectures, we chose the VAX as the representative *Complex Instruction Set Computers* (*CISC*) because it is so different from MIPS and yet still easy to understand. By seeing two such divergent styles, we are confident that you will be able to learn other instruction sets on your own.

At the time the VAX was designed, the prevailing philosophy was to create instruction sets that were close to programming languages in order to simplify compilers. For example, because programming languages had loops, instruction sets should have loop instructions. As VAX architect William Strecker said ("VAX-11/780—A Virtual address Extension to the PDP-11 Family," AFIPS Proc., National Computer Conference, 1978):

> A major goal of the VAX-11 instruction set was to provide for effective compiler generated code. Four decisions helped to realize this goal: . . . 1) A very regular and consistent treatment of operators. . . . 2) An avoidance of instructions unlikely to be generated by a compiler. . . . 3) Inclusions of several forms of common operators. . . . 4) Replacement of common instruction sequences with single instructions. Examples include procedure calling, multiway branching, loop control, and array subscript calculation.

Recall that DRAMs of the mid-1970s contained less than 1/1000th the capacity of today's DRAMs, so code space was also critical. Hence, another prevailing philosophy was to minimize code size, which is de-emphasized in fixed-length instruction sets like MIPS. For example, MIPS address fields always use 16 bits, even when the address is very small. In contrast, the VAX allows instructions to be a variable number of bytes, so there is little wasted space in address fields.

Books the size of the one you are reading have been written just about the VAX, so a VAX appendix cannot be exhaustive. Hence, the following sections describe only a few of its addressing modes and instructions. To show the VAX instructions in action, later sections show VAX assembly code for two C procedures from Chapter 3. The general style will be to contrast these instructions with the MIPS code that you are already familiar with.

The Big Picture

The differing goals for VAX and MIPS have led to very different architectures. The VAX goals, simple compilers and code density, led to the powerful addressing modes, powerful instructions, and efficient instruction encoding. The MIPS goals were high performance via pipelining, ease of hardware implementation, and compatibility with highly optimizing compilers. The MIPS goals led to simple instructions, simple addressing modes, fixed-length instruction formats, and a large number of registers.

E.2   VAX Operands and Addressing Modes

The VAX is a 32-bit architecture, with 32-bit wide addresses and 32-bit wide registers. Yet the VAX supports many other data sizes and types, as Figure E.1 shows. Unfortunately, VAX uses the name "word" to refer to 16-bit quantities; in this text a word means 32 bits. Figure E.1 shows the conversion between the MIPS data type names and the VAX names. Be careful when reading about VAX instructions, as they refer to the names of the VAX data types.

The VAX provides 16 32-bit registers. The VAX assembler uses the notation r0, r1, ..., r15 to refer to these registers, and we will stick to that notation. Alas, 4 of these 16 registers are effectively claimed by the instruction set architecture. For example, r14 is the stack pointer (sp) and r15 is the program

Bits	Data type	MIPS name	VAX name
8	Integer	Byte	Byte
16	Integer	Halfword	Word
32	Integer	Word	Long word
32	Floating point	Single precision	F_floating
64	Integer	Doubleword	Quad word
64	Floating point	Double precision	D_floating or G_floating
8n	Character string	Character	Character

FIGURE E.1 VAX data types, their lengths, and names. The first letter of the VAX type (b, w, l, f, q, d, g, c) is often used to complete an instruction name. Examples of move instructions include movb, movw, movl, movf, movq, movd, movg, and movc3. Each move instruction transfers an operand of the data type indicated by the letter following mov.

counter (pc). Hence, r15 cannot be used as a general-purpose register, and using r14 is very difficult because it interferes with instructions that manipulate the stack. The other dedicated registers are r12, used as the argument pointer (ap), and r13, used as the frame pointer (fp); their purpose will become clear later. (Like MIPS, the VAX assembler accepts either the register number or the register name.)

VAX addressing modes include those discussed in Chapter 3, which has all the MIPS addressing modes: *register*, *displacement*, *immediate*, and *PC-relative*. Moreover, all these modes can be used for jump addresses or for data addresses. Chapter 3 also has *autoincrement* and *autodecrement* addressing, mentioned in section 3.8.

But that's not all the addressing modes. To reduce code size, the VAX has three lengths of addresses for displacement addressing: 8-bit, 16-bit, and 32-bit addresses called, respectively, *byte displacement*, *word displacement*, and *long displacement* addressing. Thus, an address can be not only as small as possible, but also as large as necessary; large addresses need not be split, so there is no equivalent to the MIPS lui instruction (see page 125).

That's still not all the VAX addressing modes. Several have a *deferred* option, meaning that the object addressed is only the *address* of the real object, requiring another memory access to get the operand. This addressing mode is called *indirect addressing* in other machines. Thus, *register deferred*, *autoincrement deferred*, and *byte/word/long displacement deferred* are other addressing modes to choose from. For example, using the notation of the VAX assembler, r1 means the operand is register 1 and (r1) means the operand is the location in memory pointed to by r1.

There is yet another addressing mode. *Indexed addressing* automatically converts the value in an index operand to the proper byte address to add to the rest of the address. Recall the swap example from Chapter 3 (page 125); we

Addressing mode name	Syntax	Example	Meaning	Length of address specifier in bytes
Literal	#value	#−1	−1	1 (6-bit signed value)
Immediate	#value	#100	100	1 + length of the immediate
Register	rn	r3	r3	1
Register deferred	(rn)	(r3)	Memory[r3]	1
Byte/word/long displacement	Displacement (rn)	100(r3)	Memory[r3 + 100]	1 + length of the displacement
Byte/word/long displacement deferred	@displacement (rn)	@100(r3)	Memory[Memory [r3 + 100]]	1 + length of the displacement
Indexed (scaled)	Base mode [rx]	(r3)[r4]	Memory[r3 + r4 × d] (where d is data size in bytes)	1 + length of base addressing mode
Autoincrement	(rn)+	(r3)+	Memory[r3]; r3 = r3 + d	1
Autodecrement	− (rn)	−(r3)	r3 = r3 − d; Memory[r3]	1
Autoincrement deferred	@(rn)+	@(r3)+	Memory[Memory[r3]]; r3 = r3 + d	1

FIGURE E.2 Definition and length of the VAX operand specifiers. The length of each addressing mode is 1 byte plus the length of any displacement or immediate field needed by the mode. Literal mode uses a special 2-bit tag and the remaining 6 bits encode the constant value. If the constant is too big, it must use the immediate addressing mode. Note the length of an immediate operand is dictated by the length of the data type indicated in the opcode, not the value of the immediate. The symbol d in the last four modes represents the length of the data in bytes; d is 4 for 32-bit add.

needed to multiply the index of a 4-byte quantity by 4 before adding it to a base address. Indexed addressing, called *scaled addressing* on some computers, automatically multiplies the index of a 4-byte quantity by 4 as part of the address calculation.

To cope with such a plethora of addressing options, the VAX architecture separates the specification of the addressing mode from the specification of the operation. Hence, the opcode supplies the operation and the number of operands, and each operand has its own addressing mode specifier. Figure E.2 shows the name, assembler notation, example, meaning, and length of the address specifier.

The VAX style of addressing means that an operation doesn't know where its operands come from; a VAX add instruction can have three operands in registers, three operands in memory, or any combination of registers and memory operands.

Example

How long is the following instruction?

```
add13 r1,737(r2),(r3)[r4]
```

The name `add13` means a 32-bit add instruction with three operands. Assume the length of the VAX opcode is 1 byte.

Answer

The first operand specifier—`r1`— indicates register addressing and is 1 byte long. The second operand specifier—`737(r2)`—indicates displacement addressing and has two parts: the first part is a byte that specifies the word-displacement addressing mode and base register (`r2`); the second part is the 2-byte long displacement (`737`). The third operand specifier—`(r3)[r4]`— also has two parts: the first byte specifies register deferred addressing mode (`(r3)`), and the second byte specifies the Index register and the use of indexed addressing (`[r4]`).

Thus, the total length of the instruction is 1 + (1) + (1+2) + (1+1) = 7 bytes.

In this example instruction, we show the VAX destination operand on the left and the source operands on the right, just as we show MIPS code. The VAX assembler actually expects operands in the opposite order, but we felt it would be less confusing to keep the destination on the left for both machines. Obviously, left or right orientation is arbitrary; the only requirement is consistency.

Elaboration: Because the PC is one of the 16 registers that can be selected in a VAX addressing mode, 4 of the 22 VAX addressing modes are synthesized from other addressing modes. Using the PC as the chosen register in each case, *immediate* addressing is really autoincrement, *PC-relative* is displacement, *absolute* is autoincrement deferred, and *relative deferred* is displacement deferred.

E.3   Encoding VAX Instructions

Given the independence of the operations and addressing modes, the encoding of instructions is quite different from MIPS.

VAX instructions begin with a single byte opcode containing the operation and the number of operands. The operands follow the opcode. Each operand begins with a single byte, called the *address specifier*, that describes the addressing mode for that operand. For a simple addressing mode, such as register ad-

Byte address	Contents at each byte	Machine code
201	opcode containing add13	c1$_{hex}$
202	index mode specifier for [r4]	44$_{hex}$
203	register indirect mode specifier for (r3)	63$_{hex}$
204	word displacement mode specifier using r2 as base	c2$_{hex}$
205	the 16-bit constant 737	e1$_{hex}$
206		02$_{hex}$
207	register mode specifier for r1	51$_{hex}$

FIGURE E.3 The encoding of the VAX instruction addl3 r1,737(r2),(r3)[r4], assuming it starts at address 201. To satisfy your curiosity, the right column shows the actual VAX encoding in hexadecimal notation (page 175 describes hexadecimal notation). Note that the 16-bit constant 737$_{ten}$ takes two bytes.

dressing, this byte specifies the register number as well as the mode (see the rightmost column in Figure E.2). In other cases, this initial byte can be followed by many more bytes to specify the rest of the address information.

As a specific example, let's show the encoding of the add instruction from the example on page E-7:

```
addl3 r1,737(r2),(r3)[r4]
```

Assume that this instruction starts at location 201.

Figure E.3 shows the encoding. Note that the operands are stored in memory in opposite order to the assembly code above. The execution of VAX instructions begins with fetching the source operands, so it makes sense for them to come first. Order is not important in fixed-length instructions like MIPS, since the source and destination operands are easily found within a 32-bit word.

The first byte, at location 201, is the opcode. The next byte, at location 202, is a specifier for the index mode using register r4. Like many of the other specifiers, the left 4 bits of the specifier give the mode and the right 4 bits give the register used in that mode. Since addl3 is a 4-byte operation, r4 will be multiplied by 4 and added to whatever address is specified next. In this case it is register deferred addressing using register r3. Thus bytes 202 and 203 combined define the third operand in the assembly code.

The following byte, at address 204, is a specifier for word displacement addressing using register r2 as the base register. This specifier tells the VAX that the following two bytes, locations 205 and 206, contain a 16-bit address to be added to r2.

The final byte of the instruction gives the destination operand, and this specifier selects register addressing using register r1.

Such variability in addressing means that a single VAX operation can have many different lengths; for example, an integer add varies from 3 bytes to 19 bytes. VAX implementations must decode the first operand before they can find the second, and so implementors are strongly tempted to take one clock cycle to decode each operand; thus this sophisticated instruction set architecture can result higher clock cycles per instruction, even when using simple addresses.

E.4   VAX Operations

In keeping with its philosophy, the VAX has a large number of operations as well as a large number of addressing modes. We review a few here to give the flavor of the machine.

Given the power of the addressing modes, the VAX *move* instruction performs several operations found in other machines. It transfers data between any two addressable locations and subsumes load, store, register–register moves, and memory–memory moves as special cases. The first letter of the VAX data type (b, w, l, f, q, d, g, c in Figure E.1) is appended to the acronym `mov` to determine the size of the data. One special move, called *move address*, moves the 32-bit *address* of the operand rather than the data. It uses the acronym `mova`.

The arithmetic operations of MIPS are also found in the VAX, with two major differences. First, the type of the data is attached to the name. Thus `addb`, `addw`, and `addl` operate on 8-bit, 16-bit, and 32-bit data in memory or registers, respectively; MIPS has a single add instruction that operates only on the full 32-bit register. The second difference is that to reduce code size, the add instruction specifies the number of unique operands; MIPS always specifies three even if one operand is redundant. For example, the MIPS instruction

```
add    $1, $1, $2
```

takes 32 bits like all MIPS instructions, but the VAX instruction

```
addl2  r1, r2
```

uses `r1` for both the destination and a source, taking just 24 bits: 8 bits for the opcode and 8 bits each for the two register specifiers.

Number of Operations

Now we can show how VAX instruction names are formed:

$$(\text{operation})\,(\text{datatype}) \begin{pmatrix} 2 \\ 3 \end{pmatrix}$$

The operation add works with data types byte, word, long, float, and double and comes in versions for either 2 or 3 unique operands, so the following instructions are all found in the VAX:

addb2	addw2	addl2	addf2	addd2
addb3	addw3	addl3	addf3	addd3

Accounting for all addressing modes (but ignoring register numbers and immediate values) and limiting to just byte, word, and long, there are more than 30,000 versions of integer add in the VAX; MIPS has just 4!

Another reason for the large number of VAX instructions is the instructions that either replace sequences of instructions or take fewer bytes to represent a single instruction. Here are four such examples (* means the data type):

VAX operation	Example	Meaning
clr*	clrl r3	r3 = 0
inc*	incl r3	r3 = r3 + 1
dec*	decl r3	r3 = r3 − 1
push*	pushl r3	sp = sp − 4; Memory[sp] = r3;

The *push* instruction is the last row is exactly the same as using the move instruction with autodecrement addressing on the stack pointer:

    movl -(sp), r3

Brevity is the advantage of pushl: it is one byte shorter since sp is implied.

Branches, Jumps, and Procedure Calls

The VAX branch instructions are related to the arithmetic instructions because the branch instructions rely on *condition codes*. Condition codes are set as a side-effect of an operation, and they indicate whether the result is positive, negative, zero, or if an overflow occurred (see page 176 in Chapter 4). Most instructions set the VAX condition codes according to their result; instructions without results, such as branches, do not. The VAX condition codes are N (Negative), Z (Zero), V (oVerflow), and C (Carry). There is also a *compare* instruction cmp* just to set the condition codes for a subsequent branch.

The VAX branch instructions include all conditions. Popular branch instructions include beql(=), bneq(≠), blss(<), bleq(≤), bgtr(>), and bgeq(≥), which do just what you would expect. There are also unconditional branches whose name is determined by the size of the PC-relative offset. Thus brb (*branch byte*) has an 8-bit displacement and brw (*branch word*) has a 16-bit displacement.

The final major category we cover here is the procedure *call and return* instructions. Unlike the MIPS architecture, these elaborate instructions can take dozens of clock cycles to execute. The next two sections show how they work, but we need to explain the purpose of the pointers associated with the stack manipulated by `calls` and `ret`. The *stack pointer*, `sp`, is just like the stack pointer in MIPS; it points to the top of the stack. The *argument pointer*, `ap`, points to the base of the list of arguments or parameters in memory that are passed to the procedure. The *frame pointer*, `fp`, points to the base of the local variables of the procedure that are kept in memory (the *stack frame*). The VAX call and return instructions manipulate these pointers to maintain the stack in proper condition across procedure calls and to provide convenient base registers to use when accessing memory operands. As we shall see, call and return also save and restore the general purpose registers as well as the program counter.

Figure E.4 gives a further sampling of the VAX instruction set.

E.5 An Example to Put It All Together: swap

To see programming in VAX assembly language, we translate the C procedures `swap` and `sort` from Chapter 3; the C code for `swap` is reproduced in Figure E.5. The next section covers `sort`.

Just as we did in section 3.9 of Chapter 3, we describe the `swap` procedure in these three general steps of assembly language programming:

1. Allocate registers to program variables

2. Produce code for the body of the procedure

3. Preserve registers across the procedure invocation

The VAX code for these procedures is based on code produced by the VMS C compiler using optimization.

Register Allocation for *swap*

In contrast to MIPS, VAX parameters are normally allocated to memory, so this step of assembly language programming is more properly called "variable allocation." The standard VAX convention on parameter passing is to use the stack. The two parameters, `v[]` and `k`, can be accessed using register `ap`, the argument pointer: the address `4(ap)` corresponds to `v[]` and `8(ap)` corresponds to `k`. Remember that with byte addressing the address of sequential 4-byte words differs by 4. The only other variable is `temp`, which we associate with register `r3`.

Instruction type	Example	Instruction meaning
Data transfers	Move data between byte, halfword, word, or doubleword operands; * is data type	
	mov*	Move between two operands
	movzb*	Move a byte to a halfword or word, extending it with zeroes
	mova*	Move the 32-bit address of an operand; data type is last
	push*	Push operand onto stack
Arithmetic, logical	Operations on integer or logical bytes, halfwords (16 bits), words (32 bits); * is data type	
	add*_	Add with 2 or 3 operands
	cmp*	Compare and set condition codes
	tst*	Compare to zero and set condition codes
	ash*	Arithmetic shift
	clr*	Clear
	cvtb*	Sign-extend byte to size of data type
Control	Conditional and unconditional branches	
	beql, bneq	Branch equal, branch not equal
	bleq, bgeq	Branch less than or equal, branch greater than or equal
	brb, brw	Unconditional branch with an 8-bit or 16-bit address
	jmp	Jump using any addressing mode to specify target
	aobleq	Add one to operand; branch if result ≤ second operand
	case_	Jump based on case selector
Procedure	Call/return from procedure	
	calls	Call procedure with arguments on stack (see section E.6)
	callg	Call procedure with FORTRAN-style parameter list
	jsb	Jump to subroutine, saving return address (like MIPS jal)
	ret	Return from procedure call
Floating point	Floating-point operations on D, F, G, and H formats	
	addd_	Add double-precision D-format floating numbers
	subd_	Subtract double-precision D-format floating numbers
	mulf_	Multiply single-precision F-format floating point
	polyf	Evaluate a polynomial using table of coefficients in F format
Other	Special operations	
	crc	Calculate cyclic redundancy check
	insque	Insert a queue entry into a queue

FIGURE E.4 Classes of VAX instructions with examples. The asterisk stands for multiple data types: b, w, l, d, f, g, h, and q. The underline, as in addd_, means there are 2-operand (addd2) and 3-operand (addd3) forms of this instruction.

```
swap(int v[], int k)
{
    int temp;
    temp = v[k];
    v[k] = v[k+1];
    v[k+1] = temp;
}
```

FIGURE E.5 A C procedure that swaps two locations in memory. This code is a copy of Figure 3.18 on page 136. This procedure will be used in the sorting example in the next section. Appendix D shows the C and Pascal versions of this procedure side-by-side (page D-5).

Code for the Body of the Procedure swap

The remaining lines of C code in swap are:

```
temp = v[k];
v[k] = v[k + 1];
v[k + 1] = temp;
```

Since this program uses v[] and k several times, to make the programs run faster the VAX compiler first moves both parameters into registers:

```
movl r2, 4(ap)          ; r2 = v[]
movl r1, 8(ap)          ; r1 = k
```

Note that we follow the VAX convention of using a semicolon to start a comment; the MIPS comment symbol # represents a constant operand in VAX assembly language.

The VAX has indexed addressing, so we can use index k without converting it to a byte address. The VAX code is then straightforward:

```
movl r3, (r2)[r1]           ; r3 (temp) = v[k]
addl3 r0, #1,8(ap)          ; r0 = k + 1
movl (r2)[r1],(r2)[r0]      ; v[k] = v[r0] (v[k + 1])
movl (r2)[r0],r3            ; v[k + 1] = r3 (temp)
```

Unlike the MIPS code, which is basically two loads and two stores, the key VAX code is one memory-to-register move, one memory-to-memory move, and one register-to-memory move. Note that the addl3 instruction shows the flexibility of the VAX addressing modes: It adds the constant 1 to a memory operand and places the result in a register.

Now we have allocated storage and written the code to perform the operations of the procedure. The only missing item is the code that preserves registers across the routine that calls swap.

Preserving Registers Across Procedure Invocation of swap

The VAX has a pair of instructions that preserve registers `calls` and `ret`. This example shows how they work.

The VAX C compiler uses a form of callee convention. Examining the code above, we see that the values in registers r0, r1, r2, and r3 must be saved so that they can later be restored. The `calls` instruction expects a 16-bit mask at the beginning of the procedure to determine which registers are saved: if bit i is set in the mask, then register i is saved on the stack by the `calls` instruction. In addition, `calls` saves this mask on the stack to allow the return instruction (`ret`) to restore the proper registers. Thus the `calls` executed by the caller does the saving, but the callee sets the call mask to indicate what should be saved.

One of the operands for `calls` gives the number of parameters being passed, so that `calls` can adjust the pointers associated with the stack: the argument pointer (ap), frame pointer (fp), and stack pointer (sp). Of course, `calls` also saves the program counter so that the procedure can return!

Thus, to preserve these four registers for swap, we just add the mask at the beginning of the procedure, letting the `calls` instruction in the caller do all the work:

```
.word ^m<r0,r1,r2,r3>     ; set bits in mask for 0,1,2,3
```

This directive tells the assembler to place a 16-bit constant with the proper bits set to save registers r0 though r3.

The return instruction undoes the work of `calls`. When finished, `ret` sets the stack pointer from the current frame pointer to pop everything `calls` placed on the stack. Along the way, it restores the register values saved by `calls`, including those marked by the mask and old values of the fp, ap, and pc.

To complete the procedure swap, we just add one instruction:

```
ret                       ; restore registers and return
```

The Full Procedure swap

We are now ready for the whole routine. Figure E.6 identifies each block of code with its purpose in the procedure, with the MIPS code on the left and the VAX code on the right. This example shows the advantage of the scaled indexed addressing and the sophisticated call and return instructions of the VAX in reducing the number of lines of code. The 17 lines of MIPS assembly code became 8 lines of VAX assembly code. It also shows that passing parameters in memory results in extra memory accesses.

Keep in mind that the number of instructions executed is not the same as performance; the fallacies on pages 147 and E-21 make this point.

MIPS versus VAX

Saving register	
| ```
swap: addi  $29,$29, -12
      sw    $2, 0($29)
      sw    $15, 4($29)
      sw    $16, 8($29)
``` | ```
swap: .word ^m<r0,r1,r2,r3>
``` |
| **Procedure body** | |
| ```
      muli  $2, $5,4
      add   $2, $4,$2
      lw    $15, 0($2)
      lw    $16, 4($2)
      sw    $16, 0($2)
      sw    $15, 4($2)
``` | ```
      movl  r2, 4(a)
      movl  r1, 8(a)
      movl  r3, (r2)[r1]
      addl3 r0, #1,8(ap)
      movl  (r2)[r1],(r2)[r0]
      movl  (r2)[r0],r3
``` |
| **Restoring registers** | |
| ```
      lw    $2, 0($29)
      lw    $15, 4($29)
      lw    $16, 8($29)
      addi  $29,$29, 12
``` | |
| **Procedure return** | |
| ```
      jr    $31
``` | ```
      ret
``` |

FIGURE E.6 MIPS versus VAX assembly code of the procedure swap in Figure E.5 on page E-13.

Elaboration: VAX software follows a convention of treating registers r0 and r1 as temporaries which are not saved across a procedure call, so the VMS C compiler does include registers r0 and r1 in the register saving mask. Also, the C compiler should have used r1 instead of 8(ap) in the addl3 instruction; such examples inspire computer architects to try to write compilers!

E.6   A Longer Example: sort

As in Chapter 3, we show the longer example of the sort procedure. Figure E.7 shows the C version of the program. Once again we present this procedure in several steps, concluding with a side-by-side comparison to MIPS code.

Register Allocation for sort

The two parameters of the procedure sort, v and n, are found in the stack in locations 4(ap) and 8(ap), respectively. The two local variables are assigned
```

```
int v[10000];
sort (int v[], int n)
{
    int i, j;
    for (i = 0; i < n; i = i + 1) {
        for (j = i - 1; j >= 0 && v[j] > v[j + 1]; j = j - 1) {
            swap(v,j);
        }
    }
}
```

FIGURE E.7 A C procedure that performs a bubble sort on the array v. This code is a copy of Figure 3.20 on page 139. (See Appendix D for a Pascal version of sort.)

to registers: i to r6 and j to r4. Because the two parameters are referenced frequently in the code, the VMS C compiler copies the *address* of these parameters into registers upon entering the procedure:

```
moval    r7,8(ap)           ; move address of n into r7
moval    r5,4(ap)           ; move address of v into r5
```

It would seem that moving the *value* of the operand to a register would be more useful than its address, but once again we bow to the decision of the VMS C compiler. Apparently the compiler cannot be sure that v and n don't overlap in memory.

Code for the Body of the sort Procedure

The procedure body consists of two nested *for* loops and a call to swap which includes parameters. Let's unwrap the code from the outside to the middle.

The Outer Loop

The first translation step is the first *for* loop:

```
for (i = 0; i < n; i = i+1) {
```

Recall that the C *for* statement has three parts: initialization, loop test, and iteration increment. It takes just one instruction to initialize i to 0, the first part of the *for* statement:

```
clrl     r6                     ; i = 0
```

It also takes just one instruction to increment i, the last part of the *for*:

```
incl     r6                     ; i = i + 1
```

The loop should be exited if i < n is *false*, or said another way, exit the loop if i ≥ n. This test takes two instructions:

```
for1tst: cmpl    r6,(r7)   ; compare r6 and memory[r7] (i:n)
         bgeq    exit1     ; go to exit1 if r6 ≥ mem[r7] (i ≥ n)
```

Note that `cmpl` sets the condition codes for use by the conditional branch instruction `bgeq`.

The bottom of the loop just jumps back to the loop test:

```
        brb    for1tst  ; branch to test of outer loop
exit1:
```

The skeleton code of the first *for* loop is then:

```
        clrl   r6        ; i = 0
for1tst: cmpl  r6,(r7)   ; compare r6 and memory[r7] (i:n)
        bgeq exit1       ; go to exit1 if r6 ≥ mem[r7] (i ≥ n)
               . . .
               (body of first for loop)
               . . .
        incl   r6        ; i = i + 1
        brb    for1tst   ; branch to test of outer loop
exit1:
```

Exercise 3.11 on page 157 explores writing faster code for the similar loops.

The Inner Loop

The second *for* loop is

```
for (j = i - 1; j >= 0 && v[j] > v[j + 1]; j = j - 1) {
```

The initialization portion of this loop is again one instruction:

```
    subl3   r4,r6,#1      ; j = i - 1
```

and the decrement of j is also one instruction:

```
    decl    r4            ; j = j - 1
```

The loop test has two parts. We exit the loop if either condition fails, so first test must exit the loop if it fails ($j < 0$):

```
for2tst:blssexit2          ; go to exit2 if r4 < 0 (j < 0)
```

Notice that there is no explicit comparison. The lack of comparison is a benefit of condition codes, with the conditions being set as a side effect of the prior instruction. This branch skips over the second condition test.

The second test exits if $v[j] > v[j + 1]$ is *false*, or exit if $v[j] \leq v[j + 1]$. First we load v and put $j + 1$ into registers:

```
    movl    r3,(r5)       ; r3 = Memory[r5] (r3 = v)
    addl3   r2,r4,#1      ; r2 = r4 + 1 (r2 = j + 1)
```

Register indirect addressing is used to get the operand pointed to by r5.

Once again the index addressing mode means we can use indices without converting to the byte address, so the two instructions for $v[j] \leq v[j + 1]$ are:

```
    cmpl    (r3)[r4],(r3)[r2]; v[r4] : v[r2] (v[j]:v[j + 1])
    bleq    exit2                ; go to exit2 if v[j] ≤ v[j + 1]
```

The bottom of the loop jumps back to the full loop test:

```
        brb     for2tst         # jump to test of inner loop
```

Combining the pieces, the second *for* loop looks like this:

```
        subl    r4,r6, #1       ; j = i - 1
for2tst: blss   exit2           ; go to exit2 if r4 < 0 (j < 0)
        movl    r3,(r5)         ; r3 = Memory[r5] (r3 = v)
        addl    r2,r4,#1        ; r2 = r4 + 1 (r2 = j + 1)
        cmpl    (r3)[r4],(r3)[r2]; v[r4] : v[r2]
        bleq    exit2           ; go to exit2 if v[j]v[j+1]
        . . .
        (body of second for loop)
        . . .
        decl    r4              ; j = j - 1
        brb     for2tst         ; jump to test of inner loop
exit2:
```

Notice that the instruction blss (at the top of the loop) is testing the condition codes based on the new value of r4 (j), set either by the subl3 before entering the loop or by the decl at the bottom of the loop.

The Procedure Call

The next step is the body of the second *for* loop:

```
        swap(v,j);
```

Calling swap is easy enough:

```
        calls   #2,swap
```

The constant 2 indicates the number of parameters pushed on the stack.

Passing Parameters

The C compiler passes variables on the stack, so we pass the parameters to swap with these two instructions:

```
        pushl   (r5)    ;  first swap parameter is v
        pushl   r4      ; second swap parameter is j
```

Register indirect addressing is used to get the operand of the first instruction.

Preserving Registers Across Procedure Invocation of sort

The only remaining code is the saving and restoring of registers using the callee save convention. This procedure uses registers r2 through r7, so we add a mask with those bits set:

```
        .word ^m<r2,r3,r4,r5,r6,r7>; set mask for registers 2-7
```

Since `ret` will undo all the operations, we just tack it on the end of the procedure.

The Full Procedure sort

Now we put all the pieces together in Figure E.8. To make the code easier to follow, once again we identify each block of code with its purpose in the procedure and list the MIPS and VAX code side-by-side. In this example, 11 lines of the `sort` procedure in C become the 44 lines in the MIPS assembly language and 20 lines in VAX assembly language. The biggest VAX advantages are in register saving and restoring and indexed addressing.

Elaboration: The optimizing VMS C compiler did several tricks to improve this code, including replacing the call of the `swap` procedure with the body of the code inside the `sort` procedure, thereby avoiding the overhead of procedure call and return. Actually, the MIPS C compiler uses a much more efficient register save/restore convention than the one shown in Figure E.8, so the number of lines of code for each architecture is much closer than the figure suggests. Both compilers also use more efficient loops. We show them in this form to make the code easier to follow.

Fallacies and Pitfalls

The ability to simplify means to eliminate the unnecessary so that the necessary may speak.

Hans Hoffman, *Search for the Real*, 1967

Fallacy: It is possible to design a flawless architecture.

All architecture design involves trade-offs made in the context of a set of hardware and software technologies. Over time those technologies are likely to change, and decisions that may have been correct at one time later look like mistakes. For example, in 1975 the VAX designers overemphasized the importance of code-size efficiency and underestimated how important ease of decoding and pipelining would be ten years later. And almost all architectures eventually succumb to the lack of sufficient address space. Avoiding these problems in the long run, however, would probably mean compromising the efficiency of the architecture in the short run.

MIPS versus VAX

Saving registers		

	`sort:    addi $29,$29, -36`
	`         sw   $15, 0($29)`
	`         sw   $16, 4($29)`
	`         sw   $17, 8($29)`
	`         sw   $18,12($29)`
	`         sw   $19,16($29)`
	`         sw   $20,20($29)`
	`         sw   $24,24($29)`
	`         sw   $25,28($29)`
	`         sw   $31,32($29)`
		`sort:   .word ^m<r2,r3,r4,r5,r6,r7>`

Procedure body		
Move parameters	`move $18, $4` `move $20, $5`	`moval  r7,8(ap)` `moval  r5,4(ap)`

Outer
loop
	`          add  $19, $0, $0`
	`for1tst:slt  $8, $19, $20`
	`          beq  $8, $0, exit1`
		`          clrl  r6`
		`for1tst:cmpl  r6,(r7)`
		`          bgeq  exit1`

Inner
loop
	`          addi $17, $19, -1`
	`for2tst:slti $8, $17, 0`
	`          bne  $8, $0, exit2`
	`          muli $15, $17, 4`
	`          add  $16, $18, $15`
	`          lw   $24, 0($16)`
	`          lw   $25, 4($16)`
	`          slt  $8, $25, $24`
	`          beq  $8, $0, exit2`
		`          subl3 r4,r6,#1`
		`for2tst:`
		`          blss  exit2`
		`          movl  r3,(r5)`
		
		`          addl3 r2,r4,#1`
		`          cmpl  (r3)[r4],(r3)[r2]`
		`          bleq  exit2`

Pass parameters
and call
	`move $4, $18`
	`move $5, $17`
	`jal  swap`
		`pushl (r5)`
		`pushl  r4`
		`calls #2,swap`

Innter loop	`addi $17, $17, -1` `j    for2tst`	`decl  r4` `brb   for2tst`
Outer loop	`exit2: addi $19, $19, 1` `       j    for1tst`	`exit2: incl  r6` `       brb   for1tst`

Restoring registers		

	`exit1:  lw   $15, 0($29)`
	`        lw   $16, 4($29)`
	`        lw   $17, 8($29)`
	`        lw   $18,12($29)`
	`        lw   $19,16($29)`
	`        lw   $20,20($29)`
	`        lw   $24,24($29)`
	`        lw   $25,28($29)`
	`        lw   $31,32($29)`
	`        addi $29,$29, 36`	

Procedure return		
	`jr   $31`	`exit1: ret`

FIGURE E.8 MIPS versus VAX assembly version of procedure sort in Figure E.7 on page E-16.

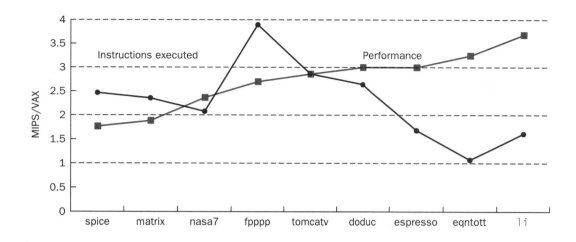

FIGURE E.9 Ratio of MIPS M2000 to VAX 8700 in instructions executed and performance in clock cycles using SPEC89 programs. On average, MIPS executes a little over twice as many instructions as the VAX, but the CPI for the VAX is almost six times the MIPS CPI, yielding almost a threefold performance advantage. (Based on data from "Performance from Architecture: Comparing a RISC and CISC with Similar Hardware Organization," by D. Bhandarkar and D. Clark in *Proc. Symp. Architectural Support for Programming Languages and Operating Systems IV*, 1991.)

Fallacy: An architecture with flaws cannot be successful.

The IBM 360 is often criticized in the literature—the branches are not PC-relative, and the address is too small in displacement addressing. Yet, the machine has been an enormous success because it correctly handled several new problems. First, the architecture has a large amount of address space. Second, it is byte addressed and handles bytes well. Third, it is a general-purpose register machine. Finally, it is simple enough to be efficiently implemented across a wide performance and cost range.

The Intel 8086 provides an even more dramatic example. The 8086 architecture is the only widespread architecture in existence today that is not truly a general-purpose register machine. Furthermore, the segmented address space of the 8086 causes major problems both for programmers and compiler writers. Finally, it is hard to implement. It has generally provided only half the performance of the RISC architectures for the last eight years, despite significant investment by Intel. Nevertheless, the 8086 architecture—because of its selection as the microprocessor in the IBM PC—has been enormously successful.

Fallacy: The architecture that executes fewer instructions is faster.

Designers of VAX machines performed a quantitative comparison of VAX and MIPS for implementations with comparable organizations, the VAX 8700 and the MIPS M2000. Figure E.9 show the ratio of the number of instructions executed and the ratio of performance measured in clock cycles. MIPS executes about twice as many instructions as the VAX while the MIPS M2000 has almost three times the performance of the VAX 8700.

E.8 | Concluding Remarks

The Virtual Address eXtension of the PDP-11 architecture . . . provides a virtual address of about 4.3 gigabytes which, even given the rapid improvement of memory technology, should be adequate far into the future.

William Strecker, "VAX-11/780—A Virtual address Extension to the PDP-11 Family," *AFIPS Proc., National Computer Conference*, 1978

We have seen that instruction sets can vary quite dramatically, both in how they access operands and in the operations that can be performed by a single instruction. Figure E.10 compares instruction usage for both architectures for two programs; even very different architectures behave similarly in their use of instruction classes.

A product of its time, the VAX emphasis on code density and complex operations and addressing modes conflicts with the current emphasis on easy decoding, simple operations and addressing modes, and pipelined performance.

With more than 600,000 sold, the VAX architecture has had a very successful run. As this book is being printed, DEC is making the transition from VAX to Alpha, a 64-bit address architecture very similar to MIPS.

The Big Picture

Orthogonality is key to the VAX architecture; the opcode is independent of the addressing modes which are independent of the data types and even the number of unique operands. Thus a few hundred operations expand to hundreds of thousands of instructions when accounting for the data types, operand counts, and addressing modes.

Program	Machine	Branch	Arithmetic logical	Data transfer	Floating point	Totals
gcc	VAX	30%	40%	19%		89%
	MIPS	24%	35%	27%		86%
spice	VAX	18%	23%	15%	23%	79%
	MIPS	4%	29%	35%	15%	83%

FIGURE E.10 The frequency of instruction distribution for two programs on VAX and MIPS.

E.9 Historical Perspective and Further Reading

VAX: the most successful minicomputer design in industry history . . . the VAX was probably the hacker's favorite machine . . . Especially noted for its large, assembler-programmer-friendly instruction set—an asset that became a liability after the RISC revolution.

Eric Raymond, *The New Hacker's Dictionary*, 1991

In the mid-1970s, DEC realized that the PDP-11 was running out of address space. The 16-bit space had been extended in several creative ways, but the small address space was a problem that could only be postponed, not overcome.

In 1977, DEC introduced the VAX. Strecker described the architecture and called the VAX "a Virtual Address eXtension of the PDP-11." One of DEC's primary goals was to keep the installed base of PDP-11 customers. Thus, the customers were to think of the VAX as a 32-bit successor to the PDP-11. A 32-bit PDP-11 was possible—there were three designs—but Strecker reports that they were "overly compromised in terms of efficiency, functionality, programming ease." The chosen solution was to design a new architecture and include a PDP-11 compatibility mode that would run PDP-11 programs without change. This mode also allowed PDP-11 compilers to run and to continue to be used. The VAX-11/780 resembled the PDP-11 in many ways. These are among the most important:

1. Data types and formats are mostly equivalent to those on the PDP-11. The F and D floating formats came from the PDP-11. G and H formats were added later. The use of the term "word" to describe a 16-bit quantity was carried from the PDP-11 to the VAX.

2. The assembly language was made similar to the PDP-11's.

3. The same buses were supported (Unibus and Massbus).

4. The operating system, VMS, was "an evolution" of the RSX-11M/IAS OS (as opposed to the DECsystem 10/20 OS, which was a more advanced system), and the file system was basically the same.

The VAX-11/780 was the first machine announced in the VAX series. It is one of the most successful and heavily studied machines ever built. It relied heavily on microprogramming (Chapter 5), taking advantage of the increasing capacity of fast semiconductor memory to implement the complex instructions and addressing modes. The VAX is so tied to microcode that we predict it will be impossible to build the full VAX instruction set without microcode.

To offer a single-chip VAX in 1984, DEC reduced the instructions interpreted by microcode by trapping some instructions and performing them in software. DEC engineers found that 20% of VAX instructions are responsible for 60% of the microcode, yet are only executed 0.2% of the time. The final result was a chip offering 90% of the performance with a reduction in silicon area by more than a factor of five.

The cornerstone of DEC's strategy was a single architecture, VAX, running a single operating system, VMS. This strategy worked well for over ten years. Today, DEC is in the midst of a transition to the Alpha RISC architecture. Like the transition from the PDP-11 to the VAX, Alpha offers the same operating system, file system, and data types and formats of the VAX. Instead of providing a VAX compatibility mode, the Alpha approach is to "compile" the VAX machine code into the Alpha machine code. The transition will be fun to watch.

To Probe Further

Levy, H., and R. Eckhouse [1989]. *Computer Programming and Architecture: The VAX,* Digital Press, Boston.

This book concentrates on the VAX, but includes descriptions of other machines.

E.10 Exercises

E.1 [3] <§3.2, 3.9, E.4> The following VAX instruction decrements the location pointed to be register r5:

```
decl (r5)
```

What is the single MIPS instruction, or if it cannot be represented in a single instruction, the shortest sequence of MIPS instructions, that performs the same operation? What are the lengths of the instructions on each machine?

E.2 [5] <§3.2, 3.9, E.4> This exercise is the same as Exercise E.1, except this VAX instruction clears a location using autoincrement deferred addressing:

```
clrl @(r5)+
```

E.3 [5] <§3.2, 3.5, E.5> This exercise is the same as Exercise E.1, except this VAX instruction adds 1 to register r5, placing the sum back in register r5, compares the sum to register r6, and then branches to L1 if r5 < r6:

```
aoblss r6, r5,L1 # r5 = r5 + 1; if (r5 < r6) goto L1.
```

E.4 [5] <§E.2> Show the single VAX instruction, or minimal sequence of instructions, for this C statement:

```
a = b + 100;
```

Assume a corresponds to register r3 and b corresponds to register r4.

E.5 [10] <§E.2> Show the single VAX instruction, or minimal sequence of instructions, for this C statement:

```
x[i + 1] = x[i] + c;
```

Assume c corresponds to register r3, i to register r4, and x is an array of 32-bit words beginning at memory location $4,000,000_{ten}$.

Index

X

Y

Z